Street Therapists

Street Therapists

Race, Affect, and Neoliberal Personhood in Latino Newark

ANA Y. RAMOS-ZAYAS

The University of Chicago Press   Chicago and London

ANA Y. RAMOS-ZAYAS is Valentín Lizana y Parragué Endowed Chair in Latin American Studies and professor of black and Hispanic studies at CUNY–Baruch College. She is the author of *National Performances: Race, Class, and Space in Puerto Rican Chicago*, also published by the University of Chicago Press, and coauthor of *Latino Crossings: Mexicans, Puerto Ricans, and the Politics of Race and Citizenship*.

The University of Chicago Press, Chicago 60637
The University of Chicago Press, Ltd., London
© 2012 by The University of Chicagos
All rights reserved. Published 2012.
Printed in the United States of America

21 20 19 18 17 16 15 14 13 12   1 2 3 4 5

ISBN-13: 978-0-226-70361-9 (cloth)
ISBN-13: 978-0-226-70362-6 (paper)
ISBN-10: 0-226-70361-4 (cloth)
ISBN-10: 0-226-70362-2 (paper)

Library of Congress Cataloging-in-Publication Data

Ramos-Zayas, Ana Y.
    Street therapists : race, affect, and neoliberal personhood in Latino
    Newark / Ana Y. Ramos-Zayas.
        p. cm.
    Includes bibliographical references and index.
    ISBN-13: 978-0-226-70361-9 (hardcover : alkaline paper)
    ISBN-13: 978-0-226-70362-6 (paperback : alkaline paper)
    ISBN-10: 0-226-70361-4 (hardcover : alkaline paper)
    ISBN-10: 0-226-70362-2 (paperback : alkaline paper)
    1. Latin Americans—New Jersey—Newark—Social conditions. 2. Newark (N.J.)—
Social conditions.   I. Title.
    F144.N69L387 2012
    305.868'073074932—dc23

                                                                        2011034664

♾ This paper meets the requirements of ANSI/NISO Z39.48-1992
(Permanence of Paper).

Contents

Acknowledgments

I have to confess that one of the parts of writing a book that I most look forward to is the acknowledgments section. This is also the section that I first turn to when I pick up a book, in the hope of finding out more about the author, her affiliations, her inspirations, her friendships, and whatever other chismesito might appear between the lines. Ultimately, the acknowledgements sections of books are a form of affective expression and it is from that perspective that I want to thank the many individuals and institutions that have enabled me to complete the long process of producing this manuscript.

I was at Rutgers University–New Brunswick for the ten years that it took me to get to know Newark. I am grateful to the colleagues in the Department of Anthropology and the Department of Latino and Hispanic Caribbean Studies who gave me substantive feedback on various portions of this manuscript and the published articles that have emanated from this ethnographic project. In particular, I would like to thank Ulla Berg, Carlos Decena, Milagros Denis, Zaire Dinzey-Flores, Peter Guarnaccia, Aldo Lauria-Santiago, Kathy López, Fran Mascia-Lees, and Edgar Rivera-Colón, as well as the administrative assistance of Ginny Caputto, Monica Licourt, Penny Murphy, Toni Napier, and Sarah O'Meara-González. At Rutgers–Newark, Kimberly DaCosta-Holton, Tanya Hernández, Asela Laguna-Diaz, Clement Price, Maura Sidney, and Olga Waggenheim provided encouragement and various forms of data and guidance throughout the research process. In addition, the participants in my two graduate seminars—"Urban Ethnography" (spring 2004) and "Race, Migration, Citizenship" (spring 2006)—were any professor's dream students whose incisive questions and genuine curiosity sharpened my own intellectual process. The same can be said of the undergraduate students in my "Latinos and Whiteness" (spring 2002) and "Latino Youth" (spring 2008) seminars. To all of them, my gratitude.

Other groups at Rutgers also facilitated the undertaking and completion of this project, by providing financial support and scholarly space. These include the Center for the Critical Analysis of Contemporary Cultures (2003–4), especially Linda Bosniak; the Institute for Research on Women (2004–5) under the stellar leadership of Nancy Hewitt; the Bildner Fellowship (2005–6) administered by Isabel Nazario; the Henningberg Civic Fellowship (2010); and the staff of the Center for Latino Arts and Culture.

From its inception through the fieldwork and writing stages, this project has benefited from the thematic, theoretic, and cosmetic suggestions of people who have become much more than colleagues, journal co-authors, writing buddies, long-term mentors, panel co-organizers, or conference co-participants, even though they have been that, too. Some of them are Carlos Alamo, Frances Aparicio, Aimée Cox, Nicholas De Genova, Micaela di Leonardo, Virginia Domínguez, Jorge Duany, Arlie Hochschild, John Jackson, Katherine S. Newman, Suzanne Oboler, José Raúl Perales, Sonya Ramsey, Mérida Rúa, Ann Stoler, Deborah Thomas, Arlene Torres, Vilna Treitler, Ingrid Vargas, and Carlos Vargas-Ramos. T. David Brent at the University of Chicago Press also published my first book, *National Performances* (2003), and has been once again a delight to work with. I got some of the best recommendations for revisions from one of the two anonymous readers of this manuscript; the second reader provided mostly a much-needed ego boost. Thanks to all!

This project's intimate entanglements with the city of Newark required the energy, patience, and continuous support of many Newarkers, like my former student Melissa Delrios and her family, who introduced me to their North Newark neighbors and invited me to several hospitality breakfasts at St. Michael's Church; the teachers, staff, and students at high schools and community agencies in North Broadway and the Ironbound, who generously revealed their quotidian concerns, joys, and amazement to me; the staff at the Newark Public Library, particularly librarian extraordinaire Ingrid Betancourt, and of the New Jersey Historical Society and the Newark Museum who directed me to critical archival and media sources. Above all, such a project required the generosity of the Newark residents and "street therapists"—activists, not-for-profit organization staff and workers, high school students and teachers, small-business owners, graphic artists, journalists, creative writers, spiritual leaders, beauticians, and morticians—whose strong voices and sharp analytical skills resonate throughout this volume. I cannot thank them enough because they certainly gave me more than I could ever convey or reciprocate. The anonymity codes of ethnographic research prevent me from thanking them by name, but I hope that I have done justice not only to their words but, perhaps more important, to that which is beyond semantic grasp.

Halfway through my fieldwork, I realized that, as transnational subjects, many of the interlocutors in this project developed their perspectives on Newark, affect, and race, elsewhere. Two of these "elsewheres" were Brazil and Puerto Rico. While most of the data that I collected in the cities of Santurce, Puerto Rico, and Belo Horizonte, Brazil, will have to wait for a future project due to space constraints with this one, I do want to thank the individuals who facilitated my ethnographic research in both places.

No Brasil, eu sou muito grata ao pessoal e os estudantes do Colegio Magno, particularmente Ronaldo Maciel e Ibsen Cunha, e da Escola Municipal Imago em Belo Horizonte, especialmente Cleide Maselli. Agradeço também a: Fabiano Maisonnave do jornal *Folha de São Paulo*; Moacyr Novaes da Universidade de São Paulo-CAMPINAS; Paula Miranda Ribeiro da Universidade Federal de Minas Gerais-Belo Horizonte e a sua família; Consolação Penha da Biblioteca Pública de Belo Horizonte; e a R P Vieira pelo convite a participar na Conferência de ABRALIC em Rio de Janeiro em agosto de 2006. Minhas boas amigas Bernadete Beserra da Universidade Federal do Ceará e Paula Botelho, que mudou-se para Belo Horizonte depois de alguns anos nos Estados Unidos, leram partes deste trabalho entusiasticamente e também compartilharam comigo seus próprias pesquisas. Finalmente, fico agradecida aos acadêmicos brasileiros nos Estados Unidos que criaram espaços interdisciplinarios importantes onde apresentei meu trabalho. Clémence Jouët-Pastré e Letícia Braga organizaram a palestra de "Imigração Brasileira aos Estados Unidos" em Harvard em março de 2005, e editaram o volume subseqüente que saiu da conferência. Os membros do grupo cibernético NEBIRG compartilharam informação muito útil sobre comunidades brasileiras pelo mundo todo. Obrigadinha!

En Puerto Rico, quiero agradecer el apoyo y entusiasmo de los maestros, estudiantes y administradores de la Escuela Bilingüe Padre Rufo y del Colegio La Piedad, en especial Puchita, a quien conozco desde hace más de veinte años y quien me puso en contacto con varios estudiantes.

También quiero agradecer al Dr. César Rey, sociólogo y Secretario de Educación al momento de mi investigación, y al personal de la biblioteca y archivos del Departamento de Educación Pública de Puerto Rico, por ayudarme a navegar el proceso burocrático y tramitar los permisos correspondientes. La Universidad Interamericana me proveyó hospedaje durante parte de mi estadía en Puerto Rico; la mayor parte del tiempo estuve en casa de mis papás que viven frente por frente a una de las escuelas en Santurce. Mil gracias!

By the time this book comes out, I will have officially accepted the position of Valentín Lizana y Parragué Endowed Chair in Latin American Studies at the City University of New York. I am excited to get to know my new colleagues at Baruch College and the Graduate Center, and look forward to the creative possibilities that my new position will bring, in terms of community partnerships with NYC Latino neighborhoods, vibrant intellectual spaces, and working with a talented and diverse student body. I am tremendously honored to occupy an endowed chair that is named after the beloved grandfather of someone whose values I respect and admire.

My family—by birth, by law, and by choice—have always provided the base from where I venture into any academic and personal endeavor. I am tremendously appreciative to the most important women in my life—my mom, Ana Hilda, and my Aunt Yolanda. My friends say that in my family the women "llevan la voz cantante" and I absolutely agree. I am also grateful for my stepfather, Vicente, and my Uncle Manuel, who have steadily supported those women whose unwavering presence, hard work, and passion allow me to do what I love. Así mismo, Magali y Javier Sánchez siempre son una gran inspiración para mí porque hacen de tripas corazones sin perder la motivación de querer echar para adelante siempre. In addition to my family by birth, I am appreciative to my family by choice: my comadre, Aixa Cintrón, her partner, Julie Burch, and the nieces they allow me to love and spoil, Ino and Amelia Cintrón-Burch; my close friend and almost sister, Clara Castro-Ponce, because regardless of mounting work and life commitments, we still manage to spend hours and hours on the phone; and to mi hermano del alma, Oscar Blanco-Franco, who is there through all that our friendship was, is and shall grow into. In the past few years, I gained family in Australia, England, and India and I am grateful for them; particularly my stepson, Christopher Abraham, sisters-in-law Premila Hoon and Lavinia Abraham, their sons Jay Hoon and Alokk Abraham, and my brother-in-law Peter Abraham, as well as the Alnemri, D'Souza, Farias, and Fernandes families in New

Jersey and Pennsylvania. What better excuse to get to know all world continents and enjoy great holiday hospitality throughout the year!

As the people whom I met in Newark, Belo Horizonte, and Santurce well knew, urban life can only be navigated with a deep appreciation for emotive entanglements. As this project unfolded, I went from being a happily, unencumbered single woman to being an even happier, perfectly partnered married one. It took someone like Thomas Abraham to convince me of the merits of this transition. We have enjoyed an exciting, refreshingly unorthodox domesticity ever since. Throughout the writing and revising of this manuscript, Tom has offered the practical support, necessary distractions, provocative interventions, and consistent encouragement that allowed me to gain an even greater appreciation for the lessons learned in the researching and writing of this book. Often undertaking more than his share of household tasks, Tom co-piloted our family with determination and enthusiasm and engaged in intellectual debate with brilliance and passion. I could not have envisioned a better partner with whom to share life's adventures. Perhaps one of the most exciting of these adventures was the birth of our son, Sebastián Abraham-Zayas. Sebastián was born exactly two weeks after I walked the manuscript to the local post office and shipped it to my editor. I can't claim that our respective timings are always as well synchronized, but what I can say is that Sebastián continues to charm those around him with his great disposition, contagious laugh, and curiosity about strangers. It is to Tom and Sebastián that I dedicate this book.

Preface

I did not set out to study the world of affect, sentiment, or
emotion when I first began this project in 2001. In fact, for
a long time into my fieldwork I shied away from examining
emotions in terms of the Latino and Latin American populations who had been the subjects of my past work. After all,
Latinos and Latin Americans have been generally construed
in ways that either flattened their affective worlds or as emotionally excessive and hyperaffective; affect, emotion, and
sentiment had been used to legitimate subordination, a primacy of culture over structural factors involved in culture
of poverty arguments, and critical to popular stereotypes of
"Latin" culture. Given this context, I was very torn when I
encountered the first few "street therapists" whom I met in
Newark, New Jersey.

"I'm a lawyer, a therapist, a cop, a nurse, and a social
worker at this job!" remarked an evidently exhausted Amarilis Guzmán in reference to her position as full-time security guard at Newark's University Hospital. When I first met
her, she was a student at a high school in North Broadway,
a predominantly Puerto Rican neighborhood in Newark. At
the time, Amarilis also worked as a stacker in Home Depot
and part-time security guard for an insurance company in
downtown Newark. Whenever I would ask Amarilis about
her school and work experiences, she would do what most
other informants did: Engage in a psychological analysis of
the individuals with whom she came into contact as a way

of explaining that there was an emotional landscape unique to Newark and a process of racial formation that oftentimes existed beyond semantic availability. A question about how she got along with her coworkers at the insurance company, for instance, would lead to comments on how white workers were "neurotic" and "obsessive compulsive" over a drip in the bathroom faucet or how black workers were "angry" and resentful of Latinos or how Puerto Ricans lacked "self-esteem" or how recently arrived Latin American migrants were prone to "depression." Spaces were likewise characterized in psychological terms, as "stable" or "aggressive," and their populations were collectively assumed to be "driven" or "crazy" or "withdrawn" or "explosive."

While I return to Amarilis's life later in this volume, she is somewhat representative of the individuals whom I came to see as "street therapists." In their participation and interpretation of urban interactions, particularly those involving racial difference and racialization practices, these were individuals skilled at rendering some encounters with race as diagnostic of racism, while allowing other encounters to go unnoticed or undermined in the registry I term "cartography of racial democracy." In fact, the encounters that were registered and analyzed were the ones more closely associated with the affective world and ensconced in the connection between this world and material, neoliberal projects. These street therapists had figured out a way to articulate racial difference within the constraints of urban neoliberalism, by opting not to publically denounce racism not because they didn't believe racism existed, but because they lacked trust in society and government to attend to racism and racial subordination. Instead, intimate relationships were where beliefs about racial difference played out.

Drawing from a popular Latin American and Hispanic Caribbean ideology of racial democracy, some Latin American migrants and US-born Latinos altered the interpretation of racial encounters in a predominantly black city, particularly in instances over which they would otherwise have little control. Rather than passively feeling emotion, these individuals became street therapists who actively analyzed and interpreted emotion and affect in themselves and in others, and related to their surroundings accordingly. A particular interpretation was more or less enduring depending on an individual's skill at orchestrating perceptions of a given racial situation. Affect motivated individuals to attend more carefully to their environment and their social encounters. The more disempowered or marginalized an individual felt in a certain situation, the more likely he or she was to pay careful attention to the affect and emotions of others and to develop judgments about them. How do we explain this connection between power (or a sense of powerlessness) and this increased attention to affect as a tool for judging everyday social interactions? Under neoliberalism, economic relationships become deeply emotional, just as intimate relationships increasingly influence economic models of exchange, acquisition, and negotiation. Street therapists realize that emotional vocabularies constitute sets of glosses for negotiating understandings of interpersonal relations, including processes that overlap with learning about race in translocal contexts.

Although a focus on these urban psychological dynamics was not the initial impetus for this ethnography, the empirical centrality of this theme led me to examine how the "interior" world of feelings, affect, and emotion come to inform individuals' perspectives on everyday social interactions, economic prospects, and political potential. It allowed me to examine how certain historical events and political economic structures come to mark cities and generate a visceral perception of cities in light of emotion and sentiment. Urban spaces became, in very explicit ways, humanized and the humanity of city residents became contingent upon the adequate manifestation of affect and emotive practices.

In some ways, this volume engages a long-standing interest on how different forms of human capital–including emotional insight, affective displays, and comportment—are valued in particular political, social, and economic contexts, as well as on how they fluctuate from "alternative" to "mainstream." The volume also contributes to our understanding of how migrant populations and US-born minorities—particularly those from Latin American and Caribbean countries—learn and relearn racial etiquette in the United States and straddle multiple translocal racial formations in an effort to become neoliberal subjects. Initially, I wanted to limit the research to Brazilians and Puerto Ricans, the two populations that were demographically salient in the two main Newark neighborhoods where I conducted fieldwork—the Ironbound and North Broadway, respectively. To a degree, these populations are still salient in this volume, and I even included some aspects of the fieldwork I conducted in the cities of Santurce, Puerto Rico, and Belo Horizonte, Brazil, among Puerto Rican and Brazilian return migrants. However, as is the case with ethnography, these initial parameters quickly blurred as other populations—African Americans, Portuguese, other Latin Americans, and Latinos—either asked to participate or simply were integral in the processes I came to examine. This complexity adds to the examination of affect, race, and neoliberal personhood in Latino Newark.

On a spring day in 2003, and after weeks of passing by the Botánica La Estrella on my way from a high school in the Ironbound neighborhood to Penn Station–Newark, I decided to go into the storefront building. At the entrance to the botánica was a dusty glass window displaying candles, aromatic oils, and ceramic images of Virgin Marys and saints, along with a handwritten sign stating: "America is immortal and she will recover. She's going through difficult times and will rise again. We have to be good citizens. This country has given many riches and asylum to many immigrants and we need to pay back."

Once inside I waited as Osorio, the seventy-something-year-old Cuban owner, instructed a Brazilian woman and young adult son to be careful with envy: "You may not know it, but others may be envious of your apartment or of your girlfriend or of some other aspects of your life." This seemed to make sense to the mother and the son, who remarked that jealousy ran rampant in their Newark neighborhood. In some form of Portuguese-Spanish code switching, what I came to see as a staple of the area, Osorio urged the mother: "Explícale a tu hijo lo que es la envidia [envy, in Spanish] . . . enveja [envy, in Portuguese]. Háblale sobre eso. Así es como los jóvenes aprenden [Explain to your son what envy is. Talk to him, talk to him about it. That's how young people learn]." When the young man asked if there was any other bath concoction which was better smelling than the one Osorio had offered, Osorio was visibly mortified and simply responded: "You don't like it? Don't buy this! Just go ahead and buy whatever you have on that list of yours and that's it." The mother promptly accepted the product, regardless of odor, and gave a sharp look to her son, as they both left the store.

It was my turn. As I asked Osorio for an interview, he warned, "I do not read cards or do predictions for the future. I only carry out consultations. Go on and do your school project and come back some other time, not so close to Holy Week." Like so many other small businesses in the area, the botánica shut down shortly after. I never got to interview Osorio, but I always wondered if he anticipated the challenges of a project that aimed to reconcile the intangible and the concrete, the interiority of the material and the materiality of the interior. I suspect that, a street therapist himself, he probably did.

Street Therapists: Race, Affect, and Neoliberal Personhood in Latino Newark

The first thing that I learned here [in the United States] was the trouble with black people. You are looking at someone and they're like "What you looking at?" Very antagonistic, aggressive. They are like that, with that attitude, and they are proud of it! I never saw something like that in Brazil. I never saw people like that there, with that attitude. People are afraid of black people here. Because it's like they are going to hit you out of nowhere. And don't think it's the guys I'm talking about. . . . Noooo, it's the women! And you can't show them you're afraid, because they'll fight you even more, they're like guys.
ANA TEREZA BOTELHO, 19, BRAZILIAN LIVING IN IRONBOUND

I think Hispanic families are very open. They will accept anyone as long as they give us respect . . . because we are ourselves [racially] mixed, so we're used to that. My aunt is married to a black guy and my family is crazy about him. He eats our food, dances salsa, he says a few words in Spanish. . . . It's harder with the [black] women, because they get very jealous of us. They think we steal their men, because you see more couples of a black man and a Puerto Rican woman than the other way around. That we're prettier, have prettier hair. They do give you a lot of attitude, to see what you do. They can be very aggressive, like they live on an edge and you have to analyze the situation, which way it's going to go. MIGDALIA RIVERA, 18, US-BORN PUERTO RICAN LIVING IN NORTH BROADWAY

I met Ana Tereza and Migdalia while doing fieldwork at the high schools they attended in two neighborhoods in

1

Newark, New Jersey—the Ironbound, a largely Portuguese area with a growing influx of Brazilian migrants, and North Broadway, a predominantly Puerto Rican neighborhood with a significant presence of African Americans and Caribbean and South American immigrants. Like the other US-born Latino and Latin American migrants with whom I shared spontaneous conversations, structured interviews, and focus groups, Ana Tereza and Migdalia consistently raised, without any prompting, the volatility, uncertainty, and illegibility that characterized their everyday relationships with and affective perceptions of African Americans, particularly African American women.[1] Most of them emphatically condemned African American women's "attitude" as vulgar, unfeminine, and contrary to an aesthetic of self-care and comportment to which both Latinas and Latin American women aspired, and to which they attributed success in all aspects of life, from securing jobs to finding boyfriends. They offered characterizations of black women's affective inadequacy, excessive kinetics, vulgar mannerisms, and over-the-top or flashy fashion, hair, or nail styles.

Like other Newark residents with whom I spoke over the years, Ana Tereza and Migdalia formulated a surprisingly cohesive characterization of "Blackness" as a deeply emotive and gendered idiom, appraised in a visceral and spectacular way, not unlike an audience's response to an over-the-top, exaggerated television talk show. Through quotidian observations, these young US-born Latinos and Latin American migrants assessed the interactive styles of African American women in ways that were surprisingly congruent with mainstream corporative and managerial views of "emotional intelligence," a prerogative of the upwardly mobile, productive individual (Illouz 2008, 66).[2] There was a general sense that the emotional style of African American women was more difficult to commodify because of their presumed inability to hide temperamental outbursts, a quality that would render them unmarriageable and unemployable in most of the service-sector, customer-oriented jobs available to working-class women of color in Newark. Likewise, among recent Latin American migrants, a politicized black consciousness elicited feelings of anger rather than appreciation for the United States. In the cosmologies of many of these migrants, a black/white US racial model, which in their view was obsessed with race, was to blame for the emotional handicap—the "aggressiveness"—of African Americans and, consequently, their presumed material failure in a city like Newark.

Nevertheless, young Latinos and Latin American migrants also acknowledged the importance of acquiring a form of racial knowledge that would enable them to better navigate Newark's urban landscape. They *very analytical - brittle.*

recognized that African Americans possess that desired form of "urban competency," and the modernity, hipness, and cosmopolitanism globally associated with Blackness. Acquiring and internalizing the knowledge of how race operates in social exchange became a deeply emotive process for Latinos in Newark, as individuals both phenomenologically experienced these emotions and projected them onto others, particularly African Americans, as a way to render them legible. Quotidian interactions in schools, neighborhoods, commercial venues, or the streets and public transportation oftentimes propelled a therapeutic (and psychoanalytical) engagement, a heightened gaze of black bodies and mannerisms. These interactions and the historical, political, and economic contexts that enabled them constitute what I have termed "urban emotional commonsense."

Even though this initial ethnographic material and discussion highlight antiblack sentiments among Latinos and Latin American migrants, this volume is not rigidly circumscribed to those populations. The very terms "Latinos," "Latin American migrant," and "black" are in fact quite complex and I very attentively try to capture some of that nuanced production of difference in subsequent chapters. While this project began and continued to be mostly about the experiences of Puerto Ricans, most of whom were US-born, and Brazilians, a largely migrant population, as it is generally the case with ethnography, other groups insisted that their presence be noted in my fieldnotes and here. It is no longer possible, in US eastern cities like Newark, to artificially confine research projects to this or that nationality group. Instead, while paying attention to the unique migration and settlement histories of Puerto Ricans and Brazilians (and their distinct positions in the global economy), I stopped to listen and include the voices of the Peruvians, Colombians, Mexicans, Dominicans, Cape Verdeans, Iranians, African Americans, West Indians, and Portuguese groups who shared the physical space, material resources, and emotive landscape of Newark, New Jersey. For the purpose of simplifying an already complex context, I oftentimes use "Latino" in reference to individuals of Latin American or Caribbean ancestry who were either born in the United States or who arrived as infants. While most of the Latinos in Newark were Puerto Rican, there was also a growing number of Dominicans, Cubans, Ecuadorians, and Colombians or people of mixed Latino ancestry. When I use the term "immigrant" or Latin American migrant, it is more often in reference to Brazilians and, to a lesser degree, to other recent arrivals from Ecuador, Peru, and Colombia, the countries that supplied the largest proportion of Newark's Latin American populations. Throughout this volume, I try to identify individuals by nationalities, unless I am trying deliberately to note ideological or epistemological distinctions between US-born minority and Latin American "immigrant." A limitation of this project is that, while I met and spoke with African Americans, Portuguese, and other non-Latino populations, I did not do so in any systematic way and those voices have, therefore, remained outside the purview of this project. Ultimately, this work is about how US-born Latinos, particularly Puerto Ricans, and Latin American migrants, particularly Brazilians, view African Americans and engage (or not) with modernist conceptions of Blackness in their process of becoming neoliberal subjects.

In the context of the diversity of populations indicated here, and trying to highlight whenever possible the specific sociopolitical, historical, and economic conditions that accounted for the distinct migration and settlement of each of these nationalities in Newark, I still found myself seeing the role of "street therapist" as a critical thread. The role of street therapist is one rooted on the political economy and history of Newark, rather than being circumscribed to decontextualized perspectives on difference that focus on "culture" or "identity" (cf. di Leonardo 1984, 1998; Williams 1973). Examining "street therapist" allowed me to consider how, under neoliberalism, when projects of capital accumulation dictate urban development, everyday perspectives on "race" were ensconced in interpretations of individual and group affect; likewise, I note how, when allusions were made to sentiments or feelings, they were usually followed or analyzed by discussions of interracial relations. These epistemologic and analytic connections guided my interest in further examining the connection between race, affect, and neoliberalism and, in particular, my inquiry into a largely understudied side of capital accumulation. Urban neoliberalism has come to be influenced by the enforcement of an emotional commonsense that heightens a process by which race is psychologized and affect is racialized. In such an urban emotional landscape, neoliberal personhood requires that certain individuals act as street therapists. Not only did street therapists think in the words their diverse languages assigned to feelings or emotions, but these inchoate, unconscious affective worlds became conscious in connection to quotidian expectations and when they were glosses for articulating experiences of race, racialization, and racial difference.

Because the individuals whom I met held affective predispositions that influenced their feelings for and judgment of individuals as group members, perspectives on a social group affect oftentimes influenced how interpersonal trust developed. By acknowledging the nuanced interactions among various groups—not just Puerto Ricans or Brazilians alone or even how these groups viewed African Americans only—I focus on how these processes operated in alignment with market exigencies. The psychologizing of racial difference oftentimes hid the structural roots of distress. Instead of blaming a widening class polarity, segregation, and the geopolitics of transnationalism for individual and group material conditions, street therapists frequently blamed these individuals and groups (oftentimes themselves) for being too aggressive or too passive, incurring in unnecessary spending, or not finding a better paying job.

In Newark aggression frequently served as a meta-sentiment that dominated quasi-therapeutic readings and assessments of emotional adequacy. Fred Myers (1979) uses the term "meta-sentiment" to refer to a specific regulatory emotion that some communities place outside the person, as a "control feeling," to teach individuals what to feel and what not to feel, what kind of self to be and not be. In this sense, distinctions between emotions at a micro (social psychological) level oftentimes get confused with emotions at a structural and cultural level. Latin American migrants and US-born Latinos deployed these readings in their everyday encounters with, visual attention to, and narrative understanding of African Americans.[3] Certain urban emotional experiences condensed bodily and social experiences, since "it is through the body as a seamless, multidimensional domain of emotions, thoughts and social relationships that the impact of loss and conflict is both absorbed and reframed" (Kirmayer 1992, 339).

Significantly, however, reading this urban meta-sentiment cannot be reduced to learning what Elijah Anderson (2000) calls a "code of the street"; rather, reading affect in an urban context also requires an assessment of how quasi-therapeutic scrutiny and emotive analysis in fact propelled the resurrection of alternative racialization practices, including, in the case of Latinos in Newark, the deployment of a Latin American ideology of "racial democracy." It was through the articulation of a US-based cartography of "racial democracy" that Latin American migrants and US-born Latinos alike assumed a higher moral-emotive ground in contradistinction to a presumed African American "aggressiveness" (or "having attitude"), or the "blandness," traditionalism, and lack of sensuality attributed to whites. I thus look not only at how racial knowledge is produced in relation to an urban emotional commonsense, but at what people actually do with that knowledge, at how they produce pragmatic meanings that "work" in different contexts and social spheres. The interaction of three main concepts—urban emotional commonsense, cartography of racial democracy, and neoliberalism—provides the foundation for the theoretical framework introduced in this study.

This volume examines how neoliberalism attempts to more closely align emotions with the imperatives and needs of state and market. This alignment has reinvigorated the discourse of personal responsibility in everyday racial encounters. A key question that will be addressed is: How can paying attention to emotion, such a highly subjective, invisible, and personal experience, be helpful to the social scientific research on urban racial practices and neoliberal projects, a research topic that is chiefly concerned with objective regularities, patterned action, and large-scale institutions? There is much to be gained by analyzing the impact of political economy and urban history on emotions, affect, and sentiments. This approach counters the forces of naturalization and reification by introducing "the intimate" as critical, rather than peripheral, to state and city projects of surveillance, regulation, and uneven capital accumulation. An emotional commonsense operates in tandem with racialization practices of the state, and yet social scientific approaches safely render emotion as the terrain of therapists and psychological experts, and outside the purview of urban politics and policies.

I highlight how a politics of emotion, race, and the economy operates in a predominantly black city in which US-born Latinos and Latin Americans are required to actively learn about their own racial and class subjectivities. Untangling the social institutions, historical conditions, and political practices around which such urban commonsense operates enables a closer examination of what is meant by "emotions" in the context of quotidian urban encounters. In fact, examining the foundation and operation of such an "emotional commonsense" in cities may furthermore supply new empirical and epistemological tools to capture the depth and intensity with which both US-born Latinos and Latin American migrants approach the process of learning race and racial etiquette in the United States, how they situate themselves and are situated in a black-white racial paradigm, and the potential implications of urban neoliberal processes in the future of intraminority relations. Ultimately, a reframing in our understanding of Latino antiblack attitudes enables us to examine what happens to individuals' emotional lives, affect, and sentiment under urban neoliberalism, when capital accumulation is viewed as a virtue of self-regulation that reactivates a politics of respectability and prescribes "proper" public behavior. As I argue in this volume, attaining the appropriate mood in a city—the "feel that sells" (chapter 1)—requires that the poor, particularly poor youth of color, are displaced, deconcentrated or repositioned in "nonthreatening" ways, if not entirely removed from increasingly desirable real estate areas, so that capital accumulation and real estate aspirations can be met.

Throughout this volume, I demonstrate not only how neoliberal projects are largely rooted in emotional styles and expectations, particularly among the most marginal urban populations, but also how this emotional landscape effectively fragmented racialized populations by encouraging them to engage in minority-minority (horizontal) racialization practices that generated new kinds of exclusion. Under neoliberalism, racialized groups were incited to develop complementary scales to measure their marketability, attractiveness, and desirability, as well as their "worthiness" of US citizenship (Ramos-Zayas 2004; chapter 2), in accordance with the urban renewal goals of cities and surveillance projects of the nation-state. Variously racialized populations assessed their own emotional style against the emotional competency of others, so that groups were able to explain particular material conditions as consequences of the "attitudes" or "way of being" of other minority groups, rather than the structures on which these conditions were played out. Because of the multilayered nature of emotions, these assessments were prone to creating a slippery sense that political economy did not really matter. The illusion of "immediacy" and "intimacy" that derived from emotions rendered them powerful tools in advancing neoliberal objectives.

Affective Conceptions of Practice: Themes and Terminology

The concept of "street therapists," as established in the title of this book, serves as an efficient shorthand for the theoretical contribution of this volume, by enabling the preliminary formulation of an emotion-based theory of practice that is grounded on relational affect and knowledge sharing. Relational thinking, and the bridging of subjective knowing and material structures, is at the heart of practice theory and provides a particularly suitable dynamic approach to analyze how everyday practices are the locus in the production and reproduction of power relations under urban neoliberalism. While "therapist" is a term usually applied to professional clinicians dealing with psychological illness or distress, I use the term in a more popular way to refer to the heightened attentiveness and relational learning that takes place in social settings, where individuals act as apprentices who are required to analyze, observe, and interpret each other's actions, behaviors, and sentiments. I specify that these are *street* therapists, as opposed to a conventional form of therapy that might happen in traditional institutional settings, to highlight how all individuals involved in the therapy process implicitly viewed themselves, others, and the nature of their relation as historically constituted and constituting and as provoked or enabled by material practices and urban social hierarchies. Thus conceived, the concept of "street therapist" is an intervention to address a long-standing dichotomy between practices that are inspired by Marxist thought (and fundamentally historical, structural materiality) and those that are more phenomenological (and focused on the exploration of human consciousness and patterning of signification).

In this volume, an emotion-based practice theory—built upon historically grounded conceptions of neoliberal personhood, affect, and a cartography of racial democracy—aims to establish that assessing consciousness and intentionality is not a zero-sum game, but a process that can only be appraised by a focus on degree. Rather than a dichotomy between consciousness-based (phenomenological) perspective and a nonconscious habituation (practice theory), I am attentive to the ways in which variation and reflexivity can happen even within habitual behaviors and how consciousness does not always involve a fully intentional ability to produce verbally mediated representations. This volume, thus, demonstrates that recognizing affect as a visceral constituent of racial practices and racialization as rooted on affectivity to advance the interests of capital enables us to focus on the degrees of autonomy within experiences of consciousness and intentionality. Not all nondiscursive content of consciousness (including feelings, emotions, bodily processes) are beyond an individual's conscious control and even habitual practices can be infused by verbally mediated representations; rather, any focus on consciousness or intentionality must be rooted in an understanding of social structures and political projects that provide the context for the moments in which phenomena develop and are appraised or not.

Street therapists are not mere observers, but are affectively engaged in the tacit and explicit social knowledge that constitutes the practices of the multiple relations in which they become involved; as they gradually master these practices, and perhaps become practitioners themselves, their legitimacy and competency in urban spaces increase. This process of observation, analysis, and learning, however, does not refer to some monolithic, preordained acquisition of a "culture"; rather, it is an inconclusive, historically grounded, and continuously unfolding process that includes a continuous engagement with what others do; how they talk, walk, and act; what they need to do to be successful in the elusive process of belonging in a local, national, and international scale.

The concept of "practice" is widely invoked in social theory to identify the background understanding or competencies that enable individuals to follow rules, obey norms, and articulate or grasp meanings. Theories of practice also encourage an empirical focus on publicly accessible performances, rather than private mental events or states (Rouse 2006, 504), and attend primarily to "outward" behaviors rather than "inner" beliefs or desires. In this sense, human performances and activities are meaningful in themselves, so that rules, norms, and concepts get their meaning and normative authority from their embodiment in publicly accessible activity. What could an emotional, affective formulation of practice add to how practice theory is currently conceived? One could propose that practices also get their meaning and normative authority from embodied forms of materially grounded affect, so that pre-existing external structures are not only internalized (as Bourdieu's concept of *habitus* states), but also experienced viscerally with various degrees of consciousness and reflection.

In this volume, I focus not only on the publicly accessible performances that are at the center of theories of practice, but also on the visceral and affective components that might escape semantic expression.[4] A reason why emotions fit so well in this conception of "practice" is that affect animates desires, intentions, and motivations, but does this within an internalized understanding of possibility derived from concrete historical and material conditions. An emotion-based practice could contribute to rendering aspects of individual interiority legible, while recognizing that such "interiority" is inseparable from the entanglements and power hierarchies of a social and cultural political economy. As I argue here, by examining not only individual action or behavior, but also the affective realm and reflection on affective social processes, one is able to shed light on the intricacies of social history and enduring political economy. While practices are composed of individual performances, these performances nevertheless take place against a more or less stable background, including a background of other performances that respond to experiences of intimacy and affect. This emotion-based practice does not use "practice" as a replacement for social structure, as other theories of practice sometimes do, but rather affirms the centrality of a social structure sustained in part by enduring and transmissible forms of inequality that impact individual and collective "interior" worlds.

Practice theory is particularly pertinent to examinations of affect because it offers a radical challenge to any psychological reduction of social practices to which concepts like "affect," "emotion," "feeling," or "sentiment" might be susceptible. Those practice theorists who emphasize the role of bodily skills (especially Dreyfus 1991) deny that there need be any semantic psychological intermediaries between the description of bodily action at the biological level and its description in terms of socially and culturally situated practices. Thus, practice theories effectively claim that ordinary perception and action often have no appropriate description at the intermediary "psychological" level, but are appropriately described in practice-theoretical terms. Individual beliefs, desires, and affective responses do not require a cognitive-psychological "level" of interpretation, but their ascription is part of a complex, socially articulated discursive practice (Rouse 2007). By challenging the autonomy of psychological explanations, practice theory presents an opportunity to situate affect, emotion, feeling, and sentiment—historically attributed to the world of human psychology—in the social realms of power, hierarchy, and materiality. This is a way of re-engaging affect, emotion, sentiment, and feelings without recreating the "culture of poverty" and models of mental deficiency used in the social sciences to legitimize the subordination, oppression, and colonization of racialized populations in the United States and throughout the world.

Social and cultural structures exist only through their continuing reproduction in practices, but affect could exist both within the realm of "practice" and as a mediator between such realm and the material context by allowing us to attend to the *degree* of stability in the structures that practices sustain. Structuring structures (Bourdieu's habitus) are very strong and enduring partly because they are affectively appraised and, therefore, introduce variability at the most intimate level, thus making their articulation and interpretation difficult and easily manipulated. An emotion-based approach to practice theory introduces an appeal to the visceral, without falling into reductionist conceptions of "nature" or the "natural," and thus, begins to address the long-standing concern with how patterns of social practice supposedly govern, influence, and constitute the actions of individual practitioners. By examining affect, and situating it as constituted by and constitutive of the world of capital and materiality, one is able to better understand how patterns of social practice are sustained both through imitation, training, and sanctions on the one hand, and through human understanding and rationality on the other (Rouse 2006). Affect involves both imitation and reflection, but both of these are partial and not always predictable or leading to the same forms of reproduction; in this way, examining affect as integral to and constitutive of structuring structures addresses long-standing concerns with the transmission of patterns of practice. Since the ability to learn how to participate in a practice must involve a grasp of other performances, and because these performances have to be rendered meaningful without individuals needing or even being able to spell out explicitly what they have grasped, a consideration of affect and social interactions in light of intimacy opens up another vehicle to examine the production and transmission of practice.

"Practice" offers a particularly suitable theoretical tool to frame phenomenological questions of affect and the emotive without undermining processes of social reproduction and inequality. Theories of practice recognize the coexistence of alternative practices within the same cultural milieu, differing conceptions of the same practices, and ongoing contestation over the maintenance and reproduction of cultural norms (Rouse 2006, 506), thus avoiding an anthropological inclination to view "culture" as rigid or monolithic. While practice theory provides additional resources for understanding cross-cultural interactions brought about through migration, political domination, or trade relations, it also recognizes localized practices of interpretation. Moreover, an important theme in practice theory has been the central role of human bodies and bodily comportment (Rouse 2006, 511–15). Theories of practice view the human body as both causally affected and effective object in the natural world, while also taking into account the body's unified capacity for self-directed movement and expression that can be "inculcated"; in this sense, human bodies are conceived as the locus of agency, cultural expression, and the target of power. This focus on inculcation, as best articulated in the concepts of *doxa* (Bourdieu 1977, 166; 1990, 68) and *body hexis* (Bourdieu 1977, 124), aim to account for conscious and unconscious bodily practices that become accepted as unquestioned. Nevertheless, at times this appraisal of bodily practices is sometimes limited when attempting to understand how the visceral, that which may or may not be beyond perception and action, operates. An emotion-based conception of practice could more adequately appraise the visceral, not necessarily by viewing it only as imitation or reflection, but by attending to the space where imitation stops and reflection has not quite begun.

Affect effectively reframes a perception of "practical knowledge" that is embodied without being only located in the body. While kinetic performances involve the coordination of bodily movement with a receptive responsiveness to one's surroundings, a focus on affect allows a better assessment of the degree or spectrum of connectedness between perception and action, bodily kinetics and material, social historical, political economic context. In this sense, the body is not merely interactive with its surroundings, but "intimately"—rather than just "interactionally"—involved with macro structures, hierarchies of power, and immediate economic and social conditions (Rouse 2006, 513n8).[5] At the most basic levels of bodily performance, human agency is realized through participation in practices that are "'ours' before they can be 'mine'" (514);

however, these practices are not "ours" in the same way, because they are always already produced in an intimately hierarchical constitution of power and difference, as these are materially and affectively recognized. In this sense, individuals themselves keep track of the commitments or entitlements accrued by fellow participants in a given practice, and each subsequent performance might call for a revision of that participant's discursive score and overall balance of commitments and entitlements (Brandom 1994). As argued in this volume, these processes by which "practical knowledge" is framed in affective terms cannot be divorced from the interests of capital and neoliberal practices.

One of the primary interests of and requirements for successful capital accumulation in urban spaces is the establishment of an emotional commonsense—a series of tacit understandings of appropriate affect, expressing adequate public emotions, and controlling the display of private emotions in public. Civilizing or harnessing, rather than coercing or repressing, "the passions" was one of the feats of liberalism in the nineteenth century, as a growing recognition that the culture of the self and of the body politic went hand in hand (cf. Hirschman 1998, 16; Foucault 1972). Under twentieth-century neoliberalism, narratives that had historically been trademarks of the realm of psychology, self-help, and corporate managerial cultures (e.g., Illouz 2007), and which had been formerly associated with middle classes in the West, have trickled down to frame everyday interactions in working-class, racialized communities. More significantly, the manifestation of public affect is related to the strength or weakness of the racialization of particular groups, so that the affect of whites, whose racial identity is generally neutralized, is perceived to be highly individualistic, whereas the affect of blacks is examined as a feature of African Americans as a collective. Affect in US urban contexts has become—particularly in an allegedly "postracial" era—a salient criterion of judgment and political critique, as well as a central component of how dominance and subordination have been complicated in proliferating majority-minority contexts, like the city of Newark.

Postindustrial economic transformations have had a significant impact on how racism has been viewed increasingly in light of emotional projections, evaluation (and projection) of the emotions of others, subjective emotional experiences, and the expression and performance of emotion. This has endowed interracial encounters with unprecedented forms and meanings. Emotions depend on personal (and political) elements that to a large degree are common to members of a group living in similar circumstances. They are shaped through cultural stereotyping of experience as well as shared expectations, memories, and fantasies, and they can provide a "reading" of one's own responses, and a judgment of those who don't share in those similarities. The success of neoliberal projects has increasingly come to rely on alternative forms of capital, particularly those forms that are measured in terms of qualities of modern personhood, such as "attitudes," "feelings," and other determinants of emotional "adequacy."[6] These assessments of emotional adequacy tend to hide structural aspects of inequality. More significantly, rather than being experienced as a top-down coercive judgment on the part of government authorities or corporations, such emotional adequacy is assessed in everyday interactions among equivalently disenfranchised populations, including Latinos and blacks in postindustrial Newark.

Judith Irvine (1982) powerfully argued that there was a "sincerity problem" in how members of different social groups distinguished "true" from "deceitful" affective displays, and how the role of public emotional displays in attributing a particular affective state to someone "depend[ed] not only on that someone's behavior, but also on context" (35). The question of how individuals and groups frame events in which emotions can be talked about and what role these events play in the social life of communities remain central to this project, as does the issue of whether more covert affect indexes, which easily escape normative scrutiny, can in fact be used to communicate feelings, such as anger, in everyday interactions. Key to such discussions is how to examine the inherent indeterminacy of many affect-encoding devices.

In an attempt to address the empirical and epistemological concerns that arise from examining affect, which has been associated with individual "interiority" and, thus "unmeasurable" qualities, I have developed a theoretical framework rooted on three main concepts: the "emotional commonsense" or "feel" of urban spaces, the "cartography of racial democracy" that encompasses processes of transnational racial systems (in the United States and Latin America/Caribbean countries), and the behavioral exigencies of "neoliberal personhood."

Urban Emotional Commonsense

From a variety of theoretical perspectives, emotions have been understood as complex categories suggestive of experiences learned and expressed in the body in social interactions through the mediation of systems of signs, verbal and nonverbal.[7] The examination of emotion in anthropological thought generally shows that meaning about emotions emerges through interpersonal processes (Rosaldo 1984; Abu-Lughod 1986), particularly dialogue, and that the opposition between cognition and emotion is a dominant Western construct (Lutz 1988) rooted in traditional philosophical and psychodynamic perspectives that have historically insisted on such dichotomy.[8] In some anthropological studies, a catalogue of emotions often supplies the labels for feelings, while the active manifestation of emotion is viewed as communicative process.[9] Through emotion we enact cultural definitions of personhood as they are expressed in concrete and immediate but also socially defined relationships.[10] I am particularly drawn to Eva Illouz's definition of emotions as "cultural meanings and social relationships that are very compressed together" and her contention that this compact compression confers them their energetic and hence their prereflexive, often semiconscious character. In this sense, "emotions are a deeply internalized and unrefined aspect of action, but not because they do not contain enough culture and society in them, but rather because they have too much" (2007, 3). The power of emotion largely relies on the fact that emotive worlds do not fit into a meaning (cognitive)/feeling (bodily) dichotomy, but are instead both affective and felt associations. In that sense, the concepts of "feelings," "affect," and "sentiment" have also been central to the study of emotion.

A physiological, broad category of person-centered psycho-physiological sensations, "feelings" are presumed to put individuals in touch with their intersubjectivity and intercorporeality as they ease a presumed opposition between the social world and individual interiority. Feelings are also information-gathering experiences, of a polyvalent quality, that generate judgments about a particular target or situation. The involuntary, almost-automatic character of emotions generally suggests a deeply ingrained, overlearned habit, or a process of chunking and organizing a situation, while sometimes also viewing emotion as more or less pre-social or outside the material world.

This book examines the implication of taking "affect," "feelings," "emotions," and "sentiments" as integral aspects of everyday urban practices, and explores the intersubjective ways through which individuals acquire knowledge about how "race" operates and, particularly, how it operates as a practice that works through embodiment and is situated in the world of experience and politics. For instance, a judgment of "inappropriate affect"—the perceived emotive dissonance in quality, intensity, or dimension between what one feels and what one "should" feel—contributes to the positive or negative evaluation of a particular practice, behavior, or idea concerning a racialized subject or group. The strength or weaknesses of the racialization of groups—that is, the various degrees of integration into or marginalization from a nation-state, which in the case of the United States is premised on white supremacy—determine a collectively oriented emotive urban landscape. This emotive urban land-scape is underscored by competing ideological perspectives on US racial relations, emotionally assessed, as well as by transnational perspectives on race which, in the case of Latino populations, tended to draw from a Latin American ideology of racial democracy.

In the context of Newark, Latinos oftentimes attributed negative emo-tions to African Americans and assumed that the "race" of blacks as a social unit explained "aggression" or perspectives on "having attitude" in ways that increased distrust and uncertainty in everyday interactions. When Latinos evoked positive emotions toward African Americans, these positive emotions were not automatically attributed to the group's "race," but rather, individual subjectivity was evoked (e.g., "he's not like most blacks"). In the rare instances in which these positive emotions were attributed to African Americans as a social unit, a positive view of the affect of racial others led to a "minority consciousness" (solidarity) that engendered assessments of whites as Other. These rare instances decreased, at least temporarily, a sense of uncertainty and increased trust between blacks and Latinos, and contributed to a condition of trust, al-beit one still characterized by volatility and uncertainty.

The academic discourse of feeling tends to assume as a starting point a normal human being in a "neutral" state, in a state of "normal" emo-tionless abstraction, rather than entangled with others and infected by the social exchange of feelings. The actors assumed by racialization the-ory are unemotional, instrumental, information-processors, even when dispositions, satisfactions, and deprivations are not optional extras, but variously built into the human condition, into historically endur-ing structures of social relations shaped through discourses, practices, and experiences. My theory introduces an emoting actor, who responds emotionally to exchanges and attempts to understand the source of her or his emotions and feelings. This assumes that actors are motivated to interpret such global emotions and that specific context in which such interpretations takes place points them in the direction of a racialized social unit in Newark.

As illuminated in conversation with Ann Stoler, examining the inter-section of an urban emotional commonsense, racialization, and neolib-eralism requires that an epistemological distinction be drawn between projecting emotion onto others, experiencing emotions oneself, and performing emotions. Taking into consideration these distinctions, a central question that this project takes into account is: What are the emotions that are dominant and what are the political critique possi-bilities of emotion? An emotion may set the horizon against which we see the world. The way in which people experience events emotionally influences judgment about what kind of people they must be in order to participate in the events, while creating an impression of powerfulness instigates emotions of mastery. Likewise, although interrelated, talk or writing about emotions is different from the interweaving of emotions and discourse. This is the distinction between what is articulated/represented about feelings (and how) versus the phenomenological experience of feelings (or observable emotions). The distinction also allows us to examine how sensibilities are part of the constitution of social locations and hierarchies; in fact, one can oftentimes map class or other forms of social location through emotions in a way that expands traditional analyses of inequality.

How one straddles the intersection of one's own emotions and those that are projected onto others is a central aspect of the "emotional energy" that constitutes the less-examined side of everyday social interactions and racial encounters. Randall Collins (2004) defines "emotional energy" as the type of energy we accumulate from a series of successful interactions with others and that holds interaction rituals together. It is, therefore, an important aspect of sociability and generates the self-confidence an individual gets from repeatedly gaining a sense of belonging in a status quo. Collins claims that people with that emotional energy are likely to assume a position of leadership because they derive energy from the group that can, in turn, embody the group. Because, in this sense, emotional energy is accumulated through past membership, questions that remain are: What happens to those who have not tested their belonging or who have tested it unsuccessfully? What is the alternative situation of lacking such emotional energy like?

More important, emotions function as a form of capital not only because they derive from one's social bonds and one's position within those bonds, but also because emotional habitus is defined by one's social position and social identity and that, in turn, defines it. In this sense, "not all forms of emotional energy can function as social currencies and be converted into social capital" (Illouz 2008, 214–15). A rowdy and exuberant energy will not get very far in most neoliberal settings (service sector economy, the military), where certain emotional styles—greater perceived docility or "friendliness"—are more likely than others to be converted into capital. For instance, the lower ranks of the service sector demand complex emotional work that is attuned to the emotional aspects of interaction, while being in full cognitive control of them; this is an example of the shifting demands of the postindustrial economy. These demands are experienced even by (or *especially* from) its youngest racialized workers who are required to possess the symbolic and emotional skills to cope with a variety of situations in complex markets in a new form of "connectionist capitalism" (Boltanski and Chiapello 1999). Luc Boltanski explained that in this form of "connectionist capitalism" the "class habitus of the dominant classes can no longer rely on its own intuition. This habitus needs to know how to establish relationships between people who are geographically and socially distant from oneself" (176). An "emotional capitalism," to borrow Eva Illouz's term, has thus "realigned emotional cultures, making the economic self and emotions more closely harnessed to instrumental action" (2007, 23). In this sense, emotional competence has become a formal criterion for measuring and quantifying competencies—that is, "for ascribing a monetary value to a person's emotional make-up"—so that a certain emotional habitus is increasingly a prerequisite for entering into more and more fields, even "surpassing traditional forms of cultural capital" (Illouz 2008, 214; cf. Bourdieu 1977).

Practices have a crucial tacit dimension, a level of competence or performance that is oftentimes assumed to be prelinguistic or perhaps even inaccessible to verbal articulation; practice theory is particularly sophisticated in its examination of "what can be shown but not said" or the competencies that can be enacted without verbal mediation. However, an emotion-based focus on practice would nuance the way in which this tacit dimension is grounded on the presumption of shared presuppositions. A sense of shared presuppositions grounds the intelligibility of social practice and the way that practice might be tacit and commonsensical; however, an emotion-based focus on practice would illuminate forms of tacit intimacy enabled by the skillful know-how underlying social practices, even in instances when processes involved in the transmission of such practices might require leaving rules behind in order to achieve a distinctively bodily capacity, as the conception of "urban competency" in this volume suggests.

Emotive urban interactions are technologies of self-management relying extensively on language and the mastery of "proper" racial etiquette and racial-talk, a challenge for Latin American migrants who sometimes consider engaging in race-talk as a racist act. Manifesting an emotional commonsense that was suitable for the Newark urban context required, among other things, that Latinos become racial experts and "street therapists" dedicated to scrutinizing, analyzing, and selectively emulating features of a cosmopolitan urban Blackness, while carefully avoiding an overidentification with African Americans and, in the case of Brazilians living in the Ironbound, even with working-class Portuguese whites.

Moreover, most Latinos and Latin American migrants read their own emotions and those of strangers as a barometer to appraise concrete state projects, including those related to urban "development," the installation of surveillance cameras in schools, and the recruitment of youth of color to the US military.

It is important to note that, as many Latinos developed their own readings of the racialization of African Americans, they also came to view blacks, to various degrees, as their models of what to do and not do when it came to racial etiquette in the United States. Most of the US-born Latinos and Latin American migrants with whom I spoke conveyed the importance of presenting oneself as emotionally different from blacks, not only because they viewed blacks as emotionally defective but, more significantly, because only by attaining an "adequate" (i.e., neoliberal-friendly) emotional style would they be able to benefit from certain aspects of the Newark Renaissance, including urban corporate investment in local jobs or a profitable neighborhood-based commercialization of culture (how cultural products, displays, and practices are packaged and marketed to be palatable for mainstream consumption), especially in the "ethnic" area of the Ironbound. Likewise, being emotionally different from blacks would presumably allow them to sidestep conditions of heightened policing and surveillance.

Emotion has traditionally been seen as an aspect of human experience that is primarily "intimate" or "personal," and the one most exempt from the material world, including the social world of racial, class, gender, and sexual subordination. Sartre (1957) argues that an emotion is an active transformation of the world that we imaginatively perform in the face of an obstacle to desire; thus, emotions are defenses against those aspects of the world that challenge our desire. Likewise, Damasio's conception of "somatic marker" (1996) renders emotions an essential part of practical reason, which gives the individual a sense of how the world relates to her or his goals and projects. Some people become "race experts" and internalize how to talk (or not) and feel about racial difference, as well as how to communicate emotionally "appropriate" manners in potentially volatile racial situations which, in turn, affect the real estate/urban development viability of a city.[11] Emotions, affect, and sentiment are indispensible tools to understanding the process by which individuals become racial subjects and racial experts—who attribute deep meaning to a brush against someone's skin on the bus or to the outcomes of holding someone's gaze for a few seconds too long—as well as how they are marginalized and neglected in ways that appear justifiable and deserving.

A postindustrial economy in which racial relations are structured around perspectives of "appropriate" and "inappropriate" affect provides a context for examining how emotions are not only organized within the market, but have themselves become commodities of a market that exacerbate rather than destroy them (cf. Illouz 2003; Stoler 2004; Hochschild 1990). Thus, we cannot presume that the realm of commodity and capitalism debases the realm of sentiment, but quite the contrary. These new models of emotionality have furthermore altered modes of racial sociability and self-awareness among US-born Latino and Latin American migrants and have reshuffled the cognitive and practical emotional boundaries regulating how social difference is produced. By reducing personality and emotions into new forms of social classification, many Latinos and Latin Americans contribute to making emotional style (historically the professional realm of psychologists and the medical profession) a social currency—a form of urban competence—while articulating a new language of racial selfhood that dovetails with urban "renewal" needs. The emotive becomes an analytic tool that is deployed to make moral claims to citizenship, while racial knowledge becomes a form of social capital that structures belonging, mobility, and subject formation in US cities.

This ethnography embarks on the ambitious process of disentangling the complicated emotional aesthetics (or "commonsense") that racialized working classes in US cities develop to navigate spaces of capital accumulation, test their own proximity to social mobility and Americanization goals, and assess potentially explosive moments of everyday urban tension.

Cartography of Racial Democracy

A highly developed emotional idiom sustains notions of racial difference among US minorities who articulate, reinforce, and recode positive and negative social exchanges, imagined personhoods, and self projections. In the case of US-born Latinos and, especially among some Latin American migrants, conceptions of "race" result not only from stock theories of civil rights movements, with which they were relatively unfamiliar, but also from previously held folk theories of race drawn transnationally.[12] This combination of understanding "race" and racism by drawing from multiple, often competing, racial systems is part of what I refer to as "cartography of racial democracy."

A cartography of racial democracy transforms coded emotions into public objects to be exposed, discussed or argued over. I use "cartography" in both a metaphoric and pragmatic way, as it refers to the symbolic, historical, and cognitive roadmaps that US-born Latinos and Latin American migrants deployed to navigate everyday racial situations that seemed tenuous, illegible, and potentially volatile. In the context of urban "renewal" and safety in a predominantly black city, "racial democracy" served as an ideological and even moral cartography to plot and trace an individual's market value within the broader neoliberal objectives of capital accumulation.

Thus, racial democracy did not so much describe a landscape but untangle or chart it through codes and symbols that represented social reality. As David Harvey notes, cartographic identifications—locating, positioning, individuating, identifying, and bounding—are operations that play a key role in the formation of personal and political subjectivities, so that there are mental and cognitive maps embedded in our consciousness that defy easy representation on some Cartesian grid (2001, 219–21). A key question that this book tends to is: How is the competency to manage those maps formed? Like geographical maps, a cartography of racial democracy orients US-born Latinos and especially Latin American migrants within the intricate and oftentimes illegible terrain of US racial relations, as these very relationships were transformed by homeland mental maps of class, gender ideologies, and racial practices that were resurrected, modified, and deployed to accommodate transnational differences.

A central epistemological concern that must be addressed from the start is: Why is "racial democracy" the lens through which I examine urban emotional aesthetics in Latino Newark? Racial democracy as a perspective through which to communicate emotion emerged organically from the fieldwork; its connection to emotions is a central question in every chapter of this volume, even though it was not a part of the initial conception of this project. Nevertheless, a cartography of racial democracy is useful when describing the ideological and communicative practice that *emotionally* and affectively marks everyday urban interactions in the predominantly black urban context of Newark, locating racial situations in terms of feeling tones, affective resonances, or associations among Latin American migrants and US-born Latinos. The emotions that "racial democracy" codifies are not action per se, but the inner energy that propels individuals toward an act and prompt a particular "mood" or "coloration," in Illouz's words. Emotions are thus "energy-laden sides of action, where that energy simultaneously implicates cognition, affect, evaluation, motivation and the body" (2007, 2).

Among many US-born Latinos and Latin American migrants in Newark, the emotions involved in the practices of racial knowledge, particularly in the process of racial learning itself, continuously led to views of race akin to the Latin American ideology of "racial democracy." The comments by Ana Tereza Botelho and Migdalia Rivera that open this chapter have to be situated in light of several conversations we had in which they insisted that US Latinos and Latin American migrants possessed different perspectives on "race" than did African Americans; that they were more accepting of racial difference than blacks in the United States or did not even consider "race" as a valid analytical category to begin with; that they had "every race [racial group]" represented in their own families and kin networks; or that their very nationalities were a product of three ancestral bloodlines, as evidenced by the various combinations of "looks" common in one's countries of origin or ancestry. These claims resonate in obvious ways with long-debated and quite normative views of Latin American "racial democracy." What was perhaps different about the comments above, and those gathered through much of my fieldwork in Newark, is how discussions of "racial democracy" were activated by the perceived volatility, uncertainty, and general "illegibility" of everyday racial situations involving African Americans. In a "majority minority" city, US-born Latinos and Latin American migrants activated discussions of "race" that drew from the racial democracy tenets of erotic racial "mixture" and, I argue, emotive desirability. More significantly, Latinos deployed these ideologies of racial mixture to highlight a higher emotive and affective modern personhood that was viewed as radically different from the presumed inadequate affect of African Americans, particularly of African American women.

In many ways, Newark is a premiere site to examine racial democracy in the United States because of the particular attachment that local populations—Brazilians, Puerto Ricans, other populations from Latin America and the Caribbean, Portuguese, and Spaniards—have to racial democracy ideologies, and how these ideologies emerge in an urban context that had historically consisted of African Americans from the south and whites who understood race in bifurcated, black-white terms.[13] My main goal, however, is not to contribute directly to the robust literature on "racial democracy" in Latin America, but to consider the everyday ramifications that some of the postulates of this ideology have on the everyday experiences and interpretations of US-born Latinos and Latin American migrants living in working-class urban areas.[14] The view that Latin America is a "racial democracy" has been challenged for decades, but what most scholars are still struggling to explain is why does such a

concept of race relations, and its various tenets, still hold so much discursive, imaginative, pragmatic, and symbolic power—as well as material and social mobilization repercussions—into the twenty-first century?
The potential activation of "racial democracy" discourses in the United
States calls us to analyze how domains oftentimes considered outside the
purview of traditional social scientific inquiry are increasingly drawn into
perspectives on subordination and implicated in the experience, articulation, and managing of social inequality. I am particularly interested in
the elements of racial democracy that situate "sentiment" and "affect"
not in conflict with reason, but serving the exigencies of a specific racial
reasoning that indicates a social recognition of expectations and a rich
evaluative vocabulary of social critique (Stoler 2004). A power-evasive
reduction of racial discrimination from the social to the private operates
in tandem with a growing neoliberal emphasis on self-regulation, surveillance, and development.

We must thus consider the multiple discursive, ideological, and pragmatic realms in which individuals make sense (and generate a "commonsense") of their own marginalization. Many of the young Brazilians
and Puerto Ricans with whom I spoke in Newark revealed an emotional
aesthetics built upon neoliberal forms of "racial democracy." This cartography of racial democracy rendered "race" unacceptable and morally
reprehensible as an analytical category, while also creating a hyperconsciousness of "race" that induced individuals to repackage themselves, to
become more desirable to the nation, by rejecting associations with both
Blackness and whiteness in the United States. It not only complicated
rigid racial binaries, but put forth other conceptions of "difference," including emotive difference.

Moreover, in the context of Newark, a cartography of racial democracy operated like a series of "folk theories of race," giving emphatic behavioral glosses to racial practices, so that an individual was presumed
to belong to a racial group because he or she "acted" *and* "felt" in accordance with the behavior attributed to that group (cf. Jackson 2001).
Certain aspects of "racial democracy," particularly those that created the
impression that one could alter racial politics and racism not necessarily
in the terrain of rights or official politics, but in the affective and emotive
terrains, were compatible with urban neoliberal goals, such as bringing
more local tourism to Newark and encouraging real estate investment.
These folk theories of race, coded in the ideology of "racial democracy,"
enabled Latinos to mobilize their own schema of presumably "unique"
habits, ideas, and dispositions (a sort of Bourdieuan habitus, since these

schemas are subjectively lived and communicated as personal identity and taste despite being objectively determined by one's position in the hierarchy of cultural, social, and economic capital) to respond to contradictions and predicaments of being Latino in a black/white context.

This cartography sustained a classic interest of neoliberalism: to displace "big" problems into the realm of individual affect (cf. Rabinowitz 1997). The terms of antidiscrimination struggles enabled by this cartography were fundamentally different from (and at times incompatible with) classical civil rights–inspired antiracism discourse. In fact, many Latin American migrants and some US-born Latinos oftentimes viewed such denunciations as symptomatic of emotional or even psychological "inadequacy" (e.g., being "lazy," "tener complejo," having low self-esteem or "too much anger," or being "too aggressive by nature"). This is not to say that denunciations of racial discrimination, discursively attributed to African Americans, were outright rejected; in fact, these were necessary to sustain views of a more racially harmonious Latin America, distinct from the "real racism" of the United States. Rather, "racial democracy" served as a cartographic guide to the seeming contradiction between a fundamentally racist, unequal US context, on the one hand, and a narrative that conditions the "immigrant" experience in general and the experience of Latin Americans in particular on the other—that is, the narratives of meritocracy and social mobility that justify the risks, family separations, enduring state violence, and personal sacrifices that characterize the lives of many migrants. In this sense, this cartography was also a particular strategy of *class* differentiation among some Latin American migrants. A critical element of this "cartography of racial democracy" was that the nation-state and US racial history did not provide the critical lens through which Latin American migrants or many US-born Latinos viewed "race" or racism; instead, the realm of affect and intimate knowledge were the narratives supplied as leading evidence that "racism does not exist among Latinos" or that denunciations of antiblack racism in the United States had to do with the "inadequate" character or emotional flaws of African Americans. In this sense, "racial democracy" discourses in the United States call us to analyze "intimate frontiers" (Stoler 2001) and how the workings of intimate domains are also implicated in the managing of white supremacy, subordination, and difference in a highly militaristic homeland security state.

I do not explicitly examine the contentious academic debates around "racial democracy," but consider the impact of tenets attributed to racial democracy and how they supplied the ideological and mythological tools that US-born Latinos and Latin American migrants produced as they generated folk theories of race that were pragmatic, dogmatic, and attentive to quotidian social interactions. The "cartography of racial democracy," in this sense, served to identify, catalogue and organize multiple systems of understanding "race" and racism in everyday contexts. It oriented the individual not only in terms of adequate behavior or action, but also in the readings of intimate, quotidian encounters, development of an affective decorum, and the management of difference. At times, in fact, it rendered race a valid analytical category *only when* it was deployed in the terrain of affect, emotion, and intimate knowledge—outside the purview of the nation-state, political economy, and structural inequalities.

Race has become a critical lens of everyday social analysis through which US-born Latinos and Latin American migrants in Newark navigate, negotiate, and alter the emotive landscape of this predominantly African American city. While oftentimes viewed as detached from the immediate political economic projects of cities, these emotive evaluations of race, which draw heavily from a racial democracy paradigm, are in fact fundamental to the effectiveness of most neoliberal projects; they create ideas of "proper" looks and behaviors, of environments "safe" for middle-class consumption. Analyzing this phenomenon advances the study of the intersection of capitalism and affect, particularly those explorations that examine how global economic processes, like neoliberalism, impact the everyday, intimate, and emotive lives of individuals and the sentimental landscape of cities.

Neoliberal Personhood

"Neoliberalism"—along with "late capitalism," "economic globalization," and "postindustrialization"—has served as a buzz term to describe the particular economic transformations that began to take place in the latter part of the twentieth century (Chomsky 1999; Comaroff and Comaroff 2000). By "neoliberalism" I mean the conglomerate of economic urban development policies that aim to attract capital accumulation through private investment, and selective state deregulation in favor of free-market approaches. Some neoliberal urban projects have commercialized culture in order to attract tourism to ethnic enclaves by implementing "security" and surveillance technologies to create spaces that appear safe to real estate investors and corporations, and showcasing shopping and cultural events that might appeal to the lifestyles of affluent (and usually whiter) consumers. I am especially concerned with the use of "emotion"—as it appears in a malleable language of personal responsibility, manners, family values, respectability, shame, aggression—in the formulation and appraisal of these neoliberal urban projects.

More precisely, I examine how neoliberal leaders use emotion in public discussions to render working-class racialized populations alternatively hypervisible and invisible when it comes to benefiting from any material outcome of such economic initiatives. For instance, the theory that new retail will generate new jobs for poor and working-class Newark residents has been questioned in the media on the grounds of employee readiness or lack of "soft skills" (Ferguson and Gupta 2002, 989). As a *New York Times* writer notes, the chronically unemployed "needed the most basic training: how to dress for an interview, how to speak to an employer and how to handle disputes without storming out the door."[15] In this sense, these willing Newark workers were considered unequipped to work even when the jobs were loading and unloading cargo at the waterfront or handling baggage at Newark airport.[16] A main inquiry of this volume, then, is how urban projects associated with neoliberalism—including urban "revitalization" initiatives, corporative involvement in community development, and the uses of culture in strategies of capital accumulation—configure perspectives on emotional styles, racial difference, and evaluations of behavioral and psychological "adequacy" that render some individuals "good" or "bad," "deserving" or "unworthy," depending on their ability to generate capital or at least appear as if they had the potential for generating capital.

Vivian Rovira, a young and outspoken Puerto Rican woman who had been born and raised in Ironbound, explained her perspective on some of her Portuguese neighbors:

Being that I work around here to me I feel that the Portuguese think that they are bigger than us. 'Cause they look at me and they can have the same nappy hair as me, they can have the same complexion, and they just like throw me the money on the counter, instead of saying thank you and have a nice day. They just look at me like [expression of disgust].

And she continued:

The Portuguese are stuck up. . . . You have people pretending to have a lot of money when they're really broke. They would tell one group of friends, "I'm buying a $500,000 house," and then they tell another group, "I'm so broke." And I'm like, if you live in Newark, you're not buying a $500,000 house. Not here. For that you would move to the suburbs, and you ain't. You as poor as me. You live across the street from me. But the Portuguese are very spoiled. Their parents are like "You got an F? Here, let me give you a car." My mother would be like "Hell no, if you want a car, go work!"

Because style, behavior, and consumption patterns were assumed to represent the real self in neoliberal fashion, they were oftentimes viewed as an effective means of rendering strangers legible in everyday racial interactions. Moreover, Vivian's perspectives on her Portuguese neighbors and the clients she met at the store where she worked as a clerk were suggestive of an authentic emotional culture that whites and even whites-in-the-making, like the Portuguese, were presumed to lack. The emotional paucity that whites were ascribed was a "compensatory racial fantasy" (Rivera-Colón 2009, 154) that affirmed, in a counteridentificatory manner, the emotional complexity and sophistication of Puerto Ricans, who refused to concede whiteness any type of superior or even interesting social aesthetic in the realm of an intimate, inner world. People judged their class identities and that of their neighborhoods in a dense social idiom that attended to both demographics and gossip, but also to the ability to purchase an urban cosmopolitan (or cosmopolitan-*like*) lifestyle that served as linchpin to a neoliberal personhood. When Vivian accused her Portuguese neighbors of faking their class and status, the Portuguese claim to a less-privileged socioeconomic position was not always validated. On the one hand, the neighborhood presumably located Vivian and her neighbors in the same class position while, on the other, this class position was viewed as rooted in parental inadequacy (how Portuguese parents overindulged their children). Such an illegible or ambivalent class similarity was undercut by racialized psychological readings. Whites, including the Portuguese neighbors, were framed as lacking a sophisticated affective capacity and lacking an inner depth that Puerto Ricans possessed. Because of this, they could engage at a superficial communicative level, but were seldom taken into one's inner circle of trust. As Edgar Rivera-Colón (2009) argues, the idea of keeping white people outside the circle of trust is a preventive form of defense in a white supremacist society that is not strictly based on personal interactions, given the intense and increasingly policed residential and social segregation of majority-minority cities like Newark.

In Vivian's case, consumption was a vehicle of both inclusion and exclusion into Newark's racial-*cum*-class order. A racialized logic of neoliberal consumption of public space aimed to produce increasingly larger segments of Newark "safe zones" for the more affluent, white residents that were leaving Manhattan for Newark's Ironbound, a twenty-minute train ride from Midtown and still a "white looking" area in an otherwise predominantly black city.

The personhood that neoliberalism requires is that of a solitary achiever, able to succeed without the intervention of the state. It harkens back to numerous "rags-to-riches" tales reminiscent of a Horatio Alger–like American dream mythology, and that privileges a white European experience over that of "welfare dependent" or "parasitic" US minorities—including African Americans, Puerto Ricans, and other US-born Latinos—that did not live in culturally commodifiable "ethnic enclaves," but in criminalized and segregated "ghettos."

In March of 2005, Paula Pereira, a twenty-two-year-old Brazilian resident of the Ironbound, and I met at Pão de Açucar, a bakery café on one of the Ironbound's main commercial arteries. As we both sipped our cafés com leite and Guaranás and ate a couple of brigadeiros, Paula mentioned reflectively, alluding to the Bohemian-style café with heavily draped chairs and vintage lamps: "In Brazil, these types of places, going to a café to eat a pastry or drink a coffee, is only for the rich. Most people cannot afford it. I had never been to a place like this before coming here. I used to sell candy in the streets! Here, anyone can go and just sit and buy something to eat. That's what I like about being in this country." When I mentioned that I hadn't seen many coffeehouses like this one in Newark, outside the Ironbound, Paula responded: "That's because of the work the Portuguese have done. I have to give them that. . . . The people here are foreigners and very hard-working, strong families, the Portuguese, the Brazilian, and even the other Hispanics that live here. They are hardworking people. Here is not like the rest of Newark." The significance attached to being able to go for a "café and pastry" resonates with García-Canclini's claim that "It's in cities that the global is imagined, and where a cultural cosmopolitanism in consumption exists along with a loss of jobs" (1995, 13).

Although Paula's family eventually had to move to North Broadway because the Ironbound was too expensive for them, her attachment to the Ironbound continued to be associated with an everyday perception of social mobility, evidenced mostly by lifestyle consumption practices *in the public sphere*, as well as her ability to draw on her own parents' narrative of overcoming obstacles in Brazil and, especially, in the United States. Without much prompting, Paula engaged in a narrative of family "overcoming" that became a staple of most formal and informal conversations with (and among) Ironbound residents and which contributed to the sentimentality of culture in the neighborhood. Pain, sacrifice, and US nationalism were impossible to disentangle in the Ironbound; having undergone pain through individual sacrifice and economic hardship rather than the "easy" route of welfare "dependency" associated with US-born minorities was a leading criterion of belonging and deservingness. The case of Portuguese, and some other migrants, in the Ironbound resonated with Veena Das's claim that "suffering mould[s] human beings into moral members of a society" (in Kleinman, Das, and Lock 1997, 71). While pain may signal the failure of social and cultural systems to alleviate suffering, it also marked individuals as moral subjects by marking an acceptance of disciplinary procedures and rules. Narratives of the self drew upon collective, national narratives, values, and scripts that saturated stories of neoliberal personhood in Newark. Stories of individual and family struggle, particularly those associated with Iberian populations who arrived in the Ironbound penniless, placed such narratives of overcoming squarely in the historical tradition of middle-class respectability regardless of material status.

Neoliberalism personhood in the United States is an extreme realization of the priority of market principles, which are now invading all areas of social life and exposing citizens to new levels of risk, as the current fiscal crisis further demonstrates (cf. Ong 1996, 211). Whose culture is deemed "commodifiable" and suitable for urban economic goals increasingly depends on emotional attributes that introduced new forms of classification and distinction (cf. Bourdieu 1984). Emotional style has become a social currency, and a new language of selfhood that seizes capital has been articulated. Emotional capitalism is the progressive fusion of market repertoires and the languages of self during the twentieth century (Illouz 2007, 108); it has imbued economic transactions and most social relationships with an unprecedented cultural attention to the linguistic management of emotions. These goals were sustained and sustaining of Newark's neoliberal aspirations and "emotional regime" (Reddy 1999).

Neoliberalism has impacted the widening class divide both nationally and globally. This volume aims to highlight the centrality of political economy by noting the role of emotion, in a variety of forms, as a less recognized phenomenon in the creation and strengthening of social difference. Evaluations of race and racism in the terrain of affect or intimate realms document the immediate, everyday ways in which neoliberalism, with its ability to reduce "big" issues to personal events, may flatten and depoliticize the public sphere and effectively keep subordinate populations at bay more effectively, even, than outright coercion (cf. Gramsci, Hoare, and Nowell-Smith 1999; Rabinowitz 1997). Everyday forms of social ambiguity, like the "glance" or pulling away when someone brushes against one's skin on the bus, frequently gave credence to particular inter-pretations of subordination; such interpretations privileged the affective qualities, feeling rules, and the emotional or sentimental realm, while oc-culting or undermining the impact of the political economy conditions on which experiences of poverty and marginality are grounded. There are different layers and rules that operate between macro accounts of the neoliberal, on the one hand, and the everyday intimate occurrences, on the other. In a postindustrial economy, the spheres of public and private, intimacy and commerce, and consumption and competency have inter-penetrated one another and have become mutually transformed, making the consumer marketplace one potential arena for securing authentic, yet bounded, forms of interpersonal connections (cf. Bernstein 2007, 21).

Epistemological Considerations

Two critical epistemological questions arise from a project in which an examination of emotion is so central: One concerns emotions as socially valid objects of knowledge (i.e., How can they be known?) and the other concerns the nature of the knowledge that emotions provide us with. A unifying assumption behind these two questions is that, just as emotions are notorious for their supposed irrationality, they are also generally held to be subjective, to tell us nothing about the outside world, to be analyz-able only within a therapeutic setting, and to be less epistemologically feasible than other tools of social analysis.

To address the first question, I demonstrate how emotions provide in-formation on the intention or orientation of those onto whom the emo-tion is projected, as well as reveal one's own affect. Thus, the information that emotions provide is always grounded in a broader social context and may enhance or diminish racialization processes among minorities in a neoliberal microsocial order. In this sense, emotions are helpful analytical tools precisely because they contribute to the "objectification" of relations and groups, yet remain largely unexplained as a key component of the ra-cialization process. Emotions have been central to the dynamics of social life and even propel everyday commercial exchanges and social experi-ences; they are the subjective barometers to judge one's own relationships to institutional structures and conditions of power and subordination.

Therefore, understanding the social production of "emotion" and related concepts like "feelings," "affect," and "sentiment" supplies im-portant, yet relatively unexamined analytical tools for social scientists concerned with how notions of difference are learned and communicated. I am in no way suggesting that examinations of power and inequality ought to be reduced to the "intimate" at the expense of broader structural levels of subordination, as Gutiérrez's (2001) critique of Stoler suggests. Quite the contrary: I am suggesting that "the intimate"—in its immediate interpersonal relations, misrecognition, and speculation— seems increasingly to be one of the few realms to which the working-class Latinos and Latin Americans in Newark had access, and in which they could vie for claims to citizenship, and express or conceal broader social justice and civil rights concerns. This is critical to a contextually driven emotional evaluation of (racialized) others. The volatility of race in everyday life has been lost in metatheorizings on race; yet, race is lived in ways that are oftentimes incomprehensible when systems of racial logic are illegible across ethnoracial groups.

Emotion norms or rules, including those behind everyday interpretations of racial systems, are produced by and function to sustain dominant institutional arrangements. If it is true that societies develop nuanced vocabularies for certain feelings, complex ideologies about emotions, and folk beliefs about affective development, my main concern in this project is how emotional knowledge and racial expertise are mutually constitutive, particularly under an urban neoliberalism. My focus, therefore, is not on the Freudian tradition of describing the "subconscious" meanings of an individual's comments or statements. Instead, I consider how emotion becomes socially produced around neoliberalism-friendly assumptions of racial difference in "temperament," "affect," "sensuality," or "desirability," and, more significantly, on how working-class Latinos and Latin American migrants educate themselves about the proper distribution of sentiments and desires. I aim to understand and decode the emotional expressions that are shaped in anticipation of how they will be perceived, or in terms of how they have been reflected on after a particular experience, and focus on the embodiment of conduct as it relate to racial learning.

Rather than a "top-down" production of affective knowledge, I am examining the "horizontal" processes that "minority" groups deploy in educating themselves and each other about the "proper" use of sentiments, affect, and desires. I argue that this is largely accomplished through a process of racial teaching and learning. More significantly, these lessons are directly related to Latino and Latin American perspectives on African Americans. Acquiring knowledge about the appropriate "feeling rules" (Hochschild 1990) associated with racial learning can be particularly challenging in transnational contexts, where individuals subscribe to competing ideological referents to understand their position within a social structure (e.g., racial democracy, biracial dyad). As racial expertise becomes a leading requirement in the Americanization process, I also take into account how Latin American regional groups are positioned differently on the grading scale.

It is important to note that "racial democracy" was simultaneously an inductive and deductive concept. Only when a majority of the US-born Latinos and Latin American migrants with whom I spoke began to describe traits associated with Brazilian "openness" to racial difference or to Puerto Ricans being "a result of three races," and to interpret everyday racial situations in light of such "cultural" distinctions, did the resonance of these comments with the tenets of racial democracy compel me to examine the term more closely. Only two Puerto Rican adults in North Broadway used the term "racial democracy"; hence, while the descriptive aspects of racial dynamics in Newark resonated with traditional conceptions of Latin American racial democracy, the term as such is, ultimately, an "ethnographer's choice." The fact that the main populations in this ethnography—"Puerto Ricans" and "Brazilians"—have been central to academic and popular discussions of racial democracy in the Caribbean and Latin America, respectively, makes them particularly suitable for the terminological choice, however. Considering that the very term "racial democracy" is an academic, top-down term, I am using it consistently with how it has come to be understood in Latin America and the Spanish-speaking Caribbean. Nevertheless, I also take into account, as a central aspect of my work, the instances in which these understandings of "race" did not match or did not entirely subscribe to what conceptions of Latin American racial democracy might have dictated, or instances in which interpretations varied along nationality, regional, class, or gendered lines. I center more concertedly on how certain tenets of Latin American views of "racial democracy"—particularly those around "racial mixing"—influenced African American–Latino relations, particularly those related to the area of emotion, affect, and intimacy.

This volume proposes that an emotional aesthetics, reinforced by a reinvigorated cartography of racial democracy, has effectively become a powerful site through which state racializing, surveillance practices, and urban neoliberal aspirations are coded in predominantly minority contexts, like Newark. At the community level, emotions must be examined in the context of particular regimes of power, and how race and class compositions of neighborhoods complicate emotional management within its institutions. A key finding was that racism in the US context (given the Brazilian and Puerto Rican tendency to leave discussions of "race" outside the realm of discourse) has been constructed as a problem of "affect," not structural discrimination, in the minds of many Latinos and Latin American migrants (cf. Oboler 1995, 23). Even the most blatant discussions of segregation or slavery eventually focus on the "feelings" of individuals or on "self-esteem" issues. How and why does that happen? In Latin America, the notion of *mejorar la raza* places race in the realm of the private and renders it "changeable" (88). This has also become common among Latinos in Newark, where racism is often viewed as a "self-esteem" issue or racial openness revealed in dating choices. A focus on a cartography of racial democracy, as is intended in this volume, provides the opportunity to engage in an analysis of race and affect that recognizes the privileged role of colonial, imperial, and neoliberal structures in enabling intimate knowledge (cf. Stoler 2001; Gutiérrez 2001).

An emotional urban aesthetics, and its related affective or sentimental meanings, is constituted through a broad range of communicative and linguistic practices, but is not circumscribed exclusively to language; instead, the emotional urban aesthetic that I propose cannot exist without a concurrent investigation of the nature of categories of social difference, power inequalities, and a clear understanding of state objectives. Most commonly in everyday life, emotions are alluded to rather than overtly described and require a decoding task, a process of "reading" complex covert messages. For real dangers such as those noted in Newark, the narrative mode of the account is factual, realistic, detailed, and sequential, while feelings are hidden behind the factuality. To capture not only the descriptive aspect of these events, but also the deeply emotional aspects of racial processes, I've adopted a largely phenomenological approach. In an effort to avoid artificially separating scales of analysis, I focus on the identifications and terms that are important to informants, and when and how they utilize more than one scalar or identity concept simultaneously, such as immigrants discussing their sites of origin across the sea as both intimate and transnational, or using both "American" and "foreign" as national markers in their self-conceptions. This technique follows a tradition of scholarly work on embodiment, which considers different facets of experience as occuring simultaneously rather than as neatly separable, and which draw from phenomenology, as they consider subjects' intimate, shifting, and in-motion experiences of their lives as the key starting point for scholarly analysis (Husserl 1970; Merleau-Ponty 2004). Recently, anthropologists have turned attention to embodiment and the senses as a way for scholarly analyses to more closely mirror informants' experiences (Stoler 2001). In an era of globalization, this has evoked new interest precisely because, unlike starting from "social position," it allows access to experiences of movement and the simultaneity of different facets of subjectivity (Massumi 1993). This approach is uniquely well suited for analyzing experience in volatile and highly dynamic contexts, where multiple identifications are constantly deployed.

My framework analyzes urban emotional episodes, particularly those saturated with racial meaning, by considering the affective phenomenology of the experience; the environmental antecedents that led to the incident; the implications of those antecedents to the self; the social valuation of the experience; the self-management habits that become activated and the symbolic means of communicating the experience. Although I did not set out to focus on a specific emotion, the episodes that were more salient and created the greater template for discussion were those that highlighted some behavior—particularly, the one considered "aggressive." This does not deny the fact that specific emotions generate specific forms of knowledge, but it does suggest that my own emotional attention gravitated toward incidents that could be potentially explosive or misapprehended. This claim begs a discussion of methodology that focuses on how the epistemological concerns discussed here are addressed in practice.

Some Notes on Method

Witnessing people's lives—their life transitions, everyday interactions, and their contact with institutions and strangers—provides the cornerstone of ethnographic research. From the spring of 2001 through the summer of 2007 I conducted the various phases of this ethnographic research in the two predominantly US-born Latino and Latin American migrant areas of Newark, New Jersey: the Ironbound, where almost half of the population is Brazilian, and the predominantly Puerto Rican North Broadway neighborhood.

While Puerto Ricans consisted mostly of a second- or even third-generation US-born population in Newark, Brazilians began arriving in significant numbers in the late 1980s and 1990s and are thus considered "New Latinos" in transnational studies parlance. My methodological approach is designed to expand on our knowledge of "New Latinos," while also focusing on a population (Brazilians) that has existed at the fringes of this very Latinidad, but which, in Newark, also contend with living in a city where "Latino" generally means "Puerto Rican." Partly because of their lower numbers and more contemporary migration patterns, but also due to language differences, Brazilians have chosen to position themselves either as black or as white, while avoiding a "Hispanic" identity, which they associate with "immigrants" from Spanish-speaking countries. Although I do, to a degree, note the significantly different access that "Brazilians" and "Puerto Ricans" *as groups* have to institutional and commercial arenas in Newark (chapter 1), my project is not intended as a contrast between two discrete groups. Rather, I am more concerned with how "groups" (and "discreteness") emerge in the first place and how populations get racially marked and position themselves in new and conventional ways according to predictable and unexpected outcomes of urban neoliberalism.

Between the summers of 2001 and 2002, I began archival research at the Newark Public Library and the New Jersey Historical Society on the history of Puerto Rican migration to Newark. I also conducted archival work at the Ironbound Community Corporation, since I was interested in how the two predominantly Latino or Latin American areas of Newark—North Broadway and the Ironbound—had come to occupy such different positions in the citywide urban development projects. I also conducted preliminary interviews with the leadership, staff, and clients of three community organizations in North Broadway and one organization in the Ironbound. In North Broadway I attended ESL, GED, job readiness, and citizenship classes, where I was able to meet a diverse group of Latinos, all residents of Newark. In the Ironbound, there were fewer not-for-profit organizations, so I attended the Uncle Sam Institute, where Brazilian and Brazilian American youth could take Portuguese language and Brazilian history courses that met the requirements of the Brazilian Department of Education, so that they would not fall behind in school should their families decided to return to Brazil. I met the parents of many high school students and their concerns over urban development and safety almost always centered on a preoccupation with "violence" in public schools and street "aggression" in particular neighborhoods; African Americans were frequently viewed as the perpetrators of such "aggression," and many of the parents whom I interviewed early on relayed how their own children would tell them about how violent "even the [black] women!" were.

By the spring of 2002, I came to view high schools as "points of entry" into the lives and community experiences of Latin American migrants and US-born Latinos in these two neighborhoods. My research mostly centered on the students, parents, teachers, and communities related to the two public high schools with the highest Latino and Latin American student populations in Newark. The project was not about "schooling," however, in the sense that I did not focus on curriculum, bilingual education, and administrative structures (though these are very pertinent top-ics).While my initial connection was with Brazilian migrants and US-born Puerto Rican youth in East Side High School (ESHS) in the Ironbound and Barringer High School (BHS) in North Broadway, I also interviewed and spoke informally with adults who interacted with the young people, as well as with friends around their own age who did not attend these two schools. I realize that public schools are important citizen-making in-stitutions and have increasingly become implicated in neoliberal urban projects in and of themselves, and I take these considerations into ac-count when pertinent. Nevertheless, the main role of the public school in this ethnography is a methodological one, a way to identify a population of youth more or less representative of their respective neighborhoods.

Despite notable exceptions of instances of Latino-black friendships and solidarity, the interactions between Latinos or Latin American mi-grants and African Americans were usually riddled with suspicion and mistrust and these young people often lacked the public space and tools to examine what was hastily read as black "aggressiveness." Concerns about safety and the need to figure out one's relationship to a chang-ing urban context generated great socioeconomic insecurity, emotional exhaustion, and cognitive struggles. Because young people are usually excluded from discussions of urban development but central to concerns about public safety (as perpetrators of violence, rowdiness, or disruption) the main ways in which my informants engaged these discussions in-volved great emotional investment into disentangling racial situations that felt uncertain or unfamiliar to them. It is important to note that, while I got to meet many of my informants while they were still in high school, a significant part of our interaction took place once they had graduated; hence, while "youth" was an important analytical category in the beginning of my project, the fact that the data presented here pertains more often to these young people's post–high school lives, their work experiences, family relations and friendships, and community con-nections, makes it inaccurate to understand this as an ethnography of "youth" or "youth culture" in any traditional sense.

More specifically, I engage in participant observation and the analy-sis of "diagnostic events" (Moore 1987) that are attuned to how people move through space, identify emotionally charged situations, use ob-jects around them, dress, and carry themselves, a technique of collecting detailed habitus descriptions (Bourdieu 1977, 1984). Between 2002 and 2007 I conducted participant observation, semi-structured life history interviews, and focus groups with youth, parents, staff, and community activists and merchants whom I had met through the two public high schools. At ESHS I attended bilingual (Portuguese and Spanish) classes about once a week and also volunteered to help the teacher of a "job readiness" class; the class was loosely defined and oftentimes the teacher allowed me to conduct the sessions as "focus groups" on a variety of topics related to the concerns of this study. I also attended talent shows, sports events, and faculty meetings, although most of the interactions with students took place outside the school, particularly after the first year of the fieldwork. These interactions included going out to eat at local places, attending church services, street festivals, family get-togethers, weddings, and funerals, going on immigration-related errands, and visiting workplaces. While ESHS prides itself for its diversity of nationalities, the physical structure of the school—according to which each one of the four floors has a particular "character," so that the second floor is the "ghetto floor," the third floor is the "immigrant floor," and the fourth floor is the "Brazilian floor"—predictably dictated individuals' relationship to one another. I take these distinctions into consideration in my research.

From the beginning, I felt I had greater access to BHS than to ESHS and, initially, I attributed it to me being Puerto Rican, a valued "bond" among many of the Puerto Ricans I met in North Newark, and being from Rutgers, where the principal had gone to school in the 1970s. Eventually, I wondered if it had more to do with the fact that the school is so marginalized and criminalized that anyone showing care or concern is well received. At BHS I volunteered to facilitate a "girls' group," direct senior-year projects, and to help with the creation of a parent-teacher group. BHS's student body is predominantly Puerto Rican—both US- and island-born—although there is a significant presence of Dominicans and African Americans. While I participated in a number of school events, most of the follow-up interactions with students took place outside of the school. It is important to note that most of the students with whom I ended up in closer contact were graduating seniors at the time I met them, so oftentimes my relation with them continued to unfold after they graduated and were either in college and/or pursuing jobs.

In the summer and fall of 2004, I extended my fieldwork to the cities of Belo Horizonte, Brazil, and Santurce, Puerto Rico, where some of the Brazilians and Puerto Ricans whom I met in Newark had either lived prior to migrating or had extended relatives and school contacts with whom they had stayed in touch. Although most of the data from this portion of the fieldwork has not made it to this volume, some aspects of it—those concerning how young people in two public and two private schools in Brazil and Puerto Rico viewed "Black America" and "return migrants" from the United States (and themselves assumed therapeutic readings of these populations)—are introduced in various sections of this book.

From the spring of 2007 through the spring of 2010, I conducted follow-up focus groups and individual interviews in Newark. I was able to track many of the students whom I had interviewed back in 2001. I also taught an undergraduate seminar at Rutgers titled "Latino Newark" in which college students were able to become familiar with the city and I was able to connect many of the students in that university seminar, as well as other students at Rutgers, with some of the high school students whom I had met through my fieldwork with the hope that some mentorship relationships could emerge. Toward the end of my fieldwork, Newark acquired some national notoriety in the media and popular culture. The city's charismatic mayor, Cory Booker, who had been the central character of an award-winning documentary film based on his electoral race titled *Street Fight*, also appeared on the *Oprah Winfrey Show* as a quasi-spiritual leader of an otherwise dilapidated city. This was followed in the fall of 2009 by *Brick City*, a seven-hour documentary series produced aired on the Sundance Channel under the executive endorsement of Forrest Whittaker and which was compared to the fictional HBO series *The Wire*. Weeks later, a reportedly friendly bantering between Cory Booker and Conan O'Brien also ensued as part of the comedy lineup of NBC's *The Tonight Show*, in which O'Brien criticized Newark and Booker defended the city. Mainstream news channels were covering Newark in unprecedented ways. This popular notoriety, in the context of devastating poverty, unemployment, and the 2008 foreclosure crisis, also points to the complexity and multilayered quality of US urban areas.

Cities like Newark have several kinds of sites, demanding a different brand of multisited ethnography based not only on geographical distance but also on the complicated dynamics of what Katherine Morrissey (1997) calls "mental territories," places where social, economic, political, and cognitive factors have a part to play in the construction of spatial identities and the creation of "socially meaningful cartographies" (Jackson 2001, 9). The field site stands as the empirical ground of anthropology as a discipline, as the anthropologist is forced to create boundaries and forge distinctions between "here" and "there" to circumscribe the area of his or her fieldwork and downscale the terms and scale of analysis. In a number of ways, this project contributes to the growing number of so-called multisited ethnographies.[17] While the primary site of the study is Newark, New Jersey, the project examines different neighborhoods within the city and follows individuals as they navigate distinct social and cognitive maps. This multisited ethnographic project invariably highlights the ambiguities, ambivalences, and misapprehensions that are common in all ethnographic encounters; these are heightened in light of other power and economic differentials—including one's institutional affiliations to Rutgers University—but also in a context in which notions of belonging are measured by subjective readings, behavior, and mannerisms, and what I came to understand as elusive forms of urban cosmopolitan competencies (as examined in chapter 6). Attending to such asymmetries is critical to examining the methodological and practical decisions made and addressing the research process and configuration of the production of ethnographic knowledge.

An Ethnographer's Craft: Representation and Self-Positioning

I would have never guessed [that you are] Puerto Rican. Around here [in the Ironbound], you're either Portuguese, if you're pasty white, or Brazilian if you're a little darker. I would have guessed [you were] Brazilian . . . or from South America somewhere. But you really don't look Puerto Rican. Not at all! SPANIARD, IRONBOUND RESTAURANT MANAGER, THINKING HE'S PAYING ME A COMPLIMENT

You're the first person from Rutgers University that sets foot in this school in years; That's why our students go into the Marines instead of going to the State University of New Jersey. PUERTO RICAN HIGH SCHOOL PRINCIPAL IN NORTH BROADWAY, REPROACHFUL OF RUTGERS AND OF ME FOR BEING AFFILIATED TO THE UNIVERSITY

Filmmaker Jean Renoir poignantly states: "You are never so revealing about yourself than when telling someone else's story" (quoted in Garner 2006). My interest in how neoliberal projects, particularly those related to urban development and concerns with "safety," come to influence the emotive or intimate aspects of human experiences and personhood in cities has been largely fueled by two seemingly unrelated personal conditions: not having relied on a car for the past twenty years and, my sorely lacking—by most Latino youths' standards—urban or cosmopolitan competency.

Not having a car made me, sometimes unwillingly, privy to the way in which urban spaces and "security" stage interpersonal encounters. I became intrigued by how situations became "about race," even as (or because) they were articulated in terms of affect or evaluations of someone's "aggressiveness" or "attitude." Shouting matches between individuals in the streets, bus stops, or school hallways were legible according to radically different points of reference, and the flattening of political solidarity in favor of pathologizing racial difference along affective lines seemed to be a strong common ground framing this urban stage. The inevitability of eavesdropping into personal conversations, witnessing moments of tension that escalated or dissipated almost unexpectedly, along with direct or indirect institutional or commercial interventions regulating how people navigated streets, train platforms, or public buildings, all became part of a pedestrian cosmology of the city. Navigating Newark, largely on foot or by public transportation, made me more acutely aware of how the horizontal (minority-minority) operations of race were evaluated, silenced, and understood in ways that effectively concealed vertical (minority-majority) forms of subordination. Perhaps predictably, tensions and conflict were rarely sparked by philosophical debates about subordination or inequality, but from assessments of seemingly imponderable subtleties—a glance, a gesture, a posture. I became intrigued by how these interpretive repertoires were generated by spatial formations, in often rough, disjointed correspondence with neoliberalism, urban development, concerns with safety, and national political discourse.

My lack of "urban competence"—which I later came to see as an alternative form of capital or cosmopolitan competency—was first noted by Amarilis Guzmán, a Puerto Rican student at a public high school in North Broadway, who was surprised by my insistence in looking for a motivation behind an incident in which girls "jumped" other girls in Newark: "I bet you've never been in a fight. . . . I can tell you haven't punched nobody . . . in your life!" She intuitively knew that I was unlikely to be able to fight anyone, to fend for myself, or be an asset to anyone who needed an extra pair of fighting arms. After the initial curiosity about my occupation, place of birth, and motivation for wanting to talk to them, most of the people whom I met remarked on my being "too girlie" or not tough enough. Being "too girlie," particularly when lacking an evident ability to "be street," was always uncool.

Ironically, of all the contexts in which being street savvy is valued, the academic world of urban ethnography is right at the top. In the case of urban ethnographers, being capable of tapping into one's own street credentials and approaching authenticity by highlighting one's ability to be a real "homeboy" confers significant degree of intellectual and academic capital. Male urban ethnographers, in particular, reap personal and professional benefits from their entry into "dangerous" fieldwork settings—mastering the rudiments of boxing in fraternal and competitive "ghetto" spaces (Wacquant 2004; Venkatesh 2008), running with street-gang members (Hagedorn 1998) or displaying bravado by declaring that one is ready to fight or punch if called upon (Sánchez Jankowski 1991).

There are numerous instances of the pursuit of masculine-gendered affirmation through ethnographic research and reinforce their own and others' perceptions of them as enviably "hip" or macho (cf. Bernstein 2007, 241n27).

I am enthralled by stories of strong girls who can fend for themselves, and who have the kind of alternative capital that I lack. In this sense, my own emotional and affective schemas came into play and were manifested in the form of respect and admiration for the many young women whom I considered self-reliant, strong, and fearless, as well as a sense of personal inadequacy as I recognized my own lack of urban competency. These (perceived or real) personal inadequacies mark the embodied practices of my work on feelings, racial democracy, and urban neoliberalism. When considering the kinds of affect and sentiments called forth by this ethnographic project, therefore, context-based conceptions of emotional adequacy and urban competency are central to the epistemological questions addressed here.

Ethnography is always an imperfect, and some claim futile, attempt to portray an elusive everyday reality that overpowers or outdoes any form of representation. The ethnographic project, as most anthropologists have come to recognize, is not a series of unadulterated reflections of what has been observed or represented in static portraits. Rather, the data generated from fieldwork is also a reflection of what the researcher brings into these sites, as well as how the sites, people, and circumstances determine the trajectory of certain aspects of the project. They are a reflection on personal, material, and ideological transactions that sometimes do not make it to the final text. In my case, the transactions were many and spanned across various neighborhoods, cities, and countries; more often than not, they were revealing of privilege and inequality in and of themselves. These exchanges involved, among other things, the challenges of learning new languages—literally and metaphorically—so that exchanges took place not only in English, Spanish, and Portuguese (or Spanglish, Portinglese, and Portunhol!), but also in light of class, racial, gender, and institutional positionalities.

As indicated in the quotes at the beginning of this section, being judged on "looks" was important in the Ironbound, whereas town/gown distinctions—the fact that I was from Rutgers, an institution that was responsible for uprooting hundreds of Puerto Rican families from the Central Ward in the 1960s and 1970s (chapter 1)—were critical to how I was received in the predominantly Puerto Rican area. Nevertheless, while not an unproblematic genre, ethnography still provides a uniquely textured engagement with data. It is arguably one of the few tools we have to gauge the intimate, everyday impact of broader social and economic policies in the lives of individuals and formation of communities.

Structure of the Argument/Organization of the Book

This book is organized around a series of "ethnographic episodes" that, when taken together, provide insight into Newark's emotional and racial landscapes. Each episode or vignette is reflective of how emotive characterizations of race and racialized forms of affect intersected and mutually constituted fundamental aspects of neoliberal personhood in the political economy of the city. As examined through the theoretical framework outlined above, the socially polarizing impact of neoliberal projects often remained hidden behind (albeit interconnected with and dependent upon) the effective naturalization of an emotive common-sense. In the context of this urban emotive commonsense, Latinos and Latin Americans became street therapists. They analyzed, evaluated, and interpreted racial situations, oftentimes by imbuing race with affective glosses and developing a cartography of racial democracy that drew from US and Latin American racial projects. An important objective of center-ing on ethnographic episodes in the following chapters is to trace the quotidian interactions that have the potential to unearth what is buried, not only examine what is evident, in the intersection of race, affect, and neoliberalism.

Building upon the theoretical framework outlined throughout this introduction, subsequent chapters situate six ethnographic episodes that are then deconstructed, analyzed, and situated in broader political eco-nomic and historical contexts. Rather than following a chronological order, the ethnographic episodes highlight a series of themes that, when taken together, provide the empirical base of the theoretical framework proposed in this volume.

Chapter 1 begins with an interaction that took place in the lobby of a federal building in Newark between an African American Department of Homeland Security officer, a white delivery man, and a Latin American woman with a teenage son going through the security search process. This incident provides the point of departure for an analysis of how each party might relate to Newark's social history and the foregrounding of the city's "emotional regime" (Reddy 2001). Drawing from archival docu-ments, newspaper articles, and fictional and social scientific literature written about "Newark," this chapter shows how "aggression" became a meta-narrative of emotion in Newark. The chapter traces the "feel" of the city from industrial era to the present, by focusing on how African Americans become associated with dictating the "mood" of the city and what that means for other residents of Newark.

Chapter 2 documents the showing of a movie about the participation of Puerto Rican soldiers in the Korean War at the Newark Public Library, and the subsequent conversation between a Puerto Rican mother who did not want her son to enlist in the military versus an Ecuadorian migrant mother who thought that would be the only way to ensure discipline among young Latino men in the Puerto Rican neighborhood of North Broadway. The chapter focuses on the "delinquent [US] citizenship" of Puerto Ricans in light of the development of a "politics of worth" that ultimately demands that only through death or the proximity to death can some populations acquire value as neoliberal subjects.

I explore how highly emotive perspectives on trust, intent, and respectability influence the relationship between African Americans and Puerto Ricans, and how black and Latino youth and adults understood US citizenship, "deservingness," and "self-help." In particular, I focus on how the recruitment strategies of US military personnel in North Broadway high schools and the proliferation of self-help organizations highlight the "delinquent citizenship" (Ramos-Zayas 2004) of Puerto Ricans in ways that interrupt black-brown alliances.

Chapter 3 begins in a Brazilian beauty salon in the Luso-Brazilian area of the Ironbound. When an African American middle-class client comes into the salon to get her eyebrows done, one of the Brazilian stylists jokes about how the black woman is so dark that it is pointless to even notice her eyebrows. This episode launches a discussion on how systems of race and color in Latin America and the United States converge under a "cartography of racial democracy." It also considers the role of a globally exoticized "Brazilian culture" on ethnic marketing. Centering on the everyday social interactions between Luso-Brazilians, "Hispanics," and African Americans in the Ironbound, the chapter focuses on perspectives on "color," the self-packaging of an emotive persona, and a sensorial form of affect grounded in particular forms of racial humor. The ability to create commercially profitable "cultures" and package oneself accordingly becomes fertile ground for resurrecting views of "racial democracy," especially those that link racial mixture to intimacy, attractiveness, and a higher emotive and moral ground. The Latino identity of Brazilians is critically examined here.

Chapter 4 describes how a teary-eyed Brazilian woman approached me at a bakery in the Ironbound where she declared what became a common Ironbound narrative: that Portuguese women were jealous of Brazilian women because they thought that all Brazilian women were after their Portuguese husbands. This chapter focuses on the gendered and sexualized aspects of the urban emotional commonsense of cities and neighborhoods. Examining attraction and desire as neoliberal feelings, this chapter also connects how a gendered "stereotype of the tropics" associated with certain groups of women in fact sustain a budding New Jersey sex work industry.

Chapter 5 begins with Amarilis Guzmán, a young Puerto Rican lesbian resident of North Broadway, being visibly agitated when another Puerto Rican friend of hers is jumped by a group of African American women. This chapter explores how discussions of young women being jumped or jumping other young women are constructed in light of how aggression and anger are neoliberal feelings associated specifically with images of black lesbians in Newark. While the previous chapter examined notions of sexualized femininity, this chapter focuses on a masculinization and criminalization of black women, according to highly heteronormative and classed codes of comportment. Moreover, the chapter examines the nationally documented 2007 schoolyard shootings of four African American college students by a group of mostly undocumented Latin American migrants, and the ambivalence in reading this crime as an "anti-black" versus "anti-gay" hate crime.

Chapter 6 begins with a young Brazilian woman commenting on how an Ecuadorian male classmate of hers has gone from being "a happy immigrant kid" to becoming a "depressed thug." This final chapter shows how mastering negative affect—particularly, certain performances of depression, seriousness, being withdrawn—is a fundamental aspect of the Americanization process among certain Latin American groups. Shedding an image of "backwardness" or "rural," associated with some Latin American immigrants, in favor of becoming an urban competent neoliberal subject was critical to the successful Americanization of certain migrant populations. At the center of this chapter is the process of "racial learning," as a way to understand how US-born Latinos and Latin American migrants oftentimes become street therapists, that is, speculators that delve into the emotional lives of African Americans, as they theorize and learn about US racialization processes. Despite the connections of Blackness with aggression in Newark, this chapter highlights particular contexts in which Blackness is associated with a high level of urban capital and cosmopolitan competency. The valorization of this urban knowhow or implicit social knowledge, associated with a selective desire for Blackness, nevertheless, did not require (and in fact sometimes impeded) a productive relationship between Latinos and African Americans. This chapter highlights the acculturating power of Blackness, as well as how, for many Latinos, the Americanization process involved not "becoming white," something to which they realized they did not have access, but of "making Blackness right."

The conclusion to the volume considers some of the implications of an increasing focus on a neoliberally friendly form of personhood, and what this transition from a focus on material and structural conditions to a focus on interiority and affect does to racial relations and urban life. Rather than arriving at a facile political view that renders a focus on structure as positive and a focus on affect as negative, the conclusion suggests a more nuanced state of affairs: one in which both structure and affect are mutually constitutive of one another and provide effective spaces for social critique among the most disenfranchised urban residents.

ONE

The Feel that Sells Newark: From "Aggressive" City to Neoliberal-Friendly Emotional Regime

Anyone can become angry—that is easy. But to be angry with the right person, to the right degree, at the right time, for the right purpose, and in the right way. That is not easy. ARISTOTLE

On a cold mid-January day in 2003, as I waited for a friend of mine to come down from his office, I stood by the security checkpoint of the federal building that houses Newark's Department of Homeland Security. While waiting, I witnessed an everyday occurrence that caught my ethnographer's eye. As an obviously overworked, heavyset African American female guard tended to a lanky, white delivery guy while simultaneously directing visitors through the scanning devices, a Latina woman and two teenage boys tried to enter the lobby through a nonfunctioning glass door. "Do not use that door! Do. Not. Use. That. Door!!!" the guard shouted. "Don't you see the sign?" she impatiently asked. The Latino woman nervously fumbled through some papers to show the guard what seemed to be an official letter. The guard directed her to pass through the metal detector and someone else informed the woman where to go. "This gotta be America!" proclaimed the white delivery guy in what sounded like a heavy Brooklyn Italian accent. Looking at the African American security guard expecting a degree of complicity, he added with obvious disapproval, "Only in America can't people understand English. Here, if you can't speak Spanish, you better get out!" The guard shook her head in agreement, then paused, seeming to refrain from verbalizing her agreement. With what I perceived as hesitation, she looked my way, as I had obviously been paying much more attention to the exchange than she may have thought natural or even appropriate. I looked slightly away and, shortly after, spotted my friend and headed out to lunch. This quotidian episode is not very remarkable, yet it provides a good point of entrance into Newark as a material, symbolic, and emotive space.

Emotions are an integral part of the historical unfolding of politically significant events, institutions, and practices in Newark, New Jersey. In this study I focus on moments of heightened emotional exchange and analyze how they sustain or challenge the interests of the marketplace under neoliberalism. In Newark, "anger" and "aggression" became dominant emotions, or "meta-sentiments," inscribed through the interpretation, narration, and policy outcome of salient historical events in Newark's urban landscape (Myers 1986).[1] The neoliberal policies of the 1980s and 1990s implicitly required that a normative style of emotional management—in which characterizations of the city as aggressive or angry were concealed or redressed—be instituted if attractive real estate, well-attended artistic venues, and the promotion of tourism were to be successful urban-development strategies. Therefore, examining the emergence and control of aggression in Newark requires an analysis of historical moments that aimed to solidify particular social structures; in this sense, it also requires an examination of how old and new forms of capitalist development entered into synergistic interaction with a politics of individual agency.

Rather than presenting a traditional history of Newark, a task that others have already done masterfully (e.g., Price 2008), I examine Newark in relation to two major themes that characterize the modernist public sphere: the social production of the city and the regulation of emotions. Henri Lefebvre (1991) notes how references to the image of most cities are often ensconced in a language that depicts some inherently pathological social condition, a putative sickness of society, while obfuscating the fact that the modern city is a product of a capitalist or neocapitalist system (City of Newark 1959).[2] This perspective is central to popular images of Newark, as well to the everyday lives of residents, workers, and visitors. I want to add to Lefebvre's discussion, however, by suggesting that Newark's perceived pathology is not based on just any form of illness but specifically on *mental* illness and an emotional inadequacy projected onto its racialized populations. An emotional regime was established in Newark according to which the welfare of certain populations, particularly the black "underclass," was attributed to their inappropriate emotional style—an embodied form of the city's aggressiveness.

"From Riot to Respectability": Historicizing Anger and the Emotional Style of the Newark Renaissance

Visions of racial violence and urban decay that crystallized in our collective memory around the time of the 1967 riots still dominate the popular imagination and function as a dividing line in Newark's collective historical consciousness.[3] Carmen Morales, a Puerto Rican parent-volunteer at a public high school in North Broadway, was one of many Newark residents who lamented Newark's falling from grace:

Newark used to be a great metropolis. Like New York. Theatres everywhere. You could walk out on a Saturday night and there were thousands of people on the streets. But, they destroyed everything. You could hear the snipers at night. Some people had to show an ID to get into their own houses. After the rebellion, all the stores and theatres were destroyed . . . and to this day, many buildings are still abandoned. . . . Every part of the city was affected. Every part of the country knew about Newark and Newark got a bad reputation. All they saw was angry blacks. The violence, aggression. Big companies, like Borden, eventually ended up closing because they couldn't lure employees. If they wanted to transfer someone from Chicago to the Newark branch, people would be like "Newark? No way I'm going there!" Many jobs were lost. Blacks were not qualified to take up those vacant jobs. They didn't have the skills needed.

Lefebvre's "logistics of visualization and of metaphorization" (1991) provide a good lens through which to understand how Carmen Morales' phenomenological experience of Newark, past and present, involves the codification of particular scenes and actions from her everyday life and an awareness of how they have changed over time. As suggested in Carmen's recollection, as well as in multiple conversations I had with other Newark residents, everyday social exchanges, memories, images, and daily uses of the built environment in Newark frequently evoke images of the "riots" or the "rebellion," as well as speculations about "those [former Newark residents] who left" or "angry blacks." Those who stayed came to witness an urban change that altered most, if not all, aspects of their lives and identities at a most intimate level. To them, the riots provided the precise date to affix to the death of Newark. Very few cities have experienced events that are as radically embodied—experienced not only at a cognitive, but also at a sensorial, and even moral, metaphysical level. As was also the case in other US cities, incidents of conflict and particularly the racially marked "rioters"—the angry blacks in Carmen's narrative—were retrospectively viewed as the cause of decay, even when the riots were, in fact, the culmination of long-brewing racial tensions, restricted employment opportunities, residential segregation, and the lack of a social infrastructure to provide adequate housing, public health, and education dating back to the post–World War II period.[4]

Rarely was "slum clearance," rather than the 1967 riots, the entry point into everyday narratives of Newark's "decay" (Hayden 1967). Nevertheless, Newark has been rightly called "a living laboratory for nearly every bad planning idea of the twentieth century."[5] Accounts of the lived experiences of space must consider how place is produced and conceived in light of citywide policies, urban planning, and, in the case of Newark, the "slum clearance" in the 1950s and 1960s.[6] Urban renewal attempts within the city destroyed whole neighborhoods, replacing low-rise, vernacular residences with mismanaged public housing projects. The new interstate highways linking Newark to adjacent suburbs cut the city into pieces, dividing and isolating neighborhoods, and increasing levels of segregation.

Led by the Newark Housing Authority (NHA), Newark was the first city in New Jersey and among the earliest in the United States to begin an urban renewal program under the 1949 Title I Act of the Federal Housing Authority.[7] As Newark historian Clement Price (2008) has documented, following World War II, veterans who lived in Newark took advantage of the GI Bill to attain a college education and, eventually, their upward mobility led them to the nearby New Jersey suburbs. The NHA monopolized the sources of federal funding, as the Newark Economic Development Committee, a rival group composed of downtown business owners, advocated increased investment in Newark's downtown at the expense of residential neighborhoods (Kaplan 1963, 94).

Corporations like Prudential Insurance tried to help restructure the city after the 1967 riots by building fortress-like towers, connected to Penn Station–Newark and to other corporate buildings, bypassing the streets below. The city developed a policy of granting generous tax breaks to major institutions—colleges, universities, museums, libraries, hospitals, churches, and government properties—resulting in the majority of Newark's most valuable properties being tax exempt. Throughout the heyday of "slum clearance," a major characteristic of Newark's urban-renewal program was that those groups that urged central planning were the same groups that demanded fiscal control, tax reductions, a city-manager government, and an end to public housing.[8] The mayor effectively controlled the local communities, so that, for example, entire neighborhoods could be designated as "blighted" and targets of clearance whenever necessary, and oftentimes without much evidence or consensus about what constituted "decay" (Kaplan 1963).

The somewhat arbitrary designation of a community as "blighted" suggests that this targeted clearance was about rendering invisible a particular kind of undesirable (poor and black). The NHA's plan was to concentrate public housing construction in "Negro areas," with private redevelopment in the less-dilapidated areas to the west. Blacks would be relocated from the areas set for redevelopment to massive public housing projects that became spaces of racial containment.[9] The most important substantive norm guiding slum clearance was that "anything bringing new capital into Newark was good, and the most important procedural norm [was] the requirement that 'conflicts be settled through informal bargaining, not through overt attacks or public agitation" (Kaplan 1963, 167). Agitation was the background against which social policy was drafted and implemented.

Along with most major industrial centers in the United States, Newark had fallen from grace by the 1960s. Images of "angry blacks" dominated Newark's representation in the national media, obliterating historical evidence of urban decay that predated the riots. The centrality of these images that permanently attached anger to black bodies led to multiple levels of discourse—from national narratives to everyday conversations among people like Carmen and her neighbors—and contributed to a particular kind of emotive inscription or feel associated with Newark.

Since the 1980s, and once again inspired by the interest of corporations and private developers, the Newark city government made the development of a downtown—under the banner of the "Newark Renaissance"—a priority. Unlike other midsize cities stumbling from the loss of their manufacturing bedrock, Newark's location ten miles from Manhattan, its surrounding wealthy suburbs, expanding seaport, international airport, and commuter rail lines were commonly cited as blessings that could allow the city to become an urban renewal success. Newark began to be marketed as an important gateway in the heart of the most economically powerful metropolitan region in the United States.[10]

In the 1980s and 1990s Newark became a prime example of an aspiring neoliberal city. Selective state retrenchment and deregulation, along with the privatization of public spaces and privileging of free market approaches to development, provided the basis on which arguments for efficient technologies of government were fostered under neoliberal economic and urban policies.[11] Despite the dismantling of a social welfare state that is suggested as evidence of state shrinkage, it would be a fallacy to indiscriminately equate neoliberalism with a lack of government intervention or laissez faire market policies (Chomsky 1999; cf. Caldeira 2000b).[12] Instead, it is important to trace the qualitatively different kinds of intervention that neoliberal policies enable, particularly in light of cultural industries, private corporations, and business interests that in fact thrive on government subsidies. Gentrification, a cultural and tourist industry of museums, stadiums, and other entertainment venues, and a selectively commercialized cultural and retail market become central aspects of the process of resignifying the "inner city" under neoliberalism (cf. di Leonardo 1998).

The opening of the first Starbucks in Newark in 2000 became evidence of governmental success, as documented in an article that describes how the mayor at the time, Sharpe James, "christened an espresso machine during the opening of a Starbucks on Broad Street, [while] 40 travel agents toured the city's sites [sic] and sounds. The two separate events merged when agents stopped to have samples of mango tiazzis, mochas and lemon and chocolate sweets at the trendy coffeehouse."[13] Like downtown revival projects in other US cities, the Newark Renaissance has largely relied on the promotion of the arts to ameliorate the deeply seeded consequences of deindustrialization and recession by creating a profitable commercial machine focused on leisure, tourism, and conspicuous consumption as an antidote to urban decline.[14] In January of 2002, the US Department of Housing and Urban Development designated Newark a "Renewal Community," making it eligible to share in an estimated $17 million in tax incentives to stimulate job growth, promote economic development, and create affordable housing (Dumenigo 2002, 15). The celebratory tone of the Newark Renaissance is evidenced in multiple print media.[15] Like other urban centers, Newark compensated for its rapid deindustrialization through growth in the service sector, promoting high-end financial and business services, pursuing the arts, entertainment, and tourism, and a reformulation of the real estate industry, either through subsidies or deregulation.

Neoliberal urban policies were instituted in the context of a decentralized and partially dismantled welfare state that left governments with a lack of redistributive resources, provided legitimacy to redevelopment of any kind, including the kind that aimed to deconcentrate poverty and attract middle-class residents without caring much about eradicating poverty (Crump 2003). In Newark, these urban development goals worked in tandem with an increasing reliance on technological devices aimed to promote "safety" through surveillance. Everyday efforts to render "the poor" invisible (through physical surveillance of youth who don't act, dress, or behave appropriately, and through the codification of such actions as part of an emotional handicap) are intended to convince prospective wealthier, whiter buyers that they can come in and not feel threatened.

Urban development and safety discourses are central to the neoliberal agenda in cities, particularly in cities with large concentrations of racialized populations, like Newark. The goal of "return[ing] people to the city's streets," as a *New York Times* op-ed piece suggests, further highlights how invisible the people who in fact *are* (and have always been) "on the streets" really are in the eyes of a mainstream, middle-class public.[16] In such a context, the reduction of vacant lots or more visceral signs of decay are noted, while the rates of poverty, unemployment, and violence remain the same or escalate. A production of space rooted in an aesthetics of visibility and respectability depended both on decisions about what should be visible and what should not, as well as on views of comportment and emotive appropriateness. Additionally, moral codes were employed that operated as criteria through which to market Newark in terms of obvious middle-class consumption practices, lifestyles, and emotional regimes; concepts of order and disorder; and the "strategic interplay between aesthetics and function" (Zukin 1996, 81).

I am inspired here by Raymond Williams's (1973) dynamic integration of two seemingly oppositional phenomena: "feelings" as a kind of experience that is inchoate and derives from who we are without us being able to articulate it, and "structure," which suggests that this level of experience has an underlying logic rather than being haphazard. Williams introduces the term "structures of feeling" to distinguish the lived experiences of a community from the institutional and ideological organization of society. He shows that the relations of production and the pursuit of a hegemonic cultural configuration relied on the systemic or institutional regulation of individual emotion, as well as on the emotive articulation of those very regulatory systems. The institutional operation of the Newark Renaissance, like other urban development projects that privilege real estate, commercial, and touristic interests, requires that cities are associated with a right (middle-class or neoliberal-friendly) emotional style for their success. Neoliberal measures coexist with certain antipoverty government initiatives and together constitute the operational aspects, institutional components, and emotional requirements of the Newark Renaissance.

Communities and political regimes systematically seek to train emotions, idealizing some and condemning others, subjecting them to a normative judgment that would readily allow for their control or manipulation. As William Reddy (1999, 256) demonstrates, under such normative styles of emotional management emotions are enhanced and habituated in such a way that emotional meaning systems reflect social relations and, through emotion's constitution of social behavior, structure them.[17] An absence of such a social structure would force particular kinds of sentiments to cultural prominence (Fajans 1985).[18]

Establishing an Adequate Emotional Regime in Postindustrial Newark

Whereas other scholars have examined the institutional aspects of the Newark Renaissance (e.g., Newman 2004, Sidney 2003), I focus on the neoliberal-friendly emotional style on which these policies rely for their successful operation. At a citywide level, three main premises have dominated the efforts to establish an adequate emotional regime in Newark since the 1980s. The first premise is that whites were abandoned by the neoliberal aspirations of the city and were called to establish a context of white victimhood from very early on in Newark's neoliberal process. The second premise, which I examine by focusing on the emotional style behind the image of a black political elite, is that adequate behavior, comportment, and feelings are the leading conduits to a middle-class lifestyle, and the uplifting of an impoverished black "underclass." Finally, the third premise is that a recharacterization of Newark as a multicultural city, rather than as a predominantly black city, aims to offset the relationship between Blackness and aggression. Latinos, as the fastest growing population in the city, constitute these multicultural others that are, in turn, called upon to distance themselves from blacks and cooperate with the capital accumulation process. These three premises are examined in the remainder of this chapter.

Whiteness and Meta-Narratives of Aggression in North Broadway: Italian Mafia Lords, Jewish Landlords, and "White Trash"

In the 1970s high schools were premier sites of tension between African American students and the largely working class, European whites who had remained in Newark. At Barringer High School in North Broadway, white teenagers, who comprised about one-fourth of the student body in 1972, reportedly found themselves "engulfed by a whirlwind of black-ness," as they experienced a curriculum that now included black history and literature, and Black Pride cultural events, including the playing of Swahili music over the school's public address system (and which some white students found "as offensive and threatening as blacks would find 'Dixie'") (Shipler 1972, 79). Fatima Teixeira, a Portuguese teacher whom I interviewed in the Ironbound, recalled what it had been like to teach at a predominantly black high school in 1970s Newark:

Right out of college, I applied for teaching jobs in Newark and the only position avail-able at the time was at Malcolm X Shabazz, which at the time was also going through its own revolution [drawing metaphorically from a previous discussion of the Newark riots], and at that time it was almost all black. The year before they had changed it to Malcolm X Shabazz. It used to be the South Side High School. So it was into that, that interim thing, well, I had doubts [about whether to accept the job]. It was a culture shock. Most of the teachers were white, which was unusual considering the area, but a lot of Jewish teachers were still in that area. The kids were fine. You know, kids will be kids. I tended to pick up their language, though. On the weekends when I would hang out with friends and stuff, they'd go, "you're talking differently," and I would say, "yeah, well that's what comes from hanging out with . . ." At the time it was very "Hey, Man . . ." The little idioms started to creep into my vocabulary. But I was only there a year.

Most of the teachers in Newark at the time remained white, despite the rapid change in the student body composition, and this raised fears among them at several levels, including a fear of coming across as insensi-tive for not using the right language and "appearing racist." The sense of "walking on racial eggshells" contributed to a "racial paranoia" (Jackson 2006) among whites that continues to characterize Newark's emotional landscape and which is central to the politics of racial learning. As a white minister from the predominantly white Vailsburg neighborhood explained, "Now it's a problem of trying to convince the black majority [of Newark as a whole] to be more humane and just toward the white minority" (Shipler 1972, 80).

In a 1972 article that appeared in *Harper's* magazine titled "The White Niggers of Newark," David Shipler provided a nuanced discussion of whiteness in postindustrial Newark by portraying disgruntled white, pre-dominantly Italian, youth whose families did not have the resources to leave the city and were forced to contend with the federal aid initiatives aimed at ameliorating institutional racism and inequality. This dwin-dling white minority resented that colleges came into the city to recruit blacks and that federal job and recreational programs were established to aid black areas of the city. They also felt negatively about the emergent romantic Black Pride and Black Nationalist vision of Newark. At a time when celebrated poet and playwright LeRoi Jones adopted the African name of Imamu Amiri Baraka, the cultural strength and political power of blacks frightened many whites who saw "in the dashikis of the black councilmen, the clenched-fist salutes of the Board of Education members, and the black-liberation flags in the schools the symbols of a new racism." "These kids are part of a dwindling white minority in Newark, New Jersey. . . . Black power has been converted into reality with such headiness, and the outside white establishment has applauded the turnabout so vigorously, that many whites in Newark have been left with a corrosive sense of invisibility" (77, 78).

Newark white ethnics represented what Michael Novak (1972) called "the rise of the unmeltable ethnics," a European nationality pride that emerged in the 1970s in response to civil rights achievements and what whites viewed as a totalizing Black Pride movement. Similarly, in his article, Shipler describes a Newark resident who reaches back to his Italian roots, arguing that as a minority ethnic group, Italians should be given the same kind of representation on public bodies and in federal programs that blacks have won for themselves in cities where they are the minority. This same man condemned middle-class Italian politicians whom he called "Uncle Marios who think black" (1972, 81). These early manifestations of what later might have been labeled in reactionary circles as "reverse discrimination," inspired "emotional, hate-filled" conversations in the Italian social clubs of North Broadway in the 1970s, as well as heated discussions about employment prospects in a perilous city.

In a city where race relations had been configured according to a southern-style black-white dyad, the arrival of Puerto Ricans, the first Latinos to arrive in significant numbers in Newark, altered the racial landscape of the city. Old-time Puerto Rican residents continuously recalled the great tensions between Italians and Puerto Ricans, and felt that Italians had an even harder time accepting Puerto Ricans as they did relating to blacks. A Puerto Rican man who lived in a house adjacent to Barringer High School spontaneously initiated a conversation about his memories of life in the North Ward. He recalled:

I remember one day when I was a student at Barringer, when I went into Icy Spring, an Italian ices store on Broad Street. I knew that that store was almost forbidden to us. We knew not to go in there. But that day, I was just so focused on getting a lemon ice. I really wasn't thinking about anything else. So I went in. When I was about to order, it struck me, "Uh-uh. Bad move." It hit me that I shouldn't have been there, but I had to go on and order so I did. When I was leaving the store, I heard a shuffling of chairs. And I knew the Italians were going to run after me. I decided to go into Branch Brook Park. They didn't catch me, but in retrospect, going into the park was not a good idea. If they had killed me in there, nobody would have ever found me.

Throughout these early impassioned discussions about power, deserving-ness, and suitability, Puerto Ricans began appearing, along with blacks, as the purported beneficiaries of new local and federal initiatives. In specu-lating about the job openings that would result from the construction of Newark Airport, an Italian interviewee complained that "they held up construction for a year already . . . being that it's being built in Newark they want 50 percent of the working force minorities, if they're qualified or not, because they're black or Puerto Rican. That means if I'm a quali-fied man, a bricklayer, I'm gonna lose a fuckin' job because I'm gonna be replaced by a shine that has no qualifications" (Shipler 1972, 81).

As David Roediger illustrates, "both 'becoming American' and 'be-coming white' could imply coercive threats to European national identi-ties. . . . The pursuit of white identity, so tied to competition for wage labor and to political citizenship, greatly privileged male perceptions. But identity formation, as Americanizers and immigrant leaders realized, rested in large part on the activities of immigrant mothers, who entered discussions of nationality and Americanization more easily than those of race" (2002, 167). In Shipler's *Harper's* article, the author quotes an Italian teacher at Barringer High School:

We're the niggers now, that's what's happened. . . . The blacks aren't so sophisticated with their racism. They're just learning what power is about, what America's about. They're more overt, and so are we—we're not sophisticated about our racism as Ital-ians. We're amateurs too. . . . We're not acting like other whites, 'cause we're . . . clawing and punching and kicking in the balls and all the rest. . . . And of course we look bad because we're cursin' and swearin', and we say "nigger" all the time, and the people in the back always said "Negro" when that was right and now "black." They talk the right way. (1972, 78–79)

White youth and their parents saw themselves in double jeopardy for be-ing a "minority in their own city, yet too urban and too Italian to be part of the American mainstream, which they characterized as suburban and WASP." As the daughter of a white foreman, a student at Barringer in the 1970s described her experience with those suburban whites in college: "you come from Newark and you're caught in the middle: you're not rich enough to be really a white person, but you're not poor enough to be a colored person" (Shipler 1972, 80).

While Shipler acknowledges white ethnics' antiblack racism, he also urges his readers, presumably a white middle-class elite, to look beyond this working-class "anger and hurt":

These are working men who generally make under $10,000, own $8,000 brick or wooden row houses on dingy streets. . . . Many understand that they and blacks are equal victims of the rampant block-busting being attempted in white neighborhoods of their city, where they are barred by letters and phone calls from real estate agents who spread fear and urge sales at low prices so that the houses can be sold at inflated levels to black families. (1972, 81–82)

While some of these families "stuck it out in Newark" and even put up signs declaring "This house is NOT For Sale," these decisions caused great rifts in families who "have lived all their lives in Newark, their parents having arrived there from Italy, but their block has become mostly Puerto Rican, and crime has increased in recent years" (82). As if in a cat-and-mouse race, an Italian man who disagreed with his wife about moving out of North Broadway told Shipler:

There's no magic in black skin, and some of us are beginning to realize you cannot run. Because if you run from Wakeman Avenue today, you're going to run from Mt. Prospect Avenue tomorrow, and if it's from Mt. Prospect Avenue tomorrow, you're gonna run from Llewellyn Park, which is an exclusive suburban residential area, the following day. When do you stop running? . . . For you, son, this is okay. I'm staying in Newark because I simply do not want someone pushing me out. I do not like the idea that I am running away. (82)

For working-class whites, a social and economic attachment to Newark, an inability to move to the suburbs, and the renegotiation of their own identity as racial minorities marked the limits of their whiteness and white privilege in deeply emotive ways. In a dramatic conclusion to his article, Shepler muses: "The city wallows in the swath of stinking factories that belch filth from the Jersey flats into the shadow of the Statue of Liberty. It has also tarnished the other symbols of America by making hatred look like honesty, by making old dreams laughable" (82). For whites who remained in the city, especially those in the decimated inner-city areas, the significance of race has been drastically altered (cf. Hartigan 1999, 20). "White enclave" represents the prevailing depiction of the Ironbound, even though area whites tried to counter this representation by developing contrasting attention to the relative degrees of whiteness in the suburbs of Newark; thus, they argued against this image by pointing to other places that were "whiter than we are."

In conversations with residents of North Broadway and the Ironbound, Italians were rendered visible in Newark's history in their roles as corrupt politicians and, more frequently, as somewhat picturesque "Mafia lords," roles that were never mutually exclusive and in fact were often convergent. "I'm not sure if I should talk to you about the Italians," warned Antonio Guzmán, the father of a Newark High School student and long-time resident of Newark's North Broadway. He continued: "Because they still have their people in place around here." Drawing from his experience growing up in the 1960s, Antonio recalled:

They hated us! They still hate us. They think the Puerto Ricans took their neighborhood away from them. And they feel that's a slap in the face, because it is because of them that this area exists and was not as destroyed as the Central and South Wards. Let me tell you: As soon as the riots started, one of the mafia lords got a truck, almost like one of those military trucks and equipped it with arms. He claimed he'd be firing if the blacks entered the area [of the North Ward]. Someone told him that that was illegal, to have a truck like that. But, nobody really messed with those guys. I mean . . . they're mafia, they're connected to the most higher up people. And he [the mafia lord] just said: "If they come here, I'm going to have the arms to defend myself." Everyone was afraid of them. Someone, the principal of a school Down Neck [in the Ironbound] appeared dead, in front of his own school. People were afraid of them. So the blacks were kept out of the Ironbound by the rail tracks and from the North Ward by the Italian Mafia!

The characteristics attributed to Italians activated an internal logic similar to what John Jackson (2001) and others have described as "conspiratorial thinking" (Turner 1993; Fenster 1999) or a form of "populist paranoia" (Hofstader 1955).[19] "Off-the-record" requests were common among many of the old-time Latino residents with whom I spoke, although references to "the Italians" and images of the mafia lords as welcomed protectors of the areas of North Broadway and the Ironbound dominated most of the narratives I heard throughout my fieldwork.

When Abel Cabrera, a Puerto Rican resident of North Broadway and the uncle of a student at Barringer High School, who had been a nationalist activist in the 1970s, warned me that he wanted to say something "off the records," he didn't even wait for a response: "Well, I'm going to tell you something off the records. If you mention I told you, I'll deny it.

But what happened was that, after the riots, all the wealthy Jewish people living in the mansions in the South Ward left. They collected the insurance money for their businesses and, instead of reinvesting in Newark they headed out and never returned." Abel was possibly referring to the fact that by 1972, barely five years after the Newark riots, only 6,000 Jews remained in Newark out of a total of 100,000 Jewish residents in Essex County (Helmreich 1999, 32).[20]

The salience of particular historically inspired narratives, including hyperbolic stories of powerful but benevolent mafia lords and prosperous but malevolent Jewish deserters, have captured individual and community imaginations and contributed to an emotional commonsense in/of the city. The riots and "slum clearance" projects not only consolidated a black political elite, in light of increasing white suburbanization, but also revealed competing tensions and steep class divisions among European ethnics in their connection to the privilege of their whiteness. At the time of Kenneth Gibson's mayoral victory in 1970, many of the white residents who had remained in Newark, as well as those who had moved to the suburbs but perhaps maintained occupational ties to the city, "expressed great panic at the possibility that 'angry Blacks' would 'take over'" (Chase 2005, 63). According to an account in the New York Times:

The City of Newark [is] angry and anguished as Negroes take over political life amidst bitter racial tensions. . . . Negroes are now 60% of the population, with an ever-increasing white minority of mostly Italians, so that Newark may become the first all-black major U.S. city. . . . Puerto Ricans and Cubans are 10% of the population but have been politically passive.[21]

Likewise, in the 1950s the city of Newark witnessed an increase in the number of blacks living and working in the city. Sociocultural factors and sanctioned everyday practices influenced individual subjective understandings of an urban emotional landscape. These subjectivities are also important in tracing structural and phenomenological aspects of the emotional aesthetics attributed to "Newark" historically. The dominant image of Newark, reinforced by the media, is one of poverty, disease, violence, and danger, all coded as "black."

These configurations and repositioning of whiteness and white privilege made an inadequate emotional persona the main cause of Newark's poverty and decay. As seen in the previous section, the Newark Renaissance aimed to redress these racialized images of aggression by adopting a message of respectability, as key to generating in Newark a "feel that sells," an emotional landscape that is attractive to potential white, middle-class investors. Among Puerto Ricans in North Broadway, this urban emotional commonsense was met through the development of not-for-profit service organizations that have largely relied on "self-help" or "building self-esteem" rhetoric in order to challenge a perpetual view of Puerto Ricans as "delinquent citizens" (Ramos-Zayas 2004; chapter 2). Among Brazilians, a commercialization of "Brazilian culture" was deployed in the context of ethnic restaurants, stores, and festivals, as well as in the circulation of life stories of overcoming and conquering hardship (chapter 3). Capital accumulation and a therapeutically influenced narrative of "conflict resolution" became intertwined for good: In Newark, an enduring emotive commonsense was established partly as a result of the images of racial rebellion and the policy control over neighborhoods through market-driven projects.

From Black to Multicultural City: Elite Emotional Styles and the Latinization of Newark

An important component of neoliberal policies is that they foster new definitions of "good citizenship" that oftentimes disconnect the citizen from the state (Maskovsky 2001) and establish personal responsibility and emotional adequacy as the main qualities necessary for improving urban life. In Newark Mayor Cory Booker embodies, to various degrees, the success, respectability, *and* psycho-social adequacy to which a predominantly black city like Newark should aspire in order to combat its aggressive national image. Booker's public persona and image, as it has been circulated and promoted in Newark and nationwide, illustrates the critical characteristics expected of a quintessential neoliberal subject. These characteristics, rather than centering on professional achievements, public accomplishments, or even lifestyle, are, in fact, more directly concerned with overall emotional adequacy, quasi-spiritual values, and appropriate affect. Elected in 2006 and again in 2010, Cory Booker ran on a platform that stressed "safety" and "development" as key concerns, while characterizing his government in light of accountability and transparency, in contradistinction to the levels of corruption of the Sharpe James administration.[22] Throughout his campaigns and election, Booker was described as an "Ivy League–schooled, Buddhist-inspired, vegetarian major who was raised in an affluent Bergen County suburb."[23] This set of psychosocial and quasi-spiritual attributes of a good citizen, although largely undertheorized, is critical to visions of an effective neoliberal city.

On October 10, 2007, Cory Booker appeared on the Oprah Winfrey Show as a personal guest of Gayle King, better known for her status as

Oprah's best friend and the editor of O magazine, who commented that she would sometimes get calls from an exhausted Booker narrating his daily struggles in Newark. Under the theme of "The Gift of Giving Back," Booker was praised for having taken on the daunting task of straightening up "a small city with a high crime rate." The tone and topic of the show rendered Booker's decision especially commendable given that he had more lucrative options due to his corporate law and educational credentials from Stanford, Oxford, and Yale, as well as his wealthy New Jersey suburban background. A puzzled Oprah asked him why he decided to run for mayor, to which Booker responded: "I feel like this is my calling. . . . How lucky is it in life to be able to wake up in the morning and feel like you're doing what you were meant to do, with people who inspire you every single day?"

One of Booker's "hooks," for the purposes of Oprah's show, was the fact that "Unlike most politicians, Mayor Booker doesn't live in a big house in an exclusive neighborhood. He calls one of Newark's poorest housing projects home." And, as the Oprah show website further explains, "For the past eight years, Mayor Booker has lived in Brick Towers, a housing project in one of Newark's most violent neighborhoods. Though the Housing Authority declared his apartment building 'unlivable,' Mayor Booker wanted to live like the people who need him most." Oprah, consistent with the wellness and spiritual focus of her show, frowned on critics who called Booker "too idealistic." For instance, established black activists and public intellectuals like Amiri Baraka, the poet, longtime Newark resident and Booker's neighbor, saw Booker as a patronizing outsider whose very authenticity was questionable: "It's all a romantic fantasy. It's a politician's hooey, part of the mythmaking."[24]

Oprah, however, listened attentively as the Newark mayor assured millions of spectators worldwide: "We are going to make Newark, New Jersey, the national example of urban transformation. . . . I'm in this fight, and we can do it. This country's whole history is a perpetual testimony to the achievement of the impossible." Although most of the day's show was dedicated to Cory Booker, two short segments appeared at the end—one dedicated to "Faith," a rescued mutt dog who could only walk on her two hind legs due to an accident, and another one to "today's giveaway," which was Oprah's gift of $1,000 and a DVD handycam to every member of the studio audience, including Mayor Booker, so they could each donate the money to a charity of their choosing. Said Oprah, "You're going to open your hearts, you're going to be really creative, and you're going to spend it all at once on one stranger or spend a dollar on every person. . . . Imagine the love and kindness you can spread with $1,000" (Illouz 2003).

The Oprah show was not the first time that a narrative of spiritual journeys and wellness had characterized the Booker campaign and election. One of the most widely circulated narratives of this kind focused on how the newly elected mayor compassionately but firmly became mentor to two black teenagers who had written "Death to Cory Booker" in a high school hallway. To introduce these "underclassed" youth to a middle-class sensibility, Booker is said to have escorted them to suburban bookstores, treated them to paella in the city's Portuguese Ironbound, and arranged for tutors from Rutgers University. The only caveat was that they had to abide by the mayor's strict rules:

The first thing I said is, "You've got to dress properly. You've got to cut your hair. . . . People judge you on how you present yourself. And you have to speak proper English. I can't deal with the double negatives and the slang. You have to speak the English of Frederick Douglass, W.E.B. DuBois [and] Booker T. Washington."[25]

These anecdotes of personal growth focus on self-improvement through the activation of a cosmic lifestyle that does not appear inconsistent or inaccessible to anyone, since, after all, there's now a Starbucks on Market Street and Mayor Booker lives in the projects. In this neoliberal, emotionally driven context, a politics of respectability and comportment becomes the foundation of financial success. A very cursory illustration of this is a response to Cory Booker's *Oprah* appearance that was posted on the Newark-based online magazine *Black Voices*.[26] The writer of the post warned some (presumably anti-Booker) participants:

I watched the oprah show with corey booker on it however, please stop trying to blame him for what is going on with your kids in newark. corey booker is not responsible for your children's actions. you train up and raise up your children the appropriate way at home and stop looking for someone to blame for your kids violent behavior. your kids have built up anger behind something you did or didn't do. therefore, blame yourself for what's going on in newark take back your own kids because we can't do it for you.[27]

Cory Booker's charisma—and, more tacitly, his interpersonal style, palatable Blackness, and emotionally and spiritually healthy lifestyle—has been credited with reinvigorating Newark's Renaissance, and prompting national discussions of "psychic rebirth" and "Newark's moment" that are aimed at luring investors and prospective homebuyers to the city.[28] Anybody reading current articles about Newark, including those titled "Two Miles in Newark that Run from Long Decline to Rebirth" and "From Riots to Respectability," would think that Newark is quickly becoming a prosperous US metropolis.[29] During the early months of the Booker administration the mainstream media quickly focused on real estate and commercial growth, retail investment opportunities, and lifestyles that included health clubs, the arts, Whole Foods, and Starbucks. All of this was available to the intrepid "pioneers" and "the young, the creative, and with time, the well-heeled" who dared cross to the other side of the Hudson River.[30] Unlike the "politics of respectability" that traditionally served as a strategy to uplift the black middle class, refracted through the eyes of a white intermediary lens and a focus on appearance, the more contemporary version required that not only appearance, but also, and possibly more important, emotional style and comportment also functioned as urban marketing tools when attracting capital to the city.

Cory Booker, for instance, devoted most of his hundred-minute-long State of the City address in 2007 not only to enhanced law enforcement, but to preaching the virtues of personal responsibility, calling on Newark residents to take care of their city, their neighborhoods and their own families: "We must cease looking for blame in this time of crisis and begin to accept collective responsibility. . . . We must begin by looking at parenting."[31] Implicated in such "family values" statements is the effect of the new modality of government, which functions by creating mechanisms that work all by themselves, as notions of individual responsibility "empower" subjects to discipline themselves (Burchell 1996). Neoliberal urban processes have, in fact, transferred the operations of government (in Foucault's extended sense) to nonstate entities, via "the fabrication of techniques that can produce a degree of 'autonomization' of entities of government from the state" (Barry, Osborne, and Rose 1996, 11–12). These nonstate entities operate in tandem with city-sponsored urban programs, particularly in generating an appeal to emotional "appropriateness," aesthetic sensibility, and moral respectability. In Newark these regulatory operations are intended to reassure private investors, tourists, and potential middle-class homeowners that Newark is safe; more significantly, these disciplining and regulatory mechanisms are discursively framed around the visibility of urban youth, in particular.

Poor and working-class residents, particularly US-born Latino and African American youth, are simultaneously invisible and hypervisible in contemporary "security" discourse, a neoliberal tendency exacerbated in the case of a majority-minority city like Newark. When the Booker administration learned that the state government would pay for the installation of fifty surveillance cameras across the city, the mayor enthusiastically received the news and expressed his interest in also reactivating a police helicopter to increase surveillance capabilities.[32] Likewise, Panasonic donated state-of-the-art surveillance cameras (with some discussion of incorporating an audio feature) to be placed throughout Barringer High School. For Newark's most disenfranchised urban residents, who live at the outskirts of the safer development zones, this surveillance trend has not gone unnoticed. A part-time African American security guard in her late twenties commented: "All my life, the politicians have been calling this place the Renaissance City. I think the renaissance is for suburban people who go downtown. If they have their way, people like me would just disappear."[33] Implicit in this statement is that, with its emphasis on building and revitalizing the city's downtown, the Newark Renaissance created divisions between this downtown area and its surrounding neighborhoods.[34]

A neoliberal emotional persona—of which Cory Booker is a highly visible representative—and the urban development and security initiatives behind the Newark Renaissance, represent efforts to redress the meta-sentiment of "aggression" that continues to characterize Newark in the national imaginary. Another such effort involves promoting Newark as a multicultural city, as opposed to what was (and still is) a predominantly black city.

In a *Star-Ledger* article on the topic of ethnic diversity and Newark electoral politics, the people cited, as well as the author's tone, conveyed a strong sense that African Americans were losing numbers to "Hispanics" or foreign-born populations:

Each of our communities is slightly different, but in Newark, [Latinos] are seeing they have the critical mass to do something. We are in the same position the African-American community was 30 years ago," said Rafael Collazo of the U.S. Hispanic Leadership Institute. . . . The East Ward, the smallest in terms of registered voters, has been a focus of the campaign as Booker and James compete for Portuguese, Brazilian and Spanish voters. . . . Booker said he's been learning to speak Portuguese. "It's very important that a leader can communicate with the people of the city," he said. While the Portuguese and Latinos have enough numbers and political prowess to elect members of their own ethnic groups, other ethnic communities like the Ecuadorians in the North and East Wards, Ghanaians in the South and Central Wards, and Russian Jews and Haitians in the West Ward were also hoping to be courted in political campaigns.[35]

Although Newark remains one of the few US cities with a majority black population, the presence of some European ethnic groups, particularly the Portuguese in the Ironbound and some Italians in North Broadway, and the increasing numbers of Latin American migrants and US-born Latinos, has been critical in the effort to promote that city as "multicultural."[36] Latinos and new Latin American migrants have been credited for halting the population decline that Newark faced since the 1960s. In fact, the Latino population grew substantially, even in the 1970s and 2000 when the city's overall population declined. North Broadway and the Ironbound, the two neighborhoods where I conducted fieldwork, reflect the effects of Newark's crisis, from its depopulation to the steady economic deterioration, but they are also noted for their role in the possible resurgence and repopulation of the city, with their steady stream of newcomers from Latin American and Caribbean countries.[37] As a Cuban client at one of the local Portuguese bakeries once told me, with evident neighborhood pride, when she was trying to figure out if I spoke Spanish or Portuguese: "Aquí se habla de todo menos inglés [Here everything is spoken but English]." Rather than a political statement about language learning, she was hinting at how the Ironbound was a poster for what Charles Hale (2005) calls "neoliberal multiculturalism"—neoliberal politics that do not negate but selectively recognize ethnic claims in order to safeguard dominant relations in the nation.[38]

By 2002, Hispanics represented 30 percent of Newark's population, growing from 61,254 in 1980 to 80,622 in 2000. In the North Broadway neighborhood, the percentage of Latinos grew from 40 percent in 1990 to 62 percent in 2000. About a third of North Broadway residents were black in 2000, a decline from 56 percent in 1990 (Sidney 2003, 10). Of the states with large Latino populations, New Jersey has the largest percentage of South Americans who constitute 21 percent of the state's Latinos, although the state's largest proportion of Latinos continues to be Puerto Ricans (30%) (Pew Hispanic Center, March 2004). In 2000 Newark had a population of 273,546 and one of the highest population densities anywhere in the United States. The city also had the largest black and Latino populations in the state, the second-largest "multiracial" population, and the fifth-largest white population.

Newark shares a heavy-handed reliance on top-down marketing of ethnic culture with other multicultural neoliberalisms, particularly in the Ironbound neighborhood. However, in Newark, this cultural marketing exists against a demographic background which continues to be predominantly black. This combination of top-down cultural marketing, particularly in largely Latin American neighborhoods, combined with the formation of Latino and Latin American identities vis-à-vis African Americans provided fertile ground for the resurgence of the Latin American ideology of racial democracy. In chapter 3, I introduce and analyze what I call "cartography of racial democracy," a navigational set of ideological and pragmatic social tools that enable the repositioning of a growing US-born Latino and Latin American migrant population in a long enduring white-black racial dyad. What is more pertinent to the current discussion, however, is that the image of a "multicultural" Newark, in its intention to eradicate or at least dissipate the city's predominantly black demographics, draws on "Latinos" to interrupt long-held associations between Blackness and aggression. Moreover, this multicultural image simultaneously homogenizes and culturalizes groups of Latin and Caribbean Americans across nationalities. The present work, with its focus on Puerto Ricans and Brazilians, aims to highlight such distinctions and convergences.

As David Harvey eloquently argues, cartographic identifications such as locating, positioning, individuating, identifying, and bounding are operations that play a key role in the formation of personal and political subjectivities (2001, 219–21). As colonial subjects, Puerto Ricans have become equivalent or at least more proximate to African Americans in the imagination of many Latin American migrants. In October of 2005, for instance, the Brazilian consul in New York advised the Brazilian community of Danbury to "keep their distance from the cucarachos [cockroaches in Portuguese]" because "Brazilians do not need to participate in a story that is unrelated to them, the West Side Story," in reference to the violence associated with Puerto Rican gangs in the film.[39] Likewise, in areas like Framingham, Massachusetts, one of the cities with the highest Brazilian concentration in the United States, Brazilian migrants are credited with "revitalizing" an area that had deteriorated due to the lack of "entrepreneurial spirit" of old-time Puerto Rican residents, who have in turn been associated with welfare "abuse" and criminality (cf. Sales 1998).[40] These are important distinctions in how populations become racialized differently in response to the circumstances of their arrival, forms of capital they carry, and the relationship between the United States and particular countries of origin.

Moreover, as examined in the next chapter, spatial differentiations connect places like the Ironbound to their putative opposite—the ghetto, the 'hood, the no-go areas where the urban "underclass" resides (cf. Kobayashi and Peake 2000, 396). Thus, representations of space and place involving metaphors that reflect dominant ideologies reinforce difference and by default devalue places associated with racialized people, but with some deal of variety even within racially marked populations, as is the case of majority-minority cities.

Emotional-Cultural Schemas in Newark: Whose "Golden Age"?

Instances of "micro-aggression," defined as subtle, often automatic or unconscious insults directed toward people of color remain compromised under what William Reddy calls an "emotional regime." This set of tacit rules of reward and punishment insists that the unity of a community and the progress of a city depend on the implementation of a coherent set of prescriptions about the adequate display of discordance, while determining what constitutes an "emotion-charged cultural schema" (1997, 330). Thus, to cure Newark of a putatively inherent aggression and anger, which became the dominant "meta-sentiments" (Myers 1986, 120) of the city, particularly after the riots, a new form of civic engagement—one that relied on institutions, rather than public outcry, as vehicle of change— was put in place. Despite the racial segregation, infrastructural inequalities, and increasing labor subordination that predated the Newark riots, the individual and personal readings that circulated around the post-riot period tended to overshadow or contain political economic concerns. Newark experimented with what Raymond Williams terms "structures of feeling" (1973), as the interpretation of urban historical events gained salience only in light of an individual's everyday experiences and subjectivity (cf. Cristoffanini 2003).

As examined in some of the following chapters and hinted at in the opening of this one, seemingly spontaneous tension or outright hostility in Newark cannot be disentangled from a preceding historical moment. This is particularly the case when such moments highlight the prominence of race as excessive and violent, while predicating the success of "urban renewal" and personal safety on the establishment of a neoliberal-friendly emotional style ensconced in a politics of respectability and personal responsibility. Without this kind of adequate emotional style, Newark would continue to exist in disadvantageous contrast to its surrounding suburbs, where inhabitants have presumably mastered these everyday relational skills and embodied "emotional capital" (Illouz 2007). Ever since the mid-twentieth century, the suburbs have become the material and symbolic site where emotionally "adequate" Newark residents go to escape the unlivable conditions of the city; in fact, as I demonstrate below, the most widely disseminated literary and anthropological representations of Newark have been those in which the suburbs serve as a naturalized subtext.

In *The Country and the City*, Raymond Williams eloquently demonstrates how the contrast between "the country" and "the city" is an enduring modernist form through which "we become conscious of a central part of our experience and of the crises of our society" (1973, 289). Poets, novelists, and essayists—in Williams's case, those of eighteenth-century England—represent "the city" as a symbol of capitalist production, labor, and exploitation, or as the "dark mirror" of the country. By tracing the development of this city-versus-country duality in his cultural analysis, Williams shows that the country and city are inextricably related (and even constitutive of one another), when one looks at the historical, lived experience of a community as distinct from the institution and organization of the society. Structures of feeling arose from a given state in capitalism that requires the pursuit of a hegemonic cultural configuration to justify and organize productive forces and relations of production. The country as idyllic served, therefore, to explain the city's corruption as a consequence of a social malaise and cultural deficiency. The racialization of neighborhoods—and emotive and classed correspondences between race and space—in Newark highlighted a comparable distinction to Williams's city and country, with Williams's city being Newark's urban areas and his country being Newark's suburbs.

Just as suggested in Williams's cultural analysis, poets, playwrights, novelists, and even social scientists have played a critical role in documenting the urban/suburban divide in Newark in ways that sediment structures of feeling and the hegemonic cultural configuration Williams references. Williams identifies the novels he analyzes as "knowable communities," in the sense that authors depict people and their relationships in essentially knowable and communicable ways that place the country and the city within a single tradition (1973, 163). Two Newark writers who have come to occupy a premiere role in documenting such "knowable communities" are novelist Philip Roth and anthropologist Sherry Ortner. Without going in depth into either of their prolific literary and social scientific production, I want to show that, epistemologically, these authors' allow us to focus on the relationship between emotional performance and political authority, and to examine their respective positionality as former Newark residents.

Philip Roth's literary reputation has been advanced partly through the proposition that he has "universalized his Newark cityscape comparable to Joyce's Dublin or Faulkner's Yoknapatawpha County" (Stone 1998, 38; cf. Schwartz 2005). As Schwartz pointedly argues, however, Roth's Newark renders the Jewish neighborhood of his childhood as representative of the city, particularly of what Roth views as the city's golden era. in ways that remain disturbingly uncritical of race: "the hard-edged, thoughtful, and ironical realist, becomes a conservative 'utopian'—too much caught up in the interplay between his liberal, civil rights conscience and his sentimentalizing of Weequahic [the Jewish neighborhood of his late-1940s adolescence]" (Schwartz 2005, 1). As Roth recalls his driving through the streets of black Newark in a 1998 interview, he considered Newark as an "intensive-care case" and added: "Over the years I went back to visit by myself, walk around. When it became too dangerous to walk by myself I'd go with somebody. . . . I was mesmerized by the destruction of this place. . . . And I knew all the streets and I knew what they had looked like and I knew how people lived."[41]

Roth's willingness to stereotype post-riot Newark as a crime-ridden burnt-out city of blacks, in contradistinction to the nurturing Jewish urban community life of his youth, and Roth's own ideological contradictions, provide important analytical tools for examining how perspectives on Newark's history have always required a deeply emotive, racialized narrative. While Roth understands that apartheid flourished in Newark, he "does not make the connection between the enclave that was Weequahic and the exploitation of Black immigrants," nor does he recognize that industrial decline began much earlier than the 1960s or that once wartime manufacturing ended, the Black community was left with no work and "inhabiting one of the most congested and run down ghettos in the country" (Schwartz 2005, 15).[42]

Both Philip Roth and Sherry Ortner link anecdotal accounts to bigger historical events in order to add meaning to the individual lives of their predominantly Jewish literary characters and anthropological informants respectively. In a methodologically innovative ethnography, Ortner (1993, 2003) examines the lives of the members of the Weequahic High School Class of '58 in the decades following their graduation. Although a couple of years apart, both Roth and Ortner attended the same high school and lived in the same neighborhood. In "Comment: High School Classmates Revisited: Sherry Ortner and Philip Roth," Jonathan Schwartz (1998) examines the intersection of anthropology and fiction in Newark through a comparison of these authors' publications. What I would like to accentuate here is the centrality of a particular kind of emotional landscape that has all but vanished in contemporary descriptions of Newark:

"nostalgia," "loss," "sadness," and "longing" poignantly characterize the lives that Roth and Ortner depict, albeit in different ways.

While Roth's longing is rooted in the public space (e.g., the built environment, the way life used to be lived in terms of neighborhood), Ortner notes that, for her upper- and upper-middle-class former classmates, the recollections are reflective of a public sphere that has become more intimate as private matters of sexuality (and perhaps a sexual angst associated with high school class reunions), morality, and family become key issues to be projected onto one's memories (cf. Berlant 1997). The family and friendship groups become primary sites to negotiate the usage of the city. As the world of 1950s Newark broadens with increasing population heterogeneity, the role of the city's Jewish population grows smaller symbolically. The possibility for attaching one's identity to the urban landscape is challenged in light of the documented vulnerability experienced by these upwardly mobile, future suburbanite Jewish social actors (Helmreich 1999). A retreat to the private and even a formulation of citizenship that consists of a social membership rooted in personal acts and values, rather than on political rights and radical struggles, appears as a means to counteract the insecurity that many white families faced in their pursuit of a suburban, racially neutral existence. The nostalgia and grief that both Roth and Ortner note are, therefore, the emotional underside of a process through which the group subjectivity that had constructed multiple meanings and levels of access to the city became delimited by a racial reconfiguration that rendered particular urban sites no longer accessible.

The prominent public role and national recognition conferred to the Newark-based works of Phil Roth and Sherry Ortner, while undoubtedly well deserved, should be considered in light of the knowledge production and perspectives that have been invisible in literary and anthropological representations of "knowable communities" and "structures of feeling" in contemporary Newark. Particularly pertinent are the works of African American playwright and poet Amiri Baraka and Puerto Rican social worker Hilda Hidalgo.[43] These authors' works enable a closer understanding of emotional transformations behind particular historical moments. Baraka's and Hidalgo's perspectives supply phenomenological perspectives of the lives of two populations that are nearly absent from the works of Roth and Ortner: a politically militant African American contingency and a newly emergent population of Puerto Ricans arriving in Newark.

Amiri Baraka's work draws from an Afro-centric tradition in Black Power, Third World nationalism, and anticolonial struggles to interpret

Newark. It has been conventionally argued that the further back a person reflects, including a reflection on ancestral stories about running from a slave lynching a century ago, the less immediate is the sense of bodily fear and the more strategic those recollections actually become (cf. Forde 1997). Nevertheless, Baraka's deployment of the past, while certainly mediated by a sense of distance, still becomes situated in a deeply phenomenological narrative of racial oppression that draws from a long canon of black radicalism rooted in emotional and affective links to such a past. There is not a sense of longing for a pre-riot era or even a particular marking of a critical moment—for example, the riots—as a turning point. Instead, one can examine his work in light of Heidegger's phenomenology for its great concern with epistemologically challenging issues such as what it is like for black subjects to be in the world; how black gesture and bodily orientation might be useful in recalling histories of sensations and the body in a racially segregated society; and how such questions could offer a good approach to the history of feelings, affect, and politics in the African American community.

The little-known monograph by Hilda Hidalgo and her students, published barely three years after the riots (discussed more explicitly later in this chapter), prominently features riots and disturbances, not to distinguish a nostalgically saturated era from a context of post-riot decay, but rather to portray critical historical moments in the consolidation of a Puerto Rican community in Newark (Hidalgo 1970). Among the Puerto Ricans whom Hidalgo describes, the formation of an institutional life of social agencies, and the socialization of emotions through the development of not-for-profit organizations, played a major role in how people interpreted community and evaluated community building success. While Hidalgo considered the riots an "epidemic of anger," she situated the incident in the context of a longer history and memories of fear and danger. Such fear and danger were so deeply a part of Newark's pre-riot fabric that they no longer required words to articulate their existence. A structure of feeling operated as a complex blend of short-term and longer-term memories for Hidalgo's informants—Puerto Ricans being chased by Italians with knives down Branch Brook Park and absentee Jewish landlords that hoped their properties would burn down so they could collect insurance. Heightened emotion, drawing on such memories, came to define the ensuing days of spontaneous violence.

The fears of the time are most easily catalogued when transformed into stories told to serve various purposes including plain information, serious reflection, personal anguish, or even entertainment. In contradistinction to the narratives of longing and nostalgia so central to Roth's novels and Ortner's informants, Hidalgo highlights how newly arrived Puerto Rican informants were always entangled with others and infected by the social exchange of feelings, dispositions, satisfactions, and deprivations that were woven into historically enduring narratives that have remained outside the purview of dominant literary and social scientific accounts.[44] Taken together, the works of Baraka and Hidalgo offer great insight into the transformation of Newark's emotional landscape in the mid- and late-twentieth century, when the city ceased to be a promised land for blacks and Puerto Ricans.

Neoliberalism and Emotional Regimes in Historical Perspective

Referring back to the episode that began this chapter, it is critical to situate the characters involved within broader political economic and historical contexts. The white (Italian?) ethnic working-class guy and his statement, bordering on white victimhood. The complicity-*cum*-hesitation of the black guard in her reaction to the white guy and to me. The nervous Latina fumbling through official papers in a perhaps unfamiliar language. The white, nativist space of Homeland Security in post-9/11 United States. Underlying this episode is an active process making spatial sites significant. Michael Taussig (1987) considers that the culture of colonialism is inscribed in the body and meaning is produced in the bodies of the dominated. Prejudices and derogations not only are verbal but also reproduce themselves in rituals of suspicion and investigation at the entrances of public and private buildings.

This active transformation of space into place involves the investment of subjective value and the attribution of meanings to components of the socially constructed environment. One's sense of place is the product of a particular proximity and familiarity with the environments of one's routine circulation; nevertheless, these practices of everyday life also consist of minuscule details that may be overlooked due to their apparent insignificance (Forman 2002). It is important to note that neither the individual subjective affiliation nor the collective inhabitation of proximate spaces can be reduced to a simple "sense of community" in any romantic sense. Individual and collective identities are connected to place, although rarely to a single place and never in a pure and unmediated way, given current transnational processes. As Norman Fainstein argues in his study of the logic of large development projects: "[The] built environment forms contours which structure social relations, causing commonalities of gender, sexual orientation, race, ethnicity, and class to assume spatial identities. Social groups, in turn, imprint themselves physically on the urban structure through the formation of communities, competition for territory, and segregation—in other words, through clustering, the erection of boundaries, and establishing distance" (1994, 141).

In his fieldwork among the Dou Donggo of eastern Indonesia, anthropologist Peter Just (1991) notes the impact of the lack of privacy in communal life on the expression of passionate affect. Among this Indonesian community, there was no space to experience private sentiments in public space; neither was there the discourse nor dialectic between private and public, for they simply did not exist in the same universe (294). Spatial density provides a critical component to the context in which affect is publically expressed in Newark and how constraining "aggression" becomes, in some instances, an "other-control" intervention. In the context of Newark, there was at times a sense that too much restraint might be socially dangerous, that an emotional openness should allow people to know where they stood in relation to one another and that this openness was preferable over too much restraint.

The image that emerges from this understanding of affective expression and social restraint was one in which individuals saw themselves as tough but fair; whose "aggression" was dictated by values of righteousness and securing just treatment, not by someone deliberately going out looking for trouble. Once expressed, anger was presumably released into the social world, where others could sometimes be counted on to tame it, domesticate it, and socialize it (cf. Just 1991). There was a general regard of human nature as more or less unpredictable and punctuated by strong, even violent, emotions openly displayed. These "tactical uses of passion" (Bailey 1983) were preferable and more respected than, say, whining. In fact, in Newark there was a general intolerance of whining and self-victimization, and forcefully discouraged even among young children, which was very much in agreement with self-management expectations under neoliberalism. Extravagant or even flamboyant, but selective, emotional public displays, coupled by physical restraint, usually socially exerted restraint, were patterns of public exchange noted in Newark.

These tactical uses of passion were oftentimes designed to convince participants in consensually ratified disputes and the community at large of the sincerity of the speaker, and these emotions, publicly displayed, were analytically distinct from internally experienced feelings. Thus, the display of strong emotion was not only a public act, but also a social act and "the emotion, its display, and its domestication [usually by others] were all inseparably bound together in a single processual whole"; these were at times collaborative, social, communal efforts of other-control, so that self-control was not always the idiom of civility or the fundamental of a moral order, unless it was done in alignment with neoliberal goals. In this sense, emotions like "anger" were in fact "civic emotions" (Just 1991, 299, 301).

Newark became popularly conceived as a premiere site of "aggressive" and antagonistic social exchanges.[45] When Latinos described Newark, anger and aggression in the city were embodied in interpersonal relationships involving African Americans and various forms of casual everyday interactions that appeared as spontaneous, disconnected incidents, rather than as the product of a longer history of subordination and inequality, as was the case with the Latina woman entering the Homeland Security building and the African American female guard receiving her. The feeling conveyed by many of the Latinos with whom I spoke appeared shaped by memories of fear and danger, which no longer required words because everybody understood the players involved as hostile and aggressive. Furthermore, this feeling was encapsulated in specific memories and stories that acquire material significance in individuals' everyday routines—passing through the building where such-and-such a store used to be (before the riots), the club where one met one's spouse or went on a first date, and so on. Many Newark residents recalled how moving vans picked up residents and businesses from Newark's neighborhoods to move them west into the New Jersey suburbs.

Emotional styles themselves become forms of capital that ought to fit market goals and symbolism, and neoliberal aspirations are partly enabled through a prescribed set of white middle-class everyday practices, affective expressions, and ideological imaginaries that are intimately connected to the formal political field, even when whites constitute a numerical minority, as is the case with Newark (Berlant 1997; Illouz 2007, 2008). In her critique of the clinical use of "emotional intelligence," Eva Illouz illustrates how the system of equivalence between emotions and professional performance is "enabled by this notion (of emotional intelligence) [which] suggests an unprecedented process of commodification that makes it possible to ascribe a monetary value to a person's emotional makeup, and even to convert one into the other" (2007, 214). Moreover, "the emotionalization of economic conduct and the rationalization of intimate relations have given rise to a form of selfhood in which strategic self-interest and emotional reflexivity are seamlessly interconnected" (239). There has been a pursuit of hegemonic cultural configurations to justify and organize productive forces and individual relationships to production, as well as grassroots mechanisms of resistance.[46] But what are the everyday, pragmatic, and intimate consequences of such an emotional regime? I want to propose here that in addition to supplying a "civilization-of-manners schema" (Elias 1982) through the increasing disciplining of behavior and bodily functions of "angry blacks," Newark's neoliberal emotional regime takes on the qualities of classed, gendered and racialized subjectivities. These subjectivities are certainly identified according to the specific material and capital concerns of urban projects, which render them in terms of individuals who are either considered "safe" or "unsafe," "productive" or "parasitic," "aggressive" or "well-behaved," "legal" or "illegal."[47]

Some scholars have noticed how rational concepts like neoliberalism or development have depended on the denial of an affective basis and offer forms of knowledge that are organized around the denial of emotion (Game 1997), even when they activate and rely upon aspects of "observable behaviors" that are emotionally coded and interpreted. Moreover, urban neoliberalism has effectively operated to depoliticize any criticism of racialization practices, and a variety of problems previously defined as social or political, by situating racial and social differences in the terrain of emotions and comportment, under the heading of particular meta-sentiments, such as "aggression" in the case of Newark. Precisely because everyday life in poor racialized areas is saturated with structural risks and agonizing uncertainities, these meta-sentiments and the meta-narratives through which they are articulated become more deeply rooted in a public sphere that is increasingly intimate, as intimacy and feelings also appear more real and easily identifiable in the exercise of power (Illouz 2003, 2008; Trabasso and Ozyurek 1997).

Through the repetition of images and representations over time, spatially inscribed emotions in Newark worked to produce a sense of inclusion (and exclusion) along criteria of consumption and emotional style. Emotions in such context became a property that could be attached to certain places, objects, and experiences, but which needed to be actively preserved, documented, and circulated in everyday narratives and popular expression.[48] Thus, emotions delineated and provided legibility to culture by rendering it an object and, subsequently, attaching market and symbolic values to it, albeit in differential ways depending on whose culture was on the line.

Racialization of space takes place in two very different ways for the Newark Latino populations inhabiting and producing the space: Puerto Ricans needed to be disciplined through military recruitment, and Brazilians became culturally excessive, the subject of chapters 2 and 3, respectively. Neoliberal efforts in Newark have in fact highlighted the distinction within the city, as the case of a criminalized North Broadway and a quaint Ironbound suggests. Not surprisingly, these neighborhood characterizations, rather than centering on economics, tend to focus on the culturally dominant ethno-racial groups in a given area and culture—or rather, the viability of a particular "culture" and sometimes individual "life histories"—to be commercialized or showcased. A prevalent idea is that Newark, and the two neighborhoods alluded to here, are a product not of the capitalist or neocapitalist system but rather of some putative "sickness" or "hard work" of specific segments of society. In such a scenario Latinos can help by producing change—whether by subscribing to a culture of self-help or assessing the economic and moral marketability of their culture.

Despite increasing efforts to describe Newark as a "multicultural" city, it is critical to recognize that the few white ethnic and growing Latino and Latin American residents alike developed "socially meaningful cartographies" or "cognitive maps" of urban life that were necessarily constituted against a centrality of Blackness in which African Americans alternatively represented both a powerful political elite and a highly stigmatized "underclass."[49] In many ways, Newark was experienced by its Latino and Latin American residents in radically different ways than it was nationally imagined.[50] For these populations, the city was lived at the scale of more immediate neighborhoods, or even certain streets or "mental territories" within neighborhoods. Neighborhoods within Newark reflected a new geography of centrality and marginality directly related to a strategic construction (and destruction) of the built environment and the racial tensions that emanated from the historical and contemporary urban "renewal" projects and white flight, discussed earlier.[51] Therefore, as a city, Newark cannot be treated as a discrete spatial unit in which neighborhoods are mere physical and institutional arrangements; in Newark, neighborhoods are proxies for racial and class distinctions and views of stability, community, and commercial viability and, more often, of crime, decay, and waste.[52] Social relations, in a most fundamental way, were regional relations.[53]

In the next two chapters, I focus on how two such "communities"—Puerto Ricans in North Broadway and Brazilians in the Ironbound—carved their respective positions in the context of a meta-sentiment of "aggression" associated with Newark. Historical conceptions and contemporary productions of space continue to inform perspectives on "renewal," "renaissance," "good areas," and "bad areas" to generate enduring narratives of heroism that continue to shape racial formations in Newark, although in decidedly context- (or even neighborhood-) specific ways. Labels like "protective Italian mafia lords," "defective southern blacks," "degenerate Puerto Rican poor," "Jewish deserters," and "hardworking Portuguese" have great emotional resonance in a city with such extreme social and economic inequalities. Henri Lefebvre insists that produced space "serves as a tool of thought and action that, in addition to being a means of production, is also a means of control" (1991, 26). Neoliberal aspirations of cities like Newark, New Jersey, impact the configuration and articulation of transnational racial ideologies and everyday structures of feeling. The highly developed idiom of emotion in Newark, likewise, includes readings of aggression through a deeply racialized (and classed and gendered) popular epistemology, as I explore in the next chapter.

TWO

Delinquent Citizenship: Self-Help Organizations, Military Recruitment, and the Politics of Worth in Puerto Rican Newark

In the summer of 2003 I attended the premiere of Noemí Figueroa's film *The Puerto Rican Soldier: The Story of the 65th Infantry Borinquen-eers* at the Newark Public Library. The documentary chronicled the story of "the only Hispanic-segregated unit in the U.S. military" that began as a "volunteer regiment" in 1899 and participated in the Korean War and in Vietnam. As the promotional flyers stated, the film aimed to "tell the inspiring stories of heroism and tragedy." Many of the people whom I had interviewed or whose children I knew through my involvement as a volunteer at Barringer High School were part of the audience. The mother of one of the students I knew proudly told me that her own uncles had participated in the Korean War and were now living in Puerto Rico. In a spacious room filled to capacity despite stormy summer weather, the mood was celebratory. The event was a tribute to heroism and patriotism, a pleasant surprise for those unfamiliar with the Borinquen-eers, and evidence that Puerto Ricans had contributed as much to the United States as any Americans. Some of the veterans attending the event tearfully recalled the stories of compatriots who had been casualties of war.

The film noted that while Puerto Ricans represented only one-eightieth of the US population at the time, one out of eighteen of the soldiers in Korea and one out of every forty-two casualties of war were Puerto Rican. Narratives of Puerto Ricans who were soldiers on their own terms and for their own reasons, as well as the "volunteer" status of their involvement, were emphasized. For instance, a jovial Puerto Rican soldier recalled how one of his comrades had carried his guitar to entertain the troops ("we won't be fighting all the time!"), while another man mentioned that being a soldier was an aphrodisiac for "seducing the ladies." The film was intended as a tribute to Puerto Rican men who, in the view of their families and communities, were unrecognized heroes. The fact that the island-based Puerto Ricans who were drafted could not even vote for the US president, or that Puerto Rican soldiers were placed in the most dangerous combat positions and racially segregated in their own battalion, only increased the sense of indignation that propelled a characterization of these men and, by patriotic association, of all Puerto Ricans as deserving and courageous US citizens. The exceptional circumstances surrounding Puerto Rican soldiers, and their erasure from mainstream records, only rendered them more generous and worthy of any federal benefit to which they might be entitled as veterans.

When I asked Julia Cabrera, whose son and daughter attended Barringer High School, about her thoughts on the event, she commented: "It made me cry to watch that movie! Because I had an uncle who was in the 65th Infantry, he got a medal and all." I asked her if she thought that these veterans were patriots, and she responded: "Absolutely. It's a part of our history that people don't know about. And it was a whole group of Puerto Ricans, but people don't see that part about us. I didn't even know much about it before the movie."

In North Broadway, Puerto Ricans oftentimes displayed a self-defensive patriotism—a patriotism that had to be continuously narrated back into official documents and everyday conversations, and which served to challenge a criminalization of the predominantly Puerto Rican area of Newark. The discussions that ensued from the film have to be contextualized in a broader politics of worthiness, deservingness, and respectability that aimed to challenge a dominant characterization of Puerto Ricans as "delinquent citizens" (Ramos-Zayas 2004). These politics were most salient in relation to Puerto Rican youth and they reflected the great personal affliction and community conflict that the parents of US-born Puerto Rican youth faced when asked to defend the social worth of their children's "deviant" lives in North Broadway.

A few months after the film event, during the fall term at Barringer High School, I ran into Julia Cabrera again at the school, where she served as a parent-volunteer. When I asked her about Joel, her son who left the high school the previous semester, in his junior year, Julia showed visible concern. "I keep telling him, you need to go back, finish high school or get the GED, but he says school is not for him. I just don't like the friend-ships he's hanging out with. Son unos vagos . . . son malas influencias, tú sabes [They are lazy . . . bad influences, you know]." Since leaving Barringer, Joel worked at a warehouse for a large home repair company until quitting after a disagreement with his boss. He'd also done odd handy work in the neighborhood. "He's a good kid, you know, pero lo que le gusta es el relajo, como decimos nosotros [what he likes is to joke around]," Julia told Elisa Elizondo, an Ecuadorian parent, and me, as if sensing that some people would label Joel an "unproductive" young man with a lack of personal value and worth.

"He is. He probably just hasn't found something that grabs his atten-tion yet," I said, trying to be reassuring.

Elisa then added, apparently in reference to several previous conver-sations she and Julia had, "Well, you know what I've already told you about that. The military! You cannot be supporting a lazy bum. He needs to be straightened out, to take responsibility, do something with his life and help you. For some kids that's the only way." And, addressing me, Elisa added, "I think some kids need the military, because some of them are just doing nothing with their lives, even the girls around here, get-ting pregnant, babies having babies, doing drugs, gangs. They need to be taken off the streets, because they're out of control. And there are a lot of those [kids] here." Julia seemed uneasy as she slowly disengaged and looked away in silence.

When I finally had a chance to approach Julia in private, she admitted that several people were trying to get her son to join the military, includ-ing some military recruiters who had been calling her house: "He doesn't want to, and I don't want him to go, but I feel like people assume that he needs to go, to make something of himself, to be worth something. I don't know what to do. . . . I've never had problems with my son, but this woman [Elisa] is always telling me that I should make him join [the military] to get him off the streets." Julia explained, "My son is this tall and husky Puerto Rican kid and people immediately assume . . . that he's trouble. . . . But, you know, even if my son got into trouble, God forbid, I'd rather have him do nothing than send him to Iraq to die. Maybe that's the wrong attitude, but as a mother, I can't."

Coming from Julia, who had been visibly touched by the 65th Infantry event, I was acutely aware that her confusion did not stem from a lack of "patriotism" or even a liberal antiwar activism. Instead, Julia was simply serving as a faithful advocate for her son and was conflicted about having to explain Joel's worth against dominant neoliberal narratives of labor market productivity, academic or professional drive, or the normative capitalist and familial desires for a family, mortgage, and white-collar career. "I'm not going to kick my son out because he's not working, but that's what people tell me to do. [To give an ultimatum] Either you get a job or you join the military or whatever or you're out of my house. I can't be like that, because he's a good kid, he loves his sister, his aunts. He's a very affectionate kid, a good kid. He tells me, 'Mami, I'm going to cook arroz y habichuela for you today.'"

When Julia talked about her son's situation, I recognized the struggle of many Puerto Rican parents—how to engage in an alternative form of making meaning for lives that are imagined as unproductive because they don't subscribe to standard neoliberal measures of mobility, productivity, reproductivity, or ambition (cf. Cacho 2007, 191). This is not only a mother who cares for her son, although there is certainly an alternative attribution of worth that is inherent in a narrative of affect and caring. There is a deeper recognition that conventional notions of productivity are not as definitively within the reach of some racialized young people. Like other Puerto Rican mothers, Julia mobilizes notions of home as a place of specific forms of affective capital and symbolic labor, but also as a place where outside frames and practices of "productivity" are not necessarily relevant or even welcomed.

Joel—who later told me that what he most enjoyed was cooking for his family, but did not want to pursue cooking school (which had been my suggestion)—was challenging the attitudes, values, desires, and work ethic that would lead him to the life of a productive neoliberal subject. Cathy Cohen notes the irony: "[T]hrough these attempts to find autonomy, these individuals, with relatively little access to dominant power, not only counter or challenge the presiding normative order with regard to family, sex, and desire, but also create new or counter normative frameworks by which to judge behavior" (2004, 30; Fuery 1995). There is the expectation that kids are supposed to have certain seminal life experiences (a family, a job, a house), making it impossible to ascribe value to life choices that don't comply to normative goals of capital accumulation, productivity, and heteronormative family units (Cacho 2007, 202; Ingraham 1996). Julia inadvertently narrated her son's worth by ascribing human value to a devalued life in a way that did not depend on a logic of deserving/undeserving, while still struggling to self-defensively question the dominant racialization of Puerto Rican youth and the questioned value of Puerto Ricans' US citizenship.[1]

The emotional contexts behind a politics of social worth, deservingness, and respectability offer important insights into the role that Puerto Ricans, as racialized US citizens, played in Newark neoliberal projects and urban aspirations. By focusing on the militarization of Latino neighborhoods, the criminalization of schools, and urban surveillance practices, this chapter provides an ethnographic portrait of how the neoliberal emotional regime theorized in the introduction and situated historically in chapter 1 impacted the everyday relationships among Puerto Ricans, African Americans, and South American immigrants, particularly in the predominantly Puerto Rican North Broadway neighborhood. The emotional styles in North Broadway that were compatible with Newark's neoliberal aspirations were those that situated Puerto Rican youth—materially and discursively—in three distinct ideological spaces of interactions in relation to South American migrants and an African American population.

First, despite a numerical dominance in the area, Puerto Ricans have been branded as "delinquent" or "deviant" by other South American residents, who have been assigned the role of ideal neoliberal subject—a version of what Bonnie Honig (2001) terms "the supercitizen immigrant." Two main responses that Puerto Ricans have historically adopted to challenge images of delinquency are creating social service organizations and joining the military. At a broader community level, the prominence of social service organizations premised on psychologically influenced notions of "self-esteem" and "self-help" served as defensive strategies to establish the national belonging of otherwise delinquent citizens. Newark is one of the cities with the highest concentration of Latino social service organizations, most of which were founded and staffed by Puerto Ricans. Tracing their genesis to the civil rights era, these organizations have embraced notions of individual empowerment through sociopsychological and "mental health" capital (e.g., notions of "pride" and goals of "increasing self-esteem" among youth).

These practices did not allow for Puerto Ricans to be scripted out of their deviance, or considered socially worthy, not only because of their race, but also because of their inability to perform the respectability, productivity, and domesticity required of citizen-subjects under neoliberalism. At an individual level, perspectives toward military recruitment in light of conceptions of street violence, welfare, dependency, and teenage motherhood are likewise particularly salient in reinforcing heteronormative capitalist goals that Puerto Rican youth can only aspire to by subscribing to self-defensive accounts that render them as individual exceptions to an otherwise "delinquent citizenship." These perspectives also function to produce an ideal neoliberal subject, whose rags-to-riches story supports capital accumulation, and who is better embodied in the image of the docile and more readily exploitative "immigrant" rather than an "aggressive" domestic minority.[2]

A second ideological space, one shared by Puerto Ricans and African Americans, required the activation of a working- and middle-class African American politics of respectability, which in turn privileged trust, sincerity, and intent as the lenses through which Puerto Ricans viewed African Americans in Newark and evaluated their social and affective interactions. In the case of Puerto Rican youth, the distinction between "getting along" with African Americans and determining "who has your back" becomes critical. As simultaneously "unproductive," "reproductive," "lawless," and "parasitic to the system," Puerto Ricans were subjected to various surveillance and containment practices—including the implementation of Panasonic-donated security cameras at Barringer High School. While African American youth have also been subject to these criminalizing narratives, the existence of a consolidated black political elite in Newark at times tempered the association of black with crime.

Finally, Puerto Ricans existed within a logic of worth that rendered them visible only when they could be placed in a dyad of productive versus unproductive, good citizen versus bad citizen, socially mobile versus underclassed that corresponded to ideas of emotional adequacy (or, more often inadequacy). Only by appealing to alternative forms of meaning-making were Puerto Rican parents able to defend the value of their children and themselves, as the funeral of Sujeiti Ocasio, an eighteen-year-old Barringer High School student, demonstrates at the end of this chapter.

Puerto Rican "Delinquent Citizenship" and South American "Supercitizen Immigrants"

The conversation between Julia Cabrera and Elisa Elizondo revealed both Julia's difficulty in narrating her son as a worthy individual and Elisa's inability to understand how one could allow a family member to "do nothing with [his] life."[3] It was not that Elisa, as an Ecuadorian migrant, was an uncritical cheerleader for the American dream, but she could not fathom the possibility that upward mobility could, in fact, be beyond the reach of someone like Joel—an English-language-speaking US citizen. And, although Elisa genuinely liked Julia, she wondered about Julia's parenting skills and leniency. She could not understand why Julia was not more proactive in getting Joel to work "at *a-ny-thing!*"

It is important to note that Julia and Elisa met through their involvement at Barringer High School, a school that draws its predominantly Puerto Rican student population from the North Ward. In the United States, high schools provide a unique site for examining the production and reformulation of processes of "becoming" and "unbecoming American," as well as of creating understandings of citizenship, "immigrant" identity, and race.[4] Social theoreticians of education have demonstrated that the values, assumptions, language skills, behaviors, and parental involvement encouraged and rewarded in schools are not only biased in favor of white, European American, middle-class, patriarchal values, but in fact are the foundation of such values (Bourdieu 1977). In this context, Barringer High School, like other public high schools in the United States, provides an important ideological subtext to the construction of "social worth" and how Julia, Elisa, and other parents, students, and school staff refined those perspectives.

The Newark public school system is the largest in New Jersey, with over 44,000 students enrolled. Newark is also one of New Jersey's thirty Abbott school districts—districts that receive state money under a 1997 state court decision that attempts to balance the financial and educational inequities between affluent suburbs and poorer urban and rural areas. Abel Cabrera, a graduate of Barringer and long-time Newark resident, who was a nationalist and civil rights activist in Newark in the 1970s, described how the quality of Newark high schools was never independent of the racial composition of the neighborhood and student populations they served:

East Side and Barringer were perceived to be Newark's good schools, because they had the largest white populations in the 1970s. It was mostly Italian back then. Shabazz [High School], which was known as South Side, was Italian, Weequahic was Jewish at one time, but then, about 30–40 years ago, it started turning African-American. So Weequahic, Shabazz and Central were the black schools and were not viewed as anywhere near as good as Barringer or East Side. Now Barringer is supposed to be the bad school, where all the gang members and the crazy Puerto Ricans are. The black and Latino kids come here acting just like the Puerto Ricans, so that's bad. We have kids who live in this ward, but the parents will send them to East Side High School. They won't send them to Shabazz or the West Side or Central, which are closer, because those are black schools. They send them to ESHS, because that's as white as you can get in Newark.

Since the 1980s, East Side High School in the Ironbound and Barringer High School in North Broadway have been the two public schools with the most significant US-born Latino and Latin American migrant student populations in the city and, because of this, they were often-times described in relation to one another. Barringer occupies a two-story building sprawled over a large city block located across from Newark's Gothic Cathedral of the Sacred Heart and bordering Branch Brook Park. Throughout the 1970s Barringer's demographics changed; Puerto Ricans and African Americans replaced Italians who had either moved to the suburbs or began attending local Catholic schools. In this same era, East Side, a large building across from Van Buren Park in the Ironbound, saw an increase in its Portuguese population and, in the 1980s, in its Brazilian and other South American student body. With comparable enrollment of 1,438 and 1,776, respectively, in the 2001–2 academic year, East Side and Barringer were known for their language diversity. At Barringer, 65 percent of the student body considered English to be its primary lan-guage, while 35 percent were Spanish-speaking. The student population at Barringer was 68 percent Latino in 2002, mostly US-born second- or third-generation Puerto Ricans, although there were also some Domini-can and other South American students, particularly Ecuadorians. When-ever I would mention to anyone familiar with the Newark public school system that I was doing fieldwork at Barringer High School, people would warn me that that was a "bad school," of "too many gangs," in an area through which I shouldn't walk at night. Barringer High School is the third-oldest high school in the United States and the first one to test a state-of-the-art Panasonic surveillance system.[5] The teachers and staff at BHS (especially the younger ones) stood, in many ways, in contradistinc-tion to the ESHS teachers, who oftentimes denied both that racial sorting occurs in the school system and that there is discrimination embedded in the fabric of public education.[6] Barringer's language diversity, although considered linguistically diverse for Newark, was not as significant as what one would find at East Side, where only 15 percent of the students were English-dominant in 2002. Of the rest, 42 percent considered Por-tuguese their primary language, 38 percent were Spanish-dominant, and 1 percent were French-dominant. There was a great rivalry between the two schools, including in the area of sports, particularly baseball. "The only two schools that have good baseball teams are Barringer and East Side High School," Rodolfo, a parent-volunteer mentioned, alluding to the stereotype of Latinos as better baseball players than their African America counterparts.

More significant, and relevant to framing Julia and Elisa's conversation, was the fact that comparisons between Barringer and East Side included coded statements about the spatially inscribed dimensions of Puerto Rican "delinquent citizenship" that was oftentimes deployed in contradistinction to "immigrant values," "decency," and "morality" attributed to Latin American migrants and Portuguese residents of the Ironbound (cf. Ramos-Zayas 2004). Ada Reyes, a Puerto Rican woman who worked in the ESL program at East Side, had migrated from Puerto Rico as an adult and considered herself more similar to other Latin American migrants than to the US-born Puerto Ricans whom she had encountered in her twenty-five years working in the Newark public school system. A resident of a New Jersey suburb about twenty miles west of Newark, Ada continuously deployed her identity as a Puerto Rican "Islander" instead of a "Mainlander" (Ramos-Zayas 2003). In a conversation I had with her, she was particularly vocal about the distinction between Barringer and East Side High Schools:

Ada Reyes: Uff . . . That school [Baringer] is so horrible, horrible. The entire area is horrible, so of course the school will be too. I worked there for four years. There is a lack of respect, a welfare culture in that school. You talk to the parents and you see that they tell their kids: "you better go to school, or else you won't get welfare!" [mimicking a "street" accent]. Students are having babies, and that goes on for generations, babies having babies. If you reprimand a student in the hallway [of BHS], they are defiant. Not like here. Here the student tells you, "I'm sorry." There they look at you like "You can't tell me what to do." And that school, the whole area, there's a lot of illness. . . .

Ana Yolanda (AY): Illness?

Ada: Yes, syphilis and who knows what else. . . . It's all so disgusting.

AY: Why do you think the schools are different?

Ada: Well, the communities are very different. This [Ironbound] is a more stable community. It's an immigrant community; they have immigrant values. [At Barringer] the kids come from the projects. Sometimes you can't even contact the parents when you need to talk to them. The parents are in jail. Here [at ESHS] kids learn what hard work is. Most of them came here from other countries, or even came here when they were babies, but their parents have a work ethics, morals. They know what it's like to live in a house, in a family environment. They come here to work, save money, move to the suburbs. And they get to do that. North Newark, the people who live in the projects there have lived there for generations. They never go anywhere. They don't make a better life for themselves.

As Bonnie Honig argues, "exceptionalist accounts of American democracy are inextricably intertwined with the myth of an immigrant America" (2001, 74), a discourse that solidifies the treatment of the most vulnerable immigrants as the fictitious antithesis of the domestic poor. This form of pro-immigrant conservatism, in its exaggerated praise of immigrant "family values" and traditional patriarchal structures, is intended to mobilize the immigrants symbolically to discipline the native-born racialized groups into traditional heteronormative roles (81–86). A deployment of the foreigner to model the American dream does not offset xenophobic reactions, but in fact generates them. In particular, because the foreigners are depicted as "passive" and too invested in their everyday routines and family lives, and are too busy pursuing the American dream, they are praised for a perceived political apathy and passivity.

Such highly emotive, affective, and visual conceptions of "the immigrant" or "the foreigner"—in their enjoyment of the rewards for their hard work—contribute to sustaining urban neoliberal aspirations by equating citizenship and a language of rights with consumption, materialism, and capital production, so that commercial (not political) incorporation is most notable among the foreigner, the immigrant, and model minorities. Conceptions of such a "supercitizen immigrant" (Honig 2001, 77) are so powerful and compelling, deeply seeded and emotive, that they render impossible an alternative way to narrate certain populations—including Puerto Rican youths like Julia's son Joel—out of their "deviance" in ways that would valorize them in light of an inherent self-worth or humanity, unless such valorization can be attached to mainstream definitions of a productive existence.

In relation to Puerto Rican youth, moreover, productivity was measured not only in terms of dominant forms of cultural, symbolic, and economic capital (Bourdieu 1977), but also in terms of emotional capital that Puerto Ricans (and, as examined in chapter 5, African American women) presumably lacked and which rendered them unincorporable at all social levels, even in terms of a broader South American–based Latinidad in Newark. A main component of such emotional capital included Puerto Ricans' presumed inability to be "grateful" or "appreciative." Almost invariably, in conversations with Portuguese, Brazilians, and other South Americans in Newark, the tense relationship between recognizing discrimination and being "grateful for the opportunities" in the United States emerged. While these populations sometimes recognized discrimination in relation to African Americans, and pointed to slavery as leading evidence, discussions about Puerto Ricans focused almost exclusively on their "ungratefulness."

Albert Rodríguez, a vivacious and energetic graduate of Barringer High School who still did odd jobs at the school, was one of many Puerto Ricans who noticed the emotional inadequacy that other Latin Americans projected onto Puerto Ricans. When I asked him if he noticed many friendships or relationships among Latinos of different nationalities, he commented with an uncharacteristic:

There are some but, to tell you the truth. . . . I don't know, for some reason, siempre nos están tirando [they're always taking a shot at us]. [They criticize] the way we speak and they're always making fun of us. So I'm not really, really tight with them because I don't like that. They feel they're more educated than us and that's not true. I think the issue of them not being US citizens plays a part in all that. My Puerto Rican friend from Lares [a town in Puerto Rico] married a Colombian girl and she's always saying, "Oh you guys are lucky and you guys don't appreciate what you have" and she's always, siempre está tirando. [Saying] "Here I am I just came here two years ago I'm going to go into the army and I'm in college now. You guys don't appreciate how much this country has done for you."

"Siempre nos están tirando" suggests how insults become things that can be thrown around—like balls or bullets, depending on the intensity—and which would presumably be caught and thrown back from the other side or simply self-defensively dodged. Albert shifted into Spanish when describing the interaction with other Latinos, particularly the South American wife of a good friend of his, using the phrase "siempre nos están tirando," as he conveyed the boundaries of trust with some South American migrants. I envisioned the physical manifestation of that phrase in relation to both Puerto Rican "ungratefulness" and linguistic "inadequacy" often, and noted how the emphasis on an inadequate Puerto Rican emotional style was profoundly tied to conceptions of Puerto Rican linguistic disorder (Urciuoli 1996). When a student complimented a Puerto Rican boy at an ESL class at East Side, the boy turned toward an Ecuadorian girl who had been making fun of him and told her, "Ves? Yo también tengo celebro." Another one of the Ecuadorian girls in the class immediately laughed at him for saying "celebro" instead of "cerebro," a linguistic mistake commonly attributed to Puerto Ricans (the substitution of an *l* for an *r*). The boy was embarrassed but simply said, "Well, I still was able to remember what happened in the other class."

Javier Otero, who had graduated from Barringer in the 1990s and worked at a social service agency, noted how this was a common perspective that many "people who are not citizens" had of US-born minorities. Javier recalled,

Some of these [Latin American] immigrants have degrees from their countries. They never experienced discrimination [in their countries of origin]. They never experienced prejudice. My baby's mother, she's a green-eyed, light-skinned person. She never experienced discrimination [in Colombia]. She used to think it was a problem that we Puerto Ricans had . . . a complejo [complex]. Until, she was around African American and dark skinned people who treated her differently. That's when she had to deal with it. And she said this is ridiculous.

Javier highlighted a perspective of prejudice that was common among many South American migrants in Newark (further examined in chapter 3): African Americans were the bearers of the greatest anti-Latino prejudice in Newark. What is also relevant in Javier's quote is the fact that, at least initially, this young Colombian woman assumed that Puerto Ricans were "acomplejados," who subscribed to a culture of victimhood and misread other people's attitudes as racism. In the end, when she herself, a white Colombian, experienced prejudice from blacks, then she acknowledged that racism existed, even as she apparently remained unable (or unwilling) to recognize racism on the part of whites.

Jennifer Flores, a Puerto Rican graduate of Barringer High School who worked at a North Broadway social service agency when I met her, recounted an experience she had with a young Peruvian woman who had begun to attend one of the agency's GRE classes:

I had this Peruvian kid once telling me que "Los latinos son malagradecidos a los americanos, que ellos no quieren aprender inglés y si uno va al país de otra persona uno tiene que aprender su idioma" [that "Latinos are ungrateful to the Americans, that they don't want to learn English and that, if one goes to another person's country, one has to learn their language"]. And I'm looking at her like ¿Qué te pasa a ti? [What's wrong with you?]. And I got pissed off. I told her, "What are you going to tell the Chicanos and Puerto Ricans, knowing that the U.S. came over and took their lands? And all the Puerto Ricans that get sent to the front lines to get killed, are you going to tell them that?" And she was like, "Well you know, things are like that, and that was a long time ago. And they get taken off the streets." And I'm looking at her like . . . [with disapproval]. All her friends were white. . . . And, by the way, I don't believe all white people are bad and I don't think our people are always the best either. But for her, having her own issues being from South America, being accepted by estos rubios [these light-skinned people] was important. Because she had this need to be accepted, she looked down on all other Latinos. And that's not uncommon. I've heard it all over and over from the barrio to the suburbs. "No, no, no, estamos aquí. Qué buenos son los americanos. Ellos nos recibieron [No, no, no, we're here now. The Americans are great! They allowed us in]."

Jennifer serves as a street therapist in this instance, when she concludes that this South American woman had a "need to be accepted" (and presumably relies on external conditions for validation); this is how Jennifer reclaims a degree of worth from this interaction in a context where her existence, as a Puerto Rican subject, is presumed to be rooted in being "ungrateful." Ungratefulness is symptomatic of emotional inadequacy and this influences, in very precise ways, neoliberal goals in Newark. Implied in this statement is also that there is a connection to a different take on racial democracy—one cannot be South American and rubio (blond, light skin), even though there is an awareness of a diversity of appearance among South American populations.

Puerto Rican "ungratefulness" acquired a particularly strong spatial grounding in the context of social service work, where Puerto Ricans and other South American clients were marked by the particular kind of service they requested. As Mario Ruiz, a worker in one of Newark's Hispanic social service agencies explained when I first met him, the agency's clients were divided between "welfare students," who consisted mostly of Puerto Rican women, and "the general public," who were mostly recent migrants from other Latin American countries. After explaining this distinction and without any prompting, Mario commented, "I don't know why the populations are divided that way. Maybe it's a difference in work ethics. I don't know if it's growing up under a colonial type of situation with the United States that leads to some kind of low self-esteem, I don't know what it is." Although Puerto Ricans continue to be the single largest group of Latinos, a South American subgroup has collectively become the larger percentage of the Hispanic population. Many of the older Puerto Rican residents are returning to the island after retirement; many other Puerto Rican residents still live in the city, while other educated and professional Latinos—who are moving up the corporate ladder—are moving to the suburbs or migrating to Florida. Since the 1980s, a growing number of Dominicans, Ecuadorians, and Colombians have also settled in North Broadway. According to a study by the Lewis Mumford Center, in New Jersey, by the mid-1990s, Puerto Ricans had already been "outnumbered for the first time by New Latinos (over 500,000)" and about half of the state's "New Latinos" are from South America (Lewis Mumford Center 2002).

The son of a Puerto Rican father and an Ecuadorian mother, Mario identified as Ecuadorian because his father was never part of the picture, as he described a presumed incomplete framing of what a complete family life should be. Mario continued to draw from his own personal experience to explain the distinction between Puerto Ricans and other people from Latin America not only as a distinction between "welfare abusers" versus "hard-working people," but as one between people who were "dependent," as a stigmatized substance abuser would be, on the one hand, and people who were clear-headed, focused, self-motivated, and mentally adequate, on the other. He explains:

I've seen immigrants who come here from South America, even from Haiti, and they come here and some of them that actually could go on welfare, don't. They'd rather take that five dollar fifteen an hour job than be on welfare. . . . Welfare is almost like a drug, because you get dependent on it. It's a very nasty cycle that runs in many Puerto Rican families. . . . My mom [who's Ecuadorian] was on welfare, but she was very well educated. She didn't know the language and my father was not in the picture, that's why she received welfare. But still my mother stressed education for my brother and I. . . . And I ended up going to college and my brother ended up going to the [military] service. I know that the students who are coming from Latin America don't think a whole lot of the Puerto Ricans, because of the whole welfare dependency thing.

Although Mario, like most other social service workers in North Newark, nodded to the "colonial type of situation" of Puerto Ricans, the message was still the same. Puerto Ricans suffered from emotional inadequacy, subpar mental capacity, low self-esteem, and an inability to focus or care for one's life, all attributes required for social mobility and progress. Seductive images of immigrant self-sufficiency overshadowed most political economic interpretations of the "poor work ethic" or "low self-esteem" of Puerto Ricans, because such images were also saturated with subjective readings of mental health and emotional stability. That is why Mario's own mother, who did indeed receive public aid, appeared exempt from a "welfare queen" prototype; she was able to display her emotional adequacy by stressing education and military service, instilling self-esteem in her children, and keeping a patriarchal family structure despite the absence of the Puerto Rican father. For other South Americans, like Viviana Amaral, a Brazilian resident of Belleville, a working-class neighborhood adjacent to Newark's North Ward, the issue was not so much about Puerto Ricans receiving "welfare" as such, but about working. In describing the difference she noticed between North Broadway and the Ironbound, an area where she had lived upon arrival in the United States in 1989, Viviana commented, "Puerto Ricans have a welfare mentality, but the Brazilian never had that mentality. Even if a Brazilian could get welfare, they would accept to take the welfare, they wouldn't reject it, but they would continue working to save twice as much!"[7]

Latinidad supplied descriptions of an identity—related to Spanish-language commonality, an "immigrant" identity, and, ironically, a status of "illegality"—that excluded many Puerto Ricans and their English-dominant US citizen children. Interestingly, even spaces where concerted efforts toward a "Latino ethnic consciousness" (Padilla 1985) appeared to successfully transcend attitudes toward this Puerto Rican exceptionalism, a subtext of intimate ambivalence and constant assessments of emotional adequacy persisted. "Here we are the United Nations," Isabel Hernández, a Puerto Rican woman born and raised in Newark, claimed in a celebratory tone at a brunch sponsored by a Catholic parish in North Newark. As she introduced me to a group of people sitting at a nearby table, Isabel mentioned both the names and the nationality: "Pedro and Marissa Fernández are Cuban. They have a seven-year-old grandson who's half-Cuban and half-Portuguese. Mariana is Dominican. And we are Puerto Rican. We all work together and have known each other since our kids were babies." About twenty minutes later, as I was walking to get a coffee refill, Armando Zapatero, a Salvadoran man, stopped me to ask about my project. When I vaguely answered that I was interested in learning more about the Latino community in Newark, he categorically stated: "There's very little collaboration here among Hispanics. Puerto Ricans are losing political clout and the older politicians, they're all Puerto Ricans, don't want to let younger candidates of other groups emerge. They have a lot of resentment." Two older Puerto Rican women who were standing behind the cafeteria counter nearby overheard Armando's comment and looked disapprovingly at him. One of the women later told the other, "You see? They're always discrediting all the work that Puerto Ricans do here."

When I described these conversations later to the Brazilian priest who conducts the Spanish mass at the Catholic church, he explained matter-of-factly: "The other groups see Puerto Ricans as the beggars of America." And he added, as if distancing himself from those people who harbored that negative image: "The deeds of one or two people color how everyone else is perceived. That's not fair, but it happens to Puerto Ricans here . . . just one or two that fit the stereotype and everyone else pays for it. Because here everyone assumes that, if you're Puerto Rican, you're on welfare, you're waiting to take a knife out, violent. But most Puerto Ricans are really very peaceful, generous people that want to raise good families." Emotional adequacy was the leading criterion to determine which Puerto Ricans fit the stereotype, and also became critical to explaining or justifying intimate relationships one might have with Puerto Ricans. For instance, a day in late November 2004, as I was riding the New Jersey Transit train into Newark–Penn Station, I overheard a mobile phone conversation between a Brazilian woman in her late twenties and her mother in which the young woman was talking about a Puerto Rican man she had begun to date. I overheard the young woman defending her boyfriend: "Mãe, ele é de Porto Rico, Boricua. Ele é americano. Nasceu em Nova Iorque [Mom, he is from Puerto Rico, Boricua. He is American. Was born in New York]." She explained how Puerto Ricans are "really American" and how he was "born in New Jersey." Was the mother urging her daughter to date an "American" and was she not clear as to whether a Puerto Rican would fit the bill? In reference to a past conversation that the Puerto Rican boyfriend apparently had with the Brazilian woman's mother, the daughter commented:

Mãe, ele fala espanhol. Ele falou português com vôce, mais ele fala espanhol. vôce esta nervosa e não entende, mais ele tentou falar português com vôce. Se ele presta atenção, ele entende português. Todos os americanos falam português muito estranho, é engraçado. [Mom, he speaks Spanish. He spoke Portuguese with you, but he speaks Spanish. You are upset and don't understand, but he tried to speak Portuguese with you. If he pays attention, he understands Portuguese. All Americans speak Portuguese awkwardly, it's funny.]

Apparently, the boyfriend had spoken with this woman's mother earlier and had joked by calling her "sogra" (mother-in-law). The woman defends the boyfriend: "Ele é uma boa pessoa, mãe. Me pergunta: 'Usted llamó su mamá hoje'? [in sort of Spanish or Portunhol]' Ele é lindo, sim. [He's a good person, Mom. He asks me: "Did you call your mom today?" He is so cute.]"[8]

Several remedial strategies were deployed as tools for the social defense of Puerto Ricans, even by people who were not themselves Puerto Rican, like the woman on the New Jersey Transit train. In the context of US high schools, like Barringer and East Side, such strategies were manifested in different ways. At Barringer, a form of disciplined desperation prevailed. From the first time I set foot in the high school, I felt a sense of impossibility. When I requested an appointment with the principal, a Puerto Rican administrative assistant whom I began to see as a key gatekeeper conveyed how difficult any contact with the principal would be. He was very busy. She needed to know what exactly I wanted from them. Did I have all the permissions needed by the Board of Education and, if not, did I realize how long something like that would take? "Really, are you sure you want to do your school project here?" And then one day, after weeks of canceled appointments and being stood up, it all became miraculously easy. I met the Puerto Rican principal, who shared his own experiences with Rutgers and took the time to introduce me to the staff. "She's from

Rutgers. She's Puerto Rican. No, no, she's not a student. She's a professor there." He allowed me to have as much contact as I wanted with the students and he asked me to help with various programs to bring more parents into the school. I began to learn that my being Puerto Rican was read as evidence that I would not be one of those people who "siempre nos están tirando" [they're always attacking us], and being from Rutgers meant that they could finally get the State University of New Jersey to care about Newark high schools. The initial sense of impossibility, however, was a form of Puerto Rican self-defensiveness that I would come to encounter many times over at other North Broadway institutions.

At East Side, the remedial strategies were mostly promoted by some concerned white, Portuguese American, and Latino faculty members in reaction to what they interpreted as a need to establish a process of cultural recognition and pride that would challenge dominant negative views of Puerto Ricans in the school. Upon learning about my interest in the experiences of Latino students, several Portuguese and Italian teachers would invariably show me graffiti writing (a couple of scribbles that could not have been more than two inches long) behind the school stairway or relay their suspicions about specific students being gang members. A "Puerto Rican Show" was put in place to counter such images. A Portuguese American parent volunteer explained: "For the Puerto Rican Show, the parent-volunteers and I sew a large Puerto Rican flag, and then put the palm trees and golden sand and a little boat." And she added: "I was wearing a Puerto Rican shirt with palm trees and stuff, not with the Puerto Rican flag, and a student was telling me 'But you're not Puerto Rican.' And I told him 'I am today! We're all Puerto Rican today.'" Laura McCarren, a white teacher who had participated in the struggle to build Puerto Rican studies at Rutgers in the 1970s, described the reason for having a Puerto Rican show at a school with only fifty or sixty Puerto Rican students:

At the time, there had been instances of graffiti, and other writings that some people viewed as gang-related or violent. All fingers were pointing to the Puerto Rican kids. People around the school were accusing even before investigating or even understanding the problem. So I felt the kids needed to do something to regain their voice back and to show others that there are other dimensions to being Puerto Rican.

Adamaris and Leila, two Puerto Rican students who had learned to dance Bomba, an Afro-Puerto Rican folkloric dance, for the show described what the activity had meant to them. Adamaris explained, "The woman who taught us how to dance Bomba, at Aspira, made sure that we understood also the political aspects of Bomba. How it was a form for blacks and Puerto Ricans to defend themselves." Leila added, "In this school people think that all Puerto Ricans are on welfare or in gangs, and there are a lot of people who are, but there are other aspects to being Puerto Rican and the show started with that, with the stereotypes." When I asked Laura McCarren if she sensed that others students had changed their view of Puerto Ricans as a result of the show, she said,

They [the Puerto Rican students] felt they could defend themselves better when allegations were made against them. . . . Puerto Rican kids are very helpful, but they're also a bit passive. They always want to be helpful to others, don't complain too much. They are in this school because their parents think this school is better than Barringer. Some parents have a relative in this area, so they use that address to matriculate the kids here, so they don't feel such a strong sense of ownership or that their culture is understood here.

There is a process of erasure of the social worth of Puerto Rican and black youth in these predominantly white/multicultural spaces that South American immigrants, even the undocumented, were still able to avoid. Even caring teachers struggled but failed to ascribe value to the lives of Puerto Rican and black youth, largely because they could only measure these lives vis-à-vis dominant ideas of respectability, productivity, opportunities, and hard work into which it was difficult to accommodate or narrate Puerto Ricans as individuals who had a presumably tremendous advantage—US citizenship and English-language dominance—that South American and other immigrants lacked.

While occasional remedial strategies centered on displays of cultural pride rooted in a reappraisal of a rich quasi-mythical history of struggle, virtuosity, and resistance, as was the case with the Puerto Rican Show at East Side, it was the development of community organizations and US military enrollment that became the leading institutional responses to two critical concerns of urban neoliberalism: first, getting youth of color "off the [gentrifying] streets" and imparting "self-esteem" and, second, reestablishing normative gender and sexual values that could be consistent with a form of quaint patriotism that would be more in alignment with Newark's changing demographics and real estate and "security" interests. Both of these concerns required that youth and their guardians become convinced that the only way for them to acquire emotional adequacy was to abandon the crime-ridden streets and their tenuous productive (and invariably reproductive, as in "unwed mothering") future. I now turn to the two main strategies suggested here: the historical transformation of Puerto Rican organizations from a strategy of political militancy to a psychologically influenced "self-help" focus and the targeted military recruitment of Puerto Rican youth.

From Political Militancy to Self-Help Strategies: The Branch Brook Park Disturbances of 1974 and Puerto Rican Social Service Organizations

The North Broadway neighborhood is an example of how "self-help" often becomes rhetoric of choice in discussions of improving a neighborhood through not-for-profit organizations and increasing "self-esteem" among youth; these are rooted in visions of empowerment and pride that have characterized Puerto Rican communities throughout the United States (Ramos-Zayas 2003). This is exacerbated in Newark, a city that has one of the highest numbers of Hispanic not-for-profit organizations in the United States. The role of the self-help industry and its psychoanalytic culture has received some attention among social theorists interested in interrogating the manifestation of inequality and subordination in structures of affect and capital (Hennessy 2000). Emotional and economic discourses and practices mutually shape each other thus producing what Eva Illouz (2007) views as a sweeping movement in which affect is made an essential aspect of economic behavior and in which emotional life—in Illouz's case, that of the (white) middle classes—follows the logic of economic relations and exchange.[9] A rationalization of feelings and the commodification of emotions are key themes in these processes. It is important to examine the conditions that led Puerto Ricans to embrace a self-help culture in Newark, channeled through a variety of social service groups, from very early on in the formation of a Puerto Rican community.

The arrival of Puerto Ricans in Newark in the 1950s coincided with the heyday of "slum clearance" in the city, and there seems to be a sense of longing among Puerto Ricans for an "ethnic enclave" that never really blossomed (Hidalgo 1970). In the 1950s agricultural workers were recruited from Puerto Rico to work on farms throughout New Jersey as part of the federal and commonwealth-sponsored program of rapid industrialization known as Operation Bootstraps. In addition to agricultural workers, a "second wave" of Puerto Ricans arrived (some from Puerto Rico and others as a second-stage migration from New York) directly to Newark in the 1950s and 1960s. Attracted largely by factory jobs, they were informally recruited through the networks developing within the small but significant community of Puerto Ricans already established in Newark. After World War II, Puerto Ricans occupied the industrial jobs that war recruits had left in cities including Perth Amboy, Paterson, and Newark. The chain migration by which family members would inform other relatives and friends of jobs available accounted for entire communities to be settled mainly by people from one or two towns in Puerto Rico. As a woman interviewed by a New Jersey newspaper mentioned: "On island towns like Guayanilla, the shout was: 'Nos vamos para los Amboy [We're going to the Amboys].' As a result, most of the people in Perth Amboy came from that town" (in Hidalgo 1970).

The first Puerto Rican migrants to Newark settled within the two-block area of the old Plane Street (now University Avenue), but they were displaced from this area when Rutgers University built its Newark campus.[10] By 1956, under Louis Danzig, the director of the urban renewal program, the city was ready to market its land and engaged in promotional campaigns to generate the interest of developers, eventually encouraging several firms to make bids on auctioned-off lands.[11] The auctioning of this land coincided with the early stages of Puerto Rican community development and, ultimately, led to Puerto Rican displacement. After the urban "renewal" programs were underway, the Puerto Rican population, viewed in the segregation literature as a buffer racial group between blacks and whites (e.g., Massey and Denton 1993), was being resettled in the North Ward, a predominantly Italian area. The North Broadway neighborhood is part of the North Ward. Landlord abuse and open discrimination against Puerto Ricans in rental practices resulted in Puerto Ricans being "the most exploited group in the city in reference to housing" at the time (Hidalgo 1970, 12).

When the first slum-clearance project, which consisted of the edification of the Columbus Homes in North Broadway, was announced in 1952, Joseph Melillo, a North Ward Italian lawyer, organized mass rallies, petitions, and protest marches, and requested audiences with the mayor through his Save Our Homes Council.[12] Melillo's initiative was partly a response to the fear that the public housing phase of the North Broadway project, the Columbus Homes, would increase the number of black families in the predominantly Italian area and eventually serve as "an opening wedge for a Negro invasion of [the predominantly Italian] North Broadway" (Kaplan 1963, 152). In fact, the movement of black and Puerto Rican families into North Broadway's Columbus Homes generated an opposition to urban renewal programs that had, for the most part, been dormant in Newark.[13] Prejudice against blacks among Newark's white residents, most openly voiced by Italian Americans, became most salient in light of increased southern black migration, even while images of Newark as a black paradise had been attracting southern blacks during the Civil War (Price 2008).[14]

Even when Newark had a large low-income housing program that had built over 3,700 units since the late 1950s, the city had already evicted over 12,000 families for "renewal" purposes and highway construction. This was also a period of heightened Puerto Rican settlement in Newark, and the "renewal" projects in fact truncated many community-building efforts in the newly emergent Puerto Rican community. By 1960, at the height of Puerto Rican migration, Newark's Central Business District was 33 percent Puerto Rican, while the Ironbound had a Puerto Rican population of about 6 percent. Very few Puerto Ricans (under 2 percent) lived in the North Ward at that time and those who did lived in the Columbus Homes, which were constructed in 1952. About 9 percent of Puerto Ricans lived in the South Broad section of the South Ward and 2 percent lived in Weequahic (Kaplan 1963, 149).

By the mid-1960s, many Puerto Ricans had already been displaced from the central districts of the city to North Broadway, which a decade later was considered a predominantly "Spanish area" of Newark. Around this time a significant number of Puerto Ricans also lived in the Ironbound, an area that was already considered more "traditional" and more "ethnic" than the other city neighborhoods. In fact, it was thought that Puerto Ricans and Cubans would displace the few early Portuguese and Spanish residents who lived in the area at the time. In an article titled "Latin Influence Rising in Newark" (1966) reporter Josephine Bonomo documented the growing influx of Puerto Ricans and Cubans:

There are blocks in Newark today where young children speak no English, where housewives shop for mangos and plátanos and frijoles, and teen-agers read comic books whose covers advertise "Action [sic]! Sorpresas! Suspenso!" . . . Although there has been a small nucleus of Spanish and Portuguese families in the Ironbound section for many years, recent arrivals from Puerto Rico and Cuba have more than doubled the group. . . . Some of the newcomers have gone to the Ironbound, the city's traditional melting pot, while others have settled in both the north and south ends of Broad Street. . . . In Ferry Street, heart of the Ironbound business district, there are Spanish clothing stores, photographers, furniture stores, tuxedo rentals, barbers, beauty parlors and bakeries and even a Cuban-owned pizzeria. There are Cuban interns and nurses in several local hospitals and Cuban and Puerto Rican doctors in private practice. . . . Stores owned by non-Latins cater to the Spanish trade. . . . There are magazines from Spain and paperback books and greeting cards printed in Spanish. . . . An even more important sign in a Pacific Street television shop announces "Aquí se instala el Canal 47."[15]

The 1960s Ironbound, where Puerto Ricans and Cubans settled, was described with images similar to those deployed later to describe the Portuguese-dominant Ironbound of the post-riot (particularly the 1970s) and contemporary eras. Theatres showing movies in Spanish and foods reflecting Spanish taste—"even selling frozen Mexican dinners of tamales, frijoles and rice"—served as evidence of the changing look of Newark in the 1960s. These depictions are telling because they constituted an area as productive, upwardly mobile, commercial viable, and culturally excessive—an area of "hardworking" and "family oriented" people—in contradistinction to other parts of the increasingly fragmented city, including the other "Spanish area" of North Newark.

The Ironbound was the only area in which Puerto Ricans, like other "immigrants," were able to pursue entrepreneurial interests.[16] The space of the Ironbound, almost irrespective of the population occupying it, appears to generate images of productivity, cultural richness, and "immigrant values," largely because it is viewed as physically and even morally separate from "the rest of [black] Newark." In Bonomo's article, Puerto Ricans and Cubans are treated as earlier generations of European arrivals, who have the same reasons for migrating, "lack of opportunity at home."[17] Puerto Ricans like José and Margarita Martínez, shopkeepers who had operated a grocery store at 84 Ferry Street in the Ironbound since 1959, and José Soto, who had, in 1966, taken over an Italian grocery store in the North Broadway area of South Broad Street, were quoted as examples of Puerto Rican productivity in a way that appeared almost entirely absent a decade later.

Between 1960 and 1970 the Newark Puerto Rican population had increased by 75 percent, and by the 1980s Puerto Ricans were the fastest-growing ethnic group in the city, with a growth of 150 percent.[18] By the 1970s Newark Airport already received at least four daily weekday flights from Puerto Rico and even more flights on weekends and high-peak harvest and holiday seasons.[19] To meet the needs of this rapidly growing community, many Catholic churches became centers for the dispensation of social services. Mario Muccitelli, a Catholic priest at the Our Lady of Perpetual Help Center in North Broadway's South Broad Street, counted 1,000 families in the area near the parish, most of whom were Puerto Ricans who had arrived from the island and lived in the Archbishop Walsh and Christopher Columbus homes. Father Mario is cited as saying: "We don't want them to lose their Spanish background or language. The language is a great asset to them. We tell them 'Each person is worth the number of languages he knows. If you're worth two people, why should you be worth only one? We don't want them to be ashamed of their tradition and heritage. They should be proud of it."[20] Puerto Rican and Cuban children entering Newark public schools without English-language skills received help from special teachers in Lafayette School in the Ironbound and McKinley in North Broadway prior to the formal institutionalization of bilingual programs. Spanish-language maintenance was likewise a way of retaining an identity as "immigrant," and part of a group which the Catholic Church was aiming to recruit as members.

For Puerto Ricans who arrived from the Bronx and Brooklyn in the 1970s, New Jersey represented the American dream of suburban (or suburban-looking) houses, rather than the crowded tenement buildings in which they had grown up. At a time when the so-called Puerto Rican problem—the belief that there were "too many" Puerto Ricans in New York and the negative public portrayal of these migrants—led government officials to redirect Puerto Rican workers to other US production centers including Chicago (cf. Padilla 1985; Ramos-Zayas 2003), Newark became a secondary area of residence for New York Puerto Ricans. In many ways, Puerto Ricans who had lived in the most deplorable areas of the Bronx and Brooklyn, as well as the predominantly Puerto Rican areas of Manhattan, like Spanish Harlem and Loisaida (the Lower East Side), viewed New Jersey as one step closer to fulfilling their desire for better, more spacious housing, greater safety, and more consistent employment opportunities. These Puerto Ricans oftentimes settled in Teaneck, Hackensack, Englewood, and North Bergen. For some time, it seemed as though Puerto Ricans living in the southern part of the state and those in the more prosperous north did not communicate with one another, and various statewide social service agencies, at the time motivated by the era's civil rights struggles, aimed to change that.[21]

In the case of Puerto Ricans in Newark, social service organizations have served as a vessel for the articulation of neoliberal aspirations, not necessarily by engaging in direct techniques of capital accumulation, but by adopting a culture of self-help that attempts to convey to other Latinos and Latin American migrants an emotional style that is consistent with those aspirations. A sort of emotional assimilation involves, in particular, not only the avoidance of affiliations with "angry blacks" in a post-riot Newark, but also the recognition of a Latinidad that is not white and which, more specifically, would not represent a threat to political and corporate elites. As Illouz (2003, 136; 2007) notes, while factory work had been directed at introducing bodies (particularly European ethnics) to capitalism in the early twentieth century, not-for-profit organizations focused on helping the subjects that capitalism had, by the middle and latter parts of the century, left out, by creating a different meaning of the term *self-help*. This institutionalization of social networks under different versions of the self-help banner becomes evident in the insistence on "emotional health," "self-esteem," and "self-reliance" that characterizes the racialization of Puerto Ricans in Newark.

On September 1, 1974, a Hispanic service organization known as FOCUS, a multiservice agency established by a predominantly Puerto Rican staff in 1968, sponsored a Labor Day celebration at Branch Brook Park, in the predominantly Puerto Rican area of North Broadway. Festivities came to an abrupt halt when several mounted white policeman entered into conflict with a group of Puerto Rican attendees, who were either vendors or illegal gambling sponsors, depending on who was asked to describe the scene. Raúl Colón and Carlos Santos, two Puerto Rican community leaders, reported that the trouble started when someone threw a bottle at the policemen, but other accounts of the original cause of the violence also exist.[22] Rumors that a four-year-old Puerto Rican girl was trampled to death by one of the policemen's horses began circulating and were printed in hundreds of anonymous handbills later distributed through the Puerto Rican neighborhood. This incident became yet another example of police brutality against the Puerto Rican community. Everyone agreed that afterwards a "riot" erupted, in which hundreds of Puerto Ricans and the entire white Newark police force fought each other. The fighting soon escalated and extended from the park to the North Broadway streets (Chase 2005). A former teacher at Barringer High School recalls: "The cops went on horseback into the school cafeteria during the riots. Can you imagine? They brought horses into our cafeteria downstairs!" When it came to explaining the conflict, issues of inadequate housing and police brutality, however, were downplayed by a consolidated black political elite. For instance, Mayor Gibson stated: "The reason we had a disturbance in Newark is because we had 10,000 people in a park. It had nothing to do with bilingual education, housing or any other socio-economic factor."[23] In total, at least forty-two people were arrested, forty-seven people were injured, and three men, all Puerto Rican, were admitted to the hospital with gunshot wounds.

The events in Newark were of such national importance that the *New York Times* ran numerous articles, one on its cover page. The mayor responded to Puerto Rican demonstrators by saying: "My door is open, and I hope people will come through the door rather than through the window."[24] These "disturbances," as the incident was called, also coincided with an increased visibility of militant anticolonial organizations seeking the independence of Puerto Rico in Newark in the 1970s.[25] Puerto

Ricans began to approach an emotionally over-the-top image akin to that of African Americans, except that "emotions" rather than "race" became a leading category of exclusion and social difference in their case. As William Reddy (1999) notes, "As a category of exclusion, emotion has an unusual status. The political implications of exclusion on the basis of gender, race, sexual orientation, ethnicity, or mental capacity have constantly remained of paramount importance to researchers. But the political implications of different cultures of emotion have not always been clear." Nevertheless, "emotion is a category of exclusion that overlaps and informs other such categories. . . . What is emotional is not rational or scientific; and persons categorized as incapable of reason have invariably been seen as especially emotional" (257).

As a result of the Branch Brook Park incident, the underlying issues that prompted the riots were downplayed or distanced from earlier militant political activism in favor of a new "culture of self- help," rooted on sociopsychological strategies—such as communicating, focusing on youth self-esteem, and solving conflict through dialogue. For instance, Jose Rosario, the board chairman of FOCUS, stated: "After the civil disturbances involving our youth in 1974, I envisioned an auditorium in which communication could be opened among ethnic groups and where the various nationalities could exhibit the artistic accomplishments of their youth. . . . The racial revolution we are living today is of great concern to all of us, but if we can guide our youth into loving instead of hating his fellow brother, there won't be too much racism in the years to come."[26]

Puerto Ricans denounced the deplorable educational conditions of Latino youth, in contradistinction to the educational opportunities extended to white and black youth at city public schools, and ensuing demonstrations demanded bilingual education in Newark public schools along with more support for community-based programs that would serve the extracurricular needs and interests of Puerto Rican youth. La Casa de Don Pedro, an ancient brick factory construction turned into a youth service organization by Puerto Rican youths, was an example of such a community-based program. The director of Casa at the time commented:

Our kids construct most of what we need. . . . The philosophy behind La Casa de Don Pedro was born some three years ago, yet it did not make any real impact with the adolescents until after the Labor Day Weekend disturbances in 1974. . . . After the Labor Day disturbances, I had to get involved. I decided that the Puerto Rican and Hispanic teenagers in my neighborhood were going to have an educational-recreational center of their own. . . . I discovered that the best way lies in offering them a sense of belonging, ownership and pride.[27]

The Branch Brook Park incident confirmed for many Puerto Ricans that power and authority were unevenly distributed throughout society, with space and the neighborhoods that people navigated, claimed, or avoided emerging as one important vector among many for the expression of dominant-subordinate relations within the hegemonic order. This is also what Henri Lefebvre refers to as "spatial practices" that project space onto "all aspects, elements and moments of social practice" (1991, 8). These spatial practices appear to be mobilized as various social boundaries are renegotiated and transformed; therefore, space does not possess an inherent capacity to dominate, but rather is oftentimes invested with power and becomes part of an apparatus of domination (cf. Foucault 1977; Harvey 2001). A leading spatial practice that Puerto Ricans have adopted to pursue community development goals through not-for-profit agencies, as it turns out, is particularly receptive to broader neoliberal techniques and aspirations, including a focus on a culture of self-help and emotional adequacy.

By 2007 foreclosures of residential properties in working-class and poor areas of Newark, particularly in the predominantly Puerto Rican and Latino areas of North Broadway and Roseville, could no longer remain concealed behind Renaissance projects (Newman 2004) Predatory lending practices, along with other unforeseen financial circumstances and misunderstandings about complex mortgage transactions among first-time homeowners, partly explain the fact that more than 40 percent of Newark homeowners spend more than half their income on housing, one of the highest percentages in the New York metropolitan region and among the highest in the United States. A 2007 New York Times article, "Behind Foreclosures, Ruined Credit and Hopes," describes how debt is forcing thousands of Newark homeowners to take multiple jobs and even rent rooms to avoid what appears as an inevitable home loss to foreclosure.[28] While in 2007 New Jersey had a low foreclosure rate, remaining at less than 2 percent of all outstanding mortgages, these numbers mask the reality of the conditions faced in lower-income, heavily minority neighborhoods like Newark, where signs announcing "Avoid Foreclosure" and "Sell Your House" decorate lampposts. Community groups in contemporary Newark lack direct access to federal funds; to access such funds, nonprofits now have to go through the city, which controls federal block grants (Newman 2004, 46). In Newark nonprofits do not challenge the neoliberal development agenda because they are "co-opted with 'side payments' . . . in the form of federal grant funds so their leaders . . . do not challenge the prevailing economic arrangements" (Schulgasser 2002, 15).

Amarilis Guzmán, a Puerto Rican woman in her early twenties whom I met when she was a student at Barringer High School, picked me up at Newark's Penn Station to show me her new home in North Broadway. Once we turned onto her street, Amarilis explained that when she was younger, everyone in the area was Puerto Rican or Italian, but now the area's composition had changed and more Dominicans and Ecuadorians had moved to the neighborhood. "You notice it in the businesses. We don't have Puerto Rican businesses here. Bodegas, los colmados son dominicanos o ecuatorianos [stores are Dominican or Ecuadorian]. Most of the neighbors are still Puerto Rican, but you know, it's changed. People come from Latin America and in a day they open their business. But that doesn't happen with Puerto Ricans." I asked her why she thinks that is, and Amarilis responded: "To be honest with you, it has to do with self-esteem. Because Puerto Ricans are very proud, the flag, the 'Yoooo, Boricuaaaa!' But they don't have self-esteem. There's a lot of complejo, insecurity, plain laziness. That's what I'm trying to change with the kids I work with." Amarilis had begun running her own youth-mentoring sports group when she was barely eighteen years old. Like other Puerto Ricans with whom I spoke, Amarilis saw such organizations as a natural strategy to "build self-esteem" among Puerto Rican youth. Self-esteem was the requirement for social mobility in this narrative.

Social service organizations in North Broadway also highlighted, initially, the distinctions among Spanish-speaking groups that began to arise as the Latino population in the area became more diverse (this was especially prominent at a time when many politically militant Puerto Rican activists viewed most Cubans as capitalist deserters of a newly instituted revolutionary government).[29] Although Puerto Ricans still constituted the largest Latino population in Newark in 2010, and most of the social service organizations in North Broadway were still directed and staffed by Puerto Ricans, eighteen years earlier, in 1992, 85 percent of all Latino businesses in the city were owned by Dominicans.[30] Most Puerto Ricans blamed a lack of self-esteem for what they viewed as a collective failure at entrepreneurship and adopted a psychological language of "complejo," chip on their shoulder, depression, insecurity and laziness. Social service organizations, mostly staffed by a group of working- and middle-class Puerto Ricans, considered eradicating these conditions one of their main goals. Tacitly this aimed to remedy the emotional inadequacy of Puerto Ricans, especially of Puerto Rican youth. These conceptions of emotional (in)adequacy need to be situated in an enduring historical context of colonial governance and tension (cf. di Leonardo 1998; Stoler 2004).

The making of race, the management of empire, and the congruence of imperial projects about the globe—and, as I argue here, in the context of nation-state racial projects in the United States—have always been central constituents of the workings of the intimate affective domain. By shaping appropriate and reasoned affect, by directing affective judgment, by severing some affective bonds and establishing others, by adjudicating what constituted moral sentiment—that is, by educating the proper distribution of sentiments and desires, the emotional economy of colonialism was always central to strategies of labor control; this is what Stoler has termed the "management of the intimate" (2004; see also my introduction). In this sense, the role of the state is not only in the business of educating consent, in the Gramscian sense, but such concern is possible by the shaping of appropriate and reasoned affect, and placing "affective knowledge" at the core of political rationality (8). This emotional economy of colonialism is also reflective of the broader political and ideological (and economic) context in which formal and quotidian Puerto Rican self-help perspectives are ensconced.

Social service organizations, premised on ideas of self-help, contribute to the emotional regimes behind urban neoliberal projects. Such a psychologically influenced language permeates individuals' everyday lives, transforms their thinking, and engenders new forms of sociability and emotionality critical to the creation of a new emotional style, as feelings are also historically reconfigured in ways that are ideological interreferential; in this sense, reference to Latin American racial ideologies coexist with discussions of race in a new US urban context. Formerly Puerto Rican–founded and –staffed agencies were now faced with the challenge of expanding programs to be "more inclusive of Latin immigrants coming from Ecuador, Colombia, Chile, Brazil, Argentina and Mexico," and were in charge of addressing these immigrants' "culture shock" and "sense of alienation," according to many accounts.[31] As the Puerto Rican executive director of a large multiservice social service agency in North Broadway remarked:

The new immigrants bring their own layer of "I'm lost and scared. I don't know what to do, or where to go, I don't want to get involved. I just want to go on with my daily chores and be safe." But from an organizational perspective, I understand that, I understand that we could be . . . in many respects we are a community based organization, we are also an institution. And the main thing is how do I keep this organization relevant to this community? . . . You have to see the needs for support, and don't think I just mean finding them an immigration lawyer. That's not even the main issue most times. It's about directing them to psychological counseling for depression, marital issues, domestic violence. . . . Because they don't know how Newark works, and we have to help them cope.[32]

Puerto Ricans have succeeded in building social service organizations and have even extended community services to the more diverse Latino populations in Newark, and this service has become, in light of new funding requirements and expectations, heavily geared toward teaching new migrants an emotional style that would help them to navigate (or to "cope") in Newark. David Engle (1984) identifies two kinds of individualism: a rights-based kind (through which individuals note injustices in terms of their individual rights as citizens) and self-sufficient individualism (through which individuals view their welfare as something of their own doing, separate from institutions and the context of rights. Puerto Ricans in Newark, particularly those who were active in the civil rights movements of the 1960s and 1970s, tended toward an individual or even collective rights–based approach, which appears in contradistinction to the self-sufficient individualism oftentimes embraced by more recent Latin American migrants.

After many years as a client and later staff member of a Puerto Rican not-for-profit organization, Amarilis began her own youth group to use karate as a way to "keep kids off the streets" and "raise their self-esteem." With such language, the material and symbolic space of the streets of North Broadway almost predicts the emotional health goal of finding an institutionalized way of enhancing individual well-being through self-esteem. This is a metaphoric rendering of what neoliberalism requires, and which will be further considered in the next section, as I consider another significant way in which North Broadway streets become undesirable and keeping kids off the streets becomes a racial project of the nation-state under neoliberalism.

Enlisting Deservingness: US Military Recruitment and the Broadening Boundaries of "Illegality"

Military hiring practices are premised on promises of vocational opportunity and social mobility, but also conceived as preventive or disciplinary measures for taking "at-risk" youth off the streets. Keeping these youth "off the streets" is a coded term for lessening their involvement with illicit substances and activities or preventing pregnancy, in the case of women, but it goes beyond that: It is also a way of removing the "human surplus" (Harvey 2001) from public view. The military serves to institutionalize and convey characteristics of whiteness (e.g., discipline, belongingness, conformity) and presumes to make the benefits of whiteness available to everyone; thus, the military is proposed as an equalizing institution, not only in terms of narrowing the employment gap but, perhaps more relevant to the case of youth of color, by narrowing a perceived moral and emotional gap between mainstream and minority cultures. In this sense, the military serves a role equivalent to that of the US public school and social service agencies. It frames certain key concerns that Latino youths and families have, based on their own social locations and migration histories. In the case of Latin American migrants, for instance, it capitalizes on concerns with "illegal" status and lack of citizenship/deportation, while in the case of US-born minorities a main promise is to reduce street violence/delinquency, and provide well-remunerated employment at some (undetermined) point in the future. These strategies contribute to making the ghetto neoliberally friendly and appealing to potential investors and gentrifiers.

In some ways, the US military is guided by a need to meet the demands of what David Harvey (2001) has termed a New Imperialism, by helping to dispose of an urban poor that is unincorporable, a surplus humanity under post-Keynesian forms of capitalism. The threat of a rebellion by this surplus humanity is monitored through an urban emotional style of fear, as well as technology.[33] The intention here is not to evaluate whether joining the US military is good or bad; rather, I am refocusing military recruitment and targeting in light of a different guiding question: To what degree do the ideological and material claims promoted by military recruitment, particularly around granting social worth to devalued "deviant" youth of color through the imposition of normative lifestyles and expectations, reduce those very lives to a perpetual form of delinquency?

Hector Colón, a Puerto Rican military recruiter in downtown Newark, noted how he had to tailor his recruitment efforts depending on whether he was trying to attract the mostly South American and Portuguese "immigrant community" in the Ironbound or the predominantly Puerto Rican youth in North Broadway.[34] A soft-spoken man in his mid-twenties, Hector had been the army recruiter of Newark's Latinos for three years. According to Hector, people in Newark, and particularly black Newark residents, were very antimilitary. He commented, "Blacks here in Newark have organized numerous protests against the war on Iraq and the army. They don't want us [no nos quieren]. They say, 'I'm not going to follow George Bush's orders.' They can't separate Bush from the military." Hector and other military officers in charge of recruiting in Newark recognized not only a difference in how whites, blacks, and Latinos viewed the military, but also between perceptions of the military in the Ironbound versus North Broadway.[35] He explained:

In the East Ward [Ironbound] you can see the American flags, the yellow ribbons, the [signs of] "We Support Our Troops." But that also depends on the Hispanics and on the area. In the East Ward [Ironbound], at the high school, teachers let you do your job. I could go right now and set up a table, pull students aside to talk about the army and all that. And they're very welcoming. That's very different from Barringer [High School] in the North Ward. I don't even go to Barringer anymore! They have a counselor there who don't like us. And she's Boricua [Puerto Rican] too. And she be like "No, you're not gonna talk to the students here at school. If you want to talk to them, do it outside the school." And she be telling the parents to sign so that we can't get their phone numbers, telling them that their children will be going to war. Stuff like that. But Barringer is the only school where we've had problems . . . besides the private schools that is, but that's another world altogether.

Military service is almost a naturalized dimension of Puerto Rican life on the island of Puerto Rico and in the United States. When I asked Hector whether he had ever encountered a Puerto Rican who had joined because of patriotism, he did not have to ponder the question: "Never. Not once have I encountered that in the six years I've worked here. . . . Blacks and Puerto Ricans are very narrow-minded when it comes to the military."[36]

Despite the proportionally higher recruitment of Puerto Ricans and Latinos living in predominantly Puerto Rican areas into the military, it was the South American migrants and white ethnics who were viewed as particularly patriotic. Even in a predominantly black city like Newark, whites still dictated the terms of patriotism. During the time of my field-work, it became apparent that the US military as an institution, ironically, contributed to the criminalization of Puerto Rican spaces precisely by generating a discourse that introduced military recruitment as the only way out of an otherwise "underclassed" existence for Puerto Ricans and Latinos living in areas like North Newark. Rather than a testament to Puerto Rican patriotism or even an effort to pursue a career, the recruitment of Puerto Ricans to the military was viewed as a corrective measure against "the [Puerto Rican] streets." By deploying culture of poverty arguments to characterize Puerto Rican spaces, military recruitment supplied a discourse that, consequently, accentuated the "delinquent citizenship" of Puerto Ricans oftentimes in contradistinction to the super-citizenship of more vulnerable Latin American immigrants. This was particularly prominent in the context of Barringer High School, often characterized as a minority school, in opposition to East Side High School, which was characterized as an "immigrant" school.

The first time I entered the college counseling office at East Side, I noticed that two men in military uniform were waiting to speak with students. A second team of a man and a woman were heading to the cafeteria to set up a table with US military recruitment materials. Since this was the first time I visited the ESHS counselors' office, I assumed that this military personnel were preparing for a special activity. Later I learned that their presence was part of a consistent and federally imposed initiative that targeted public schools in Newark and throughout the United States. When I asked Eugenia Segato, one of the Portuguese American college counselors, if there was a special event at the high school on that day, she responded:

After the "No Child Left Behind" [educational reform] law was implemented in Newark, the military recruiters can have access to any part of the school they want. One day is the army, the other day the Navy or the Marines or Air Force. They move around the school and they don't have to ask for an appointment or anything. Not after the "No Child Left Behind" law.[37]

The career counselor commented that recruiters from Rutgers University and other area universities were not visiting the school as much as they had in the past. At ESHS, teachers and staff attended "We Support Our Troops" vigils, US flags and yellow ribbons decorated the school hallways, and open statements of feeling proud of being an American abounded. T-shirts stamped with the photographs of young men and women recruits against the backdrop of the US flag, or of enlistees of Portuguese descent who had been casualties of war, also sold at stores down Ferry Street. This was particularly noticeable in comparison to Barringer, where an ESL teacher had been commended by the administration for her insistence in notifying parents that they could opt out of having their children's information be released to military recruiters; in fact, many parents had written letters demanding that their children's information would not be released. Nevertheless, as a Latina teacher at ESHS noted:

It's so weird because you see people here talking about patriotism all the time, and being very pro-military and the whole thing. You hear things like "Bomb 'em, nuke 'em, kill 'em! Kill Saddam, kill bin Laden!" But when it comes down to the people that are actually going [to the military], the white kids are ending up not going. And those are the patriotic people, the ones that don't go! Military recruiters and school counselors target the kid with the bandana, the kid with the attitude, and those always turn out to be the Hispanic and the black kids.

The tone of my conversation with the Portuguese American counselor at ESHS was very different from the comments I heard from the students and staff at Barringer, where discussions about the military were frequently ensconced in displays of racial consciousness. An interview with Migdalia Rivera, a Puerto Rican student at Barringer who remarked on the high volume of military personnel that came to recruit at the high school, illustrates this point:

To me, it looked like "Ok, let's take the little niggers and the spics and let's take them out there. They're going to die anyways." People tell me, "But you're an American." And I'm like "No, I was born and raised in the States." I guess that would technically classify me as an American, but honestly I think Americans are too well-fed in a way that I don't identify with. . . . Just because something like 9/11 happened, everybody wants to be patriotic, enlist in the army, go fight a war, go shoot Iraqis, and if they die, they want to imagine that glory. And some of the people that are going are going because they come from other places and they're afraid of being stoned to death here! It's their way of fitting in. And of course the army is like "Sure, come join!" [They think]: "Hey, what the hell, you're going to be a low-life, unemployed person" or "Well you are poor and on welfare, might as well kill you off."

Residents of North Broadway had a very ambiguous relationship to US military service; on the one hand, they usually recognized the questionable racial and class politics on which the military is sustained; on the other hand, regardless of this awareness, the military was still viewed as the only alternative available for youth of color to attain social mobility, not only because of its offer of a paid-for education, but also because of its commitment to inculcate dominant cultural values. In fact, for generations of Puerto Ricans, achieving middle-class status has been circumscribed to joining US military service.[38]

Who is patriotic, and the very assumption that being patriotic is a good thing, varied significantly within neighborhoods and communities. At Barringer, faculty and staff often commented that military recruiters would be more successful targeting South Americans, because "South Americans like all the ritual, the protocol, the uniforms." In a conversation with the parent of a Puerto Rican senior at Barringer, a well-liked Puerto Rican school secretary mentioned: "I think that many Latin American . . . especially South American . . . people like the military. They like the protocol and are used to seeing the military as powerful and special in their countries of origin, so they come with that vision." Likewise, Jennifer Flores, a Barringer graduate who worked at a social services agency in North Newark when I interviewed her, stated:

When you're young and want to belong to a country that's successful or at least appears to be successful. If you're Colombian you're losing, if you're Nicaraguan, you're losing. Go into Colombia as well, the people there feel this small. If you say you're an American citizen, they say, "Do you want us to kiss your feet?" So kids whose parents are migrating here and are getting born and raised here want to join because their parents encourage that U.S. patriotism. . . . The South American populations that are here now, including the older generations, were in their countries of origin during the Vietnam War. They don't know what this government is doing. They don't know that services were cut back in the educational system to deprive minority children or poor people. They never question why it is that Puerto Ricans and blacks are so overrepresented in the military . . . and are angry.

Many of the people with whom I spoke at Barringer perceived white and South American populations at East Side High School to be more "patriotic" than Puerto Ricans or African Americans in the rest of Newark. They attributed the heightened patriotism to their experiences with the military in their countries of origin (somewhat stereotypical images of South American dictatorships, "banana republics"), the need to "belong" in the United States, the lack of a historical awareness of 1970s civil rights struggles, and even the idea that the military would protect them from discrimination in the streets.

More recently, the US military has also become involved in dispensing citizenship status, previously the realm of the Department of Homeland Security (formerly the INS), to young migrants from Latin American countries who have been casualties of the war in Iraq.[39] The notorious case of Guatemalan José Gutiérrez, who was granted US citizenship posthumously, after being a casualty of the US invasion of Iraq, is the most renowned example.[40] This has not gone unnoticed among Latin American immigrants in the Ironbound or the North Ward. As Arturo Souza, a Brazilian high school student in Newark, told me in the weeks following the dispensation of the Guatemalan man's citizenship: "Sometimes I think of joining the army so I can get the US citizen faster and be able to bring my mom from Minas [Gerais]. But I don't think they give it [the citizenship] by just joining. I think you have to be sent to war . . . or do you have to actually die in war? I'm not sure." This comment resonated with what Father Carlos, a Brazilian priest in the Ironbound, had told me in April of 2003: "I've recently heard more Brazilians wanting to join the military, because that's the only way they foresee for becoming citizens. A young man recently told me: 'Father, sometimes I wish I could just go to the military and be sent to war, so that I can be given the citizenship and be able to bring my mother here!'"

The engagement of Latinos and Latin American immigrants with the US military in the context of a North Broadway public high school suggests that the citizenship of US-born Latino youths in general, and of Puerto Ricans in particular, effectively approaches the illegality traditionally attributed to undocumented immigrants or noncitizen populations. The presumed "illegality" of Latin American immigrants becomes more contingent on the degree to which these populations are likely to view the militarization of public education as a desirable path toward whiteness. This federal production of citizenship contributes to the racialization of some Latinos as criminal and others as having "good immigrant values" in ways that praise the subordination of youth to dominant views of US patriotism and, thus, white supremacy.[41] The spectacle was different from how the domestic poor were viewed as deviant and in need of the military to "strengthen up" their lives. The domestic poor were not going "beyond the call of duty," but rather were being brought up to par in their otherwise useless lives as "parasites of the system." In the case of Puerto Ricans, military participation was corrective of an otherwise delinquent citizenship.

"It's a greater glory to get killed in Iraq than in the streets of Newark, you know," assessed Amarilis, who also noted how many of her classmates at Barringer had joined the military because "everybody expected them to be nothing" and "to die on the streets" through illicit activities. Only death and a community-wide mourning may, in the end, accrue the social worth that Puerto Rican youth are denied on the streets of Newark. Not any death, but a patriotic death becomes the way of being narrated back into existence, of falling into the "good citizen" side of the dyad according to which Puerto Ricans can become visible in a context of subordination. In these almost-formulaic conversations, "the streets," rather than well-funded military recruitment strategies, Newark's postindustrial crisis, or American patriotism, had led Puerto Ricans and other Latinos in "Puerto Rican"-ized North Newark areas to join the military. When the story about the value of lives cannot be told, the visual (e.g., a roadside memorial, commemorative murals, and so on) can be an alternative mode of expression (Cacho 2007, 190). Such performances of mourning are also central to African American culture, as Karla Holloway (2003) notes: "Their visual excess expressed a story that African America otherwise had difficulty illustrating—that these were lives of importance and substance, or that these were individuals, no matter their failings or the degree to which their lives were quietly lived, who were loved" (181). As Lisa Marie Cacho (2007) shows in the case of the deaths of three young men of color in San Diego, an alternative archive of feeling or caring ascribes value to these young men's lives "through their friends and relatives' public mourning, their performances of explicit caring, profound pain, and deeply felt depression, desperation, and despair" (191).[42] I would argue that, in the case of Puerto Rican youth in Newark, death and a politics of worth operated both as an "archive" and a "repertoire" of personhood.

Performance studies scholar Diana Taylor introduces the concepts of "archive" and "repertoire" as methodological tools needed in the study and analysis of the slippery subject and process in the field of performance. Taylor describes "archive" or archival memory as the documents, maps, texts, archaeological remains, and any items presumably resistant to change and which works across distance, time, and space to separate the source of knowledge from the knower. Conversely, "repertoire" refers to embodied memory, including performances, gestures, orality, movement, and acts usually thought of as "nonreproducible knowledge." The "repertoire" requires people to participate in the production and reproduction of knowledge by being there, since the actions of the repertoire never remain the same, but in fact transform "choreographies of meaning" (2003, 19, 20). To have a chance to acquire personhood and humanity in a context of social (disenfranchisement) and physical death noted in North Newark, Puerto Rican youth needed to inscribe themselves in light of both "archival" and "repertoire" processes that would legitimize their human experiences,

As a Barringer High School Puerto Rican administrator commented, a dominant view in Newark was that

for Puerto Ricans, the second and third generations, go into the military because they see it as a way of becoming a 'tough guy,' and we're taught that that's a good thing. What I've seen here is that the top 10 percent of African American men and women in schools, the valedictorians and all that, they go on to college after high school. Same with Puerto Rican women. They go on to Kean [University] or even Rutgers. But the highest 10 percent of Puerto Rican men go into the Marines, not college. I think it's not only because the counselors push them in that direction, but also because that's what they hear from their families, their communities. A lot of kids need the military as a vehicle to straighten out their lives. A lot of children see this all around them and want to get out of Newark. They don't think they are college material or don't want to go to college so the military gets them out of here.

It is the repetitive quality of these narratives that make them suitable for emotional scrutiny. Repetition both in enunciatory and behavioral registers are, according to some renderings of psychoanalysis (cf. Rivera-Colón 2009), traces of trauma that remain outside of conscious narrative incorporation. The repetitive thought, behavior, and/or statement point toward a trauma that needs to be worked through discursively. When historical traumas of misrecognition, invisibility, criminalization, and neglect among populations of color in the United States are the source of these traces, then the repetitive narratives (the "talking cure") must be enacted in both ethical and political contexts that "go beyond the couch and into the streets" (Rivera-Colón 2009), but even institutional settings in these neighborhoods, such as not-for-profit agencies, aim to become clinical settings that have taken up community scrutiny, mobility, and a politics of self-esteem and respectability.

I was particularly surprised with how the military became a vehicle toward self-worth in a narrative that resonated with middle-class views of wellness and physical fitness among some Latino youth in North Broadway. Nelson Miranda, a Puerto Rican and Salvadoran man in his early twenties, was contemplating going into the Marines. I asked Nelson to tell me more about the factors he was taking into account in making his decision. He said: "My main motivation [to join the military] is that I like the training. The little training I got [in the army reserves] I liked a lot. I just love to train, pushing my body to get stronger, endurance, and weight training. I love . . . that part of it."[43] Juan Gorbea, the Puerto Rican director of a not-for-profit agency in North Broadway, also alluded to military training as a working-class equivalent of going to a health and fitness club. He commented: "Some of these girls are big girls, strong girls, and they are like 'I want to get in shape.' There's also that feeling of 'I know I can take on any guy.' That type of attitude. . . . Many of these kids are motivated [to join the army] by that." When I spoke with some young women who had either joined the military or knew of other women in their families and friendship groups who had, I heard many stories of how "getting out of a bad relationship" or preventing future relationship abuse and getting in shape and becoming physically stronger were leading motivations for their decision.

For Marisol Padilla, a young Puerto Rican woman who was considering enlisting in the Army, joining the military service represented one of the few paths to challenging both old-fashioned notions of traditional Latina femininity and dominant perspectives on welfare "abuse." Marisol, an articulate and self-reflective woman, explained:

One thing that my grandmother always told, and Mami too, was to be a strong independent woman. . . . We know that men are not reliable. But also, I just don't see myself with the husband, 2.6 children, white-picket fence, 9-to-5 job. It's not for me. The military . . . is not just the money. For me it wasn't. It was more knowing that you can take care of yourself, you can defend yourself, because they teach you to fight, and people don't mess with you. You get to travel, train. One girl I knew wanted to have her own clothing line and the military gives loans [to the enlistees] for that, and she was telling me, "Mary, I see myself as a businesswoman, designing, selling clothes." It's that feeling of getting respect, feeling strong and comfortable in your own skin.

Roderick Ferguson (2004, 11–18) notes that diverse gender and sexual practices within communities of color are produced by the needs of a capitalist economy, yet these same practices are pathologized and criminalized because they diverge from US ideals of domesticity and respectability. Although capital requires that racialized groups transgress the ideals of gender and the norms of sexuality (such as intimate relationships outside reproductive marriage), the US state names those transgressions "deviant" and "un-American," legitimating various state regulations that have been imposed upon communities of color. In this way, "surplus labor becomes the impetus for anxieties about the sanctity of 'community,' 'family,' and 'nation'" (Ferguson 2004, 17). This is the case even when cultural and political discourses that naturalize "the family" actually recruit people into relationships of exchange that often become involuntary relations of economic dependency. The state, complicit with capital, asks "the family" to do all that it cannot do in terms of making sure the basic needs of the citizens are met (cf. Ferguson 2004, Rivera Colón 2009; Ito 1985). A key question that arises from the discussions around military enlisting is: How do we create alternative frameworks for judging behavior, particularly for individuals like Marisol who want autonomy but have little access to (or interest in) dominant power or who might not take a standard nine-to-five job even in the off chance it was available to them?

When I asked Marisol why she had ultimately decided against joining the military, she mentioned, with a mixture of the cynicism and wit that characterized her: "Why would I fight for Bush. . . . What the hell, I'm a lesbian! [laughed]" And she added: "If I told my mother 'I want to join the army,' she'll be like 'That you want to do *what*, pendejita? Qué tú te crees? que tú te mandas? [what do you think? that you are the boss of you?].'" Marisol, who considered herself first and foremost a creative writer, and who would show me fragments of a novel she had been hand-writing over several college-ruled notebooks, was undoubtedly among the most insightful, critical-thinking young people I have met in my life. In addition to mentioning being a lesbian, in light of military hostility against homosexuality, and her mother's opposition, Marisol placed military recruitment in the context of a Newark economy familiar to her:

You know why I would never think of joining? Because I know a lot of people who have done so much for this country and they're working freaking eight-dollar-and-fifty-cent jobs. You fought for this country, you lost friends, you lost family, you lost wives, and you're stuck working eight-dollar-and-fifty-cent jobs? C'mon now. I'm sorry. If I'm eighteen and I'm busting my ass and I got my leg shot, when I come back to the States you can rest assured that I'm going to sit my ass in a bar and be like "I want a beer!" You can all kiss my ass.

The expectation that young people like Julia's son Joel, or Marisol are supposed to have seminal life experiences, like buying a house, getting married, and having children, made it impossible to ascribe value to alternative life experiences beyond the normative goals of production and reproduction. This was felt, at a deep level, not only as "an exclusionary way of knowing social life [but also] a violent and paralyzing one" (Cacho 2007, 202). A politics of deviance enables us to rethink how value is ascribed to lives and deaths because it is invested and interested in "redefining the rules of normality that limit dreams, emotions, and acts of most people" (Cohen 2004, 38). In this sense, deviant behavior and attitudes are forms of "definitional power," which can potentially create alternatives to established US norms of gender, sexuality, respectability, and domesticity.

The citizenship of Puerto Rican parents at Barringer was usually questioned, particularly in instances in which disenfranchised parents exerted their right to challenge the recruitment of their sons and daughters, especially sons and daughters perceived to be "troubled," into the military, as was the case with Julia and her son Joel, in the opening to this chapter. Likewise, Carmen Morales, the Puerto Rican parent-volunteer whom I met at Barringer, told three other parents and me that she was getting annoyed at the many military recruiters that were calling her house trying to get her son, a graduating senior, to join the Marines. "My son was like 'Mom, do you think I should join the military? They say they'll pay for this and that and school.' And I grabbed the phone from him and cussed the [military recruiter] out. I was like: 'Don't you fucking call my house again!' and hung up on him. And my younger daughter was looking at me like 'Wow, you said fucking' and I'm like, 'Yeah I said fucking. It deserved it.'" The demands of minority parents were oftentimes viewed as divisive and as posing the threat of fragmenting the nation state (see Honig 2001, 85; cf. Ngai 2004). And, in fact, when it comes to the recruitment of Latinos to the military, military recruiters have explicitly identified "the Hispanic family," and specifically "the Hispanic mother," as the main ally or hindrance in their recruitment efforts.[44] The state complicit with capital asks "the Hispanic family" to do all that it cannot do in terms of making sure the basic needs of the citizens are met in true "an Army of One" ("an Army of Juan," as it is joked about) fashion.

Any possible critical engagement by Puerto Ricans against US military recruitment, including strong parental opposition to recruiters calling their homes to talk to their high school–age children, was viewed as further evidence of Puerto Ricans' "ungratefulness to the U.S." Puerto Ricans (and eventually US-born generations of Latinos that inhabited Puerto Rican–ized spaces) became the antipatriots who must prove themselves over and over again to claim any type of belongingness in the United States. A Puerto Rican high school administrator at Barringer noted how such "ungratefulness" contributed to an everyday antagonism between Puerto Ricans and African Americans at the high school:

We have an ESL counselor that made sure she sent letters to her students' houses informing the parents that they could demand that their children's information not be released to the military. But because she's an ESL teacher, and most Puerto Ricans are not in the ESL program, many of the Puerto Rican students' parents did not get as much notice. Some of the black teachers who are in charge of the Puerto Rican students, who are mostly US-born, are not as sensitive. Because they see the military as a good thing for disrespectful kids . . . that's who the rich people in their families are, the ones that joined the military. The Colin Powells of the world! So you had Latino parents saying, "No, my child is not going to the military" and that's it. And that was looked down upon. Not only by the South Americans who like the pomp and ceremony of the uniforms in their own countries, but also by the blacks here, for other reasons.

The militarization of public schools like Barringer was not only grounded on visions of social mobility, vocational opportunities, or moral character, but also along an axes of "illegality," "lawlessness," and "discipline" illustrative of how US citizenship, as a racializing institution (De Genova and Ramos-Zayas 2003), is federally enforced and locally configured at the level of urban neighborhoods. An everyday politics of "worthiness" required that racially marked populations continuously demonstrated their deservingness of inclusion into the US nation-state. Of course, this rhetoric omits the fact that this whitening process has been sold to the very people on whom the nation-state relies for cheap labor (migrants) and for providing the "Blackness" against which the state's very whiteness is measured and sustained. Given that citizenship in the United States has historically been and continues to be not only a white supremacist institution, but also a set of legal statures invested in producing and reproducing "race"—in light of a white-compliant versus white-disobedient formula—as a natural, taken-for-granted set of attributes superimposed on humanity, a question that begs attention is: How do these politics of social worth impact the relationship between the two groups that are most abject in the US national imaginary and who come together within the walls of Barringer High School, a predominantly Puerto Rican school in a predominantly African American city?

Military recruitment taps into a politics of deservingness that stipulates that the only way in which "noncitizens" and "delinquent citizens" can aspire to the benefits of whiteness is by enlisting in the military and learning the basic premises of white culture. Recruitment strategies of US military personnel in North Broadway high schools in fact highlight the "delinquent citizenship" (Ramos-Zayas 2004) of Puerto Ricans in ways that interfere with any form of black-brown alliances, while resurrecting Puerto Ricans' racialization of African Americans in light of "racial democracy" discourses and repositioning discussions of the "welfare queen" and "respectability." Highly emotive perspectives on trust, intent, and respectability frame the relationship between African Americans and Puerto Ricans, and how black and Latino youth and adults understood US citizenship and deservingness in North Broadway, where working-class and poor Puerto Ricans frequently came into contact with middle-class African Americans.

Trust, Intent, and the Politics of African American Respectability in Puerto Rican Newark

One morning in late February, I walked into a confrontation between a security guard, an African American woman in her late fifties, and two Latino students who were carrying their babies and strollers into the lobby of Barringer High School. All I heard was the guard saying, "At least I was married when I had my children." The young women dismissed the guard's words with some profanity, and the guard added, "Be careful where you leave those strollers, or you may never see them again," refer-ring to the strollers the two women had just left next to the guard's desk. One of the young women retaliated defiantly, "If something happens to them, we'll come after you!" Then the guard, talking to another African American staff member who had come to help calm the situation, com-mented, "Look at those cheap strollers. The one we gave at the baby shower last week even had a watch on it and stuff."

I had the opportunity to talk to the African American part-time secu-rity guard, who insisted that everyone call her "Mrs. Johnson" (nobody even seemed to know her first name). Like many other African American women whom I met in North Broadway, Mrs. Johnson described herself as a "Christian woman" and a "God-fearing woman." Mrs. Johnson was one of several African American women, ranging from their early thirties through their late sixties, who were teachers, counselors, administrators, health care, and security staff at Barringer High School. Although not all of these women articulated their identity around their religious involve-ment, they all happened to subscribe to a politics of African American respectability hinted at by Mrs. Johnson's moral judgment on single par-enting. Mrs. Kennedy, a well-liked African American teacher who had been at Barringer for nearly two decades, for instance, said, "This is one thing I teach them [pointing to the photo of a group of well-dressed Latino youth taken on a field trip to Washington DC]: I teach them to dress for success. The power of dressing right. They need to learn that. They need to learn to know that speaking two languages is a sure route to making lots of money and being successful in this country. They have value for who they are." When Rhonda. Clayton, an African American social worker in her early thirties, heard Karina, a Puerto Rican junior, calling me "Ana," she reprimanded her. "What did you just call her? No, you need to refer to her as Ms. Ramos." I assured her that I was fine with Karina calling me by my first name and, not very convinced, she then stated, "Well, then you have to call her Ms. Ana." Disapproving of my informality, she warned Karina so I could hear it, "And don't let Mrs. Pay-ton [another African American counselor] hear you calling her Ana!"

These politics of respectability operated according to regional, reli-gious, and racial cosmologies that served as subtext for a particular kind of black-white interaction at Barringer High School. There were efforts on the part of both old-time African American and white teachers in the school to convey their acceptance of each other, even though these efforts came across as overly eager, awkward, and rarely smooth at all; it was almost as if, in their mutual effort to pretend that race did not matter at all, it mattered a whole lot. For instance, when an African American teacher sensed that a white teacher, the only white person in the faculty lounge at the time, appeared uncomfortable with a brief reference to a PBS documentary on the trans-Atlantic slave trade that another teacher had seen the previous night, she immediately commented, "Well, that was a very long time ago . . . like the Holocaust, and how all the people were opposing Mel Gibson's movie. People get too sensitive about these things." Even though I never heard of friendships between African Americans and whites that extended beyond the school day, or about African American teachers or white teachers who visited each other during weekends, for instance, African Americans performed a great deal of "emotional labor" (Hochschild 1990) in their everyday interactions with whites. This appeared unique to a Black-white pattern of interaction at Barringer and in other public institutions in Newark, and very seldom did I see the same level of emotional labor between Latinos and African Americans. Such a manifestation of "emotional labor" involved an insertion of a politics of respectability that suggested not so much a willingness to be situationally "colorblind," but an actual appreciation of middle-class values that were presumed to produce an inherent bond between whites and blacks and that excluded Latinos. These situational forms of "colorblindness," normativity, and appeal to a universal emotive narrative describe the relational styles of black-white interactions at Barringer and, at times, enabled a modicum of managed intimacy between whites and blacks in a predominantly Puerto Rican context. Moreover, such managed intimacy created tacit conceptions of belonging or common "unbelonging" that generally was not available to Puerto Ricans and other Latinos at the school.

Black-white affinity, therefore, drew from common understandings and recognition of a Goffmanian "situational propriety," or rules that were only partial guides of conduct that required that the individuals involved had a sense of local, immediate context of the tacit and practical knowledge necessary to perform or narrate appropriate behavior (cf. Goffman 1959).[45] Such situational propriety codes a form of class identity and respectability that was not just based on education or occupation, income or wealth, since many of these conversations included African American teachers as well as parent-volunteers, counseling staff, and security personnel, but on a perceived lifestyle or aspiration to a lifestyle understood to require specific skills, social competencies, and cultural practices that the Latino working class lacked (cf. Durrenberger and Doukas 2008). The appeal to a universal (mainstream) emotional style among African Americans like Mrs. Johnson was, therefore, also a claim to a "culture of the middle class" which she attributed to some of the white teachers in the school, but which was also irreducible to annual income or other easily quantifiable variables; it was more akin to "status," a presumably more subjective, individualized, and variegated category, and which required a reimagining of "race" as a leading determinant of difference.[46]

In stratified societies, social groups are frequently perceived as having different affective styles and class (racial) identifications that rest in part on the individual's affective demeanor. Conveying an appropriate emotional style that connected individual experience with historically derived group cognitive and moral structures became an important aspect of how many African American teachers and personnel viewed their role, particularly in relation to African American students, at Barringer.[47] An instance of this emotional "project" of African American teachers was evident when Brenda, an African American freshman, commented that in her other school one of the teachers was a "cracker." "A what?" Mrs. Clayton contended, visibly upset and shocked. "Well, he's a white person . . . whatever," Brenda responded, equally upset, perhaps because she had expected some kind of complicity from Mrs. Clayton. "You don't use that kind of language," Mrs. Clayton insisted. "You don't know who may be offended. There could be white people in the room," the social worker insisted and seemed to be referring to me, even though she knew I was Puerto Rican. Puzzled, obviously not even considering the possibility that I may have been white, since she seemed to view me just as she views her Dominican light-skinned close friend, Brenda replied: "Sorry, sorry, for having used the word. I don't want to offend anyone. But he [the white teacher in question] needs to be respectful to me, too."

Although in the 1970s, inspired by the militancy of the civil rights era, blacks and Puerto Ricans embraced Kenneth Gibson, the first black mayor of Newark, in perhaps the only substantial African American–Puerto Rican coalition in Newark's political history, such alliances were rare and short-lived. In part, this was because the city's $65-million debt and lack of revenue sources limited the mayor's plans to improve Newark and ultimately generated greater interracial tensions and competition between these very political contingencies (Chase 2004). Abel Cabrera, a Puerto Rican teacher and activist who self-identifies as Afro-Latino, reflected on his own racial awareness while also emphasizing how he was different from African Americans in Newark:

Abel Cabrera: The black migration in Newark came directly from North Carolina, southern black folks, folks who had their own vision of black and white. There were no Puerto

Ricans in this vision. So they think [imitating a reaction of confusion] "This people . . . wait a minute, they look like white people and they couldn't be minority."

Ana Yolanda: But did they consider them white, did they consider Puerto Ricans white?

Abel: I think they dropped that idea eventually. . . . From my experience, it depends on what blacks you are talking about. In New York you have a West Indian population that is very forward thinking, much more than the southern black population here in Newark. Here the blacks are in power, but these are blacks who are from the segregated South. . . . They don't understand how Latinos fit into this.

Abel's response resonated with the betrayal that long-term Newark Puerto Rican residents expressed regarding a well-established Newark black political elite. As the dark-skinned Puerto Rican father of a Barringer High School student recalled: "Blacks don't care about us. They will only care for their own. That goes back all the way to the election of Gibson. After all the support that Puerto Ricans gave [black mayor Kenneth] Gibson, he did nothing when he got elected." More significantly, however, for Puerto Ricans, a perspective on race that drew from a Latin American ideology of racial democracy, rather than a US black/white racial polarity, also offered distinctive grounding to notions of self-help and the psychological language of self-actualization in social service organizations.

Hilda Hidalgo and her Rutgers research team had already noted the early formulations of a cartography of racial democracy that Puerto Ricans deployed to circumvent the black-white polarity that characterized Newark in the 1970s:

Newark is a city engulfed in racial conflict. . . . The racial conflict is further complicated by ethnic conflicts. The Puerto Rican is caught in the middle of these two conflicts. Both blacks and Puerto Ricans are responsible for the misunderstanding and attitude that adversely affect their relationship. Blacks do not seem to understand that "Puertorricaness" supersedes race or color for the Puerto Rican. The black culture as expressed by black Americans is as foreign to the majority of the Puerto Ricans as is the white Anglo-Saxon culture. Blacks often are guilty of trying to force Puerto Ricans to give up their culture and adopt black American culture, at times forcing a rift between black Puerto Ricans and white Puerto Ricans. Relations between blacks and Puerto Ricans are usually strained. . . . In addition, Latin-European minority groups in Newark are constantly trying to ally "white" Puerto Ricans to their constituency and split the Puerto Rican community. . . . [As they claim]: "Puerto Ricans resent the fact that, when 'blacks and Puerto Ricans' are lumped together, the result is that blacks are served; *Puerto Ricans are left out*" (emphasis in original; Hidalgo 1970, 14).[48]

It is important to notice that Puerto Ricans narrated themselves as New-ark residents through an insistence on the particularities of their Latin American–influenced Blackness, as racially distinct from the Blackness they came to associate with African Americans in the United States. These Latin American perspectives on race were also highlighted by an intimate awareness of everyday racial segregation in cities. When I asked Amarilis Guzmán where, besides North Broadway, she went in Newark, she commented:

I stay in North Broadway. I stay in my little box and, if I left my little box, it is to get as far away from Newark as I can, not to go to other parts of the city! When I was younger, the majority of the people seemed Puerto Rican to me. Now the blacks that are in North Broadway are between Broadway and Route 21, McCarter Highway. And they stay in that area. It's only like two or three blocks from here, but that's like a total different place, like another South Newark. . . . My father is a black Puerto Rican and he himself says he won't go there. Not out of racism. I mean, he's black, you know [laughs]. It's not that. He's been called "molleto," which is like "nigger" in Spanish. It's just a differ-ence that you know shouldn't be there, because we're all people and I see everyone as just people, but . . . you know, it still is there, sadly. Because they don't know what to do with us. We're not black, but they can't call us white, and that confuses them.

These different kinds of "Blackness" played a big role in the emergence of a cartography of racial democracy in Newark (chapter 4). "Molleto" be-came a word that many Puerto Ricans used in reference to dark-skinned Puerto Ricans or to Puerto Ricans whom they viewed as "acting black." This complementary racial vocabulary not only indicated discriminatory practices among Puerto Ricans, but also suggested how these discrimina-tory practices operated according to a different Latin America–influenced racial formation than the dominant Newark-based or even US-based one. These racial vocabularies supplied the cognitive, emotive, and symbolic tools for a cartography of racial democracy that dissociated race from skin color and a common trans-Atlantic history of slavery in favor of a cultur-ally constituted moral view of race as unimportant or at least marginal to other categories of subordination.

Schools—like neighborhoods and totalizing institutions, including the military—impacted how Puerto Ricans and African Americans judged social relations around key concepts like "trust" and "sincerity," and evaluated specific actions and behaviors in terms of a perceived "inten-tionality," a politics of respectability, and competing understandings of "race." Ross, Mirowsky, and Pribesh (2001) argue that in neighborhoods mistrust arises from a combination of personal disadvantage and community disadvantage developing among individuals with few resources who live in places where resources are scarce and threat is common. Disadvantage magnifies mistrust in such contexts of material scarcity, so that perceived neighborhood disorder and an overall lack of respectability influence interpersonal mistrust directly and indirectly by increasing perceptions of powerlessness among residents. As examined in chapters 5 and 6, in Newark Latinos reported the sexuality and appearance of African Americans, particularly the racial language and posturing of African American women, as cues of social disorder. Conceptions of "trust" (and, more often, mistrust), operating in tandem with perspectives on "respectability" and an emergent cartography of racial democracy, unfolded in North Broadway, a largely Puerto Rican neighborhood in a predominantly African American city. In doing this, at least two racial systems always operated in tandem: one with origins in the racial economy of the US South and the other in a presumably more "fluid" Caribbean or Latin American racial system. It is thus imperative to introduce an examination of individual emotional subjectivity and multiple racial systems into analyses of structural neighborhood inequality.

The main explanation for why a black-white alliance was more probable than a "rainbow coalition" between Latinos and African Americans had to do with what Puerto Ricans viewed as a fundamentally incompatible perspective of how "race" operated. While African Americans allegedly were "more comfortable with" structuring their everyday racial relations in ways that were informed by a historical black-white southern-style dyad, Latinos perceived race in more descriptive, colorist, and culturalized ways that took into account other individual qualities, including place of birth, looks, lifestyle, emotive style, and other criteria that also became coded in very classed and gendered ways. The ability to freely refer to skin color in individual descriptions or to privilege humor in sustaining boundaries appeared as critical aspects of how Puerto Ricans, and other Latinos, experienced racial dynamics in everyday life.

Yesenia Almonte, a Barringer student who had recently arrived from the Dominican Republic, once asked me, "Se dice African American or Afro-American? [Does one say American African or Afro-American?]." I told her that I usually said "African American" or just "black," and asked her why she wanted to know. And she explained, as if drawing from a puzzling past experience, "I know they don't like us to say it in Spanish, to say Negro. That's the one that's a bad term here. You can say Moreno, but not Negro, right?" This brief conversation also offers a glimpse into the process of racial learning, of the trial and error that can be emotionally taxing if one "gets it wrong." But these conversations and the foundational black-white social exchanges at Barringer High School were also suggestive of the emergence of a dynamic cartography of racial democracy in Newark, according to which Latinos attribute intentionality and judge sincerity in their everyday interactions with African Americans.

Many Puerto Ricans drew on a conglomeration of group members' selective historical recollections, partial information of events, and socioeconomic conditions—what Yamamoto (2000) calls "stock stories"—to draw speculations about the future and deploy a lens through which to read other racial groups. While some Puerto Ricans acknowledged, at least in passing, that African American politicians frequently also neglected the black poor, in individual perspectives of everyday social interactions this awareness became secondary to a dominant impression that blacks could not be "trusted" because even the black poor who might share one's material and structural concerns were likely to "take out" the emotive consequences of their subordination against Puerto Ricans. Individuals drew on stories of past and present structural and political inequalities to interpret behavior and racially code what were often economic arguments into folk theories of race.

Even though there are only about 7,500 Italians living in the North Ward, and only a handful of Italian students at the school, many of the Puerto Rican staff and faculty felt that blacks and Italians were likely to unite with each other against Puerto Ricans. Delia Torres was one of the people who, while still convinced that African Americans and whites were more likely to unite against Puerto Ricans and Latinos more generally, believed there were exceptional cases in which some African Americans could be considered trustworthy. Delia commented, "An African American teacher, one of the good ones, not the ones that attack us Puerto Ricans all the time, told me that an Italian teacher had told her, 'Now that you have the Puerto Ricans in charge of this school, you'll know what we [Italians] felt back in the 1970s [when Italians were assumed, in popular historical accounts, to have been displaced by a growing number of African Americans and Puerto Ricans]. You better align with us or else you're really going to be screwed!'" A question that emerges in such exceptional cases is: What makes some African Americans, like the teacher Delia referenced, "one of the good ones"? How do members of different social groups distinguish sincerity from deceitfulness and how does such a distinction impact displays of affect and emotion (or, in Goffman's [1959] terminology, "exuded expressions" versus "guided doings")? Such questions are partially premised on emotions as both (and simultaneously) individual experiences and interactional constructs that play key roles in the attribution of intentionality across racial groups, and which become central to how groups render certain behaviors as transparent to emotional interpretation while others are viewed as suspect of insincerity.

In the case of the African American teacher who is "one of the good ones," as well as in the case of intergenerational, interracial engagement that I turn to now, the concept of "tough love" becomes central to interpretations of sincerity, caring, and intent. On a winter day in 2004, the Puerto Rican principal at Barringer and the African American basketball coach scheduled an "intervention" with Rashad Johnson, a charming and articulate seventeen-year-old African American student who had been suspended from school for two days and expelled from the high school's basketball team. The interaction between Rashad, the school principal, and a few other administrators involved in determining Rashad's future was very revealing of the ways in which "tough love" becomes one of the strategies of interracial collaboration. The immediate and long-term repercussions of student actions invited the collaboration between black and Puerto Rican staff, in this case, in which a common sentimentality almost assured a sense of sincerity and trust, as long as it was rooted in narratives of "self-esteem," "self-knowledge," and more existentialist New Age styles.

"What did I tell you last week, Rashad?" Rafael Cordero, the high school principal, began after introducing me to Rashad. "I told you to look at yourself in the mirror. What did you see? What do you see when you look in the mirror?" Knowingly, yet hesitantly, Rashad responded: "That I'm black . . . African American." "But do you really know yourself? Do you really know what that means? Do you know what happens to young men like you when you go to Bloomfield or Belleville and get into trouble?" continued the principal, being very self-consciously pedagogical. "They get suspended from school . . . ?" Rashad speculated. "No, they go to jail. That's what Italian Americans do out there, because they don't give people like you a second chance." Rafael cited statistics about the racial composition of jails in New Jersey versus the low college graduation rates for men of color.

While Mr. Cordero spoke on the phone with a parent, Mrs. Simmons, an African American administrator in her late fifties, walked in, and asked Rashad, "What are you doing here?" "They're trying to help me out, because I've been getting into trouble," Rashad explained. Unconvinced, Ms. Simmons commented in a commonsensical tone, "So just stop getting into trouble. Whose fault is that? You're the one getting into trouble, so why don't you just stop?" "I know it's my fault. I'm admitting my responsibility, but they're helping me with my future," Rashad commented. Mrs. Simmons appeared suspicious of treating what she viewed as a student's lack of self-control in such a "communitarian" level. An advocate of tough love and believer in individual responsibility and self-reliance, Mrs. Simmons was obviously doubtful of the need for what she viewed as a "touchy-feely" babying of students. A middle-class woman who had moved to Newark from North Carolina in the 1950s, Ms. Simmons shared a very traditional family values rhetoric attributing student misbehavior to parental deficiency.

I want to describe another incident that reconfigures conventional alliances at Barringer, and then highlight a pattern I read from both situations. During the time of my fieldwork, I witnessed and volunteered in various initiatives to get more parents involved in the high school. One such initiative was a teacher-parent event that featured a workshop titled "My Teen Self." The main goal was to give parents a greater understanding of their children's lives by encouraging them to reflect on their own adolescence through a series of open-ended questions. One of the Puerto Rican parents had not attended high school; others commented on how difficult their teenage years had been. Mrs. Johnson (a security guard) grew up in North Carolina and commented, "Back then, if you did something, your neighbor could smack you and then your parents would find out what you did and would smack you, too." Mrs. Johnson agreed. They seemed to think that this was a better time, and that tough love was the way to go. Everyone seemed to agree that needy kids gravitated toward parental or mentor figures at the school. In an "it takes a village to raise a child" fashion, an African American parent mentioned that it was up to the communities to enable their youth's social well-being and mainstreaming. She added, "When we were young, if someone saw you getting into trouble, they'd call your parents and you'd get a whipping. . . . Sometimes they'd give you the whipping themselves, because that's how much your parents trusted them to do that!" While many African American parents invoked this kind of community-focused disciplining, they also tended to be on their children's side when they were called into school to solve an issue concerning their sons or daughters; this was in counterdistinction to many of the Latin American parents whom I saw coming to the school, most of whom usually stood on the teacher's side. Moreover, the African American parents whom I met tended to bring in their own negative memories of school and teachers into their interactions with school personnel. Many of the Latin American parents had little first-hand understanding of the US public education system, so they tended to assume that it was fair and that, if their child had been reprimanded, he or she deserved it.

Dialogues about a common expectation of tough love abounded at Barringer High School. They were intended to counteract a dominant "claim to victimhood" (Robert Hughes in Illouz 2003, 221–22) and created the most tangible, albeit relatively infrequent, moments of cooperation between Puerto Rican and African Americans at Barringer. The conversation with Rashad and the workshops at the parent-teacher event were among the many interventions that I witnessed where discussions of racial subordination and material inequality were framed in light of motivational rhetoric, self-help language, and wellness narratives. A common aspect of such popular psychology and counseling narratives was the implicit reference to a culture of victimhood, the view that US-born Latinos and black youth secretly enjoyed being victims because victimhood entitled them to undeserved rewards and privileges.

Interestingly, the endorsement of tough love as the only possible strategy to weed out the youth of color who had "potential" from those who were a "lost cause" resonated with a criticism that many South American migrants, like Elisa in the introduction to this chapter, launched against Puerto Ricans and African American youth and their parents. For many of the South Americans with whom I spoke, a claim to victimhood was a representation of a suffering that lead to overindulgence, un-deservingness, and laziness. In the cases considered here, of Rashad and the parents' workshop, the intention is to produce a self that is deeply institutionalized and regulated.

Quasi-therapeutic interventions like those described here sustained and even propelled broader neoliberal institutional initiatives, including the possibility of having the ROTC in the school and determining which students were so "beyond intervention" that they needed to be sent off to the military to be "straightened out." I only saw three white people—all of them representatives of either the Board of Education or the superintendent's office and two of them graduates of Barringer in the 1950s—attending the parents' events that were scheduled for the 2003–4 academic year. One of the white men recalled nostalgically, "When we went to school, kids had dressed-up Friday and, if you didn't show up with jacket and tie, you were left back in a classroom and were not allowed to even show up at the auditorium." To this, the African American representative of the Board of Education added, "I think kids nowadays don't have a sense of what is appropriate. I hear them cursing in the hallways as if they were on the streets. There's an appropriate time and place for everything."

Although such a comment may be emblematic of generational differences that may transcend racial lines, class, and segregated neighborhoods, the consequences that being a "misbehaved" kid—a kid who does not know what "appropriate" is—carries are radically different in North Broadway than in white, middle-class areas. In North Broadway the quotidian experiences of Puerto Rican youth were inextricably linked to disciplinary structures that imparted lessons in citizenship and forms of subject-making through disciplining and surveillance (cf. Foucault 1977). Puerto Rican subjectivity is produced through abjection, as Puerto Ricans and other US-born minority youth focused on avoiding a "failure" that was defined according to prevalent stereotypes of their own groups.

As Cacho (2007, 185) notes, the recreational practices of young people of color—as well as the individual work or educational activities they may lack—mark them all as "lazy" and "immoral," potentially "criminal," and always "illegal." Lives that were not presumed to be on the road to middle-class status, suburban living, heterosexual marriage, property ownership, or full-time employment lacked the ideological codes for normative (socially valuable) existence, and justify a desire to discipline and monitor deviance. Of course, this is not unique to Newark, but draws from a historical legacy of criminalizing Latino unemployment and recreational activities (e.g., 1855 Vagrancy Act and the Zoot Suit Riots) by expanding the state's definition of crime and extending its realm of punishment so that young people's social practices are not only "delinquent" but increasingly coded as criminal.

Legal scholar Devon W. Carbado's concept of "racial naturalization" is pertinent here. Carbado masterfully disaggregates American citizenship from American identity and pointedly argues that one does not guarantee the other, since racial naturalization produces inclusionary forms of exclusion. In the case of African Americans, Carbado argues that Blackness might be thought of as an insular identity; "like Puerto Rico, blackness is foreign in a domestic sense [in reference to the Insular Cases that characterized Puerto Rico as neither foreign nor a part of the United States]" (2005, 639). This racial liminality is at the center of what Carbado terms "racial naturalization." Carbado claims that racism is a naturalization process through which people become American, that historically the law has structured the racial terms of this naturalization, and that naturalization is at once a process of inclusion and exclusion.

In Newark Barringer was the first high school where Panasonic-donated "security cameras"—reportedly with audio features—were tested.[49] The celebrated joint venture between Panasonic and city government is important as it is emblematic of how state and nonstate governmentality operate as part of a common frame through which it becomes possible to pose the question of the spatiality of contemporary practices of government as an ethnographic problem (cf. Joseph and Nugent 1994). Security discourses, when presented in the mainstream media in relation to Puerto Rican or black youth, do not acknowledge particular racialized tragedies as collective loss. Public sympathy for youth in surveillance discourse was only rarely expressed, but was in fact explicitly refused under a journalistic "performance of explicit non-caring" (Taylor 2003, 147). As Lisa Marie Cacho notes, "such a refusal makes it necessary to juxtapose the limited 'official' archives of the written, recorded accounts of [racialized young people's] deaths with the ephemeral performances of their friends' and relatives' mourning, explicit performances of love, care, and grief beyond words." Privileging "anecdotal and ephemeral evidence grants entrance and access to those who have been locked out of official stories and, for that matter, 'material reality'" (189–92). The limits of what constitutes "evidence," thus, becomes clearly visible when we attempt to describe and imagine contemporary identities that do not fit into a single pre-established archive.

While many of the students whom I interviewed claimed to know how to tamper with the surveillance device and laughed at their effectiveness, while also describing instances of open bribery of security personnel, part of the work that navigating a city and existing in an urban context required for them was also dictated by learning to "relate to" surveillance mechanisms. During the summer of 2005, I met with Amarilis to catch up and see how her life had been in the year after graduation from Barringer. A brilliant and charismatic young woman, Amarilis found a job working as a security guard at a downtown corporate building right after graduating, while also teaching karate at an academy she co-owns with her girlfriend. On this particular summer afternoon, Amarilis met me at Newark's Penn Station after finishing her shift and, instead of taking me up on a lunch invitation, she asked me if it would be okay to talk at her house instead. Amarilis guessed I would be using a tape recorder for our follow-up interview and, as she later explained, "There are too many cops in Newark and, if you work in security and are wearing a uniform like mine, they look at you like 'Why is she talking onto that tape recorder,' you know?" Sounding more annoyed and irreverent than truly concerned, Amarilis added, "Everyone is so stuck in this period of fear, you know? They think that anyone can be about to put a bomb in the building, anyone will blow up the trains. They want to be doing drills all the time."

The principles of public order and "security" render the police as actors who are under the obligation to decide on a case-by-case basis that zone of indistinction between violence and the law (Agamben 1993). As a security guard herself, Amarilis was aware of how even surveillance and security are negotiated on an individual, often affective basis:

When I was at Barringer, they had cameras there. Out of a hundred, eighty didn't work [laughs]. If you're going to do stuff like that, you have to hire the right people. They all hire security who are young kids, like us. Let me tell you something, you can't put a bunch of young people monitoring eighteen-year-olds, because they're going to beat you up outside. Or you bribe them. "I'm going to the corner bodega. Let me go and I'll bring you a sandwich." What the hell, you grew up with these kids!

With the African American female security guards, on the other hand, one could not engage in this level of intimate negotiations, of affective relations, and hence one's agency was undermined under a politics of surveillance and security.

Concerns with trust and intentionality, examined above in relation to African Americans and Puerto Ricans, become more clearly illustrated in the case of Newark's Latino populations, in terms of how an inter-Latino intimacy emerges in relation to a cartography of racial democracy. Dominican–Puerto Rican relations in North Broadway are especially illustrative of this. In North Broadway, as perhaps is the case in other North-eastern urban neighborhoods (Grosfoguel 2003), certain Latino groups become racialized based on their proximity to Puerto Ricans. Dominicans in Newark constitute such a group. In a Goffmanian sense, trust—along with normal appearances, stigma, and frames—is a device for endowing social order with predictability (Goffman 1959), so that a search for stability in any social order requires the reduction of complexity and deployment of trust as a "lubricant for cooperation" (Scott 1992). People use certain rules of interaction to make themselves readable to others, so that the qualities which groups attribute to one another are primarily related to a perceived intent, the assumptions of conspiracies or ill intentions, and social trust is a critical issue to this (Rabinowitz 1997).

For instance, Dominicans complained that upon meeting a Puerto Rican, they almost expected to be called "plátano" or be made fun of for their accent or backwardness (an assumption that Dominicans were country bumpkins of sorts; chapter 6). Sometimes Dominicans interpreted this teasing as evidence that Puerto Ricans were just jealous of them because there were more Dominican businesses in the predominantly Puerto Rican neighborhood or because the Puerto Ricans felt that Dominicans were "taking over." Puerto Ricans also experienced a great deal of distrust in Dominicans. Marisol Padilla, a Barringer graduate, commented:

There are a lot of differences [among Dominicans and Puerto Ricans]. In your face, they are like "Hi, how are you?" [faked friendliness], but behind your back they talk, [they say] that we're lazy, that we don't want to work, that everything is given to us for free. . . . That's why when a Dominican, or someone who's not Puerto Rican, calls me, "Ah, you, Boricua," I tell them, "No, I am Puerto Rican." Because I'm only Boricua to other Boricuas. I find it disrespectful when other groups call us that.

Although such stipulation of boundaries—questioning the sincerity of a greeting, establishing who was allowed to use the colloquial term Boricua, and so on—may be expected in a context of material scarcity and demographic change, what is perhaps surprising is the great intimacy that such boundaries, misconceptions, and stereotypes generated among Puerto Ricans and Dominicans in North Broadway. A poignant illustration of this was when Dominicans themselves would deploy Puerto Rican characterizations of them against other Dominicans or when they would use these stereotypes to distinguish between US-born and recent immigrant Dominicans. Hence, it was not unusual to hear US-born Dominicans refer to recent arrivals as "plátano" or make fun of their accents or inability to speak English.

More significant, however, was how some Dominicans would view each other through the eyes of their own Puerto Rican neighbors, thus ironically displaying a great deal of dis-identification with Dominicans in their identification with Puerto Ricans. I was especially surprised to hear a Dominican female restaurant owner in North Newark referring to her Dominican husband, who happened to come in drunk to the restaurant early one morning, in an insulting fashion by calling him *dominicano* (with obvious pain and about to cry). As I was having a coffee-and-toast breakfast, the woman's husband came into the otherwise empty restaurant and a domestic fight ensued. A visibly frustrated wife kicked out the husband by telling him: "Vete de aquí dominicano. Esto no es un bar. Vete a la casa a que se te pase la borrachera! [Leave this restaurant, Dominican. This is not a bar. Go back home to get rid of your hangover!]." After the man left, the woman continued talking to her Dominican and Ecuadorian employees, complaining about how hard she worked just to have her husband spend the money on liquor. In some instances, stereotypes supplied the building blocks of narratives that were altered and dialectically modified self-representations and views of otherness. Legibility of order allowed Puerto Ricans and Dominicans to impose a modicum of legibility on the irregularities of a shared social reality that bound everyday experiences of the world in a readable and meaningful whole.

Relationships between Puerto Ricans and North Broadway residents who are African American, ethnic whites, and Latinos of other nationalities exist in a cosmology characterized by a political realm in which a Black elite of elected officials is viewed as dominant and neglectful of the interests of the residents of the predominantly Puerto Rican neighborhood in the city. Notwithstanding these perspectives on a black elite, however, readings of "race" among Puerto Ricans and between Puerto Ricans and other racialized populations gained salience in the realm of the intimate—of communities of affect, conceptions of trust and intent, of views of "tough love" in tending to the needs and experiences of area youth. It is in the tension between these two mutually constitutive realms that Puerto Ricans also address the delinquent citizen status to which they have been historically subjected (Burnett and Marshall 2001) and aim to produce, with varying degrees of success, an alternative politics of worth.

Mourning Youth: Failed Neoliberal Subjects and the Politics of Elusive Worth

Disentangling a politics of emotions requires an understanding of the ways in which the individual submits to emotional regimes and why. In particular, what is at stake for the individual in submitting to political authority, in accepting and feeling the emotions prescribed by specific organizations, in embracing emotional styles (a collectively constructed emotional commonsense) that render them humble, obedient, deferential or aggressive, independent or arrogant? Strategies of Puerto Rican containment—including the military and surveillance—shape Newark's neoliberal goals. This happens not only through the actual presence of totalizing institutions and surveillance devices, but through the emotional regimes that those institutions and devices generate; for instance, by creating African American "respectability" and Latin American "supercitizen immigrants." A critical question that guides the conclusion of this chapter centers around the visual and embodied performances of explicit caring and the "archive of feelings" that Puerto Rican parents and relatives were propelled to deploy to construct their "deviant" children not so much as people who were not productive, but rather as people who were not useless, so that the possibility for an alternative making of meaningful lives and understanding of worth could at least be considered (Cacho 2007, 193, 194, 200).

A neoliberal emotional regime aims to evoke universal emotions—emotions that newcomers and gentrifiers can relate to—while also creating a climate that is particularly receptive to disciplining racialized forms of "deviance" and "difference" that could threaten the normative social relations and structures at the base of capital accumulation. Under neoliberalism, this requires that the subject is narrated as either already productive or as having the potential and desire to be productive (and reproductive) in a normative, patriarchal way. Only those subjects who can trace their worth or potential worth to conventional measures and meet that criteria are viewed as deserving of compassion and esteem, so that value is ascribed to lives and deaths to define the rules of normality that limit the dreams, emotions, and acts of most Puerto Rican youth and parents in Newark (Cohen 2004, 38; Cacho 2007, 203).

Despite Julia's love for her son Joel, Joel could never be an ideal neoliberal subject. Instead, she viewed her son's life, as she did the lives of the soldiers in the film, through what Ann Cvetkovich (2003) calls an "archive of feeling," that is, as part of an archive constituted by the lived experiences of mourning and loss, ephemeral evidence that is anecdotal, rather than part of the "official archive." The lives and deaths of "unproductive" youth of color function primarily to repudiate these young people for not fulfilling mainstream work and familial expectations. Nevertheless, in contexts of structural subordination, an archive of feeling—in the form of documentaries, street side memorials, commemorative murals, and narratives of young men who are "good kids" even if they are not "good [neoliberal] citizens"—provides an alternative way of measuring value. As Cacho (2007) notes, such archives of feeling attempt to accomplish what mainstream news narratives do not: To make the grief or joy of family members in poor communities universal, so that the specific and particular of a given young person's life, rather than her or his self-promotion or "contribution to society," is all that matters. In this sense, family and friends create their own publics to witness the emotional lives of these young men and women and render their parental pain or joy universal.[50]

The film event at the Newark Museum, described in the introduction to this chapter, is akin to the visual elements deployed to incarnate feelings of a worthy life in burials and street memorials (Cacho 2007, 191), including the ones erected to commemorate Sujeiti Ocasio, an eighteen-year-old Puerto Rican woman who was shot in front of her house a few hours after her graduation from Barringer High School. In Sujeiti's case it was precisely the normativity of her life that most highlighted the deviance of Nicole Guyette, the eighteen-year-old Puerto Rican woman who shot her. Sujeiti had graduated from Barringer High School a few hours prior to her death, a fact that dominated the mainstream media's account. Not only had she graduated and intended to attend Essex Community College, but she had actually been the first one in her family to accomplish this. Attention was given to the fact that Sujeiti's mother was thirty-three years old and, in multiple blogs that resulted from the tragedy, bloggers bothered to calculate that the mother was fifteen and single when she gave birth to Sujeiti.

On the night she was shot, Sujeiti had invited a couple of friends over for pizza, as a preamble to a graduation party she would have that Sunday. It was right in front of her house—on a "tree-lined, residential street predominated by Puerto Rican families"—that Sujeiti and Nicole "exchanged words."[51] As a friend of the young women described to a reporter, "She [Sujeiti] said, 'Let's shoot a fair one,' you know, let's fight." And added, "Sujeiti went into the middle of the street and then bang." Depending on the account, Nicole had gone either to her own house, across the street from Sujeiti's, or to her boyfriend's house, also on the same street, to get the gun that she used to shoot her neighbor and former classmate. A friend of Sujeiti told WABC news that "She got shot for no reason. . . . I was trying to tell them to stop arguing, but the girl [Nicole] just shot her out of nowhere. They was just [arguing] over nothing. Name calling, over nothing. She got shot for no reason."[52]

After the shooting, Nicole allegedly was at large for a couple of days, during which "Wanted" signs were posted around the area. Eventually, Nicole turned herself in, perhaps moved by her grandmother's plea, "Nicole, please, this is Grandma. I want you to come home. I want to see you. You are not alone." When Nicole turned herself in, the main outcry in the community was "They got her! They got her!" A makeshift memorial—of candles, flowers, stuffed animals, and balloons, as well as photographs of Sujeiti—was put in place "in memory of a girl who her family says was a popular, beautiful teenager with a bright future."[53] And, indeed, the ultimate, more effective neoliberal subject is the one who is able and interested in "redeeming" him/herself from "deviant" behavior using the tools of capitalism.

Sujeiti Ocasio was immortalized as the antithesis of Nicole Guyette, despite living on the same street, having attended the same school, and having loving families that were willing to stand by them no matter what. The distinction between them was rooted on one basic aspect of their lives: Sujeiti had graduated high school and was on her way to becoming productive (attending community college and the prospect of leaving Newark), whereas Nicole had dropped out of high school and had no known employment prospects. Many reporters and even some of the people attending the wake speculated that maybe Nicole was jealous or had "an inferiority complex" because Sujeiti reminded her of the success and accomplishments that she, as a high school dropout, would never have. Interestingly, the initial response by those unfamiliar with the girls was to assume that this "bitch fight" had to do with "fighting over a ghetto boy," as I heard a middle-age African American woman comment on a bus. Once the possibility that this could be a crime of passion was discarded by new information that showed that both girls had their own boyfriends, a new explanation that was also in accordance with Newark's emotional landscape surfaced: aggression, jealousy, and low self-esteem were to blame. The head shots that circulated in the mainstream media portrayed a hardened Nicole—a light-skinned girl, wearing gold-loop earrings and curly brown hair—next to the graduation picture of an almost angelical Sujeiti, with straight black hair, ample smile, tanned complexion, and bare bronze shoulders. As a blogger noted, "I wonder where that picture of Nicole is from. She looks like she has some serious attitude problem. I worked with a woman who had that attitude and every day of work was a nightmare. You never knew from one minute to the next when she was going to explode."[54]

Sujeiti's wake was held at the Alvarez Funeral Home in North Newark, not far from the family's Lincoln Avenue home. Several police patrol cars were parked in front of the funeral home and the presence of about a dozen police officers, some of them paying respects and others consoling Sujeiti's family, obviously affected friends. "Take it one day at a time. One day at a time," a tall African American officer told a heavyset Puerto Rican girl who was bent over crying in a corner of the funeral home. "Now kids go from zero to killing," commented the parent of a Barringer High School sophomore who attended the funeral. And he continued, "It's as if they don't experience the range of emotions, you know, going from being pissed off to getting that gun. In our generation, you'd first get annoyed, mad, pissed, cussing, a fist fight or name calling. Now it's 'go shoot you.'" A teacher and community activist pointed to "technology"—in an almost formulaic way—as a potential way of making sense of senseless acts. "A kid can write, 'I'm going to kill you,' in a text message or MySpace page, so that when he says it to someone's face it doesn't really mean anything."

As I entered the room where Sujeiti's open casket laid surrounded by flower arrangements, cap-and-gowned stuffed animals, and posterboards of Sujeiti in various outfits and alluring poses, I also spotted some EMT workers. Apparently, Sujeiti's grandmother had collapsed. The grandmother was ushered back into the room where the casket was, as she promised her son, Sujeiti's uncle, and daughter, Sujeiti's mom, "Me voy a portar bien. Déjenme, no me agarren [I'm going to behave well, Leave me alone, don't tug on me]." Young men and women from the neighborhood and from Barringer attended the wake, sporting T-shirts with Sujeiti's photo, promises of remembering her forever, and digital cameras, which some of them used to take pictures of the open casket. Several parents approached the casket, cajoling their hesitant adolescent sons or daughters. "Yo no la quiero ver. I don't want to see it!," a young man cried, as his father assured him that he needed to—in fact, it was almost imperative that he saw the body.

"I know the grandmother of the other girl. I think she's at her other son's house."

"I gave Sujeiti's boyfriend a ride the other day. He's friends with my grandson. If the boyfriend or my grandson had been present, they would have prevented this from happening. This would not have happened because they would have stepped up."

"I think the other girl is with the police. She escaped once. They won't let her go, because she'll escape again."

These were the comments I heard as I sat contemplating the way in which people mourned, informed, and transformed their relationship to Sujeiti's family and their neighbors. The death was rendered not only untimely, unnecessary and tragic, but also provided a register to greater narratives: narratives of "degenerate youth," of "violent girls," of low self-esteem and uncontrolled anger. Because Sujeiti's life, but particularly her death, was a testament to something else: Of how, in the case of Puerto Rican youth, narratives of success and social mobility were never too far from those of delinquency, deviance, and degeneracy. In the United States, Puerto Ricans are rendered visible only according to a duality of existence, in which they can either be good or bad, productive or lazy, lawful or delinquent.

Ubiquitous manifestations of emotional control in the public arena were influenced by self-help perspectives—the need to overcome complejo (having a chip on one's shoulder), to "work at *a-ny-thing*," to be "grateful" for living in the Land of Opportunity—and establishing oneself as resident of a neighborhood of "good family values" were strategies that helped sediment Puerto Rican experiences in a predominantly black city. The conditions that continue to render US-born Puerto Ricans, across several generations, among the poorest of the poor remain concealed under narratives of emotional (in)adequacy in Newark. While self-help organizations and military recruitment served as strategies against a deterministic delinquent citizenship attributed to Puerto Ricans in Newark, South Americans, particularly Brazilians, relied on developing a highly productive commercial sector in the Ironbound. As this chapter has shown, in the racialized context of an aggressive Newark, Puerto Ricans engaged in the project of proving a collective "deservingness" or "worthiness," deployed in connection to military service, social service organizations, and renditions of African Americans as "untrustworthy." In chapter 3 I examine how Brazilians, on the other hand, claimed a higher moral ground, based on transnational perspectives on racial democracy, attitudes toward colorism, and the use of humor in discussions of race.

THREE

Cartography of Racial Democracy: Cultural Excess, Racial Play, and Universal Sentimentality in Luso-Brazilian Newark

On a late afternoon in March of 2008, in one of the several beauty salons in the Ironbound, an African American woman wearing a dark-green tailored suit and heels complained that a Brazilian worker had missed a hair in the eyebrow waxing she had just gotten done. As the African American woman inspected her eyebrow in the mirror, the Ecuadorian manicurist called out to the Brazilian worker: "Ursula! Ursula! She wants you to fix her eyebrows."

Ursula quickly fixed the eyebrow situation and the client was promptly on her way, when another Brazilian manicurist sitting nearby commented: "I don't know how she can even see that hair . . . she's so dark you can barely see her eyebrows at all!" This provoked laughter throughout the small hair salon.

A Brazilian manicurist doing my nails remarked in a lower voice, in Portuguese: "They like to complain, complain, complain, about everything. And for what? Why be in that state of mind?"

The Ecuadorian manicurist at the next table, as if to explain or clarify what everyone seemed to agree on, and perhaps to test my own solidarity with the statements that were being circulated remarked, in Spanish: "Es que son muy peleonas las morenas, verdad? Se quejan mucho ellas [Black women like to fight, right? They complain a lot]."

A bit unsure about how to respond or even if a response was expected from me, I replied with a question, "Usted cree? Se quejan mucho entonces? [Do you think so? They complain a lot then?]."

"Qué es usted? De dónde es? [What are you? Where are you from?]," she replied, with a very basic question that in Newark can mean nothing or be quite loaded, depending on context, characters, and circumstances.

"Soy puertorriqueña [I'm Puerto Rican]."

And she added the last significant, "ideologically situated" (Bakhtin 1981, 271) utterance of our exchange: "Uhmm . . . " By now, and in seamless back-and-forth bantering in Portuguese, Spanish, and English, the predominantly Brazilian and Ecuadorian staff in the small beauty salon was sharing stories about their experiences with other black clients. One of the young Brazilian hairstylists talked about another African American client who had come to the beauty salon earlier that week to color her hair. "She wanted to color it blonde!" the Brazilian hairstylist laughed, "and she was even darker than me."

There was collective laughter at the presumed absurdity or, at the very least, bad taste, of such a request. "Did you? Did you color it for her?" another Brazilian worker who was sweeping the floor asked.

"Of course! As long as she pays, I do it. And tell her that she looks pretty too . . . with a smile on my face!" she responded, showing pride in her own business savvy, even while aware of how it might border on deceit. Everyone laughed.

More seriously and reflective, Ursula, who had done the wax job, commented: "I agree with Paula, because . . . you know how you see them [black women] coming in with that face [mimics a serious or stern, or even angry look] and you think 'Uff.' But sometimes they have a better attitude when they leave. Life is too short, não é? Why be like that?" Resolving conflict without dispute in the Ironbound oftentimes took the form of gossip, joking, and other forms of verbal play and nonverbal cues.[1]

A US-based "cartography of racial democracy" is characterized not only by the use of humor, bantering, and nonverbal cues, but moreover, by a particular sensitivity to evaluations of adequate affect, emotional competency, and life skills. This sensitivity has a destabilizing effect on the status of "race" as an identity marker in everyday encounters; it creates interactions in which color and racial terms are switched even within the same conversation and reflects a general apprehension to ascribe racial labels and engage in explicit race-talk in public (cf. Sheriff 2001; Godreau 2002; Duany 1998).The possibility of constructing race through language is carefully monitored, as can be seen by the constant inquisitiveness and attentiveness to other people's reactions to one's comments about color or race. A sign of discomfort, such as a shift in one's posture, a glance, or a change in tone, would have ended the conversation very quickly, particularly if it came from a client. Developing a sense of awareness of limits in such bantering became a critical step to learning US racial etiquette among Latin American migrants, particularly for those in the service and personal care sectors. The significance of race under racial democracy is oftentimes communicated in indirect forms—through jokes, tacit references, coded silences. Given the particularity of everyday discursive etiquette in Latin America and the Spanish-speaking Caribbean, when migrants from these countries felt compelled to verbalize commentaries on "race," an otherwise unspeakable subject to many of them, there oftentimes was awkwardness, hesitation, and discomfort.[2] Nevertheless, even in light of an avoidance of explicit racial talk or denunciations of racism, there was an explicitly communicated hyperfocus on color, that is, on using color terms to describe individuals in particular interactions.

Latin Americans in the Ironbound often felt that it was their role to transform Newark racial relations from "aggressive," associated with African Americans, to "playful"—a type of racial interaction that focused on "good manners" and getting along, and which was central to commercial productivity in the neighborhood. Carefully managing interactions with African Americans that were interpreted as potentially inflammatory was viewed as critical to preserving conviviality. Just like a "politics of worthiness" regulated Puerto Rican relationship with African Americans, a "politics of conviviality" characterized Brazilian and South American life in the Ironbound. Certain tenets of Latin American racial democracy ideology provided the discursive tools to sustain this politics of conviviality. As shown in the beauty salon episode, the Ironbound's emotional landscape introduced perspectives on the appropriate self-packaging of an emotive persona and a heightened (a)esthetics of personal "self-care" and capacity to be "light" or "humorous," and not be militant or "angry."

Moreover, the centrality of the figure of African Americans, particularly African American women in this case, is indicative of two important elements of this "cartography of racial democracy." First, the focus on "complaining," and its attribution to the African American client, as well as to African Americans more generally, illustrates how discussions about "race" in light of a common oppression or subordination become compromised by a rendition of "race" as insidiously situated in a defective psyche or emotive world of blacks. Second, this African American figure is always already classed and situated in discourses of respect and respectability. In a neighborhood characterized by a highly visible service sector—of ethnic restaurants, specialty stores, and body services, like beauty salons, waxing and massage services—the relationship between Latin Americans (particularly Brazilians) and African Americans is often one of worker-client, with the African American usually being more securely middle class and the Brazilian more working class. What remains hidden from these perspectives on race as affect and manners, and which served as a concealed context for the beauty salon episode, is how "whiteness" acts as an invisible constitutive element to the production of antiblack attitudes among Brazilians, as well as how it impedes the production of a Latino identity between Latin American migrants and US-born Latinos.

Inspired by this quotidian episode to trace the production of this "cartography of racial democracy" and to examine the simultaneous centrality and invisibility of Blackness in the Ironbound, the only predominantly white neighborhood in Newark, I begin this chapter by giving a brief background to how the Ironbound and its residents are imagined in media and popular culture. I then look at the African American presence in the neighborhood and situate the beauty salon episode in the context of broader Brazilian perspectives on US Blackness. In particular, I consider how Brazilians see African Americans in ways that highlight their classed identities, as well as presumed character defects, their inclination to "appropriate" certain aspects of Brazilian culture, and their general inability to abide by the "racial democracy" ideologies that blacks in Brazil presumably embrace. In this way, I examine how Brazilians navigate a pragmatic terrain between Brazilian-ness as "cultural excess" and as "racial invisibility. Moreover, inspired by the "Uhmm . . ." that followed when I answered that I was Puerto Rican, this chapter also focuses on how Puerto Ricans become constitutive outsiders for groups who relate to the "Hispanic" category with great trepidation, as is the case of Brazilians. The question "Are Brazilians Hispanic?" is central here. While Puerto Ricans, along with Mexicans in other parts of the United States, including Chicago (De Genova and Ramos-Zayas 2003), are viewed as central in discussions of Latinidad or Hispanic identity in the United States, Brazilians occupy a very tenuous and ambiguous position. Many of the Brazilians with whom I spoke capitalized on this ambiguity by viewing themselves as possessing certain emotional qualities that other groups—including other Latinos—did not have, including life skills. One example is their presumed ability to weather problems with an optimistic attitude, as illustrated by the "Life is too short, não é?" question in the beauty salon. Considering Brazilian migration and settlement in Newark's "Portuguese enclave," I show how individual and family narratives of overcoming become critical to producing a sentimentality of culture that solidifies multicultural neoliberalism (Hale 2002).

Finally, this chapter examines how whiteness, embodied in images of the Portuguese and other Iberian ethnics, provided the unidentified grid for how racial relationships between Brazilians and Latin American migrants more generally, on the one hand, and US native minorities, particularly blacks and Puerto Ricans, on the other, were manifested in the Ironbound. As I demonstrate, a phantom of whiteness regulated the ways in which race was ignored or reformulated, even in the absence of white people.

"Not Like the Rest of Newark": A Sensual Space and the Sentimentality of Culture in the Ironbound

The neighborhood of the Ironbound, in the East Ward, has been the historically Portuguese "enclave" of Newark, a productive area that generated great revenue to the city largely because of its successful commodification of culture in the form of restaurants, specialty stores, ethnic festivals, and cafés.[3] In the early 1900s, Portuguese from Lisbon and Spanish, primarily from the province of Galicia, followed other European ethnics who had settled "Down Neck."[4] Although immigrants from Portugal had been arriving in Newark's Ironbound since the turn of the century, Portuguese immigration increased in the post–World War II period and reached its peak with the onset of Portugal's colonial wars and political unrest and the change in US immigration laws in 1965. The 1974 military coup in Portugal and the Portuguese government's mandatory army draft and war in Angola further sparked a new migration of urban professionals, tradesmen and entrepreneurs to Newark (Holton and Klimt 2009).

By the mid-1970s, the Italian and Cuban shops that had lined Ferry Street gave way to a burst of Portuguese investment. The incoming Portuguese immigrants acquired cheap land deemed undesirable after the 1967 riots and, since then, have been credited for using their carpentry, handiwork, and commercial skills to rebuild the Ironbound.[5] As was asserted in a *New Jersey Business* article: "Everybody in the Portuguese Ironbound community works, even teenagers after school. . . . The U.S. Portuguese community is not listed by the federal government as a minority. General Salazar, years ago, refused to go along with the U.S. government's suggestion on this, believing that the Portuguese could go anywhere in the world and make it on their own."[6] The wide array of churches of all denominations and nationalities in the Ironbound are oftentimes viewed as testament to the common images of "stable immigrant life." Most Portuguese Ironbound residents saw themselves as faithful to Newark because, unlike the residents of predominantly Jewish areas, they had not abandoned the city after the riots.

An unevenly shaped triangle encroached by railroad tracks and highways, the Ironbound is viewed among Newark residents and outsiders remotely familiar with Newark as the most commercially viable area in an otherwise "deteriorated" black city.[7] In Newark the Iberian ethnics were viewed as "technicians of space" (Foucault 1984; cf. Dinzey-Flores 2006), credited with displaying loyalty to Newark and saving the Ironbound neighborhood, brick by brick. The fact that the Ironbound was spared the construction of massive housing projects like those in North Broadway and the other Newark neighborhoods was rarely considered in the credit given to European ethnic technicians.

Space-making in the Ironbound relied on a commercialization of sensual experiences. Media and popular descriptions of the area invariably focused on the smells and tastes of Iberian cuisine, the sounds of "foreign" languages in the streets, the sight of colorful tiles on local homes, and ethnic festivals in the summer. Reporter Diana Rojas describes the area in a way that has become de rigueur in most journalistic accounts:

In this side of the Atlantic, there's a place where you can feast on paella and sangria to the serenades of traveling troubadours called atunas. Where you're more likely to hear "bom dia" than "good day." Where locals regularly crowd into lively cafes to people-watch, while leisurely sipping a gallão. Welcome to the Ironbound a cultural treasure tucked away in Newark's East Ward. . . . Disguised by the unremarkable facade of an urban working class community, the neighborhood puts on an authentic display of Iberian culture unrivaled in this area—from restaurants, cafés, and bars, to ethnic sidewalk produce and fish markets and multilingual newsstands. . . . While many of the older immigrants are moving back to Europe or out to the suburbs, more Spanish and Portuguese are replacing them—and more and more Brazilians are making their mark. . . . With the lowest crime rate in the city, the neighborhood that is demarcated by a long stone wall off Route 21 poses no serious safety problems. . . . Despite the occasional, colorful wall tiles on the aluminum-sided houses, the Ironbound is not a visual treat. What it does offer is an opportunity to experience a foreign culture for a day, or preferably an evening, without having to go too far from home. . . . Although the ethnic makeup of the Ironbound is in flux, its soul is still deeply rooted 3,000 miles away on another continent, fueled by a communal sense of saudade—a word unique to the Portuguese language that connotes a longing for home, family, and friends.[8]

The "city of cultural consumption" (Zukin 1996) and the "nonplace urban realm" (Rutheiser 1999) are references to instances in which cities are packaged as commodities to create the "city of scenographic sites" (Boyer 1996). As Lori Baptiste (2008) argues, foodways in the Ironbound are "dynamic, embodied practices that individuals use to self-reflexively determine, evaluate and potentially change their relationship to each other and the world." In fact, through the act of "remembering, talking about, shopping for, preparing and eating certain foods, Portuguese speaking immigrants in Newark use food to express and change social and economic relations."[9] Such images generally focused on the restaurants, cafés, and produce markets on Ferry Street, the commercial thoroughfare of the Ironbound, almost to the exclusion of the surrounding housing projects or the fragile working-class neighborhood life threatened by increasing taxes, toxic waste, and overcrowded public schools. This focus was also suggestive of how certain renderings of "culture" and social capital became defined by market possibilities and demands. More significantly, however, a particular kind of emotional landscape sustained this particular production of space.

The Ironbound ethnic foods and goods market was fiercely defended against the US service sector, of which the opening of a Dunkin' Donuts on Ferry Street became emblematic. The opening was a highly contested event, which ultimately led long-time Portuguese and Spanish residents to shift from an emphasis on the importance of European establishments in the area to a position of sponsoring any "non-American" business, including a growing number of Brazilian and Ecuadorian businesses. The US service sector was associated with a low-brow fast-food industry typical of Newark's "inner-city"; some Ironbound residents felt that allowing such businesses would devalue the Ironbound or diminish the neighborhood's caché and touristic appeal. Only by advocating on behalf of local European- or European-inspired business would the area maintain its non-inner-city *feel* in an otherwise "decrepit" city like Newark. Dunkin' Donuts was an expression of a bland or generic American-ness associated with a lack of culture and the inferior emotive persona associated with Americans. Their view of American-ness as affluent, but also as cultureless and even bland or uncommodifiable, partly explained the insistence with which Iberian ethnics monitored their own identities and preferred to straddle a middle ground between being white Americans, on the one hand, and being regarded as closer to US-born blacks and Latinos, on the other.

Vicente Alonso, a US-born man of Galician parents and the father of a student at ESHS, grew up in the Ironbound and worked as manager in one of the main supermarkets in the area when I met him at a parent-teacher activity. Vicente was one of the people who vehemently objected to the opening of a Dunkin' Donuts on Ferry Street stating: "We need to keep this area different, with good restaurants, European. It's okay if some other Hispanic businesses come into the area, but we can't have this be now about McDonald's and those white trash places." Prior to moving to Newark, Vicente had lived in a town in Florida where most of his neighbors were, in his words, "white trash." Vicente explained: "These were people from Kentucky, from other small rural areas of the United States. They were uneducated, kept their houses dirty, and never even traveled anywhere."

Vicente's vehement opposition to the opening of more "American restaurants" was not only a legitimate concern over the destitution of small, family-owned businesses in the area, but also the fear that the Europeanized, working-class Ferry Street would eventually be mistaken for either a "white trash" area or an "inner-city" neighborhood. An Iberian identity—or any culturally saturated identity, for that matter—was deployed as a way to avoid a much-stigmatized yet very immediate reality of poverty among US-born generations of European parentage in Newark; thus, Vicente's proclamation that "even Hispanic" businesses should be favored over American ones.[10] In that sense, Vicente, a third-generation working-class man himself, grabbed onto his European identity, as conferred to him partly by the space where he grew up and settled, in order to avoid the proximity of what he viewed as the even more stigmatized fate of the unhyphenated American poor. Whose culture was to be promoted and spatially inscribed was not an insurmountable point of contention in the Ironbound, as long as the area preserved an overall "feel" of "not being in America," and such a "feel" could propel further commercial development, increase real estate value, reinforce moral and emotive superiority, and accentuate the image of the Ironbound as different from the rest of Newark.

In the late 1980s the demographic dominance of the Portuguese began to shift, as more Latin American migrants, especially from Brazil and other parts of South America, began to arrive in the area.[11] When Brazil's electoral college met in 1985 to choose the country's first civilian president, Brazil was in the midst of a severe economic recession that would only get worse in the later part of the 1980s and 1990s. The middle classes saw their savings evaporate as the annual inflation rate climbed to 1,000 percent in 1986 with a projected annual rate of 2,000 percent in 1988. Not only middle-class migrants, but also migrants from the Brazilian working classes began leaving Brazil (see Kathryn Gallant in Bueno 2003). Unemployment had reached 25 percent, while wages were 40 percent lower in real terms than they had been two years prior.[12] While some Brazilians had arrived in the United States in the early 1950s through a connection with mica mines in Belo Horizonte, a commercial jewelry and gem trade with the Orthodox Jewish merchants in Midtown Manhattan's Diamond district, and a fascination with Disney World among the Brazilian middle class since the 1970s, the migration of greater numbers of Brazilians from working-class and middle-class backgrounds occurred in the 1980s and 1990s (Meihy 2004; Margolis 1994; Tosta 2004, 579; Werneck 2004).

Most of the Brazilian adults with whom I spoke in the Ironbound were parents, teachers, or relatives of students at ESHS. Initially, they had been drawn to the Ironbound because of family and work connections in the area, in addition to the predominant use of Portuguese language in everyday life and employment possibilities of the neighborhood. Once in the Ironbound, they felt that it was a good community to raise children. Many of them expressed a mixed attraction for Manhattan as a good place "to visit" and some of them had relatives in Queens, whom they also liked to visit occasionally. The few single and childless Brazilians whom I met in Newark had an ambivalent perspective on the city. Mariela, the twenty-six-year-old aunt of Paula Pereira, a student at East Side High School, encapsulated some of the main issues raised by other young and single Brazilians about Newark. Although Mariela had decided to come to Newark because her sister and her sister's family lived there, she insistently mentioned that she wished she lived in New York. In a letter she had written to a friend back in Belo Horizonte, Mariela described Newark in light of a trip she made to Florida:

When I was in the airplane coming back from Florida, the first thing I thought to myself was: I'm back in this detestable land [terra esquisita]. But here I am, perdida no fim do mundo onde Judas perdeu as meias [lost at the end of the world, where Jude lost his socks]. . . . Newark is a very strange city. It's only fifteen minutes by train from Manhattan and yet it seems like another country. For one, EVERYBODY speaks Portuguese (from Brazil and from Portugal) and sometimes they don't understand each other . . . it's hilarious. . . . I know people who have lived in Newark for over ten years and they don't speak English or have ever been to Manhattan. The houses are old and some of them are falling into pieces. . . . I don't want to pay a high rent for an apartment that is barely better than a favela. I bet that Rocinha [a favela in Rio] has better places than those I've seen in Newark, and cheaper, too. Other houses that are not as old were constructed by the first Portuguese that arrived here and have a style with tile of images of Catholic saints under the windows. . . . [But] regardless of how pretty Florida is, I was finding everything crappy and I was missing Newark. . . . This is the first place where I was able to live on my own, to have some independence. . . . So Newark is dirty, old, and full of people from Governador Valadares and rude and ignorant Portuguese people, but at least they have French bread, arroz com feijão in each corner.

The Brazilians with whom I spoke in the United States and in Brazil alike seemed to either conflate New Jersey and New York as the same area, by noting the physical proximity of New York's Little Brazil and New Jersey's Ironbound, or emphasize the cultural distinctions between both areas, as was usually the case with middle-class Brazilians in New York.[13] A staff at the Brazilian consulate stated: "Even within the jurisdiction of the New York consulate, there are enormous variations between Brazilians who are in New Jersey and Connecticut and those in New York. Nobody is going to say that he lives in New Jersey or even if they live in New York, they will say they live in Manhattan rather than Queens. It is much more fashionable to say that one lives in Manhattan." While Brazilians in New York seem to be overwhelmingly young, single, and professionally trained in Brazil (see Meihy 2004; Werneck 2004), many Brazilians in Newark were married, had children, and had been working class or working poor in Brazil. When Camilo Siqueira, a writer for a Brazilian newspaper who had lived in Kearny, learned that my research would focus on Brazilians in Newark, his first response was to encourage me to also interview Brazilians in New York. In a very low voice, so as not to be overheard by the other Brazilians sitting at the table next to us at the cafeteria where we were having lunch, Ricardo Lima, a Brazilian freelance writer whom I met at an event sponsored by a language school in the Ironbound, mentioned: "The Brazilians in New York are sophisticated, well educated. That's not the case in Newark. In Newark, the Brazilians are laborers. They don't have an education. They are simple people. You really ought to interview people in New York." While the earlier migrants to Newark tended to be from small towns in Minas Gerais, particularly Governador Valadares, the most recent migration was more geographically diverse, with many migrants hailing from urban areas including São Paulo, Rio de Janeiro, and especially Belo Horizonte.

In 1990, 70 percent of the Brazilians in the United States were presumed to be undocumented.[14] The Brazilian 2000 Census divulged by the Palácio do Itamaraty placed the figure of documented and undocumented Brazilian living in the United States at 800,000. Unofficial Brazilian sources, however, have used a much higher figure—1.5 million (Meihy 2004). As Maxine Margolis notes: "By 2001, nearly 2 million Brazilians were living abroad; of those between 800,000 and 1.1 million were in the United States, according to the Brazilian Ministry of Foreign Affairs, but only 212,000 were counted in the US Census" (2006).[15] Seventy-five percent of US Brazilians lived in only six states in 2000: Massachusetts, New York, New Jersey, Florida, California, and Connecticut. According to the Brazilian American Cultural Center in New York, 500,000 Brazilians lived in the New York–New Jersey–Connecticut tristate area in 2003. According to the Brazilian Immigrant Center in Boston, the largest settlements of Brazilians are on the East Coast, particularly in New York, which has an estimated 80,000–150,000 Brazilian immigrants (mostly in Astoria, Queens). Newark's Brazilians are sometimes included in New York area statistics and are numbered, in official counts, at 65,000.[16]

Many old-time residents of the Ironbound considered the neighborhood to be an example of an "illegal" immigrant life that was open, drew little security, and was virtually indistinguishable from that in the legal world (Martins 2003).[17] In 1995 the Portuguese were the largest group of "illegal immigrants" in New Jersey, with a population of about 17,000. According to a *New York Times* article, however, their "illegality" was quite invisible, at least at the time of the article. Paul Quintela, a bar manager in his thirties who came to the United States illegally in 1990, is quoted as saying: "We are totally invisible. . . . No one knows about us. Being illegal is just a label that doesn't mean anything." He stated that he never thought of himself as an illegal immigrant, but that "from the beginning, he was the image of middle-class America—a maître d'hotel at a tony French restaurant in Morristown, with a nice home in the suburbs and a new Volkswagen sedan parked in the driveway." He added: "In a lot of ways, this is more home to me than Portugal. It was built by people like me."[18]

By the year 2000 a growing number of Brazilians began arriving to the United States through the Mexican border, rather than overstaying their tourist visas, as had been the case of previous migrants. Although for a while Brazilians were considered an "invisible minority," by 2005 Brazilians were used by the Bush administration as evidence of the effectiveness of US immigration policy. As a BBC Brazil article suggested, US President George W. Bush emphasized the reduction in illegal Brazilian immigration as an example of his government's successful immigration policy, which speeded deportation.[19] This was a pat on the back to the Mexican government for requiring visas of Brazilians. Until October of 2005 Mexico did not require visas of Brazilians, and many prospective migrants had access to the clandestine routes across the US-Mexico border. After October of 2005, and under significant pressure from the United States, Mexico discontinued this agreement with Brazil, thus inducing many Brazilians to pursue routes through Guatemala. According to a *New York Times* article of June 13, 2004, the Mexican government was informed of an increase in the number of Brazilians that arrived to Mexico City by plane and then crossed the border by foot.[20] The annual number of Brazilians detained by US immigration agents jumped from 439 in 1997 to 3,485 in 2001, according to INS statistics. A *Folha de São Paulo* article reported that between October 1, 2004, and September 30, 2005, over 31,000 Brazilians were arrested at the US-Mexican border.[21] Nevertheless, in 2005 Brazil only occupied the fourth place in the ranking of arrests (from fifth in 1999), after Mexico, Honduras and El Salvador.[22]

Since the 1980s the Ironbound has been configured as a touristic stronghold of Newark.[23] Many of the businesses on Ferry Street, the neighborhood's main commercial artery, attempted to accommodate the area's linguistic diversity by hiring personnel that spoke at least the area's three main languages—Portuguese, Spanish, and English. In the Ironbound, a commercially viable place-making requires presenting culture not only as an object, but also as a fundamentally sensorial and emotive form of interacting with the built environment, a "feel" of community that related to a longing for a distant home—some used the Portuguese term *saudade*. Appealing to a universal sentimentality that purportedly transcended social constructionist perspectives on group differences, the Ironbound was decidedly experienced through a heightened emotionality conceived in a quasi-biological, sensorial way through smells, sights, sounds, touch, and tastes, available to anyone regardless of race, ethnicity, class, and nationality. Moreover, this sentimentality of culture in the Ironbound included a privileging of individual and familial life histories. These life histories—of hardship, sacrifice, pain, and overcoming—complemented most media coverage of the neighborhood. They were framed according to a perspective on Iberian ethnic assimilation that was always (and protectively) selective and incomplete (sometimes strategically so).

As Pine and Gilmore (1999) convincingly show, place identity plays a large role in shaping how the economy is experienced viscerally, so that particular identities of place can provide a large surplus value; in this sense, place identity is manipulated to encourage consumption. These experiences of place in the Ironbound involved creating the emotive conditions that allowed consumers not only to buy cultural objects, but also to elicit from them a sense of belonging, however temporary, to a communal past of good values and family unity, a central trope of US ethnic history. The manipulation of place identity is not solely a tool for urban regeneration and economic allure. It is also used to represent a certain vision of social worth and individual values that only a few communities appear to possess. In the case of the Ironbound, for instance, the neighborhood is modeled on an ideal image of what a neighborhood should be like. In this ideal the neighborhood is a community, a socially integrated area characterized by tightly knit (heteronormative) families with good values. The idealized neighborhood stands as the opposite of the supposed downfall of community in the problem-ridden "inner city" Newark; the Ironbound looks not only aesthetically more desirable than those neighborhoods (e.g., cleaner, quaint), including the Puerto Rican area of North Broadway, but also more peaceful, friendlier, and welcoming to (white, middle-class) outsiders.[24]

Images of such universal sentimentality in the Ironbound were anchored in modes of consumption and domesticity that reflect changes in the processes of capital accumulation and labor disciplining in the United States since the 1970s. As the state aligns more closely with market imperatives and withdraws the social base, the cost of social reproduction shifts more to the middle and working classes. A reinvigorated discourse of individual responsibility and family values sorts out people into those who are "productive" citizens and those who are "underclassed." Spaces like the Ironbound are representative of the former just as North Broadway is emblematic of the latter. Space-making in the Ironbound is fundamentally conceived, in popular media and everyday life, as a contrast between middle-class respectability and an underground deviant identity, thus truly making "home" into a "foreign place."

Potential chauvinistic competition among nationalities over area business and resources in the Ironbound have been tamed, if not entirely resolved, through a common emphasis on cultural objects and practices that are intended to appeal to a universal, quasi-biological aspect of human existence: the senses. As long as the culture produced has an appeal to such universalized features of human existence—through taste, smell, sound, visual, and tactile appeal—it was generally well received, in contradistinction to a cultureless perspective of things American. This emotive, "feel" aspect resonates in some ways with what Phil Cohen terms "multicultural capitalism," a capitalism based on the re/production of cultural diversity and the marketing of exotic commodities and which, by being "at the cutting edge of globalization" (1999, 322), serves a new cosmopolitan elite that both produces and consumes cultural diversity on a global scale.

In the case of Newark, however, space-making through a cultural excess that privileged forms of sensual/sensorial marketing enhanced the appeal to middle-class gentrifiers and suburban white visitors in a predominantly black city. The emphasis on the senses contributed to a condition not only of shared feelings, but to an imponderable but palpable thickness in the air, or an atmosphere that was different from that noted in the rest of Newark. These feelings were not only produced from a heightened or lessened tension, as those noticed in the beauty salon incident, but sustained from those interpersonal tensions; in fact, "emotions in their very intensity involve miscommunication, such that even when we feel we have the same feeling [about a place as someone else would], we don't necessarily have the same relationship to those feelings." This is the process that Sara Ahmed describes as "the objects of emotion that circulate, rather than emotions as such," since emotions move through the circulation of objects, rather than remaining static (2004, 10).

Rather than the well-documented process of cultural commodification typical of a multicultural neoliberalism (Hale 2002, 2005), cultural objects and practices in the Ironbound were saturated with affect and often became sites of personal and social tension, misinterpretation, and gossip. They were also deployed as evidence of intimacy and betrayal, pain and overcoming. The process of ascribing emotional referents to cultural objects and practices has, over time, accumulated affective value, so that such value is sometimes cultivated through an erasure of a more troubling history of production and labor. This local process of cultural excess is characterized not only by a commodity fetishism, in a classical Marxist sense, but by *person* or *life history* fetishism: it is not only the cultural commodities that seem divorced from those who produced them, but people and life stories that seem divorced from the commodity logic that produced them (cf. Illouz 2003; Marx and Engels 1998). It is not so much that emotions are erased, but that emotions themselves are produced as fetishes or qualities intrinsic to cultural objects and practices without a consideration of the history of their production and circulation (cf. Ahmed 2004, 11). These stories were oftentimes rooted on what Kleinman, Das, and Lock (1997) term "social suffering," that is, a process by which suffering is already socially situated and interpreted before we can even express it. Eva Illouz terms this a "culture of victimhood" (2003, 111–19), according to which a conjunction of therapeutic, humanistic, and liberal discourses makes pain—or the management of pain—the crucial dimension along which identity is formed and along which the individual builds his or her relationship to social institutions and makes claims on them.

The Ironbound is imagined and represented in ways that solidify a working-class image in the United States as quintessentially European. African American, Puerto Rican, and other Latino area residents are generally excluded from such views of labor/productivity (Roediger 2002). These images and representations gained salience and valence against the backdrop of Newark, a city whose name alone connotes images of chaos, destruction, decay, racial riots, and angry blacks. A space imagined as the material manifestation of the American dream mythology and foundational meritocratic discourse in the United States, the Ironbound was created—or transformed from space into place—in ways that could accommodate a necessary ambiguity inherent in most ethnic enclaves. Ethnic enclaves can only retain their authenticity as long as foreign-residents remain, perpetually (and passive), "immigrants"; however, paradoxically, these areas can only work ideologically if those "immigrants" become upwardly mobile enough to be able to leave the area for the suburbs. In fact, leaving the place of entrance (or having the opportunity to do so) is the very ideological core of ethnic enclaves like the Ironbound, where US-born racialized generations—in all their polluted, criminalized, and corrupted existence—were regarded with suspicion.

Precisely as the city of Newark became the epitome of de-industrialization, the Ironbound was constructed as evidence of working-class ethnic stability and the currency of American dream and meritocratic discourses. Nevertheless, a sense of passivity was also tacit in many of these narratives. On a rare occasion in which this was mentioned, Moacyr Gil, a Newark native of Portuguese descent who is a businessman and the director of a community service agency, states: "We don't have a high rate of students getting a college education. . . . The majority of people are involved with their church, their work and their home. They are close-knit and don't get involved in issues." Repeatedly, the Ironbound was laudable for the emotional work of its families and residents, rather than their logical political savvyness or militancy. The neighborhood was regularly described as "an island of prosperity in a city known for decay," as "prosperous but isolated," as having "the atmosphere of a small village . . . [in which] ethnicity is the area's common thread," and as "an insular society, 910 acres in the city's East Ward that are more European than American."[25] In fact, the Ironbound served as a staging area that was visible as long as new immigrants replaced those moving on, because that also gave the illusion of the temporality of poverty, and how any individual with the right work ethics could eventually attain the American dream.[26]

Before turning to a discussion of the role of "cultural excess" in light of the formation of what I term a "cartography of racial democracy" among Latinos in Newark, I want to highlight here that it was largely the Portuguese abstention from whiteness, and the continuous reassertion of such abstinence, that enabled Portuguese residents to produce space in the postindustrial era, and reconfigure the Ironbound as Newark's tourist stronghold. Fredrick Jameson (1991) argues that late capitalism has a distinctive cultural logic that is reshaping the form and functioning of the city. The Ironbound became the only area of Newark where deindustrialization did not lead to ghettoization, partly because incoming Portuguese residents were given the opportunity to become homeowners very early on, and largely because the very commercialization of Iberian culture interrupted a presumably de facto ghettoization process in the 1960s, thus avoiding the "culture of poverty" and "underclassed" depictions of other regions of Newark, including North Broadway. Narratives of overcoming hardship and attaining upward mobility were true staples of Ironbound conversations. References to the hard work of the Portuguese and one's own family's migration struggles existed in alignment with urban neoliberal projects and capital accumulation goals. Furthermore, multicultural neoliberalism projects (Hale 2005), singled out Latinos and Latin American migrants so that these populations—who were presumably more amenable to real estate and commercial development goals and less threatening to incoming affluent whites that visited or moved into the area—became "healers" of an otherwise aggressive context associated with black Newark.

Brazilian Perspectives on US Blackness and African Americans: Class, Color, and the Perceptions of Aggressive Cultural Appropriation

Certain aspects of the beauty salon episode suggest that interactions between Latin American migrants, particularly Brazilians in the case of the Ironbound, and African Americans might produce potentially volatile moments of great individual anxiety, miscommunication, and personal negation. In this particular episode, such moments of potential volatility were framed by four ways in which Brazilians read African Americans in the Ironbound: the view of African American as a classed identity; evaluations of "complaining" as an African American character defect; a perception that African Americans wanted to appropriate Brazilian culture; and African Americans as emblematic of a failed US racial system. It is important to highlight that these readings of African Americans, and of the US racial system more broadly, were drawn in contradistinction to a perspective of Latin America as a "racial democracy" a concept that, since its inception, implicated a relational racial logic that existed mostly in contradistinction to a US segregationist logic.[27]

African American Classed Identity

The African American client at the beauty salon was read in terms of race, but also in terms of her classed identity and performance (most evident in having the purchasing power to seek beauty salon services and her professional dress style). For Brazilians and other Latin Americans, some interactions with African Americans sustained and were congruous with Latin American social conventions and class locations, while others were distinctly reflective of a life trajectory that might involve downward mobility, undermined social status, or other forms of class-based changes that have resulted from migration.[28] In the Ironbound, middle-class African Americans oftentimes interacted with Portuguese, Brazilian, and Latin American migrants by "wearing their class" to distance themselves from the predictable stereotypical images that some residents had of all blacks. The political hegemony that African Americans maintained in Newark was read by Portuguese, Brazilians, and other Latinos in the city in ways that alternately stressed or deemphasized race, accounting for a hyperconsciousness of race in the city that remained palpable despite the worked-on or deliberate racial invisibility that was pursued at the neighborhood level in the Ironbound.

Ironbound merchants, including beauty salon personnel, wait staff, and store clerks, played an important role in maintaining racial civility, despite the fact that even small events in Newark could trigger polarizing racial discord. Sociologist Jennifer Lee (2002) analyzes how civility serves as a way to orchestrate racial tension among Korean merchants and their African American or white clients in New York. Likewise, in her study of Korean nail salons in New York, sociologist Miliann Kang (2003) notes that in salons where Korean manicurists tend to a black clientele, the failure to perform appropriately respectful emotional labor can quickly erupt into shouting matches that take on racialized and anti-immigrant overtones, illustrating how the race and class of the neighborhood complicate the processes of emotional management inside the salons. On the other hand, however, Kang also notes that when the clientele is predominantly black, the Korean service providers invested less energy in displaying and creating convivial feeling states (which they did in the case of white and affluent customers at a more upscale salon). In some cases, that allowed for "a genuine affinity with Black customers and less of a sense of burnout from the effort involved in the manufacture of falsely convivial feelings." Of course, these patterns of "body labor" conform to the racial and class positions of the customers and the associated "feeling rules" (Hochschild 1983) that defined their service expectations, so that these types of labor expectations, "while enacted at the micro level, reflect the social conditions of the neighborhoods in which the salons are located and the clientele they serve" (Kang 2003, 831, 832, 835). Race was very well managed in the Ironbound; it was silenced or engaged with tremendous trepidation when referencing African Americans, while articulated in very particular ways in relation to Brazilians, Puerto Ricans, and other "Hispanics," as I examine later in this chapter. Once race (including whiteness) was raised, situations and relations became untenable for many of the Latin American migrant and Portuguese ethnic residents, who were not accustomed to such explicit assessments of (their) racialness or even the racialness of others (cf. Hartigan 1999, 162, 203–5).

Commercial success was also explained as a result of adequate emotionality. Brazilian women's contribution to the host society was attributed to their ability to find more joy in life, and have a more positive relationship to their own femininity, than non-Brazilian women. Malleability, the ability to adapt without complaining while also not being passive, became a salient aspect of these life skills. By noting how emotions themselves became critical commodities in a cultural market that strove for the production of a universal sentimentality—a widespread emotive appeal—one can begin to analyze social structures as dynamic ways of being and practice. "Even the ones that have a lot of money are still angry. They don't know how to live," remarked a young Brazilian woman in reference to the African American clients that came into the clothing store where she worked. Adequate emotionality and cultural excess were mutually constitutive in the minds of many of the Brazilians with whom I spoke. This is also noted by Bernadette Beserra (2006) in her study of Brazilian samba dancers in Chicago. These dancers viewed their alegria de viver (joie de vivre) and "Brazilian femininity" as strategies to help other (mostly white American) women to find their feminine strength. Non-Brazilians were viewed as not being in touch with their femininity, but the Brazilian female teachers emphasized the importance of sinterse muito bonita (to feel pretty). Brazilians, especially women, felt that an important contribution they made to life in the United States and

US society in general was their ability to show people how to live well, joyfully, and avoid getting depressed.

Adequate emotionality becomes the main contributor that Brazilians bring to Newark, a city of complaint or aggression. But this emotionality had to be manifested publically (and commercially) to acquire salience and grounding. This focus on emotions allows us to address how subjects become invested in particular structures (tight-knit families, stable communities) and helps us understand why the demise of some of those heteronormative structures can be felt as traumatic, sad, and a loss, while also examining how these feelings sustain or legitimize privilege, entitlement, and white supremacy. The image of an African American political elite in Newark metaphorically served to highlight status losses and downward mobility for Latin American migrants more than any other factor. The impression among many Latin American migrants was that, even blacks, who occupy the lowest class echelons in many areas of Brazil and Latin America, were doing better or had more spending power in Newark than they did.

It is important to note that Brazilians oftentimes read the class background and performances of African Americans through the lens of personal experiences with class inequality in Brazil, as well as among Brazilians in the United States. For instance, when asked if she thought there were differences among African Americans in Newark, Paula Pereira answered by stating that in the United States she saw more rich people than she had seen in Brazil. "In Brazil we call them *patricinhas*. I don't know what the Americans call them. I guess like a rich girl, you know, like those twins, Mary Kate and Ashley. I met one girl like that here. Now she's in Brazil. Her parents are in a very good economic situation. So she's like those girls." Then, as if in an afterthought, she added: "I also met some of those girls at the volleyball club where I used to play in Brazil. . . . Oh my god, they were so annoying! I had a fight with one of these girls. Because there was a bad call in the game and she looked at me from toes to head and she punched me. And I wanted to punch her back, but I didn't."

Instances in which Brazilians saw their compatriots as untrustworthy, racist, disloyal, or even provincial abounded. For instance, Ellen de Souza, a Brazilian woman who taught Portuguese language and Brazil history classes at a Brazilian not-for-profit educational organizations in the Ironbound, told me that the first thing a Brazilian friend of hers had advised when Ellen arrived in Newark was, "Don't trust the Brazilians here." Ellen continued to explain, "There is a lot of competition among Brazilians, even in Brazil, but it gets even more intense in Newark. I don't notice that competition among the Spanish or the people from other Latin American countries. Because Latin Americans, they come here poor and illiterate, and they just want to work twenty-three hours a day, and rest only one, to make money and go back to their countries or send money. They have no time for gossip or competition with each other, like the Brazilians do. Brazilians wish ill on other Brazilians."

While the African American middle-class clients in beauty salons and restaurants in the Ironbound appeared to be, for the most part, nonresidents of the area, the few African Americans (and many Puerto Ricans) who did live in the Ironbound appeared confined to the housing projects at the outskirts of the neighborhood. As the Portuguese American parent of a student at the Ironbound high school recalled:

There were a few, a few black families [in the Ironbound in the 1960s]. Because I remember in my elementary school class, there were probably, let's say there were twenty-five of us, there were only three. And those were families who had been here many, many years. As you go further out, you have two housing projects. There's one that . . . is close to Penn Station. And there is another housing project that goes when you're going that way down to the Pulaski Skyway, so they were on the fringes.

In this sense, Blackness in this commercially viable Newark space was generally contained, spatially and symbolically, to two housing projects. As one drew closer to the imagined (and physical) limits of the Ironbound, conceptions of space were more prominently influenced by perspectives on race that did not share the same classed complexity noted, in contained ways, within the Ironbound.

African American "Complaining"

The second way of interpreting the volatility of interactions with African Americans involved Brazilian comments on color and character defects, such as "complaining." The joke around not noticing an eyebrow on such dark skin pointed to the centrality of color (sometimes, but not always, as proxy to race) in verbal play and interpersonal exchanges. Such comments, furthermore, generate attributions of "complaining" as a character defect of black women, presumably in contradistinction to the acceptance of one's life condition attributed to Latin American migrants. Framing most allusion to discrimination, prejudice, and racism as "complaining" placed race in the category of the individual, thus making it hard to recognize the political dimensions of racial subordination.

Emotion thus becomes a form of place-making in the Ironbound that allowed both for simultaneous racial hyperconsciousness, manifested as cultural excess, and a deliberately produced insistence on racial invisibility. The very fact that the Ironbound was relatively successful and productive (unlike the rest of Newark) because people did not complain, but were rather "hard working" and entrepreneurial, was public evidence of this. The idea of a black elite experiencing discrimination was unimaginable for many Brazilians who associated financial power with emotional contentment, or at least with something that would shield the individual from allowing racism to impact him- or herself at an intimate level. It is not necessarily that these Brazilian Ironbound residents believed that having money would make others less racist toward them, but that even when they were racist, one could choose not to care about it emotionally. Cristina Andrade, an ESL teacher in the Ironbound, for instance, viewed the Portuguese as racist toward Brazilians but still situated this racist comportment in the realm of emotions—as evidence of Portuguese "jealousy"—because even though Cristina describes herself as "preta" (black), she had a coveted job at a local boutique, owned a car, and had been successful in a shorter time. Despite noting anti-Brazilian Portuguese attitudes, however, associating "complaining" with African Americans overrode any explicit racial solidarity that Cristina, as a racially or color conscious Brazilian woman, might have developed with other blacks. A focus on jealousy or complaining, as character defects, reflected a more general apprehension that Brazilians had over ascribing racial labels, at least in public, to others. Nevertheless, this strategy of a developed or worked-on racial invisibility also left open the possibility of constructing different interpersonal relationships among those implicated in the social exchanging including distance, solidarity, respect, empathy, and so on. It was an expression of emotional capital that sustained particular personal and commercial aspirations among service sector and body-work employees and business owners in the Ironbound.

Among some workers in the service sector, particularly those who had lived in the United States for many years, there was a persistent concern that their comments, jokes, and actions were susceptible to being read as racist. Race provided both pretext and context in a powerful, somewhat reductive fashion for locating the meaning in an unkind remark taken "the wrong way," or a misstep, an abrupt impropriety. Anthropologist Kathleen Stewart (2007) refers to this form of "ordinary affect" as the constant possibility of misinterpretation, transgression, and betrayal animating the realm of everyday life. Rather than a set of fixed beliefs, which also existed, "race" was negotiated through rhetorical identities, verbal bantering, and psychological labels. The ability to deflect racial instigations usually involved depersonalizing the context and an investment in keeping race outside the language and avoiding polarizing rhetorical ground. This tactic served to defuse a range of potentially explosive situations, while providing a fertile context for discussion, banter, and even gossip. The ruptures of an idealized middle-class decorum—a measured calmness or rational detachment or civility in matters of public debate— were evident in loud, emotionally charged instances (cf. Lee 2002; Hartigan 1999; Harris-Lacewell 2006). Merchants in the Ironbound—from business owners to employees—were called to cultivate the style and dispositions of the new middle classes or individuals whose primary identity is one structured around visions of upward mobility. The work lives of individuals who were located in intermediary positions of exerting some control and being controlled required a careful management of the self and were highly dependent on successful collaborative and service work (Hochschild 1983; Bourdieu 1977).

African American "Appropriation of Brazilian Culture"

A third element that provides context for the volatility of situations involving African Americans and Brazilians (and other Latinos) involved reframing the "aggression" attributed to blacks in Newark`s emotional landscape as the African American "appropriation" of "Brazilian culture." Many of the Brazilian youth whom I met in Newark's Ironbound understood that there was a global image of "Brazilian culture" that was highly commodified in visceral and emotive terms. Evidence of this included Mary J. Blige's skirt on MTV, as well as postcards of landscapes and sensual bodies, which were all hardly an expression of the human reality that many of the working-class Brazilians in Newark recalled as part of their lives in Brazil. Such images became fetishized not so much as cultural objects, but as individual feelings and emotions attributed to Brazilians, which rendered them particularly suitable as employees in social service contexts and the area of sex work (see chapter 4).

"Cultural excess," the representational, ideological, and emotive practices through which certain bodies are viewed as overflowing with meanings and never naturalized, provides the condition under which culture matters in the everyday quotidian designations of some words, comments, and attitudes as racial, while other aspects of racialized encounters are misrecognized. This form of cultural excess existed in the Ironbound in tandem with conceptions of "racial invisibility," and it contributed to the articulation of the Latin American ideology of "racial democracy" as a cartography and tool of racial learning. Brazilian cultural excess or the global appeal of Brazilian culture is not an entirely new proposition. Anthropologist Roberto Da Matta coined the term "o jeitinho brasileiro" to describe "um estilo, um modo de ser, um jeito de existir que, não obstante estar fundado em coisas universais, e exclusivamente brasileiro [a style, a way of being, a form of existence that, despite being grounded in universal concepts, is exclusively Brazilian]" (in Tosta 2004, 580). Nevertheless, in the case of Brazilian life in Newark, this "jeitinho" is not only a way of being, but also a strategic way of presenting oneself affectively, as an individual who possesses great social and emotional skills and psychological savvy, and who would make a good worker who adapts well to local labor demands. In the United States cultural excess was a complementary and dialectical social position that many Brazilians deployed to get *closer* to a locally constituted form of American-ness, while still drawing on the potential advantages of being bearers of a globally exported and highly marketable jeitinho. Brazilians understood and promoted their own placement in the Ironbound cultural market though a narrative that, rather than being premised on traditional "ethnic values," as was often the case with Iberian ethnics in the neighborhood, in fact gained its appeal from a claim to modernity, racial-ness, inclusivity, and an image of Brazil in cosmopolitan terms distinct from other Latin American nations. Brazil, in fact, possessed a unique "soft power," the power to export ideologies and practices.

Brazilian cultural excess became symbolic capital precisely by retaining a nonthreatening, folkloric, commodifiable quality, and avoiding a more explicit articulation of racial inequality ("complaining"), like the one utilized in the discourse around Latinos and civil rights. In the hallways of East Side High School in the Ironbound, Maura Silva and I had one of many conversations about "Brazilians' culture" and "how we Brazilians are as people." As we walked to Maura's locker, on the fourth floor, where the Portuguese bilingual program was housed, Maura pointed to a female student wearing a plaid short skirt with a Brazilian flag print. "Do you know who Mary J. Blige is?" Maura asked me. "She was wearing that same Brazilian flag skirt on an MTV show. Just like that one!" Not having seen the show myself at that time, I asked her why she thought that Mary J. Blige had chosen that outfit and Maura explained that Brazilian things were very popular, citing rubber flip-flops and t-shirts with the Brazilian flag that she had seen Americans wearing. And then she explained:

Because you have American people saying we're really hot. Not only really hot as in attractive, but more like that we're caring people. When you meet someone, we hug, we kiss. And that's really true. Because the American people, the black people, they're really. . . . I never saw an American going to their friends and hugging them, kissing them, you know. They don't do that like we do. And they see that as something that is Brazilian, Brazilian culture. I think they like that. They have an image of Brazil, and it's all the good things of Brazil. They don't see any of the poverty or crime, just the beach and Carnival, Rio!

At the time of this conversation, Maura had been fired from working part-time as a barmaid in a Portuguese-owned bar in the Ironbound when the owner became concerned that Maura was both undocumented and underage, and many off-duty police officers were frequenting the bar. Like many other Brazilian youth who worked in the Ironbound service sector, Maura remarked that it was precisely because Brazilians were warm, caring, friendly, and pretty that bar and restaurant owners were willing to bend the employment, legal, and age requirements to hire them. "We make people want to come back, because they feel well received," she commented when I asked her why she thought her former Portuguese boss had been willing to hire her in the first place. Maura also acknowledged that being so emotionally expressive and warm was not always an asset: "Teachers at our high school could never understand why we [Brazilians] always had to greet each other with a kiss on each cheek and do that in the hallways. If they could have drawn a rule against it, they would have! At one point they say that we were taking too long in the time between the change from one class to another because we were kissing each other!"

More significantly, an emphasis on Brazilian culture introduced harmony and a universal sentimentality, with a focus on how, at the emotional and sentimental level, all people have equal opportunities to achieve their life objectives. Such insistence on a universal sentimentality existed in contradistinction to the racial defensiveness, "obsession with race," or "taking race too seriously" attributed, especially, to US blacks. In Newark's Ironbound, a neighborhood in which Luso-Brazilian, Hispanic, and African American populations are not only shaped by their relationships with state institutions but also judged by their contribution to capital accumulation, the ability to create commercially profitable cultures and package oneself accordingly became fertile ground for resurrecting views of "racial democracy," especially those that link racial mixture to intimacy, harmony, attractiveness, and a higher emotive moral ground.

In this context of Brazilian cultural excess, and because of a perceived or actual power attributed to African Americans in Newark politics, Brazilians accused African Americans of co-opting Brazilian culture. This is another variant of the "aggression" that has been historically attributed to Newark residents, once the city became a majority-minority urban space (chapter 1). Among many Brazilians, there was a perception that (middle-class) African Americans might have a specific investment in imagining Brazil in their own Afro-centric terms, in relation to a trans-Atlantic Blackness. While not always explicitly articulated in such terms, views of African American appropriation of Brazilian culture appeared occasionally in conversations about commercial activity in the neighborhood. The relatively low but noticeable number of African Americans who consistently shared in the cultural and commercial life of the Ironbound was oftentimes viewed with suspicion. For instance, Maura noted: "Black Americans like to take capoeira, Samba, eat our foods. They think we are pretty, and that's why the [African American] women don't like us. I see them at the [eating] places around here. I went to a capoeira school once, because a friend of mine was trying to get a job with them, and they looked at us like they were the Brazilians and we didn't belong there." I asked her why she thought this was and she responded: "They think they're more Brazilian than we are, because they think that only if you're dark, you can be Brazilian, you know? And I'm a little dark, but not very. But in Brazil you also have blonde [hair], blue eyes too! I never went there again."

Marta Braga, a young woman from São Paulo who admitted to having been mistaken for African American, described her experience taking a computer class at a community college in Newark: "[They would say] 'Hey, my brother; hey, my sister.' All serious . . . emotional! [laughed]. And I would have to try not to laugh, because sometimes I can barely understand what they say, their handshakes, but it sounds funny with their accent." Many Brazilians articulated these potential pan-Africanist alliances with African Americans as verbal play or joking; in particular, this was an instance in which African American affect—their emotive approach to racial unity—was rendered inappropriate or illegible.[29] Even Brazilians who themselves identified as "black" or knew another Brazilian who identified as "black" explained that this was because Blackness could be seen not only as marker of American-ness, but also of a type of "super Brazilianness" grounded in globally circulated Afro-Brazilian cultural practices, such as samba or capoeira. The presumable claim to a trans-Atlantic bond around Blackness was viewed as a misrecognition or false assumption that certain emotions were shared.

When African Americans participated in the Brazilian cultural expressions of the Ironbound, they were viewed as trying to capitalize on their Blackness to draw connections to Afro-Brazilian populations in

Brazil, while questioning the authenticity and integrity of a "color-blind" Brazilian-ness.[30] Some Brazilians were genuinely puzzled by African Americans' interest in Brazilian culture, even when racial relations in Brazil (or how these were allegedly imagined among some African Americans) were idealized or regarded very favorably in relation to US racial relations. Despite the interest of many African Americans in Newark and adjacent towns in Brazilian cuisine, music, dance, religion, and the martial-arts practice of capoeira, a potential pan-African coalition was curtailed by the fact that most Brazilians who lived in Newark at the time of my field-work did not consider themselves "Afro-Brazilians." To many Brazilians, when African Americans (and even Puerto Ricans) talked about racism, the act of talking about this issue was viewed as the very source of (not a reaction to) racial inequality; as if talking about racial subordination is what in fact created that very subordination (cf. Sheriff 2001). However, a more notable issue here is that in the Ironbound, a Portuguese stronghold for several decades, Brazilians have a particular investment in distancing themselves from other racial minorities.

An investment in Brazilian "racial invisibility" emerges as a counterpoint to narratives of "cultural excess," particularly in institutional contexts in the Ironbound. Among Latinos in Newark, and particularly among Brazilians in the Ironbound, "cultural excess" and "racial invisibility" existed in tandem and were a reflection of the processes that took place when multiple systems of racial identification became simultaneous points of reference that were highly dependent on context.

East Side High School, the only public high school in the Ironbound at the time of my research, provided the context in which Brazilian youth experimented with navigating "cultural excess" and "racial invisibility." The atmosphere of ESHS seemed predicated on a contrast between a multicultural or even internationalist image that the administrators aimed to promote, on the one hand, and a quintessential all-American high school experience that many Brazilian students sought in their efforts to claim a "racial invisibility," on the other. Even though the school was regarded as an "immigrant" school in an "immigrant" neighborhood, or a "little United Nations," as a teacher mentioned, teachers and staff frequently commented on the demographic changes the school had witnessed in recent years.[31] As Fátima Teixeira, an ESHS teacher and Portuguese resident of the Ironbound commented, "I've noticed a difference in the demographics of the school. It used to be more European, now it's more South American. And sometimes you get students from Ecuador that come from a military academy with great schooling, and they move right into the middle class. Other times you get a kid from Honduras, very poor, and you practically have to teach them everything."

In the absence of a fully articulated political discourse on class and a dominant discourse that naturalized racial inequality, oftentimes students of color appeared to be blamed for the pain and social mobility anxieties of the neighborhood's white working class. Throughout the time of my fieldwork, the Latin American population at East Side High School consisted mostly of migrants from Brazil, and the white population was largely immigrant and second-generation Portuguese (162 Portugal-born students and 164 US-born students of Portuguese parents). In Newark, Brazilians occupied, along with Dominicans, the lowest level of educational attainment according to the 2000 Census (Mara Sidney's presentation). About 10 percent of the students at ESHS were black, although most Latin American students inflated these numbers and believed that about half the student population was African American. Notwithstanding these segregated institutional arrangements and uneven school demographics, many Brazilians still perceived the appropriation of Brazilian culture by African Americans as a threat to well-crafted attempts toward racial invisibility in the Ironbound. In fact, attempts toward achieving a sense of "racial invisibility" among Brazilians and some other Latin American migrants were framed by contexts of racial segregation and normative institutional constructions of American-ness.

During the first few weeks I spent at ESHS I did not see many African American students at all. It was not until I went to the second floor of the annex building that I noticed that most of the students in the hallway were African American. When I asked a US-born Brazilian student about this, she explained what other people would later comment on: There was an internal division in the high school building according to which Brazilian students in the Portuguese bilingual program occupied the fourth floor, other Latin American students in the Spanish bilingual program were on the third floor, and the second floor—the so-called ghetto floor—consisted mostly of US-born minorities, mostly Puerto Ricans and African Americans, and a few US-born Portuguese students. This division across floors was viewed as a logical and logistical consequence of having bilingual programs separated from mainstream academic programs, not as something particularly problematic. As a Portuguese American teacher explained: "There is a division in the building. It did not happen on purpose, but it has happened."

I asked Silvana Pereira, a junior from Minas Gerais, if she thought that students from different backgrounds got along at the school and she noted:

In grammar school they did [get along], not here in high school. They actually have a kind of a problem wherever you are from. Like a lot of the black kids have problems with the white kids. But take this school. You'll see we are separated by floors. I don't like that whole separation thing, but in high school you have your own mind and you are going to have problems with people. In that sense, it's kind of better that we are together but separated from them, so you don't have that many problems . . . with safety. . . . It's rare to see a Portuguese kid in the ghetto group, because you think of a Portuguese kid as all nice and proper because of their parents. They are the more naïve ones.

At ESHS, racial and class divisions were frequently elided behind meritocratic views of schooling according to which all students were equally positioned to participate and succeed; "color-blindness" represented a higher moral ground linked to ending prejudice and racism, and there was some anxiety about disturbing the delicate balance that would unfold from an explicit acknowledgment of racial segregation in the building. Although the specific role of Blackness and urban culture are the main subject of chapter 6, it is important to note here that the spatial distribution of students both highlighted perspectives on cultural uniqueness and concealed the role of "race" as a criterion of social differentiation—as most students explained it, social difference had to do with "the floors" rather than with race.

When considered in relation to other Newark public schools, ESHS was perceived as an "all-American high school." This image aimed to evoke universal sentiments associated with teenage life in terms of differences in popularity, intellect, and fashion, that appeared disconnected from social distinctions related to race, class, and nationality. In fact, ESHS was one of the few "American" (and "Americanizing") spaces to which Brazilians and other South American migrants had access, even if (or perhaps precisely because) "real Americans"—that is "unmarked whites"—were absent. A particular American high school experience has been exported globally through various media and it has been constructed as a white space, even though this was also one of the most distinct spaces where Brazilian youth were confronted with US racial logic. This was the space where "cultural excess" came into contact with a highly segregated high school experience that, in its efforts to endorse a multiculturalism, in fact maintained the racial invisibility of white students while racializing Latinos and blacks.

A discourse of racial democracy was articulated in tandem with long-held and media-filtered views of the "American high school experience." Maura Silva, who was a junior when I met her, and Silvana Pereira were involved in multiple activities at the school. They were part of a group of Brazilian girls who were considered very popular. The group varied in size, averaging about ten students or so, and in some ways consisted of the overlapping of multiple groups that shared in common their involvement in school, athletic ability, sense of fashion, and school spirit. What stood out more dramatically about this particular group of girls, whom I got to know over a period of about a year, was that they represented in many ways the image of a 1950s suburban, "All-American" high school experience as it has been portrayed in US popular imagination and circulated in teen movies and television shows like *Grease, Happy Days, Beverly Hills 90210, Saved by the Bell,* and the *Brady Bunch,* all of which Brazilian students both in Newark and in Belo Horizonte, where I also conducted research, were familiar with and considered to be "typical American culture."[32] Discussions about prom dresses and dates, comments on trying out for cheerleading or team sports, and concerns about appropriate fashion and hairstyles dominated the conversations among these girls in ways that seemed at times awkwardly self-conscious, hyperperformed, forced, or modeled after some imagined caricature of the "American high school experience."

What made this intensive performance even more puzzling was the fact that most of the Brazilian students whom I met led quite unconventional, un-American high school lives outside of school. The contradistinction between their almost-caricaturesque American high school identities and their everyday lives, which included helping to support their families financially, holding full-time jobs that allowed little time for extracurricular activities, serving as their parents' translators in issues concerning immigration, and, quite frequently, being active in the neighborhood evangelical churches, was extreme. When I asked Silvana if she planned to apply to college, she mentioned in an endearingly cynical and practiced mature way: "But I'm tired. I'm tired out of my mind; it's not going to work if I go because I have to, I have to want to go. I've been in school since I was four years old and I'm tired. [laughter from those around her, comments of agreement] I'm serious, I'm really, really tired. Can I take a nap, go on vacation, do nothing?"

In some ironic way, the imagining of a typical (i.e., media produced and globally exported) American high school experience provided one of the very few spaces in which Brazilian youth, and perhaps Latin American students more generally, could live a "traditional"—if highly imagined, fictional, and mediated—American life, the one they probably imagined prior to migration. If these young Brazilian migrants were so determined to preserve or create an image of a traditional American high school experience, and if the school became the only space for the performance of American-ness, how would discussions of diversity and multiculturalism and the presence of nonwhite bodies be addressed in this imagery? As examined in chapter 6, images of "American"-ness also suggest that Blackness is viewed as a way of gaining a sense of belongingness and authenticity.

African American as Emblematic of a Failed US Racial System: Everyday Comparisons of Race Relations in Brazil and in the United States

The final element that provides context for the volatility of situations involving African Americans and Brazilians (and other Latinos) involved the deployment of race relations in Brazil and other parts of Latin America and the Caribbean in contradistinction to US race relations. Perspectives on race relations in Brazil and other parts of Latin America were frequently deployed as evidence of how racial difference could be successfully managed as long as one possessed the implicit social knowledge and emotional capital to monitor the expression of race. Racial readings of manners and affect were central tenets of racial democracy ideology in the United States, so that instances of racial conflict and subordination were explained in terms of "bad manners" or "bad attitudes" in Newark, in contradistinction to the intimacy of race in Latin America. For the most part, the ability to "know" the presumed difference between a form of racism that generated laughter, and one that was repudiated and rendered "really racist," was a quality that a deeper understanding of Latin American racial democracy conferred, but which was missing in a still unfamiliar US racial system.

Paula Pereira, who was originally from Belo Horizonte, remarked on a common racial harmony mythology attributed to Brazil in light of a fundamental distinction she noted between black people in Brazil and black people in the United States. Paula stated, "In Brazil we have a lot of black people. Really black. Blacker than the ones here. Here they are black by their nature. In Brazil, too, they're black by their nature, but with the sun helping us, you know. But those problems didn't exist there. The groups in Brazil were more mixed. Whites, blacks, yellows, everyone." When I asked Paula to explain what she meant when she said that blacks in the United States were "black by their nature," she elaborated,

You see my color? I have black in me too. My sister is lighter than me, but she still has black in her. But it's not like the blacks here. There are blacks here, American blacks, that are lighter than me, but they're still black. They themselves say they're black and other people say they're black. That's their nature. But in Brazil if you're a little lighter, you don't call the person black. Black people in Brazil, even if they are very, very dark, you can look back, maybe to their grandparents or great-great-great grandparents and they have someone who was lighter. They're mixed, even if they are very black.

"So, does that difference mean that blacks in Brazil are treated differently than blacks in the US or . . . ?," I asked her, trying to make sense of a complicated, but surprisingly common racial logic among Brazilians.

She explained,

There is racism in Brazil. Definitely. And there's racism here. But the difference is that there we still get along. We know there's racism, but we don't jump people when they look at you the wrong way or feel superior. They're not talking, complaining, complaining all the time about racism. Everyone tries to get along, even if you know there's racism and, after you get along with the person for a while, you don't even notice the color anymore. It doesn't even cross your mind. Here you always notice the color, grab your purse, get scared when you see a black person. I'm not proud of that, but that's how it is and I've talked to other friends of mine about that and they also feel the same way.

For many US-born minorities, an acknowledgment of racism was a prerequisite for establishing what Paula views as meaningful relationships or "getting along." For many of the Brazilian and other Latin American migrants whom I met, on the other hand, colorblindness was almost a precondition for any meaningful relationship. Ironically, the ability to ignore, dismiss, or rationalize away racial remarks was viewed as a form of eradicating racism, even when potentially great pain could result from such pretending.

Like Paula, many other Brazilians in Newark highlighted a difference between racial relations in Brazil, which they felt were characterized by a high degree of intimacy, and race relations in the United States, where racial relations involved "aggression," "bad manners," "complaining," and a lack of life skills to deal with interpersonal conflict. This distinction was characterized by what Costa Vargas (2004) identifies as the simultaneous existence of a hyperconsciousness of race and its negation. The same distinction was suggested in a conversation I had with Ellen de Souza, the Brazilian teacher of Portuguese, A former English teacher in São Paulo, Ellen taught a group of about ten children ranging in age from eight through twelve. Most of Ellen's students had been living in Newark for at least three years, but they had all been born in Brazil and spoke Portuguese with various levels of fluency. Their parents, some of whom I met at Imperial Institute social events, wanted their children to learn grammar and Brazilian history and, through an arrangement with the Brazilian Consulate, get credit for these courses in Brazilian schools should they decide to go back.

While teaching a course on the topic of "Deslocamento e População" (Displacement and Population), Ellen directed her young pupils to the map of Brazil she had glued to the wall of the small room that served as her classroom, and said, in what is almost a classic example of a belief in racial democracy:

In Rio Grande do Sul, there are many groups from Europe. People from Parana have lighter skin . . . peles mais claras, não é?. In São Paulo there's one of the largest Italian populations, most immigrants who were Italian live there. That's why paulistas speak like this [imitating a paulista accent]. In Brazil there is a lot of racial mixing, like in the U.S. But it's not like in the U.S., where you are either preto ou branco [black or white]. One can find Blacks of German ancestry and combinations like that . . . go figure! And everyone gets along. People know how to get along there.

Ellen then pulled out black-and-white photographs of her own parents and grandparents to further stress that Brazil was not only a country of multiple races and migrations, but one in which such diversity was evidenced by noting color variation *within families*. Ellen explained that on her father's side her grandparents were African and Portuguese, and on her mother's side they were Danish and Swiss. She subscribes to what Donna Goldstein (1999) terms "color-blind erotic democracy," the view that interracial sex (and the offspring of such unions) are "proof" of the fact that Brazil does not have a racial problem. In this sense, a key question around which racial democracy is articulated in everyday life is "How can we be racist when so many of us are mixed?"[33] It's important to note here that both Ellen and Paula have admitted to experiencing discrimination, both along class and racial lines, in Brazil and the United States. What they viewed as a difference here was a certain negation of the pain that such discrimination might have caused in them, a process which required a great degree of emotional work.

Important for clarification purposes is that myths are not necessarily untruths or statements of truth; rather, they are stories and belief systems that help people navigate their social context and justify specific cultural values and social (and emotional) rules. For most of the twentieth century the Latin American ideology of "racial democracy" and its caveats of "racial mixing" (mestizaje/mestizagem) and "whitening" (blanquea-miento/ embranquecemento) served as a benchmark of racial tolerance, deployed in academic and activist circles in contradistinction to a le-gally segregated and racially intolerant United States. Brazil, in particular, became emblematic of "antiracialism" as the "racialism" of the United States insisted on the existence of discrete—largely black or white—racial groups (Telles 2004). In Latin American and Caribbean societies, some of the basic tenets of "racial democracy" included the belief that, to one degree or another, all subjects are inherently mestizo (racially mixed), thus drawing from the fable of the three races in which the body of the nation resulted from the combination of African, European, and native indigenous bloodlines.[34]

Phenotype and "color," rather than hypodescent or "race," were the predominant factors in how people were classified racially. The possibil-ity of whitening through miscegenation rendered "race" mutable and not as easily legislated as it was under the US legal system. In fact, the concept of *mejorar la raza* ("to improve the race"), common throughout Latin America, urged people to choose sexual partners that were of a lighter hue, placing race in the realm of the private and rendering it changeable (cf. Dzidzienyo and Oboler 2005, 88).[35]

Ellen deployed a "cartography of racial democracy" in which Brazilians occupied a higher emotive ground on issues of race, and offered direc-tions to Brazilian and maybe to other Latin American migrants on how to navigate Newark's racial landscape, a process particularly challenging for individuals socialized on deeply rooted racial ideologies that intended to dilute difference.[36] This does not suggest that some Latin American groups are "blind" to understandings of race or that they do not under-stand the discriminatory bases of inequality. In fact, when I asked Ellen if any dark-skinned Brazilians in the United States develop forms of col-laboration or solidarity with African Americanism, she replied:

Ellen de Souza: You don't really have many black Brazilians here for some reason. I actually know of one and she says that, you know, she doesn't know why but she doesn't' know a lot of black Brazilians here.

AY: Here in Newark you mean?

Ellen: Uh, in the United States, actually. If you think about it. Because the darker of Brazilian people you have here, they are from Minas. Those people are kind of dark but they are not black. Because in Brazil the black people they are in a really bad condition unfortunately, so they can't even come here.

Ellen, who told me that African Americans sometimes thought she was "one of them," was aware that the ability to migrate to the United States in the first place was dependent upon access to economic and information resources mostly unavailable to black Brazilians. Rather than being oblivious to, or in denial of, racial subordination, Ellen and other Brazilians oftentimes subscribed to what Stanley Bailey (2004) has termed "social dominance theory." According to Bailey's conclusions, although in the United States blacks and whites look at the world in fundamentally different ways, that is not the case in Brazil or other parts of Latin America. Instead, as Bailey states, race in Brazil would be more equivalent to gender in the United States, insofar as gender was not a determinant of beliefs about gender discrimination, while race was a decisive determinant (in the United States) of beliefs about racial discrimination. Denise Ferreira da Silva's "racial boundary salience" (1998) and Marvin Harris's "ambiguous racial calculus" (1970) are useful to explain Latino racial ambiguity in Newark, a context where skin color dynamics may be characterized by a lesser degree of group membership salience or racial subjectivity. Among many Brazilians there is an ability not only to deny, but also to avoid, their own racial identity because of the tremendous depth of the racial democracy ideology, not necessarily as a belief that is gullibly accepted, but as a preference for avoiding discourses of race altogether (Sheriff 2001).[37] From a sociolinguistic perspective, Jennifer Simpson (1996) argues that many Latin Americans of color, in an attempt to undermine racism, engage in "white talk": the active attempt to ignore, forget, or deny racism through "selective hearing," "creative interpreting," and "complicitous forgetting"(377; cf. Warren 1997).

Furthermore, there was also a tendency, as seen in the beauty salon episode, to subscribe to a language of "reverse racism" to diminish not necessarily the significance of color, but racial subordination more precisely. When I asked Giselle Coutinho and Mariana Oliveira, two Brazilian students at ESHS, whether they saw a difference between blacks and whites in the United States, Giselle drew vaguely from historical accounts of US slavery: "Oh yes! There's a lot of racism. I was talking about that with some friends. Because everything started in the 1600s. The slaves coming from Africa and all that. In Brazil there were slaves too, but we had the emperor living there at one point, so they view Brazil as their home, not so much as their colony." She continued: "And after slavery here . . . well, you see that the black people are the poor people. The really white people are very racist, because they don't want to be around black people. They see that the black people are troublemakers, rob them."

Mariana contributed: "But black people are racist, too. Because the black people sense that racism from white people, so they feel rejected and hurt. They have a lot of anger, even if that happened thousands of years ago. So they are really racist because of that, they are very hurt, they feel inferior. This is different about the US."

Despite cursory references to the cruelties of US slavery, a dominant reading of African Americans occurred in relation to feelings—of how African Americans felt rejected, hurt, angry, or inferior. These dominant readings of African Americans rendered racism as something that could be "managed" by the individual, as long as he or she had the adequate emotional tools not to allow discrimination to penetrate his or her psyche. Even though some vague historical context is referenced in Brazilian discussions of racism in the United States, the focus of these interpretations tended to be on current, present-day effects, *in psychological terms*, of such history (Godreau 2008).[38] Such landscape was premised on the view that, deep down, all individuals "feel" and "experience" an environment in emotional and sensorial terms that sre universal, while also establishing criteria by which to judge the emotional adequacy of those individuals or groups who do not meet (neoliberally friendly) standards of civility. A translocal emotive and neoliberal ideology constituted around a "cartography of racial democracy" situated discussions of racism in the realm of affect and intimate knowledge; references to "racial diversity" within families, interracial romantic relations, and emotive or comedic interactions, instead of political manifestos or denunciations of discrimination, for instance, offered the leading everyday evidence that racism "does not exist among Latinos."

These narratives thus tempered denunciations of antiblack racism in the United States by developing an everyday idiom about the "inadequate" character or emotional flaws of African Americans and how African Americans "complained too much about racism," in contradistinction to a working-class Latino pragmatism and emotional commonsense. More often than not, discrimination against African Americans, while often acknowledged, was always qualified by statements about how open prejudice was a "thing of the past," how "blacks also discriminated against whites," and, especially, how blacks had "a chip on their shoulder" or allowed discrimination to be overdeterministic of their condition. A key aspect to note here is that being black and being African American were viewed by many migrants as different things.

Brazilians and youth from the Spanish-speaking Caribbean in Newark seemed highly aware of the notion of Latin American racial exceptionalism and, even though rarely did they use the academic term *racial de-*

mocracy, they nevertheless alluded to how their countries, or even Latin America and the Caribbean as sociogeographical regions, were "more accepting of all people regardless of race" or how the populations from these regions were "very mixed."[39] Among many Brazilians in Newark, narratives abounded about how Brazil was, like the United States, a "country of immigrants" and how, unlike the United States, the concept of segregation—social or spatial—did not exist. The hyperconsciousness/ negation of race dialectics allows us to understand how a system that is on the surface devoid of racial awareness is in reality deeply immersed in racialized understandings of the social world.

It is important to emphasize as a critical component to my argument that this "cartography of racial democracy" in the United States—that oftentimes considered denunciations of racist practices as pointless or even unacceptable in the public realm—could not be simplistically explained away as a lack of racial consciousness or a "false consciousness" among Latin American migrants and many US-born Latinos. Rather, it suggests that these populations generally did not look to the state to eradicate racism or create racial equality in the way that African Americans and many US-born Latinos who lived through the civil rights movement did. They simply did not see how the US nation-state (or any state, for that matter) would be invested in eradicating discrimination and, from this pragmatic (rather than ideological) perspective, it "made no sense" to denounce racism.

The articulation of a US-based perspective on racial democracy in the Ironbound relied on two main conceptualizations of "racial invisibility": the decentering of "race" as a primary lens through which we can interpret urban subordination; and the transformation of race-talk from the "aggressiveness" associated with African Americans (see chapter 1) to a playfulness narrative around joking, bantering, and verbal play. Race was rarely invisible, but its hyperconsciousness oftentimes required that intergroup tensions be understood in the terrain of affect, emotions and aesthetics, not political economy or neighborhood politics (cf. Costa Vargas 2004).

"So, Are Brazilians Latinos?": Playing with Ambivalence

Inspired by the "Uhmm . . . " that followed when I answered that I was Puerto Rican in the mostly South American beauty salon, the second section of this chapter focuses on how Puerto Ricans become constitutive outsiders for groups who relate to the "Hispanic" category with great trepidation, particularly Brazilians.

A key question that served as discursive subtext to multiple spaces in the Ironbound, including the beauty salon and the high school mentioned above, is: What does it mean to have to learn racial etiquette—the appropriate choice of racial identity labels, deployment of color categories, and engagement in forms of verbal play and racial bantering in everyday social encounters—in a new country, particularly when racial talk is not part of one's everyday social repertoire? For most Brazilians, and many other Latin Americans, racial democracy is a pragmatic concept and a historically conditioned national commonsense that tended toward ambiguity rather than subjective racial definitions (cf. Bailey 2004). At times, this ambiguity prevents race-based political mobilization (Hanchard 1994), but in other instances it also offered maneuvering opportunities for nonwhites (Bailey 2004; de la Fuente 1999). The very silence surrounding racism throughout Latin America is evidence of a view of race not only as a system to categorize according to descriptive codes (i.e., who is of what color or color gradation), but also for its power as an often unrecognized yet highly *pragmatic*, everyday cognitive practice (contextual meaning and intention behind a particular racial reference). The US-based cartography of racial democracy I noticed in Newark shared in this pragmatism. Highlighting Brazilians' ambiguous relationship to the "Hispanic" or "Latino" labels, the question of "Are Brazilians Hispanic?" is central to this section. While Puerto Ricans, along with Mexicans in other parts of the United States, such as Chicago (De Genova and Ramos-Zayas 2003), are viewed as central in discussions of Latinidad or Hispanic identity in the United States, Brazilians occupy a very tenuous and ambiguous position.

"What do you think I was, when you first met me?" asked a Brazilian graduate of ESHS, in what would be a common question among many Brazilians whom I met over the course of my fieldwork. I paused, realizing that in this instance the question was more rhetorical than anything, since she knew I had known all along that she was Brazilian. She continued: "People would not look at me and automatically say, 'Oh she's Brazilian.' I'm not dark enough; I don't have Latin features. Americans get shocked to know that you can be Brazilian and look like me, because they don't know we have European people in South America, so they have a different image." Brazilians navigated the "Latino" and "Hispanic" identities with great trepidation, by using the Portuguese language as a key element in their avoidance of a racial category they associate with "illegality" and disenfranchised populations in the United States.

It is not my intention here to focus on the question of Brazilian Latinidad, particularly given that other scholars have approached the problematic of panethnic labels for *all* Latin American populations in their work (Oboler 1995; Calderón 1992). Rather, I am interested in the structural commonalities and differences that working-class Brazilians in Newark share with populations racialized as "Hispanic" or "Latino" in the United States. What is key here is not whether a label—"Hispanic," "Latino," "Brazilian"—is embraced or rejected, or even whether embracing or rejecting such labels leads to social mobility or to avoiding marginality in the United States. I am more interested in how populations are pitted against each other and used to discipline one another in discussions of "Hispanic" or "Latino," and how capitalizing on one's own ambiguity became strategic. Many of the Brazilians whom I met in Newark occupied low-paid occupational niches like those of other Latinos and were, at least outside the Ironbound, assumed to be "Latino" or "Hispanic." However, the Portuguese language and global marketing of all things Brazilian also allowed space for maneuvering such racialization.

While many Portuguese viewed Brazilian "cultural excess" as evidence of their "primitivism" (akin to how whites view blacks, or colonial powers viewed their subjects), other migrants from Latin America and the Caribbean viewed Brazilians as "Hispanics" or approaching Hispanic, based on their level of urban identification. Puerto Ricans, in particular, did not see the Portuguese language as a barrier to a Latinidad that presumes Spanish speaking, given that many Puerto Ricans, being second- or third-generation US-born, did not speak Spanish themselves and did not reduce the Latino identity to the Spanish language. In such cases, colorism became central to Brazilian racialization in a way that was not entirely the case for other groups, like Puerto Ricans, who were oftentimes considered "nonwhite" regardless of phenotype. Ingrid Diaz, a young Puerto Rican resident of North Broadway, explained: "I think with Brazilians, it depends on their color. Because you can have, you know, the blue eyes, blonde, and they're Brazilian. But the Brazilians that would hang out with my cousin and I went to Science [High School in North Newark] and they were Hispanic like us." Likewise, sharing community services provided contexts in which presumed commonalities were highlighted. For instance, Ingrid's grandmother, who had lived in the Ironbound section before moving to North Broadway, still sought medical services in the Ironbound, even though all the doctors there spoke Portuguese. Likewise, Brazilians sometimes sought legal services from Puerto Rican–led social service agencies that had developed areas to counsel clients on immigration issues.

In a nuanced perspective on the question of Brazilian relation to a Latino identity, Ana Cristina Braga Martes (2000) notes that most adult

Brazilian immigrants enter the United States thinking of themselves as "white" in the more expansive Brazilian sense of the term, even if not in the more restrictive American sense of the term.[40] Brazilian immigrants usually identify as "whites," "blacks," or "Latinos" based on the meanings these labels carry for them outside the United States, and they reject these labels if their meanings are not adequately recognized in the United States—that is, if they are treated derogatorily or if internal diversity within these groups is not acknowledged. For Brazilian children, speaking English, spending time in the United States, participating in US customs, and more important, being a US citizen are markers of "American" identity. They justify their sense of being "Latin American" by having migrated to the United States and becoming "American." As Clémence Jouët-Pastré and Letícia Braga (2009) found in their study of Brazilian youth in Boston, by the second generation fewer Brazilians identify as "white." Moreover, in his analysis of Brazuca or Brazilian American literary and cultural production, Antonio Luciano de Andrade Tosta (2004) argues that the participation of Brazilians in Latino struggles for rights has been constrained by the temporary nature of earlier Brazilian migrations and the prejudice Brazilians harbor toward other Latin American populations. In this sense, Tosta concludes, Brazucas pose no threat to the national order of the United States because they deploy the very stereotype that dominant US culture has of Brazil. Thus, Brazilians have been "a part apart" from the Latino group, occupying an in-and-out position (2004, 576).

Most Brazilians whom I met in Newark engaged in practices of cultural ambivalence that allowed them to simulate—and dissimulate—identity, which was not only a strategy for establishing and negotiating belonging, but also a modality of practice through which they claimed disparate forms of social and cultural capital and attachments to the global order.[41] In a conversation with Maura Silva, I asked her whether she thought that Brazilians were Latinos, and she replied:

Maura Silva: Hmmm . . . I don't know. Well, we are Latinos, too, because it's South America. Because Latino includes also Central America and those other little places too, right? Dominicana Republica, Puerto Rico, Jamaica . . . no, not Jamaica. I don't know, the little islands, Cuba, you know. So they're the same, but when you start going to South America, we're all Latin. . . .

AY: Do you feel that other Latin groups see Brazilians as Latino as well?

MS: I think they see Brazilians as different. The difference is that we understand their language, but they don't understand Portuguese.

Maura considers herself "Latina" because to her Latinidad was a geographical identity, rather than necessarily a political or sentimental one (cf. Marrow 2003). "It is where I'm from, but like from the continent. From the country, no. I'm Brazilian. But I think all South Americans are Latinos." And she added: "Sometimes I speak more Portuguese than English. The one thing that distinguishes Brazil is because we are from the Portuguese. If we all completely spoke Spanish, then we would all be a mess. No one could tell us apart. I think that's what distinguishes us, the language."

Nevertheless, even when Maura felt that language was the main distinguishing feature that separated Brazilians from "Latinos" from other parts of South America and "the little islands," one can see how asserting the Portuguese language in contexts where Brazilians ran the "risk" of being confused for "Hispanic" became important to her:

Brazilians only started getting here about twenty years ago, so Americans are still getting used to them. . . . But I think they have the same feeling like they have toward Spanish people, because I think Americans have a whole notion about Spanish people. And they present everyone as Spanish. . . . Sometimes some American people, in their really broken Spanish, they come and talk to me. And I'm like, I understand it, but I say, "I don't understand, because I'm not Spanish, you know, I'm Brazilian." . . . Some people are kind of ignorant about it, they just put us all together and we're not. We are totally different people.

Many Brazilians noted that other Latino groups were more invested in displaying their national culture, whereas Brazilians expressed their Brazilian-ness in a longing for Brazil (a saudade) and a desire to return, rather than constantly manifesting their national pride. Eulália Freyre, the mother of a Brazilian student at ESHS, explained that she had moved to Newark from a small town in Paraná, where she used to work as a teacher. Her daughters, who are ten and fourteen, have received full scholarships to attend a private school in a nearby suburb. Eulália mentioned that, like other Brazilian parents, she notices the widening generation gap between herself and her daughters and commented on how this gap is accentuated by the girls' "Americanization."

If you ask other groups, Mexicans, Peruvians, Ecuadorians, Bolivians, Uruguayans . . . well, not Uruguayans, but . . . if you asked any of those other groups, they'd tell you that no, they want to stay in the United States, they don't want to go back to their countries. But with Brazilians, they all want to go back. They suffer a lot here. They get depressed, they cry. They want to make money and go back, but that can be difficult, because they don't know the language and many of the Brazilians that come here are illiterate in both languages [Portuguese and English].

Eulália, who immediately after she knew I was from Puerto Rico declared herself to have been a fan of Menudo, the Puerto Rican boy band popular in the 1980s, said: "Puerto Ricans carry that pride in their sleeve. They wear the flag, the coqui." "Boricuaaaaa!," a Brazilian priest who worked with youth in the Ironbound commented. And he added, "The Brazilians really don't understand that. They don't understand why you need to do that if you're in America." Although there could be a number of potential explanations for this difference—including the racial, phenotypical, socioeconomic, and regional variation noted among Brazilians both in Brazil and in the United States—another important aspect of this "malleability" has to do with the idea that Brazilian emigration is an aberration, whereas the emigration from other Latin American countries to the United States has been naturalized. The view that "Brazil is a country of immigrants" operates in tandem with what writer Nélida Piñon writes in *A República dos Sonhos* (2004, 123):

[Os emigrados] foram sempre brasileiros sólidos, originários de um país sem o costume de expulsar a seus patriotas. . . . Jamáis portando à testa o sinal de imigrado. [The emigrants were always established Brazilians, from a country that does not have a tradition of expulsing its compatriots. [They] never carried the mark of immigrant in their face.]

Moreover, as Tosta (2004) shows, Brazilians have also succeeded in creating a second-generation Brazuca identity that is not as stigmatized as that of other US-born groups, including the "Nuyorican" (Ramos-Zayas 2003) and "Chicano" (De Genova 2008). Some of the same anxiety over language loss is tempered by an enduring association between linguistic assimilation and economic mobility among Brazilians.[42]

Despite some spaces where a tenuous form of Latinidad developed, Brazilians tended to view themselves as different from those whom they considered "Hispanic." For Brazilians, whose cultural capital rested in global and highly marketable images of Brazil, a sense of belonging did not rely on claiming space in Newark or creating pride in a spatial (Newark-based) identity, as might have been the case for other groups. Instead, Brazilians strove for a racial invisibility, which at times appeared to curtail any collective form of strategic essentialism and activism. Nevertheless, Newark's Ironbound, with its insistence on a commercialization of culture, presented a more complicated case than the most frequently studied Brazilian areas of Massachusetts (e.g., Marrow 2003; Martes 2000) or California (e.g., Beserra 2003, Ribeiro 1997).[43] Whereas Newark Brazilians emphasized that they were not "Hispanic," a term in fact associated with racism and social stigma, and only used "Latino" selectively, to suggest a common geographical area or foreign status, they also avoided being considered "white." In the context of the Ironbound, where cultural excess opened commercial niches and social opportunities and being "just white" was considered undesirable, "ethnicity" and "culture" carried considerable clout.

Variable positions regarding the "Hispanic" and "Latino" identification among Brazilians and other Latin American migrants point to a connection between the creation of a cartography of racial democracy and perspectives on US citizenship. The cartography of racial democracy that I am proposing does not assume that all Latinos and Latin Americans subscribe to one, homogenous idea of the ideology of racial democracy, but rather that there are alternative perspectives on race that are historically grounded in a very localized political economy in which people's neighborhood experiences and intimate lives are ensconced. These perspectives on racial democracy are also influenced by transnational experiences and familial imaginaries. Conceived as such, a cartography of racial democracy raises questions about whether Latinos are always defining themselves vis-à-vis blacks or whites, whether views of racial democracy subvert/sustain a US black-white binary, and whether conceptions of Blackness more closely approach notions of citizenship than views of "immigrant"-ness, among others. When an Afro-Brazilian reporter from Rio de Janeiro asked me about an incident in which an African American man was hitting a Mexican immigrant on Ferry Street in the Ironbound, her concluding question was: "Why do people hate immigrants so much here?" The awareness of nativism in the United States has led many Brazilians to conclude that attaining formal citizenship is panacea against anti-immigrant discrimination in the United States..

Although in Newark Brazilians showed ambivalence toward the "Latino" identification and generally assumed that the label "Hispanic" applied only to Spanish-speaking immigrants, the connection between race, citizenship, and the labels "Hispanic" or "Latino" was more complicated than a unilateral avoidance of classificatory terms.[44] Rather than simply viewing US citizenship as emblematic of political power and rights, in relation to racial minorities who were US citizens Brazilians and other

South American migrants oftentimes saw certain forms of citizenship as racialized and racializing. When in reference to US racial minorities, these migrants sometimes insinuated that these minorities had abused the responsibilities of a (neoliberal) citizen and violated the tenements of the American dream; citizenship, in such cases, was rendered legible only through a "culture of poverty" language (e.g., being "lazy" or welfare "dependent,"). Brazilians and other recent Latin American migrants considered the citizenship of these US racial minorities as decidedly delinquent.

From "Aggressive" to "Playful": Puerto Ricans Contribute and Racial Learning

Puerto Ricans violated the racial sensibilities of other Latinos, particularly Brazilians, by communicating race through the use of ethnoracial labels and, second, by challenging the goodness or American-ness of whites. For Brazilians, being antiracist oftentimes meant viewing "Brazilian"-ness as a nationality that captured all colors, whereas Puerto Ricans generally understood it in light of connections with African Americans and other Latinos.

In the Ironbound, arguably more so than in other parts of Newark, Puerto Ricans were perceived as privileged Hispanics who sometimes interrupted the marketable Europeanness of the Ironbound, because of their proximity to "Blackness." Puerto Ricans embodied a complicated conception of privilege, in relation to other "immigrant" groups—when such privilege was assumed to come from US citizenship, English language skills, and place of birth—since most Puerto Ricans in Newark were second- and third-generation US born. They also embodied the Blackness associated with being urban and were known to get along with Blacks and live in areas considered tough and "ghetto." They were considered to be versed in an urban vernacular often connected to African Americans in media and hip-hop culture, and were associated with "culture of poverty" discourses, including welfare "abuse," "laziness," and moral decay. Most Brazilians considered both blacks and whites to be "American," while they considered Puerto Ricans as "American" only selectively.

In the northeastern United States, Brazilians have frequently settled in areas of significant Puerto Rican presence, leading to the view that Puerto Ricans were the nemesis of what Brazilian immigrants would become. In her study of Brazilians in Framingham, Massachusetts, Teresa Sales (1998, 67) cites John Stefanini's claim that in addition to contributing to the revitalization of Framingham's downtown with their businesses Brazilians possessed an "entrepreneurial spirit" that Puerto Ricans lacked:

a sector of the Brazilian population that is coming here consists of people with high qualifications, that I would characterize as entrepreneurial. The Puerto Rican community lives here, for instance, for two or three generations and still has not set up businesses, whether these are family businesses or companies. Already the Brazilian population, that has been here for only ten years, they have opened companies, family businesses, they are doing things, not necessarily in the same fields in which they used to work in Brazil. . . . I'd say they are more educated and entrepreneurial people, opening businesses, taking risks, working hard. (My translation, 67–68)

This Puerto Rican exceptionalism or ambiguity was revealing of how neoliberalism creates subjects based on evaluations of productivity and the ability to accumulate capital; in fact, some research has revealed that when Puerto Ricans constitute a high percentage of "Hispanics" in an urban area, white flight tends to increase (Sacks 2003).

The heightened stigmatization of Puerto Ricans in the United States has also been a theme of seminal Brazilian politics and fiction (Tosta 2004). The declaration made by Júlio César Gomes dos Santos, Brazilian consul in New York, at an immigration support rally in Danbury, Connecticut, regarding "Hispanics" was but one of the most recent efforts to incite Brazilians to sever ties with other Latino groups. The Brazilian consul stated:

A maioria dos nossos são illegais—não para nós, para eles. Se houver uma relação, é pior para nós. Deixa os cucarachos lá. Não deixem que essa mistura aconteça. O West Side Story é para eles. [Most of our people are illegal—not illegal for us, but for them. If there were a way to align ourselves with them, it would be worse for us. Leave the cockroaches over there. Don't mix with them. West Side Story is for them.][45]

In *Febre Brasil em Nova Iorque*, Norma Guimarães remarks:

A raça que começou a "sujar na estaca," foi a protejida do titio—os porto-riquenhos, considerados os "bugs" (baratas) da América (ou "cucarachas"—hablando en español). Dai, todos os que chegam falando espanhol serem considerados "cucarachos." Mas o americano não distingue muito o que é brasileiro do que é mexicano, argentino, peruano, colombiano ou porto-riquenho. Para ele tudo é "latino." Mirou, é gato. E assim entramos também para o rol dos "bugs." [The race that began to "dirty the pond" was the protegees of Uncle Sam—the Puerto Ricans, considered the "bugs" of America (or cockroaches in Spanish). From then on, all those that arrived speaking Spanish would be considered "cockroaches." But Americans do not distinguish much between who is Brazilian or who is Mexican, Argentine, Peruvian, Colombian, or Puerto Rican. For them, everybody is "Latino." And that's how we also fall into the role of "bugs"]. (Guimarães, quoted in Tosta 2004, 580)

Likewise in Roberto Athayde's *Brasileiros em Manhattan* (1996), the author notes: "among those who come to the disco Cathedral in New York are the ralé (scum), composed of porto-riquenhos, negros e desabrigados (Puerto Ricans, Blacks, and the destitute)" who are described as "starving to death and impolite" (quoted in Tosta 2004, 581). Drawing from Silviano Santiago's *Stella Manhattan* (1994), Tosta describes how the author differentiates between Brazilians and other Latinos by placing the former in a position of superiority when he states: "O rosto do chefe se descontrai de verdade e deixa entrever simpatia pelo brasileiro, bem diferente dos outros latinos com quem tinha lidado. Especialmente os do Caribe [The boss's face truly softens and allows for some kindness toward Brazilians, very differently than toward other Latinos with whom he had dealt with. Specially those from the Caribbean]" (Santiago 1994, 220). Yet, in Newark, Puerto Ricans were the Latino default category, and Brazilians (and other Latin American migrants) were very conscious of this.

Puerto Ricans were masters in distinguishing "racismo de verdad," the one that merited a response and a challenge, and "racismo de relajo," the use of racial labels to assert solidarity through the emphasis on racial difference. A conversation with Amarilis Guzmán was one of many instances in which Puerto Ricans aimed to "soften" what they viewed as racial overdeterminism with a form of communicative (verbal and nonverbal) play. After graduating from Barringer High School, one of the part-time jobs that Amarilis took was as a receptionist at the Prudential building in Newark's downtown. When I asked her about the people whom she met through her job, Amarilis commented: "The white people that come by our building, they don't know the differences between Latinos. If you're caramel-skinned, brown eyes, curly hair, you're automatically [assumed to be] Puerto Rican. No matter if you're Brazilian or Dominican or whatever." When I asked her about her work experience, Amarilis described the environment by noting the emotional styles and humor among a seemingly diverse workforce:

I work with Brazilians, Dominicans, Haitians. . . . A girl that's half-French along with Puerto Rican and African mixed in. In my job we're always talking about people's background, bantering and joking around. We have to do that, because we have nothing better to do at that stupid job. The people there are like 25 percent Puerto Rican, 25 percent mixture, and then 50 percent black. So it's funny because I have this black friend and we're talking and I ask her, "Why is it okay for a black person to call another black person "nigger," but if a white person said it, it's fucked up?" And she's like, "I don't fucking know." And I'm like, "But don't you take offense to that?" And she's like, "Hell no, because there *are* niggers down here." [laughed]. So she told me, "Some black people don't like other black people down here. Because you have your ghetto black and then you have your black." And I'm cracking up laughing as she's telling me that, you know. So I asked her if she considered herself African American, and she's like: "Hell no! My family's from Virginia. What the hell do I know about Africa!" But you have the people that wear the African colors all over and they don't know anything anyways. It's just a fashion to them. The 25 percent that are not Puerto Rican and black sitting there looking at us, like, "You guys are stupid!" We just get into these stupid jokes, though they are serious to some people. My black friend would be like, "Hey, you habichuela [bean] come here," and I'll be like, "Stop playing nigger naps." We just look at each other and laugh. Because, are you really that stuck on everything that happens that you can't laugh at things? And the other people [who are not black or Puerto Rican] look at us and they're like [with concern], "Oh my God, she just called her nigger!" thinking that there's going to be another riot, you know.

Puerto Ricans oftentimes understood race as a knowledge system, as the context-based distinction between racismo de verdad (real racism) and racismo de relajo (humor racism). This distinction relied on a "softening" of discussions about race and race-talk—through jokes, comments on color, and individual neuroses—in favor of a universal sentimentality. Most Latin American migrants and US-born Latinos recognized racism as a very real social malaise, particularly when racial discrimination rendered them "illegal," for instance. Nevertheless, the distinction between forms of racial interpretation—between a racism that was presumably more real or tangible than another—also pointed to an alternative form of racial knowledge, one that distinguished between an individual's emotional ease and stiffness in racial talk. The ability to joke about color without subscribing to a US racial etiquette ironically gave a false sense of greater racial tolerance.

While most Brazilians seemed to have a positive impression of white Americans, even though (or precisely because?) they had very limited interaction with unhyphenated whites in their everyday lives, Puerto Ricans subscribed to an image of the "neurotic Caucasian" to explain their interactions with white people. Following up with her comment of the white co-worker being paranoid by the racial bantering and name-calling between Puerto Ricans and blacks, Amarilis continued:

But it's hysterical because we do it to a lot with the Caucasians there, too. Most of the people that work at the Prudential offices are Caucasian and there's this lady that works with us that . . . Caucasians are neurotic, you know. She sees a water faucet dripping, and she goes crazy. "I'm from Morristown [a more affluent area] and where I live we're not even allowed to water our plants or clean the sidewalk to economize water" and we just laugh at her, because you see that this woman will lose sleep over this drip, you know? . . . You have also some Caucasians that walk around as if they were VPs, but the beauty of my job is that I have access to a lot of information. I can type in their names and find out whether they are really VPs or the assistant of the assistant of the assistant, you know? [laughed].

"Knowable communities" is a term Raymond Williams (1973) uses which is similar to Michael Taussig's (1987) "implicit social knowledge" or Michael Herzfeld's (1997) "cultural intimacy." These terms are suggestive of the importance that some communities attribute to knowing what not to know in public and to the recognition of those aspects of cultural identity that are considered a source of external embarrassment but that nevertheless provide insiders with their assurance of common sociability.

The distinction between racismo de verdad and racismo de relajo is tangentially rooted in what Isar Godreau (2008) has termed "slippery semantics" or the

recurrent linguistic inconsistency in racial identification processes that takes place when people use different systems or logical grids of racial classification during a single conversation; such grid can include the use of multiple racial terms to describe the same individual, the consistent use of binary black/white terminology, or the use of the same racial term to describe different "types of phenotypes" during a single narrative event. (7)

Such linguistic pattern in Puerto Rican racial talk is shifting, highly dependent on context, and defies rigid dichotomization made between black-white binary forms of classification, associated with the United States, and more ambiguous forms or racial terminology associated with Latin America. The tendency toward polyvalency and inconsistency produces a destabilizing effect on the status of "race" as an identity-marker during the course of everyday conversations.[46] This slippery effect enables different interpersonal relationships among those implicated or involved in the conversation indexing solidarity, intimacy, distance, or respect among speakers. In that process, social identities that go beyond race, including being workers in a tedious job or a criminalized subject in the streets of Newark, come into play, making racial meaning dependent and conflated with the social cleavages they summon during the conversation.

Code switching, jokes, gossip, ritualized insults, boasts and other (often competitive) banter or verbal play are critical linguistic and ethnographic components of any analysis of affective and emotional life among Latinos and Latin American migrants in Newark. The micro-organization of talk (and silences, withdrawals, and other nonverbal communication) can in themselves serve as vehicles for interpreting affect in an ethnographic context (e.g., Briggs 1988; Limón 1982). The affective function of many verbal and nonverbal communication practices demonstrates how emotive meaning is constructed interactionally and interreferentially, as different affective indexes can also key "contradictory meanings" (Farr 2004, 19, 22).[47] Among migrants and "minority" populations in the United States, the "double-voicedness" (Bakhtin 1981) and ambiguity of these communicative practices are suggestive of identity constructions both in the United States and in one's country of origin. In fact, by resisting inclusion in either nation's racial categories, these populations affirm their difference from both nations' dominant identities as the internalization of meanings from the jokes remains partial and incomplete and opened for innovation in daily practices (cf. Farr 1994, 2004). Relajo and verbal play served as a barometer of emotional competency and racial knowledge. The ability to be playful regarding race, of not taking racial and color comments "too seriously," signaled a commercially and personally valuable ability to carve a space to experiment with a racismo de relajo or racismo de brincadeira. By its very description, this form of racial play excluded most African Americans and some whites in Newark, who were viewed to be too invested in "being angry" or "being really racist." Nevertheless, in the context of intimate friendships or collaborative work relations, as the one described by Amarilis, Puerto Ricans and blacks tacitly understood their racial bantering to be qualitatively and experientially different from the true racism of whites.

As in the beauty salon episode, this distinction between forms of racism emphasizes a changing etiquette governing speaking rules and verbal content in public discourse among different groups. When and how certain situations or comments are regarded as racial rendered some instances commonsensical and visible, while masking others. What counted as racial was much more reduced among some groups, particularly recent migrants like Brazilians, and more extensive among other US-born Latino groups, like Puerto Ricans. Puerto Ricans considered more exchanges to be racial and race was a more central lens to view certain events. As a Brazilian college student whom I met in Newark told me: "When I first got here, I did not think about racism or know very much about it. I did not know that when a white person commented on what a good worker I was and told me that she had always assumed that Brazilians were more focused on 'partying' and 'carnival' than work, that that was racist. But when I talked more with other friends, Puerto Rican friends, they explain this to me. And I see what they mean." As this student also admitted, she had only read the comments by African Americans—particularly comments in which race figured explicitly in the conversation—as truly racist and aggressive.

Portuguese residents were perceived to be defending the neighborhood's "Iberian"-ness against black incursions, but also against newer Brazilian and Latin American residents. Portuguese racism, however, was already situated around questions of "rudeness" and "bad manners." Brazilians engaged race through disengagement even amid heightened attention to the pernicious effect of Portuguese anti-Brazilian discrimination. This was done in two main ways: first, by articulating Portuguese discriminatory practices as "rude" (rather than explicitly racist) and, second, by emphasizing good manners and adequate public behavior.

Whiteness as Manners: Race, Comportment, and Portugal Day

In the beauty salon episode, good manners among the staff constituted part of the emotional labor that was essential to generate a broad and racially diverse clientele. Many of the Brazilians with whom I spoke capitalized on their ambiguous position in Newark by viewing themselves as possessing certain emotional qualities that other groups—particularly Portuguese and black groups—did not have, such as life skills, the ability to weather problems with an optimistic attitude (e.g., "Life is too short, não é?" in the beauty salon episode). In relation to the Portuguese, many Brazilians commented on how their Portuguese neighbors were always serious and rude to them and, in emphasizing Portuguese rudeness, Brazilians also highlighted how "Brazilian culture" supplied psychological, affective and life skills that other groups, particularly African Americans, but also the Portuguese and other Latinos, lacked.

In their interaction with one another, Brazilians and Portuguese, in particular, created a liminal state of not-quite-whiteness and reshaped this space in ways intended not only to avoid Blackness, but also to distance themselves from downward mobility from a working-class perspective. Images of an Iberian ethnicity aimed, at times, to avoid being considered "white trash" partly by rejecting conventional notions of unhyphenated or cultureless American whiteness. In some instances, the Iberian populations of the Ironbound preferred to feel suspended in what John Hartigan calls "a conviction of racelessness" or "the race of no race" (1999, 205), and perceived their ethnic categories to be more relevant to the composition of their own interests and actions. However, as the population of Brazilians and other South Americans increased in the neighborhood, a dominant spatial logic of racefullness, or having "the race of all races" developed as a US variation of Latin American "racial democracy."[48] The Iberian residents of the Ironbound were regarded in light of what Thomas Guglielmo terms a "racially encoded (in)visibility" (2003, 97). Being Portuguese in Newark, for instance, required constant alteration and mending, and a continuous investment in the fiction of stability and self-containment the identity had come to epitomize.[49]

Ellen was one of the many Brazilians who spontaneously commented on the tense relationship between the Portuguese and the Brazilians in the Ironbound, and she specifically noted the role of Newark, as an emotionally saturated space—what she refers to as "something in the air." Ellen explained, "In Brazil we have Portuguese too and we don't have any problems. I think the problems here have to do with Newark. . . . There's something in the air here. I don't really have an explanation for that, but you can almost feel it, sense it." Whenever Brazilians commented on their relationship with the Portuguese or even with people from other nationalities and even "races," they highlighted the fact that Newark was unlike any other city where they had lived. In Ellen's case, upon further reflection, she speculated: "It could be that [the Portuguese] are jealous of the role of Brazil as a country that has developed a lot faster. But the Portuguese still want to see the Brazilians as their creatures and they see themselves as the creators. They still have that colonial mentality, even if that happened centuries ago."[50]

The colonial referent in everyday conflicts between Brazilian and Portuguese residents in the Ironbound oftentimes introduced, either explicitly or tacitly, the connection between the Portuguese ascription to the view of "Luso-tropicalismo," on the one hand, and the Brazilian perspective on "racial democracy," on the other. Gilberto Freyre's (1956) Luso-tropicalismo introduced the "benevolent Portuguese" colonial narrative which regarded the Portuguese as responsible for the harmonious construction of a new tropical civilization in Brazil that was very different from the conditions of other colonial empires; after World War II, Portuguese miscegenation in the colonial era was viewed as evidence of such harmonious integration with the natives and, its outcome, Brazilian "racial democracy," signaled the special capacity of the Portuguese to re-late to populations in tropical regions intimately. Sex between Portuguese men and native women was eroticized and idealized for it represented the culprit of racial tolerance and genesis of Brazil's "racial democracy." Thus, the Portuguese were attributed a special capacity to relate to other peoples, especially in their tropical colonies, and consequently, a capac-ity to serve as a connection between cultures. As José de Renó Machado (2003) notes, "Portuguese Luso-tropicalism reissues the idea of Brazil as the grand product of the richness of the Portuguese soul, restructuring Brazil's position in the actual Portuguese imagination: if Brazil is its grand creation, it is subaltern; if it is subaltern, its citizens are in an inferior posi-tion in the hierarchy of otherness" (5).

Moreover, in Newark, discussions of colorism and whitening between Brazilians and Portuguese resonated with what Machado (2003) notes among Brazilian immigrants and Portuguese in Porto, Portugal. The con-flict between the two racial orders—Portuguese Luso-tropicalismo and Brazilian racial democracy—limited the way in which Brazilian miscege-nation was deployed as an ambiguous strategy that made racial classifi-cation more flexible and disguised deep racism. Among the Portuguese, there was no ambiguity about the "mixed" identity of Brazilian migrants; one was either white or not. In Machado's study, Brazilians were mixed and, as such, were placed below white Portuguese and above blacks and African populations in Portugal. In fact, in Portugal, Machado argues, white Brazilian immigrants experience a lessened racial status than they had in Brazil, whereas mestiço and black Brazilians had a chance to be "equal" to Brazilian whites.

Although the Portuguese and Brazilians usually related to each other on a daily and consistent basis, especially in Portuguese-owned construc-tion and cleaning companies, "the Portuguese" as metonymic shorthand for institutional and social power were never to be trusted entirely. Many Brazilian youth and adults alike commented that dealing with Portu-guese in a tactful way required a great deal of work, and, even when a reasonably good relationship could be built over time, the Portuguese rarely admitted them into an inner circle of trust and intimacy. Brazilians in Newark continuously asserted that the Portuguese were "backward," "rude," "emotionally (or sexually) repressed," or "ignorant," and came from a nation that had no role in the international order or even in the European Union. Instances of "technical rudeness" were far more com-mon than situations involving yelling and profanity in the descriptions given by Brazilians about their treatment by the Portuguese. Rudeness, in this sense, could be made visible not just through the content of people's remarks, but in disattention to the procedures whose tacit recognition provided for trust and a sense of security (Anderson 2000). Oftentimes Brazilians framed the Portuguese as lacking an affective sophistication that, in turn, required that whenever Brazilians worked for Portuguese bosses or clients, they were required to perform a significant deal of emotional labor (Hochschild 1983).

The emotional paucity of white people and the "rudeness" that the Portuguese were ascribed served as "compensatory racial fantasy" that both affirmed, in a counteridentificatory manner, the emotional complexity, depth, and sophistication of Brazilians and some US-born Latinos in the Ironbound.[51] Looking at the creation of these emotive characteristics and the "folk theories of race"—everyday perspectives on racial difference that draw heavily from the association between racial authenticity and particular behaviors (cf. Jackson 2001)—into which they are ensconced is important, not because they accurately describe "what white people are like," but because they reflect the interests, concerns, and material conditions of the US-born Latinos and Latin American migrants responsible for producing the them.

It is important to note, however, that despite all the ways in which the whiteness of the Portuguese was challenged, when it came to claiming neighborhood space, the Portuguese constituted the invisible grid on which Latinidad and black-Latino alliances tended to disintegrate. Even though there was no Portuguese participation in the beauty salon episode, the context of the Brazilian beauty salon still supplied racialized tools that relied on notions of emotional inadequacy when it came to US-born racial minorities. Such perspectives were evident in other public spaces in the Ironbound as well, including ethnic festivals.

Although in 2008 Portugal Day came close to being canceled for lack of city funding, a new agreement was reached that made the festival organizers responsible for financing future festivals through their own fundraising. While the festival typically drew in excess of a quarter-million people over a weekend, the organizers and city officials expressed frustration at their inability to turn the event into a sustainable business. More critically, they were frustrated at their inability to attain the level of "civility" and "appropriate behavior" to which they aspired.

While most of the young people with whom I spoke about the festival did not know the specifics of the funding troubles, they had heard that the festival was in a precarious situation. Giselle Coutinho, who worked as a clerk in a bakery, told me that many Portuguese costumers were in fact glad that the festival would be canceled because they felt that "it was not a Portuguese festival anymore. That the feast has turned into a ghetto event." Giselle explained, "I've heard people saying that it's now a feast of Brazilians, Puerto Ricans, and all the other Hispanic from other countries. They want it to be only Portuguese because other cultures disrespect them. I've heard things like that. That they were shocked to see that last year there were kiosks selling South American flags and foods and people wearing t-shirts from other countries. And they always complained that people can't behave."

Emília Ribeiro, a Brazilian student at East Side, who joined Giselle and me on her day off from her work as a boutique clerk, added, "My mom's boss, she's Portuguese. She's the owner of the [cleaning] company, and she was talking to another Portuguese woman saying that now that these other groups were in the festival, it had become violent. Gangs, drunk people, men grabbing the women, fighting, things like that. That the food was different, not Portuguese."

Giselle commented, "That's what they say and I understand that it is their day and people have to show respect. But they don't see that there are Portuguese guys, younger guys, that also get drunk and grab women! It's their own children!"

Emília confirmed, "Yeah, it's not only the other people, but that's not what they see. They always say that it's the Puerto Ricans or the Hispanics and the Brazilians. But everybody does that."

When I asked them if they felt the Brazilian festival was any different, they both agreed that many of the same issues of people getting drunk and grabbing women were there. There was one exception, as Emília saw it. "I'm not saying we're perfect, but I have to say that we accept everybody, every culture, every race, no matter what they are. We don't think that people need to be in one area, like the Hispanics here, the blacks there, the Portuguese there, the Brazilians, all separate. That's how other people see it in Newark."

Giselle interjected, "The people here are just rude. They go over their limits and push against someone or step on your foot or whatever and instead of saying 'Sorry,' they turn around and look like it's your fault that they stepped on you. That's really how the fighting starts, and that's with all the groups."

Emília agreed and commented, "The Portuguese are very close minded about the Brazilian culture, and even more about the Hispanics. With the Puerto Rican and the blacks . . . uff! . . . forget it, they can't even deal with those groups!"

In 2008 the Portugal Day celebration and the Puerto Rican Day Parade in Newark took place on the same weekend in June. Comments about

Brazilian indecent exposure and unruly behavior dominated the pages of local newspaper editorials and Internet chat boards, alongside similar comments about Puerto Ricans "taking over" Ferry Street, even when the Puerto Rican parade was held downtown, in Newark's Central Ward. Vivian Rovira, who was born and raised in the Ironbound and attended ESHS, told me that she was offended by comments she heard from some Portuguese who complained about Puerto Rican presence in the Portugal Day events. "I've heard people saying things like 'This is not Puerto Rico day, this is Portugal Day. We don't go to Puerto Rican Day, so why do they have to come here. Puerto Ricans should go to celebrate in New York.' [They say] Stuff like that. And I'm like, what the hell, I've lived here my whole life, even longer than most of them have. So, I'm like, screw you, I'm Puerto Rican and I'm going, and if I feel like waving the most giant Puerto Rican flag, I will. It's something to do after the Puerto Rican Day Parade!"

In April of 2006, the Ironbound Improvement District organization hired off-duty police officers to "address student rowdiness" on Ferry Street, the main commercial artery of the neighborhood. The organization was concerned about "large numbers of students from ESHS harassing shoppers, littering, and damaging property on Ferry Street as they wait to catch buses on their way home after school *to other parts of the city*." The emphasis on how these students "did not belong" or "did not live" in the Ironbound appeared throughout the organization's communiqué; in the context of the Ironbound, out-of-placeness invariably suggested nonwhite so that the bodies criminalized on the streets, those who interrupted neoliberal commercial aspirations and the wellbeing of "the shoppers," were those of young men of color.[52] Following Toni Morrison (1992), I want to highlight "invisibility" to denote ostensible absence but actual presence, when analyzing belongingness in the Ironbound. While the Ironbound has traditionally been considered a Portuguese "ethnic enclave," it is necessarily constituted in light of "the rest of Newark." The play of stereotypes sustained and was sustained by neoliberal views of the city and who fit and who did not, into specific symbolic and material territories—about which bodies were productive, able to consume ("the shoppers"), valued, decent, and "legal," and also white. An extension of this discussion of "illegality"—in terms of migrating without documents as well as becoming part of an underground economic niche—can be traced to the connection that the local media and Portuguese public officials drew between violence in the Ironbound and increased Brazilian migration to the area.

José Inácio Werneck argues that, unlike Colombians, Muslim/Arabs, Russians, and other immigrants, Brazilians are not perceived as particularly "problematic" in the US imaginary. Whether a group is considered problematic or not oftentimes has to do with the historical relation between the two countries involved (2004, 28). In the United States, a country where the politics of difference is dominated by a white Anglo-Saxon elite, ethnic segments aim to draw from their distinct cultural heritage to become visible and to acquire distinction and accumulate symbolic and political capital as actors in the politics of identity. Through cultural manifestations, political-cultural actors demonstrate not only the exuberance of their cultures, but also their numbers and presumable political and economic weight. A strong element of this constrangement is the image of the culture of a people that is received and diffused (Ribeiro n.d., 18). Identified as energetic, happy, sensual, and exuberant, Brazilians who were discovering what it meant to be inserted in a position as a minority faced new concerns regarding identity politics in discussions of "illegality" and "inappropriate behavior" and reinterpreted "racial democracy" in a racial landscape that was largely unfamiliar. These modes of learning to navigate a US racial landscape and the emotional basis on which such a process was established appeared most notable in the context of public institutions, like the public school.

Paula Pereira, the Brazilian student who commented on how class distinctions had been manifested in the volleyball clubs to which she had belonged in Brazil, perceived "racial invisibility" as the conduit to racial harmony. This perspective was not only akin to a US-based version of the Latin American ideology of "racial democracy," but was furthermore a particular denunciation of African American racial consciousness, which she (and many other Brazilians and Latin American migrants) viewed as a basis for (rather than a response to) racism in the United States. Perceptions of Blackness, particularly a politicized perspective on race as threatening and militant, oftentimes drew from Newark electoral politics.[53] More often, however, these perspectives were manifested in the realm of expressive culture, of which the Portugal Day festival was a leading example. As many New Jersey Portuguese viewed this celebration as the symbolic consolidation of their national identity, claims over space, belonging, and racial difference acquired behavioral glosses, centered on emotional style, and threats to the images that contributed to narrating the Ironbound as Newark's commercial jewel. Street festivals, particularly the Portugal Day celebration, were central to the racial marking of Brazilians in the Ironbound, because such racialization relied on a Portuguese deployment of "shame" that required witnesses—an audience—that could spot how Brazilians failed to live up to the community's moral, behavioral, and emotive standards (cf. Ahmed 2004, 108; Keeler 1983). In such celebrations, Brazilian renderings of "racial invisibility" were challenged, as the Portuguese engaged in practices that racialized Brazilian migrants as "closer to" US Hispanics, particularly Puerto Ricans, the largest Latino group in Newark.

In some ways, "racial invisibility" served as a strategy to fight a form of shaming Brazilians, and interrupted more benevolent or less politicized notions of cultural excess (cf. Ahmed 2004, 107). In an editorial piece that appeared in the *Brazilian Voice*, one of the multiple Portuguese-language newspapers in Newark, around the time of the Portugal Day festivities in 2003, Brazilians were urged, somewhat paternalistically, to be well-behaved during a celebration that was not their own. It stated:

This weekend . . . Newark will be celebrating the Luis de Camões Day, the largest Portuguese feast in the U.S. The event will also count with the presence of the Brazilian community, which feels very honored to be able to participate in such an important date for our Portuguese brothers. Alert to the Brazilians: We are simply guests at this feast. Let's eat, drink, and have fun in moderation. It's Brazil on Ferry Street on Portugal Day. Obrigadinho, pá!!![54]

Brazilians' strategy of "cultural excess," while contributing to an unthreatening and highly commodifiable Brazilian-ness in the United States, did not exempt Brazilian residents of the Ironbound from being racially marked by local Portuguese residents and even claimed by other Latino and African American populations alike. Brazilians in Newark appeared to inhabit an imperfect space in which they constructed themselves as "culturally excessive" (rejecting an American blandness, but producing a nonthreatening hypercultural self-image), while other residents, particularly the Portuguese, constructed Brazilian-ness in explicitly racial terms.

The failure to live up to an ideal of adequate behavior was a way of taking up that ideal and confirming its necessity. In the case of Brazilians in the Portuguese Day festivities, a denunciation of inappropriate behavior was emblematic of an instance when shame confirmed the commitment of some community members to normative ideals of respectability and domesticity. Shame likewise reintegrated Brazilian subjects (Braithwaite 1989), like the writer of the editorial piece, despite a collective Brazilian failure to live up to a Portuguese communal ideal. In some ways, Brazilian "cultural excess" scrambled moral categories and made it difficult to inscribe moral certainty and closure. If Brazilians are viewed as amoral in the Portuguese imagination, it was not because they have forsaken morality but because "they contain all moralities and rarely offer a higher foundational principle to order them" (cf. Illouz 2007, 76).

Shame or the failure to approximate "an ideal" forged through normative social practices also served to racialize Brazilian as more akin to other abject US-born minorities. For instance, similar claims about inappropriate behavior were made of African American participation in the festivity. However, most commonly, it was the behavior of Puerto Ricans and Brazilians that were singled out as inappropriate. In fact, the Portugal Day festivities became an instance in which Brazilians approached Puerto Rican–ness through a highlighted politics of shame, and such racialization was experienced as the affective cost of not following the script of normative existence. In this sense, shame became a domesticating feeling (Ahmed 2004, 106–7). Many contingencies, including residents, business owners and government officials, had highly vested interests in what the Ironbound looked like and how the area was represented to others, particularly potential consumers; such a stake in the neighborhood's image increased the policing of both the Ironbound vis-à-vis other areas of Newark and, internally, where belonging was not always based on who had resided in the area or for how long, but rather who was more effectively involved in the capital accumulation process.

Social Regulation and the Cartography of Racial Democracy

The beauty salon conversation is suggestive of how joking, verbal race play, and emotions were critical not only in preserving civility, but also in reducing the "militancy" and "anger" associated with African Americans in Newark by introducing a perspective on racial democracy that highlighted the "playfulness" of race among Brazilians, as well as among other Latin American migrants in the Ironbound.[55]

Everyday forms of social regulation—the emphasis on class distinctions and contrast between US and Brazilian racial dynamics, the role of whiteness as a tacit grid in local racialization processes, and the ambivalence between "cultural excess" and "racial invisibility"—constitute what I call a "cartography of racial democracy." This cartography of racial democracy required that "(racial) difference" be reconstituted as differences in emotional style and affect in everyday urban interactions. This inscription of race in a language of emotion was not difficult to establish, since whites had already begun the process around the time of the riots, when they began to view Newark as a city of "aggressive blacks" and "angry mobs" (see chapter 1). More significantly, the fluid perspectives on racial difference assumed under a "cartography of racial democracy" repositioned a growing Latino and Latin American population in a long enduring white-black racial dyad. It served as a navigational tool through which these populations identified certain emotional styles as more effective for capital accumulation than others. The salience of emotions and affect capital became fundamental to a politics of conviviality that largely undermined a political engagement of race and subordination. Such a cartography highlighted differences between race in the United States and in Brazil (and Latin American or US-Latino communities more broadly) and led to a deepened sense of racial relativism that, in fact, was compliant with neoliberal objectives in the Ironbound (of marketing the area for tourism, a budding service industry, and real estate investment and promoting it as "quaint," "safe," and where middle- and upper-class whites are welcomed).

The Ironbound's emotional landscape introduced perspectives on the appropriate self-packaging of an emotive persona and a heightened (a)esthetics of personal self-care and capacity to be "light" or "humorous," or not be militant and "angry." Sustaining such a landscape required the simultaneous pursuit of both "cultural excess" and "racial invisibility," but also the promotion of a context in which Portuguese traditionalism and conservatism would not be unappealing to middle-class, professional, white couples buying real estate in the area. Brazilian "modernity" complemented ideas of Portuguese traditionalism to promote a sense of universal sentimentality accessible to all residents, new and old.[56] While Newark's neoliberalism shares in common with other multicultural neoliberalisms the heavy-handed reliance on top-down marketing of clearly contained versions of ethnic culture, it also provides a fertile ground for the resurgence of Latin American ideas around racial democracy. Straddling strategies of "cultural excess" and "racial invisibility" involved a singular dialectic of embodiment and disembodiment that was ultimately determined by where one stood in the chain of social relations linking the sphere of production and the public sphere.

Part of the power of race discourse is its ability to take a variety of forms and to adapt to a variety of circumstances, which is partly why the cartography of racial democracy outlined here encountered a fertile ground in US Latino and Latin American communities, particularly those in predominantly black areas. The popular images of the Ironbound signify qualities of the landscape that directly associate people and place, not merely in the creation of interesting cultural formations but as a significant manifestation of the ways in which territory bespeaks power.

Racialization is as much about absence as presence of people or color. Near silence on issues of racialization suggests an overwhelming inattention to the details of racial practices, a silence, thus, dominated by whiteness. Oftentimes concepts of racial difference are legitimized and nonwhite areas, like the projects in the "periphery" of the Ironbound, are mapped into marginality and subordinance (Kobayashi and Peake 2000, 397–99).

"Racial invisibility" in such a context required an appeal to a universal sentimentality. Every single conversation about "culture" in the Ironbound pointed to several of the issues outlined here: First, issues of cultural excess: space-making through an appeal to the senses/universal sentimentality; Portuguese traditionalism and Brazilian modernism as key not only to the heightened commercialization of Brazilian culture, but also to the unwhiteness of the Portuguese; and not only racelessness, but having all races through the idea of tropicalismo or racial democracy. Second, to issues of racial invisibility issues: how racismo de verdad versus de mentira were articulated and how multiculturalism served as a way of conveying Brazilian modernity. The one topic that came up in every single interview with Brazilians and Portuguese alike, and which will be elaborated on in the next chapter, was the inherent difference between Brazilian women and Portuguese women at the crux of the intersection of cultural excess and racial invisibility, and how they viewed gender relations, sexuality, morality, self-care, and body expression.

FOUR

Real-Life Telenovelas, Self-Care, and Stereotypes of the Tropics: Sexing Race and Emotion in the City

Brazilian women "stealing men" from Portuguese women was a recurring theme in many of the real-life dramas that were related to me by adults and young adults in Newark. One of these stories came to me from Marcela de Souza, a Brazilian woman in her forties, and one of the few people I met in the Ironbound who was not connected to the public high school in some way.[1] I met Marcela somewhat unexpectedly, when I was having lunch and writing "fieldnotes" at a small Brazilian bakery on Ferry Street. Marcela struck a conversation with me, by asking, in Portuguese, if I was Brazilian. I responded, also in Portuguese, that I was Puerto Rican. Then, as if my response was inconsequential to her own thread of consciousness, Marcela almost broke down into tears, telling me how much she missed Brazil and how cruel every Brazilian and Portuguese person she had met in Newark had been to her since she first set foot in the Ironbound nearly six months prior.[2]

I asked Marcela if she knew anyone in the area, and her despair, frustration, and sadness became even more evident as she explained that she knew some people at a Portuguese-owned bar where she used to work, "The owner is Portuguese, a good Portuguese man, unlike all the others here, who are so rude to you when they know you're Brazilian. . . . I was friends with one girl who worked there, but she was fired. She was fired because a crazy Portuguese woman got in her head that my friend was trying to steal her husband. It wasn't true, but she thought it was. She got my friend confused with someone else."

"Why did she even think that?" I asked, trying to show support with a tone that pointed to the absurdity of the thought.

"They all think we want to take their husbands, all the Portuguese women think that!" Marcela said, and continued to explain that the disgruntled Portuguese wife would call the bar over and over again, threatening to call Immigration to have Marcela's friend deported. She added, "The owner of the bar got tired. He said he didn't want any problems, that he didn't want his bar to get a bad reputation, because the woman would follow her home and then she even showed up at the bar and made a scene and accused my friend of being a slut. My friend got so tired that she is talking about going back to Brazil."

By the time Marcela finished talking about her "friend's" experience, one of the Brazilian women working behind the counter of the tiny cafeteria had joined in the conversation to validate the fact that Portuguese women were rude to Brazilian women because they felt threatened. "It is not our fault if Portuguese men like Brazilian women, but they think it is. They are very prejudiced. The other day the manicurist from [one of the beauty salons in the area] told me that she had heard a Portuguese woman saying that Brazilians were sluts because we waxed the pubic area, the Brazilian bikini. But then, this same woman wanted to know how much it cost!"

Although the conversation on that day ended on a humorous note, Marcela's story was actually very complex, and I will come back to it later in the chapter.

In Search of a Stereotype to Love: Affect, Cultural Sampling, and Desire

Particular demographic configurations and segregation in cities and neighborhoods influence how stereotypes of affect and folk theories of race—the everyday behavioral glosses associated with the member of a racialized group—become part of everyday racial situations, and how some neoliberal projects benefit when instances of subordination are reconfigured as questions of individual inadequacies. Since affect can also be used and manipulated across contexts, it is important to pay attention to how the presentation and representation of emotional processes—for instance, talk (or writing) about desire, rumors about dating, conflict in interpersonal relationships—contribute to the interweaving of emotion and discourse. In regard to my research on Newark, the ambiguity of situations characterized by emotion and desirability allowed greater maneuvering and oftentimes required that US-born Latinos and Latin American migrants viewed "race" and "racism" as something that could be addressed in the terrain of individual action, while undermining political economic structures.

As political scientist Michael Hanchard notes in his examination of race relations in Brazil, "stereotypes are one of the currencies of social life. They represent long-established prejudices and exclusions and, like nationalist ideology itself, they use the terms of social life to exclude others on cultural grounds. They render intimate, and sometimes menacing, the abstraction of otherness. They are thus the building blocks of practical nationalism (my emphasis)" (1999, 72). Hanchard views stereotypes as rhetorical images that are instrumental in the representation of rapidly changing political relations. Stereotypes around race and sexuality, in particular, have historically become a central mechanism for assessing and guarding racial membership in the United States. In their transition from Negro to quasi-white, for instance, the Mississippi Delta Chinese severed their sexual and marital relationships with black women, cutting off ties with both Negro kin and any Chinese who violated this proscription (Loewen 1988). Likewise, the Irish exerted claims to whiteness through the sexual separation from blacks, which required that they sever sexual relations with blacks and bring their sexual behavior in line with Anglo norms (Barrett and Roediger 1997). While the stereotype of insatiable, exotic women of color has served to justify their degradation, women of color have used their own images of sexual restraint and purity to position themselves as morally superior to "loose white women" (Le Espiritu 2003); in fact, images of the virginal or matronly ethnic woman suggest how the responsibility for maintaining an ethnic community's valence has been placed on women's sexual integrity (di Leonardo 1984). Feelings, affect, and sentiment likewise are produced by and give meaning to racial belief and assessments of national belonging.

An outgoing eighteen-year-old resident of the Ironbound, Giselle Coutinho, arrived from Belo Horizonte with her mother almost six years before I met her at East Side High School. Like other Brazilian migrants with whom I spoke, Giselle felt it was a bit ironic that, even though she now lived in the United States, most of the people she came into contact with were still Brazilian. "There are many groups in this country, but you don't really get to know them that well. Even in dating, there is some mixing, but for the most part people stay within their own group," she once told me. And, in several of many conversations about who she planned on marrying, a topic surprisingly common among many Latin American migrants, Giselle commented:

I don't see myself with an American or a Hispanish or a Portuguese guy. Maybe that's a prejudice, but I think that Americans are too cold and I don't like the Hispanish, Hispanic men. I ask forgiveness from God, but I don't like them. I'm walking down the street and they are standing there in the corner, on Murray Street, and I know they're going to say something [like] "Miraaa, bonitaaaa, ese culo!!!" . . . . Portuguese men are not so strange to me, because my mom dated this Portuguese guy and he was so nice. But for the most part, Portuguese guys are rude. They think that women should be property. People say that Americans are not like that, but there are no real Americans here in Newark.

To Giselle, dating and the sphere of intimate relations provided one of the few templates where genuine openness to difference could be measured. The comment on "Hispanish" men, and the very awkward vacillation between "Hispanish" and "Hispanic" also reflected the ambivalence that many Brazilians felt about their own slippery position in regard to "Hispanic" or even "Latino" identity, an identity which generally privileged the Spanish language.[3]

In a Derridarian sense, her language contained a trace of that which it excluded. In this particular context, Giselle's ambivalence—and invocation of God's forgiveness—was underscored by the association of "Hispanic" men with day laborers who stood in various areas of the Ironbound hoping to get hired for an array of manual work, some within the sophisticated construction work and informal handyman economy that was mostly controlled by Portuguese immigrants and Portuguese Americans (cf. Dines 1991b; Feldman-Bianco 1992). In addition to straddling a hyperconsciousness and negation of race, and examining racial tensions in the terrain of affect, as suggested in Giselle's case, a critical aspect of the Latino folk theories of race produced in Newark involved the virtual reduction of difference to "morality" and "values" so that racial readings were, above all, value judgments, oftentimes unaffected by even the most visible local concerns.

Giselle's attitudes toward other groups were rooted not only in broad statements about people's temperaments (e.g., Americans being "too cold"), but in the immediate, everyday connections that were formed through her incorporation, as a young woman, into Newark's public sphere and of her mother's own dating experience. The lack of familiarity with "Americans"—whom she had met only occasionally as the clients in her mother's housecleaning jobs—accounted for a more general statement about this group, in contradistinction to specific, immediate references to men of other groups. Discussions about dating were not only central in configurations of race but also of gender ideologies. There was a common tendency to engage in a somewhat futile identification of a behavior as either determined by gender or by race, even when conceptions of race were always-already gendered, as conceptions of gender are always-already racialized.

The fact that African Americans were absent from Giselle's narrative cannot be easily dismissed as a result of the Ironbound having the lowest concentration of blacks in Newark; there are very particular readings of Blackness and, in particular, of black women and blacks in political power, that Ironbound residents made and which will be discussed below. Likewise, it cannot be assumed that young Ironbound residents never left the iron-clad triangle that "contains" the "Portuguese enclave."[4] Like most of the other Brazilians with whom I spoke, Giselle described daily routines that involved great mobility to other parts of Newark and New Jersey. There were instances of "politicized feelings" in which emotions could not be regarded as truths but as feelings produced by larger societal structures (cf. Hennessy 2000). Stereotypes of affect, such as the "coldness" attributed to "Americans" in the quote above, were oftentimes based on individual ventures outside the neighborhood. They were likewise manifested in satires and other forms of "hidden transcripts" (Scott 1992) about the inadequate emotional style of white Americans, as members of a dominant group "somewhere out there," a common form of resistance found among many socially disadvantaged groups (Basso, quoted in Besnier 1990, 426; Scott 1992).

What is significant to notice is that qualifications of a group's stereotyped racial affect required a connection that was emotively charged, and grounded in ambiguous readings of the political economic context in which they unfolded. In this context, I understand "racial affect" as the process of locating individual interpretations of the racial projects of the nation-state in the terrain of emotion and sentiment, while privileging individual behavior and practice over considerations of social and material inequality in cities.[5] Interracial attraction was turned into an essential, highly erotic feeling that physiologically arises from a body removed from a sociocultural context. The only "real Americans," as Giselle called white suburbanites, were the people whose houses her mother cleaned.[6]

Giselle's mother worked for a Portuguese-owned cleaning service whose owner hired mostly undocumented Brazilian and Ecuadorian (and sometimes Mexican) women, and assigned them to suburban houses that were on her list. This owner would drive the women in a van to different houses throughout suburban New Jersey, where they would clean from ten to fifteen houses on a given day, before being picked up by the Portuguese employer at the end of the day.[7]

Multiple layers of subordination and misrecognition conditioned the exchanges between the domestic workers and the Portuguese owner, and further accentuated the very tenuous and highly controlled relationship with the "real American" suburban homeowners (cf. Fleischer 2002).[8] As Giselle once told me, at one point her mother had tried to build her own clientele, separate from the Portuguese company owner. In an effort to do this, she had asked one of the homeowners, who was white but whose rudimentary knowledge of Spanish Giselle's mother interpreted as a greater willingness to value other cultures, if she knew of anyone who might be interested in her services. The white woman eventually accused Giselle's mother of being "unprofessional" and reprimanded her for putting her in an "uncomfortable situation." Should something like that happen again, she said, she would be forced to alert the Portuguese owner.

This incident was read by Giselle's mother and by Giselle herself as a "betrayal," but also made Giselle and her mother question whether their "reading" of the white woman, who had seemed "so nice," had been wrong. The partial inclusion of the Portuguese owner into an expansive whiteness further relegated Giselle's mother to a racialized space akin to that of the other "Hispanic" workers. The fact that Giselle's mother had a greater level of formal schooling than the Portuguese supervisor, who was reportedly illiterate, further accentuated the complexity of this situation. This was compounded by the fact that Giselle's mother worked alongside "Hispanic" women, and that even the Portuguese language was not a significant marker of difference (neither for the English-dominant employers who oftentimes did not distinguish by language, nor for the Spanish- and Portuguese-speaking employees who understood each other surprisingly well), also limiting the separation that many Brazilians wanted to emphasize between themselves and the presumably more stigmatized Spanish-speaking Latino groups. Another critical aspect of Giselle's articulations of a racial affect that insisted on the "coldness" of (white) Americans and her preference for other Brazilians as dating partners was the omnipresence of Blackness in its very absence (cf. Morrison 1992).

This emotive stereotype of white people as "cold" oftentimes took place in the context of exploitative work conditions. What frequently remained unquestioned was why such a lack of familiarity with white Americans and virtual lack of interaction with them happened in the first place, or how class structured various conditions of difference, subordination, and segregation in Newark. Giselle described the incident with the suburban white woman as one that caused great "pain" to her mother; in fact, "pain" displaced other potential metaphors in discussions of subordination, privileging the biographical so that suffering was located in the psyche rather than structural employment and residential segregation (cf. Illouz 2003, 101). Giselle's perspective about the "real Americans" being "cold" and the view among Ironbound and North Newark residents that Portuguese-Brazilian and Puerto Rican–Dominican arch-rivalries were due to essential temperamental differences suggest that oftentimes the barometers of racial tensions or collaboration in Newark were viewed in light of stereotypes of affect that undermined greater political economic contexts, while depoliticizing a variety of social problems by psychologizing them under "pain" and "betrayal."

Such a psychologizing of experiences with racial difference frequently emerged in discussions of dating outside one's group. Separate conversations with Mildred Irizarry, Michelle Sánchez, and Renata Cunha—all students at ESHS—highlighted a "transformation of intimacy," which Anthony Giddens (1992) describes as a type of neo-utilitarian relationship that is at once anomic and democratic, subject to a new range of pathologies (e.g., codependency, sexual addiction), but also the site of emancipatory potential; that is, "these are pure relationships entered into for its own sake, for what can be derived by each person from a sustained association with another" (58). A topic that emerged in every single interaction with young Latinos and Latin Americans in Newark was interracial dating in light of manifestations of desire and desirability, attractiveness and unattractiveness, and sexual performativity, aberration, and prowess. Mildred, Michelle, and Renata expressed a desire to date people from outside of their group and, to some degree, even avoid dating men from their own groups. They specifically interpreted this desire in terms of personal discovery, intellectual growth, and as a symbol of change in one's life, respectively.

Mildred Irizarry (Puerto Rican, North Broadway resident, commuted to ESHS): I like to date people from other places, not only Puerto Ricans. Because, you know, you're Puerto Rican and, all of a sudden, you go out with someone who is Dominican or something other than Puerto Rican. And you're like, "Wow." It's so different and yet it's so alike. I'd date anyone as long as they know how to treat a girl.

Michelle Sánchez (US-born, Puerto Rican and Dominican, Ironbound resident): I've always dated Brazilian guys. My ex-boyfriend is Brazilian. My current boyfriend is Brazilian. Everybody thinks he's Puerto Rican and Dominican. We met in eighth grade. He and my ex-boyfriend and I all went to the same grade school, to Wilson. They were in my same class.

AY: So was this a coincidence or do you look for Brazilian guys when you date?

Michele: I like Brazilian men. I have something for them. I don't know. When my boyfriend talks, when he talks Brazilian, I'm like, "Oh." It's such a nice language. When I met him, he was a star at the school, because he was Brazilian and played soccer. I knew he was Brazilian because we had bilingual classes at Wilson, so I noticed that he was in the Portuguese bilingual class. And Fabio, my boyfriend, was too dark to be Portuguese and his accent was different than the other Portuguese that I had met in the neighborhood.

AY: Did you have a particular impression of Brazilians before dating your first Brazilian boyfriend?

Michele: I was always interested, but I became more interested in my boyfriend's life. Like I wanted to get to know what's Brazil about, what's going on in Brazil, the different cultures and stuff, like the Carnival and all and everything. When I go to my boyfriend's house, his family cooks me a Brazilian meal and they make all this big deal on Brazilian holidays. They put on the Brazilian channel for me and they make me watch the Carnival and watch shows. I've gone with them to the Brazilian feast in New York, and all the different stuff.

AY: Have you ever dated a Dominican or a Puerto Rican guy?

Mildred: Never. Not interested.

Renata Cunha (born in Belo Horizonte, Ironbound resident): I don't want to end up with someone who is Brazilian. I don't want to marry a Brazilian guy.

AY: Why not?

Renata: Because I came from Brazil. And I'm going to come all the way here [to the United States] to end up with a Brazilian guy? I want someone from another culture. But I was talking the other day to some of my friends, and I was telling them, my family only speaks Portuguese, so if I end up with an American guy, how are they going to talk to each other? My family doesn't speak English at all, only a little bit. And, unless the guy learns Portuguese . . . that would take a long long time.

AY: So you would like someone who speaks Portuguese?

Renata: Yeah. Only for my parents.

AY: But you wouldn't like him to be Brazilian. So would you like him to be from Portugal?

Renata: Portugal, Italy, French. I've always been interested in those countries.

In Michelle's case, the boyfriend's family became a source of curiosity and the embodiment of characteristics associated with a "Brazilian culture" that was both static and manipulable, and which Michelle enjoyed as a form of competency—what she saw as her valuable ability to "get along with" someone from a "different culture." Stereotypes of affect in fact provided spaces for experimenting with such forms of competency and occasionally gave the illusion that boundaries of "otherness" were fluid, rather than static, and that all one had to do was to learn to behave in an adequate manner to be able to acquire such forms of intergroup competency.

For Renata, the interest in dating anyone from outside of one's group had to do not necessarily with an avoidance of compatriots, but a "background view of desire" (Pettit and Smith 1990), a desire that was a symbol of greater incorporation into the United States. Dating a Brazilian, when one was from Brazil, simply did not "make sense." According to this logic, one of the perceived expectations and advantages of migrating was the possibility to become competent and fluent in a new sociocultural context, and dating or intimate relations were the most definitive ways of testing such competency. The dilemmas of detachment and attachment, in Renata's case, also affected her educational choices, as she explained her decision to pursue a career in language and translation at Bloomfield College. There was also an aspiration to an urban cosmopolitanism, particularly after Renata was more exposed to Latino groups in college.

Reflection on potential romantic partners and dating more generally sometimes provided a porous sense of belonging and opportunities, at times challenging rigid views of "insider" and "outsider," precisely because of the inherent ambiguity of such emotionally charged contexts. Positions of "incomplete" or "almost" belonging insinuated good behavior and an adequate attitude could nudge racial boundaries; thus, emotional adequacy more so than structural factors was privileged in discussions of segregation and inequality. Group boundaries could therefore be altered by someone's *intimate* knowledge of another person's culture. For instance, Mariana Oliveira, who was one of the most valued players on the ESHS volleyball team, commented about a beloved Portuguese coach: "Coach is Portuguese, but he's married to a Brazilian girl. He is with Brazilians all the time because he is a bilingual teacher and the whole volleyball team, the males and the females, all Brazilians so he knows a lot about us. He fell in love with a Brazilian and he knows her family, friends." Such moments represented a space of possibility in an otherwise tense relationship between Portuguese and Brazilians.

Many young Latin American migrants appeared to appreciate other (particularly white American) people's "interest in our culture." The group boundaries, in such instances, could be altered by someone's *intimate* knowledge of one's culture.[9]

Nevertheless, these instances of "cultural intimacy" (Herzfeld 1997) or "cultural sampling" did not necessarily disrupt dominant racial hierarchies; intimate knowledge was severely compromised by a gendered politics of respectability and a moral economy according to which one's participation in capital accumulation was evaluated. In the Ironbound, where Mariana lived, Portuguese women portrayed themselves as "decent" and "respectable," not only in traditional female roles as mothers and wives, but also in their capacity as owners of housecleaning businesses that hired Brazilians and other Latin American women as domestic workers. Portuguese women's respectability in the productive realm was also evoked in contradistinction to the "indecent" jobs of barmaid, dancer, or sex worker more often associated with Brazilians in Newark.

In Newark's "cartography of racial democracy," relationships among social groups viewed as "different" accentuated how US-born Latinos and Latin American migrants possessed a "hyperconsciousness of race" that existed in tandem with the negation of race as a valid analytical category; this perspective resembled a form of racial democracy common in Brazil and throughout Latin America (Costa Vargas 2004). An example of this, analyzed in chapter 3, was how some Brazilians viewed African American participation in Afro-Brazilian activities, like capoeira or samba classes, as a form of cultural co-optation, while African Americans may have framed these events in light of pan-African identification.

In anthropology, "endogamy" and "exogamy" are terms used to examine how inter- and intraracial marriages preserve, expand, or modify the boundaries of a presumably discrete social, racial, ethnic, or religious group. The assumption is that some groups prefer their members to marry within the group, so that "culture" or "status" is preserved; marrying outside of the group is sometimes presented as a potential threat to group cohesiveness, but also as an opportunity for "upward" mobility, depending on the groups in question, historical moment, and social context. Discussions of endogamy and exogamy have thus centered on "marriage" (or some other culturally specific equivalent) as a key unit of analysis. Even among adults in Newark, romantic relations were among the most frequently deployed idioms of racial differences and similarities, through which the racial nuances of daily life and perspectives on familiarity and foreignness were rendered meaningful. People were censored or praised for whom they dated, whom they disliked, and any perceived temperamental or cosmetic transformation they might experience as a result. This was clearly reflected in the comments of Ed Castro, a Puerto Rican teacher, and Raquel Carrillo, a Dominican community worker, both residents of North Broadway:

Ed Castro: I hear Puerto Rican women saying "I'll never go out with a Puerto Rican guy. Puerto Rican guys are this that and the other." And I would hear from Ecuadorian women: "No. I will only go out with Puerto Ricans. I will not go with Ecuadorians because they're this that and the other stuff."

AY: What reasons do they give for not going out with people from their own background?

Ed: They never have a specific reason, but this doesn't start here. It starts even before coming to the US. There was this really attractive Colombian woman in the *Cristina* show, the Latino Oprah. She had never been to the US, but yet she wanted to marry only an American man. Why? She went off on how Latin men are womanizers, whereas American men are more homebodies. And that's what people think throughout Latin America. As an anthropologist, you're probably familiar with the term *mejorando la raza* ["improving the race"], marrying up. That's what's behind all this.

Raquel Carrillo: There is a cultural issue, an issue of familiarity. Sometimes we think that looking outside of our group we can resolve the problem. You have some women, even some of the Dominican women who come here, who are very liberated, especially if they've already lived here for a while. They come here and the last thing they want is to end up with a Dominican [man]. I myself feel that way sometimes! They'd rather end up with a Puerto Rican, an Ecuadorian, but not a Dominican. It's like a phobia. Because we perceive that machismo in Dominican men, so we avoid them. Because deep down Dominican women are not as assertive, when it comes to their rights, as Puerto Rican women are. There are many Dominican women that end up in abusive relationships, we see that a lot. Dating someone who's not Dominican is viewed as a way to avoid that, you see?

It was also in such racializations of romantic relations that the interstices of competing and complementary folk theories of race—of Latin American views of racial democracy and US-dominant systems of racial polarity—became most salient, discursive, and debated. While dating generated statements about a presumed familiarity and comfort with members of one's own group, as well as suspicion toward members of other groups—particularly among those groups considered "archenemies" in the popular imaginary (e.g., Puerto Ricans and Dominicans or Portuguese and Brazilians)—it also revealed the power of intimate connections and the desire to pursue mobility, belonging, and recognition.

Practices of "cultural sampling" or venturing into relationships partly motivated by the culture of the other contributed to the perception that culturally distinct affective styles existed, and that class or racial identification rested in part on the individual's affective demeanor (cf. Besnier 1990, 435). The very understanding of intimate relationships through the creation of affective stereotypes, and discussions of romantic relationships and desire in which confirmation of those stereotypes were shared, supplied the templates to deal with emotionally charged racial situations and to explore intimacy in the racially saturated political economy of Newark. Meaning-making, a main goal of stereotyping, involves a kind of energetic engagement of the self in a social context through processes of upholding, defending, and performing the values, core symbols, and morality plays of the cultural community. Among Latinos in Newark, the very indeterminacy of emotive relationships and cultural sampling became a communicative resource. In such cases, communicative signs indexed several affective experiences ambiguously, as the multifunctionality of affective experiences sometimes became a resource rather than a problem. In other instances, particularly when "race" surfaced as a critical analytical category in a situation or discussion, the illegibility of the situation was accentuated. "Cultural sampling" challenges conventional views of a stereotype as a static portrayal, by noting how people play with stereotypes—at times being more conscious, at times less so, of the simplicity of the representation as such. Among young Latino and Latin American migrants in Newark, these stereotypes were always-already gendered productions that enabled interactions among strangers and generated a discursive emotive space without the need to examine the veracity or reality of an individual's life or her or his social plane. The individual was thus ensconced in the greater terrain the stereotype, in its very creation, provided. The creation of "affective stereotypes" offered a glimpse into the distinction that Maurice Bloch (1992) makes between "what is said about social difference and what goes without saying," the nondiscursive practices that structure apprehension of social difference.

Affective stereotypes were valuable not only as static portrayals of presumably discrete cultural groups, but as emotively charged renditions of desirability, productivity, and even "illegality" and citizenship claims among US-born Latinos and Latin American migrants in Newark. In particular, the investment in a "color-blind erotic democratic" (Goldstein 1999) required the search for a stereotype to love in ways that selectively undermined discriminatory practices or, at the very least, rendered these practices as something people of color, not whites, "did" to each other. However contextually diverse and discursively particular, affective stereotypes allowed US-born Latinos and, particularly, Latin American migrants to simultaneously navigate a "hyperconsciousness of race" alongside a "racial negation," as a way to manage "race" as an analytical construct and forms of racial learning that raised great moral discomfort (chapter 6; cf. Costa Vargas 2004). Even when race was explicit in the depiction of a particular situation, the immediate interpretation of the incident or relationship required that any tension be understood in the terrain of affect and emotion, of an individual's innermost world, which was presumably autonomous from a broader political economy or even neighborhood politics. Difference would be engaged as long as it was constructed in terms of behavior and "feelings," so that racism and national tensions were above all disjunctions predicated on the actions of "moral" versus "amoral," "hard-working" versus "lazy," "good citizens" versus "illegal others."

The way in which urban displacement was psychologized away in terms of the amorality of certain populations was an example of these processes. The relationships between Brazilians and Portuguese in the Ironbound and between Dominicans and Puerto Ricans in North Newark, for instance, were singled out in both neighborhoods to illustrate how presumed temperamental, emotive, and moral differences between the groups were ultimately responsible for the changing demographic configurations of these communities. Likewise, these relationships served as a barometer of the state of intergroup relations, as they were suggestive of both hostility and collaboration across racial and ethnic lines. Everyday folk theories of race and relationships focused on how these groups' animosity toward one another could be traced "back to colonial times," in the case of Brazilians and Portuguese, or to moments of "taking over" local business or a Dominican "invasion" of Puerto Rico, in the case of Puerto Ricans and Dominicans. Despite the clear competition for local resources, and their marginality for broader urban development projects, dominant interpretations of the conditions of these groups focused on differences in affect and temperament, especially through the lenses of gender and sexuality. Mirta Arroyo, a Puerto Rican ESL teacher in her sixties who taught for more than ten years at ESHS before moving to Barringer High School, compared the two schools by saying:

To tell you the truth, they have the same problems at ESHS that we do here [at Barringer]. When I was there the problems were not as bad. Most of the students there were Portuguese. But now more Brazilians are coming in. . . . And Brazilians are very sexual, very loose, you know. . . . In that sense, they have the same problems that we have with Dominicans here. Dominicans are very sexual too. I've heard these students talking about things that even older people don't talk about. Many Portuguese are leaving after the Brazilians started coming, just like many Puerto Ricans are leaving Newark because of the Dominicans.

The stereotype of questionable sexual mores, presumably applicable to both Dominicans and Brazilians in North Newark and the Ironbound, respectively, yielded the same result: old-time Portuguese and Puerto Rican residents were leaving the area, finding Brazilians and Dominicans to be unacceptable neighbors. Although the particularities of the relationship between Brazilians and Portuguese or Dominicans and Puerto Ricans have been discussed elsewhere (see Feldman-Bianco 2001; Duany 1998), these interactions were continuously reformulated, malleable, and highly contextual.[10] In both neighborhoods there were hierarchies that rendered some groups as hypersexual and primitive; Dominicans in North Newark and Brazilians in the Ironbound occupied equivalent positions in the ways in which they were racialized by North Newark Puerto Ricans and Ironbound Portuguese, respectively. This logic of urban erotics provided the possibility to transgress endogamous expectations that were otherwise still inspected and regulated by families, communities, and peers.

Emotions are often experienced viscerally, "a connection to the external world vibrating in individual bodies" (Cavell 1998), while also representing the world as being a certain way. Thus, the emotive has shifted to a public sphere, not only accessible to but, more important, also constitutive of neoliberalism and capital accumulation.[11] Rosemary Hennessy (2000) re-evaluates the intersection of affect and capitalism, in terms of consumption and pleasure, as it is rearticulated through contemporary global formations such as neoliberalism. She highlights how neoliberalism mystifies its own forms of producing knowledge and power through contemporary values such as entrepreneurial spirit, self-help culture, volunteerism, and forms of morality rooted in free will and personal responsibility. Likewise, Dennis Altman (2001) and Elizabeth Bernstein (2007) argue that globalization is altering patterns of intimacy; while Altman focuses on the shift from arranged marriages to marriage for love and the heightened commodification of women of color's bodies in global sex trades, Bernstein coins the term "bounded authenticity" to highlight the desire for authentic intimate sexual encounters informed by service work, the global information economy, and "postmodern" families. More significantly, against the grain of contemporary sociological studies of culture that associate the infiltration of capitalism into everyday life with utilitarian capitalist transactions devoid of emotional content, Bernstein argues that the desire for intimacy grows as feelings of alienation intensify. Market-based cultural repertoires shape and inform interpersonal and emotional relationships as they become intertwined with the language of psychology. Together, these idioms offer new self-management techniques and meanings that incite new forms of sociability. An increasingly valued "racial expertise" and "urban competence," two concepts central to my work, further illuminate how these new forms of self-management and sociability unfold among a population that has traditionally being excluded from the "self-help" and psychological culture literature: working-class youth of color in US urban areas.

Dating sometimes provided a porous space in which to acknowledge partial forms of belonging, rather than sustaining rigid views of "insider" and "outsider," precisely because of the inherent ambiguity of emotionally charged contexts. Oftentimes, positions of incomplete or almost belonging insinuated certain recognition of how folk theories of race at times challenged rigid group boundaries.

Despite the encouraged individualistic stance in the interpretation of racial situations, affect stereotypes responded to neoliberal forms of highly gendered and sexualized cultural markets so as to engage a form of self-packaging that addressed the demands of particular market niches for these "exotic at home" (di Leonardo 1998). These forms of self-packaging required that Latino and Latin American migrants, particularly women, deploy nonmarket strategies that relied on normative perspectives of physical *and* emotional attractiveness to insert themselves in local job markets. As discussed below, self-care—both in terms of taking care of one's appearance and one's safety—became an organizing theme in the context of specific market niches that required forms of body and emotional labor. Thus, affect stereotypes mediated the insertion of young US-born and, particularly, some Latin American migrant women into labor niches that were highly susceptible to essentialist views of culture.

Looking Pretty, Getting Jobs: The Economy of Looks and "Self-Care"

When Myrian Caldeira and I arrived at the small boutique in the Ironbound where Emília Ribeiro worked, Emília had already done the daily accounting and folded the clothes that customers had tried on, and was in the process of ironing out the more delicate gowns with a hand vaporizer. It was almost the end of her workday and Emília, a tall, slim, and very stylish young woman who had arrived from Belo Horizonte as a young child, seemed happy with the commission she would be getting from selling a prom dress to an ESHS classmate that day.

Let me tell you, a Hispanish girl came to buy a dress today. That's something I notice with Hispanish girls, they don't see that they wear those tight dresses and the fat is going to form like little rolls hanging. She asks me, "Do you like this and that?" And I'm thinking, you look fat, but you like the dress and I just want to sell her the dress. She goes to this school and she's going to be wearing this dress to go to prom. But, what could I say, right? "Yes, yes, that looks beautiful on you!" I mean, let me tell you, this dress had a deep cleavage and no lining! [She points to her own body to show the exact pattern of the dress.] So she buys this dress . . . and now she'll be wearing that to our prom.

Ironically, though perhaps not entirely surprising, Emília and her mother, a bartender and waitress at a local bar, lived in an area of the Ironbound that was poor and predominantly black and US-born Latino. Whereas for Myrian being considered "Hispanic" did not necessarily imply losing status and, in fact, at times, when connected to the "right" (non-Mexican or Ecuadorian) Latinos, even enabled the acquisition of a much-valued urban competency, Emília avoided a "Hispanic" identity as a form of preserving a modicum of cultural capital in the United States.

Myrian, who was one of the Brazilian students most interested in exploring friendships with "Hispanics," would always intervene whenever something potentially insulting was said about a Latino, maybe because she sometimes wondered if I would be offended by a particular comment. This time, she focused on the irony in Emília's description of the "Hispanish" customer in the skimpy dress: "Emília, what are you talking about? Our school's very dress code was instituted because of the skimpy clothes you wear!" Somewhat offended that Myrian and I could not help but chuckle at the idea that this was the very person who inspired East Side's institutionalized dress code, Emília retaliated: "But you [to Myrian] were the one who gave me the skimpy shirts when you got into the church!" After many years of wearing clothes similar to those Emília wore, now Myrian wore baggier clothes and tended to be more conservative, attending some of the numerous Christian youth group events in the Ironbound. In a no-nonsense fashion, Emília attempted to end the conversation by adding: "Plus, I come from hot weather!"

When Myrian suggested that Emília dressed in the same provocative way as the "Hispanic" women she was talking about, Emília accentuated the inappropriate behavior of "Hispanics" (e.g., fashion sense, unwelcomed advances by the men). Talk of style and fashion supplied a generative symbolism with which to articulate other things that were perceived as wrong or bad, but for which no consensus of interpretation existed, including other kinds of loss, such as lack of citizenship or full citizenship, "illegality," and changes in the neighborhood. Talk of fashion and style added to the drama of the narration of events that may have otherwise been intangible or unremarkable, but whose consequences can be distressing. Emília made it clear that she did not so much object to the type of dress, but to the type of body on which the dress would be displayed. This became more evident when I asked her and three other Brazilian students at ESHS, during part of a focus group interview, about their impressions of how Brazilians saw other Latinos. Emília and Myrian entered into the following discussion:

Emília: We see them all the same. We can't really tell the difference between Uruguayans, Colombians. . . . Hispanics have the same shape [tem a mesma forma]. They have a bad body shape [tem mala forma]. They are short, round, short necks, no butt.

Group: [Laughter]

Myrian: Those are the Mexicans and the Ecuadorians only. They have that short square body.

Emília: You see them walking down the street and you just know who they are. They stand at the corner of Market and Ferry, right there, and the men scream at you. "Mamiiiii, mamiiiii!" They scream even when I'm walking with my boyfriend. Like they have never seen a woman before! Very disrespectful.

AY: Is that only with Hispanic guys? Do other guys do that too?

Emília: Hmm. . . . No, black guys are more like "I'm cool" and they have that attitude, like they are tough, they won't pay attention or call things out. They act like they own the street. They're just walking with that style [mimicks hip-hop/rap-like poses].

Myrian: Puerto Rican guys are like that, too.

AY: What about white guys?

Emília: We don't have white guys here.

Myrian: They live in other towns.

These young women depicted a politics of streetcorner interactions that were decidedly gendered racialized, and which informed their everyday perceptions of desirability, racialized embodiment, and respectability. These politics of streetcorner interactions were never too distant from a perspective on self-commodification and one's marketability as worker. Those Hispanics who had a mesma forma or uma mala forma would not get the job at the boutique that sold "dental floss" bathing suits and thong underwear. As Emília often noted, their backs were "too broad" and they "nao tem bunda" (had no butt). A focus on body shape also rendered these Hispanics almost androgynous, as the same comments on the body applied to women and men, even when the lack of respectability (acting "as if they had never seen a woman before") was specific to these young women's experiences with Hispanic men. When I probed into the racial specificity of these streetcorner interactions, a focus on African American men's ownership of space appeared in tandem with the absence of whites (which here specifically meant unhyphenated whites, suburban Americans and excluded the Portuguese). Ultimately, these politics of streetcorner interactions were never far removed from the emotional adequacy that was required to gain employment in the Ironbound.

Emília was one of the workers who could be considered to have a high degree of emotional capital that served her in the "emotional body labor" (Kang 2003) she performed at the boutique. When Mildred Irizarry, a Puerto Rican student at East Side High School, explained to her friend Vivian Rovira, who was also a Puerto Rican Ironbound resident, that she had applied for the same coveted job at the boutique where Emília worked, she explained the fact that she didn't get the job by saying that "Emília has a better look to be clerk at that store." "That's a great job," Vivian acknowledged. To these two young women, who had extensive experience working in retail and were confident in their ability to navigate Newark, it made "perfect sense" that Emília had been the chosen candidate not only because of her personal attractiveness, but also because she was a "people person" and her Brazilian nationality was globally recognized in various gradations of "exotic beauty." From early on, US-born Latinas recognized the professions in which "exotic" led to employment, boutique work sometimes being one of them. Emília entered an employment niche that required that she induced in customers positive feelings about their bodies, a trait common in jobs that required a great deal of body emotional labor. Mildred and Vivian recognized that Emília—like many of the other "pretty" and "nice" Brazilian students with whom they attended high school in the Ironbound—had those qualities.

Miliann Kang's study (2003) of "body labor" reformulates Arlie Hochschild's (1983) concept of "emotional labor" to dramatize that the "feeling rules" governing its exchange are shaped by interlocking oppressions that operate at the macro level (cf. Hill Collins 2000) and then emerge as different styles of emotional service at the micro level. In her seminal study of flight attendants, Hochschild (1983) coins the term "emotional labor" to describe instances when the emotional style of offering a paid service is part of the service itself. The workers providing such services are required to learn and enact the feeling norms, in the form of publicly observable facial and bodily displays, associated with a prescribed appropriate intensity, duration, and target of emotions in specific social situations of exchange. Emotional labor is sold for wages and, therefore, has exchange value (Hochschild 1983, 11, 19; cf. Hochschild 1990). "Body labor" involves exchanges of body-related services (e.g., beauty salons, spas, personal trainers) for a wage and the performance of physical and emotional labor in this exchange (Kang 2003, 826). Three distinct kinds of "body labor" include a high-source body labor involving physical pampering and emotional attentiveness; expressive body labor involving artistry in technical skills and communication of respect and fairness; and routinized body labor involving efficient, competent physical labor and courteous but minimal emotional work. In Kang's study of Korean nail salons in New York, the specific demographics of the neighborhoods where the salons were located dictated the pattern of body labor required of the Korean employees. The concept of "body labor" serves to explore the embodied dimensions of emotional work and investigate the intersections of race, gender, and class in shaping its performance. Kang retheorizes emotional labor to have greater applicability to the gendered occupations dominated by racialized immigrant women. She highlights emotional management regarding bodily contact in service interactions. The dynamics of extended physical contact between women of different racial and class positions complicate and intensify the gendered performance of emotional labor (823).

Latino and Latin American young adults in Newark were highly responsive to work conditions, sustaining evidence that people are more sensitive to environmental forces at the time they acquire a new role, like becoming a main contributor to the household. As Shanahan, Finch, Mortimer, and Ryu (1991) found in their study of adolescent work experience, work experiences affect depressive moods, even when adolescent workers are more emotionally independent from their parents than nonworking adolescents. In light of these findings, young Latinos in Newark paid great attention to the personal characteristics, body aesthetics, embodied mannerisms, and social skills valued in the labor market niches available to them. They are genuinely therapists of street interactions, who are able to engage in a practiced discernment of neoliberally favored forms of being in public.

To be successful in service sector jobs that involved body work, an employee must master a display of feelings (Goffmanian "surface acting") that may or may not be in alignment with her private experience of emotion itself ("deep acting"). Workers involved in such forms of emotional and body labor are continuously invested in avoiding and negotiating conflict with customers that could quickly become racialized into heated confrontations and even neighborhood-wide conflict; thus, this form of emotional labor, was also critical in maintaining "civility in the city" (Lee 2002). The race and class of the neighborhood complicates, in this sense, emotional management within its institutions (Lasch Quinn 2001).[12] If the transmutation of private sentiments into public acts involves such great emotional and body labor, critical questions that emanate from such a body of literature and which receive some attention in subsequent chapters are: How do immigrant youth and youth of color in the United States get prepared to engage in the emotional and body labor demanded in the predominantly service sector jobs that await them under neoliberalism and to what degree has acquiring racial knowledge and developing "appropriate" affect become forms of social capital among many Latin Americans and US-born Latinos? A more troubling aspect to such questions concerns the degree to which cultivating those forms of social and cultural capital (a neoliberal-friendly attitude) among Latinos and Latin American migrants in fact require the detachment from the "inadequate" affect of blacks.

Not one of the many young men or women whom I interviewed in Newark alluded to the fact that maybe "beauty is in the eye of the beholder"; attractiveness was never viewed as subjectivity but as commodity. In fact, there was surprising degrees of consensus about who the attractive people were, partly because beauty was oftentimes conflated with notions of popularity and friendliness that have been noted to be classed and racialized (e.g., Bettie 2003). What was perhaps more noteworthy, however, was the fact that a hierarchy of attractiveness was not solely dependent on "looks" in the aesthetic physical sense, but also on appearance more broadly defined to include self-care, mannerisms, friendliness, and, ultimately, one's potential to become a "good worker" and get a "good job." A hierarchy of attractiveness that was surprisingly consistent among US-born Latinos and Latin American migrants, particularly in the Ironbound, was articulated by Michelle Sánchez. Michelle was one of the many US-born Latinas who definitively stated: "The most attractive people in this school are the Brazilians. All the guys agree that the Brazilian girls have great bodies, that they are hot. We see the Portuguese as unattractive." I also heard comments by teachers at ESHS claiming that sometimes Portuguese girls tried to "pass" for Brazilians to get the attention of some of the guys, just like some Portuguese guys were hoping to become more desirable by pretending to be Puerto Rican.

While US-born Latino girls like Mildred and Vivian were able to read discrimination and favoritism when a Portuguese classmate got hired for a job to which Latinos or blacks had applied in the Ironbound, they thought it made perfect sense that Brazilians would get jobs "because they're attractive." In fact, Brazilians' ability to be seductive was partly narrated and presented as evidence of Brazilian women's superiority; among US-born Latinas, Brazilians were praised for having a valued form of sexual capital that Portuguese women presumably lacked:

Michelle Sánchez: Emília is the prettiest girl in this school. Emília and Maura. Definitely. And they're both Brazilian.

Migdalia Rivera: My cousin dated a guy who lived Down Neck [in the Ironbound] and now goes to Montclair State [University]. Everybody thought he was really hot. My cousin was so nervous when he went to college, because she was still in high school and, you know, he has all these women interested and she being in high school and all. They couldn't see each other as much. He was Brazilian so, you know, they are very attractive people.

Vivian Rovira: When the Brazilians won the World Cup in 2002, there was this girl on Third Street walking around with a Brazilian flag painted on her body with nothing on. Just the painted flag, no clothes. And she's walking around with the Brazilian flag paint. All the guys were just throwing water at her and she's just smiling and laughing. She had an amazing body, because she was, you know, curvy but thin with a butt and . . . We are like, "Go put some clothes on! You'll make all of us look bad!" [laughed] But there are many images of Brazilians, because you have the ones who are athletic, on the volleyball team, and then you have this other one that may be slutty or really smart. All guys think Brazilians have beautiful bodies, no matter what, all guys think that. They can be a little vain sometimes.

What seemed quite clear among most of the US-born Latino students with whom I spoke in Newark, and which appeared more ambiguous among some Portuguese adults in the Ironbound neighborhood, was that the image of Brazilian attractiveness appeared to be recurrent among high school youth and very well protected by many Brazilians transnationally. For instance, when the *New York Times* published a photograph of three "overweight" women on the beach in Ipanema to illustrate a report on the rise of obesity in Brazil, numerous postings appeared on an online Brazilian website in the United States criticizing the article. The ultimate vindication happened when it was later discovered that the women in the photographs were not even Brazilian, but Czech tourists visiting Rio de Janeiro. The three women threatened to sue the newspaper for the embarrassment, but many Brazilian readers focused on the fact that a US newspaper would describe Brazilian women as fat when they viewed the United States to have an even more serious issue with obesity.[13]

When I mentioned the article to Paula Pereira, a Brazilian student at East Side and Ironbound resident, her father, an outgoing and boisterous man, overheard us talking and said: "I have never seen as many fat people as in the U.S. Here everybody's so fat! I gained a lot of weight when I got to this country, because I wasn't exercising and the change in foods. But here that's an obsession. . . . E o *New York Times* para limpar a bunda! [and *The New York Times* to clean one's ass!]."

We all laughed, but it was never entirely clear what the specific material gains from being considered "beautiful" or, more precisely, desirable were, or why the image was so protected. Could being invested in the creation of this Brazilian stereotype be viewed as a way of avoiding the Hispanic stigma without necessarily diverting to an assimilation into the US mainstream that would perhaps be an impossibility?

Emília confessed to falling into a severe depression after migrating to the United States. She attributed the depression to having gained weight, because all she was doing to make herself feel better was eating and not exercising. Rather than seeing perhaps a more dialectical connection between emotional eating and depression, Emília assumed that her weight gain was the cause, not symptom, of her depression. While the propensity of eating disorders among white women have frequently been attributed to a pressure for "thinness" encouraged in popular media, one of the most striking findings in Becky Wangaard Thompson's (1992) study of eating problems and race was the range of traumas associated with the origins of eating disorders among Latina and black women, including the central role of poverty, heterosexism, class injuries, acculturation, and abuse. This analysis of racial distinctions in the onset of eating disorders among women provides a better context for the centrality of concerns with body image, nutrition, and exercise that I noted in Brazilian migrants like Emília. More important, though, while body consciousness among the many working-class Latinas whom I met in Newark was not centered on an aesthetic of thinness (as is the case among white women of middle- and upper-class backgrounds), it did provide a basis for reading "sexuality" in very particular racialized ways. In particular, as discussed later in this chapter, many US-born Latinas and Latin American migrant women read black women's sexuality in terms of body shape; references to black lesbians or "aggressive" black women were almost always premised on a "look" of an overweight or big-boned, masculine-looking woman who was careless about her appearance and had a volatile temperament. In fact, discussions that connected sexuality, temperament, and appearance were emblematic of ways in which psychologizing is no longer the realm of professionals, but also unfolds in everyday therapeutic discourses that have reached and conditioned neighborhood-level interactions. As Lauren Berlant's discussion of a "new public sphere" reveals, citizenship appears "as a condition of social membership produced by personal acts and values" (1997, 5), as private matters constitute the public realm.

What many US-born Latina and Latin American migrant women appeared to view in light of attractiveness and desirability also has to be situated in an aesthetic of "self-care" that existed at the neighborhood and even city level in Newark. According to this urban aesthetic, "taking care of oneself" had at least two equally loaded complementary meanings: caring for one's safety in the Newark streets (i.e., being street smart or competent) and caring for one's appearance. This urban aesthetic is different from Bourdieu's "ethos of self-cultivation," the characteristic of the upwardly mobile petite bourgeoisie, which Bourdieu sums up as "the dream of social flying, a desperate effort to defy the gravity of the social field" (1984, 370). As Foucault reminds us in *History of Sexuality*, the care of the self, cast in medical metaphors of health, paradoxically encourages a view of a "sick" self in need of transformation, so that "health" could be mobilized as a motif for the legal apparatus to legislate over the mad or the perverse (Foucault and Hurley 1990). Moreover, however, to be psychologically healthy came to mean being a competent member of a liberal society. Eating habits, personal hygiene, and overall "appearance" were criteria that had the power to characterize some US-born Latinas and African American women as psychologically damaged, while rendering others as competent workers.

"Self-care" was predicated on tacit forms of emotional capital, as illustrated by a sign I saw on the window of a restaurant in North Broadway: "Se solicita mesera con buena presencia [Waitress wanted with good appearance]." "Buena presencia" refers, I argue, not only to physical look or appropriate attire, but also to the ability to express "caring" and "emotional attentiveness" to customers in ways that are heteronormative—measured by flirtation, charm, and other imponderables. What is required is not only the ability to serve food and take orders efficiently, but also the ability to turn the dining (or drinking) experience into a form of subtle pampering. The ability to dissimulate emotions means that emotions are also tactical resources, employed by social actors to gain power and respect. Although I did not meet anyone who applied for the job advertised on the restaurant window, I did ask many of my interviewees if they had ever sensed that employers were looking for a particular "type" when they hired someone. Overwhelmingly, the young US-born Latino and Latin American women provided examples that confirmed this. What they most frequently noted was that employers sought someone who "took care of themselves," a loaded term that served multiple descriptive functions. The positioning of race, gender, and sexuality in the terrain of affect and self-care served as an example of how new liberalism, with its ability to reduce "big" issues to personal events, thus flattening and depoliticizing them, could prove even more effective in keeping subordinate populations at bay than collective hostility (cf. Rabinowitz 1997, 184).

While some forms of "self-care"—like frequenting hair and nail salons—could be considered a form of luxury among young women of color, these were also aspects of "upkeeping" that were central to getting a job but always outside any consideration of the relationship between adolescent employment, migration, urban life, and stress levels, including eating disorders among working-class women of color. Practices of enhancing bodily appearance have, in this sense, selectively been repositioned from private households into new forms of public urban space. Perhaps the most dramatic manifestation of this in Newark consisted of the "Brazilian bikini wax," which was a heightened version of body labor: This very intimate process was possibly a most direct illustration of how formerly private regimes of personal hygiene are established in the service economy; this can generate highly charged feelings on both client and service provider and the closeness to someone else's private body parts is really hard to interpret. These are emotional and embodied interactions reflective of larger systems of status and power; by "rewriting the unspoken feeling rules of these interactions, women can take small but important steps in the creation of more equal relations with other women" (Kang 2003, 837).

Although the sexualized Brazilian woman and, more recently, the gay Brazilian man, have been in the US popular imagination at least since the New Deal, these images have been transformed in Newark (Santiago 1994). Despite the evaluation of these stereotypes of the tropics and seductiveness as alternative forms of cultural capital among US-born Latinos, however, many Brazilian women actively aimed to disassociate themselves from an image of hypersexuality and, more generally, of leisure that other Central and South American migrants and Portuguese Ironbound residents attributed to them. Among some of the young Brazilian women whom I met in Newark, processes of conversion, deliberate transformation, and refashioning of the self were oftentimes in tacit dialogue with the broader image of Brazilian "cultural excess" (Ramos-Zayas 2008). The cases of Myrian Caldeira, Emília's friend and a devoted member of an evangelical youth group, and of Erika da Silva, a Goth student who had just moved from the Portuguese bilingual program into the "mainstream" curriculum at the Ironbound public high school, illuminated these "conversions."

Myrian told me that she had begun attending a local Brazilian evangelical church as a result of a brush with the police when, at fourteen, she was caught attending a club, a few weeks after arriving from Belo Horizonte. She was at the club, accompanied by some of her parents' friends, in an effort to fight off a severe depression she experienced upon migrating to the United States and gaining a lot of weight. I was never fully clear about how to interpret Myrian's connection to this particular club, because in another instance she mentioned that she had worked as a barmaid and had gotten "involved with men" just a few months after arriving in Newark, but she never connected the two incidents and I always refrained from probing into what I sensed was a very sensitive topic.[14] Myrian made several comments about having "talked about the Lord" to a group of prostitutes that circulated near the area where she lived. Whereas religious converts like Myrian were usually viewed as judgmental and even ashamed of their own culture—which was viewed to revolve around music, dancing, and even wearing provocative clothes—secular converts presented themselves as more hyperindividualistic and assimilated.[15] Myrian's "conversion" narrative resonated with what has been documented about young Latinas in Union City, New Jersey, who explained that a positive by-product of their conversions to Islam was the increasing respect they gained from men in the streets when they wore the hijab. They avoided undesired whistling and felt less pressured to subscribe to fashion trends that favored revealing or provocative clothes.[16] Interestingly, while being serious, withdrawn or depressed was oftentimes associated with being Americanized and urban (chapter 6), the happiness of religious converts was viewed as authentic and qualitatively different from the fake cheerfulness associated with naïve migrants or white Americans.

Erika da Silva viewed her transformation to Goth in light of broader familial expectations she sensed from her parents and relatives while growing up in Paraná and Newark, and which required that she transformed herself to conform to more traditional gender roles directed at guarding perspectives on sexual autonomy whenever she would go to visit her family in Paraná. Erika explained:

I never liked to wear what other girls were wearing or to be looking all pretty, you know. I started going to the vintage stores and seeing things that I liked, whatever clothes made me feel better. . . . In the beginning, my mom would tell me, "You'll never find a boyfriend dressing up like that." But she leaves me alone, except when I go to Brazil, to visit family. Then she tells me, "Tone it down." I don't like to be pigeon holed, you know. I'm my own person.

AY: Do you feel . . . do you identify as Brazilian or do you . . . ?

Erika: I don't care or not if they say I'm Brazilian. It's not something that I announce, "I'm Brazilian, I'm Brazilian." If someone asks me, I'd say, "Sure, I am." Sometimes people try taking guesses at what I am. [They guess] Italian, German. . . . Nobody guesses American. They also never guess Brazilian. Because a lot of people here have this misconception about Brazilian people. They think the girls are like, I don't know, they think they are really loud and they want attention and they wear these skimpy clothes and, you know, that they just go out with lots of guys, stuff like that. I'm not like that. And even some of the Brazilian girls here are very smart and they have been here for a while, so they are not as in touch with the whole Brazilian thing. I also think that I'm not like that because of where my family is from. Paraná is very different from the rest of Brazil. In Paraná we even have people that are German. They still speak German in their daily lives.

Ironically, while Goths generally take pride in their sexual experimentation and flaunt their rejection of sociosexual mores (Wilkins 2008), in Erika's case Brazilian-ness meant complying with gendered norms related to sexuality. She was not necessarily rejecting Brazilian presumed hypersexuality, but the normativity of such hypersexuality. Erika identified the simplistic and always-already gendered stereotype of Brazilians, but she adopted a somewhat passive stance in relation to a presumed Brazilian identity (unless she's directly asked, she won't state that she's Brazilian or see this as a source of pride to be articulated openly). However, because Erika had developed a kind of sensitivity to generalizations, given the marginality that she had occasionally experienced by being Goth in mainstream contexts, she immediately emphasized that neither she nor many Brazilian women fit into the stereotype (using "very smart" in contraposition to "want[ing] attention" or wearing revealing clothes). She then proceeded to reshape or rearticulate the stereotype by explaining the seeming discrepancy between the stereotype and the reality by saying that the stereotype doesn't fit a particular subgroup of Brazilians (those who "have been here for a while" and, therefore, "are not in touch with the whole Brazilian thing").

Although Erika continued to sustain the Brazilian stereotype by explaining how some people did not fit into it (and thus presumed others did), she proceeded to challenge stereotypes of the tropics at an even more fundamental level, by removing Brazil (and some Brazilians like herself) from the tropics in the first place, by introducing "Paraná": There are Germans in Brazil and the regional racial variation was viewed as a stance from which to launch a critique of the stereotype of the tropics, which are then presumably more in line with other areas of Brazil, particularly Rio de Janeiro and Salvador da Bahia. It is also interesting that the fact that nobody ever "guess[ed] American" in their description of Erika was viewed by her as positive; she had repeatedly commented, in relation to whites, that Americans were "too bland."

When Myrian commented on the fact that the dress code at ESHS had been instituted because of her friend Emília's revealing dress style, Emília's immediate response—which was both tongue-in-cheek and somewhat serious—was that she was "from hot weather." The fact that Emília knew that Myrian, who was originally from Salvador da Bahia, and I were both from "hot weather" suggests how Emília's own explanation for wearing revealing clothes was less an effort to distinguish herself from us and more a rearticulation of a "moral-climatic idiom" (Livingstone 1993, 139) that dominated the Ironbound's gendered landscape and which, by its naturalization of racial difference according to climatic classifications, placed those of "the dark races"—in the case of the Ironbound, the Brazilians and, to a lesser extent, the other Latin Americans and Latinos—at the bottom of geography's moral terrain (cf. Kobayashi and Peake 2000, 399). Nevertheless, this moral-climatic idiom operated in tandem with an alternative scale of desire that valued images of seduction that were situated in the urban erotics in which Brazilian and Portuguese in the Ironbound were implicated. Every single comment I heard during the five years of my fieldwork, from Brazilian and Portuguese alike, as well as the mainstream media rendition of life in the Ironbound, ultimately reduced any conflict between the two groups as having to do with differences in "dress codes," "temperament," "the weather," or gender ideologies. The narrative by Marta Lima, a Portuguese parent-volunteer at ESHS, was somewhat typical of this:

The Brazilians are a whole different group, even different from the Hispanics, you know. They are South Americans, but they have their own joie de vivre. It's just a whole other concept that they have. I think it definitely comes from the climate, because it is so hot, so humid there. They wear appropriate dress for that type of climate except that they want to bring it over here. . . . We're more conservative and they come from a warm climate or from an Island, in the case of the Hispanics. Showing belly and being dressed in a certain way comes natural to them because of the climate. It's just natural to them. But [Portuguese] parents don't understand that.[17]

Differences between Portuguese and Brazilians were generally attributed to variations in the Portuguese language, "temperament," "dress style," and "looks," and they overshadowed the internal variation of these populations which were viewed as discrete, somewhat homogenous groups.[18] Moreover, an urban erotics operating here accentuated how Brazilians were viewed as having the potential, by their virtual increasing presence in the formerly "Portuguese" space of the Ironbound, not only to racialize or challenge the whiteness-in-the-making of the Portuguese residents by introducing some gendered elements associated with US working-class "minorities"—the loudness, revealing clothes, racial markedness—but also to possibly increase the vulnerability of undocumented Portuguese with an increased surveillance by the state. And yet, there is another element to be considered in the otherwise largely negative moral assessments of Brazilians by most Portuguese residents of the Ironbound: the valorization that most US-born Latinos attributed to the image of seductress they associated, somewhat enviously, with Brazilian women.

A "stereotype of the tropics" dominated discussions of Brazilian exceptionalism in the largely Portuguese Ironbound neighborhood, while similar conceptions of Latina women as seductresses were deployed in contradistinctions to views of black women as "aggressive." Brazilian cultural excess was highly predicated on the actual and perceived exposure of young women's brown bodies in spaces historically marked as "Portuguese," including Ferry Street, the main commercial thoroughfare of the Ironbound. When describing the Brazilian Independence Day celebrations in New York or festivities around the World Cup soccer victory, what many Brazilian and non-Brazilian spectators alike noted was that Brazilian women were "walking around with just the Brazilian flag painted on their naked bodies." As Gustavo Ribeiro notes in his study of the Brazilian carnival celebration in San Francisco, "Brazilian women that, in some cases, would not go to a Carnival ball in their hometowns [in Brazil] wearing minuscule costumes, do so in front of a crowd and TV cameras." As Ribeiro's analysis suggests, these women are "showing Brazilian culture." In fact, he further argues, "while some cultural workers feel there is a need to promote other visions of Brazilian culture, most of them agree that it is the sensuality of the bodies and of the dancing that calls attention to their work and allows them to sell Brazilian shows in an ethnically segmented cultural market" (Ribeiro 1997, 14).

The precarious line between playfully seductive and inappropriate moral conduct always seemed to permeate discussions of Brazilian "temperament" and difference. The racial composition of Newark neighborhoods influenced notions of attractiveness and desirability and produced "economies of desire" (Hennessy 2000) in ways that reproduced neoliberal versions of "racial democracy" among Latinos and Latin American migrants. The process transformed stereotypes from rigid and inevitable categorizations to an ideological fascination and creative template on which to rearticulate one's own relationship to a highly stigmatized urban space and its oftentimes corrupt or tacit racial politics. A component of these urban erotics, however, also involved sustaining the impression that one could alter racial politics and racism not necessarily in the terrain of rights but in the affective and erotic terrain, despite consistent evidence to the fact that racism had deeper structural and political economic roots in the United States.[19]

The Telenovelas of Everyday Life: Brazilian "Husband Stealers" and Latin American Narratives of Forbidden Love

My encounter with Marcela de Souza was partly facilitated by her saudade, a common Portuguese language word to describe homesickness or longing for one's country. In later conversations, Marcela mentioned that she had left Brazil because, in her town, one was considered old if one was hitting fifty. "I still feel young, but they would consider me an old woman," she explained. Her two children were grown and she had been divorced for over ten years. She wanted to find "adventure." She wanted to go to Spain, but she knew nobody there, and ended up going to Portugal. Marcela was still hopeful that she could go back to Europe to live, even if she had to be there by herself. She proclaimed: "If you make it in the US, you can make it *anywhere*, because life here is so difficult. Everything is difficult here." One of Marcela's close friends had been in the United States for eight years and "still works at a coats factory." The fact that that friend, who had married a Puerto Rican man and was now a US citizen, still had to work long hours and was barely able to save any money, further convinced Marcela that life in the United States was inordinately difficult.

As I later learned over a period of several months of interacting with Marcela, Marcela's story was more "autobiographical" than she had initially admitted. Marcela had been the one to be "pursued" by the Portuguese woman's husband, though she always maintained that she never gave in to his advances.[20] Originally from the town of Governador Valadares, in Minas Gerais, Marcela was quite frank about other aspects of her life, including a brief involvement in the "entertainment" industry as an exotic dancer and sometimes "girlfriend" of the Brazilian owner of a bar in Portugal, where she had met the relative of the Portuguese owner of a bar in Newark who seemed to have been instrumental in gaining her migration to the United States later on.[21] There were several conversations that suggested Marcela's involvement in sex work without really explicitly labeling it that, a tendency that seems in itself very reflective of sex work—the fluid boundaries, the slippage between certain kinds of employment niches and prostitution, and distinctions between sex work as employment or even occasional employment versus sex work as an identity added to the ambiguity (cf. Comissão Parlamentar Mista de Inquérito da Emigração 2006).[22] All these issues account for the slippage in employing "sex worker" as an analytical category. And yet, it was a category referenced in the gendered racialization of Brazilians in Newark, especially by the Portuguese. I never heard of other Latin American migrants or US-born Latinos characterizing Brazilian women in any way that suggested immorality or promiscuity, which only highlighted the particularity of these characterizations to the relationship with the Portuguese and, likewise, the very vulnerability that led Portuguese to use these characterizations to distance themselves from the precariousness associated with being a racial minority in the United States.

Gossip about adultery and infidelity oftentimes segued into discussions of Brazilian prostitution in Newark. Faviola Costa, a graduate of ESHS who had become very involved in a predominantly Brazilian evangelical church in the Ironbound, seemed very troubled by the recurrent discourses she encountered regarding Brazilian women in Newark. After mentioning that she sensed that people looked at her and assumed she would just "run around naked" because she was Brazilian, Faviola mentioned that Portuguese women had generated these images of Brazilians' "lack of morals." Faviola explained:

There's a lot of problems between the young [Portuguese and Brazilian] people. Because sometimes . . . not sometimes, always . . . the Portuguese women think we're going to steal their men. Both the young and old Portuguese women think that. Because you always see a young Brazilian girl with an older Portuguese guy. And sometimes the Portuguese women say that those girls are a go-go or work as bar maids, but they're really not. The Portuguese women just say that. They are always frustrated. They always think, "Oh, the Brazilians are putas" or bitches. And that's not true. It bothers me a lot they think that.

Faviola also mentioned that, at the bakery where she had worked, she heard of a Brazilian woman who had married a Portuguese man and they had become the talk of the town because she used to be a barmaid when they met and, depending on who one asked, some claimed they met at a massage place where she worked and which was associated with prostitution. "This woman would cry all the time, because she felt judged by everyone. All that she wanted was to leave this neighborhood," Faviola explained with sympathy, but also as an almost cautionary moral tale.

Faviola's concerns were also represented in media coverage of the Ironbound, even as a moral assimilation of sorts. In an article titled "Assimilation through Penetration: Cultures Collide in Ironbound," journalist Mary Jo Patterson insists that the "city's Portuguese and Brazilians find life is a lesson in tolerance."[23] The article narrates the story of Silvio De Souza, owner of the *Prazilian Press*, one of numerous Portuguese-language newspapers in the Newark area, who, like many other single Brazilian men, arrived in Newark in 1985, as a "22-year-old seeking a better future than he could find in Brazil." As the articles states:

Along the way, [De Souza] fell in love and married. He and his wife have two children. That's what is happening to many young Brazilians, and it is creating a more stable, family oriented community that is likely to change Portuguese attitudes, he said. "There's competition. They like to say Brazilians are lazy, don't like to work, and that Brazilian girls are bitches- though they all love them— but it's changing," he said.

Infidelity, amorality, and sensual prowess were the subject of many conversations in which Portuguese attempted to define themselves in contradistinction to the Brazilian migrants.[24] The stereotype of the tropics, particularly in relation to Brazilians, acquired a dangerous dimension in the context of a budding sex-work industry in Newark and surrounding areas. Domestic minority and international women were actively recruited, oftentimes through deception or coercion, by falling prey to ambiguous job descriptions, seduced by the possibility of leaving poverty, and a general sense that any job—as domestic workers, hairstylist, bartender, and so on—could lead to a life in sex work. One's highly exoticized nationality always had the potential to be a money-generating device in a neoliberalism highly sensitive to identity politics in the United States (Comissão Parlamentar Mista de Inquérito da Emigração 2006, 336–37). Likewise, these stereotypes, while exploitative to the most vulnerable women, were magnified in the context of the Ironbound, where "Brazilian"-ness was always-already a gendered referent to "temperamental" and "moral" distinctions from the more "traditional"

Portuguese women. Everyday social dramas in the Ironbound offer a means to analyze how members of a group frame events in ways that enable talk of emotion to emerge. But, what roles do these events play in the social life of the community and what triggers them? Moreover, what are the contexts and situations that allow emotional displays in ritualized versus abrupt manners?

Among many Ironbound residents, particularly though not exclusively among the Portuguese, there was a persistent belief that Brazilian women were the main players in a growing acceptance of prostitution in Newark. As Fátima Teixeira, a Portuguese teacher and Ironbound resident, commented: "Now that New York doesn't want them, they dump them here in Newark." Upon further discussion, I realized that Fatima was alluding to the "cleaning up" of sex shops in New York's Time Square, and was insinuating that Brazilian sex workers had been displaced onto Newark, where "go-go dancing" bars and prostitution were less heavily castigated (Delany 2001). Hence, in Newark, and I suspect in other cities in the United States, the glamour or exoticization of Brazilian women's bodies existed alongside a criminalization of Brazilian sexuality. These social dramas were emblematic of the dominant global racialization that circumscribed Brazilian (and other) migrant women either to domestic work or sex labor, depending on the exotic demands of the market, and which likewise intersected with a national political economy in which US-born minority women were viewed as a liability to the state.

The sex industry in New Jersey is large and concentrated in big cities and suburbs, one of those high-density locations being Newark (Raymond, Hughes, and Gomez 2001; cf. Laumann 2004).[25] After New York created more stringent laws regulating sexual work in the 1980s, more strip bars and their clients moved to New Jersey, particularly Newark, where the laws are more permissible (Meihy 2004, 184). "Some people claim that many of the women that used to dance in New York's bars now come to Newark because New York laws are getting tougher, but in New Jersey anything goes," João Soares, a Brazilian clergy working at an evangelical church in the Ironbound, commented to the reporter of a *Star-Ledger* article. Many Brazilian and US newspaper articles sustained the presumed "cultural predisposition" of Brazilian women toward various forms of entertainment industry work, including sex work, in Newark, and oftentimes tended to draw these characterizations in contrast to Portuguese "traditionalism."[26]

In her ethnography of Brazilians in New York, Maxine Margolis sees go-go dancing in New York and New Jersey as a primarily Brazilian ethnic employment niche for women, even when most Brazilian women were more likely involved in domestic or restaurant work than in any other occupation.[27] Margolis interviewed Brazilians who described continuous sexual harassment on the part of patrons and clients, and who acknowledged the complex connections between go-go dancing and issues with prostitution and drugs. According to Margolis, Brazilians constituted 80 percent of the 2,000–3,000 "exotic" dancers in the greater New York metropolitan area, including New Jersey (1994, 158, 165, 166). The connection between Brazilian go-go dancers in Newark and the town of Governador Valadares in Brazil was believed to have further sparked an export business of Brazilian-made string bikinis to dancers in New York, New Jersey, Connecticut, and Massachusetts in the 1990s (Dines 1989, 89). Several agencies, including some owned by Brazilians, booked mostly Brazilian go-go dancers for bars and nightclubs, while other dancers operated independently and contracted with bars alone. A significant number of dancers worked in Newark, Elizabeth, and other towns in New Jersey that had Portuguese-speaking clientele and numerous bars through the 1980s and 1990s (cf. Margolis 1994, 163). A news article about Brazilian immigrants in Newark suggests that the only jobs available to Brazilian women there are as domestic servants, go-go dancers, and barmaids.[28]

When Ursula Gomes arrived from Brazil in the late 1990s, she was placed in seventh grade, but then was moved to eighth grade after a week because she was "too tall." She recalled her initial experiences at a public middle school in the Ironbound:

It was really hard, because I had never liked this language. I was placed in bilingual classes, but now I think that was a disadvantage. I got here [to high school] knowing no English, so I struggled a lot in my first and second years of high school. My sister got here in the fifth grade, and now she speaks English much better than I do. That school was one of the weakest schools here. Because the teachers there are all Portuguese, so if you have any difficulty speaking English, they speak to you in Portuguese and that's okay, they don't care.

Then Ursula added:

By then I had met some girls, all of them were from Brazil. It was three girls. One of them was from Belo Horizonte and the other ones were from Valadares. All I wanted was to be wild, to party. I didn't want to study. I was so young. I don't know how my parents let me do all this partying. I would beg them to let me go out with friends, to go to parties. And because they didn't want me to be lonely and depressed [as she had been when she first started school], they'd let me go out. I had been very depressed when I came to the United States. I missed playing volleyball in Brazil [where she had played volleyball in a civic league and in the streets] and became very fat with the food here, even if we had a lot of the same food that we did there. I would beg and beg and they'd let me. My first few months here had been so terrible; I had gotten fat, I wasn't playing volleyball, I didn't have any friends here, only me and my sister. It wasn't good at all. So then I started meeting people and started to go out. It's still hard to explain to people back in Brazil that you speak Portuguese all the time even in America.

Ursula had this to say about her work trajectory:

I work every Sunday at a little supermarket right here, called Emporium. I worked there in the deli. My first job was in a bar. I had a fake ID to work there. Then I worked at that bakery Delicias, the corner of Jackson, I worked there too. I worked at that little bar right outside of Iberia.

AY: What was it like, when you worked at the bars?

Ursula: At the bars I never had any problems. Only one girl, the owner, only she knew about me being underage. Her husband didn't know, but I think he suspected, because he'd always ask me many questions and I was so dumb. I didn't even calculated the date when I had to be born to be of legal age. It's easy to find jobs in bars, because they're always trying to find the young girls, who look good, and have the energy to do everything they do, but they always pay them little. The owners were Portuguese.

Whether sex work is more or less exploitative than any other employment niche available to Latin American migrants or domestic minority women is a difficult question to answer, particularly given the precarious and exploitative work conditions to which all Latin American migrants are subjected to in the United States. When Ursula described a neighborhood in North Broadway where a friend of hers lived, she mentioned liking the neighborhood and added:

The only problem is that there is some prostitution. You see in the corner, there are some girls there. You have to go and talk to them. My friend, she saw this girl in the corner, selling herself, and she went to her and talked to her about the love of God. And the girl started crying. The problem is that these girls, they don't have the clothes, they're always showing everything. I used to do that, too. I'd always show everything. These girls are always shy because they know what they're doing is wrong. They always think that someone's going to judge them, but we cannot judge them.

AY: So these women have they been there for a long time?

Ursula: Before my friend moved there, we never saw them, but now we always see one or two of them. Some of them are black girls and some of them Hispanic. Sometimes it can be dangerous, because they can be aggressive. They may not want to be bothered, you know.

Noted in Ursula's statement is the contradictory nature of moral standards and their disproportionate impact on poor women and women of color.[29] The oftentimes emotionally loaded relationships that surround sex work and the stigma attached to it, nevertheless, are very particular to this employment niche.[30] Moreover, sex work relies on racist and sexist representations to market women according to stereotypical behaviors and illusions of difference. As Raymond, Hughes, and Gomez found: "Men come to expect stereotypical behavior from the women they buy in prostitution. Also, buying women from different races and nationalities gives men the illusion of experiencing the 'different' or 'exotic.' Consequently, when men write about buying women in prostitution, they frequently mention the race and nationality of the women. . . . Brazilian was among the most mentioned nationalities" (2001, 41–42).[31] As cited in a 2001 report on the trafficking of women: "Even remotely located establishments were filled with Russian and Ukrainian women . . . and a significant number of Brazilian women."[32] Likewise, in the tourist guide *City Slicker: Newark*, Daniel Jeffreys mentions the Ironbound, not only as "the district immortalized in the Suzanne Vega song," but also as a "Portuguese and Brazilian district [in which] it is said that the descendants of pirates who live here have their own system of justice and do not tolerate gangs or street crime. But a turf war has begun between Russian and Brazilian call-girls. It seems many Brazilian men prefer the blonde Russians."[33] One article mentioned that a Brazilian couple owned a booking agency in New Jersey and were famed in the go-go dancing circles, and stated that "the Brazilian booking agents are doing very well financially" and could hardly handle all the business, they say, because "the appetite for Brazilian go-gos is insatiable" (Dines 1989, 88).

Rather than engaging in a more extensive description of Newark's sex industry, I want to focus on how gendered tensions tended to be articulated between Brazilians and Portuguese so that the sexual desire of Portuguese men became a sign of a liberal, even enlightened worldview, and not as part of an economically and racially skewed system, while Portuguese women were viewed as sexually "repressed" or as "traditional" depending on the interlocutor. The ambiguous and at times emotionally loaded work relationships in which Brazilian women were implicated (and whatever fantasy may exist behind them) depended on the creation of a context in which Brazilian women, and many other US-born Latina women, were asked to participate in their own sexual commodification partly for the purpose of sustaining an industry premised on their "ex-otic"-ness, and a widespread stereotype of the tropics. Many informants explained the existence of Brazilian sex workers in Newark and New York as a result of white and black American men favoring Brazilian mixed-race women, not only because of their "darkness" and "natural" sensuality, but also because they were not African American.[34] Hence, an exami-nation of the exoticization of Brazilian women necessitates, by its very definition, an examination of the labor market in which such images are possible, as well as the migration context that enables various forms of exploitative work conditions for these women. The work relations that developed in bars were complicated, and very difficult to disentangle, because they were also emotionally loaded with love and affect and con-flated with financial need and limited employment options.[35]

Operating here is the assumption that poor women and women of color have to build relationships that conform and suit the values of neo-liberalism by requiring that they carefully position themselves as objects of scrutiny and control their emotions, assess their choices, and choose a preferred course of action according to deeply refined calculations about intimate life and emotions. While gender becomes a sort of interactual resource and a form of social capital (Alcoff 1995), the normative femi-ninity and labor markets in which it is valued also require a form of racial learning. In the case of Latin American migrant women this is based not only on learning "the code of the streets" (Anderson 1990), but on distancing themselves from (or selectively embracing) those codes as-sociated primarily with black women (and, to a lesser extent, with other US-born minorities).

Stereotypes of affect unfolded in light of situations in which some bodies fit only in certain ways and yet, when those stereotypes were as-sumed, those to whom they were applied were still punished as "loose," amoral, and parasites of the system. These gendered stereotypes of the tropics were highly adaptable and malleable, and partly sustained by the fragility of the Portuguese's whiteness, noted in the fear that many Portu-guese expressed at the prospect of being confused for Brazilians, a group whose ambiguous standing in the US racial system still appeared to render them racially marginal, subordinate, and more likely to "assimilate" into a minority status rather than a coveted white "American"-ness. While most of the traditional stereotypes of Brazilian-ness were effectively chal-lenged in everyday life, new articulations of a US Brazilian-ness in gen-eral, and a local Brazilian-ness in particular, surfaced in Newark, a city in which urban legends were difficult to disentangle from people's loose recollections of particular incidents of "violence," "profanity," or real-life romantic drama. In this context, intrigue over infidelity, attraction, and sexual expressions were concepts commonly deployed in conversations that were really about social difference, downward mobility, and racial tension. Teasing about being a seductress and having the power to seduce any men, and multiple stories in which Latinas were presented as the object of desire of both white Portuguese and African American men, provided the context in which many of the Brazilian and Latin women whom I met racialized their own bodies, approximating an image of the "hot sexual mulata" that is part of traditional representations of "racial democracy" in Latin America, while also flirting with sexual images of black women in US media and pop culture (Ramos-Zayas 2007). These stereotypes of the tropics in fact belonged to a citywide gendered landscape in which the hypersexualized image of Brazilian women, in connection to presumptions of "sexual work," existed alongside views of Puerto Rican women as "unwed mothers" and of African American women as "violent" or "lesbians in gangs" (see chapter 5).

Love in the City: Masculinity, Illegality, and the "Welfare Mother"

Narratives of "forbidden" or "problematic" or "utilitarian" relationships were frequently life-imitating-art versions of Latin American soap operas, but also emblematic of how neither US-born Latinos nor Latin American migrants were able to make the affective narratives of their communities intelligible without tacit or explicit reference to the strong African American social currents in Newark. While imagination may have played an important role in the production and transmission of narratives around the problematic of romantic relationships, these very narratives were ensconced in traditional sociological discussions of racial difference. They were suggestive of an "emplotment of the self" (Ricoeur 1991), that is, the integration of various events in an individual's life within an overall narrative framework—a story—that carries a general social theme. Three of the most common social themes sustained from emplotment of the self included: (1) being from different sides of the tracks—how class and occupational distinctions created insurmountable obstacles in heterosexual relations; (2) ulterior motives for marriage—how marrying to gain legal status, a form of "marrying up," tainted "real love" in a form of entrapment; and (3) Romeo and Juliet–style love—when parents opposed a union usually based on race or nationality.

The first theme of real-life social dramas involved discussions akin to the trope of being "from different social strata," a typical theme in Latin American telenovelas. Such episodes foregrounded the relationships of lovers from different class backgrounds and, in its modern version, presented disheartened struggling women and men who could not be trusted. The "unreliable men" and victimized (but more mature and resilient) women narrative, in connection to conditions of class difference and subordination, were central in my conversations with Mario Ruiz and Marisol Padilla, both in their twenties and residents of North Broadway, who also worked at not-for-profit organizations in the area.

Mario Ruiz: My mom is Ecuadorian and my father is Puerto Rican, and there is a great difference in their backgrounds. My mother comes from a very wealthy family in Ecuador, very traditional. She didn't really move to the States, she escaped to the States to avoid a marriage that was being arranged for her. It's a weird story because my father comes from a very rural family, a campesino [country folk] family, in Puerto Rico. They are from Utuado, from a little barrio called Caguana, up in the mountains. My family in Ecuador, they are very formal. I remember when I was young and I visited, I had my own maid. They were from Guayaquil and Quito. My father, I later learned, didn't go to school in Puerto Rico. He was illiterate and he didn't have a trade. He was a con artist. That's what he did for a living. He would be gone for three or four days, and I would ask my mom, "Where is Dad?" and she would say, "Oh, he is on a business trip." So for the longest time I thought he was a salesman. And my mom was a welfare mom. She stayed home. For them, it was a matter of not being able to communicate, you know. They were just from two very different backgrounds."

Marisol Padilla: [The hardest thing about being a woman in Newark is] the lack of respect that the men have. It's a shame to say. I have a son. I don't want my son around some of my family members. Like, I have an uncle, one particular uncle I have. He's an asshole. You have to be barefoot and pregnant. He has no respect for women. All those guys standing in the corner. They have no respect. All they want is a big ass to walk in, to serve as their little mule. And when a girl's got her thing going on or when she's pushing her Mercedes, the first thing that comes out of their mouth is "That bitch's driving her man's car . . . you know she's not pushing her own weight." It's hard to say, though. Because a lot of women in a place like Newark don't have it in them to go out. Because I have a lot of friends who put up with their boyfriends going out with other women, beating on them, disrespecting them in every kind of way, just because they pay their rent. Then you have other women who are like, "No, I don't need a guy for that"' I think it's like that with the women our age now, because the men who are our age, they were brought up in a period where they had to hustle, where shit was brought. Because their parents had nothing or their parents were drunk. They were brought up a certain way and they're caught up in that life. The view of women as bitches.

Whenever Mario and I would be at the same community event, one of his main topics of interest was "welfare" and Puerto Ricans; particularly, he wanted to brainstorm about possible reasons why Puerto Rican women had "lost the drive" to work in the same way that newly arrived women from other Latin American countries did. He would supply evidence of Latin American women who could qualify for "aid," but had "too much pride and would choose to work hard instead." In one of his conversations, I asked him if he thought that his mother would have been able to survive and put two sons through college had she not received welfare and it was clear that he thought his mother was "very different from the typical welfare mother." Once I asked him why this was, and he answered: "My mother would not have needed to be on welfare. She was from a very rich family in Ecuador. They had maids and owned land. She had to get on welfare because of my father, but she was a well-educated woman." It was because she had "left all behind" and "ended up to marrying a Puerto Rican man" that forced Mario's mother to depend on "the system." In Mario's view, the association to welfare "dependency," in all its stigma, came from the Puerto Rican side of his family. It was because of his Puerto Rican con artist father that his mother, an otherwise well-educated and socially enfranchised woman in Ecuador, had to rely on welfare in the United States.

In these cases, transcending expectations of relational appropriateness resulted in intergroup dating and anecdotes of failed marriages or bad marital situations, and were oftentimes ensconced in narratives of family status, wealth, and inequality, as in the case of Mario Ruiz. These narratives attempted to cope with the contradictions between cultural homeland and host country; governmentality of the state and the disciplining of labor markets, and the politically imposed identities versus the politics of self positioning, that scholars like Aihwa Ong (1996) have aptly theorized.

A key component of how "race" operated in these narratives, however, also involved judgments of "inappropriate" affect. Another version of Marisol Padilla's commentary on self-sufficient strong women and the men they couldn't trust was the prolific family narrative aimed at setting the stage for a broader social critique that involved a fundamental distinction between "good woman" versus "bad woman." While the virgin/whore polarity is central to the Latin American telenovela genre, in the case of Newark it was "welfare dependency"—rather than promiscuity or virginity—that dictated where a woman would fall in this binary. In a conversation with Olga Carrasquillo, a Puerto Rican teacher, and Jen Carvajal, a Cuban American teacher, in March 2005 this became significant:

Jen Carvajal: There's definitely that idea [among female students at ESHS] that men are not reliable. And that comes from their families. Because if I look in my index cards, where the kids' contact information is, you see that the child's last name is not the mother's last name. I rarely have a child write the name of the father and the mother that's not different.

Olga Carrasquillo: There's no male at home. You see this a lot with blacks, Hispanics, some Brazilians, and some South Americans. With the Portuguese you might see the mother and father together.

Jen: A lot of my African American students are raised by a grandmother. Some of the South Americans are raised by an aunt or uncle, because they are here and the parent might be back in their countries. You have situations when the family member tells you, "That's not really my son. He's only staying here with me because his mother is in Honduras, in Salvador." I get that often, but you don't see that with the Portuguese students. It's usually the mother and father. They'll both come on parents' night for example. With some of my Brazilian students, just the mom comes.

Olga: I've always thought that to be interesting, and again, a lot of them have difficulty and they go . . . they travel back and forth a lot. I don't know if it's a question of whether the parents are not together in a relationship or they are just living in different countries. Here you have the Brazilians leaving in December for Carnival and not coming back until February, when the summer in Brazil is over.

A central assumption behind such narratives was that "family values"—automatically conferred to heteronormative marital configurations—are panacea for the social ills that plagued households.

An important underside of this version of the "good woman/bad woman" binary was the image of a consumption-based identity that defined a cosmopolitan womanhood and which was sometimes used by upwardly mobile Latinas to challenge dominant perspectives on the poor reproductive choices of "the Hispanic woman." The image of a sophisticated, cosmopolitan (*Sex and the City*–like), upwardly mobile professional woman played a role that drew on images of "the body" as critical in evaluations of affluence, but also as a material site for distancing oneself from US domestic minority women. While walking down Van Buren Street in the Ironbound, Emília Ribeiro, the Brazilian student at ESHS who worked in a boutique, noted a young woman with a baby in a snuggly. Emília commented:

The Hispanic girls, I would love to know why they have so many babies, especially here. The government gives them money. We are used to seeing them around here, one in the carrinho [stroller], two on each hand, and one in the big belly. I'm not going to have five, six children. . . . At least I've noticed that they try to stay in school. If they are in their senior year, they try to finish.

Migrants distance themselves from the image of "welfare dependency" that has traditionally been applied to African American and Puerto Rican women, but which now was also sometimes applied to immigrants that were "darkened" by their proximity to these populations, even as they worked as dançarinas ("go-go" girls) or bartenders., Images of women of color's hypersexuality as a liability to the state have been central, historically, to the way welfare "dependency" was conceived in the United States and how it emerged in relation to particular employment niches available to working-class "immigrant" women.

A second recurrent theme in the real life social dramas that were recurrent as people—old and young, US-born and migrant—explained tensions related to romantic or familial entanglements had to do with the question of "marrying up" or having utilitarian or mercenary motives to get married; in this modern case, unlike its Latin American telenovela version, "marrying up" was redefined to mean "marrying up" in the legal status scale (rather than in the conventional sense of marrying someone who is more financially prosperous than oneself). While narratives of "forbidden love" adopted multiple forms, presumptions of "utilitarian love" mostly revolved around issues of seeking "os papéis" or "los papeles." In particular instances the presumption of "illegality" impacted the most intimate aspect of young people's lives both in the Ironbound and in North Newark. Karina Milanés, a Puerto Rican and Cuban teacher at ESHS, was one of several people who commented on how Portuguese "illegality" was an underground topic that oftentimes generated ironic contradictions regarding the insertion of Latin American migrants in the life of the school and neighborhood, but that also emerged mostly in the context of romantic relationships.

Here you hear a lot from the parents of kids who are born here, whether they are Portuguese or even among Hispanics. The parents are always obsessed with, you know, if the girl is going to get pregnant just so that their son marries them. I know one of the young men who graduated from here. His girlfriend was illegal, and his mother was always telling him to be careful with her. Telling him, "She's going to want you to get her pregnant." And who ever heard of, you know, this Portuguese underworld of illegals!

It was in the context of dating that Portuguese "illegality" became a salient feature in the Ironbound, which was otherwise viewed as a picturesque ethnic enclave generally outside the interest of anti-immigrant groups. Likewise, many of the relationships involving Puerto Ricans, known to be US citizens, and other Latin American migrants were oftentimes viewed with suspicion and required elaborate narratives to "prove" that the desire, attraction, and emotive aspects of the relationship were "real." There was a rumor at Barringer at the time of my fieldwork that Ecuadorian girls liked Puerto Rican boys, but this was a rumor among the faculty, rather than among the students, who used this language to accentuate a "citizenship identity" and "illegality" (Ramos-Zayas 2003; De Genova and Ramos-Zayas 2003). Stereotypes are thus formed in narratives that, although generally undermining the sociohistorical and political contexts that shape the representations, tend to insert at some level the intimate and emotive component of these very images.

Finally, a third theme that was recurrent as people positioned themselves and others in light of a quasi-prototypical narrative around the problems of love and relationships was the "Romeo and Juliet" story. These narratives of parental opposition to young people's romantic relationships were frequent. Jen Carvajal recalled an instance in which she called a Colombian female student's house to see why the girl had been coming late to school and the first question the girl's father asked was: "Is my daughter dating a black guy? Because if she is dating a black guy, I have to come into school and do something about that." As Jen explained: "There's dating between African Americans and Hispanics. But I also get cases like this, especially with groups from South America. For him [the girl's father], this was a race issue. The father was very adamant about whether I knew of the situation, to the point of keeping the daughter away from school, if necessary." Narratives akin to those of telenovelas' "forbidden love" involved Latino and Latin American youth hiding their dating partners from their families, usually because these partners were of the "wrong race," in the parents' eyes. Conceptions of "inappropriate affect" supplied narratives of intergroup relationships leading to downward mobility, particularly when one fell for someone of the "wrong" group.

Jennifer Flores, the Puerto Rican graduate of Barringer, in her twenties, who worked at a social service agency in North Newark, provided a general view of the ways in which a form of Latinidad appeared somewhat determined by the possibility or impossibility of building romantic ties between Latinos or Latin American migrants and either blacks or whites. Jennifer commented:

You see some relationships between Hispanics and blacks, depending on the proximity, of where they live. But I think there's more of that [interrelationships] between different Latin American or Central American groups. There's almost no interaction with whites, unless you are a middle-class Cuban. Those marry whites. It's a status thing. I had a Cuban co-worker who told me explicitly: "I want to move to the suburbs so I can find my daughter a white guy to be her husband." And she actually did that. Two years later, they were divorced. But, even after that, she went on to date another Italian.

Many South American groups in the Ironbound, at least in the first gener-ation, still viewed the privileges of whiteness within their reach in a way that many US-born Latinos and even migrants from Puerto Rico and the Dominican Republic do not. Equally significant here is the question of whether romantic liaisons between Latinos and blacks offered spaces of comfort or harmony in what appeared to be, at least in the realm of urban politics, a notoriously tense relationship. Although most of the young people whom I met in Newark were more likely to feel more immediately connected to the world of romantic dating, attraction, and desire than to the realm of traditional or even alternative/grassroots politics, their ex-periences with intimate relationships were also revealing of the broader political economy of competition, limited resources, and violence.

Whenever I asked or heard spontaneous conversations about the rela-tion between African Americans and "Hispanics," the commentaries were always-already gendered, in ways that suggested that the "real problem," particularly for Latina and also Latin American migrant women, were the black women. Zaida Cintrón, a Puerto Rican student at ESHS who was often confused for African American, explained tensions with African American women as based on differences in racial desirability in a youth dating market. A heterosexual woman who had arrived from Puerto Rico about one year before I met her, Zaida viewed the possibility of a romantic relationship with an African American man as a way of becoming more familiar with the United States and the English language. The attraction some of the African American boys showed her involved, at least in the earlier stages of courtship, a need to learn English from peers in order to be able to have a relationship with them.

In Zaida's case, the stereotypes that serve as catalysts for these experi-ences are rooted on emotive expectations and feelings. These quotidian opportunities raised some important questions: Are there any moments of racial consciousness not thwarted by the search for the stereotype to love and the erotic racial democracy concepts? How are these moments of racial consciousness in fact dismissed, embraced, or altered in the con-text of Newark? How do feelings of similarity of difference in quotidian exchanges and perceptions transform, intersect, or modify a recognition of structural impediments and material scarcity? Zaida's experience was somewhat emblematic of both the intimate relationship that Puerto Ricans, more than any other group, had with African Americans, and of the great tensions that this relationship presented particularly for Puerto Rican female students. The Blackness of African American women, in contradistinction to the Blackness of some Latina women, was considered to be devoid of "racial mixture." Since racial mixture is presented as evidence of a lack of racism according to Latin American racial democracy ideologies, racism becomes more clearly projected onto African American blacks, particularly black women.

Latino and Latin American migrant discussions of city violence oftentimes accentuated the centrality of black women or even black female gangs, which sometimes served as coded or explicit assumptions about black women being "lesbians."[36] Newark is a city in which African Americans experience both a tragic crisis of structural and financial resources and a high visibility in the political arena, and it is also a city in which the diverse African American population not only consists of various generations of southern black families, but also of English- and French-speaking Caribbean and continental African populations. Given this complexity, it is even more surprising that the one commentary regarding blacks that most Puerto Ricans and Brazilians expressed focused on gendering Blackness so that the "problem" was really "the black woman."

While most US-born Latinas were generally more likely to identify the operations of "race" and express them discursively to explain everyday events, for many Brazilians and other South American female students in Newark's Ironbound, race as an analytically and moral construct seemed to acquire validity and salience in discussions of black women more than in any other context. A racialization of sexual stereotypes—of the "seductress" or "the tropics"—characterized the Latina and Latin American women experience in Newark, in ways that had very specific repercussions in the production of a fertile ground for unregulated sexual work, in which Brazilian migrants have been traditionally exploited globally. This form of exploitation, which required the preservation of images of the "exotic," existed in a context in which Latinas and Latin American migrants viewed "black women" as "violent," "aggressive," and "hypermasculine." This specific kind of "self-packaging" was largely premised on a disavowal and abjection of black women, who were associated with a form of "butch lesbian" sexuality in Newark. The logic used to develop affect stereotypes and erotic racial democracies was not the same as the ones deployed in narratives of homosexuality or "black lesbian aggressiveness." Nevertheless, each of these logics did exist in a discursive field and spatial context which made the other possible.

Neoliberalism and Stereotypes of Affect

At the time I met with Maura Silva in the summer of 2007, former New Jersey governor Jim McGreevey had declared himself a "gay American." The fact that his wife, Dina McGreevey (nee Matos), had grown up in the Ironbound further enhanced "gossip"-style discussions of this already "sexy" topic in the area. Connections to viewing Portuguese women as naïve, asexual, frigid, but also scheming, power-thirsty, and materialist gold-diggers proliferated. These were, in many popular conversations, the kind of women whose husbands might be gay and they never really find out because they don't have a passionate sex life. I was not surprised when Myrian, a Brazilian high school student who was very active in an evangelical youth group in the area, expressed her perspective on the news on marital discord, sexual "misconduct," and urban corruption. After updating me in the changes she had noticed in her life—how she did not "use" guys anymore and how she no longer went to bars or wore inappropriate clothing—Maura commented that she was "saving herself" for the right guy and marriage. Although Maura's parents' own marriage was in the brink of divorce, she viewed the McGreeveys' as a cautionary tale of how materialism, greed, and amorality were also destroying the lives of the young Brazilian women who used to be her close high school friends but with whom she no longer spent time. Almost as a rhetorical question, Maura stated:

> How could she have not known [that he was gay]? She lived with him. But you know what happens? She was too focused on her appearance. And let me tell you, I know how strong that is. Because I used to be also focused on how I looked, what I wore. She cared more about the exterior and neglected the interior. I think that happens to a lot of immigrants when they come to this country. They want to buy things, have things, instead of giving their lives up to God.
>
> AY: So you think she knew her husband was gay? That she stayed with him to keep the appearances?
>
> Maura: I think so, yes, I think so.

The McGreevey "gay American" confession is illustrative of how the realm of personal relations becomes riddled with agonizing uncertainties, with no normative rules and recipes to guide and ground people. Yet the realm of the domestic—love, sexuality, parenthood—has assumed a far more crucial role for the cultural reproduction of selfhood and identity (Illouz 2007, 114; S. Langer, in Geertz 1973, 99). The result is that the same social forces that make the realm of close relations so central and important to the self are those that undermine that realm. Precisely because modern lives have become saturated with risks (e.g., divorce, unemployment, political persecution), the need to fall on secure relations is greater. The whole McGreevey incident became emblematic, in the impression of many Ironbound residents, of a great irony: although capitalism enabled affluence and material security for a working-class Portuguese immigrant—that is, Dina Matos McGreevey—it also produced social pathologies and public suffering that appeared disjointed from an individual's particular socioeconomic characteristics. Indignation was activated by the perception that collective norms of justice have been violated; compassion is evoked by the suffering of a particular person, which may or may not have been the result of a breach in ethical norms (Illouz 2003, 92). The fact that McGreeveys' sexual history was a secret hidden in plain sight further complicated discussions: "Silvana's uncle knew somebody at the place where he works who had been a cop in Newark, and he worked with McGreevey. Everybody knew in that office."

The production of stereotypes of affect and analyses of emotion, not as truths but as feelings produced by larger societal structures, reveals the traces of that which language excludes (cf. Derrida 1998; Hennessy 2000). Oftentimes, emotions have come to displace traditional political metaphors in discussions of social evil, thus locating suffering inside the psyche (cf. Illouz 2003, 101). Not only were affect stereotypes a form of meaning-making, but also a condition for various forms of "cultural sampling" in intergroup dating, friendships, and other intimate relationships. Remarks around attraction, aggression, and desire—inherent in racial situations—were embedded in a political economic context that sustained everyday practices that generated a series of gendered prototypes, including the "aggressive black lesbian," the "Brazilian sex worker," and the "Hispanic welfare mother." Almost every single US-born Latina and Latin American migrant woman whom I interviewed attributed the overall violence in Newark to a strong presence of African American lesbians, as well as with an increased incidence of "sexual work" that some residents, specially the Portuguese, associated with Brazilian women. What increases the ideological potency of sexuality as a mechanism of social control is that regulation ultimately becomes translated into the currency of self-regulation, because sexuality has already been constructed as that which is or belongs to the realm of the private, as opposed to the social/public. This is a currency not of coercion but of desire. In the everyday life of Brazilians in Newark, the images of sensual bodies had very immediate and intimate repercussions in a broader heterosexist logic that placed women in competition for a higher echelon in an imaginary attractiveness ladder, while also straddling a fine line in relation to a social and sexual deviance embodied in a local sex work industry.

While the stereotype of the tropics and images of the "seductress" prevailed, these need to be read against a background of marginality, and specific market niches that profit from the promotion of these images. These characterizations appeared to be outside the purview of the state and the local political economy and became part of the "little things that make all the difference," because they were manifested in moments that seemed to be (were constructed as) instantaneous, unencumbered interactions that appeared isolated from a before or after, but were still very much shaped by broader tensions that may or may no longer have been defined as "racial." This seeming detachment from political economy is what makes this moment powerful, since it safeguards the "racial projects" of the state, which supply the conditions to naturalize gendered constructs of Puerto Rican welfare "dependency" and Brazilian "promiscuity," so that discussions of poverty and sexual exploitation remain obscured.

Eugenia Segato, a Portuguese counselor at ESHS and long-time resident of the Ironbound, insinuated the connection between Brazilian "promiscuity" and the "teenage pregnancy" attributed to US-born Latinas, thus signaling how stereotypes of the tropics were never innocent, but highly charged conceptions of difference and worthiness. When I asked her how she thought the Portuguese community viewed Brazilians, Eugenia explained:

Their perspective on the Brazilians is that they are very loose, they are very fast, simply because they look a certain way, which may not always be true, but. . . . Here we have some second-generation Portuguese. . . . They still maintain those traditions and even their way of raising their children. They're still very Old World. But the [Brazilian] girls . . . you know . . . the tank tops, and uh. . . . They're more *liberated*. We had, I think it was two years ago, we had this Brazilian girl. She was pregnant. We have pregnant girls here [at ESHS], not as much as they have at Barringer. I heard Barringer had a population explosion this year over there! But this girl, she was wearing a tank top and half of her belly was showing. So I said, "No, no, we can't have this." That was the end of that. So that happens too.

The narrative proceeded in the following way: First, Eugenia acknowledged the stereotype and questioned it a bit by distancing herself from what most people thought ("simply because [Brazilians] look a certain way," they are judged with no other evidence other than their look and looks can be deceiving). Second, a presumably "positive" or at least nostalgic stereotype of the Portuguese was introduced without any questioning of it (they "still maintained [Old World] traditions" and child-rearing practices). Then Eugenia moved on to provide concrete "evidence" that sustains the stereotype of Brazilian women, by introducing the comment on the Brazilian student who was attending ESHS while pregnant. Finally, Eugenia not only reinscribed a more concrete stereotype of Brazilian women in connection to "teenage pregnancy," but also rearticulated the stereotype by discussing a population who is even more prone to "unwed mothering" (an actual phrase she had used in many instances): the female student population at Barringer. Barringer was not simply a reference to a school building, but to a space racialized as "Puerto Rican."

Many Portuguese and Brazilian teachers and some parents alike commented that Brazilian migrant youth were going to "assimilate faster into American culture" (the "liberated" enunciated as a pejorative term) than even some of the US-born Portuguese. "The way Brazilians dress," a common detour in most conversations with the staff, teachers, and even students of the school, suggested that dress code and getting pregnant appeared as elements in a continuum. Whenever conversations about "assimilation," as both a desired and feared process, emerged, the assimilation of Brazilian women was described in connection to a perceived hypersexuality akin to images of promiscuity and "unwed mothering" attributed to US-born women of color, particularly Puerto Rican and African American women, in the case of Newark.

These young women engaged in negotiations around their racial identities that they believed allowed them to manage others' racialized expectations of them and this was oftentimes done through discussions of self-care, not only in terms of surviving in the streets, but also in terms of caring for one's appearance according to normative notions of femininity. There is a stereotype of the tropics, and a consequent rendition of who is "loose" and who is "traditional," in Newark that emerges from the ways in which the Brazilians and the Portuguese view one another in primarily gendered terms. Some Brazilian women appropriated the very stereotype to explain their dress style, while others deliberately distanced themselves from the stereotype by engaging in processes of "conversion" (religious or secular). This provides the template onto which US-born Latinas also sought a stereotype of "seductress" to avoid the racism involved in being racialized as "closer to African Americans," a category that suggested lack of femininity, aggressiveness, and unattractiveness among Latinos and Latin American populations in Newark. A question that begs attention is, then, how does this carve an alternative, if still subordinate, space in the black-white binary? And yet, the invisibility of race contributed to a very adaptable racial logic that insisted on a racial democracy, and intergroup dating was used as evidence. The fact that US-born Latinos were oftentimes racialized as black allowed intergroup dating to really be interpreted as interracial dating, a US version of racial democracy. What historical and social conditions preceded and sustained these gendered racializations and how are they invested in challenging black-white racial polarity?

As demonstrated in this chapter, "self-care" was a loaded concept that included caring for one's physical and emotive appearance in ways that were consistent with neoliberal market requirements, as well as developing alternative protective strategies against other forms of danger, including being hypersexualized and approaching a sex-work economy. Instances of Portuguese-Brazilian tensions and narratives of "forbidden love," confound discussions of Brazilian seduction of Portuguese men with a context associated with sex work, as Marcela's vignette at the beginning of this chapter demonstrates. From Brazilian revealing clothes to Puerto Rican welfare "dependency," the positionality of a racially ambiguous group like Brazilians, who some claim do not entirely fit into the Latino category, alters the everyday production of affective stereotypes and reframes discourses of assimilation. The rendering of black-Latino relationships in explicitly (almost exclusively) gendered and sexualized terms, alluded to here, is further elaborated in the next chapter.

FIVE

Of "Black Lesbians," Hate Crimes, and Crime Talk: The Sexuality of "Aggression" in the City

"I'm pissed! I'm *so pissed*," declared Amarilis Guzmán as soon as I got into her car to drive to a North Newark Cuban deli we both liked. Before I could even ask, Amarilis explained: "Ashley was jumped! Can you believe that? And you know how I'm with Ashley. That's my girl!" At twenty-one, Amarilis, a Puerto Rican woman who had graduated from Barringer High School and lived in North Broadway, appeared unusually mature for her age. After various stints working as a security guard for an insurance company, as a stacker for Home Depot, and a paralegal in a firm in downtown Newark, Amarilis was now teaching karate at an agency she co-owned with Isabel, whom Amarilis referred to as her "wife." They were well-respected mentors to community youth who were only a few years younger in age, but who seemed ages apart in terms of maturity. Having finally buckled my seatbelt, I had to admit that I was surprised by the news. "She was jumped? What happened?" I asked.

Stories about young women "being jumped" had become almost commonplace in my fieldwork. Ashley was a petite, reserved, studious high school student, and did not fit any of the admittedly stereotypical images of someone who could get involved in a street fight. "What happened is this," Amarilis proceeded to explain, still visibly upset:

Ashley's on the phone with me and she can hardly breathe. "Alex, Alex, they're chasing me. They're chasing me." And I'm like "What? Who's chasing you? What's going on? Where are you?" But then I hear, "They're after me. They're after me!" And a click. So I'm going crazy here, not knowing what's happening. It turned out, these girls, these morenas [black girls or women] were running after her, because one of them likes her. So Ashley was like, "I'm no gay, but even if I were gay, I wouldn't go for you!" It was four girls trying to take her down to the ground, but Ashley fought back. She did what she'd learned in karate and didn't allow herself to be brought down. If they had pinned her down, they'd have beat her up to death! Because it was four girls beating her up and then four other girls in the corner, checking to see who's coming. . . . This morning I sent someone to go by the school and the girls were expelled, but I'm still pissed off.

Talk of girls "being jumped" or "jumping" other girls, particularly black girls who were or were perceived to be lesbians, was so common among most of the Latino and Latin American students with whom I spoke in North Newark and the Ironbound, that I felt this was a good opportunity to ask Amarilis about this more explicitly. "Why would they choose Ashley in particular? Is it always the same girls that are the jumpers and how do they know who they're going to jump. I really have no clue about any of this," I confessed to Amarilis, knowing that she already suspected that I had never thrown a punch in my life.

"It's always these morenas. They had a thing for Ashley. Because . . . you don't understand, Ashley is very popular. She's pretty. She's really smart. She has so much going for her. So they fell in love with her," Amarilis explained.

"So, because they like her, that's why they jump on her?" I asked, trying to highlight the odd logic behind this.

Ignoring what I noted as an inconsistency, Amarilis simply continued: "Yup, that's what morenas are like. That's Newark for you."

Departing from the widespread idea of gendered forms of aggression, captured in notions of "jumping" or "being jumped"—as well as conceptions of "having attitude," discussed below—this chapter consider instances in which Latino-black relations were complicated by emotive readings of sexuality, particularly of queer sexualities (cf. Johnson 2007). An urban emotional commonsense in Newark is sustained through deeply phenomenological episodes of Latino-black conflict that are framed around discussions of and silences regarding Latino antiblack attitudes and widespread antigay hate crimes. In another conversation with Amarilis and Isabel, her partner of many years, the intersection between sexuality, anti-Blackness, and emotive readings of jealousy and trust captured the complicated intersection that later became relevant in my analysis of a high profile crime in Newark—the 2007 shootings of four African American college students by a group of six young men, most of whom were Latin American migrants (discussed below).

"I don't know if you noticed at Barringer, but morenas hated us," remarked Amarilis when I conducted an interview with her and Isabel about four years prior to the incident involving Ashley. "She [referring to Isabel] had this problem, too." When I asked her to tell me more about her impressions of this, a complicated series of themes around sexuality, femininity, desire, Latino-black relations, and violence unfolded. These became central themes in my analyses of hate crimes in Newark.

Amarilis: My main problem was that all these guys loved being around me. And females hated that. They hated their boyfriends being around me because I was that cool chick. "Hey, yeah, Amarilis is cool, y'all." That was me. Females hated me, the morenas. I had problems with morenas all through high school. I'd be walking down the hall and they'd give me looks. I would laugh. My freshman and sophomore year I would get into a lot of fights, until I started dating this girl who was a Blood, and she was the main meanest bitch at the school. There's always these morenas who are real girlie, who are into fashion and all that. And then there are the hood rat chicks. The ones I'd have problems with were the hood-rat chicks. The cute girlie ones were always like, "Hi Amarilis" [high-pitched, flirtatious voice]. And the hood-rat ones were giving me the dirty looks.

Isabel: I always had problems with the girlie ones, because I'm very girlie myself. They really hated me. They were jealous, because I always got along with all the popular guys. And I was one of the girls who always had a car, who would dress right, and my best friend was one of the most popular guys. He'll tell me all the time that they said I was stuck up, which in reality I'm not, when you get to know me. But nobody really gets to know each other here.

Amarilis: You see, it's not necessarily that something specific happens, but how you perceive each other, how you look at each other.

Some of the recurrent themes that emerged from recollections of episodes of girls being jumped or instances of physical violence involved a series of assessments of African Americans that focused on emotional qualities specifically attributed to black women, including "jealousy," hypermasculinity, carelessness about body or appearance, and propensity to violent outbursts. These qualities were highlighted in contrast to a highly valued Latina emotive aesthetic; such emotive aesthetic was oftentimes predicated on conceptions of "self-care" rooted on appearance and emotional capital which, furthermore, mediated the insertion of young women of

color into culturally driven labor market niches, that is, into employment in industries that relied on the marketing of culture, sensuality, and
most service-oriented jobs. Although many US-born Latinas subscribed
to what Nikki Jones identifies among African Americans as a gendered
"code of the streets" that required being "aggressive for the streets, pretty
for the pictures" (2008; cf. Weston 1995), "aggressiveness" in Newark was
a quality that had been historically associated with African Americans.
Regardless of sexuality or nationality, Latinas rarely acknowledged that
African American women could possess the emotional style and heteronormative femininity valued in a labor market that had come to praise
alternative forms of nonmarket capital. Instead, like Amarilis, other US-
born Latinas and Latin American migrant women focused on how black
women were "jealous" of Latinas for a variety of reasons ranging from
hair texture to labor market competition; on the volatile temperament
of African American women and various categories of "ocular violence"
(Anderson 2000); and on how learning race in Newark meant learning
to read body kinetics, interpret glances, and managing one's emotional
displays (e.g., not showing fear). Amarilis was indeed very knowledgeable
about the bodily gestures and the physicality of emotion.

"Having Attitude" in Black-Latino Relations: The Politics of Propriety, Jealousy, and Authenticity in the Racialization of Sexuality

The conversation with Amarilis about Ashley being jumped and her
claim that the perpetrators had been black women who seemed both
"jealous" and "in love with" Ashley prompted me to go over my fieldnotes and transcripts again, to note the numerous references to "lesbian
gangs," "aggressive black lesbians," or "black female gangs" in my several
hundred pages of research. Some of the data I had dismissed as "urban
legend," before realizing how ubiquitous these narratives of violence and
sexuality were to the fabric of systems of difference, race, affect, and relationships among young people in Newark. The emotional intensity of the
narratives also highlighted how emotions served as patterns of attention
that provided a framework for how some beliefs were showcased while
others were undermined, as well as how judgments about propriety were
made in everyday life. "Having attitude"—in all its indeterminacy—was
a central affect-encoding assessment among minority youth in Newark.
"Attitude" was understood as an individual's propensity to exhibit particular emotions, rather than aiming to control or hold these emotions

back. Moreover, having attitude also implicated a strategic or manipula-tive access to emotions; whereas it was generally assumed that one had control over whether or not to display a certain attitude, attitude was si-multaneously viewed as an intrinsic aspect of one's personality. This was particularly the case in contexts in which individuals were distinguishing themselves from others on the basis of class, race, or sexuality.

By identifying contexts in which "having attitude" became a primary social code around which various exchanges, mannerisms, actions, and personality traits were organized and interpreted, the social and emo-tional conditions that contributed to a particular gendered racialization of African American women in predominantly Latino neighborhoods can be examined. Four main conditions that enabled a reading of "hav-ing attitude" in racialized and gendered terms in Newark included: (1) A generationally specific "civilization of manners" schema of respectability that privileged a black-white perspective on race and reasserted hetero-normativity; (2) An "attribution process of emotion" that highlighted jealousy as a dominant emotion of African American women around which black-Latino relations were organized; (3) Everyday identification of "situational impropriety"—including a range of intensities, from tech-nical rudeness to ocular violence to physical altercations—that rendered African American women as "masculine" and "butch," in contradistinc-tion to the valued femininity of Latinas; and (4) A "guess work" around someone's sexuality and expectations of a "coming out" experience. These conditions are outlined below.

"She's smart, but she has a bad attitude": Generational Perspectives on Racial Respectability and Manners

Rhonda Clayton, an African American social worker in her early thirties, was asked to moderate a program for young female students at the health clinic at Barringer High School in North Broadway. The high school's health clinic included about five or six examination rooms, four beds, and a computer and media room where students and a faculty mentor met each week to watch a movie and have a discussion. The first movie Rhonda decided to show was titled *Just Another Girl*. As Rhonda explained: "The movie is about a girl who is very smart but has a bad attitude." She liked this movie because the main girl's parents "are still together and work." The themes highlighted in the discussion that followed the movie, and the response of the two African American female adults pres-ent (Rhonda and a middle-aged African American student doing the practicum for her master's in social work) to the high school students' observations were revealing of a "civilization-of-manners" schema (Elias 1982) that took decidedly classed and generational contours in Newark. There were three main storylines that generated verbal responses on the part of the African American and US-born Latino students watching the film, and which were met with a disciplining of emotions and feelings by the adults invested in civilizing manners.

In one of the earliest scenes in the movie the girl-actress denounces that "people judge us for what we wear," referring to the baggy clothes, hip-hop look. At this point, a young self-identified Puerto Rican lesbian in the audience said, "Thank you!" in agreement with the main female character's comment. "There is a time and place," commented the African American intern. "You can wear anything that is appropriate." This particular Puerto Rican girl was one of the few young women who were "out" at Barringer. She was also one of the regulars at the health clinic and presented a dilemma for the staff: On the one hand, they had great affection for her because she was charming and smart; on the other hand, she did not conform to the middle-class norms they tried to institute. Instances that validated this girl's existence—like having a leading movie character verbalize a form of prejudice that was tacit or at the very least undermined—were promptly rectified by adults. However, what was also being disciplined here was this girl's sexuality.

A second part of the plot that generated response involved a segment that began with the main female character's boyfriend saying "I love you" and ended with the girl having to make a decision about what to do with an unplanned pregnancy. As soon as the leading male character said, "I love you," there was a chorus of cynical "Oh pleeeeease!" and "Yeah sure you do!" from the audience. This appeared to be in agreement with Julie Bettie's (2003) findings among the working-class Mexican and white girls in her study, who seemed very doubtful and distrustful of any boy saying "I love you." Clearly, this reaction was also strong since the audience already anticipated (based on Hollywood's formulaic themes) that this would be the beginning of trouble for the girl.

Predictably, the main character becomes pregnant and her boyfriend urges her to have an abortion. Rhonda could not contain a disapproving shake of her head: "Uhm-uhm." The leading female character assumes an explicitly antiabortion stance and goes through with the pregnancy but, once the baby is born, she asks her boyfriend to throw the baby away. The boyfriend puts the baby in the garbage can, but then cannot get himself to throw his daughter away. In the end, the girl-actress and the boyfriend are no longer a couple, but they are both involved in raising their daughter. In the last scenes of the film, the female lead appears upbeat, despite having given up her goal of attending a four-year college and medical school. Instead she enrolls at a community college and continues her education while being a responsible parent. The baby girl is presented as a cute and healthy pink-clothed bundle. As the credits rolled, a US-born Dominican girl mentioned that her cousin—who also attended Barringer—should see this movie because "she had a kid here and then went to Dominican Republic and had another one." And, another student who seemed to know the girl in question added: "Yeah, and she didn't want to have the baby, you can tell. She always comes into school and drops the baby off at the daycare, looking all blah."

The ensuing postfilm discussion, which was initiated by an African American girl who was close friends with many of the US-born Latinas in the school, revolved around the female character's "self-confidence" and how she "stood up for herself" in her denunciation of racial discrimination. What was most remarkable about this particular discussion of discrimination was that the students in the audience were as overwhelmingly invested in it as Rhonda and the social worker intern appeared disgruntled by it. The scene in question involved a white male high school teacher talking about the Holocaust. The leading female character assertively comments that "it's fine to talk about the Holocaust, but we need to talk about the oppression that black people have undergone in this country." The white male teacher responds that this wasn't the time for doing that and the girl continues to press him to engage with the topic. In a later scene, the girl character is giving a classroom presentation on how countries where people of color predominate are presented as smaller than white people's countries on maps, and she substantiates her claim by referencing the work of a geographer. The white male teacher listens to her, seeming more sympathetic to her tacit denunciation of racial subordination. The African American girl in the audience who had initiated the postmovie discussion by noting this particular scene commented that she thought it was important to be willing to stand up by one's beliefs and "call other people on their bads." Rhonda interjected by saying: "Well, that didn't take her anywhere. She wasn't able to change his mind and all she showed was her bad attitude." And then, the intern added: "It's good that the girl had an opinion, but she would have been more successful if she had been respectful, and tamed down the attitude." A lecture on how being "respectful" would have been a better approach, instead of being "quote-unquote ghetto," ensued on the part of both adults. The group of about twelve girls became more passive listeners.

The postmovie discussions exposed the main character of the film not for the structural events she encountered in her everyday life as much as for the plots of her psychological struggles and ethical dilemmas. Each of the discussions complied with a "therapeutic narrative" —that is, stories about the self and events that have helped the self achieve health or cause it to fail—while also situating emotions on a moral terrain. Such "moral emotions" aimed to create a common template that would bind listener to storytelling through a set of assumptions about worthy or reprehensible behavior (Illouz 2008, 88, 91). This movie event and subsequent discussion unified both a moral code that bound listeners to common social norms and obligations, as they were classed and generationally determined, and a therapeutic code that focused on how individual life histories differed or corresponded to models of psychological health. These forms of communication, which included therapeutic and moralizing elements in the production of respectability or the "civilization of manners," imposed legibility on the classed-based or generational irregularities of social life and reinstituted a "normality" that at times prevented any attempt at queering heteronormativity or explicitly challenging everyday racism.

After the movie and discussion were over, Rhonda requested potential topics for the next movie event or to discuss in future meetings of what was then constituted as an ongoing "young women's group." One of the girls immediately said, "Discrimination." Rhonda sighed, obviously uninterested, "We'll see." In this sense, any attempts at displacing into doubt foundational assumptions for the purpose of scrambling moral categories or enabling critique was met with a repositioning of the original normative frame through a process of instituting respectability and civilizing manners.

"They have a bad attitude because they're jealous of us": Race and the Attribution of Gendered Emotions

Regardless of nation of origin or US-born generation, the young Latin American and Latina women with whom I spoke mentioned that the greater source of tension they had personally experienced involved "black women" or las morenas. For the most parts, many US-born Latinas explained that black women were "jealous" of Latinas, because Latinas had "better hair" or were "prettier," and black guys "preferred Latinas." Delia Torres, a Puerto Rican administrator at Barringer, mocked such relationships by drawing from popular culture: "In Newark, you see a lot of Puerto Rican women going out with black guys because the African Americans are in power. The Puerto Rican has replaced the light-skinned black woman as arm candy. They have now become the new ornament, the Jennifer

Lopez–Puff Daddy phenomenon. African American women resent Puerto Rican women." Potential moments of urban tension generated readings of social relationships that framed how feelings were attributed to particular racial groups. Emotions were assumed to have a particular trigger, which was often a gendered and racialized body. In this sense, individuals were always ready to interpret or attribute emotions based on their interpretations of specific contexts or circumstances which frequently pointed in the direction of a racialized social unit (cf. Lawler 2001).

When I ran into Marisol Padilla, a young Puerto Rican graduate of Barringer High School, at a youth event in one of North Broadway's community organizations, she was visibly upset over the fact that a Puerto Rican female administrator whom she cared a great deal about had been fired from the public elementary school where she worked for nearly five years. "They didn't like her," Marisol explained, almost with resignation. When I asked her why that was, she explained:

Because they thought she was too bossy, muy cafre [ghetto] too, that she had a bad attitude, you know. She would run through walls and I asked her not to get into ningún berrinche con nadie [trouble with anyone]. And this one Italian woman did all kinds of stuff, told all kinds of stuff to get her fired. [Marisol's friend] was a strong Puerto Rican woman, and they have a hard time with that. Even African Americans have a hard time with that, don't kid yourself! African American women see themselves displaced now by Puerto Rican women and also the issue about being next to these uppity African American men that want some Puerto Rican women. . . . And African American women are like, "Wait a minute no, no we can't have that." Black women are very, very jealous of Puerto Rican women. It's ridiculous they feel like that, but that's how it is here in Newark.

Although the emotions that arise from a reading of a situation as gendered and racialized may not be under the control of the individual, some experiences still unleashed an "attribution process" that generated more specific, object-focused emotions (cf. Weiner, cited in Lawler 2001, 328). Thus, "once an emotion is activated, whether by sensory data (e.g., pain) or by cognitive processes (e.g., appraisal, attribution), even if it is a response to a specific event, it then becomes an organizing and driving force in subsequent thought and action" (Izard 1992, 43). A level of "emotional energy" that resulted from conversations and interactions around race and gender enabled a channeling of subjective interpretations that people took from one situation to another. As Randall Collins's "theory of interaction ritual chains" claims, emotional energy is a "generalized motivational state involving feelings of warmth and confidence. . . .

Repetitive interaction is the basis of solidarity at the micro level" (2004, 346). The attribution of certain emotional reactions to African American women, which in the minds of many Latinas constituted a social unit, entailed tacit or explicit undermining of the dichotomy between disposition (an internal, unchangeable quality) and situation (external, variable quality).

Bernard Weiner (1985)'s "attribution theory of emotions" applies to the phenomenon of Latinas rendering their relationships with African Americans legible, not necessarily by engaging in more intimate interracial social networks, but by developing causal attributions for behavior that have emotional effects on themselves.[1] Emotional processes enhanced or diminished the role of social networks as a foundation for microlevel ordering, so that people who repetitively interacted developed common foci and moods that symbolized their group membership (cf. Lawler 2001; Collins 2004; Izard 1992). More significantly, though, a process of emotional learning was set in place according to which the emotional meaning of an event was evaluated even before the event was fully understood. Emotions, in fact, engaged many US-born Latinos and Latin American migrants in Newark with a racialized spatial order, rather than serving as mere internal interruptions, because they were embedded in complex personal and urban histories, memories, and associations with African Americans. As Lawler (2001) also explains through his "Affect Theory of Social Exchange," emotions are incorporated as an explicit, central feature of social exchange.

Mildred Irizarry, Evelyn Rosa, and Vivian Rovira, three Puerto Rican students who attended high school in the Ironbound, engaged in a conversation that was remarkably typical of how Latina women viewed Latino-black relations in almost exclusively gendered terms. The creation of the affect stereotypes consisted of a patterned process of identifying a stereotype, acknowledging the nuances not captured by the stereotype, and reformulating a more nuanced yet equally stereotypical image:

Vivian Rovira: I don't feel too much tension between Puerto Ricans and blacks because since I grew up around blacks all my life and I have family that is black, so I never felt the tension between blacks and Puerto Ricans. One of my aunts is half-black half–Puerto Rican so we are always together. But I think black guys like Puerto Rican women. I know that a lot of black guys who live around here have Puerto Rican or Spanish girlfriends. It's always a black guy with a Puerto Rican or Latino woman, not so much a black woman with a Puerto Rican man.

Evelyn Rosa: I think there is some tension though. My mom works for Essex County so she has a lot of African American friends, a lot, but she never trust them too much, because they talking about her. I think like some, you know like not all because I do have black friends, one of my best friends is black but I guess it goes back in time when like the [black] women used to say that all the black men liked the Puerto Ricans that we try to take their men, you know, there is kind of that thing. [The black women would say] "Oh well she has pretty hair I don't like her." They get jealous of our body shape, face, the fact we got better hair than they do, they don't have no hair. We don't wear no fake hair and they do. You know, you can do anything with this hair; they have to buy theirs. That's kind of a big deal to them.

Mildred Irizarry: It's true because since blacks have nappy hair and stuff like that and Puerto Ricans have curly and natural hair [pointing to her own curly hair].

Vivian: I still have nappy hair!

Mildred: Well, my hair isn't all that straight either, but. . . . You could manage with it rather than blacks, and blacks like have to have like weaves with curls and stuff that has curly hair.

Evelyn: Even my mom is guilty of that, like she had gotten her microbraids done and she's itching like [laughter] so "yo no se cómo esas morenas los tienen como por dos meses. Ya yo me voy quitando esta mierda! [I don't know how these black women have this on for two months at a time. I'll be taking this shit off right away!]"

Mildred: They are always like scratching.

AY: So it's all about the hair, ah?

Mildred: It really is all about the hair! [laughed]

Evelyn: We got some Puerto Rican girls here with J.Lo bodies. So the guys be like, "Wow, look at her." Brazilians have nice bodies, too, but black guys don't see them in the same way or are not as close to them as they are to Puerto Rican girls.

Mildred: Well, black girls got nice bodies, too, but us Puerto Ricans look better. We are a little bit light skinned and you could see it better.

AY: See it better?

Mildred: Well, the skin looks softer.

Through this conversation, a patterned reaffirmation of an affect stereotype emerged. It involved an initial questioning of the most simplistic forms of the stereotype ("I do have black friends, relatives"); then provided "evidence" of why the stereotype exists ("Black women used to say that black men liked the Puerto Rican [women]"); the "evidence" is used to reinscribe another stereotype, of Puerto Rican/Latina women as seductress and the undesirability of black women ("We don't wear no fake hair and they do"). The most significant aspect of the conversation happens toward the end when the evidence is on the table and there is a brief moment of acknowledgment of potential similarities between black and Puerto Rican women (when Evelyn confesses that her mom got the "microbraids," associated with black women, done and when Mildred mentions that "black girls got nice bodies, too"). Even after noticing the commonalities that emerge from the very "evidence" that purported to suggest racial difference, Puerto Rican superiority is reasserted in the end, largely because Puerto Rican women do a better job at "self-care." Issues of hair and attractiveness—often in light of knowing how to take care of one's appearance (in this instance, adopting black microbraids is an instance of self-care gone wrong)—are highlighted in the dating market, at least for women of color. Any of these girls could "pass" for light-skinned, African American women.[2] In fact, they explicitly valued the characteristics associated with black women's bodies in a way that resonates with what Donna Goldstein notes: "It is possible to see mixed-race sexual partners as ideal, even as more sensual and erotic, and yet evaluate 'black characteristics' negatively, particularly in non-erotic contexts" (1999, 567).

A central quality of this conversation is that it framed the relationship between African American and Puerto Rican women around what J. T. Irvine calls "the sincerity problem" (cited in Besnier 1990, 430). Evelyn's comment about trust, in the context of her mother's work experience with African Americans, raises the question: How do members of different social groups distinguish "true" from "deceitful" effective communicative displays ("exuded expressions" from "guided doings," in Goffmanian terms)? Moreover, to what extent is the distinction between "true" and "deceitful" affect relevant to members of a particular group? The question of sincerity in this context assumes that emotions as individual experiences are different from emotions as interactional constructs and, more important, that the attribution of intentionality has to be central to the interpretation of another person's behavior, oftentimes along racialized and gendered lines. Despite not trusting her fellow co-workers, Evelyn's mom attempted microbraids, a way to care for hair associated with African American women in Newark, just to realize that the process "itched"; "las morenas los tienen como por dos meses [Black women have this on for about two months at a time]." This, I argue, is also an implicit commentary on the personal hygiene of black women and how Puerto Rican women aim to distance themselves from what they perceived to be such poor self-care. The fact that Evelyn quotes her US-born mother in Spanish also shows how code switching offers fertile ground for affect work; switches from one language to another exploit the affective connotations of each language.

The nature of intentionality, and the fact that sometimes intention was speculated upon through subjective attribution of emotion, distinguished this emotional landscape from beliefs, desires, or ideologies (cf.

Cavell 1998); unlike beliefs or desires, emotions are total orientations toward the world and have narrative character that burrows deeply into individual histories, becoming a critical aspect of subjectivity. Susana García, a twenty-two-year-old Puerto Rican resident of Newark's North Broadway neighborhood, once said, her voice almost breaking down: "Sometimes I sit on the bus and I feel the person next to me pulling away, as if brushing against my skin would contaminate them. That happens a lot with Americans, with the whites and the blacks [morenos] both. And you feel that rejection [rechazo] and, you know, it pains me [me hiere] that they think that we're worth nothing."

Susana was not concerned with evaluating the accuracy or factual aspect of her interpretation of the situation; instead, the comment pointed to how her ability to read and make sense of the situation relied on multiple, daily experiences with difference, like the one she describes here. Sartre (1957) argues that an emotion is an active transformation of the world that we imaginatively perform in the face of an obstacle to desire. He claims that emotions are defenses against those aspects of the world that challenge our desire. Antonio Damasio's discussion of the "somatic marker hypothesis" (1996) pursues this philosophical perspective by examining how emotions are an essential part of practical reason that give the individual a sense of how the world relates to her or his goals and projects. In Susana's description, there is a sense that the emotive is an all-encompassing aspect of everyday urban situations; feelings are experienced physiologically; emotions are visible, palpable, a form of expression; and affect brings in subjectivity. All of these are dimensions that come together in a dense interpretive framework that many young women used to describe their everyday life.

Nevertheless, more than beliefs and desires, emotions are the clue to what we mean by subjectivity; they are "what makes my world exclusively mine and yours exclusively yours" (Cavell 1988, 590).[3] In many of the instances when Latinas attributed "jealousy" to African American women, their analysis of emotion and of racial difference constituted a subject-making process. Among most of the US-born Latinos with whom I spoke, "race" was rarely invisible, but the hyperconsciousness of it oftentimes required that tensions be understood in the terrain of affect, not political economy or neighborhood politics.

The complicated relationship between US-born Latinos and African Americans in Newark, a predominantly black city with a considerably heterogeneous black population, produced situations in which stereotypes of affect were constructed and managed so that specific political economic contexts were experienced as potentially volatile moments of marginalization and personal negation, as moments of great anxiety and distress. Such was the case described by Adriana González, a young Puerto Rican woman who lived in North Newark, but commuted to the Ironbound to attend high school. When I asked her to tell me about how she viewed the different groups in her school and neighborhood, Adriana mentioned:

This is a very racist city. People pretty much stay with their own I feel more comfortable . . . like, I've dated blacks and never Dominicans, but I feel I relate more to Puerto Ricans. With Puerto Ricans the family invites me. I can go to a Puerto Rican house, you know, for a birthday, and they go, *"Come, con confianza"* [eat, make yourself at home]. [With] the blacks you got to be: "Oh my God does she like me? Is she going to invite me in?" You know? I can always go into a Puerto Rican house and feel super comfortable in there.

More than accentuating "hospitality" as an essentialist Puerto Rican trait that African Americans may or may not have, Adriana highlighted the anxiety that moments of racial illegibility evoked. She also demonstrates how Latinos became speculators into the emotional lives of African Americans, as they also theorized and learned to produce racial difference. Robin Sheriff argues that women tend to be more reluctant to interpret the behaviors of others as racist than are men because they tend to encounter racism in intimate contexts that are charged with ambivalent emotions (in Goldstein 1999, 579). Although this is the case among some Latin American migrant women, most US-born Latinas vacillated between a certain level of compassion—acknowledging the suffering of African Americans as a group—and indignation—a perception that African American women viewed them as a threat and that such perceptions violated some broader collective norms of justice (cf. Illouz 2007, 92). Racial feelings, rather than internal states, are placed outside the self under racial democracy, and they dictate who to be and what to be. Structural differentiation always means a concomitant increase in opportunities to distinguish finer varieties of emotions and opportunities to have "real" feelings, neglected in other practical contexts, that find appropriate new venues for expression. The manipulation of emotion did not obviate the legitimacy of feelings, but rather reflected an individual's personal skill at managing not only others, but one's own impression of oneself. A critical question is: How do we learn an emotional vocabulary (i.e., both the semantics of the emotions and also an emotional repertoire)? As our discrimination of the situations in the world becomes finer and more various, so also may the emotions to which we are susceptible. As Marcia

Cavell (2006) notes, the link between the inner and the outer is nowhere clearer than in emotions. Emotions may be treated as something to be explained by other variables (body, social structure, socialization, experience), as something that can explain cultural institutions (hospitality, avoidance customs), or as an inseparable part of cultural meaning and social systems. The three dimensions of affect (evaluation, potency, activity) are akin to the three dimensions of interpersonal stratification (status, power, agency) For the working-class US-born Latino and Latin American migrant youth with whom I spoke, race was intricate to evaluations of intimacy and a social epistemology of emotion.

Racial learning, in segregated contexts, was oftentimes mediated by ocular interactions ("the gaze"), which generated interpretative emotions that aimed to endow the social order with a degree of predictability. Potentially explosive moments of urban tension, when an emotion was attributed to a particular social object, furthermore assumed that one's emotions had a particular racial trigger. These were moments in which the emotional repertoire could be systematized by everyday interactions to differentiate and objectify whole groups (cf. de Sousa 1990). In those instances emotions were not only reactions to what happened, but also judgments or analytical tools to interpret a situation, even when one would never have corroboration of the veracity or accuracy of one's interpretation. In Newark, and perhaps in other US urban centers, "having attitude" was a rhetorical concept that emanated from a highly developed urban emotive language.

"All fights here start with a look . . . and a bad attitude": Situational Propriety and the Gaze

As noted earlier, most references to black women's temperament involved speculation about their sexuality, alluding in particular to a presumed homosexuality. For instance, Zaida, a woman who is oftentimes confused for African American, introduced earlier, said: "I have no problem with black guys. They always try to speak a little Spanish, say 'mamichula' and things like that. They like us [Latinas] a lot. But I can't stand black women. They are arrogant and like to fight. They look at you, at the fact that you speak Spanish, and they hate you for that. They don't like your color. . . . They have their own style, way of walking, machúas [unfeminine, butch]"[4]

"What do they fight about?" I asked Zaida.

She and Lucía, a Colombian student in the same bilingual class at ESHS, answered in unison: "About everything! About stupid stuff. Yeah, everything." And Lucía added: "If you look at someone, they fight you. If you brush against someone, they fight you. The morenas are like guys. They get together with women."

Likewise, Maura Silva, a Brazilian woman who had arrived from Belo Horizonte in the late 1990s (introduced in chapter 3), explained: "The thing that I learned here was the trouble with black people. You are looking at someone and they're like 'What you looking at?' very antagonistic. That's how all the fights start, you know, because you look the wrong way." And to make sure I was following her description of the situation, she clarified: "And don't think it's the guys that I'm talking about. Nooooo . . . it's the women! And you can't show them you're afraid, because they'll fight you even more. They're very masculine. They don't look like women, the shape of their bodies are like men's bodies."

The manifestations of "aggression" and "jealousy" that US-born Latinas and Latin American migrant youth attributed to African American women could be summarized in two main dominant readings of everyday situations of tension: one of them focused on a form of privileging ocular or visual interactions in everyday emotional interpretations and the other on a rhetorical engagement with the concept of "having attitude." The notion of "having attitude" was not only a deeply racializing and gendering rhetorical tool, but also one that read or imagined "sexuality"—particularly, queer sexuality—in light of temperament, violence, and emotional volatility. Rather than requiring any form of verbal confirmation, these readings privileged sight or the ocular as a leading interpretive tool.

Elijah Anderson's analysis of the "code of the streets" suggests how tacit rules of visual engagement operate among strangers in everyday encounters. In *Streetwise* (1990), Anderson also refers to "the art of avoidance" to describe how middle-class people develop skills to deal with their felt vulnerability toward violence and crime. Having to be rude is sometimes a common strategy adopted by people who have not learned to say no or, more common in the case of working-class and poor women of color in Newark, to individuals whose "No"s do not carry much weight because of their own marginal social position. While a form of "technical rudeness" is assumed to be more common than explicit physical violence, particularly in middle-class and affluent contexts, many urban ethnographers have also noted the visual choreography that Goffman labeled "civil inattention," that is, the glances and gestures that provide the benefit of recognition while simultaneously assessing the threat someone else may pose. Many US-born Latinas and Latin American migrant women described everyday situations in which they deliberately disregarded the African American women's gaze in what they considered a protective strategy to avoid moments of social illegibility or misrecognition (Fenstermaker and West 2002).[5]

Because of the limitations of my research, which did not consider the reaction of African American women in these Latino-black encounters, it is impossible to assess how African Americans viewed such avoidance. Could it have been viewed as a lack of respect? A successful way to intimidate? A symbol of Latina vulnerability or weakness? Studies that have focused on the experiences of African American women in terms of what I identify as "having attitude" could provide a good complement to the Latina focus of my study. Nikki Jones's research (2008) focuses on how inner-city girls work Anderson's code of the streets and how new and renewed identities emerge at the intersection of categorical (race, gender, class, sexuality) and cultural (e.g., code of the streets) systems of accountability. The California (and Philadelphia) inner-city girls in Jones' study engage in a form of gendered code switching, actively embracing, rejecting, recreating, or recombining elements of hegemonic and local masculinities and femininities not only to become a particular sort of girl or woman, but also to survive in a setting where safety is never guaranteed. The intersecting systems of accountability led to the development of a worldview that simultaneously embraces and reflects "the code of the streets" and normative expectations of femininity (cf. Hill Collins 2000; Anderson 2000). This duality accounted for what Jones describes as "aggressive for the streets, pretty for the pictures."

For many Latinas, instances of ocular exchanges reinforced the perspective that African American women were dangerous and gave life to stereotypes that arose from and fed into a deep social structural separation that, in turn, impeded some black and Latino possibilities for mutual understanding and meaningful engagement. Instead, what many young women, like Zaida and Lucía above, frequently noted was similar to the ocular violence that Mitchell Duneier and Harvey Molotch (1999) referred to as "interactional vandalism." For many of these young US-born Latinas and, especially, Latin American migrant women, the "gazes" of African American women were senseless acts that, "akin to the more familiar forms of vandalism, involving assault against the taken-for-granted ordering of physical property, are also artfully constructed oppositional moves" (cf. Cohen, in Duneier and Molotch 1999, 1288). Perceiving themselves as subordinate in this visual exchange, Latinas oftentimes felt they were unable to articulate what had just happened. They fell back on emotion and feeling rules to deploy a vocabulary for what otherwise constituted a problem with no name. Many Brazilian migrants, for instance, viewed African American anger as "narcissistic," while African Americans and some Puerto Ricans viewed "anger" and "attitude" as instrumental.

Oftentimes, US-born Latinas and, especially, Latin American migrants associated African American women's "attitude"—which they interpreted as a form of vulgarity and un-feminine behavior—with a way of establishing a claim over Newark as "their territory" and even as a form of "surviving in the streets." Yet, while Latinas contemplated these alternative explanations for an "undesirable" behavior, they still focused on what they viewed as African American's women inherent inability to maintain the form of heteronormative femininity many Latinas valued as "taking care of oneself." As examined in chapter 4, "taking care of oneself" referred not only to surviving the streets, but also to maintaining feminine appearance and mannerisms in securing respect. Even in instances when Latin American migrants recognized that African Americans had been historically oppressed, they oftentimes still viewed African American "aggression" or "anger" as violating cherished values of hard work and condemned them for making illegitimate demands on the racial status quo.

Evaluations of "sexuality" focused on an aesthetics of propriety associated with "self-care" and emotional capital and downplayed other forms of structural subordination. While the bodies of African American women were more frequently described in terms of stereotypes of "butch lesbians" (or las buchas, as they were translated into Spanglish, or machúas, in Spanish), these physical representations were also associated with a careless appearance—baggy clothes, being overweight or "tough looking," wearing corn rows, and so on—and a form of militancy that was alternatively legitimized and rendered chauvinistic. Maura Silva described an incident in which she was walking past a group of "big black women." "'You think you pretty? She thinks she's all that.' They kept saying that to me, in a very aggressive manner," explained Maura when describing a situation she had encountered the previous day. Maura had gone to Essex County to check out a community college program. "Did you say something?" I asked her. "Oh no . . . I'm just not like that. They give me that look, staring and provoking me, but I just treat them as if they were annoying men down the street. That's the only way to survive, if you look a certain way."

Likewise, Susana García, who described her experience on the bus, interpreted the way that African American women reacted to her as follows:

"They think I'm stuck up. Because I like to wear certain things and take care of my hair, my nails. They wear torn clothes or faded animal print and stuff like that." And laughing at the recollection, Susana added:

I remember getting into this fight with this big morena when I was in high school. I mean, this kid was like 300 pounds, huge! Looked like a man, I swear. And she says something to me like. "Booty, where did you go?" As if my ass wasn't big enough. And I'm very proud of my ass, so I was like, "What the hell, have you looked at yourself in the mirror?" But she had her friends with her, and I knew her friends thought I was stuck up, too, because they really like me. You know, *liked me* liked me. They'd say things like "You think you're all that? You think you're prettier than us, bitch?" Stuff like that, you know. And keep staring and staring. You can't show them fear. Never.

In his excellent ethnographic study of a Spanish town, David Gilmore (1987) documents how the phenomenon of mirada fuerte (strong gaze) is related to sensitivity to shame. Looking and voyeurism are the precursors to public exposure and shaming, as they become forms of disguised, ocular aggression, which are oftentimes substitutes for actual physical aggression and are intended to maintain a status quo. As Gilmore argues, there are specific culturally approved expressions of hostility that bind communities together, including indirect expressions such as gossip and nicknames. Situations of intense ambivalence are likely in most social orders because they arrange and encourage emotional attachments or hopes that inevitably come into conflict. Instances of ambivalence can also be a nodal point of instability in a normative emotional style. By allowing women full expression of aggressiveness or strength (but no other feeling), for instance, and by treating aggression/strength as a source of honor for women, emotional conventions try to tip the balance of ambivalence. This is not a culture creating aggression, but a convention promoting certain emotional expressions. For instance, Patricia Williams (1997) notes that a "forbidden gaze" of race, to see or not to see race or difference is a political act that is characterized by doubt and confusion, so that "race matters are resented and repressed in much the same way as matters of sex and scandal: the subject is considered a rude and transgressive one in (racially) mixed company" (6).[6]

When I asked Amarilis, the Puerto Rican woman in the introduction to this chapter, if she noted situations in which the connection between Puerto Ricans and African Americans were characterized by greater collaboration than she had suggested in the case of Ashley being jumped, she declared:

Listen, my father is a black man. He's a black Puerto Rican raised by a black man in the 1970s. He went through the Newark riots, the civil rights movement, all that. Back then, kung fu movies were very popular and I think that attracted him to karate. It was also a way for him to defend himself. That's what he wanted to pass on to me, though he got to be black belt and I haven't yet. . . . You had to be tough to live in Newark back then. Now violence is of a different kind. . . . And, with all those experiences he had, he still tells me that things were not as violent as they are now.

Nevertheless, while Amarilis emphasized the tensions between African American and Puerto Rican women, she continued to develop more generalized views of urban violence in later conversations. For instance, the death of Sujeiti Ocasio and trial of Nicole Guyette, described in chapter 2, was evidence of how the militancy that characterized black nationalism (and the Young Lords in the Newark of the 1960s and 1970s) had been redirected inward, even penetrating the family circle and long-term friendships. The ambiguity of situations characterized by emotion and desirability allowed greater maneuvering and oftentimes required that Latino and Latin American youth viewed "race" and "racism" as something that could be addressed in the terrain of individual action, while undermining political economic structures.

There was a propensity in Newark to consider emotions such as "anger" and "aggression" as irrational because they were oftentimes relegated to an uncertain interpretive process among individuals who navigate the city's racial terrain evoking psychological images of adequacy, becoming or acting as street therapists. The very notion of "having attitude" framed Latinas' prolific descriptions of instances of ocular violence or perceived forms of "interactional vandalism" or "technical rudeness" (Anderson 1990). Nevertheless, as Ronald de Sousa argues in his examination of the "rationality of emotion," the faculty of emotion is in fact required for the more conventional mechanisms of rationality to function (1990). Likewise, Gilmore provocatively argues against the common wisdom that regards human aggression as maladaptive and disruptive, arguing instead that aggressive behavior can be socially useful. Individual hostility and culturally approved conflict link private emotion with public society.

As noted in the introduction to this volume, the perspective of US-born Latino and Latin American migrants, particularly of Puerto Ricans and Brazilians, are dominant throughout this research. The perspectives of African Americans, particularly African American women, toward the Latinos and Latinas whose voices appear here would provide a rich complement to the analysis of the gaze and, more broadly, the intersection of neoliberalism and affect. David Ebenbach and Dacher Keltner (1998) provide a model to analyze the effects of power and emotion upon social judgment and the social implications of power asymmetries in judgment accuracy. These authors propose that when individuals come to see each other as opponents, they are more prone to stereotype each other as extremist in terms of actions, views, and perspectives. This is the result of a heuristic effort-saving strategy and, I would add, a result of a political economy that centers around racial segregation in neighborhoods and communities. As Ebenbach and Keltner conclude, only when occupying a lower relative power position or experiencing an increased emotion is a group or individual likely to go beyond stereotypes and make more nuanced social judgments. Thus, powerful majority partisans are less accurate judges but more accurately judged than less powerful minority partisans; self-reported sense of power and reduced negative emotion were both associated with reduced judgmental accuracy. Moreover, although one might expect emotion to increase irrationality in group decisionmaking processes and set the stage for poor decisions, the opposite seems to be true: those individuals and groups who are highly emotional about a divisive issue may be more motivated to reach accurate, informed judgments than those who feel less emotion about the issue. In particular, negative emotions are believed to motivate the individual to devote attention to the object or cause of the emotion (de Sousa 1990; Keltner, Ellsworth, and Edwards 1993).

Power seems to decrease the social perceiver's inclination to pay careful attention to others and to reach accurate judgments about them. Thus, affect motivates the individual to attend more carefully to her or his environment, but also such emotion encourages accuracy by decreasing the unrealistically positive illusions that groups or individuals might hold about themselves or their group. What remains unaddressed in this analysis, however, is the role of power in intraminority (horizontal) power relations, which is what we find in cities like Newark. Such relations are highly variable in context because power continuously gets reassessed and becomes so all-consuming that it is at times dangerously intractable, particularly in cases where neoliberal projects have successfully concealed the role of the market and white supremacy in tacitly orchestrating even the most intimate and quotidian interactions. Who dominates or holds the power in Latino-black interactions in Newark? Is the social judgment of black lesbians that Amarilis, a Puerto Rican lesbian, and other Latinas develop "accurate"? When many Latinos judged black women—and assumed, sometimes accurately, sometimes not, that they were lesbian and "aggressive"—the accuracy of their heteronormative racialized assessments needed to be call into question.

"As long as they don't give me attitude, I'm cool": "Coming Out" in High School

In instances in which Latinas admitted or even bragged about having been involved in incidents of violence and fights, they emphasized that they were responding to a provocation (usually by a black woman), rather than perpetrating the act. As Amarilis suggested, even other Latina lesbians viewed black women's homosexuality as "aggressive," and, despite having interviewed several Latinas who self-identified as "lesbian," never did any of them express any form of solidarity, as a sexual minority, with black women. Amarilis, who had commented on the aggressiveness and "butch" quality of black lesbians in Newark, contrasted her relationship with African Americans to that with other Latinos:

I dated a Brazilian woman once. I met her at the Puerto Rican Day Parade. I stumbled onto her and wet her shirt accidentally. Immediately I said, "I'm so sorry!" And she said, "You don't have to be sorry" [seductively]. So I was like, "Uhm . . . I guess I won't be sorry then!" [laughed]. I ran into her at a party afterward and she and I hooked up. She stayed here for two or three months and then went back to Brazil, because she was just visiting. Eventually she came back here and she wanted to be together, to have a relationship, all that. And I just didn't want that, you know. It was a fling, that's what it was. But she allowed me to see first-hand how Brazilian women are so comfortable with their bodies, they're sexually very free, very open. That's not like black . . . or white . . . women at all.[7]

Despite comments—almost urban legends—about the role of "black lesbian gangs" or "aggressive black lesbians" in the fabric of the city, there was also a general perception that gays and lesbians were accepted and more visible in Newark than in other cities. Former New Jersey governor Jim McGreevey's self-proclamation as a "gay American" in 2004 (chapter 4) simply confirmed this perception in the minds of many Newark residents. Likewise, conversations about an increasing number of young working-class and poor Latinos and Latin American migrants "coming out" and the assumed "trendiness" sometimes associated with being gay abounded among high school students at East Side High School and Barringer alike. Among the students and faculty of ESHS in the Ironbound, there was a sense that same-sex desire and same-sex couples were more

267

accepted and visible in the schools now than in the past. Although very few students apparently identified as "gay" at Barringer in North Broadway, discussions about "black lesbians" were commonplace. As Amarilis, a Barringer graduate herself, mentioned: "Nobody was out at Barringer when I was there. Las buchas only! But those were the only ones. Everyone else came out after they graduated. So I hear stories now 'Did you know that so-and-so is gay?' But I think there has been an explosion of gays. Newark is a good place for gays."

Straight-identified students at both schools claimed that gays were very accepted, even when they qualified their own progressive mindedness, as Michelle Sánchez, a Puerto Rican and Dominican student at Barringer, did when she said: "as long as they don't mess with me, they can go have sex with anyone they want. I'm cool." An ironic twist to this is that among the Latino students who were openly gay at Barringer, a sophisticated racial consciousness was the filter through which a consciousness of oppression against sexual minorities developed. For instance, when Amarilis presented her senior project on "gay marriages," several teachers, many of whom were older Italian men and African American fundamentalist Christian women, explicitly made sounds of disgust. One of them, an African American female teacher in her forties, loudly remarked the now-cliché phrase: "God intended marriage to be between a man and a woman!" After the presentation, when a few, mostly Puerto Rican and Dominican, students asked her if she was okay after the heated reaction to her project, she remarked on how it was "always white old men and those black church women that make their ignorant comments."[8] While at Barringer, a school whose very history was intertwined with various racial riots in Newark, issues of sexuality were articulated through narratives of discrimination and oppression, at ESHS sexual orientation was sometimes viewed as a "trendy identity" that involved continuous evaluations of "authentic" versus "pretend" sexualities, and which corresponded to white middle-class engagement with "gay" as a potential market niche (cf. Decena 2008; Pascoe 2007; Peña 2008). For instance, Edwin Rivera, an "openly gay" Puerto Rican senior who worked as a part-time hairdresser in the Ironbound, echoed what other teachers and students at the Ironbound high school had told me: "Everyone wants to be gay now! It's become like a trendy thing, especially in these past few years."

Jen Carvajal, a young Cuban teacher at the Ironbound high school, commented: "You have those [students] who are legitimately gay and have come to realize they're gay. They admitted they were gay and got all the ridicule for it. A kid like Tony. He's like, 'Miss Carvajal, I don't even know how to act like a guy. I'm just feminine.'" Being "gay" was presented as an emotional stereotype that must necessarily involve trauma, frustration, and analysis, or it was not genuine. Descriptions of "legitimately gay" students appeared in contradistinction to the fact that some Latino and Latin American youth, particularly the women, selectively "performed" same-sex desire to the service of heterosexual normativity; that is, "to get guys," as Evelyn, a Puerto Rican student at the Ironbound high school, claimed. "A girl might think, 'Oh he's hot, I'm going to get with this other girl in front of him to get him interested.' Last year there was this one girl. One month she loved boys. She was like, 'Oh, I'm so in love!' Then the next month she was like, 'I'm gay.' And then the next month she was crying in the bathroom because some guy broke up with her."

Latina women who identified as "gay" could be considered either "really gay" or "pretend gay," but this fluidity was not available to black women, whose sexuality was defined exclusively in terms of a perceived "aggressiveness." In these particular cases, some teachers and fellow students failed to consider the potential dangers, or even outright street violence, that may have motivated some young women to avoid a public identity as lesbian or, more generally, the ways in which "teenage girls viewed their own sexual desire as dangerous" (Tolman 1994, 336). Likewise, with Latino and black men, particularly those who lived in the projects in the outskirts of the Ironbound, there was the general view that it was difficult to "tell" because of their "tough" demeanor. Evelyn's friend, Cristina, who is Puerto Rican and Dominican, commented: "There was this gay guy that I know and he said, 'Well, you know, other guys that you know in the projects, they try to be all tough and chop? I've had them.' Sounds like latex does make a difference. I started looking at them like, Whoa, who am I dating here?" The "ability to tell" suggested one's cosmopolitanism and "urban competency" (Ramos-Zayas 2007). But equally empowering and suggestive of an urban competency was the ability to "know what not to know" in public secrets, since this demonstrates "not only that knowledge is power but rather that active not-knowing makes it so" (Taussig 1999, 6).

A final important theme in discussions of same-sex desire in Newark involved the ways in which "being gay" acquired centrality as a public identity and was an open subject of conversation in a way in which "race" generally was not. At the faculty lounge at Barringer, a white male teacher stated: "There are a lot of gays here." Other teachers agreed with that statement. Another black female teacher mentioned: "That's why girls are afraid to go to the bathroom. Once a girl asked me for permission to go to the bathroom and I noticed that she came back really quickly, so I asked her 'Are you back already?' and she told me that there were two girls kissing in the bathroom so she hadn't gone in." The teachers responded: "Wow, imagine that. They can't even go to the bathroom." Another black teacher commented: "Yes, because girls are very aggressive. They would try to come on to other girls." The same white male teacher: "Do you know that student that is very effeminate . . . what's the name of the student you're talking about? Is he obviously gay?" The black female teacher: "No, none of them is obviously gay, you know."

An even more immediate instance in which "gay" had become a public identity involved three Latino students who attended the local public high school in the Ironbound. When I arrived at the school one morning, Michelle Sánchez, Mike Rivera, and Evelyn Rosa were rehashing an incident they had experienced the previous morning after they had left the school building to go to their respective internships as part of a "work experience" requirement. As Evelyn explained, they had stopped by one of the small cafeteria-style restaurants in the Ironbound. And Michelle continued: "So we are getting something to eat and the truancy officer [who monitors students for tardiness] comes up to Mike and moves to his side and calls him 'gay.' He said, 'No because he's gay.'"

Mike added: "But get this: There were two teachers from [the Ironbound High School]. Mr. D'Agostino and Silva and they did nothing."

Still trying to figure out the incident, I asked: "So the officer just came up to you and said 'You're gay'? Just like that?"

And Mike explained: "Yes. He said something to the effect that we were tardy or not supposed to be there, which was not even true, but . . . then he said that he was talking to the three of us, 'the two girls and the gay guy.' I just left the place. I couldn't believe it. The two teachers just sat there. They were also calling me that."

A person of color's sexuality brought marginality and conceptions of "illegality" out of the closet in a way that "race"—in its racial democratic configurations—did not. These contexts involved violence, both street violence and legal, systemic violence like a brush with the law. The most referenced of such situations was the hate murder of Sakia Gunn, a fifteen-year-old African American lesbian who was stabbed to death in the Central Ward of Newark on May 11, 2003, when she told two men who were harassing her that she was a lesbian. The men became angry and attacked her and the two women who accompanied her (DuLong 2003; El-Ghobashy 2003). Her case was evidence of violence not only against sexual minorities, but also of a strong African American lesbian presence in Newark, and the case regained attention in 2007, during the school-yard shootings, discussed in the next section.[9]

The "Schoolyard Shootings": Reading Hate Crimes in Newark

Four African American college students were shot "execution style" in a Newark schoolyard in the summer of 2007. On August 4, Terrance Ae-riel, Dashon Harvey, and Iofemi Hightower were lined up against a wall on the grounds of a Newark elementary school and shot in the head. Natasha Aeriel, Terrance's sister, was also shot in the head and left for dead, though she survived. The case sparked widespread national and international media coverage and heated debates. Even by Newark stan-dards, this particular crime became etched in the city's collective memory and dominated discussions around trust, pain, fear, and anger.[10] Rather than a broader analysis of racial tension in light of resource scarcity or a change in urban demographics and policy priorities, what took precedent in popular and official narratives was the biography of the individuals. As this section shows, discussions of the incident shifted from an initial focus on antiblack Latino violence, ensconced in a (selective) biography of African American victims and Latin American perpetrators, to a focus on what had been concealed and revealed in such early interpretations of this event: the possibility that this was an antigay hate crime.

In a city where crime was sometimes treated as a common occurrence, these particular shootings dominated popular discourse and media cover-age for several months. In the first week or so of the coverage, three main themes dominated: First, the fact that the victims were "good kids"—col-lege students, from church-going families, none having a criminal re-cord. Moreover, attention was given to the fact that the perpetrators were Latin American migrants, one of whom was "illegal," and had committed prior crimes. Finally, while official reports claimed that the motive was robbery (even when nothing of material value was stolen), rather than "gang related," in everyday conversations the discussions quickly high-lighted the fact that some of the perpetrators were affiliated with the Cen-tral American MS-13. These main themes, together, produced narratives that showcased Latin American migrants as inherently prone to commit acts of violence against African Americans. This antiblack Latino stance merits some discussion.

As the Latino and Latin American migrant population grows in formerly black areas, a rising concern about the "threats" that these newcomers—most of whom are assumed to be "illegal immigrants"—pose to African Americans dominates popular media.[11] In particular, the increasing Latino presence in longtime black cities and neighborhoods has been identified as a source of "anger" and even "black flight" among African Americans, who feel they are losing an already precarious economic grasp and political power in black communities in light of these rapid demographic transformations. For the most part, violent incidents highlighted in national media accounts compellingly dispel the myth of (or potential for) "black-brown" alliances.[12] Journalistic reports cite historical antecedents of anti-immigration streaks in the black community, along with predictable decries of competition in certain labor-market niches, the proliferation of gang-based street violence, and the reconfiguration of electoral districts along racial lines, as areas of critical conflict between blacks and Latinos in the United States.[13] More recently, mounting incidents of antiblack racism among US-born Latinos and Latin American migrant youth, particularly in Los Angeles, has been characterized as the "Latino ethnic cleansing of African Americans" and related to "the diasporic origins of [Latino/Latin American] anti-black sentiment" in a *Los Angeles Times* op-ed.[14] Although "black-brown" tensions have captured the attention and imagination of scholars and the popular media in recent years, we know very little about how US-born Latinos and Latin American migrants perceive the quality of their interaction with African Americans.

Given these interpretations of black-brown relations, the "Hispanic-on-black" crimes of the summer of 2007 provided fertile analytical terrain to examine how the intersection of race, emotion, and sexuality configure urban landscapes. Amarilis and her friend, Yesenia Almonte, were the first ones to share with me their thoughts about the shootings. "That was MS-13 . . . ah, and the girl that survived was raped. I saw when they brought her into University Hospital. I was working there that night," declared Amarilis, who had worked security jobs in various sites in Newark's Central Ward.

"But they said that it wasn't gang related," I mentioned, reciting what I had heard in the mayor's office press conference right after the shootings. I was also surprised by Amarilis's comment about the rape, which at that point had not been mentioned.

"That's what Booker says, but no, that was MS-13," assured Yesenia. And she added: "The reason why they say it's not gang related or drug related is because they're trying to bring up all that downtown area, so they don't want people to know that these things happen here. I don't know if they've caught them or what, but there was a poster up for one of the MS-13 gang members."

"What do you think the motivation was for something like this?" I asked them.

Amarilis: I bet the kids were sitting there. They probably got stupid. These were college kids, hanging out in their break, chillin'. Something happens in Newark every day. Every day something goes down. There's so much stabbing, gunshots, so much stuff going on. But many times people handle that among themselves. They don't want the police to get involved, because that means that you can't handle your own battles. Most of this stuff is over stupid shit. Sometimes somebody says the wrong shit or you're at a bar and somebody rubs you the wrong way and boom-boom-boom a fight explodes. You're in a big ass fight and get stabbed.

Yesenia: And you know what? People coming from those countries they come from, they crazy. They crazy and they don't like blacks. I'm telling you the truth. People have that big misconception that morenos [blacks] here are hard, but they're shit compared to the MS-13. They're shit compared to the Haitians, to the Africans. Those Colombians . . . let me tell you, they're crazy.

Amarilis: But they have to defend themselves. Mexicans and Salvadorans, and anybody from Central America, will get more shit. I'm not going to lie. I have boys who are Puerto Rican and Dominican and they see a little Mexican kid walking around or whatever and they don't care, they'd beat the shit out of them. That's what caused the MS-13 and the shootings.

Although the thematic focus of Amarilis and Yesenia's conversation was the MS-13, perceived as utilizing a new breed of street violence that was presumably imported from abroad and dominated over a less-sophisticated local street violence in Newark, the subtext of this discussion had to do with the role of "immigrants" and anti-immigrant attitudes in a context of antiblack violence. As hinted in this conversation, instances of extreme violence are subsumed under pressing neoliberal aspirations of reconstructing Newark—"bringing up sowntown"—as safe for real estate investment. As Teresa Caldeira notes in the case of São Paulo,

Crime supplies a generative symbolism with which to talk about other things that are perceived as wrong or bad, but for which no consensus of interpretation or vocabulary may exist. . . . In fact, it is the recurrent translation and continuous reflection of these different levels through the common vocabulary of crime and its categories that dramatize the evaluation of society's predicaments. (2001, 34)

Moreover, talks about crime not only added a dramatic effect to an individual's relatively uneventful quotidian experience, but also served as a template to denounce the improper channeling of emotions. When I asked Amarilis and Yesenia why they thought some young people joined a gang like MS-13, they agreed without hesitation: "Lack of love." I probed into this curious response, and Amarilis elaborated: "The females have such loyalty to their men. They go to any length to prove that. Latin King or Nietas . . . you're not allowed to join if you're gay. Those women that are there are either a Latin Queen, because you got initiated in it, or you're a personal queen, which means that you're the girlfriend." And she added: "Yes, ultimately, you think you do it for love to your man. You get brainwashed."

Initially, discussions around the schoolyard shootings centered on whether the influx of "illegal" Latinos into formerly black-majority neighborhoods was to blame for contributing to heightened "Hispanic-on-black" violence. As expressed by Amarilis and Yesenia, "black-brown" antagonism was connected to a growing presence of sophisticated transnational crime networks.[15] Blogs denounced Newark's status as a "sanctuary city" for migrants, and commented on government's overly "lenient" approach to immigration. In the midst of Mayor Booker's declaration that Newark needed to "heal," t-shirts with the words "US Border Patrol" were worn by a few young African American men. Whether these t-shirts were fashion statements or in fact signaled the individual's work affiliation remained unclear, but many of the Latino youth with whom I spoke felt these were tools of intimidation or retribution for the schoolyard crimes.

Nativist comments provided the more functional read of the incident, until almost two months after the crime when, in September of 2008, what had been popular rumors were captured on a letter that was sent to Mayor Cory Booker and published in the alternative media. Written by black gay activist James Credle on behalf of Newark's Lesbian, Gay, Bisexual, Transgender, Intersex, Queer and Two-Spirited Concerns Group, the letter questioned why the shootings had not been examined as an antigay hate crime, particularly given Newark's past history of antigay violence (e.g., the Sakia Gunn case, discussions of the "Schoolyard Shootings"). "Why, when so much was said about the victims, about their promise, their accomplishments, the bright futures, was this important aspect of their lives [their sexuality], their very identities, suppressed? Would that somehow diminish their value, or the tragedy of their deaths?" wrote Credle. He questioned why none of the public statements made by the mayor or police director mention the sexual orientation of the victims "despite the fact several sources including friends, boyfriends/lovers of at least one of the victims and perhaps one of the parents knew that one or more of the murdered students were gay" (James Credle's letter to Cory Booker, circulated at a community organization meeting in Newark, September 28, 2007). The friend, who spoke on condition that he not be identified, said Dashon Harvey was openly gay and was out to his family. The friend said Iofemi Hightower did not identify herself as gay but "was pretty much like a tomboy," thus accentuating and protecting the ambiguity of sexuality and intractability of sexual minorities. And, in fact, rumors proliferated about the victims' sexualities (or, in the case of Iofemi Hightower, *other people's read of their sexualities*) and the possibility that they had been targeted for being or appearing to be gay or lesbian. Amarilis, herself very involved in queers of color groups in Newark, later mentioned that a group of prominent church leaders along with the city government had agreed not to pursue the antigay angle of the crime to preserve the victims' "good [i.e., heterosexual] reputation."

Rumors and deeply emotive crime-talk led many young queers of color, including Amarilis, to look into Iofemi Hightower's MySpace page: At twenty years old, Iofemi Hightower was the oldest in the group that was shot. She had attended Essex Community College, but was in the process of enrolling at Delaware State University for the fall. She had close ties to the Aeriels since elementary school and even attended the prom with Terrance Aeriel. Her MySpace page featured a "Before and After" photo comparison of herself with Aeriel in 2006 and 2007. In the "Before" picture, the couple is dressed up in formal prom wear with matching blue and white colors. In the "After" picture, Hightower sports a baseball cap and a sweatshirt. Alternative media focused on several aspects of the life histories of the victims that merited that this crime be examined for a possible antigay hate motivation: that the victims might have been or looked gay, and were heading to a black Gay Pride festivity in Queens the next day; that one of the perpetrators was black; and that one of the victims and one of the perpetrators had gone to West Side High School together, where some of the victims had been known to be in "gay circles."

Alternative media sources eventually suggested that the mayor, who was elected as a reform candidate pledging to clean up Newark's image as a crime-ridden city, felt uncomfortable delving into the sexual orientation of the victims because at least some in the black community viewed homosexuality as a negative characteristic, and because rumors around the mayor's own sexuality were also common in Newark. The idea that examining the crime as an antigay hate crime might put families through greater pain dominated these public discussions, particularly because, in the eyes of many, these young people's sexualities could not be reconciled with the fact that they were, in fact, good kids with promising futures.[16]

The LGBT community had come to understand how violence in Newark had deep-seated homophobic roots. The most referenced of such situations was the hate murder of Sakia Gunn, mentioned above.[17] Her case was deployed not only as evidence of violence against sexual minorities, but also to illustrate a strong African American lesbian visibility in Newark.[18] Amarilis, who was an acquaintance of Sakia Gunn, commented:

It was so sad and at the vigil people were talking about the danger here in Newark and the violence. But you also have to understand that you are on a street corner of a homophobic and racist city. Why are you going to talk back to a bunch of assholes that come try to pick you up? They're assholes. They don't care about what you're saying!

AY: So you would have stayed quiet.

Amarilis: Hell yeah!

Worth noting in Amarilis's comment is how, even when it came to issues of the rights of sexual minorities, Amarilis, who was herself involved in queer social circles, situated herself as a Puerto Rican woman in contradistinction (and sometimes even in opposition) to the plight of African American lesbians, whose politics she viewed as "too aggressive" and "separatist" or, at the very least, impractical and dangerous. Nevertheless, Amarilis still viewed the visibility of lesbians of color in Newark as a direct consequence of the high profile antigay crimes that had been committed in the city and nationwide. "People heard about Matthew Shepard or Sakia Gunn and they were like, 'Oh shit, we can't stay quiet. We need to get out there,'" Amarilis explained.

In the 2007 shootings, the question was framed in a way that generated an inadequately dichotomized inquiry: Did the shootings have to do with antiblack Latino attitudes and Latino "illegality" or with antigay hate crimes? While the reading of this incident as an antigay hate crime was mostly explored by alternative media, the mainstream media and official spokespeople were more invested in doing two things. First, they downplayed any aspects of the crime that could have long-term repercussions on how Newark was viewed by potential investors. And, second, they highlighted antiblack Latino tensions so that new legislature—making it possible for "illegal" migrants to be arrested and deported on minor felonies, downgrading Newark's status as "sanctuary city" for migrants—could be more easily passed. A New Jersey prosecutor eventually declared that investigators had yet to find sufficient evidence to classify the murders as hate crimes. The inconclusive, ambiguous, and yet highly dichotomized official position on these crimes provided fertile emotive ground for forms of crime-talk that consolidated popular images of dangerous queer subcultures and "aggressive black lesbians," on the one hand, and of violent and predatory "illegal aliens," on the other.

The popular and media discussions around what became nationally and internationally known as "the Newark schoolyard shootings" in the summer of 2007 urge us to pay special attention to how individuals framed these violent events, understood triggers of conflict, and evoked emotions to discuss crime, particularly crime related to a victim's perceived sexuality, but also to issues around the "illegality" of Latin American migrants. Conflict became one of the few ways in which strangers got engaged with each other in a highly segregated urban context. The public realm of emotion led most US-born Latinas and Latin American migrant women to view African Americans in Newark in ways that rendered most, if not all, racial conflict as inherently gendered and queer.

This incident, as well as the association of black lesbians and aggression by many Latinas, informs us about the emotional landscape of the city and the role of the state, as it operates in self-protective and tacit ways to condition the horizontal power dynamics and relationships in the absence of white bodies. The incident was approached by authorities in ways that undermined the need for legislative protection for sexual minorities in a city that had a long history of antigay violence. Instead, while a meta-sentiment that did consider this history existed in quotidian conversations and painful community narratives, the state framed this tragedy in terms of a widespread dominant US narrative of migrant "illegality" (cf. De Genova and Ramos-Zayas 2003).

Reflections on Public Intimacy

As Avery Gordon (2008) emphasizes, discursive absences are crucially important because it is within the ideological spaces "blinded from view" that radical alternatives and perspectives, often those of the marginalized, "live and breathe" (193–202). Rather than discursive absences, positions of marginality in Newark are better characterized by a selective intervention in public discourse. That is, the intervention of the marginal are communicated in ways that are oftentimes inconsistent with, or even destabilizing of, official discourses, but arguably not in such a straightforward, openly resistant way. Instead, an emotional common-sense becomes an angle of political critique among some marginalized populations.

When I asked Amarilis Guzmán and Yesenia Almonte about the Newark shootings, and the discussion of these crimes as a product of antiblack Latino racism versus antigay hate crimes, they stepped back to analyze the situation from a different perspective by raising issues of trust and manners:

Amarilis: The problem here, to be honest, is a lack of trust. Nobody trust nobody.

AY: How do you mean?

Amarilis: Trust begins in that split moment. Trust begins in a moment. Because someone says something to you, and the other girl looks at you because that other person said something to you. It's that split second. It's even within a handshake. That's how fast it comes and that's how easy it can go away. It can happen with people you don't expect it to happen with. It's about who would have your back. That's how you measure it.

Yesenia: It's hard for me to trust anybody. I don't expose myself like that. Here everybody wants to know your business and that's just not me. I protect myself.

Amarilis: What caught me about her [referring to Yesenia], in terms of trust, was that she was standing this way and, when this guy came right behind her, she moved away from him. That caught my attention. She turned away from the guy. I could tell what she was about. If she would have stood there, to me that would have been an arrogance. Overstepping your boundaries to see how far you can get. Moving to the side, on this angle, is "alright, I'm moving on this angle, because if I look at you from this way, I really can't get everything. I got you on my side, I got you locked in my view, from my left to my right, front and back."

AY: So you were paying that much attention to all that?

Amarilis: I learned it because I was beat when I was young. I had to learn it quick. [Laughs] My ass was whipped a lot, so my reflexes had to kick in quick! I could hear a cop come running after me and I can tell whether they're just running up the stairs or they're about to get you. You know when to run. Aw shit! Some ass-whipping might be coming at me. That's why I wonder. I wonder how much those kids [that were shot in the playground] knew about survival skills. Because sometimes you see these tough, big morenas or tough Newark kids and you think they know this stuff. But they really don't. They don't know anything. Only if they've already been beaten up enough. Then maybe.

AY: So you feel that these kids were trusting or thought they were safe when they were attacked or . . . How exactly do you mean?

Amarilis: They saw these small Mexican or Peruvian or whatever guys, and they didn't really get what was going on. You don't know if these guys are in peace or in war, you know? You don't know if they know you're a fag or not. You don't know if they're MS-13 or not. You just don't know. So why you going to trust? You. Don't. Know. These. People!

Amarilis, a US-born Puerto Rican, and Yesenia, who was born in the Dominican Republic and arrived in Newark in childhood, were among the US-born or raised Latinos who interpreted racial relations in terms of trust, and who in fact problematized perspectives on Latino antiblack sentiment. Amarilis and Yesenia still viewed African Americans, particularly the black women whom they occasionally came into contact with in moments of queer activism, as "too aggressive." Nevertheless, at times they viewed "aggression" as synonymous with loyalty and even Americanness. In such instances, an intimate read of racial relations served also as a critique of broader urban projects, and how these projects impacted the everyday life of marginalized residents, Latinos and morenos alike:

Yesenia: There's still more commonality between Dominican, Puerto Rican, and black than between Dominican, Puerto Rican and Mexican.

AY: Why is that?

Amarilis: Maybe because they're too quiet. A Puerto Rican male will trust a black male before he trusts a Mexican male. Because the Mexican gets pushed around, they're always being bullied. A black male and a Puerto Rican guy, if they're homeboys and they're drunk, they'll go after anybody. They have each other back. And that's the main point. Who has your back. I don't have problem with moreno kids who are trying to get off the streets. But most of the morenos that I know, grew up around Puerto Ricans. Some of them even speak Spanish.

AY: What if they Mexicans are born in the US?

Amarilis: Yeah, they are a little different. I had a boy [in a youth group she directed]. You would never guess he was Ecuadorian. You would think he was Puerto Rican, because of the way he was. You're around Puerto Ricans, you start to pick that up. He carries that with him. You gotta be like that. You gotta be a chameleon. If you stick out, you hit. It's like a black fly on a white wall. It's about who's going to be there for you when all hell breaks loose, who knows the territory a little better. It's about everyone trying to get their respect.

This perspective on loyalty and respect emerged from an understanding that these interpersonal battles were ensconced in citywide demographics that require a variety of strategies of accommodation and adaptation. As Amarilis concluded:

It's always been a really big battle, because some people have a tendency to believe that they have struggled more than Latinos or more than anybody in this world. It's a power trip. So you have stubborn Latinos who are like, "Oh, no, this is our hood," and then you have morenos who are like, "We're taking over, because we struggled." Everybody from the South [Ward] hood is moving to our hood now that down there is becoming a mini–New York in prices. The rents are going up and people are asking $900 for a two bedroom, and that's uncommon in Newark. That's causing chaos. Not only that, but you have all these immigrants moving in as well. From El Salvador, Ecuadorian, Mexicans, that are coming in from the Ironbound section, too. That whole down south section is coming over here. People you don't know and you're supposed to trust them? The only option that people have is to beat each other up.

While "beating each other up" appears as a bleak outcome in Amarilis's analysis, however, these conditions also offer an alternative: Conflict is controlled through lessons, teaching, becoming racial experts, and acquiring urban competency. Implicit in contemporary debates about Latino antiblack attitudes and violent actions is the assumption that US-born Latinos and, particularly, Latin American immigrants are unreflective, unconcerned, and casual about their own racial prejudices, practices, and perspectives. Such an assumption undermines and misrepresents the complex, troubling, and intimate—indeed, emotive, affective, and sentimental—ways in which Latinos experience the process of acquiring everyday racial knowledge.

A racial learning process involves the creation of powerful feelings, which are sedimented as memories in the body of its pupil and serve as a reference point for subsequent illegible experiences. Feelings are both produced by and give meaning to racial beliefs; although they seem entirely personal, they are always experienced, and hence framed, by social conditions (Fentress and Wickham 2009, 2). This is not to say that context induces only a shift in the interpretation of feelings, but also that there is the emergence of a new way of feeling; thus, cultural context both generates feelings and provides a framework for their interpretation. Crime, danger, and aggression are vital parts of the articulation of personal belief systems in Newark. Crime mediates the relationship between the material or practical and the emotional worlds; learning racial difference, thus, is not purely practical, but also emotional. It gives way to feelings that are not merely responses to cognitive processes. It is significant that informants' descriptions of their feelings—for instance, their fear about impromptu moments of "aggression" or violence—were very similar, even when they had no way of judging whether their own feelings were the same as those of other people. There was agreement about what it felt like to live in Newark. The individual memory of a particular feeling—an experience of black women's jealousy—was collectivized in the process of establishing a common explanation of what each individual felt. Although usually lumped together and homogenized, US-born Latinos and Latin American migrants experience the process of racial learning in the US in very different nationality, class-specific, and profoundly emotive ways. This is the subject of the chapter 6.

SIX

Learning Affect, Embodying Race: Cosmopolitan Competency and Urban Emotional Epistemologies

The ghetto kids are just the wild kids you see in the hallways, with their baggy jeans, large shirts, chains . . . acting "hard." Like you have to be serious . . . not very friendly . . . to show you're tough, that they can't step on you. . . . It's just how they feel inside. If you look behind the surface, there is sadness. They try to fit in and be accepted. But they act hard sometimes for protection, not because they're really like that. It's a way for them to be cool, to pretend they're tough, even if they're not sure why they have to be. But I also know that some of these kids, specially the immigrant kids that just got here, they do that because they're afraid of blacks. That's the main reason. Maybe they never saw a black person like the ones here or . . . maybe they were picked on. They don't know how to act, so they're just serious and stay out of trouble. But it's a change you notice. You know Robert, right? He's from Ecuador, bilingual program? He was a small skinny kid and people made fun of him, but he was a sweet, friendly kid. Now you see him and he's like a different person. . . . I don't know, he used to be shy and quiet and now . . . he's still quiet, but in a more, you know, like he's in his own world and doesn't want anyone to talk to him. I personally think he's very depressed and wouldn't be surprised if he quit school and just disappeared one day. EMÍLIA RIBEIRO, BRAZILIAN STUDENT AT EAST SIDE HIGH SCHOOL

An outgoing and thoughtful student who had arrived from Belo Horizonte, Brazil, as a young child in the early 1990s,

Emília Ribeiro offered an insightful depiction of the pressure some migrant students experienced to "act hard" when I interviewed her in the fall of 2004. Like other Latin American students whom I met in two predominantly Latino neighborhoods in Newark, New Jersey, between 2001 and 2008, Emília attended to the style involved in descriptions of "ghetto kids" and, more significantly, to emotive and affective transformations that Americanization required. As suggested in Emília's narrative, the distinction between "acting hard" as a protective performance seemed almost objectless and lacking focus, while "being hard" was an almost unalterable quality attributed to an African American psyche. Like other US-born Latino and Latin American migrants in Newark, Emília identified "fear" as the primary emotion that guided Latin American migrants' reading of African Americans. Emília was one of the many students who noted that the Portuguese were considered "uncool" among other young people at the school and, because of that, many Portuguese and Portuguese American students tried to "pass for Puerto Rican." She paid attention to the performance in her descriptions of "ghetto kids"—whom she mostly associates with "Hispanics," a coded term for "Puerto Rican" at ESHS—but also to the physiological and cognitive component of emotion in the process of Americanization.

What do individuals' affective worlds tell us about multiscale experiences of race, racial ideologies, and racialization practices? What kind of emotional work do embodied practices of learning race require? How does becoming a racial subject in the United States and transnationally alter one's affective world and perspectives on the emotional and racial subjectivities of others? Under neoliberalism there has been an intensification in the cultural standardization and organization of feelings and sentiments (Haskell 1985). This organization of feelings and sentiments intersects with everyday evaluations of racial difference and ongoing processes of "racial learning," particularly among Latin American migrants and US-born Latinos. Racial learning is here understood as a behavior-contingent aspect of social action and a phenomenological experience, as well as a production of bodies through everyday disciplining and normalization in service of state and market goals (cf. Foucault 1977).[1]

The process of racial learning is inseparable from the trajectory from naturalization to citizenship in the United States. As legal scholar Devon W. Carbado (2005) pointedly emphasizes, "One need not be an American citizen to racially belong to America. To racially belong to America as a nonwhite is to experience racial inequality. To become an American citizen is often to cross the border into, not outside of, this racial inequality" (639). This is a lesson that Puerto Ricans, particularly those born in the

US mainland, know well and it is this expertise around the disjunctures of racial identity and American citizen that they teach, as racial experts, to Latin American migrants. The case of Puerto Ricans demonstrates that race is implicated in naturalization processes not only as a prerequisite or as a basis for determining who gets to become an American citizen, since all Puerto Ricans are US citizens by birth. Rather, race also determines the kind of American citizenship one occupies. Thus, "formal citizenship interacts with race to produce social citizenship, a status that attempts to track the social conditions—economic political, educational—of people's lives" (641). Carbado's concept of "racial naturalization" is invaluable in understanding the complex disjunctions between citizenship and identity.

In regards to the process of becoming American through the selective deployment of Blackness, as I describe it in this chapter, the main goal is to understand how the racial projects of the US nation-state produce racial expertise and encourages a particular transmission of racial knowledge; that is, an inherent component of the everyday practices and requirements of Americanization is the development of an epistemology about race that can be activated in accordance with the goals of capital accumulation and governmentality. That identity formation and knowledge happens, not only through the disciplining exerted by institutions of the nation state—such as the police, the educational system, the official process of "legalization"—but also in everyday evaluations of affect in light of one's experience with those nation-state disciplining mechanisms, as well as with communication with other racialized US populations. Comportment, self-discipline, and self-regulation are indispensable technologies of the self that racialized populations—who are more severely subjected to the pressures of governmentality—are required to master. Nevertheless, identifying the appropriate performance of obedience toward disconfirming or negating stereotypes can be a very complicated endeavor that requires extensive processes of scrutinizing, analyzing, and ultimately selectively mastering the behavior, attitudes, and even affect of others.

Latin American and Latino populations in urban areas of the United States navigate unfamiliar racial situations through the development of a quotidian emotional epistemology, that is, through a set of rules and assumptions about affect and its adequate expression, interpretations of how others feel or should feel, and the creation or performance of an affective persona. These rules and assumptions are informed both by US and transnational racial ideologies, social practices around performances of Blackness, socioeconomic hierarchies, and expectations of belonging on multiple scales, like the neighborhood, nation-state, and the market. Latin American migrants and US-born Latinos engage in a process of racial learning that render them street therapists of sorts. In Newark, a majority black city, Latinos filtered race through complicated affective lenses that also drew from Latin American views of racial democracy and what I have elsewhere referred to as a "cartography or racial democracy" (see chapter 3).

The internalization of racial systems, or learning how race operates in particular contexts, requires the suppression of some emotions and the performance or expression of others. Racial learning is transacted through feelings and transgressions in practice that may lead to unpleasant emotional dissonance, as feelings are produced by and give meaning to racial encounters between individuals and among individuals and context-based racial systems. Approaching what I understand as an embodied racialized affect in this way allows us to focus on the complexity of an interiority that always-already occupies a social and political space, a claim to personhood in the midst of social determinism. Rather than flattening the affect of the racialized poor, an embodied racialized affect centers on how the poor and marginal examine their affective and sentimental experiences and enter social consciousness through affect; it also might explain conditions of social subordination accordingly.[2]

I am not in search of the "essence" of emotional, passional, or attitudinal modes of consciousness; nor do I want to delineate their dynamics as if they were independent of the circumstances in which they occur. In this sense, a phenomenological approach is tempered by the political economic context in which affect is grounded, so that a "natural" or "intimate" attitude is not extrapolated from the always-already racial projects in which they are ensconced. Like Crapanzano (2004, 103–10), I question the possibility of a full phenomenological reduction given that we are embedded in a linguistically endorsed universe that prevents a prereflexive moment that is fully divorced from its endorsement. While affect may have its own linguistic and cultural logic, it is based on experiences of a socially encumbered personhood, not simply a cultural interior-focused "self." A focus on structure in relation to phenomenology allows the possibility not only for different modes of consciousness to be produced in different linguistic or cultural contexts, but to recognize that these differences are grounded and constitutive of particular political economic and historical conditions of inequality. Approaching affect through a racialization paradigm sheds light on an anthropology of the body by foregrounding a dynamic perspective on space and context (Lefebvre 1991).

By bridging discourses about affect, on the one hand, and the phenomenology of those affective states, on the other, one is able to examine the collective level of state construction of a racialized affect and the individual, visceral and experiential phenomenology of affect in everyday life (cf. Jenkins 1991). Through an analysis of individual's visceral, intimate experiences of the material environment, perspectives on embodiment can better capture where perception begins, when it constitutes and is constituted by culture, and how the very experience of perceiving might be influenced by social location and experiences of race. Indeed, it is through the study of affect and emotion that anthropology may best be fully re-embodied (Lyon 1995; Csordas 1990).[3]

As shown in the introductory vignette, Emília adopted a psychological lens to trace Robert's transformation from happy-go-lucky and almost naïve to somber, "depressed," and hardened. This is the transformation from "happy immigrant" to "depressed minority" that Americanization in the urban United States entailed. The transition from "happy immigrant to depressed minority" is articulated through an emotional epistemology that draws from national foundational ideologies, especially the American dream, and expectations of migrants in Newark. Learning negative affect has become a form of racial learning for many of the recently arrived immigrants from Latin America who have settled in Newark. Being able to be dark and having a different public mood was key to gaining urban competency and letting go of the folksy or backward ways associated with being an "immigrant" in the urban, majority-minority city. Among the poor and working poor, letting go of that happy or cheery emotional style signaled a kind of Americanization that reversed a mainstream social urging to be peppy, sunny, and cheery. It has been noted that contemporary emotional norms in the United States favor a "good cheer" (Kotchemidova 2005) or "compulsory happiness" (in Wilkins 2008) that represents a cooling of emotions and discourage any emotional intensity by expecting a sociability and exchanges of pleasantries as the everyday standard of social interactions in dominant middle-class (white) contexts (Stearns, in Wilkins 2008, 112).[4] Among US-born Latinos (and perhaps other US domestic minorities) and, to various degrees, among Latin American migrants, it has been the embodiment of various emotions coded as "depression"—as well as "anger," "aggression," and other forms of negative affect that I examine elsewhere (Ramos-Zayas 2009)—that has operated as critique of racialization practices in the United States and reracialization experiences in transnational contexts of origin, including Brazil and Puerto Rico, in my research. Rendering someone "depressed" becomes a form of tacit structural critique because it points to what is lacking or how things should be different. After all, why would a kid like Robert, who had hailed from the Ecuadorian highlands where he and his family had endured scarcity and marginality, not be happy, cheery, and grateful to "America," the Land of Opportunity? Under these conditions, how could Robert's "depression" be legitimate or justified?

In Emília's statement, there are various ways in which depression becomes a structural symbol that suggests the process by which an "immigrant" embodies race in the United States and effectively learns (cognitively and viscerally/phenomenologically) a new racial system. As Emília suggested, among Latin American migrants like Robert, race is embodied through a performance of Blackness that involves not only wearing a certain style of clothes, but performative alterations in one's affect—in particular, a shift from a happiness associated with naivete and even backwardness to a "depression" associated with hardened but also cosmopolitan urban life. In the United States, negative affect in general, and depression in particular, has been highly medicalized (Burr and Chapman 2004). Emília's insinuation that Robert may one day drop out of school and "disappear" points to how this pathological approach to negative affect is an important aspect of how some racial subjects are rendered legible. Depathologizing negative affect might allow for an examination of how global politics and history manifest themselves at the level of lived, embodied experiences (Cvetkovich 2003, 461). Nevertheless, in everyday emotional epistemologies, as individuals imagine how others must feel, depression simultaneously serves as a racializing pathology, a measure of racial learning, and structural critique.[5]

To view migrant kids who "act hard" solely in terms of negative affect would be an incomplete assessment of the emotional epistemology manifested in Emília's quote. This negative affect, which Emília described as "depression," must be situated in the context of Newark, a predominantly African American city, associated with urban decay, corruption, gang violence, and unemployment; as noted in earlier chapters, other informants described this urban emotional commonsense in terms of "anger" and "aggression" (see especially chapters 1 and 5). This context exists in contradistinction to a dominant state project that involves reinforcing the foundational mythology of the American dream (Ramos-Zayas 2003). In relation to migrants, an attitude of gratefulness has been cultivated by the nation state around the image of a "supercitizen immigrant" (Honig 2001) who is more of a citizen than domestic minorities would ever be. This reinforces the American dream mythology, notwithstanding economic crises and impossible upward mobility expectations. Among Latinos, those who cheerfully take on heavy workloads and oppressive work conditions, *without complaining or denouncing injustices,* are counterposed to those who are viewed as lazy, welfare dependent, or who have a "bad attitude" (i.e., who complain, appear "resentful," and denounce injustice in some way). Thus, as a state project, cheerfulness and appreciativeness can be exploited to serve market goals and interests in creating a tractable labor in a way that "bad attitude" might not be.

As analyzed in chapter 1, an important component of neoliberal policies—including the privileging of corporate and real estate interests, gentrification and urban development through cultural venues, and aiming to attract middle and upper-middle classes to the city through the "Newark Renaissance" (Newman 2004)—is that they foster new definitions of "good citizenship." These definitions of good citizenship oftentimes disconnect the citizen from the state and establish personal responsibility and, emotional adequacy as the main qualities necessary for improving urban life (Maskovsky 2001). In Newark African American mayor Cory Booker embodies, to various degrees, the success, respectability, *and* psychosocial adequacy to which a predominantly black city like Newark should aspire in order to combat its aggressive national image. Booker's public persona and image, as it has been circulated and promoted in Newark and nationwide, illustrates the critical characteristics expected of a quintessential neoliberal subject. These characteristics, rather than centering on professional achievements, public accomplishments, or even lifestyle, are, in fact, more directly concerned with overall emotional adequacy, quasi-spiritual values, and appropriate affect. This set of psychosocial and quasi-spiritual attributes of a good citizen, although largely undertheorized, are critical to visions of an effective neoliberal city. These affective, quasi-spiritual, and psychological practices have become critical to the differentiation of (neoliberal) citizens, regardless of actual legal status in the United States.

In Newark, many US-born and immigrant Latinos acquired racial knowledge through the continuous scrutiny of how African Americans (or even US-born Puerto Ricans) were institutionally racialized and how these US-born minorities themselves actively assumed or rejected such racialization practices; of how such antiblack subordination operated in historical and political contexts and impacted individual aspirations and opportunities; of how racial performances enhanced one's cosmopolitanism, modernity, and urban competency, while redefining gender, sexuality, class, and generational subjectivities; and how bipolar (black/white) perspectives of race in the United States converged and diverged from configurations of "race" in one's country of origin or ancestry. Depression and other forms of negative affect were ultimately associated not with just any form of Americanization, but with an urban Americanization associated with Blackness. Youth of color in Newark viewed "depression"—or more precisely, the presentation of a depressive or withdrawn persona—as evidence that a migrant possessed urban competency, had developed racial knowledge, and had become, in effect, Americanized.

While challenging ideas of immigrant passivity and backwardness, the transformation from "happy immigrant" to "depressed minority" unfolded in alignment with the material exigencies of urban neoliberalism and the creation of productive workers and consumers. Developing an appropriate emotional style—the one that strikes the body knowledge and balance to navigate a racialized Americanization and market expectations—was related to the capacity to be attuned to the emotional needs of the market. Thus an internal emotional alignment [Bourdieu's (1977) habitus and Merleau-Ponty's (1962) perception] in everyday social contexts was imperative to the process by which working-class youth of color were tacitly required to perform a great deal of emotional labor (Hochschild 1983) in the low-end service sector jobs for which they were destined under neoliberalism. In a predominantly black city like Newark, this urban "emotional regime" (Reddy 1997) required that Latinos manifested negative affect as evidence of no longer being an "immigrant," while still avoiding an overidentification with African Americans. This was a process of holding on to marketable expressions of affect. In this sense, the racial projects of the US nation-state were always-already projects of controlling the emotions of subordinate populations, of disciplining into racial subjectivity not only in the official realm of political institutions, but in the regulation of the most intimate, visceral, phenomenological quotidian forms of existence.

From "Happy Immigrant" to "Depressed Minority": Cosmopolitan Competency and Puerto Rican "Blackness" in Newark

In 2001, in the exploratory stages of this ethnographic project, I approached teachers, staff, and students at East Side High School in the Ironbound and Barringer High School in North Broadway for connections to Puerto Rican youth whom I could interview. "You definitely have to talk to Tasha and Jazmin," Leila Quiñones, then a Puerto Rican junior at East Side, declared. "They did the dance number with us," Leila reminded me, in reference to a talent show I had attended at the school that had resulted in girls being sanctioned for what teachers and staff considered to be sexually provocative moves and revealing clothes. As it turned out, while most other students and teachers at East Side agreed that I would have to include Tasha and Jazmin in my project, I later found out that neither Tasha nor Jazmin was, in fact, Puerto Rican. Tasha was Iranian and Jazmin was Cape Verdean. In an effort to unravel this attribution of "Puerto Rican"–ness to non–Puerto Ricans, I chose to interview these two young women and ended up spending quite some time with them throughout the period of my fieldwork.

An assertive and boisterous young woman, Jazmin Gonçalves had been born in Newark of Cape Verdean parents. Jazmin informed me, almost from the beginning of our exchange, that at East Side High School "all immigrants pretend[ed] to be Puerto Rican." When I asked if that was the same thing as "pretending to be black," Jazmin responded: "Sometimes those are two different ways of being, because it's easier [to get along] with Puerto Ricans." Later on, when I asked her about this in a formal interview in which Tasha Messud, Jazmin's good friend, also participated, Jazmin explained: "The ones that pretend to be Puerto Rican start speaking Spanish, hanging out with Puerto Ricans, and sometimes even waving the flag. . . . Well, I don't know if they'd be waving the flag. . . . But they'd be throwing in Spanish words, speaking like Puerto Ricans."

Tasha, an outgoing and insightful woman who had arrived from Iran with her parents as an infant, explained that fashion played a role in how "the immigrants" tried to "assimilate" to Puerto Rican. She commented: "People in this school think that you can change clothes and you change who you are, but that's not it at all." Adamantly, she continued: "We may wear certain things, but that's superficial. This is about who you are *on the inside*, how you *feel* when certain things are said, what makes you want to say 'yes, this is who I am.' Immigrant kids are pretending to know what's up, what being Puerto Rican is about and all that, but they don't have that common feeling or sense of who you are."

Both Jazmin and Tasha expressed great pride in the fact that their best friends were Puerto Rican, that they were bonded with these Puerto Rican friends by "knowing what's up," a phrase that at the time was used to suggest an implicit social knowledge that was articulated as much by words as by silences and corporeal expressions, and by knowing how to "have somebody's back," even if that intense display of loyalty compromised one's individual posturing. It was the commonality of "feeling" at an intimate, self-reflective, psycho-emotional level.

As I conveyed my interest in learning more about Puerto Ricans at the school, Edward Acevedo, the Puerto Rican principal of Barringer High School, suggested: "You may as well talk to any of the Ecuadorian girls at the end of the hallway." Noting my confusion, he added: "They know more about Puerto Ricans than anyone else here!" He later explained:

Ecuadorians *loooove* Puerto Ricans. . . . We Puerto Ricans love and embrace anyone who wants to be like us. That I have to say about us. We accept them just fine, as long as you want to be like us. . . . That's what we're really like. You want to be like us? You think we're decent, good people? Wow, we so appreciate you think that. We love you, we make you Puerto Rican! [laughed] But that's also because so many people think we're nothing, don't kid yourself about that.

A key question these perspectives raised was: Why is it that "Puerto Rican"–ness rather than (or perhaps in combination with) the well-documented strategies of "passing for white" or "passing for black" provided a more viable option for many Latin American migrants and some working-class white ethnics in Newark, a city where both Whiteness and Blackness had the potential for conferring powerful social standing? In his reading of Puerto Rican culture as open or receptive to anyone who wanted to "be like us," Edward also alluded to a Puerto Rican politics of worthiness and a delinquent citizenship that I discuss in chapter 2 (see also Ramos-Zayas 2004).

Urban competency was conflated with "Blackness" and rendered as a slick surface of images alienated from embedded social processes through commodification. Latin American migrants viewed such commodification of culture as an urban form associated with Puerto Ricans more than with blacks, partly because these immigrants had closer everyday connections and linguistic ties with Puerto Ricans. While Puerto Ricans were viewed as "closer to blacks," they nevertheless occupied an ambiguous position as US citizens and minorities, on the one hand, and as Latinos and sometimes Spanish-speaking, on the other. In a sense, "becoming Puerto Rican" meant letting go of "folksy" immigrant ways by acquiring urban competency. Moreover, for Latin American migrant youth in North Broadway, most of whom were Dominican and Ecuadorian, the deployment of an "urban" identity was less contested by blacks and Puerto Ricans than it was in the Ironbound, where Puerto Ricans and African American students monitored the boundaries of "the urban" very closely in light of a large Portuguese presence.

Racial learning and the production of racial knowledge provide an analytical framework for interpreting how US-born Latinos and Latin American migrants became speculators—"street therapists"—engaged in observing, interpreting, analyzing, and at times altering the everyday behaviors, body kinetics, and emotional lives of US-born people of color in Newark. Such forms of "racial learning" require that young people recognize not only explicit social rules, but also the implicit and ambiguous forms of social knowledge implicated in everyday exchanges (cf. Taussig 1999). Given that, as Pierre Bourdieu (1977) reminds us through his concept of "doxa," every established social order tends likewise to produce the naturalization of its arbitrariness, this was no easy task. It required strategies of learning situational incompetence—when *not* knowing how to do something in fact generated a symbolic or material gain. As Loic Wacquant argues, "knowledge is transmitted by mimeticism or counter-mimeticism, by watching others do things, scrutinizing their moves. . . . [This] sets into motion a dialectic of corporeal mastery and visual mastery: To understand what you have to do, you watch the others . . . but you do not truly see what they are doing unless you have already understood a little with your eyes, that is to say, with your body" (2004, 117). In fact, as Michael Taussig (1999, 6–7) notes, knowing what not to know in public secrets demonstrates not that knowledge is power but rather that active not-knowing or selective knowing makes it so. This likewise accrues value to the relationship between what is said about social difference and what "goes without saying" (Bloch 1992).

As street therapists themselves, Puerto Ricans were critical in measuring the level of "progress" that other Latin American migrants and working-class individuals sometimes undertook in attaining a cosmopolitan competency. In turn, these "pupils" were charged with learning about the urban doctrines of belonging, understanding the meanings of those doctrines from the point of view of the Puerto Rican (and, by association, black) "experts," believing that the doctrines were true and correct (i.e., believing in the sincerity and authenticity of those views), allowing the doctrines to structure the actors' perceptual worlds and guide their actions, and deploying such doctrines in instigating action. These levels represented an urban version of Melford Spiro's (1982) cognitive salience of cultural systems. Ultimately, the highest levels of success were measured by how these young pupils could render their racial learning legible in this urban context and through a Puerto Rican lens in a way that reflected a feeling-level emotional investment. Rather than a complete "Puerto Rican"-ization or buying into an "oppositional culture," however, many Latin American migrants and working-class ethnic whites were able to avoid the full racial consequences of the stigma associated with being Puerto Rican or African American in the United States.[6]

As this chapter shows, learning race through a "Puerto Rican" lens did not necessarily have to lead to downward mobility, as has been argued in the "oppositional behavior" literature; instead, what was critical was the selective incorporation of what was learned, including the importance of distinguishing between in-your-face and situational "attitude," the knowledge of when to appear standoffish, rude, friendly, and cheery in the context of racialized exchanges, determining who and when one trusted. I am not suggesting that the process of "passing for" Puerto Rican or even black leads to migrant social mobility, but rather that issues of mobility need to be examined in the context of political economy, not culture. While racial learning was often grounded in individual engagement with various forms of emotional experimentation, these processes also generated more nuanced distinctions between "US-born" Latino and Latin American "immigrants"; how these populations situated themselves in relationship to African Americans and their understanding of Blackness influenced by a transnational cartography of racial democracy that drew from images and memories in countries of ancestry or origin; and configurations of an "urban cosmopolitanism" that was often articulated in contradistinction to the presumed "backwardness" of migrants.

Racial learning and emotional experimentation among some US-born Latinos and, especially, among many Latin American migrants alert us to the need for reframing the seeming contradiction between antiblack Latino attitudes, on the one hand, and a desire for an urban competency associated with US Blackness, on the other. While US-born Latinos and Latin American migrants associated Blackness with "Americanness," and exerted claims to an urban competency in their effort to experiment with alternative forms of citizenship and belonging, the appreciation of Blackness among Latin American migrants generally failed to engage discussions of racial segregation, subordination, and capital inequality. I am not suggesting that such an engagement would necessarily be a sign of political consciousness or that a focus on the commercial aspects of Blackness eliminates the possibility for such a consciousness, but that "Puerto Rican" oftentimes served as a default or residual identity for many working-class migrants of color, particularly in northeastern US cities, as they engaged in the process of racial learning in the United States.[7] Judging urban competency on the basis of emotional adequacy privileged cosmopolitan and marketable elements of "multiculturalism" and "diversity," while reinscribing neoliberal forms of white supremacy, by in fact subjecting the racial projects of the state to heavily psychologized individual comportment.[8]

Central to my discussion and to the broader questions of social reproduction that are implicated in these forms of racial learning is: How does a meaning system associated with a subordinate Puerto Rican minority become desirable for non–Puerto Ricans, like Jazmin and Tasha, as well as for the Ecuadorian migrant girls that Edward described? That is, how do individuals develop knowledge—or even mastery and expertise—about the operations of a racial system and in what ways does that knowledge or "cognitive salience" (Spiro 1982) stimulate action? More important, to what degree is a desire for Puerto Rican–ness—which could arguably be conceived as a variant of Blackness—among Latin American migrants and other non–Puerto Rican working-class Newark residents also a critique of their social location in the United States? How do the state and neoliberal projects structure such conditions? In sum, when did "Puerto Rican"-ness—in itself and as proxy to Blackness—begin to serve as a benchmark of social belonging in ways that "Whiteness" or "Blackness" did not? An important claim here is, thus, that it was precisely the inconclusiveness and ambiguity that characterized the everyday exchanges between US-born Latinos and Latin American migrants that framed the production of racial knowledge. The process of learning "adequate" racial etiquette served as a form of urban cosmopolitanism that required not only an interpretation of the material world of natural and rational decisions, but more significantly of an internal world of emotional and irrational feelings in Newark, a predominantly black city considered "violent" and "aggressive" in the national imaginary.

To theorize some of the questions posed in the case of Puerto Ricans and Brazilians in Newark, I coin the term "cosmopolitan competency" to highlight the effective manipulation of a set of symbolic and material tools that US-born Latinos and Latin American migrants and working-class white ethnic residents associated with possessing the know-how and implicit social knowledge of everyday urban life. This includes not only a high consciousness of physical appearance, style-talk, fashion, and bodily kinetics, which other scholars have documented (e.g., Bettie 2003, Wilkins 2008), but also acquiring the implicit social knowledge and emotional capital to assess ambiguous or confusing racial situations and, ultimately, to project feelings onto (or speculate about the emotional adequacy of) African Americans; moreover, it entailed the effective navigation of the everyday interactions that took place in Latino neighborhoods and that undermined the social, emotional, and ethical parameters that subordinated racial subjects were expected to learn and negotiate.

Unlike an adversarial outlook associated with black "underachievement," cosmopolitan competency involves selecting elements from a "defective" Blackness and, by including references to a transnational urban competency and racial democracy paradigm, developing a more "suitable" copy of Blackness. It is, ultimately, the process of "doing Blackness right," which I analyze below. For US-born Latinos and Latin

American migrants, Blackness and cosmopolitan competency operated in tandem and served not only as emblematic of subordination, but also of American-ness or, more notably, of *non-immigrant-ness* in a time of heightened nativism and anti-immigrant sentiment, and in a context where being an "immigrant" also stood for backwardness, folksiness, an undesirable "immigrant [indigenous] look," and, ultimately, un-American-ness.[9] This cosmopolitan competency, therefore, required not only that an outright "adversarial outlook" be avoided in the "assimila-tion" process (Ogbu 1982; Waters 1999), but also that some elements of "urban"-ness be selectively rescued as an alternative form of symbolic capi-tal. The affiliation of migrants with US-born minorities might involve not only the potential for stigmatication and downward mobility, especially in the US-born second generation but, conversely, also one of the few roads to claiming an adequate American identity.

Practices of enhancing character and emotional development, racial expertise, and appearance (e.g., tough, self-sufficient) accounted for a new form of urban socialization that furthermore suggested how capi-talism in fact repositioned social reproduction from private households into public (and heavily policed) spheres, and reconfigured the unspoken feeling rules of these interactions. Controlling, expressing, and interpret-ing emotion, in such urban contexts, were critical aspects in the devel-opment of a tractable, subordinate labor, especially in the service sector, low-wage industries—the ones most readily available to working-class youth and adults—that required great degrees of compliance and emo-tional work (cf. Hochschild 1983). These contemporary emotional norms contributed to the creation of the smooth, tension-free social relations necessary for the organization of late-capitalism (Kotchemidova 2005). A "good disposition" and emotional control "contrast with stereotypes of blacks and US-born Latinos as fiery, volatile, and in-your-face" (Wilkins 2008).

People who were considered to have a great deal of cosmopolitan com-petency were oftentimes those who had become cultural polyglots, able to master both dominant and alternative forms of cultural capital, and skilled at displaying emotions with a pointed awareness of contextual propriety; they were adept at manipulating images in such a way as to both critique and mimic, and to articulate mainstream expressions when engaging with institutions. Perspectives on appropriateness—on which these views of "passing" or "acting" are ensconced—were not empty discourses; instead, they spoke of and expressed sentiments that were everywhere, even though they have often been sidestepped in scholarly accounts of adversarial youth subcultures. In this sense, scholars have turned away from a focus on sentiment as a way of dismissing the deni-grating irrationality and charged passions attributed to colonized peoples as features of colonialism's reductionist racist ideologies. As Ann Stoler argues, "attachments and affections get cast as compelling flourishings to historical narratives, but as distractions from the 'real politik' of empire, its underlying agenda and its true plot" (2004, 6). The material, political economy of urban neoliberalism makes one question a very pressing one for Latin American migrants: What is the proper packaging of oneself as an "immigrant"? How can a less-threatening racial formation be articu-lated so that one remains or becomes a neoliberal subject while navi-gating the volatile terrain of everyday urban life and in-your-face racial situations? How are people's existence simultaneously commodified and criminalized depending on their individual and group-based deployment of culture and what's the intentionality behind these performances? How does one make an effective copy of an otherwise defective self? That is, how does one make an "effective copy" of an otherwise "defective" Black-ness? Is the view of "race" as an individual character incompatible with the view of "race" as a structural, system of power inequality?

For most Latin American migrants "becoming American" was not equated with "becoming white," as has been the case for European mi-grants in the past, but more often with selectively approaching a cosmo-politan competency sometimes associated with "becoming black"—and with the stylistic and emotive forms of knowledge this implied—in a way that was mediated by an identification not with African Americans, but with "Puerto Rican." In the context of Newark, Puerto Ricans were singled out as the Latino group "closer to black." For some Latin American mi-grants, identifying with "Puerto Rican" provided an opportunity to gain status, even within a lower status group in the perspective of dominant US society. Such identification was oftentimes naturalized based on shar-ing common neighborhood spaces, as well as by drawing from emotional claims (e.g., "connecting more" with Puerto Ricans, "feeling understood" by Puerto Ricans, "just being attracted to whomever one is attracted to" and that happens to be Puerto Rican). As Erving Goffman (1959) mas-terfully notes, we often assess authenticity by conferring "special atten-tion to features of the performance that cannot be readily manipulated, thus enabling us to judge the reliability of the more misrepresentable cues in the performance" (58). In keeping with this analysis, inner lives and emotional styles are viewed as less readily manipulated than outer identity markers, even while such visible markers are also molded (cf. Wilkins 2008, 244). This is why the ability to master an emotional style and acquire racial expertise were critical (sine qua non) aspects of urban cosmopolitanism.

But how was cosmopolitan competency evaluated and by whom? Assessments of cosmopolitan competency partly relied on shifting criteria of appropriate affect (e.g., responding to jokes and bantering, displaying the adequate emotions in public), as noted in Emília Ribeiro's comment on Robert in the introduction to this chapter. But such assessments of an authentic cosmopolitan competency also relied on an implicit social knowledge of how to be modern (not "folksy") and engage in appropriate "style-talk," a term I use here in reference to the circulation of discourses about brand clothing, personal fashion styles, and mannerisms associated with a cosmopolitan urban culture. Moreover, it also involved imagined and actual perspectives on an individual's country of origin or ancestry.

Authenticity in Street Therapy: Style-Talk, Class and Urban/Rural Imaginaries

Although not always explicitly contextualized, assessments of cosmopolitan competency were generally situated in rapid neighborhood change, increasing anti-immigrant nativism and a devalorization of the citizenship of US-born minorities in Newark. "Style talk" included the everyday narratives, commentaries, conversations, and jokes that had fashion and style as their subject and aimed to accentuate social distinctions. In discussions of fashion and style, barriers were embedded not only in discourse but also, materially, in the classification of a city or neighborhood as "good" or "bad," of who was an "immigrant" and who was "American," who was a "Pepe Wetback" and who was a "thug," and even in the living arrangements and educational opportunities of individuals, and official handlings of "security" and "surveillance." Style also was rooted in a concept of "surplus corporeality" or a form of "homeboy [or homegirl] cosmopolitan" (Diawara 1998), which involved individuals in a relentlessly fashioned and performed attachment to Blackness—and less often, to an "African Diaspora"—through the adoption of the latest trends in hip-hop style, everyday speech, bodily kinetics and mannerisms. The trope that facilitated the appropriation of Blackness and the embodiment of "race" (or the racialization of the bodily space) was highly performative. Performance theorists are not only interested in how prevailing social categories are reified through conventionalized performative acts, but also on how signifying acts may enable new subject positions and new perspectives to emerge (Diamond 1996).[10] Style was a variable signifier because audiences differed in their assumptions and knowledge about fashion; in fact, the communication of group values and interests through fashion could be slippery and, therefore, assessments of style were frequently combined with other components of identity to be effective in communicating difference and belonging (cf. McCracken 1988).

When I asked Vivian Rovira, an outspoken Puerto Rican student at ESHS and long-time resident of the Ironbound, if there were people who would set a stylistic trend at the school, she explained:

To me, in this school, there are not a lot of people that set the style. Like you see some people, like for example, I have a fake Louis Vuitton [bag], so I'm like y'all, I love Louis Vuitton. I paid thirty-five dollars for something people pay a thousand dollars for. But there's some people out there who say their stuff is real, you know. I say, "Hmm, that looks just like the one I got." You know what I mean? Like those are the type of people . . . Like I know some Portuguese people who try to be all high class and whatever and in the inside they are poor. It's like you just as poor as me, cause you're right across the corner from me, in the townhouse next door. . . . They pay the real Louis Vuitton and then next thing you know they talk about being poor and how their mother can't pay rent. Go and explain.

Vivian questioned the Portugueses' whiteness—and their access to the "real" Louis Vuitton bags—and suggested that common experiences of space, of living in similar houses and being neighbors in a working-class urban area, highlighted the differences in consumption practices rather than diminishing them. Vivian's perspective was emblematic of an instance in which a subject positions herself not only in relation to modernity, but also struggles to reposition herself through the deployment of the very codes of the modern that have framed her as its other (cf. Schein 1999, 363–64). Ironically, while consumption becomes the only way to reassert difference, the distinctions between "fake" and "real" objects appeared so blurred that one had to become an expert to determine which Louis Vuitton was the "real" one. But even "real"-ness does not automatically confer a higher community status in the context of a consumerism that revels in knock-offs and wears them against the grain of societal expectation.[11]

Class distinctions when one shares the same neighborhood are very slippery and ambiguous, leading Vivian to engage two strategies commonly used by Puerto Ricans who are situating themselves not only in Newark's racial hierarchy, but also in the city's complex class dynamics:

(1) examine the Portuguese's personal qualities (pretentious, fake, uppity, prejudiced) and (2) analyze whether their material goods could justify their emotional attitudes (living on same street, having real Louis Vuitton bags that are impossible to distinguish from knockoffs). As Rosemary Hennessy (2000) argues, "new economies of desire" have unfolded hand in hand with the expansion of capitalist commodification and, indeed, the solace of commodity consumption has been perhaps the most common way of coping with the problem of bodily exclusion and the desire for positive forms of disembodiment; consuming, in Hennessy's view, represents a way of escaping the pain of embodiment or disembodiment. Commodities become a kind of access to publicness.

Class-specific styles of speech, mannerisms, and dress, are learned sets of expressive cultural practices that express class membership (Bettie 2003, 51). The self being expressed through one's relationship to and creative use of commodities (both artifacts and popular cultural discourses) is a central practice to capitalist society. Looking at the material context of emotional readings, one also recognizes the transnational lens through which class difference was always-already constitutive of one's social positionality. For instance, comments about how Portuguese youth were spoiled were echoed by Paula and Silvana Pereira, two Brazilian sisters from Belo Horizonte who understood class relations in the United States through colloquial Brazilian terms like "patricinha" and "mauricinho" in Newark. Drawn from the diminutive form of the names Patricia and Mauricio, presumably pretentious elite names in Brazil, these terms emphasized not only material affluence, but a lack of character associated with spoiled children. The same classed terms were common among the Brazilian youth in Belo Horizonte and they were equivalent to terms like "los blanquitos," "los Guaynabitos," or "los comemierdas," all race-*cum*-class terms that point to appearance as well as (affluent) area of residence in Puerto Rico.

These terms constitute part of a "cognitive baggage" (Bloch 1992; McCallum 2005) that is the practices that structure apprehension of social difference, that subjects bring to and take away from social interactions that are remembered in other contexts. The memories of these events are embodied as knowledge that may or may not shape present-time interaction. Emotions framed, transformed, and made sense of perceptions, thoughts, and activities, even when, at times, emotions resisted both understanding and rational control (de Sousa 1990, 3). In this sense, possessing emotional capital or identifying emotional capital in others gave legitimacy to an array of actions and cognitive interpretations of one's immediate condition, even when the rules of attaining that very capital were necessarily absent in public discourse. Pursuing an urban cosmo-politanism was also a class critique, revealing of how US-born Latinos and Latin American migrants devised alternative claims to a spurious US citizenship only fully available in the context of a normative white-ness, and premised on the equal rights and full membership of whites (Haney López 1996). Latin American migrants and US-born Latinos re-formulated, to various degrees of success, alternative routes to belong-ing that were influenced by competing media representations of what "American"-ness looked like, and also by public opinion concerning "im-migrants," transnational affiliations, and global configurations of race and wealth distribution.

Distinctions between "urban" and "immigrant" were oftentimes ar-ticulated through a language of fashion and style, but these distinctions were always-already produced through one's position—in Newark and as a transnational subject—in a nativist context where US nation-state boundaries were increasingly policed in racialized "inner-city" neighbor-hoods. In addition to style-talk, Latin American urban/rural imaginaries also served as class critique in the United States, a country where class has been historically assumed to have little relevance to social mobility outcomes.

A folk system of evaluating urban competency and determining the authenticity of performances of Blackness was oftentimes inseparable from formulations of hemispheric geopolitical identities; there was a gen-eral understanding that some countries of origin were more "urban" (e.g., Brazil) and others more "backward" (e.g., Portugal, Ecuador) and that populations from these areas were differently positioned in the Newark urban landscape. An irony of such interpretations was that oftentimes Brazilian migrants in fact hailed from very small towns or rural areas in the Brazilian interior, albeit benefiting from the global images of Brazil rooted on the tourist areas of Rio de Janeiro or the business centrality of São Paulo, and such regional distinctions were oftentimes deployed in light of inter-personal tensions. To what degree does urban competency create winners and losers in migration? As this section demonstrates, oftentimes assessments of belonging indexed ways in which some Latin American migrants in Newark were closer to coveted ideas of "American"-ness *even prior to coming to the United States* precisely because their re-spective "home countries" were considered more urban, cosmopolitan, and modern. This was the case even when their specific region of origin in those countries were small cities or even rural areas; some migrants, thus, were presumed to have the social tools to effectively decode images, styles, and performances associated with the city, while others—those presumed to be Latin American hillbillies of sorts—had to more actively learn the tacit rules of what was considered "modern" and "urban." Among Latinos in Newark there was, in fact, a tacit understanding that "not all immigrants were created equal."

Countries of origin—and an "urban elsewhere"—frequently supplied organizing schemes to interpret the racial and spatial configuration of Newark among most Latin American migrants and US-born Latinos, thus suggesting that US urban spaces were constructed, filtered, and modified through transnational referents and multivalent imaginaries (Ramos-Zayas, work-in-progress).[12] The performance of Blackness, in its uneven development, had ideological underpinnings in the construc-tions of "immigrants" as emblematic antipode to the modernity and potential capitalist access much sought-after by US native minorities.[13] To what degree did an urban cosmopolitanism that remained transna-tional and multilocal shield conferred hierarchically organized levels of "immigrant"-ness and levels of nativist prejudice? More precisely, how are the identities behind being modern and urban in US cities shaped by "urban elsewheres," that is, by the actual or imagined urban-ness of locales of origin in other countries?

While moderating a group of US-born Latinos and recent Latin Ameri-can migrants of various nationalities, the role of Ecuadorians as target of jokes around "backwardness" or lack of modernity emerged.

Michelle (a Puerto Rican and Dominican student): You have different groups here. Puerto Ricans make fun of Ecuadorians.

Ricky (a Puerto Rican senior): Yeah, everybody makes fun of Ecuadorians in this school.

Arturo [an Ecuadorian junior]: Only if you let them!

Michelle: I'm not saying that I make fun of Ecuadorians. But there are some people, some Puerto Ricans in this school . . . who make fun of Ecuadorians. They call them *chapito* and stuff like that.

Ricky: Sometimes I question where those Puerto Ricans came from. They must have come from el monte [the hinterland]! In this school, everybody's treated like an Ecuadorian if you're from south of the border. Even if you're not Ecuadorian, you're treated like that.

Adamaris (a Puerto Rican senior): We call them Pepe Wetbags, and they have like a specific look that you see.

AY: A look? What kind of look?

Adamaris: The hair, the hair, too dead like flat. Us Puerto Ricans have this scholarly, a little bit straight, a little bit nappy, see? [Touched her own hair, which I would have actually described as straight]. And the different shapes. The Mexicans they got wide face, like a football? You can tell by the eyes, and you know, depends . . .

Amalia [an Ecuadorian girl]: That's a generalization. We [Ecuadorians] distinguish between people from the coast [de la costa] and people from the hills [del cerro]. . . .
I'm from the coast.

AY: Is one better? Is it better to be from the coast or from the hills?

Amalia: Well, the people from the hills are more festive, they are more traditional. They
are more fun to be around, but . . .

Arturo: No, I think it's better to be from the coast. You are more . . . you are more
exposed [to different situations; tienes más mundo]

The performance of modernity worked in tandem with the displacing of traditionality onto others (Schein 1999), and such traditionality, in the case of many Latin American migrants, was constructed in the form of identities bound to regions within countries of origin. "De la costa" versus "del cerro" also operated in the case of some of the Colombians with whom I spoke, although for them being "de la costa" was less desirable, possibly because of the association of the Colombian coast with Afro-Colombian populations. The distinction that the Puerto Rican students made between Brazilians, Dominican, and Ecuadorian "immigrants" was guided not only by images that in fact inscribed race onto the body and the evaluation of urban competency, but also by those bodies' relationship to the state and modernity. The "modern" (in opposition to the "backwards" or "antimodern") was thought of not as a context in which people made their lives or as a discursive regime that shaped subjectivity, but also as powerfully constituted and negotiated performance.

Many of the more recent South American migrants knew (or quickly learned) that Mexicans were the quintessential "immigrant alien" in the United States. Likewise, US-born Latino students in Newark associated "immigrant" with "Mexican," even though Mexicans were a minority in the city and its schools. Competing opinions as to whether it was Mexicans or Ecuadorians that occupied the lowest echelon in the rankings of "immigrants" abounded. For instance, Robert Spano, an Italian American teacher at ESHS, claimed: "Students may say that it's the Ecuadorians who are treated poorly here, but the Mexicans are the ones at the very bottom of the ladder. There are many Ecuadorians here, so that helps them, but there's only one or two Mexicans." Robert stated that "Even Salvadorians, having established their own gang in the area [surrounding ESHS], were viewed as better than the Mexicans."[14]

Many Puerto Rican and Brazilian students evaluated Latin American migrants based on their presumed proximity to "that Mexican look." Although most of the migrant students at ESHS were Brazilian and Ecuadorian, and most of the "foreign"-born students at Barringer were

Dominican, these migrant groups were positioned very differently in articulation of style-talk, urban competency, and belonging. For instance, in a couple of instances I heard hallway bantering sessions at both ESHS and BHS that involved a black or Puerto Rican student referring to Ecuadorian students as "Mexican" in an inflammatory way, while also deploying "positive" (if highly stereotypical) images of Brazilians.

In a conversation with Evelyn Rosa, a Puerto Rican junior at ESHS, she mentioned that "kids that are like just gotten here [to the United States] they want to be like, they want to be black, they try hard at that." To which Vivian Rovira, also Puerto Rican, agreed: "Yeah. They try to be ghetto. . . . These are mostly the Ecuadorians." When I asked them why they thought this was, they commented that these immigrant students "want[ed] to fit in, they don't want to look like an immigrant, so they'll wear baggy clothes, they . . . you know they'll do anything in their power to fit in."

Vivian proceeded to explain that sometimes these students tried too hard: "They say things like 'you go girl!' And that's so done, you know? Nobody even says that anymore! [laughed]. Like you see them, they look ridiculous, it's like eeww, what are you wearing? Like we don't set our pants down to our knees, that's not even something we do now. They let them down to the knees and it's like butt cheeks happening, you know, in daylight! Whoa."

Showing perhaps a bit more sympathy for the immigrant plight, Evelyn added: "They do that because they want to feel wanted, like they don't want to walk around in the hallway by themselves when they see a whole lot of people walking. They want to push themselves toward that group that knows what's going on, but they never ask questions! They be lost and they're too proud to ask. They analyze people, like, 'Okay, I'm going to be just like that.' So you have to dress like that to make friends, whatever."

And Vivian elaborated: "Yeah. Like they will look at blacks and at us, and they be . . . you know, 'Yo, dawg . . . ' " [hand, head posing gesture]. Really ghetto like that, but it comes out fake."

In this instance, modernity served as a form of domination characterized by strains of nationalist or even racialist superiority narratives, by the valorization not only of an "urban-ness," but of an *authentic* urban-ness never fixed or clearly attainable, but always connected with a dominant social order and modes of belonging. Perhaps more significantly, these migrants presumably lacked a shared pain and experience of US racial oppression because they were performing in a way that suggested their inauthenticity; they lacked the ability to create a self that challenged a dominant expectation of what was viewed as an artificial and even naïve "happy" and "cheerful" attitude. They, indeed, came across as if they were having fun with social experimentation, regardless of any actual anxiety such mastery might in fact be causing the migrants.

Myrian Caldeira and Bruna Almeida, two Brazilian students from Bahia and Recife, respectively, had a conversation that was emblematic of the deployment of urban identities vis-à-vis a presumed "backwardness" attributed to people from small, rural towns, or even countries whose global representations were less commercialized than the view of Brazil in US popular imagination. Bruna's boyfriend was from Governador Valadares, like most of the Brazilians who lived in Newark, and possibly in the northeastern United States, at the time of my research. A small city about 120 kilometers east of Belo Horizonte in the state of Minas Gerais, Governador Valadares is also referred to as "Valadólares," a reference to the area's reliance on remittances from the more than 40 percent of its former residents living abroad. In fact, in the literature on Brazilians in the United States, Valadares and surrounding towns have been reported to supply the greatest number of migrants to the United States, particularly in the decade of the 1980s (Meihy 2004; Werneck 2004). When Myrian and Bruna learned that I would be spending the summer in Belo Horizonte and had planned to travel to Valadares, the following conversation took place:

Myrian: You're going to Valadares? [almost shocked] The people there ride around in bikes! They don't even have cars there!

Bruna: That's not true! [with some indignation] Valadares has grown a lot, a lot. Marcelo [her boyfriend] has pictures. It's very different now!

Myrian: So, if it's grown that much, why don't they buy themselves cars? Favíola said that when she got to the airport, people were wearing no shoes, no shirt, nothing!

Bruna: That's not true. C'mon, Myrian, how can they not have shoes? That's a lie.

Myrian: Faviola would not lie about that. I swear, she said that. And her family is from there and she still said that.

Bruna [to me, ignoring Myrian]: People in those places are happy people. They can enjoy life. They're warm and care for each other, not like the Brazilians here. The Brazilians here are selfish and gananciosos [greedy].

Myrian: Well, that's true.

There was a fundamental incompatibility between the cheerfulness associated with a folksy identity and the dark cynicism of being modern. This fundamental incompatibility generated great insecurity in the proper presentation of self and the new rules of interaction in racialized situations. Being "valadarense" was almost an automatic target of jokes or proxy for a more "natural" and "cheery" way of life that was radically different from what becoming American entailed, even though Americans themselves were oftentimes made fun of for their "fake happy."

Countries of origin continue to supply the organizing schemes to interpret the spatial configuration of Newark among most Latin American migrants and US-born Latinos. For instance, some Brazilian students who had met Portuguese immigrants in Brazil and had either witnessed or heard stories about Portugal's peripheral position in Europe noted the "rural"-ness of Portugal. Hence, Portugal was viewed alternatively as European, and hence "whiter" and "superior," but also as rural, and indeed many Portuguese students had immigrated or belonged to families from poor rural areas outside of Lisbon and the Azores. Conversely, Brazil was viewed as much more urban, and students claimed association to certain regions and cities of Brazil, while rejecting others (more rural and poor) ones.

Most of the Brazilians and many of the Puerto Ricans whom I met in Newark evaluated cosmopolitan competency not only in light of an individual's disposition toward an "adequate" process of racial learning in the United States or an urban know-how associated with black America, but also based on transnational imaginaries of countries of origin or ancestry. While places like "Brazil" had come to be associated with a series of global images suggestive of urbanism, modernity, and cosmopolitanism, other countries, like Mexico and Ecuador, were oftentimes associated with backwardness. The references to such transnational elsewheres were so prominent, and the connections with countries of origin and ancestry so intimate, that three years into my field work, I decided to conduct research in Belo Horizonte (Minas Gerais), Brazil, and Santurce (San Juan), Puerto Rico, where many of the Brazilian and Puerto Rican youth whom I met in Newark had relatives or friends. Throughout the time of my research, my impression was that conceptions of "Blackness" were not rooted only on the experience of living in the United States, but that it also drew from images of modernity associated with countries of origin or ancestry. A main question that behind the research I conducted in Brazil and Puerto Rico was: How was Blackness, particularly, American Blackness, conceived in these transnational contexts and to what degree did these global imaginaries operate to sustain, challenge, or reconfigure cosmopolitan competency?

Before turning to the ethnographic aspects of the Belo Horizonte and Santurce research, I want to underscore the limitations, challenges, and opportunities that conducting research in these cities posed. First, due to time and logistical constraints, my research in Brazil and Puerto Rico only consisted of interviews with faculty and students in two private and two public schools in each city. I was not able to situate these schools on the broader and tremendously rich political, social, and historical contexts of Belo Horizonte and Santurce, or in light of the significant geopolitical disparity and distinct global positionalities of Brazil and Puerto Rico, respectively. Second, the connections that Newark's Brazilians and Puerto Ricans had to compatriots in their countries of origin were categorically different. Many of the Brazilians whom I met in Newark had attended the Belo Horizonte public school where I ended up conducting fieldwork and still had direct connections to the faculty and students in that school. This was not the case among Newark Puerto Ricans, many of whom were US-born or raised and had never attended school in Puerto Rico. For these Newark Puerto Ricans, the connection to Puerto Rico occasionally involved distant relatives and friendship networks, but more often included images of Puerto Rico as an ancestral homeland, a visceral source of pride and identity, rather than a place associated with personal quotidian experiences.

These differences notwithstanding, the intensity of transnational connections—whether in material or imaginary terms—was evident in the everyday life of both Brazilians and Puerto Ricans in Newark. Finally, the role of "migration" was qualitatively and politically different in Brazil and Puerto Rico. While Brazil still considered itself a "country of immigrants" rather than one that supplied any significant percentage of its population to the global migration flow, migration is ubiquitous in the political and economic history of Puerto Rico, and nearly as many Puerto Ricans live on the Island as they do in the United States.

Taking the above distinctions I into account, my main goal in undertaking field research in Brazil and Puerto Rico was to nuance the views on American Blackness that were so central to the everyday lives of Brazilians and Puerto Ricans in Newark, and perhaps gain a broader sense of how affect is transacted transnationally in light of perspectives on race and migration.[15] Before continuing to analyze the life experiences of Emília Ribeiro and her "depressed" classmate, as they appeared in the ethnographic episode in this chapter's introduction, I turn to the visceral and phenomenological aspects of transnational affiliations and experiences of race, affect, and migration as they were manifested in Belo Horizonte and Santurce. By examining how racial systems operate transnationally, it is also possible to gain greater insight into the intricacies of Newark's urban affect and the everyday production of an emotional epistemology among US-born Latinos and Latin American migrants in the city.

Emotional Epistemologies and Transnational Racial Systems: Return Migrants, Cartographies of Racial Democracy, and the Power of "Black America" in Belo Horizonte, Brazil, and Santurce, Puerto Rico

Learning carries within itself certain dangers because out of necessity one has to learn from one's enemies. LEO TROTSKY

The image of "black America" in Newark is suggestive of and sometimes conflated with possessing urban competency or being Americanized, as well as viewed in terms of gendered forms of aggression (see chapter 5). What is important to note is that "black America" has also become a set of images that is exported and modified transnationally and known to Brazilian and Puerto Rican migrants even prior to migration.[16] Albeit from significantly different political and historical perspectives beyond the scope of this book, the cities of Belo Horizonte (and Minas Gerais more generally) and Santurce (and the San Juan metropolitan area more broadly) have witnessed a significant degree of migration and return migration with the US northeast, including Newark, and have been important spaces in the reracialization of return Brazilian and Puerto Rican migrants, respectively. While in Newark "Blackness" is associated with urban competency, cosmopolitanism, and aggression in complex ways, in Latin America it is embodied in return migrants and circulated through popular conceptions of "America" as "black America." In Brazil and Puerto Rico, Americanization was understood through an emotional epistemology that served as an important transnational, cosmopolitan racial project in and of itself, and was experienced in contradistinction to an enduring ideology of "racial democracy" (e.g., Freyre 1956; cf. Sheriff 2001).

Drawing from ethnographic work in Brazil and Puerto Rico, the countries of origin of many of the young people whom I met in Newark and their families, I highlight the transnational racial registries from which Latino and Latin American youth come to understand their own affective worlds in the United States. In context of high return migration to Puerto Rico and Brazil, views of a "depressed American" are associated with having subscribed to a US racial system and foregoing ideologies of racial democracy that dictate, among other things, that there is a distinction between "real racism" and other, presumably more benign forms of racial difference. Negative affect becomes both a local and transnational cornerstone of a structure of feelings that is fundamental to rendering transnational neoliberal subjects emotionally legible. New Jersey, but also in Belo Horizonte, Brazil, and Santurce, Puerto Rico, two secondary sites of my fieldwork. In Newark, these characterizations were drawn in contradistinction to a cheerful, happy, or friendly disposition associated with being new to the United States, naïve, or being a "Latin American hillbilly." In Puerto Rico and Brazil the emotional shifts noted in return migrants were more complicated. At times they did signal a connection to a cosmopolitan Third World Blackness. More often, however, they intended to blame return migrants for having "bought into" a US racial system that, both in Brazil and Puerto Rico, was viewed as simplistic and counterproductive; there was a general view that in the United States all people talked about was race and that this race talk was dominated by a "constant complaining" attributed to African Americans. In this sense, the assumption in both Brazil and Puerto Rico was that, among return migrants, race had become overdeterministic of individuals' moods and personalities. In Brazil and Puerto Rico, these perspectives on race were, for the most part, associated with "black America" and the embodiment of "Blackness," in very affective terms, among return migrants.

A connection between Americanization, racialization, and negative affect among Latin American populations has been cultivated in transnational contexts. In the public and private schools that served as field sites for the Brazil and Puerto Rico components of my research, the production of a migrant Other was rooted in a view that an emotional repertoire was established, reproduced, and altered through the process of migration and return. In both Belo Horizonte and Santurce, I identified a dominant discourse that constructed migrants returning from Brazilian and Puerto Rican areas of the United States as "emotionally defective." These returnees oftentimes became a modified proxy for local images of American Blackness or what race in the United States "looks like." Characterized in terms of negative affect—as being depressed, sad, gloomy, detached, aggressive—return migrants were often read in Belo Horizonte and Santurce public and private schools as subjects of pop psychology analyses drawn from self-help literature; as populations in need of counseling or therapy; or as individuals who ranged from being disengaged to being narcissistic. For instance, Alexis Rodriguez, senior at one of the public high schools with the highest population of return migrants in Puerto Rico, said:

The thing is that some of them [students that come from the United States], they don't want to come here. Their parents forced them or they had to come because of something else, but not because they wanted to. They don't want to come here so they rebel. They don't follow rules, they don't do their work, they don't do nothing. I think it's mostly the guys that act that way. They get stupid, they don't want to do work and they think they are the shit. They get this air about them. "I'm the shit because I came from there." It's an attitude. They're like "I'm from the ghetto" and "I'm all that."

Likewise, at a public high school in Belo Horizonte, which many of my Newark Brazilian interviewees had attended prior to migrating, students also remarked on the apatía (apathy) of many returned migrants. In my notes from the Brazil fieldwork I conducted in 2004, I noted that "Mariela, Renata, and Ana Paula insisted that Marcelo, a student who had recently arrived from New Jersey, would not be interested in being interviewed for my project, because he was very withdrawn. They said that nobody knew much about him, that he kept to his own, that was depressed and could not fit in. Mariela even said: 'He's more American than Brazilian. The way he talks, never smiles. The oversized clothes. He really wanted to stay there, because he knew he would not belong here. It was his parents who forced him to come.'"[17]

While Alexis pointed to an almost chauvinistic "attitude" he noted in Puerto Ricans who had either been born in the United States or spent a significant time there, Mariela, Renata and Ana Paula viewed Marcelo as emotionally defective, as an outcome of migration gone wrong. The fact that Marcelo's family did not appear to have significantly improved their economic condition through migration was central to this psychological reading of Marcelo. What did Marcelo, or Robert, the Ecuadorian student Emília alluded to, or the students who Alexis refers to above, *feel*? Discomfort in their own skin and not knowing how to approach others back home were common ways in which return migrants viewed their own experiences. They were the kids who did not know how to be and that fear of not "getting it right" was what, when expressed, became coded as "depression" in the emotional epistemologies that circulate among their more integrated peers. These returnees experienced a form of anticipatory disorientation, a constant wondering of what might happen if their actions, behavior, and appearance did not come out right. At an affective level, the possibility of humiliation and shame were a constant threat to their dignity, and this condition of being indignant was situated in specific class and racial social locations. Although these conditions of being indignant are class specific, they are such a constitutive aspect to a broader emotional epistemology—of discomfort, awkwardness, and so on—that social location gets lost in translation and the focus becomes on questioning intent or genuineness. Descriptions of disappointment with the unmet expectations of migration in both economic and intimate ways were common among Brazilian and Puerto Rican returnees who had expected to improve their economic relationship, resolve family conflicts, and gain educational opportunities, yet had returned with little or nothing to show for their stay in the United States.

The significant geopolitical and historical differences between Brazil and Puerto Rico accounted for the ideological and political role that migration, in general, and return migration, in particular played in the social fabric of Belo Horizonte and Santurce, respectively.[18] What is important to highlight for the purpose of this chapter, however, is that when I asked students who had not migrated why they thought return migrants were depressed or withdrawn, their responses were remarkably similar in Belo Horizonte and Santurce: they claimed that these returnees not only had experienced the "real racism" of the United States but, more significantly, that they had "bought into" a US-bred understanding of race and racism that could in fact *cause* depression (or resentment or anger). While rarely subscribing to facile assumptions that the United States was "more racist" than their own countries, these Brazilian and Puerto Rican youth, across class, did view race and racism in the United States as qualitatively different in ways capable of directly impacting, not so much institutional racism, but how affect was manifested and embodied. Particularly critical to discussions of negative affect in Belo Horizonte and Santurce was the distinction most individuals drew between a "real racism" associated with the United States and a Latin American racism that was presumably "less real."[19]

While it was clear to these young people that structural racism existed (e.g., police brutality or the predominance of the black poor), they usually did not see as strong a connection between institutional forms of racism and those more overt, quotidian, or visceral forms. For instance, when I asked a Brazilian student at a public school in Belo Horizonte whether she thought that racist slurs could hurt people, she replied: "If the person is poor or their situation [well being] is depending on that person [who uttered the slur], yes. But if you're rich, what would you care what other people call you? It's just a name." In Puerto Rico, a student at a public high school in Santurce remarked: "It may hurt their feelings, but if you don't let them know [that you're hurt by their racist comments], you're not giving them the satisfaction. It really doesn't matter. It's all about how you react and stay positive. You cannot get resentful . . .

you'd go crazy!" These distinctions presupposed intense moments of emotional management. They enabled particular constructions of racism in the United States as both "more real" (than the one manifested in Latin America) and more overdeterministic (even humorless) in everyday interactions. In redrawing the parameters of what constituted racismo de verdad (or verdadeiro racismo, in Portuguese), on the one hand, and other forms of racism, discussions revolved about a question of sincerity, or being able to discern between the truth of the feeling and the appearance of the feeling behind a particular racial situation or behavior. A concern with sincerity and, likewise, with authenticity located race in behaviors, practices, and sentiments that were premised on distinctions in trust and intent (cf. Jackson 2001, 2006).

Gabriela (student at a private high school in Belo Horizonte): Here we also have some upper-class people who pretend that they are from the favela. I don't understand why they have to pretend they are poor. Maybe they think it's fashionable to be poor. They claim that their sneakers are fake, when they are the real expensive brand. It's the reverse of what you'd expect! They call it favela chic [laughed].

The favela in Brazil, or areas associated with Puerto Rican Blackness—like "Piñones," el caserío, la barriada—served as sites of contestation and reformulation of a racial hegemony in a similar way as did the US "ghetto." The very disruptions engendered by these contestations relied upon the discursive split between globalization, in terms of system of capital allocation and inequality, on the one hand, and particular localities that symbolize authenticity and valorization of alternative forms of cultural capital, especially conceived as "the street," "the ghetto," "the projects," and so on, on the other. "The ghetto" has become an international space, a space as central to images of the United States as the more iconic touristic sites officially exported by the US tourism industry, even though the glamorization of the ghetto ultimately concealed the everyday corporeal dangers faced by its inhabitants (cf. Johnson 2003; Forman 2002). These were ideological spaces, not simply context, but the producer and product of social relations (cf. Lefebvre 1991), including racializing practices of defective embodied forms in transnational contexts.[20]

What local ideological goals does faking poverty serve in Santurce and Belo Horizonte? A nationalist goal preserves foundational myths of racial democracy by focusing on Blackness as not only symbol of oppression, but as marketable commodity without much structural or historical resonance. Young people in both public and private schools in Belo Horizonte and Santurce remarked on what they view as "fake poverty" in ways that suggested that selective identification with the marginalized was a strategic requirement of a Third World cosmopolitanism. Nevertheless, although in some ways racial discrimination was acknowledged, there were numerous references to individuals who actively tried to learn to perform "Blackness" (in its commercial forms, related to fashion, music, and style) even if they were not phenotypically considered "black" or very dark-skinned to really frame a particular instance as "real racism" rather than "pretend racism." In the following quotes, the focus is constantly shifting around who the target of racism was. Racism against blacks is acknowledged, but also blackness is diversified by emphasizing a spatial and cultural complexity—for instance, being "from Pinones," showing solidarity with "rastafari," or equating black with "Dominican," in the case of Puerto Rican youth.

Frances (public school, Puerto Rico): I've noticed that overall there's a lot of racism against blacks. People saying things like "monkey," stuff like that. Some people take it as a joke. It's not only with people from the [Virgin] Islands, but also with Puerto Ricans who are black. I feel like I'm black, even though I'm not very dark-skinned. Because my mother is black and I consider myself black. Maybe it has to do with being from Piñones. . . . I chose to put "Rastafari" on my senior t-shirt, instead of my name. I've seen that in universities too, that it's an identification with black movements from the Caribbean. I think that those people that are Rastafari are very patriotic, they want Puerto Rico to be free. It's a mixture, they are Rastafari and they are nationalist. I see other people who have that conscience too. I see that in people coming from New York, from the US. You see people saying, "I'm Dominican, I'm black." I think it's because there was so much injustice there that . . . you know. But it's also a problem to say that blacks are discriminated against. Because you see a lot of prejudice by blacks against blacks

Mariela: You see all this construction going on around here? All those workers are Dominican. I think it's in the heritage. I read this work by a psychologist that said that it had to do with the type of indigenous population we had here. The indigenous population here was different from those in the Dominican Republic. . . . The Tainos here had everything accessible. They had the golden nuggets in the river, everything accessible, so they didn't have to work hard for anything. They had everything they needed right next to them.

Vanessa: Yeah, even back then they were just happy, not bugged down by those [racial] differences.

Renata (public school, Brazil, commenting regarding the Affirmative Action-like quotas begun in Brazilian public universities): "There are more blacks here now than ever. Everybody wants to be black to get into the university! . . . You hear someone say-

ing, "I'm black," and I just don't see that person as black. Maybe they do feel black
or maybe they're just saying that, to feel special.

These quotes illustrate a general perception that Blackness in Latin America "felt" different than the image these youth had of the experiences of
African Americans in the United States. While racism was acknowledged
among students in both Brazil and Puerto Rico, the targets of racism were
less readily identifiable partly because of the still-significant tendency to
focus not only on color, but more significantly on appearance, socioeco-
nomics, and spatial and symbolic markers, including "looking black,"
"being from Piñones," or identifying as "Rastafari." Most Latin American
migrants, and many US-born Latino youth, insisted that "Blackness" was
predominantly a signifier of skin color, phenotype, and cultural or folkloric practices, not primarily an emblem of structural subordination.
Renata's quote was suggestive of how claiming Blackness as such would not
be an issue as long as it conferred benefits. In the conversation between
Vanessa and Mariela, happiness and positive affects in Latin America
were implicitly counterposed to complaining, which was also equated
with depression and other negative affects. In fact, happiness and humor
became a moral sentiment implicated in the creation of certain styles
of political order. Contempt toward those who complained, including
individuals who had gained racial consciousness associated with US minorities, acted as a mechanism for ranking people based on their affect. At
times it seemed that, unless racism was expressed as open disgust, not just
contempt, it did not really count; being the object of someone's disgust
rendered racism physiological.

The tendency to perceive race as a physical property, personal posses-
sion, or emotional essence at times obscured the character of race as an
aspect of social relations and power inequalities. The closest Blackness
was to being staged, planned, and consumed and contained within a
language of emotional and psychological pathology, the more it served as
cultural capital for Latin American and Latino youth both in Latin America and the United States. In this sense, Latinos viewed African Americans
not only (or even primarily) in light of a dominant criminality discourse,
but in relation to psychiatric labels—for example, passive-aggressive, depressed, lacking self-esteem, being violent, or harboring resentment from
childhood experiences. This was also how Americanization was viewed in
the countries of origin in relation to return migrants.

While a characteristic of the contemporary public sphere might be
a denial of the body in favor of the logic of abstraction, racial learning

relied on an embodied affect and emotional epistemology that, at times and in certain contexts, appeared liberatory and a source of social critique. As Habermas's examination of "phantom bodies" and the "public sphere" establishes, individuals whose embodied identities are excluded from finding expression in officially sanctioned terms seek it through the formation of "subaltern counter-publics" which rely on "hidden transcripts" that run parallel and counter to the official transcript (Scott 1992). At a phenomenological and visceral level, longing served as an underside of depression.

Cristina (public school, Puerto Rico): I was the happiest in New York. Because my whole life is there. Because I am part Dominican, and I also consider me part Puerto Rican, but I represent myself to be from New York. That's part of my life and I'll never forget it. Every time I go back there, I feel like, "yeah, this is home.". . . . When I moved to the South Bronx, it was black people, Jamaican people, you know, there we were all together. . . . I think Dominicans and Puerto Ricans got along better than here, because there they were all immigrants. In the United States you see people of all places, so they are used to that.

When Cristina moved back to Santurce, the thing she missed the most was

having a group of Latin peoples like I used to do in New York. . . . When you migrate from another country, you have to establish yourself to those rules, you know? [When I returned to Puerto Rico] they saw me as a black girl coming from New York.

Central to Cristina's remarks are her memories of anti-Dominican prejudice in Puerto Rico and oftentimes tense relationships between Dominicans and Puerto Ricans in the United States (Duany 1998). This forms part of Cristina's own "cognitive baggage" (Bloch 1992; McCallum 2005), as memories of significant events become embodied as racial knowledge that continue to define Cristina's own affective experience.

The emotional epistemology through which the young people with whom I spoke in Belo Horizonte and Santurce emphasized the connection between "Americanization" and Blackness was thus mediated through a perceived negative affect attributed to returned migrants. According to this emotional epistemology, returned migrants were withdrawn, somber, and depressed as a result of encountering "real racism" in the United States and embracing the impact of this racism affectively. For return migrants like Cristina, however, the phenomenological experience of the migration process was quite different and they often disdained their own integration into both host *and* homeland countries. For them affect appeared as a stance for social critique.

Epistemologies of Race and Affect

I want to return to Emília Ribeiro, the Brazilian student who first commented on a peer's depression, as well as to Ricky Acosta, a Puerto Rican student who remembered how he used to try to "act hard" when he first arrived at the Newark high school where I met him. As is sometimes the case, Emília's assessment of Roberto, the Ecuadorian peer who tried to "act hard," as "depressed" was never far from Emília's own personal history. As Emília once explained in relation to her own Americanization, when she first arrived in the United States, she developed a serious depression that was manifested as an eating disorder. In Brazil, Emília had been active in various sports teams sponsored by a Catholic charity community center in Belo Horizonte. She explained that, once in Newark, her eating got "out of control"—what she described as patterns of uncontrollable overeating followed by weight gain, guilt, self-loathing, and extreme dieting. She became "depressed" and "obsessed with her weight and food" soon after her family settled in Newark, where her parents became overprotective and would not even allow her to participate in after-school organized sports. Descriptions of developing eating disorders and weight related issues were surprisingly common among Brazilian migrants in Newark, and were often reflective of a "somatic mode of attention" to the body (Csordas 1983). To alleviate her depression, Emília secretly began going to clubs while still being underage, and flirted with various jobs in a budding Newark sex industry (Ramos-Zayas 2009). Given this personal history, Emília's interpretation of Roberto's "depression" also has to be filtered through a fairly common trajectory in the Americanization process.

Likewise, Ricky Acosta was one of the Puerto Rican students whom others viewed as "trying to act hard" or "be ghetto." He himself acknowledges that: "I wanted to play tough, be quote-unquote ghetto. A little bit to scare the white kids. But then I met the people who are my friends now. We're more mature now. We have jobs, we want to move out of Newark and do something for ourselves." As I got to know Ricky better, he explained that having a "ghetto style" somewhat alleviated the prejudice to which he may have been subjected because people suspected him to be gay, even before Ricky "came out" to his closest friends. In Ricky's case, the deployment of a ghetto identity served as a tool to gain a certain respect that eventually laid a more receptive foundation for a more open expression of his sexuality.

What does Emília's subjective appraisal of Robert's "depression" and "acting hard" say about Emília herself? Was Ricky's "acting hard" instrumental or spontaneous or both? Like other "street therapists," Emília and Ricky had personal histories that were inseparable not only from their phenomenological experience of them, but from the specific political economic contexts in which they unfolded. Despite the creativity involved in "making Blackness right," the structural elements in which such a process is ensconced remain: Emília, Ricky, and many of the Newark residents whose voices appear here face the everyday realities of an urban renewal that privileges real estate and corporate interests over the wellbeing of working-class and impoverished subjects, not only in Newark, but also in Santurce and Belo Horizonte, to some degree (Ramos-Zayas, work-in-progress). They face high levels of unemployment or, at best, a service sector employment that requires the suppression of felt emotions and simulation of unfelt ones and which may contradict their very social identities in the goal of producing docile racial bodies.[21]

Their ventures into a sphere of racialized "public feelings" (Cvetkovich 2003) are suggestive of how an embodied racialized affect emerges from the managing of sentiment and emotions in the public sphere and how neoliberalism has dialectically sustained and been sustained on affective grounds. Examining affect in its alignment to the aspirations of urban neoliberalism allows us to analyze the impact of the market and class interests (the consolidation of neoliberalism at its best) on changes in cognitive style and sensibility. It foreshadows the impact of capital on people's intimate, phenomenological experience of the material environment.

For US-born Latinos and Latin American migrants, Blackness was conflated with urban-ness and oftentimes deployed in the face of tacit experiences of white supremacy that are unspeakable or unidentifiable, or experiences that would require individuals to be "ungrateful to America" or "too much complaining." The value of the urban (and its slippery mediation as Blackness) was repeatedly constructed through emotional performances that were sometimes theatrical in their repetitious and rehearsed character, and were judged in therapeutic ways. From offhanded comments in school hallways and streetcorners, to scripted acts on stage during school talent shows, students were both negotiating their locations in relation to the social categories that typed them and affirming those very social categories through their acts. Blackness has become emblematic of difference, but also, to US Latinos and Latin American immigrants in the United States, of American-ness or, more notably, of not-immigrant-ness exacerbated in a time of heightened nativism.

A culturalization of Blackness was instrumental in endorsing the belief that there were multiple and fluid (albeit hierarchically ranked) forms of Blackness, and that the status of "immigrant" or being from another country ranked a person higher, regardless or race, on the scale of desirability and marketability than being American black. In the case of an Americanization that is equated with Blackness and urban competency, the main question was not so much what "being ghetto" or "acting hard" was, but how did these ways of existing really feel and to what degree did this expression of affect suggested individual agency versus spontaneity. The performance of Blackness and urban cosmopolitanism among US-born Latinos and Latin American migrants was an alternative way of exerting claims to citizenship in light of nativist views of immigrant "illegality" and the "delinquent citizenship" associated with US-born minorities, particularly Puerto Ricans. While most Puerto Ricans could not avoid the criminal labels imposed on them based on a "delinquent citizenship" (chapter 2), many Latin American migrants and even other US-born Latinos were able to subscribe to arguably less stigmatized psychiatric self-labeling (cf. Wilkins 2008).

As this chapter suggests, there is a need for a social epistemology of emotion that engages discussions of neoliberalism and race beyond a cursory acknowledgment that emotions, as "irrational forces," have historically been attributed to racialized colonial groups as a feature of reductive racist ideologies. My work considers various levels at which emotion, affect, and sentiment operate as evaluative judgments of someone's psychological health—as presumably conveyed through emotional style, productivity as a worker, and effectiveness as a member of a normative patriarchal family—that require social validation or negotiation for their realization. These evaluative judgments are integral aspects of the structural distribution of power, including the development of racial knowledge, class consciousness, and other forms of subordination. Feelings become associated with social units, although even those social units are fluid (Lawler 2001; Weiner 1985). While identity projects may be an integral part of entering adulthood, they also have a potential to fail to be transitory and bring permanent costs, so that youth subcultures play a role in social reproduction (Willis 1977). Some new migrant youth have learned how to perform subservience that is praised in low-wage labor market hiring, but is degraded in light of alternative forms of capital. I turn to this in the conclusion.

Street Therapists as Neoliberal-Friendly Emotive Subjects: Embodying Affective Labor and Enlisting a Cartography of Racial Democracy

Se busca mesera con buena presencia [Seeking waitress with good appearance]   HANDWRITTEN SIGN ON THE WINDOWS OF AN ECUADORAN RESTAURANT IN NEWARK

Hinted throughout this volume is the idea that state and market interests generate tacit, indirect mechanisms or affective meta-sentiments (Myers 1979) that go, in most instances, largely unacknowledged in everyday racial encounters and in expressions of public feelings. Many scholars have considered the impact of the rise of capitalism (and neoliberalism)—particularly on what capitalism requires of labor—on changes in emotional styles and sensibilities (Hirschman 1998; Weber 1958; Elias 1982). The control of feelings has increased across historical time and has experienced qualitative alterations across emotional regimes (Reddy 1997). Capitalism produces a particular sentimentality and affect that govern social life and interactions; indeed, significant

318

emotional work is done through capitalism. An embodied anthropology, therefore, ought to remain vigilant to the degree of accord in the nature of affective communication and expression among multiple states and political sources and how these forms of affect sediment competing counter discourses of race and racial difference in quotidian practices.

Affect is an element of social ethos that is central to the nation-state construction of racial subjects. The inscription upon certain bodies of disciplines of self-control, particularly affective control, and practices of group discipline are often tied up with and essential to the interests of state and the market (cf. Appadurai 1996, 198; Hochschild 1983). State construction of racial subjects takes place not only in traditional political institutions, but also through everyday processes of learning how race operates and the appropriate expressions of sentiments and emotion. The search for "buena presencia," as stated in the help wanted sign mentioned above, while indexing particular class and race locations, also suggests that a good worker in the United States is someone who possesses the fine-tuned, calibrated emotional style that navigated "docility" and nonagressiveness, while also embracing cosmopolitanism and savvyness. This is the emotional style that would appeal to the affluent suburban and metropolitan whites whom the "Newark Renaissance," in all its focus on cultural events, ethnic cuisine, and high culture performances, aimed to attract during the years of my fieldwork (chapter 1). In this sense, states and market orchestrate racial projects through the regulation (and induced self-regulation) of affect; this is how neoliberal aspirations come to constitute a politics of embodied racialized affect that are essential to the very goals of capital.

Focusing on the intersection of racial projects, affective expectations, and the formation of a neoliberal personhood allows us to shed light on how changes in the discourse of individual responsibility for socially shared problems is reinvigorated in everyday life. The neoliberal projects of the last twenty years have altered processes of capital accumulation and labor disciplining in the United States so that the interests of the state and market imperatives are in greater alignment than ever. As the benefits won during the civil rights era get significantly scaled down or altogether eliminated, a resulting massive redistribution of wealth upward and in an asymmetric pattern conforms to pre-existing racial and gendered hierarchies, while requiring new forms of affective communication and expression, particularly among racialized groups.

In this political economic context the US-born Latinos and Latin American migrants whose voices appeared throughout this volume experienced unprecedented personal turmoil and almost inescapable pressures towards downward economic mobility. Almost all of my informants—including the high school students and youth whose voices appear here—were working people of a variety of lower or middle-to-lower income levels who were either full-time or part-time employed in the service sector (in fast food, ethnic restaurants, bars), low-end retail (as cashiers, stackers), construction work and security (as guards), personal services (as domestic workers, baby sitters, beauty salon workers) or the lower administrative sectors of the social service economy (as staff in not-for-profit organization). With the exception of school administrators and a few informants working in the security industry (as security guards in hospital and insurance agency buildings, for instance), none of my informants had a job with defined-benefits or pension and, in the period of my fieldwork, most of them had no health insurance benefits. These downward economic pressures and deteriorating benefits packages were manifested not only in these individuals' particular employment situations, but also in their inner worlds and the public spheres they navigated in Newark. It is the urban emotive commonsense that connects these government and market imperatives with individuals' intimate lives what has been at the core of this volume and constitutes the affective requirements of postindustrial cities in the United States (chapter 1).

This volume has examined how those practices that exist at the "edge of semantic availability" (Williams 1977, 134) are actively lived and felt, and also how they are manifested in the material and social worlds of working-class racialized subjects. In particular, in the context of Newark's emotive urban commonsense, I have identified a cartography of racial democracy that serves as a structure of feelings that is interpreted through emotional epistemologies in multiple local and transnational locations and which organizes the interactions among migrants, US minorities, and the durability of white privilege in majority-minority urban areas (see introduction, chapter 1 and chapter 4). These structuring structures, in Bourdieu's sense, are all lived experiences that change not according to rigid parameters or static categories, but in relation to how individuals see themselves, the world around them, the spaces they occupy, and the people and institutions with whom they come into contact in visceral, phenomenological ways.

In the case of Newark, a predominantly black city, whiteness operates by disciplining poor and working-class US-born Latinos and migrants of color, particularly those from Latin America, to carve a space as a distinct kind of national subject, one that cannot attain the privileges of white America, but also cannot cultivate solidarity with African Americans.

Transnational migrants approached domestic US minorities and the process of becoming US racialized subjects themselves with trepidation. They found themselves subscribing to emotional styles that allowed both a display of urban competency and an alignment with market demands for a particular form of emotional labor (Hochschild 1983). While under nativism being an "immigrant" was recognized as a bad thing, being the wrong kind of minority was oftentimes worse; these forms of personhood caused great distress, anticipatory disorientation, and performance anxiety of not getting a neoliberally friendly form of personhood and Americanization right. Racism is indeed formative, and not simply incongruent with, American democracy; for Latin American migrants, "racial naturalization" is, in this sense, "a process or experience through which people enter the imagined American community as cognizable racial subjects" (Carbado 2005, 651).

Many Latin American migrants and US-born Latinos would engage in a process of "doing Blackness right," as part of an embodied racial learning and in response to visceral and structural aspects of their affective worlds and reflections on those worlds (chapter 6). The process of "doing Blackness right" centered on the assumption that African Americans were excessively "resentful" of their subordination. Moreover, it emphasized that there were multiple forms of Blackness, based on international or distinctly Latin American perspectives on race that were more malleable and compatible with market goals in the United States. Finally, this process focused on a "public sphere" that rendered the bodies of African Americans as "phantom bodies" in the Habermassian sense. "Doing Blackness right" involved overlooking similarities with African Americans in terms of residential segregation, occupational and educational neglect by the state, and equivalent degrees of economic and political marginality, while highlighting distinctions in emotive communication and psychological makeup. In its association of black America with urban competency, cosmopolitanism, and modernity, this process was also the work of a creative imagination, of struggling and creating oneself with and against the limits of neoliberal desires.

"Doing Blackness right" required a calibration of knowledge that dictated the kinds and limits of the embodiment of a racialized affect; this entailed the capacity to know and know what not to know, simultaneously, and in multiple (seemingly contradictory) contexts like the streets of "inner-city" neighborhoods, the market, school, or country of origin. It involved making a palatable copy of an otherwise "defective" Blackness, so that Blackness among Latin Americans and Latinos was emblematic of Americanization in a neoliberally friendly, cosmopolitan way. The process of "doing Blackness right" is a critical aspect of the transformation of the body physical through physical labor and productivity/capital accumulation that Marx and Engels (1998) describe. In fact, it was the ultimate way of creating suitable workers within a racial project that involved naturalizing rules of emotive display in the interests of capital. The socialization of body and emotions, on which the process of racial learning was premised, operated to make some individuals more vulnerable to the effects of emotional dissonance, suppression, and display rules that were aligned with entry-level labor market needs.

Most Latin American migrants and many US-born Latinos continued to pursue the traits associated with a US "immigrant tale" under a precisely executed urban cosmopolitanism cloak, by becoming street therapists or experts in the community norms of appropriate emotional displays (chapters 3 and 4). These processes of racial experimentation were central to the constitution of a neoliberal personhood among racialized subjects. Selectively activating classic ideologies of Latin American "racial democracy," Latinos and Latin American migrants not only distinguished themselves from African Americans at an ideological level, but more significantly, at the emotional level, as they differentiated themselves as more desirable, marketable, and attractive to the commercial projects of the Newark Renaissance. This is a new form of competency for most Latin American migrants and even for many US-born Latinos in predominantly black cities.

In this volume, a cartography of racial democracy has served to highlight how street therapists filtered their analyses of race in the United States from an imagined or experiential memory of what race in their countries of origin or ancestry *felt like*. Giselle Coutinho, a Brazilian student and Ironbound resident, undermined denunciation of black oppression by blacks by drawing comparisons that accentuated the presumption of racial democracy in Brazil: "Why do blacks here have to complain so much about racism? Racism, racism, racism, that's all they talk about! In Brazil that's not important. We don't have to be talking about race and this and that, you know? Everybody is mixed there!" From a slightly different perspective, but also rejecting US racial categories, particularly "Hispanic," which was associated with US-born Latinos and Puerto Ricans in particular, Pedro, a seventeen-year-old from Uruguay, commented: "I don't come here thinking that I'm less than them [white Americans]. I don't come here thinking that they are superior. In that sense I'm different from some of the people here. I mean, there are times that I'm like 'Yeah, Hispanics!' [with pride] and I feel good when someone achieves things and he's a Hispanic. But I'm just me, an individual, you know." An assumption behind these comments is that most African Americans and even some US-born Latinos were excessively "resentful" of their subordination (chapters 4 and 5).

Even when most Latinos and Latin Americans acknowledged anti-black discrimination in the United States, they qualified that recognition with statements about how "reverse (black-on-white or black-on-Latino) discrimination" also existed and how the "complaining" and "resentment" was disproportionate to the level of subordination blacks experienced; even when the historical context of slavery was raised, which was always done in passing and oftentimes dismissively, connections to contemporary African American life in the United States were rarely drawn. "Resentment" and "quejarse" (to complain) were sometimes used interchangeably, but always assumed an emotional or psychological weakness. The projection of "resentment" and "aggressiveness" onto African Americans effectively reinscribed hegemonic correlations between "American" and whiteness, even in a predominantly black city, while promoting images of certain migrants as "deserving" in contradistinction to the "undeserving" US minority poor (chapter 2).

Given these visceral attachments to physical and social space at multiple scales—from the intimate to the national and transnational—this volume became necessarily more inclusive of populations and perspectives than it was initially set out to be. Exploring the intersection of a productive urban emotive commonsense, a cartography of racial democracy, and the formation of a neoliberal personhood required keen attention to analytic distinctions and political economic framing of several populations that shared "Newark"—US-born Latinos and Latin Americans of different nationalities, African Americans of different class and regional backgrounds, white ethnics who were mostly Portuguese and some Italians, and even suburban (mostly white) populations that served as constitutive outsiders (chapters 3 and 4).

In this volume, I have suggested that certain forms of emotional darkness or negative emotions were oftentimes valuable to the production of a neoliberal subject, as long as they were selectively deployed as sustainable cultural capital, so that they did not interfere with a service sector labor market that required a "good disposition" or "buena presencia." When appropriately expressed, dark emotional styles meant sincerity (one is not fake happy). Street therapists were invested in taking into account the context and situation—and hierarchical expectations of respectability. They tried to identify (and sometimes avoid) instances of emotional styles that challenged US conventions of "good disposition." In the process, painful feelings were sometimes directed toward forms of self-knowledge in the new context of racial learning, not toward a denunciation of social and structural dysfunction.

Learning these forms of emotional and affective self-management was critical in establishing new patterns of social recognition and differentiation in Newark, as these didactic processes were also ensconced in the production of enduring urban meta-sentiments. This was particularly the case when one's identity had been premised on the belief that racial talk is "impolite" and what generates racism in the first place, as was the case for many Latin American migrants who still subscribed to ideologies akin to racial democracy (cf. Sheriff 2001; Goldstein 1999). Limited embodiment was facilitated by a cartography of racial democracy that provided Latin American migrants and even some US-born Latinos with the possibility of inhabiting multiple systems of racial difference at once. Likewise, most US-born and immigrant Latinos acquired racial knowledge through the continuous scrutiny of how African Americans and, more often, Puerto Ricans, were institutionally racialized and how these US-born minorities themselves actively assumed or rejected such racialization practices; how such antiblack subordination operated in historical and political contexts and impacted individual aspirations and opportunities; how racial performances enhanced one's cosmopolitanism, modernity, and urban competency, while redefining gender, sexuality, class, and generational subjectivities; and how bipolar (black/white) perspectives of race in the United States converged and diverged from configurations of "race" in one's country of origin or ancestry.

These final remarks are a reflection on the implications of an increasing focus on a "neoliberally friendly" form of personhood, grounded in the political economy of cities and the urban emotional commonsense that sustain various forms of capital accumulation, as well as ensconced on local and transnational racial projects. It has outlined how, in everyday interactions among working-class and populations of color, there has been a transition from a focus on material and structural conditions to a focus on interiority and affect in readings of inequality, marginality, and subordination. What does this shift do to racial relations and urban life? Rather than arriving at a facile political view that renders a focus-on-structure as positive and a focus-on-affect as negative, this project has pointed to a more complex set of practices. In fact, it suggests a more nuanced state of affairs: one in which both structure and affect are mutually constitutive of one another and provide effective spaces for social critique among the most disenfranchised urban residents.

———

Hilda Hidalgo's Way COMMEMORATIVE STREET SIGN TO BE PLACED AT THE CORNER OF UNI-
VERSITY AVENUE AND NEW STREET IN NEWARK'S CENTRAL WARD

On a sunny afternoon in March of 2010 I attended an event to "Celebrate
the Life of Hilda Hidalgo," whose academic contribution to the migratory experiences of Puerto Ricans in New Jersey I analyze in chapter 1, at
the Newark Public Library. A Rutgers Puerto Rican faculty member who
conducted oral history research in Newark in the 1970s, Hilda Hidalgo
was also a prominent social worker who had left a Catholic convent to
"find her truth." As one speaker after another talked about Dr. Hidalgo,
the audience learned that she had been committed to the rights of gays
and lesbians and of working-class Puerto Rican residents of Newark. The
two great loves of Hilda's life—an African American woman with whom
she lived for nearly two decades and a white woman physician with
whom she shared the latter part of her life—occupied a central role in
the life story that was woven at the commemorative event. Hilda's sisters,
her partner, and close to 100 people—a large community of middle-age
Puerto Rican/Latino lesbians, Rutgers faculty members, and community
activists—attended the activity in Newark, even though Hilda had been
living in Florida when she was diagnosed with cancer and passed away.

"A Celebration of Life: Hilda Hidalgo, Ph.D. (1928–2009)" and a picture of an obviously vibrant woman with large-rimmed glasses and short
salt-and-pepper hair decorated the cover of the programs that had been
printed for the commemorative event. Emerita Rutgers professors welcomed the audience and talked about Hilda's life and career; Hilda's sisters and partners remembered events from Hilda's childhood in Puerto
Rico and life in New Jersey and Florida; a number of people—including a
renowned Nuyorican poet and a clown who entertained breast cancer patients at a local hospital—offered testimonials of their interactions with
Hilda Hidalgo. Toward the end of the event, a young woman who was introduced as the "first Puerto Rican archivist in New Jersey" presented an
audiotaped interview and slide show she had gathered in the last months
of Hilda's life. When the young woman had asked her if she had any final thoughts, Hilda simply stated: "I wish there were more Puerto Rican
women like you . . . women that our community can be proud of." Hilda
also lamented what she viewed as a decline in the prominence of a Puerto
Rican identity and, while she acknowledged that this was probably because, in a multicultural context, Puerto Ricans had to coexist with other
groups, she urged young people like the archivist-interviewer to cultivate
a greater "sense of justice."

When a Puerto Rican judge and activist confirmed that the city of

Newark would rename a portion of a street in the Central Ward as "Hilda Hidalgo's Way," the tongue-in-cheek appropriateness of the street nam- ing—given Hilda's very maverick nature and self-determination—gener- ated comment and laughter among those in attendance. Yes, after all, as an openly lesbian, politically active Puerto Rican woman in 1970s Newark, Hilda had really done things her way. More significantly, at least for the other young women in the audience, however, was that Hilda Hidalgo had maintained "buena presencia" throughout.

Amarilis Guzmán, the Puerto Rican graduate of Barringer HS and North Newark resident whom I identified as one of the first street therapists I encountered in the preface and who described conflicts between black and Puerto Rican women in chapter 5, came with me to the commemo- rative event. I hadn't seen Amarilis in over a year so we decided to go for lunch at a nearby place after the event to catch up. While looking for a space to park Amarilis's girlfriend's white BMW in the congested area of the Ironbound, Amarilis declared: "I admire people like that lady [Hilda Hidalgo]. What she did, how she conducted herself. Because, I'm telling you, she was able to do what she did . . . to give us pride as Puerto Ri- cans . . . by looking inside and not falling into all this Newark shit." Almost as part of the same conversation, Amarilis narrated her latest "adventures" as a security guard at Newark's University Hospital. The inability to distinguish psychiatric ward patients from everybody else, encounters with "aggressive" black women who wanted to pull knives on her, and a neurotic white receptionist who obsessed over a faucet that wouldn't stop liking were among Amarilis's colorfully narrated stories. "People think that this is a cop-for-hire kind of job, but they don't know all the emotional energy that goes into it too. Because, let me tell you, dealing with crazy people is hard work," she declared.

Despite the dramatic narratives that by now I'd come to see as char- acteristic of her vibrant personality, I immediately noticed how much Amarilis's life had changed since I had met her in 2002 and, especially, in the year since I had last seen her. In the seven years since graduating from the North Newark high school where I had first met her when she was a senior, Amarilis had metamorphosed from someone who had struggled with coke abuse and alcoholism and had spent some time in rehab to a full-time employee and her father's main caretaker. Her father had been diagnosed with colon cancer and Amarilis had moved in with him and her stepmother to help them out financially.

When I pointed out how much her life seemed to have changed, par- ticularly referring to the several years she had spent working at University Hospital, Amarilis promptly remarked: "I owe that to my spiritual practice." Amarilis and I had never talked about spirituality beyond occasional references to religion or psychological services, and I said something along those lines, that I had never heard her mentioning spirituality before. She elaborated:

The only way I've been able to survive all that's going on in my life, my father's illness, staying sober . . . and especially, staying at that crazy job in this crazy city is because of my Taino spirituality. You know how many mentally damaged people are in this city? And these are not the ones that are in the hospital, those are not as bad, because at least you know what you're going into. They're crazy and that's it. The ones on the streets, those are the real fucked up ones. The ones that come into the lobby [of University Hospital] and want to blow off on you. And you know me, I don't take shit from nobody. But you know why I've had that job for all this years? My spirituality . . . and knowing about human nature.

At the time when we met, Amarilis had lost contact with her Taino spiritual guide and was unable to get in touch with him because she had a fallout with the only person who seems to know how to contact this Taino shaman. Apparently, this woman caught Amarilis sleeping with her daughter. Amarilis was eager to reconnect with the Taino priest whom she credits with her recovery and with Taino spirituality more broadly; her father, an Afro-Puerto Rican man who is a long-time practitioner of Taino spirituality, did not want to Amarilis to get more involved in the practice because "he's afraid because I also have a dark side and he doesn't want that to come out."

I was nearly nine months pregnant at the time of this conversation and, shortly after Amarilis had dropped me off at Newark Penn Station, she texted me: "I forgot to ask you. What are you having?"

"A baby boy," I texted back.

She herself had a son with her ex-wife. "Great. Name him something strong."

"We're naming him Sebastián. With an accent. In Spanish. What's your son's name?"

"I like that name! We named him Legend, very Taino name."

The next text: "What's your husband?"

"Indian," I responded.

"That's great. U'll have a spiritual child!"

I decided not to clarify that my husband was actually Indian "from India" and perhaps not the kind of "Indian" we had been discussing.

What remained significant in this post-meeting texting session was that, for Amarilis, like for many of the other young people whose voices appear here, managing what they viewed as a affective and quasi-spiritual "dark side" was critical to remaining fully employed in a neoliberal context where jobs are scarce and in which one felt provoked to "act aggressive" and lose a sense of buena presencia.

Notes

1. "Latino" here refers to US-born or -raised individuals. "Latin American migrant" refers to individuals born in Latin America or the Spanish-speaking Caribbean or recent arrivals from those areas. In this ethnographic context, most Latinos were Puerto Rican and, to a lesser extent, Dominican, and most Latin American migrants were Brazilian, but also Colombian, Ecuadorian, and Peruvian. In most cases, I use the nationality term, rather than panethnic terms like "Latino" or "Hispanic."

2. Illouz defines "emotional intelligence" as "a form of habitus that enables the acquisition of a form of capital situated at the seam line between cultural and social capital. . . . If cultural capital is crucial as a status signal, emotional style is crucial to how people acquire networks, both strong and weak, and build what sociologists call social capital, that is, the ways in which personal relationships are converted into forms of capital, such as career advancement or increased wealth." This is related to Illouz's "emotional competence," which involves self-awareness, the ability to identify feelings and talk about them, empathize with others' positions and find solutions to problems (2007, 66–67, 69).

3. The modalities through which racialized working-class populations learn the language of popular psychology and mental health discourse is beyond the scope of this work, though some possible sources could be similar to those through which middle-class adults have learned them, including advice literature in trade books and magazines, talk shows, interaction with counselors, psychologists, school personnel, or clergy.

4. The issues of consciousness and intentionality are at the center of debates between phenomenologists and practice theorists. Bourdieu, for instance, believes that habitus is transmitted without conscious intention and rejects the view of the agent as a conscious, intentional, and rational actor. This is in part due to "the forgetting of history which history itself produces by incorporating the objective structures it produces in the second nature of habitus" (1977, 36,78–79), which also constitutes doxa, a misrecognition established through tacit consensus and "common sense." While the non-conscious aspect of habitus is an important contribution of Bourdieuian practice theory, the case of people of color in the United States requires that we draw distinctions between which groups are more likely to forget which histories; as this volume shows, people of color in the United States are forced to remember their history because of the particularities of how that history instructs their contemporary social positioning and life chances and, thus, not as easily transformed into the second-nature, nonconscious, prereflective process Bourdieu describes. Thus, Bourdieu criticizes phenomenology for its emphasis on "intentionality," which he sees as a debilitating mentalism that does not adequately account for the functioning of nonintentional somatic dispositions. The main critique that phenomenologists have against Bourdieu and other practice theorists is that they fail to account for agency and how agents can make conscious, intentional decisions (Throop and Murphy 2002).

5. It is noteworthy here that Haugeland (1999) introduces the distinction between "interaction" and "intimacy" to reject not only any clear boundary between mind and body, but also between body and world; social practices are embodied, and the bodily skills through which they are realized are intimately responsive to the affordances and resistances of their surroundings (cf. Rouse 2006, 536).

6. Despite acknowledging qualitative differences between "feeling," "sentiment," and "emotion," I will sometimes use these terms interchangeably, except when the distinctions between them are relevant to the analysis.

7. Two tendencies frame traditional studies of emotions in anthropology. The first tendency viewed emotions as bodily, physical feeling, and presumed a transcultural or universal emphasis (e.g., Levi-Strauss, Tyler), often suggestive of biological and evolutionary attributes (e.g., Edmund Leach). See Katz 2001, 345n2, for an examination of this literature. The second "psychocultural" perspective views emotion as cultural meaning and a part of cognition variously disassociated from bodily "feeling." This perspective has yielded multiple theoretical frameworks, including a focus on language and discourse, cultural constructivism, psychoculturalism, and anticonstructivist perspectives, among others. Researchers who have subscribed to this "psychocultural" approach (e.g., Obeyesekere 1990; Kleinman, Das, and Lock 1997) claim that there is a broad underlying commonality in human emotions. In addition to viewing language as a leading way to express

or talk about emotional experiences, the psychocultural perspective emphasizes how emotions are simultaneously "egocentric" and "sociocentric."

8. An exploration of emotions employing a "constructivist" approach (Rosaldo 1984; Abu-Lughod 1986; Lutz 1988) argues that "what individuals can think and feel is overwhelmingly a product of socially organized modes of action and of talk" (Rosaldo 1984, 147), and this applies to even the most intimate, individual private feelings. In her study of *liget* (anger, envy) among the Iglonot headhunters, Rosaldo realizes that the activities motivated by liget were not just cultural scripts, but resulted from a profound emotional engagement that suggested that culture operated at a deeper level than anthropologists had previously recognized. Likewise, Abu-Lughod's study of Bedouin women in Egypt reveals that even individuals' most intimate, private feelings were deeply shaped by social norms, and were already in conformity with a community's values and outlooks. Furthermore, Lutz's examination of emotions among the Pacific atoll reinforces the cultural constructivist stance while noting that outside the West, emotions are not viewed as distinct from (or in opposition to) cognition. Anthropologists who subscribe to social constructivist or interpretive perspectives argue over precisely how and to what extent emotions are influenced, shaped, or constructed by "culture," and in what ways are emotions both socially shaped and socially shaping phenomena (Lutz and White 1986; Thoits 1989). Traditional philosophical and psychosocial perspectives have examined emotions in contradistinction to cognition. Sartre examined how cognition placed the object of knowledge outside the self, while Freud focused on how in emotion the object of knowledge is inside the self.

9. Anthropologists traditionally focused on building a vocabulary of emotional terms, adopting the position that, since we can't get into people's heads and hearts, we must focus on people's definitions of emotions. This approach assumed that emotions are internal events or that affect is "too slippery" an area of language for empirical investigation. Leavitt challenges this epistemological claim by arguing that to define emotions as words or concepts was to lose the feeling side of the phenomenon and reduce it to a kind of meaning: "Emotion is expressed not only at every level of language, but also outside language that is explicitly about emotion—that is, language has a heart that is distinct from explicit cultural models and vocabularies" (1996, 522). Closer attention needs to be paid to the more covert ways in which affect suffuses language, including how groups emphasize control of aggressive displays, and how the very inherent indeterminacy of many affect-encoding devices are exploited. It is in the act of communicating in its various forms that individual "interior experiences" become objectified and observable as social phenomena and, thus, a subject of ethnographic scrutiny.

10. The role of "culture" on emotion has since been criticized as overly deterministic. Circumspect stances challenging a "pure" constructivist approach

have centered on how such approaches draws too sharp of a distinction between social meaning and relationships, on the one hand, and subjective or personal meanings on the other (Watson-Gegeo, White, and Arno 1990). Some alternative approaches that have challenged a "pure" cultural constructivist take are the following: Unni Wikan (2008), who argues that there exists a nonverbal "resonance" that allows for empathetic communication across cultural gaps; Margot Lyon (1995), who argues that emotions derive not directly from culture, but from the way in which bodies are associatively linked to social structure; and John Leavitt (1996), who views emotions not only as pragmatic acts and communicative performances, but also as bodily experience and an expressive vehicle.

11. Emotions are embedded in contexts of memory and association and are, thus, subject to learning. As Cavell (1998) states, through learning, one's emotional vocabulary can expand and become more nuanced; through this emotional learning, an individual can evaluate the emotional meaning of an event before it knows what the event is and why it might be good or bad.

12. My understanding of "folk theories of race" is inspired by John Jackson's aim to nuance the classical way in which social scientists have come to talk about race as an "ascribed characteristic" and class as an "achieved" one. In *Harlemworld* (2001), Jackson posits race as a kind of achieved characteristic, claiming that racial authenticity is often achieved through performances and practices that are oftentimes class marked. In this sense, racial identity takes work and is therefore also achieved or not achieved based on one's actions and how they are interpreted. As John Jackson eloquently explains: "Folk theories of race discover race in the doing, arrived at through specific actions and not only anchored in one's epidermis and morphology. This performative notion of race creates space for people to challenge arguments about what particular behaviors connect to which discrete races, potentially challenging all forms of 'racial realism'" (2001, 12).

13. In the context of the United States, discussions around racial democracy have centered on literary invocations of Latin American *mestizaje*—noteworthy being Anzaldúa's "mestiza consciousness" or García-Canclini's "hybridity"—an antidote to US-style logics of racial categorization (Alcoff 1995; Anzaldúa 1987; Fernández 1992). An equivalent category suggesting racial mixture, *mulataje* has also been used in the case of populations hailing from what Charles Wagley (1957) called "plantation America" to distinguish how the Caribbean and Brazil, as locus of Afro-America, had to be understood in contrast to an Indo-America centered on Mexico, Central America, the Andes, and Euro-America, represented by countries in North America and the Southern Cone. Wade (2004) challenges the more celebratory aspects of the "hybridity" suggested in discussions of US mestizaje or mulataje by noting the essentialist elements imbedded in ideas about mixture and the failure of such essentialism to destabilize racial absolutes

or shed attention on issues of class inequality and social justice. (See also Winant 1994; Marable 1995; cf. Wade 2004, 360; Vasconcelos 1997) Likewise, George Lipsitz (1998) examines the uses of mixed-race tropes to show how these have been used by neoconservative and neoliberals to represent race in the United States as personal, private, individual, and idiosyncratic, rather than institutional, ideological, collective, and cumulative. See also Domínguez 1973; Dzidzienyo and Oboler 2005.

14. The dismantling of formal segregation and the increased migration of populations who do not fit easily into rigid black-white parameters, including Latinos, are cited as reasons for an increasingly fluid racial configuration in the United States (Degler 1986; Skidmore 1993a, 199b; Winant 1994). Renowned Brazilianist Thomas Skidmore argues that Latinos in the United States, particularly those from the Spanish-speaking Caribbean, constitute an equivalent to Brazilian conception of "mixed blood." As he notes, while "some of this diverse 'Hispanic' population (especially from Cuba, Puerto Rico, and the Dominican Republic) would, by physical appearance, fall into the traditional non-white category (black or African-American), . . . the US legal system has created another category which is neither black nor white. . . . [Moreover] the US black community is itself sensitive to colour gradations" (1993a, 379). In this sense, racial democracy might seem consistent with US "multiculturalism." Conversely, a greater recognition of racial inequality (not just socioeconomic marginality) has fueled grassroots Afro–Latin American movements, antidiscrimination legislature, and "affirmative action"-like politics throughout Latin America in the last two decades. Taking into account national political, economic, and historical particularities, as well as the cultural contexts embedding the production of racial "difference," many scholars have examined the transformations of "race" in light of increased migration, globalization, and transnationalism (Silverstein 2005; Skidmore 1993b; Wade 2004; Warren and Twine 1997, 2002; Winant 1992). This presumed "convergence" of Latin American and US racial systems has even led some scholars to speculate about the possibility of a "hemispheric" perspective on race (Affigne, Avalos, and Jackson 1998; Dzidzienyo and Oboler 2005).

15. Andrew Jacobs, "Two Miles in Newark That Run from Long Decline to Rebirth," *New York Times*, January 5, 2007.

16. Specifically, Jacobs notes: "[D]own at the waterfront, where the business of unloading and loading cargo has doubled in the past decade, producing about 1,000 new jobs a year, nearly 80% of the 28,000 stevedore and truck driving positions are held by people who live outside the city. At Newark Liberty International Airport, few of the baggage handlers, flight attendants and reservation agents are from Newark. . . . As it stands, more than three-quarters of the city's 150,000 jobs are held by out-of-towners" (Andrew Jacobs, "A New Mayor Tests His Promises on Newark's Harsh Reality," *New York Times*, October 19, 2006).

17. For a critical discussion on multisited ethnography and the creation of socially meaningful empirical cartographies, see Marcus 1995.

CHAPTER ONE

1. Myers (1979) characterizes meta-sentiments as socially constructed patterns of sensations, expressive gestures, and cultural meanings organized around a relationship to a social object, another person, and groups that sustain relatively enduring social relationships as affect elicitors. An example of such meta-sentiments appears in Obeyesekere's (1990) examination of "grief" in Iran, for instance. Demonstrating how emotional states are transformed, Obeyeskere focuses on the impact of the Iranian revolution on the experience of grief; once an emblem of resistance, in postrevolutionary Iran grief became an emotion mandated by the state.

2. Understandings of particular cities must be considered in light of broader conceptions of space, inequality, and power relations. From this perspective, boundary setting within cities is more concerned with the way in which physical and conceptual boundaries are constituted and are produced and reproduced by social relations and power inequalities (Harvey 2001).

3. On July 12, 1967, an incident of police brutality against John Smith, a black cab driver, sparked five days of racial conflict that resulted in the death of twenty-six people, twenty-four of whom were African American. Focusing on the financial costs of the riots, an estimated "$8 million worth of looting and almost $2 million in property damage," the *Los Angeles Times* described: "Snipers and looters raced randomly from street to street through [Newark] Saturday night. Tense national guardsmen and police working under a state of emergency, fought to contain the fourth straight night of bitter racial violence" (July 15, 1967). Incidents of racial conflict were, of course, not unique to Newark. In the early 1960s, protests over living conditions were common in the black neighborhoods of northern cities, and racial violence surfaced not only in Newark, but also in Chicago, Cleveland, New York, Philadelphia, and Los Angeles, among many others. The most serious outbursts of widespread unrest left three people dead in Chicago, twenty-six in Newark, and forty-three in Detroit. Concentrated in the abandoned and decayed inner cities, this breakdown in civil order needs to be contextualized in rampant racial discrimination in job and housing markets, unemployment, and the disempowerment and impoverishment of urban African American populations nationwide. See also Jackson and Jackson 1972.

   Note: The first part of the section title is drawn from an article by Argelio Dumenigo that appeared in the *Princeton Alumni Weekly* 2 (2002): 13.

4. Following the national trend, manufacturing jobs declined the most in Newark during the latter half of the twentieth century. Manufacturing jobs

in Newark peaked close to 100,000 in 1953, but by 1996 employed only 16,400 workers, an 80% drop from the 1953 level. More than 72% (17,000) of the transportation jobs in Newark are tied to air transportation at the Newark International Airport. In 1994 Newark residents accounted for 13.1% of all airport employees. Newark also employed 195,600 employees in the private sector in 1969, but only 110,800 in 1991 (Newark Economic Development Corporation 1998). See also Al Frank, "Sky's the Limit as Newark Airport Looks to Future," *Star-Ledger*, December 29, 1998.

5. Julia Vitullo-Martin, "Gateway Newark," *New York Times*, October 22, 2006.

6. In urban planning practices, space is usually conceived of as a condition that is reflected *in* social practices rather than a condition that might reveal things *about* social practices and social thinking otherwise hidden from view. As Setha Low states: "The social construction of space is the actual transformation of space—through people's social exchanges, memories, images, and daily use of the material setting—into scenes and actions that convey symbolic meaning" (1996, 861). For a discussion on the locality-producing capabilities of large-scale social formations and how localities become transactions in and of themselves, see David Harvey's (2001) discussion of time-space compression.

7. Title I of the 1949 Federal Housing Act provided federal aid to urban communities for the "clearance" of "blighted" areas that would then be sold at write-down values to private redevelopers who would agree to build middle-income housing or other projects appropriate to those sites. Newark is generally presented as a case study of one highly successful city and the Newark Housing Authority, which launched nine clearance projects during its first ten years in Title I, is credited with this success. The blatant disregard for examining potentially conflictive definitions of "success" is astonishing: "'Success' is synonymously with high levels of clearance activity. . . . [It] may be measured by the number of blocks cleared, the number of new dwelling units constructed, or the total amount of funds spent. It is a quantitative, not a qualitative index; it deliberately avoids questions involving the appropriateness of particular versions of renewal policy" (Kaplan 1963, 2).

8. NHA was the second-largest (after the Board of Education) spender of funds and the largest dispenser of contracts in the city government in 1949, and Danzig had his legal staff prepared an ordinance making the NHA the city's official redevelopment agency. Nevertheless, in the search for redevelopment sites, the key question became whether a private firm could make a profit on middle-income housing in the most "undesirable" areas of the city (Kaplan 1963, 16). Under the argument that there was "no market" for middle-income housing in Newark's "hard-core slum" or "Negro ghettos," the NHA eventually subordinated "slum clearance" to site feasibility. This decision led the agency to bypass the most decayed areas of the predominantly black Central Ward in favor of "more marketable" and less

racially marked sites in the predominantly Italian North Broadway. NHA refused to reduce the size of the clearance area or to sacrifice one of the natural boundaries; instead, the agency proposed to retain redevelopment along the *outer* boundaries of the site and to fill in the middle spaces with public housing. The 1954 Federal Housing Act renewed the slum clearance provisions of the 1949 act, added a program of federal aid for local renewal activities other than clearance, and permitted local agencies to designate an entire neighborhood as an "urban renewal area." Under these new terms, NHA launched comprehensive attacks on the Central Ward.

9. Eventually, urban renewal agencies concluded that the renewal area needed to be cut down from its original 100 blocks to 60 blocks, and no area was available for redevelopment after this reduction; hence, the NHA was left with only public housing sites (in the most decayed area of the Central Ward), and later on sold the rest of the cleared space to the city, the board of education, and the Boys Club of Newark. NHA's efforts led to projects involving high-priced apartments on sites immediately surrounding the central business district and "slum clearance" became associated with the development of public housing projects. NHA also persuaded the Newark Museum, the Newark Pubic Library, and the Newark College of Engineering to join in constructing new facilities on the site. In September of 1958, NHA designated a fifteen-block renewal area, just south of the North Ward project, for the expansion of local educational and cultural facilities. Nevertheless, none of these newly included institutions was any more willing to redevelop sites in the "hard-core slums" than private builders had been (Kaplan 1963, 22, 23).

10. Jacobs, "Two Miles"; Vitullo-Martin, "Gateway Newark."

11. The literature on neoliberalism considers the operations of shrinking state responsibilities, the disciplining and tractability of labor, and the privatization of public spaces through the examination of an array of issues, ranging from the marketing uses of culture to concerns with homelessness, poverty, residential segregation, and other indices of inequality (Escobar 1995; Comaroff and Comaroff 2000; Storper 2000; Maskovsky 2001). Jean Comaroff and John Comaroff (2000) urge scholars to expand neoliberalism beyond a structural and policy-based standpoint into a culture of capitalism rooted on the belief in a "millennial capitalism" that presents itself as a gospel of salvation—a capitalism that, if rightly harnessed, is "invested with the capacity wholly to transform the universe of the marginalized and disempowered (292, 304). Lisa Duggan (2003) likewise urges a more integrated understanding of neoliberalism that examines the mutual interdependency of economics, political, and cultural fields, on which neoliberal politics is predicated.

12. Even if there's a retrenchment of the state under neoliberalism, in some areas, domination has long been exercised by entities other than the state. Governmentality refers to those relations that regulate "the conduct

of subjects as a population and as individuals in the interests of ensur-
ing the security and prosperity of the nation-state" (Ferguson and Gupta
2002, 992). The logic of the market has been extended to the operations
of state functions, so that even the traditionally core institutions of the
government (including schools), run according to an "enterprise model"
(Burchell, quoted in Ferguson and Gupta 2002, 992).

13. Carly Rothman, "Newark Welcomes Its New Starbucks, and 40 Travel
Agents," *Star-Ledger*, July 17, 2008.

14. The reconstruction of downtowns across the United States involved a
neglect of the almost-extinct manufacturing, warehousing, and freight-
handling operations, and a shift in attention and resources to the construction of offices, banks, financial firms, government agencies, hotels,
restaurants, entertainment and cultural venues, and department stores. The
artistic scene, for instance, reflects the parallel development that came out
of the Newark Renaissance: Most of the Renaissance has centered on downtown Newark, where most of the large businesses and public buildings
are located. The New Newark Foundation has focused on developing the
downtown commercial district right below Washington Park, adjacent to
the central business district, as an "arts and entertainment neighborhood,"
with a twenty-four-hour residential street life modeled after Greenwich
Village and SoHo. New Newark has purchased twenty-four large parcels of
property in an area measuring several dozen square blocks and is in the
process of renovating the buildings for use as artist studios, residences and
boutique stores. See "Director Named for Newark Development," *New York
Times*, March 9, 2000. It is also worth noting that a significant concentration of artists also emerged in the 1980s in the Ironbound, where three or
four former factories or warehouses were turned into living space, studios,
and galleries for artists. Likewise, the New Jersey Performing Arts Center
(NJPAC) opened in October 1997. The original design plan for NJPAC,
which was altered at the last minute, included a tunnel connecting the
parking garage under Military Park to the arts center, because the archi-
tects did not believe arts patrons would want to set foot on the streets of
Newark. For discussion of other artistic initiatives in Newark, see Cole 1987.

15. A cover-page article on the *Princeton Alumni Weekly* (Dumenigo 2002,
14–17), boldly titled "Newark: From Riots to Respectability," is evidence of
how various media claim that "after decades of decline and disinvestments,
Newark today is attracting national attention for its ongoing rebirth and
renewal." Allusions to the New Jersey Performing Arts Center, and to the
possibility of creating a sports complex for the Yankees, the Nets, and New
Jersey Devils teams, were presented as evidence of the phoenix-like future
of the city. See, for instance, Bettinger 2002, where the author emphasizes
Newark's location as "contiguous to the suburbs and edge cities of New
Jersey, including the robust markets and corporate centers of the state's
'Wealth Belt.'" See also Nikita Stewart's "Festival Celebrates the Spirit of

South Ward's Resurrection," *Star-Ledger*, August 20, 2000. There are notable exceptions to the celebratory Newark Renaissance narrative. One such narrative appeared under the title "City Slicker: Newark" (Daniel Jeffreys, "City Slicker: Newark—Newark, New Jersey, Has Been Designated the Crime Capital of the United States by the FBI," *The Independent* [London], December 12, 1994). The author begins by stating that "Newark, New Jersey, has been designated the crime capital of the United States by the FBI." Then he proceeds in inventory-style fashion to list "the most dangerous place: West Side Park. Serious gang territory. Police will only stop a suspicious vehicle if two police cars are present. Mostly 1950s housing projects in the brutalist style. Each corner is marked with gang colors. Gunfire and rap music are the prevailing sounds at night. . . . Favorite destination: The New Jersey Turnpike, which leads out of Newark."

16. Vitullo-Martin, "Gateway Newark."
17. When social class is indeed examined, lower-class status is seen as entailing either less emotionality, defined as personal subjectivity, or more emotionality, defined as chaotic, "over-the-top" affect rather than a more nuanced, refined sentimentality (Medick and Sabean 1984). Following Norma Alarcón's and Raymond William's works, José Esteban Muñoz (2000) argues that what unites and consolidates oppositional groups is the way they perform affect, especially in relation to an official "national affect" that is aligned with a hegemonic (upper and upper-middle) class. Muñoz proposes that difference becomes examined not only in terms of the politics of identity, but through a more nuanced engagement with feelings in all of their ambiguous (and, thus, powerful) quality.
18. According to Reddy (1997), emotives are thoughts that lie outside of language, yet are intimately involved in the formation of utterances. Emotives are like performatives in that they do something to the world (cf. JL Austin, Judith Butler). Reddy claims that neither "discourse" (Foucault) nor "practice" (Bourdieu) captures the two-way character of emotional utterances and acts. In fact, emotional utterances have a unique capacity to alter what they refer to or what they represent—a capacity that makes them neither "constative" (descriptive) nor "performative," but a third type of communicative utterance entirely with a unique capacity to alter the state of the speaker from which they derive. Reddy advocates for a conceptual framework that acknowledges the importance of management (as opposed to construction) of emotion, allows political distinction among different management styles, and permits the narration of historical changers in such management styles (Reddy 1997, 266).
19. The New Jersey–based series *The Sopranos* approaches such a conspiratorial thinking in the image of Tony Soprano, the suburban mafia lord father and husband. Part of the *Sopranos* series storyline also involves episodes of a riverfront development that resonates with the plan put in place as part of the Newark Renaissance along the Passaic River.

20. During this time, Jewish business owners transferred their stores to blacks in the post-riot era in what came to be known as "Project Transfer." These businesses for the most part failed and were eventually transferred to a new flow of immigrants from Latin America, the Caribbean, and Africa. In 1972, for instance, barely five years after the Newark riots, only 6,000 Jews remained in Newark out of a total of 100,000 Jewish residents in Essex County (Helmreich 1999, 32). This period is immortalized in Philip Roth's character of Seymour Levov, the quasi-All-American Jewish boy in *American Pastoral*, who upon returning from the Marines takes over his father's Newark Maid glove factory. After envisioning a paternalistic rage against the upheaval and black workers' "refusal to work hard," influenced by "son of a bitch LeRoi Jones" (Roth 1997, 164), the factory relocates to Puerto Rico in 1973 where labor is willing and plentiful and presumably less "contentious" that potential workers in post-riot Newark (cf. Schwartz 2005).

21. See Fox Butterfield, "Newark Held an Angry and Anguished City," *New York Times*, April 12, 1971.

22. The James administration had been notorious for operating on a patronage system that accounted for substantial profits in city real estate for the mayor, his relatives, and political allies. James had also been criticized for his close relationship with developers and conflict of interests involving Crown Bank, as well as trips to Brazil and Puerto Rico in excess of $48,000 drawn from the city budget (David Kocieniewski, "Newark City Hall Receives Subpoenas Over Land Sales," *New York Times*, November 29, 2006). See "Why Newark Matters," *New York Times*, July 17, 2006.

23. Jacobs, "A New Mayor."

24. Ibid.

25. "Cory Booker," The Oprah Winfrey website, September 28, 2006, http://www.oprah.com/oprahradio/Cory-Booker (accessed June 5, 2011).

26. *Black Voices*, advertised as "the premiere site for African-American culture and community, [consists of] African-American message boards, profiles and chats, African-American sports, African-American news, African-American entertainment, African-American style and beauty, relationship advice and more. Share your voice at BV!"

27. *Black Voices*, http://boards.blackvoices.com/n/pfx/ forum.aspx?tsn=1&nav= messages&webtag=ti-newark&tid=522 (accessed June 11, 2008).

28. One such investor, Cogswell Realty Group, is often praised for carving 317 rental units out of an art deco building that has become "a highly visible symbol of Newark's aspirations" on Raymond Boulevard, a leading commercial artery of Newark's downtown, and the area hardest hit by the 1967 riots and disinvestment (Jacobs, "Two Miles"). The realty's chief executive boasts that "more than 80% of the tenants, mostly in their 20s and 30s, work in New York City." And thus, the leading evidence of Newark's revival, in most journalistic accounts, is that "New Jersey's largest city . . . is sprouting stylish restaurants, art galleries and bars that dispense

$10 cocktails" (Andrew Jacobs, "Not Hot Just Yet, but Newark Is Starting to Percolate," *New York Times*, May 6, 2007). In his effort to recast Newark as a national model for urban revitalization, Cory Booker hired Stefan Pryor, who had led efforts to revive Lower Manhattan after 9/11, as one of Newark's three deputy mayors. Pryor has been hawking Newark to national retailers, streamlining the way City Hall doles out licenses and building permits, and trying to create a new Planning Department.

29. See Jacobs, "Two Miles"; Dumenigo 2002. Even minor Newark news is now covered by major newspapers. See also Andrew Jacobs, "Evicted from a Blighted Street, Newark's Mayor Finds Another," *New York Times*, November 20, 2006; and Jacobs, "A New Mayor."

30. See, for instance, Jacobs, "Two Miles" and "Not Hot," on how these "new arrivals bemoan "the lack of decent shopping," see themselves as "pioneers on their block," and "sometimes feel like [they are] in a foreign country."

31. Andrew Jacobs, "More Big Changes on Way for Newark, Booker Vows," *New York Times*, February 9, 2007.

32. More than 40% of Newark homeowners spend more than half their income on housing, one of the highest percentages in the New York metropolitan region and among the highest in the country. Mortgage debt, accumulated in the building boom of recent years, is forcing thousands of people to take second jobs or rent rooms, but many others have lost their homes to foreclosure. In lower-income, heavily minority neighborhoods, multicolored "Avoid Foreclosure" and "Sell Your House" signs seem to decorate most of the lampposts. See Kareem Fahim and Ron Nixon, "Behind Foreclosures, Ruined Credit and Hopes," *New York Times*, March 28, 2007, and Jacobs, "A New Mayor." Refer also to Levon Putney's "New Surveillance Cameras in Newark," WCBS Newsradio 880, July 1, 2008.

33. See Jacobs, "A New Mayor."

34. In the year and a half after the NJPAC opened in 1997, the real estate market in Newark began to take off with dramatic results for investors. See Charles Bagli's "Investors Bet on Revival for Troubled Newark." *New York Times*, July 5, 1998.

35. See Nikita Stewart and Jeffery C. May, "Opponents in Newark Mayor's Race Navigate a New Ethnic Terrain," *Star-Ledger*, March 21, 2002. The article quotes Monica Ceron, an Ecuadorian who has lived in Newark for twenty-seven years, who said she spent nights knocking on doors to register new citizens to vote. The Ecuadorian population increased to 7,611 in 2000 from 3,149 in 1990, according to census figures. It is interesting to note that most Latinos and Latin Americans (in the North and East wards) endorsed Booker, while most African Americans voted for Sharpe James in the first election, which James won.

36. Brian Donahue's "Diverse New Jersey" (*Star-Ledger*, May 31, 2002) notes that, amid the largest immigration boom in US history, the percentage of foreign-born residents living in New Jersey rose from 12.5% to 17.5% be-

tween 1990 and 2000. Significantly, during the 2000–2001 school year only 58% of Newark public school students spoke English at home. Another 8% spoke limited English, while 25% spoke Spanish and about 6% spoke Portuguese, followed by other students who spoke Creole, French, Urdu, Pashto, Bengali and Russian at home.

37. These areas are comparable when it comes to accessibility to public transportation (they are walking distance from NJ Transit stations and bus lines); percentage of owner-occupied housing units (25.6% for the Ironbound and 22.1 for North Broadway); and even the preponderance of townhouse-like edifices, which are leading criteria for assessing the occupied homes. In the 2000 census, 72% of the Ironbound population self-identified as "white"; under 6% was considered "black" or "African American." While 35% of these residents were also considered "Hispanic," only 6.8 were "Puerto Rican." In North Broadway, 39% of the population was considered "white" and 24% was "black," perhaps also suggesting that North Broadway residents were more likely to reject identifying as either "black" or "white" in favor of viewing "Hispanic" as a racial category. Of the 63% of "Hispanics" in North Brunswick, Puerto Ricans constituted almost 38% in 2000.

38. Charles Hale (2005) examines how "multiculturalism" sometimes serves as basis on which urban spatial transformations are advanced.

39. Leila Suwwan, "Para consul, hispánicos so cucarachos," *Folha de São Paulo*, October 21, 2005.

40. More recently, in *Inheriting the City*, Philip Kisinitz, Mary Waters, John Mollenkopf, et al. (2009) found that in their New York–based study of second- and later-generation immigrants between the ages of 24 and 32, 24% of the Puerto Ricans were high school dropouts, compared to 16% of the Dominicans and 13% of the South Americans, who were from Colombia, Ecuador, and Peru. See Edward Schumacher-Matos, "A Sad Epilogue for Puerto Ricans," *Tampa Tribune*, April 6, 2009.

41. http://www.houghtonmifflinbooks.com/catalog/authordetail.cfm?text Type=interviews&authorID=618.

42. As Schwartz (2005) also emphasizes, from 1920 to 1930 the number of blacks employed in unskilled factory work and domestic service in Newark doubled. For the few years prior to the beginning of the Depression, blacks were fully employed. However, the Jewish Welfare Board reported that by 1933 "the number of factories had already dropped to 1160 with total wages paid down to $40 million" (14).

43. These four critical fictional and social scientific works written about "Newark"—the works of Philip Roth, Amiri Baraka, anthropologist Sherry Ortner (2003), and social worker Hilda Hidalgo (1970)—provide a critical example of how "structures of feeling" and "knowable communities" are complicated by authorial positionality .

44. The complexity of people's feelings in circumstances of rapid urban transformation is rarely addressed in historical analyses. To remedy such

shortcomings, Wendy James urges social anthropologists to pursue the methods of the humanities, which treat language as a vehicle of conscious and critical self-inquiry into the common roots of feeling and experience. The perspective on the works cited here allows an examination, however brief and cursory, of the conventions and standards by which emotions are socially and historically evaluated and the institutions developed to reflect and encourage particular standpoints. See also Myers 1979, 1986.

45. Several authors have focused on how sentiments at a community level are able to alter the emotional state of the individual. For instance, Stearns and Stearns (1989) claim that Americans have shifted in their methods of controlling social behavior toward "greater reliance on direct manipulation of emotions and, particularly, of anger." Thus, "with an increasingly intricate bureaucracy and then the expansion of people-dealing service occupations, the primacy of economic-organizational imperatives in restraining anger becomes increasingly patent" (1989, 2, 212). See also "aggression" as quotidian aspect of community building in Andalucia (Gilmore 1987).

46. "Shame" is one of the more widely deployed tropes in discourses of social control (Myers 1986, 120). Conceptions of community convensions become real sites of the exercise of power, so that "politics is just a process of determining who must repress as illegitimate, who must foreground as valuable, the feelings and desires that come up for them in given contexts and relationships" (Reddy 1997, 335).

47. Subjectivity, in this sense, is a representation of the social system from the point of view of an individual agent, but it is also the condition of that system. It allows emotions to represent forms of judgment or means of evaluating the relationship between and individual and his or her circumstances (cf. Myers 1986). Larger disputes over respectability are also at the center of discussions involving African Americans' presumed "lack of civility" or civilized restraints.

48. See Ahmed 2004 for discussion on "emotional contagion."

49. The extent of this complexity can only be hinted at here. The fact that Newark is a predominantly black city with a ubiquitous "white ethnic" Portuguese enclave also accounts for the city's racial particularities. In this context, stereotypes are powerful codes to render everyday racial situations legible, despite (or precisely because of) the great dissimilarity indices and segregation among the city's five political wards. For Latinos in the Ironbound, the Portuguese tended to be simply racialized as "white," but this was not the case for the solidly middle- and upper-middle-class African American political leaders and residents, who still viewed them as "Portuguese." Divisions among black residents, based on US-birth versus foreign-birth, between "African Americans" and blacks from African or the Caribbean, were also central to how black populations viewed each other and how some, mostly US-born Latinos viewed them. Most Latin American

migrants, however, rarely recognized the ethnic diversity among blacks in Newark, though they generally recognized the class variations between elected officials and residents of the poorer west and south sides of the city. Puerto Ricans, US citizens by birth and generally English language–dominant, were oftentimes viewed as "more similar to black" by many South American migrants, particularly the case in the Ironbound. Brazilians, who tended to be mostly light-skinned and Portuguese-language dominant, generally rejected the "Hispanic" label and were ambivalent about the "Latino" identity, in favor of an insistence in their identity as "Brazilian," and this was sustained by the Portuguese view of Brazilians. Despite this great complexity, there was the general view that US-born Latinos and "immigrants" from South America and the Spanish-speaking Caribbean occupied an imaginary middle space in the city's racial landscape, between a homogenized "Blackness" and a the slippery Whiteness of the Portuguese.

50. In "Roth, Race, and Newark," Larry Schwartz (2005) eloquently argues that the stereotype of post-1965 Newark as a crime-ridden, burnt-out city of blacks contributes to a liberal, racist mentality about Newark as an unlivable city especially when contrasted to the "good old days" of the 1940s and 1950s, seen as Newark's "golden era." This "golden era," Schwartz rightly argues, is never examined as one built on long-term, cynical exploitation, racism, and deep, pervasive political corruption. Thus, critical here is Arjun Appadurai's claim that the capabilities of neighborhoods to produce contexts . . . and to produce local subjects is "profoundly affected by the locality-producing capabilities of larger-scale social formations" (1996, 187). The specific case of early Puerto Rican community building and disenfranchisement in Newark is approached from a journalistic perspective in Malner 1974.

51. For a discussion on simultaneity of moral panic and ethnic co-optation in white suburbs, see Kobayashi and Peake 2000, 392–403.

52. The fact that Newark's geographical boundaries have remained largely unchanged since the late 1800s, in the 23.6 miles of which the city consists, also suggests the powerful ways in which fluid racial categories can gain an illusion of stability when projected onto relatively immutable geographic boundaries. See Blanca A. Nieves, "Once Upon an Island: How N.J.'s Largest Hispanic Group Built a Community," *Sunday Record* (Bergen County, NJ), November 14, 1993.

53. This merits a brief discussion of the "official" parameters versus "subjective" notions of community and my usage throughout this volume. "North Broadway" is one of the six neighborhoods that comprise the North Ward of Newark. I do not subscribe to "official" rigid physical parameters in my analysis of "community," but rather favor a more emic approach that is more organic—one based on how people themselves define "their neighborhoods" and "their communities." Nevertheless, and acknowledging that

people oftentimes described the limits of their communities by pointing to particular streets or personally meaningful landmarks, I want to use the official parameters to describe demographics.

CHAPTER TWO

1. Some legal scholars conceive citizenship beyond the strictly political, by noting that questions about citizenship can be divided into those concerned with the substance of citizenship, its domain or location, and its subjects (Bosniak 2003, 184). These scholars recognize that the concept of citizenship does not exist in a vacuum; rather, it is "related to other aspects of a society, particularly when a society is marked and divided by racism and when race and national origin have determined who is awarded citizenship," as has been the case in the United States (Torres 1998, 172). Lauren Berlant's 1997 critique of the privatization of citizenship under the Reagan era further reminds us that the "nationalist politics of intimacy" has continued to permeate the public sphere as a space for social antagonism and struggle, reducing citizenship to personal acts and values, and reframing nationality as a question of feelings and traumas.

2. The racial readings at the core of distinctions among nationalities point to the "rationality of racism" in the United States (Bonilla-Silva 1997; Wacquant 1991). Loic Wacquant urges us to consider racism as a central part of the US system rather than as an "aberration" in that system. Bonilla-Silva (1997, 468) also argues that identity politics has aimed to make racism into a system of beliefs (rather than a structure of power), even when racism and racial systems were built on a rational foundation, not the product of irrational, crazy people. Thus, in arguing for the rationality of racism in the United States, these authors challenge perspectives that render racism a baseless ideology while failing to classify the structure of the society itself as racist.

3. The term *supercitizen immigrant*, which appears in the subhead, is borrowed from Bonnie Honig, who uses the term to describe the stereotype of the "perfect immigrant," that is, the one who is "neither needy nor threatening . . . the object of neither American hostility nor charity, but of outright adoration" (2001, 76). I extend the use of this term to highlight the ideological role that "immigrants" play in a US national imaginary, which dictates that "good immigrants" are those who avoid the "fate" of the "undeserving" US-born minorities. As Ali Behdad argues, the ambivalence of the United States toward its immigrants is worth attending to because it is a productive site for the "state's development of myriad strategies of discipline, normalization, and regulation" (1997, 175). In her examination of "the immigrant as citizen," Honig states, "The immigrant functions to reassure workers of the possibility of upward mobility in an economy that rarely delivers n that promise, while also disciplining native-born poor, do-

mestic minorities, and unsuccessful foreign laborers into believing that the economy fairly rewards dedication and hard work" (2001, 73–74). While this account presents an American democracy founded in "immigration," it neglects its origins in conquest, slavery, imperialist expansion, and annexation, which more accurately describe the experiences of blacks, Puerto Ricans, and Chicanos, for instance.

4. Lorrin Thomas's (2010) work on Puerto Ricans, race, and citizenship in 1930s New York City shows how Puerto Ricans challenged the black-white US racial binary for the first time through discussions of citizenship. In fact, the sustenance of binary racial categories preserved the white supremacist foundation of US citizenship. As US citizens at a time when African Americans were not, and as "newcomers" racialized as more similar to blacks, Puerto Ricans' ambiguous position in the racial hierarchy of 1930s New York contributed to this group's "invisible presence" in racial nomenclature and social life. Puerto Ricans were excluded from black stores in Harlem where people of the white race were not welcomed, while also holding on to a "passive" identity as law-abiding citizens (in contradistinction to the "rioting" African Americans). Although the degree to which racial invisibility was in fact strategically deployed among Puerto Ricans in the 1930s is not clear from this study, their "passivity" further inscribed Harlem as an "aggressive" African American space. In this context, Puerto Ricans, particularly the middle classes of neighboring Washington Heights, invoked long-held views of Puerto Rico as a "racial democracy" as a survival strategy to hold on to US citizenship rights even as Puerto Ricans were increasingly racialized as similar to blacks. Even back in the 1930s, Puerto Ricans' contentious relationship to US citizenship was oftentimes ascertained in connection, not only to the heightened black-white racial polarity that limited citizenship rights to whites, but also in the ideological context of "imported" views of "racial democracy."

5. Beyond maintaining a system of distinctions, narratives of crime and "crime prevention" technology create stereotypes and prejudices that separate and reinforce inequalities. As Teresa Caldeira argues in her study of gated communities in São Paulo, inasmuch as the talk of crime becomes emblematic of an extremely unequal society, "it does not incorporate the experiences of dominated people . . . rather it criminalizes and discriminates against them. . . . In the field of crime, barriers are embedded not only in discourses but also, materially, in the city's walls, in the residences of people from all social classes, and in technologies of security" (2000a, 39). These forms of prejudices and derogations not only are verbal but also reproduce themselves in rituals of suspicion and investigation at the entrances of public and private buildings and the use of surveillance technologies to monitor marginalized populations.

6. The faculty and administrators at BHS consistently acknowledged racism and subordination, and attempted to make visible the cultural perspectives

and different linguistic and national backgrounds of incoming students, rather than adopting a "color-blind" or "multiculturalist" perspective. While at ESHS race was consistently elided and impossible to interrogate, at BHS references to "race" were abundant. In my walk from the third floor to the arts classroom in the first floor, pretty much every conversation I overheard had a racial referent: "The black girls were talking to that Puerto Rican guy"; "That was the black with light skin . . . el Moreno"; "Hey, I'm Puerto Rican!"; "You my Dominican nigger." Oftentimes, students who were close to the well-liked principal at Barringer would affectionately proclaim: "You, Mr. Cordero, my nigger." Given this casualness in the use of a potentially inflammatory term, it was particularly troubling to witness an exchange that took place at ESHS on one of the days when I was about to meet with some students. I was walking on the second floor of the school, and I overheard a short white man in his early fifties screaming with a lot of fury and hate at two African American boys: "I'm not *your* nigger! Don't you ever call *me* that." The boys dismissed him and kept walking. Apparently, when the white man had asked them to go to their classrooms, they had said something like, "Okay, we're going, my nigger." Although I understood the boys to have said that phrase in a colloquial way, using "nigger" as a street referent, the white man's reaction was incredibly forceful and filled with anger. I was actually scared by hearing the emphasis on "I'm not *your* nigger" from a white man with so much hate in his voice. I tried to not pass judgment too quickly; maybe he was just trying to convey a more general rejection of the use of the term *nigger* by anyone. But, he didn't seem to be objecting to the term as much as the possibility that *he* would be considered *someone else's* "nigger." In these contrasting instances fields of local agency are channeled into a politics of performance whereby certain black bodies are used to display alternative languages of connectedness while others are used to project pathology. In this sense, blackness is a floating signifier, but its consequences vary materially depending on the space in which it is performed and the body that produces the performance (see Johnson 2003).

7. This discussion could be situated in long-held academic perspectives developed, specifically, to explain Puerto Rican poverty dating back to Oscar Lewis's "culture of poverty" (Lewis 1966) and, more recently, perspectives on the "underclass" proposed by William J. Wilson (1990) in reference to African Americans.

8. My initial response, as I could not help but eavesdrop since the tone of voice was pretty loud and I could hear both the daughter and the mother on the other end of the line, was to note the ethical and epistemological issues behind what constitutes data collection in contemporary ethnography.

9. Illouz examines Internet-based romance to make a greater claim about how romance in the United States is entrenched within self-help culture, and how these contours of emotion are intertwined with the advent of moder-

nity and capitalism. She notes the great irony behind the assault of institutions of modernity that have undermined the very basis of the formation of the self (as is apparent from increasing rates of depression and mental diseases and decline in well being), by stating: "As psychic misery increases, people feel more entitled to happiness . . . [and] the experience of suffering becomes intolerable in the face of the promises of liberal politics" (2003, 191).

10. Some Puerto Ricans began to settle in New Jersey around the turn of the century, but it wasn't until the 1940s and 1950s that they began arriving in large numbers. During the mid-1940s, an average of 4,000 contract farm workers came from Puerto Rico to the United States every year, many of whom stayed. By 1948 the Puerto Rican Department of Labor began to provide farm workers with the protection of a contract guaranteeing conditions of work, insurance, and travel. Recruited by US companies to harvest the crops for farms in the Vineland area of New Jersey in the early 1950s, Puerto Rican agricultural workers constituted the "first wave" of Puerto Ricans in Newark. Nieves, "Once Upon an Island."

11. As part of their campaign to "sell Newark," NEDC developed publicly acceptable descriptions of local renewal politics in brochures, press releases, and magazine articles, emphasizing how the shift to mayor-council government had reawakened the interest of local groups in revitalizing the city. NHA and the Central Planning Board (CPB) disagreed in their assessment of which areas in North Broadway could be considered "blighted." NHA, fearing that the CPB would find only part of the North Ward project area in need for clearance, forbade the CPB from undertaking its own independent investigation of the area. Kaplan's 1963 evidence shows that intense opposition by site residents was a feature not of the "hard-core slums [of the Central Ward]," but of areas peripheral to the "slums" (such as the North Ward), which tend to have higher percentages of homeownership and a less transient population. Both the Central Ward and the North Ward projects involved the clearance of "ethnically homogeneous" areas, yet the response of the Italian groups in the North Ward and of the African American groups in the Central Ward was very different. The Central Ward project would not change the racial characteristics of the project area, while the North Broadway project would. Blacks could potentially move into North Ward public housing, but whites probably would not move into housing in the Central Ward (Kaplan 1963, 137). More significantly, African American leaders emphasized how pointless any opposition would have been, while at the time of the North Ward project, the mayor, the chairman and the executive secretary of CPB, and the chairman of the NHA were all Italian Americans from the North Ward (Kaplan 1963, 104, 118, 136, 137).

12. Kaplan (1963) concludes that grassroots opposition would be unlikely to disrupt the NHA's arrangements with other government agencies during

the 1960s. However, even back in the early 1960s when his book was published, Kaplan qualified this statement by establishing that the increasing black migration from the south and the doubling of the black population in six years "served to inject the race issue into almost all aspects of Newark politics." He states that a NHA official said that the increased southern black migration to Newark "could blow the whole [renewal] program up in our faces." As the migrants continued to flow into the Central Ward, a breakup of "the ghetto" and the black population was no longer confined to a region of Newark (Kaplan 1963, 147–48).

13. Accepting Mayor Villani's claim that the North Ward projects would be "for the Italians," the Federation of Italian-American Societies, the *Italian Tribune*, and most city officials supported clearance in the North Ward and withdrew their support of the Save Our Homes Council. Unwilling to renege on his support for the project, the Italian mayor urged NHA to amend its plans for the North Ward by raising income limits in the proposed public housing, by guaranteeing a commercial site to displaced businessmen, and by reducing the number of stories planned for the public housing project from sixteen to twelve. NHA's later project tended to displace blacks and Puerto Ricans, who lacked influence at City Hall. Before 1949 NHA had built segregated housing projects in outlying white areas and had filled them with people from the surrounding neighborhoods. As a result, blacks, who constituted close to 40% of those eligible for public housing in 1940, occupied only 7–8% of the units. After Louis Danzig became executive director of NHA, the agency began constructing more public housing in the Central Ward, thus increasing the number of "Negro projects" and the all-white projects throughout the city were opened to eligible black applicants. Some North Ward leaders later claimed that Danzig had agreed to keep the number of blacks below 10% so as to not antagonize the already opposed Italians in the area. In November 1955 the NHA opened Columbus Homes by moving in 300 white families in the midst of protests by black leaders, who were in turn assured that "a proper racial balance in projects is best preserved when white families are moved in first; the next group moving into the project would be largely Negro" (Kaplan 1963, 152). See also Jones 1955.

14. During the Civil War, Newark had been a Southern-sympathizer city that was heavily against abolitionism and sold millions of dollars in industrial products to the Confederate army. It was not able to recover the level of income once the South lost the war in 1865, as Southern markets went to Chicago and Detroit. Although no longer the most aggressive manufacturing city after the Civil War, in the early decades of the twentieth century Newark still remained an important industrial city and its population exceeded 240,000. A historical discussion of the Great Migration of southern blacks to the North is beyond the scope of this project. However, I want to highlight that oftentimes the newest arrivals from the South were viewed

NOTES TO PAGES 97–100

as uncivilized, provincial, and "backwards," in contrast to the more highly cultured and cosmopolitan northern blacks in cities places of high African American concentration, such as Chicago, Detroit, Harlem, and also Newark (cf. Jackson 2001, 26).

15. Josephine Bonomo, "Latin Influence Rising in Newark," Newark News, July 3, 1966, 10.

16. Nieves, "From Once Upon an Island," A26–28.

17. The paradox of the Puerto Rican living on the mainland was described by Mrs. Maria González, Puerto Rico–born member of the Newark Human Rights Commission: "In Puerto Rico, we enjoy all the rights of citizens, yet here we discover that we are considered immigrants, a minority group, a separate race. But we are Americans." A graduate of New York University, Mrs. González came to Newark from New York in 1940 (see ibid., 1).

18. Frederick Byrd, "Invisibility Casts Pall on Puerto Rican Population," *Star-Ledger*, June 27, 1983.

19. In 1970 the total cost of the "quiquiriqui" flights—so called because they were flights departing at midnight or early morning and they transported poor seasonal agricultural and industrial workers—was fifty-seven dollars one way and five dollars down was enough to secure the one-way ticket (Hidalgo 1970, 11).

20. Bonomo, "Latin Influence Rising in Newark," 14.

21. Nieves, "From Once Upon an Island."

22. Robert D. McFadden, "Puerto Ricans and Police Clash in a Riot in Newark," *New York Times*, September 2, 1974.

23. Joan Cook, "2,000 Hispanic Children Boycott Newark Classes," *New York Times*, October 8, 1974.

24. "Newark Is Beset by New Violence in Wake of Riot," *New York Times*, September 3, 1974, 1; "Newark Held an Angry and Anguished City; Every Issue Becomes Racial as Blacks Increase Power," *New York Times*, April 12, 1971, 31.

25. In October 1974, for instance, the Puerto Rican Solidarity Day Committee drew 20,000 people to a Madison Square Garden rally in support of independence for Puerto Rico, and later organized itself into a permanent body in a weekend conference on the Rutgers University campus in Newark. The group said it would "work to oppose ethnocide in Puerto Rican communities here," such as abolition of bilingual programs, and other "attempts to attack the Puerto Rican national identity," as Alfredo Lopez, executive secretary of the group, stated. Noting that at the time the Commonwealth of Puerto Rico Department of Labor negotiated wage and benefit contracts for migrant farm laborers who came from the island to the mainland, the group resolved to support efforts to unionize the farm workers. The group also planned to send a delegation to an International Conference and Solidarity with Puerto Rican Independence, scheduled for September of 1975 in Havana. Ronald Smothers, a reporter for the *New York Times*,

noted that "the group, as reflected by those attending the conference, is made up largely of young white, middle-class students, and a small number of blacks." See Smothers, "Freedom Sought by Puerto Ricans: Solidarity Day Committee Forms Permanent Group at a Rutgers Meeting," *New York Times*, March 3, 1975.

26. See Charles Q. Finley, "Hispanic Group Sets Up Intercultural Center," *Star-Ledger*, November 20, 1975. Moreover, in 1989, the City of Newark designated a Jose Rosario FOCUS Plaza in the area of Broad Street, where the organization Rosario founded stands. Rosario, who at the time lived in Puerto Rico, cut the ribbon for the new plaza and accepted a copy of the street sign. Known as "El Viejo," or "the wise old man" to his many friends, Rosario, an accountant by profession, also helped establishing the New Jersey Office of Hispanic Affairs, setting up the first bilingual education program in Newark, passing a law to require Spanish-language interpreters in city courts, and developing reciprocity agreement between New Jersey and Puerto Rico allowing for unemployment compensation.

27. See Raul Davila, "La Casa de Don Pedro: A 'Home' for Hispanic Youth," *Information* (organizational brochure), July 1976. Other organizations included Aspira, Inc., of New Jersey, a private Puerto Rican educational agency dedicated to help Puerto Rican students with the college application process and acted as advocates in matters related to the education of Puerto Rican youth. Likewise, the Field Orientation Center for Under-Privileged Spanish (FOCUS), an agency funded by the Department of Community Affairs, which was already in place prior to the 1974 riots, acquired more prominence and visibility in the community by offering a wide range of programs, from job placement to elderly care, for instance. See also Cook, "2,000 Hispanic Children Boycott Newark Classes." The reporter describes an incident in which more than 2,000 Hispanic children stayed away from nine elementary schools in Newark in protest against an impending cutback in bilingual classes. Moreover, government officials and private agencies insisted that Rutgers University, the State University of New Jersey, increase its Puerto Rican staff and student enrollment.

28. Fahim and Nixon, "Behind Foreclosures, Ruined Credit and Hopes."

29. A 1976 article in New Jersey's *Star-Ledger* is particularly revealing of the broad-broached ways in which "Hispanic" had been conceived in Newark, to the point of including even Spaniards. Narrating the proclamation of "Spain Week" in Newark, the article described how Newark planned to honor "its Hispanics" in a celebration of "more than 10,000 descendants of Spanish immigrants." Interestingly, while the article considered Spaniards as "Hispanic," the image of the "Hispanic" Spaniard was significantly distinguished from that of non-European "Hispanics." The article presented "work ethic," "tradition of strong family ties," and "ethnic community growth" as "key features of the Spanish heritage," almost in contradistinction to the "Hispanics" involved in the 1974 Puerto Rican riots. European

"Hispanics" and non-European "Hispanics," most of whom were Puerto Rican, were differently racialized in Newark. Joseph Vázquez, president of Club España—the largest Spanish civic and social club in Newark—described how the club sponsored a school that emphasized Spanish language, culture, and traditions. He stated: "In the school the students are taught to have pride in Spain's role in American history. . . . Some of the key aspects include Spain's role in the discovery of the New World, Ponce de Leon's discovery of the area that is now Florida, Spanish colonists establishing the town of St. Augustine (the first permanent white settlement in the United States)." A map of the United States showing the period when Spanish influence was at its peak was put on display in the Club España. Al Post, "Newark Plans Honors for Its Hispanics," *Star-Ledger*, September 10, 1976. See also "Columbus' Patrons: Spain Week Is Celebrated in Newark," *Star-Ledger*, October 9, 1988; Elliot, Quinless, and Parietti 2000.

30. See, for instance, Reginald Roberts, "Dominicans Celebrate Homeland as Their Numbers Grow in Newark," *Newark Star-Ledger*, March 1, 1996. Roberts describes the Dominican presence in Newark. Moreover, for discussions on the role of various Latino nationalities in Newark's formal and informal economy see the following articles: "Ecuadorans in Newark to Celebrate History," *Star-Ledger*, August 7, 1992, which describes how members of the Ecuadoran Committee of Newark begun an observance of Ecuadorian Independence week and Patricia Alex's "Peruvians Celebrate Heritage: Memories, Hope, Lots of Inca Cola," *Star-Ledger*, July 30, 1990.

31. See E. Jett's "Changing Face of Latino Arrivals," *Star-Ledger*, September 20, 1980, where the reporter claims that many of the older Puerto Rican Newark residents were returning to the island after retirement and a more educated and professional group of Puerto Ricans was credited for having "moved up the corporate ladders" and relocating to the suburbs or migrating to Florida. Although Puerto Ricans continued to be the single largest group of Latinos, South Americans subgroups had become collectively the larger percentage of the Hispanic population by 1990.

32. In a way, this is a condemnation of Puerto Rican emotional inadequacy that was already noted in the earlier years of Puerto Rican community building in Newark, as suggested in a 1970 editorial, which I found at the New Jersey Historical Society's Hispanic files, titled "Newark: El sueño perdido de los puertorriqueños." The article's anonymous Puerto Rican author claims that Puerto Ricans never learned how to take advantage of what Newark had to offer when they first arrived. Directed to a solely Puerto Rican audience, and in an "it's our fault" and "self-hate-ish" tone, the author is decidedly paternalistic and encourages Puerto Ricans to approach their social marginality from a *mea culpa* standpoint.

33. Military trigger strong emotions but of different forms: among Latin American migrants, military service indicates a patriotism aimed at consolidating national belonging in the United States, whereas for Puerto Ricans and

other US-born Latinos, military service is viewed as a vehicle to raise "self esteem" and take kids off the streets. Through targeting and containment, and acting as a totalizing institution, the military conspires with other local surveillance goals.

34. As Haney López argues "under the racial prerequisite laws, this country denied citizenship to others who had served in the military, repudiated others who were long-time residents, and stripped still others of the citizenship they thought secure" (1996, 60–61). Given that citizenship in the United States has historically been and continues to be not only a white supremacist institution, but also a set of legal statures invested in producing and reproducing "race" as a natural, taken-for-granted set of attributes superimposed on humanity, a question that begs attention is: How do individual students in each of the two high schools and the relationship of the high schools to military recruitment produce claims to citizenship on the bases of a politics of worthiness?

35. Incidentally, more than an "equal access" provision, the No Child Left Behind Act fails to recognize the fact that the military has typically had a greater degree of access to schools than any other outside group. This degree of military access is particularly evident in the development of the National Defense Act of 1916 by the US Department of Defense that introduced the Junior Reserve Officer Training Corps (JROTC) into US high schools. While the JROTC does not officially self-describe as a recruiting device, 45% of all cadets who successfully complete JROTC enter some branch of the military (Bartlett and Lutz 1998). More significantly, JROTC programs are more commonly found in schools with a high population of black and Latino students, who represent 54% of JROTC cadets, and in poor schools, particularly in the rural south (65% of the units).

36. Despite this "narrow mindedness," Puerto Ricans still comprised 3,138 of the 18,453 (over 17%) Latinos in the Army in 1997. Only Mexicans had greater military representation, comprising 41% of Latinos in the military. However, considering that Mexicans represent 65% of the total US Latino population and Puerto Ricans consist of about 12% of US Latinos, the overrepresentation of Puerto Ricans in the US military is quite significant. In fact, the island of Puerto Rico is the third-ranked territory—behind California and Texas—in absolute numbers of recruits in the year 1998. About 25% of front-line casualties in Vietnam were Latinos at a time when Latinos comprised about 5% of the US population. In 1996 more than 41% of enlisted Latinos were in the lowest three pay grades in the US military, compared to 26% of blacks and 30% of whites. Latinos have become the most recent target of military recruiters, who have explicitly defined them as a specific market or recruitment niche. Changing the military's enlistment and placement Armed Services Vocational Aptitude Battery test to "eliminate cultural bias" has also been suggested as an option (Cacho 2007, 195). According to Jorge Mariscal (2005), the *Army Times* reported that

"'Hispanics' constituted 22% of the military recruiting 'market,' almost double" their numbers in the population.

37. On January 8, 2002, President George Bush signed Public Law 107-110, otherwise known as the No Child Left Behind Act. Buried deep within the law's 670 pages of text is a provision requiring public secondary schools to provide military recruiters not only with access to school premises and facilities, but also with contact information, including name, address, and phone number, for every student in the school. The section entitled "Sec. 9528 Armed Forces Recruiter Access to Students and Students Recruiting Information" grants recruiters access to information that would allow them to make unsolicited calls and send direct-mail recruitment literature to a young person's home. In fact, it is not clear whether parents can opt not to release their children's information to the military, while continuing to share this information with college recruiters, scholarship or employment programs. This is largely because the act links military recruiting with the type of access recruiters from institutions of higher education are generally given, thus equating military training to a college or university education. Rather than limiting their access to organized career or college fairs, military recruiters capitulate on the repercussions that noncompliance could have on the schools' federal funding to enter high schools unannounced and roam the halls attempting to recruit young men and women. The Department of Defense has developed a national high school database to document recruiter access and, as of October 2002, 95% of the nation's 22,000 secondary schools provided a degree of access to military recruiters that was consistent with the law. Department of Education, "Access to High School Students and Information on Students by Military Recruiters," October 9, 2002, http://www.ed.gov/PressReleases/10-2002/mrguidance .html.

38. For instance, in a *New York Times* article titled "Middle-Class Hispanics Heading for Greener Pastures" (May 20, 1979, E-6), Irvin Molotsky narrates the story of Mr. Barreto, who took what has turned out to be a popular route in his move to the suburbs: the US Army. In a celebratory tone, the article narrates how in 1950, at the age of nineteen, Mr. Barreto joined the Army and left his home in Orocovis, Puerto Rico. By the time he retired in 1970 he had risen to the rank of sergeant major. The Army provides him with a good pension. "If you have a higher degree of education, you leave the Bronx. You leave New York City." In his case he headed to New Jersey. For many Puerto Ricans, New Jersey is in fact symbol of "having made it," even if it's Newark. And a lot of this has to do with something as straightforward as architectural aesthetics: that is, living in a two-story house with a little porch versus living in "the projects," even if one's income and status don't change.

39. Many military officials have argued that Latino youth are "less hostile" to joining the military than more militant black youth. Nevertheless, military

recruiters have lamented the inability of Latino youth, particularly recent immigrants, to speak English fluently and their low high school completion rates, because these factors have reduced the pool of potential Latino recruits. Given the difficulties, the military has initiated new strategies to recruit Latinos including developing greater outreach programs by establishing partnerships with Latino community organizations, introducing younger Latinos to the military by creating JROTC and military academies in middle schools and junior high schools, and accepting alternative credentials such as the GED instead of a conventional high school diploma for admission into military service. The term *quick citizenship*, which is not the same as *automatic citizenship*, refers to a special provision of the immigration law that applies to those who have served in the military during specific times of war designated by the president. National Immigration Project of the National Lawyers Guild, December 2001–January 2002, Immigrants Consequences of Resisting Service in the Military, Y&M Online, http://www.afsc.org/youthmil/200112/immselect.htm. In 2003 the US military became one of the few organizations that was not subjected to drastic budget cuts (like the educational system was), but actually received consistent increases in federal funding.

40. See, for instance, Fergal Keane's "Guatemalan Orphan to War Hero," BBC News, UK edition, April 7, 2003, http://news.bbc.co.uk/2/hi/programmes/from_our_own_correspondent/2923209.stm (accessed June 5, 2011).

41. The image of the "immigrant"—whether white or racialized as nonwhite—continues to serve as a disciplining mechanism against the domestic minorities who have historically been criminalized. Three main interpretations of undocumented immigrants in the military sustain this image: First, immigrants validate US patriotism by demonstrating that service to the United States is something they "chose" out of deep personal conviction to the country's moral superiority; second, the value of military service is actually enhanced by their foreignness, because they are validating the host country's actions from the perspectives of the nation-states from which they hail; and, finally, if one is "illegal," the only path toward legalization (at least figuratively and in popular discourse, if not juridically) is by being willing to die for the host country.

42. An important question that is beyond the scope of this project is: To what degree is the enlisting of "unpatriotic" Puerto Ricans (and members of other groups more generally) contributes to the development of a critical, perhaps "antiwar," faction within the US military? This is why examining narratives around joining the military, as articulated at the community or neighborhood level, are critical to my discussion.

43. Lisa Marie Cacho's 2007 work on the ways in which value is not ascribed to the lives and deaths of young Latino men is critical here. The young men in Cacho's ethnographic study were not only marked as "deviant" by their

race, but also because they did not perform masculinity in ways to redeem, reform, or counter their racialized "deviance." In the case of Cacho's main subject and cousin, Brandon, his untimely death did not leave the family with any evidence to narrate him as "a productive, worthy, and responsible citizen, who had been 'unfairly' treated, 'unjustly' targeted, and 'wrongfully' accused." I agree with Cacho that it was precisely because a young working-class Latino man like Brandon could not be convincingly scripted out of his ascribed deviance that "the scripts about this death and life are important sites within which to examine the intersecting, racialized, and gendered discourses of deviancy and respectable domesticity that attribute and deny human value. By reexamining deviance, repudiating respectability, and rethinking resistance, we can . . . [get to a place] where 'deviants' do not need to be redeemed" (Cacho 2007, 184). Examining the social narratives that prevent an ascription of social value to these young men's lives is critical to understanding the pathologized practices associated with US-born Latinos in general.

44. The "Hispanic family" has been identified by the military as a main "obstacle" to recruiting underage Latino youth. The Army's advertising campaign addressing Latino parents is critical, given that many Latino youth join the military while being underaged and thus require parental consent. In fact, describing the $11.3-million Spanish-language television campaign launched by the Army, Maj. Gen. Dennis Cavin, commander of the Army Recruiting Command, stated, "You have to recognize that the mother is a dominant influence in Latino families in terms of big decisions." Greg Johnson, "Enlisting Spanish to Recruit the Troops," *Los Angeles Times*, March 19, 2001.

45. This practical knowledge served to "normalize" views of everyday events and the appropriate emotional attachment to those events. Analyzing this form of propriety, then, requires an analysis of situations where people's competencies to obey the rules come under pressure, since the role of normal and the role of stigmatized are part of the same complex and operate according to the same social rules.

46. David Halle provides an ethnographic example of this in his well-known description of some New Jersey chemical plant workers who think of themselves as working class on the job (because of the manly labor they perform) but middle class at home (because of the suburban life they lead) (1984). See also Jackson's discussion of "code-switching" and "behavior-switching" as practices that anchor a person's sense of self to his or her model of sociality and class stratification (2001, 146). The meaning and motivation by which individuals enact and interpret style and self in their daily lives require an examination of affect that gets at both the physical and symbolic aspects of hegemony, and at the political implications of local ideas and practices.

47. Discussions of communicative styles and race have focused on the role of bantering or verbal dueling, as popular practices among African Americans, particularly among African American youth. Thomas Kochman (1983) has examined the boundary between play and nonplay in black verbal dueling and argued that personal insult, long considered outside the boundaries of "play" in sounding (black verbal dueling), should be considered, in some instances, within the realm of play. In fact, Kochman aims to problematize the tendency to categorize verbal dueling as either play or nonplay, but demonstrates how there is quite a degree of overlap between both. In particular, Kochman focuses on two speech actions—accusations and denials—and how both of these structures are used in play and nonplay disputes to demonstrate more closely the nature of reciprocal influence of play and nonplay interactions. See also Boyd 1997.

48. Notions of Latinidad—encapsulated in terms like "Hispanics" and "Spanish-speaking" were being promoted and, in fact, originating at the institutional levels in the 1970s in the United States. In Newark Hidalgo and her research team argued that such panethnic terms were inadequate because they failed to recognize the heterogeneity reflected in the populations the terms aimed to represent. In particular, Hidalgo emphasizes the distinction between Puerto Ricans and the increased influx of Cuban exiles arriving in Newark in the 1960s. As she describes: "Most of the Cubans are an exiled professional middle class that came to the United States for political reasons. They were lauded and rewarded by the US government for their rejection of Communism and Fidel Castro. . . . In contrast, the majority of Puerto Ricans are in the unskilled or marginally skilled poor class. . . . They were neither invited or wanted in the U.S.A." Moreover, in addition to noting the relationship between Puerto Ricans and blacks and other "Spanish-speaking" groups, particularly Cubans, Hidalgo remarks on the relationship between Puerto Ricans and whites as one "characterized by the patronizing attitudes of the whites and the motivation to exploit and use Puerto Ricans under the camouflage of wanting 'to help.' There are organized efforts by some white groups in Newark to capitalize and actively promote and encourage a rift between blacks and Puerto Ricans" (Hidalgo 1970, 14).

49. Brian Ross, "Watchful Eye," ABC News, May 15, 2007.

50. Thus, even in the case of the tragic deaths of three "unproductive" young men of color in California that Cacho describes, "[friends and relatives] resisted the erasure of their loved ones and made the statement: these were valued young men, and they are missed. Their audiences were not given the opportunity to ask why" (2007, 191).

51. Katie Wang and Kasi Addison, "Search Continues for Newark Teen Accused in Graduate's Slaying," *Star-Ledger*, June 28, 2008.

52. http://www.wnbc.com/print/16735290/detail.html (accessed June 29, 2008).

53. Ibid.

54. baywaygirl, June 28, 2008, in http://blog.nj.com/ledgerupdates_impact/2008/06/search_continues_for_newark_te/print.html (accessed June 29, 2008).

CHAPTER THREE

1. The anthropological concept of "serious games" (Ortner 1997) is pertinent here, as this concept challenges the assumption that in games—including verbal bantering or dueling—nothing that really matters is at stake or that they are an unproductive activity. Games and play are thus considered as dispositions marked by a readiness to improvise, a quality captured by Bourdieu's habitus, but which can also lead to pernicious outcomes. See also Black 1985.

2. Among Brazilians and among some other Latino and Latin American groups, "racial talk" is viewed as a minefield. Relevant here is Robin Sheriff's (2001) study of a Rio de Janeiro favela, where she notes how racial democracy supplied patterned ways of talking about issues of color, race, equality, and inequality, as topics that were often circumscribed to the realm of discourse. Similiarly, in his ethnographic research among Dominican and Puerto Rican residents of Santurce, Puerto Rico, Duany (1998) also suggests the "unspeakable" quality of race in the Spanish-speaking Caribbean when he asks his Dominican informants what race they are. Duany finds that "Responses to this seemingly innocuous question ranged from embarrassment and amazement to ambivalence and silence: many informants simply shrugged their shoulders and pointed to their arms, as if their skin color were obvious" (157). Isar Godreau (2008) also notes how Puerto Ricans on the island shift between binary and multiple racial classification usage, even in the same conversation or even sentence. As these studies collectively suggest, under dominant ideologies of "racial democracy," individuals oftentimes try to get out of the constructions of race through language and linguistic strategies, by adopting various responses and logics of racial classification during an interaction in such a way that multiple and binary models of racial classification were deployed to establish, often simultaneously, distance and intimacy.

3. See di Leonardo (1984) for an excellent critical discussion of the problematic concept of the "ethnic enclave."

4. Historically the region enjoyed a fashionable heyday in the second half of the nineteenth century, when ships sailed on the river, and sea captains and industrial barons settled. In an article in the *Newark Sunday News* (February 5, 1956) titled "Ironbound's Bustling Industry Pours Its Products Into World's Economy," Daniel E. Durant remarks: "There's a dearth of idle hands in the Ironbound section of Newark. But that's just about the only significant shortage of record." Considering the Ironbound as the heavy

industrial stronghold of Newark and a prolific and vital force in making Newark one of the major manufacturing centers of the world, Durant raves about the thousands of tons of cargo brought daily into Newark as raw materials and taken out of the Ironbound as finished products for export. The advantages of easy transport by land, air, and sea, Durant claims, accounted for the Ironbound's busy manufacturing industry.

5. In a visit to the Ironbound in 1978, Odelma Hammond of the Committee of Churchwomen United, a national community organization conducting a study of "inner-city" problems, stated that Newark's Ironbound section could serve as a "model" for city renovations throughout the country (*Star-Ledger*; April 19, 1978, 25). Journalist Cary Herz describes how, in a three-day tour of Newark, members of Churchwomen United said "the Ironbound was one of the most unique aspects of their visit . . . because of its clean streets, colorful shops and low crime rate" (25). Sally Blackmill, a retired school principal from Cleveland quoted in the article, remarked: "The area could be a model for all urban areas. . . . It's quite different from the rest of the city, which needs a lot of work." When one of the other women in the group asked why were other parts of the city run down while the Ironbound thrived, Antonio Machado, director of the Portuguese Educational Program responded, "People in the area have pride. They want to keep this a nice, clean place to live."

6. See Jacqueline Juster, "Our Hispanic Heritage," *New Jersey Business* (May 1985): 24–28, 59, 95.

7. While I am not able to undertake an extensive discussion of Portuguese's claim to Whiteness here, I do want to note that the Ironbound is the only "white space" in Newark, but also that its residents' Whiteness is never securely inscribed and is in fact quite contested at times, as ideas of "Portuguese"-ness are oftentimes tainted with stereotypes of "backwardness" and "foreignness." See also chapter 6 in this volume.

8. Diana Rojas, "Iberia in the Ironbound: Sampling Newark's Culinary Delights," *The Record* (Bergen County, NJ), February 19, 1994.

9. In her dissertation, Lori Baptiste also considers how traditional and contemporary food practices connect Brazilians in Governador Valadares, an industrial city located in Minas Gerais, Brazil, to Brazilians in Newark, and how the Portuguese residents of Newark also maintain a relationship to Concelho de Murosa, a fishing and farming village in northern Portugal. Both of these cities have been designated sister cities to Newark. Baptiste furthermore discusses the role of cod fish (bacalhau) in Portuguese cuisine, of rice and beans (feijoada) in Brazilian cuisine, and particular ideas about health, body image, and nutrition, as well as restaurants and "eating out" in traditional Latin American, European, and American cultures.

10. In the Ironbound it is possible for the Portuguese to do without the English. Many of the workers are Spanish, and since there is a similarity between Spanish and Portuguese, everyone gets along. Most Spanish and

Portuguese immigrants in New Jersey come from the contiguous areas of northern Portugal and northwestern Spain.

11. A detailed discussion of the forces that contributed to Brazilian migration to the United States in general, and settlement in specific cities within the United States in particular, deserves more attention than I can give here. Several other works offer excellent discussions of Brazilian migration and settlement in various cities in the United States, including: Framingham (Martes 2000); San Francisco (Ribeiro 1997); Los Angeles and Chicago (Beserra 2003, 2006); New York (Margolis 1994; Meihy 2004); Boston (Marrow 2003; Sales 1998), and Miami (Souza Alves and Ribeiro 2002)

12. See Eduardo Bueno (2003) for a comprehensive discussion on the academic policies adopted by Brazilian presidents José Sarney and Fernando Collor de Mello in the late 1980s and 1990s. As Bueno notes, by the end of the decade these presidents' failed economic plans, along with the political frustration that developed in the first few years after successful struggles against the military dictatorship, pushed many Brazilians to migrate to the United States. For a discussion on the relationship between these economic policies and US economic interests, particularly during the New Deal, see Tosta 2004, 577–78. Werneck (2004) notes the connection between Brazilian arrival in the United States and the mica mining that attracted many Americans in the World War II era to Minas Gerais. Upon returning to the United States, many of these Americans brought their Brazilian servants with them.

13. As Kathryn Gallant (in Bueno 2003) noted, 59% of female Brazilian immigrants have a college degree, but 55% work as maids, housekeepers, cooks, or nannies. Among the men, while only 4% have no more than an elementary school education, over half of them work as laborers, construction workers, or busboys in restaurants. Margolis notes that the two occupations in which Brazilian immigrants in New York have an almost total monopoly in the 1960s were shoe-shining for men and go-go dancing for women, occupations that were also considered the most shameful. In Newark, where most of the Brazilians live with their immediate families, the most common work for women is domestic service and for men is construction.

14. See Wilson Loria, "Emigration: The Invisible Brazilians," *Brazzil* (November 1999); "Illegal Overstayers and Criminal Aliens," *Migration Record* 2, no. 2 (February 1995).

15. According to the Palácio do Itamaraty, the Brazilian government offices responsible for tracking demographic changes in Brazil, there were 1–2.5 million Brazilians living abroad by 2000. The Brazilian Geography and Statistics Institute adds that the statistical "absence" of 1.4 Brazilians between the ages of 20 and 44 from the 1991 census has only one explanation: emigration. During the 1980s and 1990s Brazilians migrated not only to the United States, but also to neighboring Paraguay (455,000–600,000), various European countries (total of 600,000, divided into: Germany—60,000,

Portugal—52,000, Italy—37,000, Switzerland—26,000, France—22,000, England—15,000), and Japan (254,000–280,000) (Meihy 2004, 40–64).

16. Werneck (2004, 20) states that of the 1.5 million Brazilians living in the United States in the year 2000, 60–70% were undocumented. According to the Brazilian American Cultural Center in New York, 500,000 Brazilians live in the tristate (New York, New Jersey, Connecticut) area in 2003. Brazilians rank among the top fifteen largest undocumented national-origin groups in the INS data (from personal correspondence with Helen Marrow. At least half of Brazilian immigrants to the United States have friends or relatives living in the towns where they ultimately settled, and a quarter have no plans to return to their home country, according to the Brazilian Immigrant Center in Boston. See Jerry Kammer's "Economic, Political Troubles Cited in Immigration Increase," Copley News Service, August 5, 2002.

17. José Martins, "A chegada dos portugueses," *Luso-Americano*, April 2, 2003, 35–36, 42–46, 52–56.

18. By the mid-1980s, Portugal's economy had improved and fewer immigrants were coming to the United States. Many even began returning to Portugal during the US recession of the late 1980s and early 1990s. The reporter also presents the isolated case of a man whom she names Agostinho C. and for whom the passage to the United States was not as smooth. He and his family had come to the United States in 1987 on a tourist visa and easily found work in a Portuguese construction company in Newark. But after a year, he suffered a severe head injury in a truck accident and has been unable to work since. "I never go outside of the Portuguese community," he told the reporter. Ashley Dunn, "In Newark, Immigration Without Fear: A Neighborhood Remade by Unexpected Hands," *New York Times*, January 16, 1995, B4.

19. "Bush elogia ações contra imigrantes brasileiros ilegais," BBC Brasil, November 30, 2005.

20. Ginger Thompson and Sandra Ochoa, "By a Back Door to the U.S.: A Migrant's Grim Sea Voyage," *New York Times*, June 13, 2004.

21. Oftentimes, as a strategy to stay, Brazilians would present themselves to the Border Patrol and, if there was no room at the US detention centers, migrants would be released and asked to appear for a hearing on their status at a later date, which many Brazilians did not meet. See "Estranhos no Paraíso. EUA Têm Recorde de Brasileiros Detidos," *Folha de São Paulo*, February 24, 2006.

22. See Lisa Genasci, "10% of Brazil Town in 'America'—Illegally," *Chicago Sun-Times*, November 20, 1988, 8. Brazilians were discovered stowed away amid sacks of cocoa beans and coffee on a cargo ship docked in Philadelphia. Forty were from Governador Valadares. Of the stowaways, nine escaped from US immigration officials and the rest, who were sent home, vowed to try again.

23. In fact, in a *Star-Ledger* article, Newark's former mayor, Sharpe James, is quoted as stating that "Newark is the best-kept secret in the metropolitan

area," and urging the help of businessmen in the Ironbound in foster-
ing development of the city [of Newark]." See Frederick W. Byrd, "James
Boosts Newark to Ironbound Execs," *Star-Ledger*, September 23, 1986, 27.
James's speech before the Ironbound Manufacturers' Association focused
on recruiting the help of this group in the revitalization of all of Newark.
Brad Davis, president of the Ironbound Manufacturers Association, said the
then-mayor had been invited to "foster lines of communication. Newark
is on the upswing, the mayor has a formidable task ahead of him and we
want to see if we can help." About 225 businesses in the Ironbound area
were members of the association in 1986.

24. In a way, the Ironbound neighborhood fits into the two dominant streams
of research on the ethnic city that are identified by Setha Low (1996): first,
the studies that see the ethnic city as a mosaic of enclaves economically,
linguistically, and socially self-contained as a strategy of political and
economic survival; and second, studies of ethnic groups that may or may
not function as enclaves but that are defined by their location in the occupational structure, their position in the local immigrant social structure,
their degree of marginality, or their historical and racial distinctiveness as
the basis of discrimination and oppression. Cultural and social capital are
defined by the physical vectors of the "ethnic city," such as urban space,
and by collective constructions such as social class, race, and gender; they
are dependent on physical and social location.

25. Jesus Rangel, "The Talk of the Ironbound: In a Thriving Community,
Ties That Bind Also Chafe," *New York Times*, June 28, 1988, http://www
.nytimes.com/1988/06/28/nyregion/the-talk-of-the-ironbound-in-a-thriving-
community-ties-that-bind-also-chafe.html?src=pm (accessed May 31,
2011).

26. See, for instance, Mary Jo Patterson, "Assimilation through Penetration:
Cultures Collide in Ironbound," *Star-Ledger*, May 14, 2000, 1.

27. A student of US-based anthropologist Franz Boas, Gilberto Freyre was the
author of *Casa Grande e Senzala* (1956), a seminal work in race studies
in Latin America that was both praised and criticized for turning racial
miscegenation between white male colonialists and indigenous women
into a celebration of interracial sexuality as well as into an argument for
Brazilian racial "exceptionalism" and moral superiority, particularly in relation to the United States. For Freyre, racial mixture was the key to solving
"problems of race relations" in a democratic way (1956, 98–99). The United
States has been a central counterpoint for the myth's development. Freyre's
uncritical vision of master/slave sexuality is by now dated, but the fantasy
and practice of interracial sex continue to distort both popular and elite
perceptions of contemporary race relations in Brazil and throughout Latin
America (cf. Goldstein 1999, 568).

28. Some scholars have considered the possibility that, like other European
groups in the past, some contemporary migrants—including some from

Latin America—could in fact have "Whiteness" extended to them and become "honorary whites" (Bonilla-Silva 1997) or "quasi-whites" (Gans 1999). A key question that Warren and Twine (1997) pose is: Are whites becoming a minority or will the white category simply continue to expand so that some of today's nonwhites will be tomorrow's whites? (211). They conclude that "precisely because Blacks represent the 'other' against which Whiteness is constructed, the backdoor to Whiteness is open to non-Blacks. Slipping through that opening is, then, a tactical matter for non-Blacks of conforming to White standards, of distancing themselves from *Blackness*, and of reproducing anti-Black ideas and sentiments" (208; original emphasis). Hence, "white" becomes a more elastic category, as colorism becomes an increasingly effective mechanism to sort immigrants (Bonilla-Silva 1997). This is not unique to the United States. In his study of immigration to Europe, Paul Silverstein (2005) argues that there has been a global hardening of a black-white spectrum, while social scientists like Herbert Gans (1999) and Bonilla-Silva (1997, 468) argue that contemporary immigrants to the United States are more likely to be categorized according to a "black or non-black" divide, rather than as "white or non-white" (as was the case of Europeans at the turn of the twentieth century).

29. Many middle-class African Americans viewed Brazil as a racial paradise and consumed Afro-Brazilian aspects of "Brazilian culture." This phenomenon can be situated in contemporary debates around a presumed convergence between a US bipolar (black/white) racial system and a Latin American racial system characterized by a "color continuum," the product of racial mixing. See, for instance, the debate between Hanchard (1999) and Fry (1995).

30. Interestingly, the main Brazilian national symbols exported are those associated with Blackness—feijoada, capoeira, samba, soccer, and butts (see Botelho 2006). Very few of the Brazilians in Newark could be considered "Afro-Brazilians," and yet it was evident to them that African Americans, rather than white Americans, shared a greater interest in "Brazilian culture," oftentimes associated with Afro-Brazilian cultural expression. These Brazilians seemed to sponsor a variety of notions of racial mixing, most of which were positive, and subscribed to a negative valorization of African-Americanness, which was generally conceived as an "un-mixed" (and, in this case, less desirable) type of blackness.

31. At ESHS, multiculturalism oftentimes worked as an imperative to love difference, while also elevating the national subject and points to the other's chauvinism or narcissism as a cause of injury, disturbance, fragmentation (cf. Ahmed 2004, 16). As the ESHS counselor proudly mentioned, "we have students from virtually every country, even Afghanistan, Palestine, India, and many, many European countries and a few Orientals." In 2003 the Central and South American nationalities of students were broken down as follows: 208 students were from Brazil, 125 from Ecuador, 25 from

Venezuela, 16 from Peru, 9 from Colombia, and 6 from Uruguay, as well as 24 students from El Salvador, 17 students from Honduras, 9 students from Mexico, and 2 students each from Guatemala, Costa Rica, and Panama. The Spanish-speaking Caribbean population consisted of 47 students from the Dominican Republic, 44 students from Puerto Rico (it was not clear whether these numbers included US-born Puerto Ricans), and 1 student from Cuba. ESHS took great interest in the fact that they have over 30 nationalities represented in its student body. A school administrator had made an unofficial list of the countries represented and the number of students from each country. She showed me her handwritten list, which included virtually every Latin American country plus various Middle Eastern and European countries. With an enrollment of 1438 in the 2001–2 academic year, ESHS was notorious for its language diversity. At ESHS 15% of the students are English-dominant, whereas 38% are Spanish-dominant, 1% French-dominant, and 42% consider Portuguese as their primary language. Along with Barringer High School in North Newark (chapter 2), ESHS is one of two public schools with significant Latino student populations in Newark.

32. I elaborate on this point and describe my research in two Belo Horizonte high schools—one public, one private—and in two high schools in the San Juan metropolitan area in Puerto Rico in Ramos-Zayas, work-in-progress.

33. Some researchers have paid special attention to manifestations of race and racism in intimate context, particularly how racial knowledge is produced in light of a gendered experience of racism (Goldstein 1999; Sheriff 2001; Twine 1998). Twine (1998) finds that rural upwardly mobile Afro-Brazilian women were less likely than their male counterparts to perceive racism in their everyday lives largely because of their belief that they were romantically and sexually appealing to whiter men. Both the whites and nonwhites Twine interviewed tended to conceptualize racism in terms of "practices of exclusion in the social and sexual spheres, while not considering racial disparities in the socio-economic, semiotic, educational and political spheres" (63). Nevertheless, a negative valorization of Blackness prevails in the context of the contradictions inherent in the relationship between race and beauty and race and sexuality: that it is "possible to see mixed-race sexual partners as ideal, even as more sensual and erotic, and yet evaluate 'black characteristics' negatively, particularly in non-erotic contexts" (Goldstein 1999, 567). The women whom Goldstein interviewed did not subscribe uncritically to the belief in racial democracy, but they toyed with the idea of an erotic democracy, particularly though discussions of attractiveness and sexuality. As Goldstein notes, the willingness to engage someone of another race intimately, among Latin Americans, is viewed as evidence of tolerance, even though it is possible to eroticize black culture and still consider black characteristics as negative, as I elaborate in my discussion of "urban competency" in chapter 6.

34. Even within Latin America, settler colonies developed various paths toward race. As Costa Vargas (2004) notes, at least since the 1920s and 1930s, the Brazilian myths appeared in several analogous forms throughout Latin America and the Caribbean, especially as "mestizaje" became an essentialist embodiment of the best cultural and physical traits of various ethnic populations in the Americas, and was at times attributed to a particular Iberian style of colonization and imperial expansion (cf. de la Fuente 1999; Wade 2004; Whitten and Torres 1998). Some countries, including Argentina and Chile, "pushed" the notions of the frontiers and maintained a claim to the West and Whiteness, while countries like Brazil, Puerto Rico, and Cuba incorporated the natives or imported non-European laborers into the nation and adopted, instead, a mestizo identity (Bonilla-Silva 2004, 207), as did countries where significant sectors of the black population were geographically concentrated and isolated from the national economy, such as along the Pacific coast of Colombia and Ecuador, for instance (de la Fuente 1999, 43). Likewise, I would argue, characteristics of racial democracy vary across regions of the United States with significant Latin American populations, so that popular conceptions of mestizaje in the US West Coast or Southwest may not be entirely adequate for the northeast United States. Similarly, the centrality of "the indigenous" varies among Brazilian and Hispanic Caribbean populations and some Central and South American populations.

35. Like Brazilians, Puerto Ricans and other US-born Latinos also alluded to how they came from families in which they had "everything [every racial group]," meaning that people of various phenotypes (looks) and racial groups were represented. A racial triad or three bloodlines was invoked as evidence that nobody, no matter how light-skinned or how dark, was never really "purely white" or "purely black." Although these views of Latin Americans and Latinos as "racially mixed" people were widespread among the Puerto Ricans and most Brazilians with whom I spoke, two critical issues have to be taken into account here, even if cursorily: (1) The idea of "mixture" was probably viewed very differently by Central and South American students whose racial cosmologies evolved more around an indigenous presence; for Brazilians and Puerto Ricans, the indigenous aspect of the triad appeared more as a symbolic component; and (2) The idea of "mixture" in the case of US-born Latinos oftentimes referred not only to "phenotypical" variations within a family of Puerto Ricans, but also to family compositions that included other groups, like African Americans or Dominicans, by marriage or fictive kin networks. Nevertheless, because the myth of national origin in some Latin American and Caribbean countries is based on the "three races," full Whitening is also never attainable. Conversely, Blackness, while not entirely negated, is undermined, manipulated, and confined to the "folkloric" realm to sustain the power of an elite that was predominantly white (Godreau 2002; Telles 2004; Wade 2004). The

US-born Puerto Ricans and Brazilian migrants with whom I spoke described attractive people using traditional terms by now associated with Latin America and the Caribbean, such as "tanned," "un poquito oscuro" (a little dark), "quemaito" (bronzed), "trigueño" (wheat-colored),"not too dark, not too light," "like So-and-So" (pointing to a particular person, celebrity, or to themselves). The insinuation that "all of us have some black in us" was implied in the Brazilian concept of "genipap," which has an equivalent in Puerto Rico as "la mancha de plátano" or "la raja." For instance, renowned Puerto Rican writer Enrique Laguerre published an editorial piece in 1959 praising a Brazilian novelist for articulating ideologies of racial democracy that, in his views, described the Puerto Rican racial system in the context of *Chavito Prieto*, a novel by Brazilian author Sultana Levy Rosemblatt that had just been released: "The Brazilian author, through the eyes of a foreigner living in Puerto Rico—and especially a national of a country like Brazil—focuses on that intimacy that characterizes us . . . in reality, rather than racial discrimination, we face discrimination based on color" (*El Mundo*, October 16, 1959, 2). He explicitly stated that the Brazilian model of racial democracy resonated with the Puerto Rican one.

36. Recall that Omi and Winant (1986) propose "racial formation theory" as an alternative approach to avoid treating race as a manifestation of some other, supposedly more basic, social relationship, like class. As posited by Omi and Winant, the racial formation theory perspective views race as a phenomenon whose meaning is contested throughout social life and which is an irreducible component of collective identities and social structures, as multiple actors develop "racial projects" that interpret and reinterpret the meaning of race. The question of whether "racial mixing" or "mestizaje" ("mestizagem" in Portuguese) curtails the development of a black racial consciousness has also been central to academic examinations of racial democracy (see Degler 1986; de la Fuente 1999; Skidmore 1993a, 1993b; Hanchard 1994; Fry 1995; Twine 1998; Bourdieu and Wacquant 1999; Fernandes 1965).

37. Alejandro de la Fuente (1999) contends that, in relation to Cuba, ideologies of racial democracy were not indiscriminately negative since "they created opportunities for those below, and capacity for subordinate groups to use the nation-state's cultural project to their advantage, and the fact that these social myths also restrain the political option of their own creators" (42). As de la Fuente concludes, "throughout the region, it became un-American (un-Venezuelan, un-Brazilian, un-Cuban) to discriminate openly against those perceived by the dominant sectors as racially inferior groups. . . . In systems in which racial differences are not rigidly codified and enforced, such as in Latin America under its myths of racial democracy, it is at least possible to ascend the social ladder and enter the dominant group" (46).

38. See Godreau's (2008) study of the relevance of "los sentimientos" and "Buenos modales" in racial speech in Puerto Rico.

39. There were certain instances in which Brazilians and Puerto Ricans did admit that their groups were racist, but this happened in philosophical conversations and with a lot of probing, rather than a cursory aspect of everyday life: "Yes, you see people grab their purses closer when they see a black person," mentioned a Brazilian woman. Or "Puerto Ricans and Dominicans are racist among themselves," stated a Puerto Rican high school student. Either directly or implicitly, these comments highlighted the belief that the racism identified as pertaining to black or white Americans was qualitatively different than the "dislike" that was noticed among Latino/Latin American groups themselves. I encountered several instances in which people were explaining their choice of partner by emphasizing that, even though the partner could occupy a lower rank in the scales of attractiveness or desirability, he or she was not like a "typical" member of their group. For instance, when Erika, the self-proclaimed "Goth," told me that her boyfriend is Puerto Rican and Ecuadorian, she clarified: "He was born in Puerto Rico and his father is Puerto Rican, but his mother is Ecuadorian. He doesn't really follow into the whole stereotype." The individual's "anomaly" within a group serves as a social justification to the intimate choice of dating partner.

40. Helen Marrow (2003) argues that Brazilians are becoming racialized into the black-white binary of US society, but are managing to escape the downward mobility of Hispanic/Latino categorization by becoming "American" and playing off the Spanish-language centered understanding of Hispanics/Latinos that most Americans have. Marrow uses 1990 US census data and twenty-two semi-structured interviews with Brazilian immigrant youth in Boston. A premise of this study is that Brazilian immigrants in the United States are more likely to come from middle- and upper-middle-class origins, and therefore to self-identify as "white," than the general population in Brazil (Margolis 1994). This is not necessarily the case of Brazilians in Newark, who are generally from working-class backgrounds and lack the ability to "choose" how to identify or to avoid the stigmatized job niches and residential areas occupied by other Latinos.

41. In California Brazilians have developed a particular understanding of Latinidad shaped by their interactions with Mexicans and Central Americans, as Bernadette Beserra's study of Brazilians in Los Angeles (2003) and Gustavo Ribeiro's study of Brazilian migrants to San Francisco have demonstrated (1997, n.d.). Both Beserra and Ribeiro emphasize the regional distinctiveness of the Brazilian migrants to California. In the case of Brazilians in San Francisco, most of the migrants are from the state of Goias, rather than from Minas Gerais, as tends to be the case among the earlier Brazilian migrants to Newark and the northeastern United States (Meihy 2004; Margolis 1994). In her examination of Carmen Miranda and the Brazilian Carnival celebration in Los Angeles, Beserra (2006) notes the ways in which Brazilian cultural expressions become transformed and marketed in racially

diverse contexts, such as the Hollywood Palladium. Likewise, Paula Botelho (2004) has examined the ways in which "Brazilian"-ness has gained expression in contemporary US popular media, from Carmen Miranda during the New Deal era through an always-already gendered embodiment of Brazil and Brazilians in the images of the Victoria's Secret models, Brazilian "bikini waxes," and the US media more generally.

42. See Meihy (2004, 168–69, 228–31) for a discussion on language and Brazilian-ness. See also Jocéli Meyer, "Filhos de brasileiros Perdem Cada Vez Mais seus Costumes" *Brazilian Press Magazine*, March 2003, 7–9. Meyer's article focuses on how US-born Brazilian children are "losing their Brazilian-ness," despite the efforts by Brazilian parents to instill in them Brazilian cultural roots and traditions, including language preservation, as well as considering ways in which the Brazilian Consulate in New York City has made attempts to offer "concrete conditions for immigrants to conitnue to be Brazilians in any part of the world [oferencendo condições concretas para que os imigrantes sejam brasileiros em qualquer parte do mundo]" (8).

43. Many Brazilians in Newark had close friends or relatives in Framingham, Boston, Lowell, and other cities in Massachusetts. A general perception among Newark Brazilians was that Brazilians in Massachusetts were much more organized and had developed more social service agencies than had those in Newark.

44. Based on survey research among Brazilians in Massachusetts, Helen Marrow argues that Brazilian youth view US blacks as more powerful than Hispanics/Latinos because of their birthright claims to US citizenship (which Brazilians see Hispanics/Latinos as lacking because they interpret this group to be largely "foreign," of immigrant stock like themselves), because of blacks' greater political power in the United States than Hispanics/Latinos (what some of the respondent see as the product of civil rights era legislation and public opinion for US blacks) (2003, 28).

45. Suwwan, "Para consul, hispánicos so cucarachos."

46. As Godreau (2008) notes, this is not to say that Puerto Ricans do not classify each other racially, or that they do not act according to the racist implications of such classificatory practices. Rather, what we see is a constant variance in the system of classification itself, combined with the recurrent switching of color and racial terms, and a general apprehension over the public ascription of racial labels to individual.

47. In her work on verbal play as racial critique among Mexicans, Marcia Farr shows how relajo functions as an antistructural process with the capacity for social inversion, so that "in both verbal and non-verbal play, such as relajo and fiesta, the usual norms and structures of society can be turned upside down, at least for a moment" (1994, 22–23). Limón (1982), Briggs (1988), and others further stress the creative and performative power of such play, especially verbal play, in terms of the transformative power of

language, and Farr (1994) shows that change is indeed facilitated by the critical perspectives engendered by joking.

48. In "Assimilation through Penetration," Patterson argues that as more and more Brazilians landed in Newark, Brazilians who were already in the city began to encounter prejudice. Madalena O. Ribeiro, who had moved to the city in 1983 with her husband, Helio, an engineer, was cited in Patterson's article. "At that time, there were not a lot of Brazilians here, and we were very welcome," she said. "In the Portuguese stores, we would walk in, and they treated us very well, though they could tell right away we were Brazilian." By 1988, she said, the situation had changed. "If I'd walk in a store and speak Portuguese, they'd treat me differently. If I spoke English, which I started to do, they couldn't tell."

49. As Hartigan notes in the case of white residents of Detroit: "For whites who remained in the city, especially those in the decimated inner-city areas, the significance of race has drastically altered" (1999, 20). Oftentimes the Portuguese and the Spanish argued against being considered "white" by pointing to the suburbs as the place of "real whiteness," where residents were "whiter than we are." When all residents share a working-class or working-poor background, holding on to a white ethnicity became critical in avoiding more derogatory categorizations akin to "white trash." There's no space for "white trash" in the American dream, but European ethnics are the historical pillars of the US mobility mythology. In this sense, the "ethnic card" served to counter a racial reading (157), particularly for a population like the Portuguese, who were considered "backward" and lacking a valued modernity in comparison to the Brazilians and other US-born Latinos (chapter 6), or even to their extended families and friends in Europe. While some of the Latin American migrants in Newark viewed the Portuguese as whites only in some occasions and the rest of the time assumed that "somewhere out there" there are the "real whites"—the cultureless and affluent suburban ones—many US-born Latinos constructed "white people" as such even in the absence of other types of (nonethnic) whites.

50. See also Halter 1993 for an examination of how "white Portuguese" angrily reacted to perceived racial slights and sharply drew the color line against "black Portuguese" Cape Verdeans in New Bedford, Connecticut, especially when preference in jobs and housing hung in the balance.

51. In the context of the "Ball Scene" in New York City, Edgar Rivera-Colón (2009) also noted how blacks and Latinos/as refused to concede Whiteness any type of superior or even interesting social and/or aesthetic intelligibility when it came to emotional style. In this sense, following some of the insights of Fanon, this notion creates space for affirmation, community building, and subject reconstruction that takes Whiteness on and bends it into to a "for-itself-now for-we" abject/foundation. See Muñoz 2000 for a different take on this same problematic using the field of artistic production as a site of analysis.

52. "IBID Hires Off-Duty Police Officers to Address Student Rowdiness on Ferry Street," April 6, 2006, www.goironbound.com.

53. For instance, in reference to the heated mayoral elections of 2002 in which current mayor Cory Booker ran against long-term incumbent Sharpe James, several Brazilians commented on March 25, 2002. An Ironbound resident under the signature of MDF wrote: "On the way home to Merchant Street, I had to stop because of a large group of people crossing the street. I realized that it was our Mayor Sharpe James walking with a group of supporters. Off to the side were a group of 'Cory Booker' supporters waving signs and shouting and chanting at the Mayor and his supporters. . . . I personally lean toward Cory for Mayor, my husband and the rest of the family for Mayor Sharpe James. After seeing such a poor sign of dignity, it makes me wonder if Cory Booker knows who and how these 'friends of his' are running his campaign down here?? Is this what will happen if Cory makes Mayor?? I have heard he is aligned to Black Militants (Leroy Jones son etc.) and also some very wealthy Jewish people (aren't they the ones that deserted Newark years ago and ran to the suburbs in rough times? And these people would like to come back into Newark and take over under the guise of Cory?"

54. *Brazilian Voice*, June 4–10, 2003, 46.

55. Categorizing racism as an extreme category is problematic for critical race theorists, who note that "racism is normal, not aberrant, in American society . . . and ingrained feature of our landscape, it looks ordinary and natural to persons in the culture" (Delgado, in Kobayashi and Peake 2000, 395). In such a system, whiteness is embodied and becomes desire "in the shape of the normative human body, for which 'race' provides an unspecified template" (cf Ahmed 2004, 139). This is also a defense mechanism against mainstream culture that renders minorities and working-class ethnics as the ones to blame for segregation, backwardness, and racism.

56. Gentrification remained a contested concept when applied to various "inner-city" neighborhoods as well as "ethnic enclaves"; it was applied to urban projects that seemed to inscribe the basis of class identity increasingly in spatial practices rather than the obvious relations to the means of production of the past. Such uncertainty brought to the fore the discursive aspects of class identity and distinctions, in a manner that has been sometimes overlooked in objectivist definitions of economic interests and social belonging (cf. Hartigan 1999, 169, 185). There was a distinction between a positive assertion of and interest in preserving a form of (ethnic/Portuguese) sameness and an opposite, negative reaction to (racial/white) otherness.

CHAPTER FOUR

1. Some would argue that the stereotypes of the tropics as applied to Brazilians in the United States date back to Carmen Miranda, the "lady in the tutti-frutti hat" who also served as the strategic link between Getulio Vargas'

Estado Novo and Roosevelt's Good Neighbor policy. In Newark, there was some variation along generational lines that shaped how Brazilians and Portuguese viewed these gendered stereotypes in practice. Portuguese adults were more likely than youth in any group to assume a connection between the revealing dressing style of Brazilian women and a popular image of Brazilian women as "homewreckers." For instance, Rene Ferreira, the father of a ninth-grader and the US-born son of a Portuguese merchant who arrived in Newark in the 1960s: "There was a time when people were saying that Brazilian women were getting together with Portuguese men, and the Portuguese women didn't like that. Even [getting together] with married men. You have to understand that the Brazilian and the Portuguese are very different. They come from different cultures, different climates. The Portuguese is more reserved, more conservative, the women are more protected. . . . The Brazilians are very different in that way. They are louder. They dress more provocatively and are always going to parties." See also Patterson's "Assimilation through Penetration." For other international contexts where reference to Brazilian morality has been stereotyped, see "Disney, Mickey Mouse, and Brazilian Morality," *Atlanta Journal-Constitution*, December 14, 1997, and a *New York Times* article a propos of the visit of Pope John Paul II to Brazil, in October 5, 1997, titled "Brazil Is Likely to Wink at Pope's Call to Behave." For a broader discussion on sexualized stereotypes, see Prasso 2005.

2.   See Sarah Mahler's study (1995) of tensions within immigrant "communities" and her suggestion that we understand these communities not only as folkloric entities of mutual assistance, but also as spaces oftentimes defined by competition, envy, and debt.

3.   A more extensive discussion of the relationships between Brazilians and "Hispanics" in the largely Portuguese area of the Ironbound is undertaken elsewhere (Ramos-Zayas 2009; see also chapter 3).

4.   The image of the Ironbound as a quaint ethnic enclave has most recent being debunked by an increase incidence of crime that local Portuguese officials have attributed to "people from the outside," particularly black and Latino youth presumed to be from other areas of Newark. The fact that the Ironbound has projects in its outskirts is usually erased in narratives that are invested in reifying the commercial viability and "cultural richness" of the area.

5.   As posited by Omi and Winant (1986), the analytic framework of racialization emphasizes the ways that race or racial difference cannot be presumed to be based upon the natural characteristics of identifiable groups or the biological effects of ancestry, but rather comes to be actively produced as such, and continually reproduced and transformed. Race is always entangled in social relations and conflicts and retains an enduring (seemingly intractable) significance precisely because its forms and substantive meanings are always eminently historical and mutable (Omi and Winant

1986, 64–66; Winant 1994, 58–68; De Genova and Ramos-Zayas 2003). With reference to Puerto Ricans, the concept of culture has been persistently deployed, historically, to account for poverty, marginality, and other "deficiencies" that might otherwise have been depicted in terms of shared blood (Lewis 1966). By treating "Hispanic" as an "ethnic" designation, the US Census has encouraged Latinos to identify "racially" as white, or black, or Native American—in short, as anything but Latino, while reserving "Hispanic" as an officially non-"racial" category. Nevertheless, this hegemonic "ethnic" distinction instituted by the US state, which has also relied upon biological or phenotypic notions of racial categories, has been particularly instrumental for the allocation of affirmative action entitlements, deliberately constructing "Hispanics" as an effectively homogenized minority population analogous to African Americans. Thus, the "Hispanic" status of Latinos is widely treated as a racial condition all the same.

6. In Newark, most encounters are between Latinos and Latin American migrants and blacks, rather than whites. But, despite the predominant black population, Whiteness is still maintained as an ideological norm. The normativity of Whiteness and the equation of "Americanness" and Whiteness, while perhaps not as taken for granted as in predominantly white settings, was nevertheless sustained in Newark precisely because of the limited contact that people of color have with whites in this city.

7. For an excellent study of Brazilian domestic workers in the United States, see Fleischer 2002. See also Martes 2000, 77–112; Sales 1998, 115–28; and Tosta 2004, 723nn9, 10). For an official analysis of Brazilians and work in the United States, including domestic work, see Comissão Parlamentar Mista de Inquérito 2006.

8. In her seminal work, *Maid in the USA*, Mary Romero (1992) examines how the relationships between maids and employers are always-already entangled in webs of affect that make identifying subordinate work conditions harder.

9. The concept of "ethnosexual frontiers" is also pertinent here to describe how the race and ethnicity of sexual and romantic partners, though oftentimes quite actively inspected, are frequently transgressed and sometimes conspire with "heteronormative ethnosexual stereotypes" (Nagel 2000, 113). The transgressed "frontiers" of race and ethnicity in romantic partners also lead to a great deal of attention paid to the sexual demeanor of group members (by outsiders and insiders) in inspection and enforcement of both formal and informal rules of sexual conduct.

10. What Feldman-Bianco (2001) describes in her article on "Brazilians in Portugal, Portuguese in Brazil: Constructions of Sameness and Difference," seems applicable to the images that the Portuguese have of Brazilians, which happen to oftentimes coincide with the images that Brazilians want to promote of themselves: "Central to these stereotypes [that the Portuguese have of Brazilians] were notions of the Brazilian ginga (Brazilian

swaying movement) and of 'tropical sensuality' portrayed as inherent traits of the 'mulatto woman.'" As Feldman-Bianco further explains: "These stereotypes were built upon images of Brazil readily available in Portugal because of the expanded popularity of imported Brazilian soap operas, and of the so-called 'Brazilian culture' or 'Brazilian nights' in disco bars" (615–16).

11. Some seminal works in anthropology have attempted to examine the connection between emotions and social structures of power, particularly in light of conditions of extreme poverty and duress. In her study of infant mortality in northern Brazil, Nancy Scheper-Hughes (1983) calls this disjunction a form of "death without weeping" and Donna Goldstein (1999) examines how a "different emotional aesthetic" in a Rio de Janeiro favela leads to "laughter out of place." Both of these perspectives focus on an alternative political economy of emotion to explain the reaction of informants to their terribly harsh realities with affect that may appear inappropriate to a mainstream Western eye.

12. Lasch-Quinn's study (2001) of "sensitivity trainers" in the post–civil rights era shows how these groups of professionals and experts might be responsible for the identity turn in views of difference in the United States.

13. The article was written by Larry Rotter and based on some statistics by Edilson Nascimento de Silva (*New York Times*, February 1, 2005).

14. Her friends were not terribly surprised to see her transformation, because there were several Latin American migrant women, particularly Brazilians, who had joined evangelical churches in the area. A few times I heard conversations in which "converts" judged "nonconverts" for wearing revealing clothes and "nonconverts" held on to the superiority of being Catholic (even in the case of nonpracticing Catholics) over evangelical.

15. For a context-specific, more elaborate discussion of Brazilian evangelical churches in the United States, see Botelho's (2004) ethnography study of a Brazilian congregation in Washington, DC; Beserra's (2003) analysis on an evangelical group in Los Angeles; and Martes' (2000) work among Brazilians in Massachusetts.

16. Christine Armario, "US Latinas Seek Answers in Islam," *Christian Science Monitor*, December 27, 2004.

17. This perspective was echoed in local newspaper articles, including a piece in the *Star-Ledger* that stated: "It's probably a one-generation-long conflict [between the Brazilians and the Portuguese]—friendships bloom between the children, with some Portuguese teenage girls adopting Brazilian accents to better compete for boys in both groups. . . . [W]hen the Brazilian influx into Newark started in earnest, with hundreds of single young men and women flooding the streets and looking for work . . . [t]heir language was familiar to the Portuguese, but their temperament, body language, and looks were foreign. . . . [F]or the old-time Portuguese in Newark, Brazilians represent a world full of light, laughter, and yes, bared flesh" (Patterson, "Assimilation through Penetration").

18. Language in the case of Brazilians and Portuguese adopted a similar politics to those examined by De Genova and myself in the case of Mexicans and Puerto Ricans in Chicago (see De Genova and Ramos-Zayas 2003). In that case, while both groups spoke Spanish, they used the particularities of idiomatic phrases, accents, and vocabulary to accentuate difference, rather than similarity.

19. Another key issue here is what Costa Vargas has called the "hyper con-sciousness of race" and "racial negation" (2004, 443), two concepts that operated in tandem. Race, in its negation, suggests that it lacks value as an analytically and morally valid tool; it is presumed not to play a central role in determining or explaining subordinate status. Hence, a system seem-ingly devoid of racial awareness is in reality deeply immersed in racialized understandings of the social world.

20. This has been analyzed for the impression value, but I want to emphasize the political economy of sexual work in this particular case. Not because I ever had concrete evidence that Marcela was involved in sex work in the most conventional sense of prostitution, though that may have been the case, but because she had arrived in the United States with the promise of work at a bar in which her gendered and sexualized Brazilian-ness was a prerequisite. These relationships (and whatever fantasy may exist behind them) provided a context in which Brazilian women, and many other US-born Latina women, participated in their own sexual commodification (cf. Beserra 2006). In her examination of the lives of Brazilian migrant women in Los Angeles, Beserra (2006) found that some of the Brazilian interview-ees believed that the erotic stereotype they encountered in the United States "retain[ed] their movement, promotes the idea of prostitution, and have, consequently, a negative impact," while other interviewees argued that the image was "advantageously ambiguous" and allowed a space to distance themselves from groups that were even more stigmatized, espe-cially Mexicans. These processes of exoticization of "non-Western" women restituted feelings of dominance, wealth, power, and masculinity to West-ern men, whose traditional notions of masculinity had been diminished by modern cultural expectations.

21. For a journalistic account on how Brazilian sex work has become a promi-nent industry even in small towns in Portugal, see Ripley 2003. Focusing on the remote mountain town of Bragança, in northeastern Portugal, the article describes the impact of newly arrived Brazilian sex workers on the Portuguese married couples' relationships in the town. In a colorful de-scription of jealousy and revenge, Ripley writes that "a group of Portuguese wives drew up a manifesto and brought their grievances to the mayor and the police chief, calling for a 'war on prostitution.'" Apparently, the "me-ninas" made themselves more noticeable in Bragança by sticking together and wearing sexier clothing than the traditional Portuguese women. One of the Brazilian women quoted in the article concludes by stating: "And

Brazilians—it's true—are very exotic, very sensual. It's no one's fault . . . just the logical result of a modern Latin culture bumping up against a traditional, European one, the old colony coming home."

22. See Comissão Parlamentar Mista de Inquérito (2006) for a detailed study showing how coercion, exortion, physical violence, fraud, and detention happen within migration and employment recruitment processes and even in places of work in the host society. According to the Organizacao Internacional de Migrações (junho 2004): "cerca de 75 mil brasileiras atuam na industria do sexo na Europa" (335). In June the US State Department reported that there were around 70,000 Brazilians, particularly women, working as prostitutes outside of Brazil (in Comissão Parlamentar Mista de Inquérito 2006, 340). See also a research that identified 241 routes used in the trafficking of women and children (Leal, cited in Comissão Parlamentar Mista de Inquérito 2006, 336–37), and Oliveira Silva (cited in Comissão Parlamentar Mista de Inquérito 2006, 339). This latter research demonstrated that there were as many sex workers as domestic workers in migratory routes (321, 324, 329, 336–37).

23. Patterson, "Assimilation through Penetration."

24. I don't want to overdetermine the tensions between Portuguese and Brazilians. Obviously, relationships are complicated, and just as there are instances of great antagonism, there are also instances of cooperation. Many of the Brazilians with whom I spoke were grateful to a Portuguese employer or landlord for helping them in a particular moment of vulnerability. However, my goal here is to illustrate the unusually gendered dimensions of the relationship between the two groups.

25. Raymond, Hughes, and Gomez 2001. Jersey City, East Brunswick, Red Bank and Rockaway Township—towns that are adjacent or close to Newark—were also reported to be high-density areas, but these were viewed as less appealing for non–English-speaking women than Newark was. One police official reported that New Jersey has more go-go bars (strip clubs) than any other state in the country, as well as more "discrete" massage parlors or health clubs, and thousands of residences and other locations that house prostitution venues, including some hair and nail salons that were used as front businesses for brothels. Most sex establishments in New Jersey neither advertise nor display neon signs to draw attention to what they offer.

26. Patterson, "Assimilation through Penetration"; Dines 1989, 88–92; 1991a, 1; 1991b, D3.

27. A 1991 article on go-go dancers in Newark noted a decline in earnings from tips. Where some dancers once made up to $1,500 a week, they were now earning $600 or $800. This reduction has made some former dancers enter the bikini-import business while others sew go-go outfits to be sold for $100 a piece. Dines 1991a.

28. Margolis (1994) dates the presence of Brazilian "dançarinas" in New York back to the Metropole, a go-go bar near Times Square that seemed

to employ many Brazilian women from Minas Gerais in the mid-1970s. These women might have initially arrived in the United States to work as domestics but later learned through word of mouth that they could earn significantly more in the club business (158–59).

29. For a discussion on the use of symbolic racial connotations such as "respectability" and "honor" in relation to prostitution, see Suárez Findlay 1999. Suárez Findlay exposes the contradictory nature of moral standards and their disproportionate impact on poor women of color during late nineteenth- and early twentieth-century Puerto Rico; in particular, she demonstrates how moral reform was inherently linked to the "whitening" of poor Afro–Puerto Rican women. Morality was a shifting ideal and assumed different definitions that altered the ways in which liberal activists defended women associated with disrespectability and made them "worthy of protection and capable of dignified struggle" (209).

30. In *Brasil Fora de Si: Experiências de brasileiros em Nova York* (2004), José Bom Meihy introduces the life history of a Brazilian woman from Belo Horizonte who fell in love with an American and moved with him to Elizabeth, NJ, a town adjacent to Newark. Once in the United States, the American man kept her passport and induced her into prostitution by insisting that she sleep with his friends. Eventually, the woman escaped the situation and decided to look for work at a bar in Queens (202). The challenge here is to read such a situation in the context of structural exploitation while still recognizing subjectivity and agency. Meihy does not ask the woman more specifically about the decision to move to the United States, and the degree to which other aspects may have informed the more immediate explanation of "falling in love" with an American man. Nevertheless, what is known is the widespread sexual trafficking in which Brazilians, along with other women from "Third World" countries, have been implicated. A 2006 report of the Parliamentary Commission on Emigration of the Brazilian National Congress states that human trafficking generates close to $9 billion annually, with the most vulnerable groups being women who are "illegal" migrants, subjected to sexual exploitation and new forms of slavery (Comissão Parlamentar Mista de Inquérito 2006, 324). As Kamala Kempadoo argues, while one must consider patriarchy in evaluations of the subordination of "Third World" women, this is not an absolute form of domination. Rather, this form of human trafficking is derived from capitalist, patriarchal, and racialized state relations, combined with the women's own desire to search for survival (324).

31. Many of the male clients' Internet writing that Raymond, Hughes, and Gomez analyzed mentioned the lack of English-language proficiency and recent-arrival status as characteristics sought in sex workers. In the New York metro area, the most frequently desired racial identity was "Hispanic/Latina" (32%), followed by "Black" (30%), "white" (21%), and "Asian/Oriental" (14%) (2001, 35–60).

32. According to law enforcement and social service providers, some venues were owned by prominent, local community members, while others were owned by Russian businessmen, including some who are considered member of organized crime networks (ibid., 35–36).

33. Jeffreys, "City Slicker: Newark." Most of the popular and academic discussion about Brazilian sexual workers in Newark has focused on the competition between Brazilian and Russian strippers (Antunen de Oliveira 1999). Drawing from the research of José Carlos Meihy, a historian at the Universidade de São Paulo, the article examines how Brazilian female strippers and go-go dancers are being displaced by women from Eastern Europe, usually generically referred to as "Russians." The two main reasons given for this change in the world of sexual work were that "the average American" has come to devalue darker-skin strippers in favor of "Russians," and that the most successful strippers work under the auspices of an organization, not independently. In this sense, the women from Eastern Europe, who are blonde and who are supported by local organized crime, have an advantage over Brazilian women: "The Brazilian women who would test their luck as independent strippers end up in serious situations with terrible consequences. . . . Many of them end up in networks of prostitution, pornography, forced to take an incontrollable path of drugs and alcohol, in an international crime circuit that uses dancing as the façade." According to the article, while the Brazilian strippers follow the laws governing sexual work in New York and New Jersey, the Russian workers are only bound by "the exclusive rules of the mafia of Roterdã," a criminal organization of European Jews that originated in Russia and has a base in Holland and a strong presence in the United States. One of the strippers interviewed in the article is "Luci," a woman who left her working-class neighborhood in Brazil to come to Newark, and shared a house with two other dancers in the Ironbound. Luci explained how she's confident that her two daughters will have a better life because they are "going to school" (Meihy 2004, 176).

34. As Goldstein (1999) notices, a major icon of "hot sexuality" in Brazil is the mixed-race woman, since Brazilian understandings of race and color are intimately connected with Brazilian representation of their own sexual history in Freyrian terms; an unequal (and oftentimes not consensual) "love affair" of white men and dark women that does not take into account the context of violence and rape (568).

35. Maxine Margolis noted that Brazilian dançarinas in New York were likely to tell relatives back in Brazil that they were employed as babysitters, housekeepers, barmaids, or waitresses (1994, 157), particularly if they were originally from the most "conservative" and "traditional" areas of Minas Gerais. Some of these dançarinas even lied to their Brazilian friends in New York about their profession, Margolis found, even though some of the Brazilians expressed suspicion about specific people working as "exotic dancers" (157–58).

36. Blackness becomes valuable only in specific situations where sexual com-modification and urban competency are the operational frameworks and when blackness is valorized for its consumption potential, so that in the case of African American women, black bodies were at times equated with ugliness and lack of femininity, even when they are also representations of black sensuality in the US media (cf. Goldstein 1999, 567; chapter 6).

CHAPTER FIVE

1. Weiner (1986) proposes the "attribution theory of emotions" to explain how causal attribution for behaviors have emotional effects on actors de-pending on the locus of causality, the perceived stability of the cause, and the degree that the cause is controllable by anyone. Emotions and the attri-bution processes they trigger transform relations or groups into expressive objects—that is, into a source of value. This describes an attribution process that generates more specific, object-focused emotions and tacit or explicit relational affiliation to the social unit/group/network.

2. Brazilians were simplistically associated with samba, steamy sex, and soc-cer. Nevertheless, the sensualization of a Latinidad in Newark also shaped the experience of US-born Latinas, particularly Puerto Rican and Domini-can women, whose desirability and attractiveness were framed not against that of the Portuguese women (as tended to be the case among Brazilians), but against that of African American women. Not surprisingly, these stereo-types had also been reinforced in local newspapers and advertisement for dance clubs. A *Star-Ledger* advertisement for Lancers, a club on Ferry Street: "No matter how low the temperature drops, it's always halter top weather at Lancers, a sprawling restaurant and dance hall in Newark's Ironbound district. Five nights a week, folks sweat to live salsa, merengue, cumbia and other Latin flavors. . . . Even during deepest, darkest January, Lancers is awash in July fashions. As soon as women were buzzed in the front door, they peeled away their winter gear, revealing spaghetti-strap tops, leggy skirts and sheer things. . . . Non-Spanish speakers may want to bring along a bilingual friend, although it is tough to chat over the soaring voices and furious beats." When I asked some of the young Puerto Rican women I met at Barringer what they thought of this ad, they engaged in a patterned search for stereotypes. These stereotypes were, ironically, malleable and transferable, rather than static and rigid, as stereotypes tend to be: first the young women would describe the ad as simplistic and stereotypical, then they would challenge that Lancers was even as "Latin" as the ad claimed, and finally, they would reinterpret the characteristics in the ad to sug-gest that "We [Latinos] are very warm and have the rhythm. That's in the blood, and other people want that too, but they don't have it." Another side of this visibility had to do with the exoticization of Brazilians in New York gay communities, as was mentioned by a college student I once met

while giving a talk at a small college in New England: "My mom is Puerto Rican and my dad is Brazilian. I was born and raised in the Bronx and I considered myself Puerto Rican. After I came out, I started playing up my Brazilian identity more. It's a good thing if you're Brazilian, in the gay community," this young man commented.

3. Cavell further describes emotions as a kind of sixth sense that allows individuals to perceive aspects of the world that are perceptible in no other way, and which help us know what matters to us and sometimes why. In this context, understandings of "cultural subjectivity" derive from the view that human subjects know themselves not as they are in all their human potential, but in determined forms of social being, through practical activity.

4. The word "buchas" was also used by many Puerto Ricans to describe African American women whom they assumed or knew were lesbians.

5. See also Melissa Harris-Lacewell's work (2006) on the myth of the African American superwoman and political involvement, in which she presents stereotypes as having a critical, very dynamic role in social movements.

6. See Katz 2001, 349n2, for a more thorough discussion on the gaze in the context of how emotions work.

7. See McCarthy Brown 1998; see also Bates 2001.

8. The image of "black women" as "churchgoers" is very generation-specific, so that younger black women were viewed as aggressive and older black women were viewed as churchgoers. Nevertheless, both images suggest "aggressiveness" to most Latinas. Adult African American women who worked as counselors, teachers, security guards at the schools and in other Newark institutions made moral judgment of Latinas, particularly of "unwed mothers." In several occasions I heard adult African American females making comments like "you should get married and them have a child" or "at least all my children have the same daddy."

9. This image was rearticulated when the media covered the case of a young African American lesbian from Newark who physically hurt a street vendor after the vendor made a pass at the woman's girlfriend in New York's West Village. A fistfight ensued and the young woman, who became known as the Lesbian Seven, ended up being arrested and tried. For many community members, these women, some of whom knew Sakia Gunn and were from the same small, young black lesbian Newark community, were fighting back and taking matters—and their safety—into their own hands (cf. Johnson 2007, 92). These images are part of a long tradition of representing black women as unfeminine, castrating, and sexually and economically demanding. Don Imus's remarks on the women on the Rutgers University basketball team provide a widely publicized example of this tendency. These "masculine women" were feared constantly whereas feminine women who act out in self-defense or for heterosexual men's enjoyment in popular culture are seldom feared given their femininity and nonviolence (Johnson 2007, 97).

10. Prior to this incident, most of the research and media focused their attention on cases of street violence in the West Coast, particularly the Southern California area (cf. Malanga 2008). The shooting of Jamiel Shaw, a black student, by an undocumented Latino, is an example. See Howard Blume and Mitchell Landsberg's "Locke High School in South Los Angeles Locked Down after Huge Brawl," *Los Angeles Times*, May 10, 2008.

11. Malanga (2008) cites conservative radio host and columnist Reverent Jesse Lee Peterson as calling the Newark killings and the California violence a "wake-up call" for blacks. Reflecting on the new mood, Terry Anderson, a Los Angeles talk-show host, challenged black leaders like Jesse Jackson and Al Sharpton to speak out. "If you make one simple change, and change Jose Carranza [one of the Latinos involved in the Newark shooting] to a white man," said Anderson, "I will guarantee you that [Sharpton and Jackson] would be screaming and marching in the streets."

12. In *The Presumed Alliance* (2004), Nicolás Vaca argues that the black-Latino divide has been largely ignored by the media and political leaders and recasts the 1992 LA riots in this light. Sparked by the LAPD beating of Rodney King, the riot became on the ground a black-brown confrontation in which the majority of businesses destroyed were Latino. At the same time, Vaca argues, Latino believe that, since they had nothing to do with black oppression in America, they owe blacks nothing and "come to the table with a clear conscience."

13. As Malanga (2008) states, black unease about immigration goes a long way back. In the 1870s former slave Frederick Douglass warned that immigrants were displacing free blacks in the labor market. Twenty-five years later Booker T. Washington exhorted US industrialists to "cast down your bucket" not among new immigrants but 'among the eight million Negros . . . who have without strikes and labor wars tilled your fields, cleared your forests, builded your railroads and cities." Blacks supported federal legislation in 1882 that restricted Chinese immigration to the United States. They favored the immigration reform acts of the 1920s, which limited European immigration, and also urged restrictions on Mexican workers: "If the million Mexicans who have entered the country have not displaced Negro workers, whom have they displaced?," asked black journalist George Schuyler in 1928. This anti-immigration streak subsided in the 1960s when black political leaders, in the post-1965 Immigration Reform legislation, believed that blacks and poor immigrants had much in common and could become political allies. In the run-up to the immigration bill's passage, Martin Luther King Jr. endorsed the idea of letting Cubans fleeing Castro settle in Miami and Jesse Jackson would later herald the imminent arrival of a mighty "black-brown" or "rainbow" coalition that would presumably propel him to the 1984 Democratic presidential nomination; likewise, the Congressional Black Caucus in DC became one of Washington's most vocal groups opposing immigration restrictions. In fact, in the California vote on

Proposition 187, blacks split nearly in half on the measure that would have banned government benefits for "illegals," while whites heavily supported it. See Malanga 2008.

14. Tanya K. Hernández, "Roots of Anger: Longtime Prejudices, Not Economic Rivalry, Fuel Latino-Black Tensions," *Los Angeles Times*, January 7, 2007; see also Hochchild 2007.

15. This is the case even when crimes in these areas continue to be mostly black-on-black and Latino-on-Latino. For instance, though blacks make up 9% of Los Angeles County's population, they were victims of 59% of all racially motivated attacks in 2006, while Latinos committed 52% of all racially motivated attacks. He holds gangbanging responsible for most of the violence, particularly the "500 Mexican gangs—compared with some 200 black ones—[which have] aggressively tried to push blacks out of mixed-race neighborhoods." Gang-related violence arose from blacks and Latinos sharing high schools, and seemingly innocuous issues like refusing to celebrate each others' holidays or parental resentment toward bilingual education (Alex Alonso in Malanga 2008). As high schools became more heavily policed, the resentment extended to street fighting, and gangs, including those with transnational links, proliferated.

16. As Juan Melli, a journalist for the alternative journal *Blue Jersey*, remarked: "The implication here—and without any on-the-record statements by anyone directly involved with the families or officials on this case we cannot know—is that the silence on this matter is due to homophobia and sensitivities within the black community. . . . That is playing a role in the reticence to publicly discuss the orientation of the victims (or even perceived orientations) as a motive in this crime. . . .The homophobia in parts of the black community makes this a politically unpopular issue for leaders to address. But it's a real problem and pretending it's not there only perpetuates the cycle of hate." This perspective on how the black community might deal with homosexuality appeared in contradistinction to how the mainstream media tended to glamourize gay life in suburban New Jersey. In a *New York Times* article titled "Across the State, Same-Sex Couples and Their Children Have Become Integrated Into Suburban Life. . . . But This Does Not Apply to Newark" (December 2, 2007, B23), Andrew Jacobs claims that New Jersey has become a national beacon for gay equality, boasting some of the toughest antidiscrimination laws in the United States and being one of only three states in 2007 to recognized same-sex civil unions. As Jacobs notes: The Newark Pride Alliance was established in 2004 in response to the stabbing to death of Sakia Gunn. When the Pride flag was raised in City Hall, Cory Booker was stunned by the flood of "angry phone calls" to his office. Jacobs quotes Booker as saying: "There's a lot of silent pain in the city of Newark, and perpetrators of this pain—those who promote bigotry and the alienation—must be confronted." Given this background, Newark gay activists were pressing law enforcement officials

to investigate the shootings as a possible bias crime. The schoolyard shooting incident was also framed as an instance of anti-black Latino crime and questioned the value of Newark serving as an immigrant "safe haven" city. In an undergraduate monograph, Rutgers student Emanuel Anzules (2006) also examined the complicated intersection of commercial glamourization of "Brazilian gay culture" and the everyday bigotry to which same-sex relations are subjected in Newark's Ironbound.

17. See Jessica DuLong. "Young and in Danger in New Jersey," *Advocate Report*, June 24, 2003, 26; Tamer El-Ghobashy, "Jersey Teen Killed in Gay Bias Attack," *New York Daily News*, May 13, 2003, http://www.nydailynews. com/front/v-pfriendly/story/83225p-76120c.html. At the time, almost no news reports mentioned Shani Baraka's sexual orientation or that of the other victim, her lover, until a New York Blade story.

18. The case of the African American lesbian from Newark who was imprisoned for allegedly assaulting a street vendor who made a comment to her girlfriend in the West Village, NYC, also served as an example of this.

CHAPTER SIX

1. Many Latin American migrants oftentimes attempted to learn the cultural codes that would earn them entrance into these alternative understandings of belonging in the United States. Hubert Dreyfus (1991) developed the term *expert knowledge* to describe the latest stage of a presumed continuum from being a novice through expertise. In some ways, US-born Puerto Ricans follow a "Black epistemology" (Hill Collins 2000), a way of apprehending and knowing the world that derives from accumulated experiences and cultural schemas to make sense of the experience, based on wisdom and intuition rather than on formal knowledge. Elijah Anderson (1990) introduced the term *code of the streets* to describe the set of informal rules governing public behavior, particularly violence, and which prescribe the proper way to respond if challenged. Anderson's ethnography reveals a code of the street that demands a good deal of deference in interracial exchanges in urban contexts where fights often break out because of small signals such as looking at someone for a long fraction of a second. This ostentatious toughness of the street code clashed with the normal code of Goffmanian behavior in the surrounding society (e.g., mutual politeness, shared casualness). The set of interactive rituals that constitute the code of the street generates the most emotional intensity and dominate the focus of attention so that bland politeness and mild social manners pale by comparison in the competition over public space. Ultimately, the code of the streets challenges broad categorical identities by replacing them with locally generated identities rooted in personal reputations in networks where one is known and by anonymity outside (cf. Hill Collins 2000).

2. For an excellent work that undertakes this task, see Carolyn Steedman's

Landscape for a Good Woman (1986), a memoir on working-class life and family relations in mid-1900s England.

3. Efforts to re-embody anthropology have focused on how the body is not only an object to be studied in relation to culture, but also is to be considered the subject of culture (Csordas 1990, 5). Analyses of perception (Merleau-Ponty's preobjective) and practice (Bourdieu's habitus) constitute critical aspects of social scientific inquiry that are grounded in the body. Likewise, it is the physical involvement of self, rather than an absence of rationality, that distinguishes emotion from other kinds of cognition; nevertheless, there is a need here for an examination of a socially embodied personhood, not just self.

4. An exception to the "letting go of happiness" as a way to measure American-ness was the case of several evangelical Brazilian girls whom I met in the time of my research. Some Brazilian girls preserved the "happiness" associated with immigrant gullibility by embracing an evangelical Christian identity; in this sense, these young women attributed a "true joy" to their evangelical conversion and engaged discussions about having found Jesus the Savior. See also Wilkins 2008, 110. Fake happiness, for these Brazilian youth, was distinguished from the genuine happiness they connected with their evangelical conversion. For these evangelical Brazilian girls, the happiness displayed by the youth invested in attaining a cosmopolitan competency was inauthentic and rooted in material consumption that explained their feelings of unhappiness and depression.

5. Relevant to this conception of emotional epistemology is Bourdieu's habitus (1977, 72), a system that generates ways of thinking and feeling about the world that are mediated through social experiences and structures. Dispositions toward other people and communities, which in turn influence behavior and action, are always implicated in shifts in meaning and interpretation and how individuals come to view themselves in relation to others (similar to Raymond Williams's "knowable communities"). These are grounded in the body, including discussions of taste (cf. Csordas 1990).

6. "Nondominant" or alternative forms of cultural capital—from "acting white" or "passing for white" to learning the "code of the streets" and appropriate bodily kinetics—have been at the center of analyses of minority educational success (Ogbu 1982, Carter 2005); second-generation black migrant assimilation processes (Waters 1999); and social transactions in socially mixed neighborhoods (Anderson 1990; Jackson 2001). Albeit with a number of caveats and from a variety of perspectives, scholars who have examined an "adversarial outlook" approach argue that immigrant youth compromise their social mobility by adopting the ideologies and behaviors of black Americans. When the US-born generation adopts the "adversarial outlook" that US racial minorities (such as blacks and Latinos) presumably hold toward dominant white society, the argument goes, these young peo-

ple end up experiencing downward mobility; conversely, when these migrants conformed to their parents' immigrant expectations and ethos, they
were able to do better than US-born racial minorities. Although it is not my
intention to engage in a thorough examination of the prolific literature on
"oppositional" or "adversarial" youth culture, I do want to highlight that,
for the most part, this literature has tended to undermine the experiences
of Latinos and Latin American migrants. Moreover, the literature fails to
consider how many racialized migrants may in fact *gain* mainstream forms
of capital by selectively shedding or modifying their "immigrant"-ness,
particularly in an era of heightened nativism, when being an "immigrant"
carries significant personal risk.

7.   In her ethnography of young white women and youth subcultures in
     western Massachusetts, Amy Wilkins (2008) identifies the caricature of
     the "Puerto Rican wannabe" to show how this label was applied to a
     particular kind of white girl who "rejects white middle-class cultural style,
     adopting an urban presentation of self associated with people of color.
     She wears hip-hop clothes and Puerto Rican hairstyles, drinks malt liquor,
     and smokes Newports. She adopts an attitude, acting tough and engaging
     in verbal and physical fights. And perhaps most important, she dates and
     has sex with Black and Puerto Rican men" (2008, 104). In the towns of
     Wilkins's study, "to be poor is to be Puerto Rican" (2008, 108) and Puerto
     Rican femininity was "simultaneously desired and degraded" and drew
     on historical association between women of color with exotic sexuality.
     In the case of Puerto Rican men, the concept of "homeboy" led some
     upwardly mobile Puerto Rican men, particularly those who were politi-
     cally motivated and had a strong social consciousness, toward downward
     mobility identity (cf. Wilkins 2008, 204). While Wilkins discusses why
     Puerto Ricannes is desired by these group of young white women in
     western Massachusetts, it is not clear what would motivate Latin American
     migrants—both men and women—to do this and in what ways could these
     motivations differ from those of whites (154). In Newark the Puerto Rican-
     ization of Latin American "immigrants" was both a source of pride—be-
     cause it indicated urban competency—and a source of anxiety when it
     suggested a closer proximity to "Blackness."

8.   David Harvey (2001) speaks to the contradiction between a racial backlash
     and a Western world that pretends to be cosmopolitan, multicultural, and
     raceless when he notes that the state produces geographical knowledge at
     different spatial scales as a way to fragment the multiple forms of geo-
     graphical knowledge held within the state apparatus. Through its influence
     over education, for instance, the state can actively produced national and
     local identities as means to secure its power (213).

9.   It is important to situate these perspectives on "urban"-ness or "non-
     immigrant-ness" in a discussion of dialogic performances; these performances

are sometimes source of knowledge of the Other being performed. As Fanon (1967) has argued, for instance, learning white language has historically served as a way for blacks to acquire more humanity, and de Certeau (1984) has also suggested that becoming white or "passing" implies less surveillance. Given that whiteness is implicitly viewed as prerequisite for full national membership, it is not surprising that the working-class Portuguese in Newark struggled for inclusion into the margins of the US nation-state, even when some of them were in fact undocumented.

10. I understand performativity as both discourse *and* materiality and focus on the classed and racialized spaces that constitute and are constituted by the embattled combination of performances and performativity. While performance can be viewed as the bodily experiences of embodied racial being and transhistorical subjects, performativity is seen as the historical situatedness, the fusion through discourse, words and consciousness, a sense of racial becoming. For a theoretical engagement with the concepts of performance and performativity, see Judith Butler (1993) and Marjorie Garber (1992), who analyze how acts of crossing over question the fixity and the oppositionality of the categories that confine people in certain roles.

11. As Obika Gray (2008) documents in the case of the Jamaican poor after 1980, a "ghetto fabulous" fashion associated with a different calculus of social evaluation increased the cultural confidence of the urban poor. Likewise, in reference to this ghetto fabulous fashion, John Jackson notes that "a sincerity comes through the faux and celebrates its own conspicuous alternative to middle of the road racial realities, embracing a sense of self that is irreducible to one's assumed [social] location, a way of traversing the socio-spatial margin that privileges personal and intimate privatization over market-based instrumentality." The concept of "ghetto fabulous," therefore, allowed an alternative template from which to examine the production patterns of wealth and the consumption of one's neighbors in ways that appeared consistent with racial difference, as it offered an entirely different calculus for social evaluation and "provided personal and intimate privatization over market-based instrumentality" (Jackson 2006, 59–60). In this sense, fashion-talk served as one of the media through which to communicate classed and raced self-reflexivity, cosmopolitanism, and urban competency.

12. The intriguing question of how knowledge about the United States is produced elsewhere became critical to the "cartography of racial democracy" that I was beginning to articulate around the question: How does a perception of what race or racism is like in the United States affect the racial logics of people who have been connected to a US migration stream, but have not themselves migrated or who have returned to their countries of origin (or to their parents' country of origin, in some cases)? These questions led me to conduct fieldwork in Brazil and Puerto Rico halfway into my Newark

fieldwork. This additional fieldwork allowed me to analyze how views of the US racial system shaped conceptions of race in Brazil and Puerto Rico, respectively. Although I had been to Brazil several times prior to living in Belo Horizonte the summers of 2003 and 2004, and albeit having studied Portuguese on and off, in the classroom and on my own since 1998, I had never been to Belo Horizonte or Minas Gerais. To my surprise, as someone who came late to the field of Brazilian studies and has always marveled by how prolific the English-language academic literature on "Brazil" is, most of the academic work I found centered on the states of Rio de Janeiro, São Paulo, and the northeast, particularly Bahia. A growing body of Brazil-produced literature on migration to the United States, as well as of literature on US-based Brazilian communities, has noted how most working-class Brazilian migrants hail from towns and cities throughout the state of Minas Gerais. Such was the case with most of the people whom I met in Newark, including the ESHS students through whom I got the contact information about the Escola Municipal Imago, the public school these students had attended prior to migrating to the United States and where I ended up conducting most of the focus groups and interviews in Belo Horizonte. I also conducted focus groups at a private school, Colegio Magno, in Belo Horizonte.

In the fall of 2004 I conducted similar interviews and focus groups at two schools in Puerto Rico. Although the interviews were thematically similar to those I had conducted in Belo Horizonte, my relationship to the schools in Puerto Rico represented a "homecoming" of sorts. I focused on the Escuela Superior Padre Rufo (ESPR) because I was interested in interviewing youth that had both experienced migration themselves and those who had not. I had lived across the street from the ESPR and my parents still lived in the same apartment building in Santurce. I had grown up in Santurce, still consider Spanish my native language, and was familiar with the area's history and demographic transformations in terms of gentrification, increased Dominican immigration, and "urban renewal" interests. I was, quite literally, "at home" in Santurce. I also conducted focus groups at the Colegio La Piedad, the Catholic school I had attended from kindergarten through twelfth grade. Perhaps not entirely surprising, the socioeconomic gap between the students at the public and private schools in Puerto Rico was much narrower, if at all, than the one I had noticed between public and private schools in Brazil. This could also be because, while Colegio Magno is considered among the top elite schools in Belo Horizonte, Colegio La Piedad was not a top-tier private school in Puerto Rico nor did it have the elite lineage of a handful of other private schools on the island. In fact, Colegio La Piedad was quite socioeconomically and ethnically diverse. Most of the data gathered from the fieldwork conducted in Brazil and Puerto Rico did not make it to this volume, but will be presented in a future work. In this volume, I only focus on sections of the fieldwork that add to the Newark discussion on perspectives on "Black America."

13. Ginetta Candelario (2007) notes this uneven development of Blackness in the case of Dominicans in Washington, DC, who identified with blacks more than Dominicans in New York did. Some reasons for this regional differences had to do with the fact that Blackness in DC (like in Newark) was not only associated with marginality, but also with success, given the class variation within DC's black community. Moreover, Dominicans in DC came from areas in the Dominican Republic where Blackness was associated with power because black populations in these areas were highly educated, British-accented West Indians or African Americans from Philadelphia who arrived with economic and social capital.

14. Although I was not able to confirm a gang affiliation from any specific Salvadoran group, there is a view of Salvadoran gang involvement originated from the "Salvatruchas" image in San Salvador and Los Angeles.

15. A dominant theme among Brazilians and Puerto Ricans in Newark was the view that their peers in Brazil and in Puerto Rico had a difficult time imagining "what Blacks [in the United States] were like" or what life in the United States was like when it came to issues of "immigration" for Brazilians or "race" for Puerto Ricans. This related to an extended, transnational point of reference that at times was imagined (in the case of many Puerto Rican youth who had never even visited their "ancestral homeland") and at times based on recollections from a previous life (in the case of those who had arrived to the United States as school-age children). I realized that we know very little about how "Black America" is indeed imagined abroad or how the figure of the "immigrant" is differently constructed in the "sending" or "home" countries.

16. Patricia de Santana Pinho (2005) argues that in the case of Brazil, a US-centric black experience has been viewed as the most modern form of Blackness within the African diaspora. United States Blackness is viewed as a modern and politicized racial identity in contradistinction to Brazil's Africanness which is viewed as "excess" of culture (just like Godreau argues in the case of Puerto Rico). The hegemonic project of the Afro-Brazilian movement is situated between an "African past" and a "US American future," thus introducing Pinho's main question: "Why are Afro-Brazilians urged to follow the US model of race politics that rely on a liberal multiculturalism in which the idea of diversity is inert?" Understood as such, the performance of race did away with the racialized subject and inadvertently displaced and fetishized race onto traits like hair, clothes, musical tastes, and consumption patterns; it was from these traits that many Latinos drew to create their racial presentations in Newark. In this sense, Latinos viewed African Americans not only (or even primarily) in light of a dominant criminality discourse, but in relation to psychiatric labels—for example, passive-aggressive, depressed, lacking self-esteem, being violent, harboring resentment from childhood experiences, and so on. The phenomenon of viewing "Black America" as a symbol of resistance by Afro-Latin Ameri-

cans and some Afro-Latinos has been examined by Mark Anderson (2005) in the case of the Honduran Garifunas. Especially among young men, black Americans' attitude toward racism is viewed as a stance of defiance on the part of racism's potential subjects, a stance that reverses the relation of power between purported aggressor and victim. As Livio Sansone (in Oboler 1995, 110) has argued: "For Black people outside the USA, an orientation towards the mythical 'superblacks' in the U.S. becomes a way to differentiate themselves from local white people while claiming black participation in 'modernity' and the rituals of mass consumption." This connection between US African American iconography and bodily kinetics, in relation to the inversion of a Latin American racial order, while rejecting political and personal alliances with African Americans, is central to my conception of urban competency.

17. Author's fieldnotes, August 10, 2004.

18. The role that "Brazil" and "Puerto Rico" have played in US academic research and popular interest influences how the migrants from these countries (and, in some instances, the subsequent US-born generations) are classified in Newark; as Jemima Pierre (2004) eloquently argues, the way in which immigrant countries are imagined supply the tools for the racialization of those migrants in the United States (cf. Bashi and McDaniel 1997). The role of "migration" was qualitatively different in Brazil and Puerto Rico. While Brazil still considers itself a "Country of Immigrants," rather than one that supplies any significant percentage of its population to the global migration flow, migration is ubiquitous in the political and economic history of Puerto Rico. Nearly as many Puerto Ricans live on the island of Puerto Rico as on the US mainland. In fact, in Puerto Rico, migration to the United States was central to the creation of a Puerto Rican middle class on the island in the 1940s and 1950s (and a continuing strategy for economic survival into the present).

19. A view of US Blackness as a stylistic or commercial culture provided yet another space for slippage between "real racism" and a racism perceived as more "malleable," a distinction that was coded in forms of humor, the glamorization of poverty-stricken urban spaces, the commodification of Blackness, and highlighting differences in nationality rather than race (especially in the case of how Dominicans were viewed in Puerto Rico).

20. Space is constructed in alignment with dominant racialization practices that, in turn, contribute to an emotional aesthetics of US urban contexts. An obvious example of this is the "ghetto" as a physical and symbolic space and "being ghetto" as an embodiment of such a space. Initially it was used to describe a place of poverty and pathology (e.g., many sociological studies of US urban poverty deployed this term). Then the term was applied to people who live in this places, and in the process of using the physical referent of the ghetto to describe a person residing in that physical space, the word *ghetto* became an adjective that is not only applied to "bad

areas" but also to "bad people." But there is a third or even fourth transformation of the term: The term can be taken completely out of context
and used by two people who have no relationship to the urban space of
the "ghetto" or are really always performative of "ghetto identity," to refer
to a bounded instance of "ghetto-like" behavior (e.g., as in "that was so
ghetto of you" used in an affluent context). Another dimension to this is
the ghetto as not negative, but actually a batch of authenticity, hip-ness,
belongingness, and so on. Likewise, the processes by which the characteristic of a built environment are transformed into behavior and used to create
bodies that possess those built environment characteristics deserve some
critical attention in contemporary understandings of "race," "illegality,"
and citizenship in the United States.

21. "Between Two Worlds: How Latino Youths Come of Age in America," a report from the Pew Hispanic Center,found that Latinos ages 16 to 25 (which
include all of the Latino youth in my Newark research) were satisfied with
their lives and optimistic about their futures. They valued education, hard
work, and career success, although they were more likely than other youths
to drop out of school, live in poverty, and become teen parents. While in
1995 half of Latino youths were "foreign-born," in 2009 only 34% were
(most of these youths—37%—are US born). Perceptions of discrimination
were more widespread among the US born (41%) than the foreign born
(32%). A large majority of Latino youth (76%) said that they did not see
themselves fitting into the race framework of the United States, and only
16% saw themselves as white.

References

Abu-Lughod, Lila. 1986. *Veiled Sentiments: Honor and Poetry in a Bedouin Society*. Chicago: University of Chicago Press.

Affigne, Tony, Manny Avalos, and M. Njeri Jackson. 1998. "Persistence and Transformation in the American Hemisphere's Racial Politics." Paper presented at annual meeting of the American Political Science Association, Boston, September 3–6, 1998.

Agamben, Giorgio. 1993. "The Sovereign Police," In *The Politics of Everyday Fear*, ed. Brian Massumi, 61–64. Minneapolis: University of Minnesota Press.

Ahmed, Sara. 2004. *The Cultural Politics of Emotions*. New York: Routledge.

Alcoff, Linda Martin. 1995. "Mestizo Identity." In *American Mixed Race: The Culture of Microdiversity*, ed. N. Zack, 257–78. Lanham, MD: Rowman and Littlefield.

Altman, Dennis. 2001. *Global Sex*. Chicago: University of Chicago Press.

Anderson, Elijah. 1990. *Streetwise: Race, Class, and Change in an Urban Community*. Chicago: University of Chicago Press.

———. 2000. *Code of the Street: Decency, Violence, and the Moral Life of the Inner City*. New York: W. W. Norton.

Anderson, Mark. 2005. "Bad Boys and Peaceful Garifuna: Transnational Encounters between Racial Stereotypes of Honduras and the United States (and Their Implications for the Study of Race in the Americas)." In *Neither Friends nor Enemies: Latinos, Blacks, and Afro-Latinos*, ed. Anani Dzidzienyo and Suzanne Oboler, 101–15. New York: Palgrave.

Antunen de Oliveira, Renan. 1999. "Brasileiras perdem espao entre strippers nos EUA." June 14, 1999. O Estado de São Paulo. Danarinas que fizeram a fama nos clubes noturnos estam sendo substituídas por loiras do Leste Europeu.

Anzaldúa, Gloria. 1987. *Borderlands: La Frontera, the New Mestiza*. San Francisco: Spinster/Aunt Lute.

Anzules, Emanuel. 2006. "Latino Homosexuality in the Brick City." Undergraduate monograph for Seminar in Latino and Hispanic Caribbean Studies: Latino Newark. Department of Latino and Hispanic Caribbean Studies, Rutgers University.

Appadurai, Arjun. 1996. *Modernity at Large: Cultural Dimensions of Globalization*. Minneapolis: University of Minnesota Press.

Athayde, Roberto. 1996. *Brasileiros em Manhattan*. Rio de Janeiro: Topbooks.

Bailey, F. G. 1983. *The Tactical Uses of Passion: An Essay on Power, Reason, and Reality*. Ithaca, NY: Cornell University Press.

Bailey, Stanley. 2004. "Group Dominance and the Myth of Racial Democracy: Antiracism Attitudes in Brazil." *American Sociological Review* 69 (5): 728–47.

Bakhtin, Mikhail. 1981. "Discourse in the Novel." In *The Dialogic Imagination: Four Essays*, ed. Michael Holquist, trans. Caryl Emerson and Michael Holquist, 259–422. University of Texas Press Slavic Studies 1. Austin: University of Texas Press. Originally published in Russian in 1975.

Baptiste, Lori. 2008. "Stirring the Melting Pot: Food, Identity, and the Performance of Inclusion in Newark's Ironbound Community." PhD, Northwestern University.

Barrett, James, and David Roediger. 1997. "Inbetween Peoples: Race, Nationality and the New Immigrant Working Class." *Journal of American Ethnic History* 16 (2): 3–44.

Barry, Andrew, Thomas Osborne, and Nikolas S. Rose. 1996. *Foucault and Political Reason: Liberalism, Neo-liberalism, and Rationalities of Government*. London: UCL Press.

Bartlett, Lesley, and Catherine Lutz. 1998. "Disciplining Social Difference: Some Cultural Politics of Military Training in Public High Schools." *Urban Review* 30 (2): 119–36.

Bashi, Vilna, and Antonio McDaniel. 1997. "A Theory of Immigration and Racial Classification." *Journal of Black Studies* 27 (5): 668–82.

Bates, Aryana F. 2001. "Religious Despite Religion: Lesbian Agency, Identity, and Spirituality at Liberation in Truth, Unity Fellowship Church, Newark, NJ." PhD diss., Rutgers University.

Behdad, Ali. 1997. "Nationalism and Immigration to the United States." *Diaspora* 6 (2): 155–79.

Berlant, Lauren Gail. 1997. *The Queen of America Goes to Washington City: Essays on Sex and Citizenship*. Series Q. Durham, NC: Duke University Press.

Bernstein, Elizabeth. 2007. *Temporarily Yours: Intimacy, Authenticity, and the Commerce of Sex*. Chicago: University of Chicago Press.

Beserra, Bernadette. 2003. *Brazilian Immigrants in the United States: Cultural Imperialism and Social Class*. New York: LFB Scholarly Publishing.

———. 2006. "In the Shadow of Carmen Miranda and the Carnival: Brazilian

Immigrant Women in Los Angeles." LASA XXVI International Congress, San Juan, Puerto Rico, March 15–18.

Besnier, Niko. 1990. "Language and Affect." *Annual Review of Anthropology* 19: 419–51.

Bettie, Julie. 2003. *Women without Class: Girls, Race, and Identity*. Berkeley: University of California Press.

Bettinger, Matthew. 2002. "Not Quite New York, but Newark on Rise." *The Justice* (Brandeis University). http://media.www.thejustice.org/media/storage/paper573/news/2003/03/25/Forum/Drunk.On.Hysteria.Not.Quite.New.York.But.Newark.On.Rise-398742 (accessed June 9, 2011).

Black, Peter W. 1985. "Ghosts, Gossip, and Suicide: Meaning and Action in Tobian Folk Psychology." In *Person, Self, and Experience: Exploring Pacific Ethnopsychologies*, ed. Geoffrey M. White and John Kirkpatrick, 245–75. Berkeley: University of California Press.

Bloch, Maurice. 1992. "What Goes without Saying." In *Conceptualizing Society*, ed. Adam Kuper, 127–39. London: Routledge.

Boltanski, Luc, and Eve Chiapello. 1999. *Le noubel esprit du capitalism*. Paris: Gallimard.

Bonilla-Silva, Eduardo. 1997. "Rethinking Racism: Toward a Structural Interpretation." *American Sociological Review* 62 (3): 465–80.

———. 2004. "From Bi-racial to Tri-racial: Towards a New System of Racial Stratification in the USA." *Ethnic and Racial Studies* 27 (6): 931–59.

Bosniak, Linda. 2003. "Citizenship." In *Oxford Handbook of Legal Studies*, ed. Peter Cane and Mark Tushnet, 56–59. New York: Oxford University Press.

Botelho, Paula. 2004. "In the Service of the Community: The Roles of the Brazilian American Church in Reconstructing Identity." National Association of African-American Studies and Affiliates (NAAAS) Monograph Series 2 (7): 234–59.

———. 2006. "The Construction of Brazilian and American Identities by American Art Reviewers and Newspapers." Paper presented at the Latin American Studies Association, San Juan, Puerto Rico, March 12–16.

Bourdieu, Pierre. 1977. *Outline of a Theory of Practice*. Cambridge Studies in Social Anthropology 16. New York: Cambridge University Press.

———. 1984. *Distinction: A Social Critique of the Judgement of Taste*. London: Routledge.

———. 1990. *The Logic of Practice*. Palo Alto, CA: Stanford University Press.

Bourdieu, Pierre, and Loic Wacquant. 1999. "On the Cunning of Imperialist Reason." *Theory, Culture and Society* 16 (1): 41–58.

Boyd, Todd. 1997. *Am I Black Enough for You? Popular Culture from the 'Hood and Beyond*. Bloomington: Indiana University Press.

Boyer, M. C. 1996. *The City of Collective Memory: Its Historical Imagery and Architectural Entertainments*. Boston: MIT Press.

Braithwaite, John. 1989. *Crime, Shame, and Reintegration*. Cambridge: Cambridge University Press.

Brandom, Robert. 1994. "Reasoning and Representing." In *Philosophy in Mind: The Place of Philosophy in the Study of Mind,* ed. M. Michael and John O'Leary-Hawthorne, 159–78. Norwell, MA: Kluwer Academic Publishers.

Briggs, Charles L. 1988. *Competence in Performance: The Creative Tradition of Mexican Verbal Art.* Philadelphia: University of Pennsylvania Press.

Bueno, Eduardo. 2003. *Brasil: Uma história.* São Paulo: Ática Publishers.

Burchell, Graham. 1996. "Liberal Government and Techniques of the Self." In *Foucault and Political Reason: Liberalism, Neoliberalism and Rationalities of Government,* ed. Andrew Barry, Thomas Osborne, and Nikolas Rose, 19–36. Chicago: University of Chicago Press.

Burnett, Christina Duffy, and Burke Marshall. 2001. *Foreign in a Domestic Sense: Puerto Rico, American Expansion, and the Constitution.* American Encounters/Global Interactions. Durham, NC: Duke University Press.

Burr, J, and T. Chapman. 2004. "Contextualising Experiences of Depression in Women from South Asian Communities: A Discursive Approach." *Sociology of Health and Illness* 26:433–52.

Butler, Judith. 1993. *Bodies That Matter: On the Discursive Limits of Sex.* New York: Routledge.

Cacho, Lisa Marie. 2007. "'You Just Don't Know How Much He Meant': Deviancy, Death, and Devaluation." *Latino Studies* 5:182–208.

Caldeira, Teresa Pires do Rio. 2000a. *City of Walls: Crime, Segregation, and Citizenship in São Paulo.* Berkeley: University of California Press.

———. 2000b. "Fortified Enclaves: The New Urban Segregation." In *Theorizing the City,* ed. Setha Low, 83–107. New Brunswick, NJ: Rutgers University Press.

Calderón, José. 1992. "'Hispanic' and 'Latino': The Viability of Categories for Panethnic Unity." *Latin American Perspectives* 19 (4): 37–44.

Candelario, Ginetta. 2007. *Black Behind the Ears: Dominican Racial Identity from Museums to Beauty Shops.* Durham, NC: Duke University Press.

Carbado, Devon W. 2005. "Racial Naturalization." *American Quarterly* 57 (3): 633–58.

Carter, Prudence L. 2005. *Keepin' It Real: School Success Beyond Black and White.* Transgressing Boundaries: Studies in Black Politics and Black Communities. New York: Oxford University Press.

Cavell, Marcia. 1988. "Solipsism and Community: Two Concepts of Mind in Philosophy and Psychoanalysis." *Psychoanalysis and Contemporary Thought* 11:587–613.

———. 2006. *Becoming a Subject: Reflections in Philosophy and Psychoanalysis.* London: Oxford University Press.

Chase, Sabrina Marie. 2005. "Mujeres ingeniosas [Resourceful women]: HIV+ Puerto Rican Women and the Urban Health Care System." PhD diss., Rutgers University.

Chomsky, Noam. 1999. *Profit over People: Neoliberalism and Global Order.* New York: Seven Stories Press.

City of Newark. 1959. *Newark: A City in Transition.* 3 vols. Prepared for the City of Newark, New Jersey, and the Mayor's Commission on Group Relations. [Newark, NJ]: Market Planning Corporation.

Cohen, Cathy. 2004. "Deviance as Resistance: A New Research Agenda for the Study of Black Politics." *Du Bois Review* 1 (1): 27–45.

Cohen, Phil. 1999. "In Visible Cities: Urban Regeneration and Place-building in the Era of Multicultural Capitalism." *Communal/Plural* 7 (1): 9–11.

Cole, David. 1987. "Artists and Urban Redevelopment." *Geographical Review* 77 (4): 391–407.

Collins, Randall. 2004. *Interaction Ritual Chains.* Princeton, NJ: Princeton University Press.

Comaroff, Jean, and John L. Comaroff. 2000. "Millennial Capitalism: First Thoughts on a Second Coming." *Public Culture* 12 (2): 291–343.

Comissão Parlamentar Mista de Inquérito. 2006. Brasil, celeiro de vítimas: O tráfico internacional de pessoas para fins de prostituição. República Federativa do Brasil. Congreso Nacional. Comissão Parlamentar Mista de Inquérito da Emigração. Relatório Final da Comissão Parlamentar Mista de Inquérito. Braslia.

Costa Vargas, João. 2004. "Hyperconsciousness of Race and Its Negation: The Dialectic of White Supremacy in Brazil." *Identities* 11 (4): 443–28.

Crapanzano, Vincent. 2004. *Imaginative Horizon: An Essay in Literary-Philosophical Anthropology.* Chicago: University of Chicago Press.

Cristoffanini, Pablo R. 2003. "The Representation of the Others as Strategies of Symbolic Construction." In *Intercultural Alternatives: Critical Perspectives on Intercultural Encounters in Theory and Practice*, ed. Maribel Blasco and Jan Gustafsson, 79–102. Denmark: Copenhagen Business School Press.

Crump, Jeff. 2003. "Deconcentration by Demolition: Public Housing, Poverty, and Urban Policy." *Environment and Planning D: Society and Space* 20:581–96.

Csordas, Thomas. 1983. "The Rhetoric of Transformation in Ritual Healing." *Culture, Medicine, and Psychiatry* 7:333–75.

———. 1990. "Embodiment as a Paradigm for Anthropology." *Ethos* 18:5–47.

Cvetkovich, Ann. 2003. *An Archive of Feelings: Trauma, Sexuality, and Lesbian Public Cultures.* Durham, NC: Duke University Press.

Damasio, Antonio. 1996. "The Somatic Marker Hypothesis and the Possible Functions of the Prefrontal Cortex." *Philosophical Transactions: Biological Sciences* 351 (1346): 1413–20.

de Certeau, Michel. 1984. *The practice of everyday life.* Berkeley: University of California Press.

De Genova, Nicholas. 2008. *Working the Boundaries: Race, Space, and "Illegality" in Mexican Chicago.* Durham, NC: Duke University Press.

De Genova, Nicholas, and Ana Y. Ramos-Zayas. 2003. *Latino Crossings: Mexicans, Puerto Ricans, and the Politics of Race and Citizenship.* New York: Routledge.

de la Fuente, Alejandro. 1999. "Myths of Racial Democracy: Cuba, 1900–1912." *Latin American Research Review* 34 (3): 39–73.

de Santana Pinho, Patricia. 2005. "Descentrando os Estados Unidos nos estudos sobre negritude no Brasil." *Revista Brasileira de Ciências Sociais* 20 (59): 37–50.

de Sousa, Ronald. 1990. *The Rationality of Emotion.* Cambridge, MA: MIT Press.

Decena, Carlos. 2008. "Tacit Subjects." *Gay and Lesbian Quarterly* 14 (2–3): 339–59

Degler, Carl N. 1986. *Neither Black nor White: Slavery and Race Relations in Brazil and the United States.* Madison: University of Wisconsin Press.

Delany, Samuel. 2001. *Times Square Red, Times Square Blue.* New York: New York University Press.

Derrida, Jacques. 1998. *Of Grammatology.* Corrected edition, trans. Gayatri Chakravorty Spivak. Baltimore: Johns Hopkins University Press.

Diamond, Elin, 1996. "Introduction." In *Performance and Cultural Politics,* ed. Elin Diamond, 1–12. London: Routledge.

Diawara, Manthia. 1998. *In Search of Africa.* Cambridge: Harvard University Press.

di Leonardo, Micaela. 1984. *The Varieties of Ethnic Experiences: Kinship, Class, and Gender among California Italian-Americans.* Ithaca, NY: Cornell University Press.

———. 1998. *Exotics at Home: Anthropologies, Others, American Modernity.* Women in Culture and Society. Chicago: University of Chicago Press.

Dines, Deborah. 1989. "Go-Gos: Os (As) Brasileiros (as) Entram na Dana do Dlor." *Ele Ela* 21:88–92.

———. 1991a. "Lana, Go-go em Newark, Queria Falar Ingles." *Folha de São Paulo,* June 10, D3.

———. 1991b. "Mineiros e Portugueses Disputan a Baixada Fluminense dos EUA." *Folha de São Paulo,* June 10, D1.

Dinzey-Flores, Zaire. 2006. "Technicians of Space: Dominicans and the Construction of Puerto Rico." Paper for LASA Congress, San Juan, March 15–18.

Domínguez, Virginia. 1973. "Spanish-Speaking Caribbean in New York: The Middle Race." *Revista/Review Interamericana* 3 (2): 135–42.

Dreyfus, Hubert. 1991. *Being-in-the-World: A Commentary on Heidegger's* Being and Time. Cambridge, MA: MIT Press.

Duany, Jorge. 1998. "Reconstructing Racial Identity: Ethnicity, Color and Class among Dominicans in the United States and Puerto Rico." *Latin American Perspectives* 25 (3): 147–63.

Duggan, Lisa. 2003. *The Twilight of Equality: Neoliberalism, Cultural Politics, and the Attack on Democracy.* Boston: Beacon Press.

DuLong, Jessica. 2003. "Young and in Danger in New Jersey." *The Advocate* 892:26.

Dumenigo, Argelio R. 2002. "Newark: From Riots to Respectability." *Princeton Alumni Weekly* 2 (13): 21–29.

Duneier, Mitchell, and Harvey Molotch. 1999. "Talking City Trouble: Interactional Vandalism, Social Inequality, and the 'Urban Interaction Problem.'" *American Journal of Sociology* 104 (5): 1263–1524.

Durrenberger, Paul, and Dimitra Doukas. 2008. "Gospel of Wealth, Gospel of Work: Counterhegemony in the U.S. Working Class." *American Anthropologist* 110 (2): 214–24.

Dzidzienyo, Anani, and Suzanne Oboler, eds. 2005. *Neither Enemies nor Friends: Latinos, Blacks, and Afro-Latinos.* New York: Palgrave MacMillan.

Ebenbach, David, and Dasher Keltner. 1998. "Power, Emotion, and Judgmental Accuracy in Social Conflict: Motivating the Cognitive Miser." *Basic and Applied Social Psychology* 20 (1): 7–21.

El-Ghobashy, Tamer. 2003. "Jersey Teen Killed in Gay Bias Attack." *New York Daily News,* May 13. http://www.nydailynews.com/front/v-pfriendly/story/83225p-76120c.html.

Elias, Norbert. 1982. *The History of Manners.* New York: Pantheon Books.

Elliot, Norbert, Frances Quinless, and Elizabeth Parietti. 2000. "Assessment of a Newark Neighborhood: Process and Outcomes." *Journal of Community Health Nursing* 17 (4): 211–24.

Engle, David. 1984. "The Oven's Bird Song: Insiders, Outsiders, and Personal Injuries in an American Community." *Law and Society Review* 18 (4): 551–82.

Escobar, Arturo. 1995. *Encountering Development: The Making and Unmaking of the Third World.* Princeton Studies in Culture/Power/History. Princeton, NJ: Princeton University Press.

Fainstein, Norman. 1994. "Urban Regimes and Racial Conflict." In *Managing Racial Conflict,* ed. Seamus Dunn, 141–59. London: Keele University Press and the Fulbright Commission.

Fajans, Jane. 1985. "The Person in Social Context: The Social Character of Baining 'Psychology.'" In *Person, Self, and Experience: Exploring Pacific Ethnopsychologies,* ed. Geoffrey M. White and John Kirkpatrick, 367–30. Berkeley: University of California Press.

Fanon, Franz. 1967. *Black Skin, White Masks.* New York: Grove Weidenfeld Press.

Farr, Marcia. 1994. "Echando relajo: Verbal Art and Gender among Mexicanas in Chicago." In *Cultural Performances: Proceedings of the Third Women and Language Conference,* 168–86. Berkeley: University of California Press.

———, ed. 2004. *Ethnolinguistic Chicago: Language and Literacy in the City's Neighborhoods.* Hillsdale, NJ: Erlbaum.

Feldman-Bianco, Bela. 1992. "Multiple Layers of Time and Space: The Construction of Class, Ethnicity and Nationalism among Portuguese Immigrants." In *Towards a Transnational Perspective on Migration: Race, Class, Ethnicity, and Nationalism Reconsidered,* ed. Nina Glick-Schiller, Linda Basch, and Cristina Blanc-Szanton, 145–74. New York: New York Academy of Sciences.

———. 2001. "Brazilians in Portugal, Portuguese in Brazil: Constructions of Sameness and Difference." *Identities* 8 (4): 607–50.

Fenster, Mark. 1999. *Conspiracy Theories: Secrecy and Power in American Culture.* Minneapolis: University of Minnesota Press.

Fenstermaker, Sarah, and Candace West. 2002. *Doing Gender, Doing Difference: Inequality, Power, and Institutional Change.* New York: Routledge.

Fentress, James, and Chris Wickham. 2009. *Social Memory: New Perspectives on the Past.* ACLS Humanities E-Book.

Ferguson, James, and Akhil Gupta. 2002. "Spatializing States: Toward an Ethnography of Neoliberal Governmentality." *American Ethnologist* 29 (4): 981–1002.

Ferguson, Roderick. 2004. *Aberrations in Black: Towards a Queer of Color Critique*. Minneapolis: University of Minnesota Press.

Fernandes, Florestan. 1965. *No liminar de uma nova era. A integracao do negro na sociedade de classes*. São Paulo: Dominus Editora.

Fernández, Carlos A. 1992. "La raza and the Melting Pot." In *Racially Mixed People in America*, ed. Maria P. P. Root, 126–43. Newbury Park, CA: Sage Publications.

Ferreira da Silva, Denise. 1998. "Facts of Blackness: Brazil Is Not Quite the United States . . . and Racial Politics in Brazil?" *Social Identities: Journal for the Study of Race, Nation and Culture* 4 (2): 201–34.

Fleischer, Soraya Resende. 2002. *Passando a América a Limpo: O Trabalho de House-cleaners Brasileiras em Boston, Massachusetts*. São Paulo: Annablume Editora.

Forde, Darryl. 1997. *African Worlds: Studies in the Cosmological Ideas and Social Values of African Peoples*. London: James Currey Publishers.

Forman, Murray. 2002. *The Hood Comes First: Race, Space, and Place in Rap and Hip-hop*. Chicago: Wesleyan University Press.

Foucault, Michel. 1972. *The Archaeology of Knowledge*. New York: Tavistock Publications.

———. 1977. *Discipline and Punish: The Birth of the Prison*. Trans. Allan Sheridan. New York: Vintage.

———. 1984. "Space, Knowledge, and Power." In *The Foucault Reader*, ed. Paul Rabinow, 239–56. New York: Penguin Books.

Foucault, Michel, and Robert Hurley. 1990. *The History of Sexuality*, vol. 1, *An Introduction*. New York: Vintage Books.

Freyre, Gilberto. 1956. *The Masters and the Slaves (Casa-grande e Senzala): A Study in the Development of Brazilian Civilization*. 2nd English language ed., rev. ed. New York: Knopf.

Fry, Peter. 1995. "Why Brazil Is Different—*Orpheus and Power: The* Movimento Negro *of Rio de Janeiro and São Paulo, Brazil, 1945–1988* by Michael George Hanchard / *Slave Rebellion in Brazil* by Joao Jose Reis and translated by Arthur Brakel." *Times Literary Supplement* 4836:6.

Fuery, Patrick. 1995. *Theories of Desire*. Carlton: Melbourne University Press.

Game, Ann. 1997. "Sociology's Emotions." *Canadian Review of Sociology* 34 (4): 385–99.

Gans, Herbert. 1999. "The Possibility of a New Racial Hierarchy in the Twenty-First-Century United States." In *The Cultural Territories of Race: Black and White Boundaries*, ed. Michele Lamont, 371–419. Chicago: University of Chicago Press.

Garber, Marjorie. 1992. *Vested Interests: Cross-Dressing and Cultural Anxiety*. New York: Routledge.

García-Canclini, Néstor. 1995. *Hybrid Cultures: Strategies for Entering and Leaving Modernity*. Minneapolis: University of Minnesota Press.

Garner, Steve. 2006. "The Uses of Whiteness: What Sociologists Working on Europe Can Draw from US Research on Whiteness." *Sociology* 40 (2): 257–75.

Geertz, Clifford. 1973. *The Interpretation of Cultures*. New York: Basic Books.

Giddens, Anthony. 1992. *Modernity and Self-Identity*. Palo Alto, CA: Stanford University Press.

Gilmore, David. 1987. *Aggression and Community: Paradoxes in Andalusian Culture*. New Haven: Yale University Press.

Godreau, Isar. 2002. "Changing Space, Making Race: Distance, Nostalgia, and the Folklorization of Blackness in Puerto Rico." *Identities* 9 (3): 281–323.

———. 2008. "Slippery Semantics: Race Talk and Everyday Uses of Racial Terminology in Puerto Rico." *Centro Journal* 20 (2): 5–33.

Goffman, Erving. 1959. *The Presentation of Self in Everyday Life*. Edinburgh: University of Edinburgh Social Sciences Research Centre.

Goldstein, Donna. 1999. "'Interracial' Sex and Racial Democracy in Brazil: Twin Concepts." *American Anthropologist* 101 (3): 563–78.

Gomes da Cunha, Olivia. 1998. "Black Movements and the Politics of Identity in Brazil." In *Cultures of Politics, Politics of Cultures: Re-visioning Latin American Social Movements*, ed. Sonia E Alvarez, Evelina Dagnino, and Arturo Escobar, 220–51. Boulder, CO: Westview Press.

Gordon, Avery. 2008. *Ghostly Matters: Haunting and the Sociological Imagination*. Minneapolis: University of Minnesota Press.

Gramsci, Antonio, Quintin Hoare, and Geoffrey Nowell-Smith. 1999. *Selections from the Prison Notebooks of Antonio Gramsci*. New York: International Publishers.

Gray, Obika. 2008. *Demeaned but Empowered: The Social Power of the Urban Poor in Jamaica*. Kingston:University of the West Indies Press.

Grosfoguel, Ramón. 2003. *Colonial Subjects: Puerto Ricans in a Global Perspective*. Berkeley: University of California Press.

Guglielmo, Thomas. 2003. *White on Arrival: Italians, Race, Color, and Power in Chicago, 1890–1945*. New York: Oxford University Press.

Gutiérrez, Ramón. 2001. "What's Love Got to Do with It?" *Journal of American History* 88 (3): 866–93.

Hagedorn, John. 1998. *People and Folks: Gangs, Crime and the Underclass in a Rustbelt City*. 2nd ed. Chicago. Lakeview Press.

Hale, Charles. 2002. "Does Multiculturalism Menace Governance, Cultural Rights and the Politics of Identity in Guatemala?" *Journal of Latin American Studies* 34:485–524.

———. 2005. "Neoliberal Multiculturalism: The Remaking of Cultural Rights and Racial Dominance in Central America." *PoLAR: Political and Legal Anthropology Review* 28 (1): 10–19.

Halle, David. 1984. *America's Working Man*. Chicago: University of Chicago Press.

Halter, Marilyn. 1993. *Between Race and Ethnicity: Cape Verdean American History, 1860–1965*. Urbana: University of Illinois Press.

Hanchard, Michael. 1994. *Orpheus and power: The Movimento Negro of Rio de*

Janeiro and São Paulo, Brazil, 1945–1988. Princeton, NJ: Princeton University Press.

———, ed. 1999. *Racial Politics in Contemporary Brazil*. Durham, NC: Duke University Press.

Haney López, Ian. 1996. *White by Law: The Legal Construction of Race*. New York: New York University Press.

Harris, Marvin. 1970. "Referential Ambiguity in the Calculus of Brazilian Racial Identity."
Southwestern Journal of Anthropology 26 (1): 1–14.

Harris-Lacewell, Melissa. 2006. *Barbershops, Bibles, and BET: Everyday Talk and Political Thought*. Princeton, NJ: Princeton University Press.

Hartigan, John. 1999. *Racial Situations*. Princeton, NJ: Princeton University Press.

Harvey, David. 2001. *Spaces of Capital: Towards a Critical Geography*. New York: Routledge.

Haskell, Thomas. 1985. "Capitalism and the Origins of the Humanitarian Sensibility." *American Historical Review* 90 (3): 339–61, 547–66.

Haugeland, J. 1999. *Having Thought: Essays in the Metaphysics of Mind*. Cambridge: Harvard University Press.

Hayden, Tom. 1967. *Rebellion in Newark*. New York: Vintage Books.

Helmreich, William B. 1999. *The Enduring Community: The Jews of Newark and Metrowest*. New Brunswick, NJ: Transaction Publishers.

Hennessy, Rosemary. 2000. *Profit and Pleasure: Sexual Identities in Late Capitalism*. New York: Routledge.

Herzfeld, Michael. 1997. *Cultural Intimacy: Social Poetics in the Nation-State*. New York: Routledge.

Hidalgo, Hilda. 1970. *The Puerto Ricans in Newark, NJ (Aqui se habla Espanol)*. Newark, NJ: Published by author.

Hill Collins, Patricia. 2000. *Black Feminist Thought: Knowledge, Consciousness, and the Politics of Empowerment*. New York: Routledge.

Hirschman, Albert. 1998. *Crossing Boundaries: Selected Writings*. New York: Zone Books.

Hofstader, Richard. 1955. *The Age of Reform*. New York: Knopf.

Hochchild, Jennifer. 2007. "Pluralism and Intergroup Relations." In *The New Americans: A Guide to Immigration since 1965*, ed. Mary C. Waters, Reed Ueda and Helen B. Marrow, 164–211. Cambridge: Harvard University Press.

Hochschild, Arlie R. 1983. *The Managed Heart: Commercialization of Human Feeling*. Berkeley: University of California Press.

———. 1990. "Ideology and Emotion Management: A Perspective and Path for Future Research." In *Research Agendas in the Sociology of Emotion*, ed. Theodore D. Kemper, 117–42. Albany, NY: SUNY Press.

Holloway, Karla. 2003. *Passed On: African American Mourning Stories*. Durham, NC: Duke University Press.

Holton, Kim, and Andrea Klimt, eds. 2009. *Community, Culture, and the Making of Identity: Portuguese-Americans along the Eastern Seaboard*. North Dartmouth, MA: Center for Portuguese Studies and Culture, University of Massachusetts–Dartmouth.

Honig, Bonnie. 2001. *Democracy and the Foreigner*. Princeton, NJ: Princeton University Press.

Husserl, Edmund. 1970. *Crisis of European Sciences and Transcendental Phenomenology*. Evanston, IL: Northwestern University Press.

Illouz, Eva. 2003. *Oprah Winfrey and the Glamour of Misery*. New York: Columbia

———. 2007. *Cold Intimacies: The Making of Emotional Capitalism*. Malden, MA: Polity Press.

———. 2008. *Saving the Modern Soul: Therapy, Emotions, and the Culture of Self-Help*. Berkeley: University of California Press.

Ingraham, C. 1996. "The Heterosexual Imaginary: Feminist Sociology and Theories of Gender." In *Queer Theory/Sociology*, ed. S. Seidman, 168–93. New York: Blackwell.

Irvine, Judith. 1982. "Language and Affect: Some Cross-Cultural Issues." In *Contemporary Perceptions of Language: Interdisciplinary Dimensions*, ed. H. Byrnes, 30–46. Washington, DC: Georgetown University Press.

Ito, Karen L. 1985. "Affective Bonds: Hawaiian Interrelationships of Self." In *Person, Self, and Experience: Exploring Pacific Ethnopsychologies*, ed. Geoffrey M. White and John Kirkpatrick, 301–26. Berkeley: University of California Press.

Izard, Carroll E. 1992. "Basic Emotions, Relations among Emotions, and Emotion-Cognition Relations." *Psychological Review* 99 (3): 561–65.

Jackson, John. 2001. *Harlemworld: Doing Race and Class in Contemporary Black America*. Chicago: University of Chicago Press.

———. 2006. *Real Black: Adventures in Racial Authenticity*. Chicago: University of Chicago Press.

Jackson, K. T., and B. B. Jackson. 1972. "The Black Experience in Newark: The Growth of the Ghetto, 1870–1970." In *New Jersey since 1860: New Findings and Interpretations*, ed. W. C. Wright, xxx. Trenton: New Jersey Historical Commission.

Jameson, Fredrick. 1991. *Postmodernism, or, the Cultural Logic of Late Capitalism*. Durham, NC: Duke University Press

Jenkins, Janis. 1991. "The State Construction of Affect: Political Ethos and Mental Health among Salvadoran Refugees. "*Culture, Medicine and Psychiatry* 15:139–65.

Johnson, Dominique. 2007. "Taking Over the School: Student Gangs as a Strategy for Dealing with Homophobic Bullying in an Urban Public School District." Available online at http://jglss.haworthpress.com.

Johnson, Patrick. 2003. *Appropriating Blackness: Performance and the Politics of Authenticity*. Durham, NC: Duke University Press.

Jones, Isham. 1955. *The Puerto Rican in New Jersey: His Present Status*. Newark, NJ: State Department of Education monograph, July.

Jones, Nikki. 2008." Working 'the Code': On Girls, Gender, and Inner-City Violence." *Australian and New Zealand Journal of Criminology* 41 (1): 63–83.

Joseph, G. M., and Daniel Nugent. 1994. *Everyday Forms of State Formation: Revolution and the Negotiation of Rule in Modern Mexico*. Durham, NC: Duke University Press.

Jouet-Pastré, Clémence, and Letícia Braga. 2009. "Community-Based Learning: A Window into the Portuguese Speaking Communities of New England." *Hispania* 88 (4): 863–72.

Just, Peter. 1991. "Going Through the Emotions: Passion, Violence, and 'Other-Control' among the Dou Donggo." *Ethos* 19 (3): 288–312.

Kang, Miliann. 2003. "The Managed Hand: The Commercialization of Bodies and Emotions in Korean Immigrant-Owned Nail Salons." *Gender and Society* 17:820–39.

Kaplan, Harold. 1963. *Urban Renewal Politics: Slum Clearance in Newark*. New York: Columbia University Press

Katz, Jack. 2001. *How Emotions Work*. Chicago: University of Chicago Press.

Keeler, Ward. 1983. "Shame and Stage Fright in Java." *Ethos* 11 (3): 152–65.

Keltner, D., P. C. Ellsworth, and K. Edwards. 1993. "Beyond Simple Pessimism: Effects of Sadness and Anger on Social Perception." *Journal of Personality and Social Psychology* 64 (5): 740–52.

Kirmayer, Laurence 1992. "The Body's Insistence on Meaning: Metaphor as Presentation and Representation in Illness Experience." *Medical Anthropology Quarterly* 6 (4): 326–46.

Kisinitz, Philip, Mary Waters, John Mollenkopf, et al. 2009. *Inheriting the City: The Children of Immigrants Come of Age*. New York: Russell Sage Foundation.

Kleinman, Arthur, Veena Das, and Margaret Lock, eds. 1997. *Social Suffering*. Berkeley: University of California Press.

Kobayashi, Audrey, and Linda Peake. 2000. "Racism Out of Place: Thoughts on Whiteness and an Antiracist Geography in the New Millennium." *Annals of the Association of American Geographers* 90 (2): 392–403.

Kochman, Thomas. 1983. "The Boundary between Play and Nonplay in Black Verbal Dueling." *Language in Society* 12 (3): 329–37.

Kotchemidova, Christina. 2005. "From Good Cheer to 'Drive-By' Smiling: A Social History of Cheerfulness." *Journal of Social History* 39 (1): 5–37.

Lasch Quinn, Elisabeth. 2001. *Race Experts: How Racial Etiquette, Sensitivity Training, and New Age Therapy Hijacked the Civil Rights Revolution*. New York: W. W. Norton.

Laumann, Edward O. 2004. *The Sexual Organization of the City*. Chicago: University of Chicago Press.

Lawler, Edward. 2001. "An Affect Theory of Social Exchange." *American Journal of Sociology* 107 (2): 321–52.

Le Espiritu, Yen. 2003. *Home Bound: Filipino American Lives Across Cultures, Communities, and Countries*. Berkeley: University of California Press

Leavitt, John. 1996. "Meaning and Feeling in the Anthropology of Emotions." *American Ethnologist* 23 (3): 514–39.

Lee, Jennifer. 2002. *Civility in the City: Black, Jews, and Koreans in Urban America*. Cambridge: Harvard University Press.

Lefebvre, Henri. 1991. *The Production of Space*. Oxford: Basil Blackwell.

Lewis, Oscar. 1966. *The Culture of Poverty*. New York: Scientific America.

Lewis Mumford Center. 2002. "Hispanic Populations and Their Residential Patterns in the Metropolis." University at Albany, State University of New York.

Limón, José. 1982. "History, Chicano Joking, and the Varieties of Higher Education: Tradition and Performances as Critical Symbolic Action." *Journal of the Folklore Institute* 19:141–66.

Lipsitz, George. 1998. *The Possessive Investment in Whiteness: How White People Profit from Identity Politics*. Philadelphia: Temple University Press.

Livingstone, David. 1993. *The Geographical Tradition: Episodes in the History of a Contested Enterprise*. Malden, MA: Blackwell.

Loewen, James W. 1988. *The Mississippi Chinese: Between Black and White*. 2nd ed. Prospect Heights, IL: Waveland Press.

Low, Setha. 1996. "The Anthropology of Cities: Imagining and Theorizing the City." *Annual Review of Anthropology* 25:383–409.

Lutz, Catherine. 1988. *Unnatural Emotions: Everyday Sentiments in a Micronesian Atoll and Their Challenge to Western Theory*. Chicago: University of Chicago Press.

Lutz, Catherine, and Geoffrey White. 1986. "The Anthropology of Emotions." *Annual Review of Anthropology* 15:405–36.

Lyon, Margot L. 1995. "Missing Emotion: The Limitations of Cultural Constructionism in the Study of Emotion." *Cultural Anthropology* 10 (2): 244–63.

Machado, José de Renó. 2003. "Cárcere Público: Processos de exotização entre imigrantes brasileiros no Porto, Portugal." Dissertation. São Paulo, Brasil: Biblioteca Digital de Teses e Dissertações, UNICAMP.

Mahler, Sarah. 1995. *American Dreaming: Immigrant Life on the Margins*. Princeton, NJ: Princeton University Press.

Malanga, Steven. 2008. "The Rainbow Coalition Evaporates: Black Anger Grows as Illegal Immigrants Transform Urban Neighborhoods." *City Journal* (Manhattan Institute) 18 (1): 3–7.

Malner, John. 1974. "Newark's Hispanics Still Aren't Sure Anyone Heard Them." *Herald News*, October 7, 23–25.

Marable, Manning. 1995. *Beyond Black and White: Rethinking Race in American Politics and Society*. New York: Verso.

Marcus, George. 1995. "Ethnography in/of the World System: The Emergence of Multi-Sited Ethnography. *Annual Review of Anthropology* 24:95–117.

Margolis, Maxine. 1994. *Little Brazil: An Ethnography of Brazilian Immigrants in New York City*. Princeton, NJ: Princeton University Press.

———. 2006. "Brazilian Immigration to the U.S. after 9/11." Paper delivered at the Second Conference on Brazilian Immigration to the West Coast of the US Brazilian Consulate in San Francisco, City College of San Francisco, November 4–5.

Mariscal, Jorge. 2005. "Homeland Security, Militarism, and the Future of Latinos and Latinas in the United States." *Radical History Review* 93:39–52.

Marrow, Helen. 2003. "To Be or Not to Be (Hispanic or Latino): Brazilian Racial and Ethnic Identity in the United States." *Ethnicity* 3 (4): 427–64.

Martes, Ana Cristina Braga. 2000. *Brasileiros nos Estados Unidos: Um estudo sobre imigrantes em Massachusetts.* São Paulo: Paz e Terra.

Martins, José. 2003. "A chegada dos portugueses." *Luso-Americano*, April 2, 35–36, 42–46, 52–56.

Marx, Karl, and Frederic Engels. 1998. *The Communist Manifesto* (1848). New York: Merlin Press.

Maskovsky, Jeff. 2001. "Afterword: Beyond the Privatist Consensus." In *The New Poverty Studies: The Ethnography of Power, Politics, and Impoverished People in the United States*, ed. Judith Goode and Jeff Maskovsky, 469–80. New York: New York University Press.

Massey, Douglas S., and Nancy Denton. 1993. *American Apartheid: Segregation and the Making of the Underclass.* Cambridge: Harvard University Press.

Massumi, Brian, ed. 1993. *The Politics of Everyday Fear.* Minneapolis: University of Minnesota Press.

McCallum, Cecilia. 2005. "Racialized Bodies, Naturalized Classes." *American Ethnographer* 32 (1): 100–117.

McCarthy Brown, Karen. 1998. "Mimesis in the Face of Fear: Femme Queens, Butch Queens, and Gender Play in the Houses of Greater Newark." In *Passing: Identity and Interpretation of Sexuality, Race, and Religion*, ed. Maria Carla Sanchez and Linda Schlossberg, 208–27. New York: New York University Press.

McCracken, Grant. 1988. *Culture and Consumption: New Approaches to the Symbolic Character of Cultural Goods.* Bloomington: Indiana University Press.

Medick, Hans, and David W. Sabean. 1984. *Interest and Emotion in Family and Kinship Studies: A Critique of Social History and Anthropology.* Cambridge: Cambridge University Press.

Meihy, José Carlos Sebe Bom. 2004. *Brasil Fora de Si: Experiências de brasileiros em Nova York.* São Paulo: Parbola.

Merleau-Ponty, M. 1962. *The Phenomenology of Perception.* Translated by C. Smith. London: Routledge.

———. 2004. *The World of Perception.* New York: Routledge.

Moore, Sally Falk. 1987. "Explaining the Present: Theoretical Dilemmas in Processual Ethnography." *American Ethnologist* 4 (4): 727–36.

Morrissey, Katherine. 1997. *Mental Territories: Mapping the Inland Empire.* Ithaca, NY: Cornell University Press.

Morrison, Toni. 1992. *Playing in the Dark.* New York: Vintage Books.

Muñoz, José Esteban. 2000. "Feeling Brown: Ethnicity and Affect in Ricardo Bracho's *The Sweetest Hangover (and Other STDs)*." *Theatre Journal* 52 (1): 67–79.

Myers, Fred R. 1979. "Emotions and the Self: A Theory of Personhood and Political Order among Pintupi Aborigines." *Ethos* 7 (4): 343–70.

———. 1986. "Reflections on a Meeting: Structure, Language, and the Polity in a Small-Scale Society." *American Ethnologist* 13 (3): 430–47.

Nagel, Joane. 2000. "Ethnicity and Sexuality." *Annual Review of Sociology* 26: 107–33.

Newark Economic Development Corporation and Newark Division of Economic Development. 1998. Overall Economic Development Program. Newark Division of Economic Development, March.

Newman, Kathe. 2004. "Newark, Decline and Avoidance, Resistance and Desire: From Disinvestment to Reinvestment." *Annals of the AAPSS* 594:34–48.

Ngai, Mae. 2004. *Impossible Subjects: Illegal Aliens and the Making of Modern America.* Princeton, NJ: Princeton University Press.

Novak, Michael. 1972. *The Rise of the Unmeltable Ethnics: Politics and Culture in the Seventies.* New York: Macmillan.

Obeyesekere, Gananath. 1990. *The Work of Culture: Symbolic Transformation in Psychoanalysis and Anthropology.* Chicago: University of Chicago Press.

Oboler, Suzanne. 1995. *Ethnic Labels, Latino Lives: Identity and the Politics of (Re)presentation in the United States.* Minneapolis: University of Minnesota Press.

Ogbu, John. 1982. "Cultural Discontinuities and Schooling." *Anthropology and Education Quarterly* 13 (4): 290–307.

Omi, Michael, and Howard Winant. 1986. *Racial Formation in the United States: From the 1960s to the 1980s.* New York: Routledge.

Ong, Aihwa. 1996. "Cultural Citizenship as Subject-Making: Immigrants Negotiate Racial and Cultural Boundaries in the United States [and comments and reply]." *Current Anthropology* 37 (5): 737–62.

Ortner, Sherry. 1993. "Ethnography among the Newark: The Class of '58 of Weequahic High School." *Michigan Quarterly Review* 32 (3): 410–29.

———. 1997. *Making Gender: The Politics and Erotics of Culture.* Boston: Beacon Press.

———. 2003. *New Jersey Dreaming: Capital, Culture, and the Class of '58.* Princeton, NJ: Princeton University Press.

Padilla, Felix. 1985. *Latino Ethnic Consciousness: The Case of Mexican Americans and Puerto Ricans in Chicago.* Notre Dame, IN: University of Notre Dame Press.

Pascoe, Cherrie. 2007. *Dude, You're a Fag: Masculinity and Sexuality in High School.* Berkeley: University of California Press.

Peña, Susana. 2008. "'Obvious Gays' and the State Gaze: Cuban Gay Visibility and US Immigration Policy during the 1980 Mariel Boatlift." *Journal of the History of Sexuality* 16 (3): 482–514.

Pettit, Phillip, and Michael Smith. 1990. "Backgrounding Desire." *Philosophical Review* 99 (4): 565–92.

Pew Hispanic Center. 2004. "Survey Brief: Latinos in California, New York, Florida, and New Jersey." Washington, DC, March.

Pierre, Jemima. 2004. "Black Immigrants in the United States and the Cultural Narratives of Ethnicity." *Identities* 11:141–70.

Pine, J. B., and J. H. Gilmore. 1999. *The Experience Economy*. Boston: Harvard Business School Press.

Piñon, Nélida. 2004. *A República dos Sonhos*. Lisbon, Portugal: Editorial Presença.

Prasso, Sheridan. 2005. *The Asian Mystique*. New York: Perseus Books.

Price, Clement. 2008. *The Once and Future Newark*. DVD, Rutgers-Newark Office of Communications, Rutgers University–Newark.

Rabinowitz, Dan. 1997. *Overlooking Nazareth: The Ethnography of Exclusion in Galilee*. New York: Cambridge University Press.

Ramos-Zayas, Ana. 2001. "Racializing the Invisible Race: Latino Constructions of White Culture and Whiteness in Chicago." *Urban Anthropology* 30 (4): 341–80.

———. 2003. *National Performances: The Politics of Class, Race, and Space in Puerto Rican Chicago*. Chicago: University of Chicago Press.

———. 2004. "Delinquent Citizenship, National Performance: Racialization, Surveillance, and the Politics of Worthiness in Puerto Rican Chicago." *Journal of Latino Studies* 2 (1): 26–44.

———. 2007. "Becoming American, Becoming Black?: Urban Competency, Racialized Spaces, and the Politics of Citizenship among Brazilian and Puerto Rican Youth in Newark." *Identities* 14 (1): 85–109.

———. 2008. "Between 'Cultural Excess' and Racial 'Invisibility': Brazilians and the Commercialization of Culture in the Ironbound." In *Becoming Brazuca: Brazilian Immigration to the United States*, ed. Clémence Jouët-Pastré and Letícia J. Braga, 271–86. David Rockefeller Series in Latin American Studies. Cambridge: Harvard University Press.

———. 2009. "Stereotypes of the Tropics in "Portuguese Newark": Brazilian Women, Urban Erotics, and the Phantom of Blackness." In *Community, Culture, and the Making of Identity: Portuguese-Americans along the Eastern Seaboard*, ed. Kim Holton and Andrea Klimt, 429–56. North Dartmouth, MA: Center for Portuguese Studies and Culture, University of Massachusetts–Dartmouth

———. Work-in-progress. "'They Come Back Depressed': Examining American Affect in Brazil and Puerto Rico" (tentative title).

Raymond, Janice, Donna Hughes, and Carol Gomez. 2001. "Sex Trafficking of Women in the United States: International and Domestic Trends." Coalition Against Trafficking in Women, Jersey City, East Brunswick, Red Bank and Rockaway Township.

Reddy, William. 1997. "Against Constructionism: The Historical Ethnography of Emotions." *Current Anthropology* 38 (3): 327–51.

———. 1999. "Emotional Liberty: Politics and History in the Anthropology of Emotions." *Cultural Anthropology* 14 (21): 256–88.

———. 2001. The Navigation of Feelings: A Framework for the history of emotions. London: Cambridge University Press.

Ribeiro, Gustavo L. 1997. "Street Samba: Carnaval and Transnational Identities in San Francisco." Paper presented at the BRASA IV Congress, Washington, DC, November 12–15.

———. n.d. "Vulnerabilidade e Ambiguidade. Cidadania na Situacao de Emigrante em San Francisco, California." Paper written for the Institute for Global Studies in Culture, Power and History. Johns Hopkins University, Baltimore.

Ricoeur, Paul. 1991. *From Text to Action*. Evanston, IL: Northwestern University Press.

Ripley, Amanda. 2003. "When the Meninas Came to Town." *Time*, October 12. http://www.time.com/time/magazine/article/0,9171,517712,00.html (accessed May 30, 2011).

Rivera-Colón, Edgar. 2009. "Getting Life in Two Worlds: Power and Prevention in the New York City House Ball Community." Ph.D. diss., Rutgers University, 2009.

Roediger, David. 2002. *Colored White*. Berkeley: University of California Press.

Romero, Mary. 1992. *Maid in the USA*. New York: Routledge.

Rosaldo, Michelle. 1984. "Toward an Anthropology of Self and Feeling." In *Culture Theory: Essays on Mind, Self, and Emotion*, ed. Richard A. Shweder and Robert Alan LeVine, 137–20. Cambridge: Cambridge University Press.

Ross, C. E, J. Mirowsky, and S. Pribesh. 2001. "Powerlessness and the Amplification of Threat: Neighborhood Disadvantage, Disorder, and Mistrust." *American Sociological Review* 66 (4): 568–91.

Roth, Philip. 1997. *American Pastoral*. Boston: Houghton-Mifflin.

Rouse, Joseph. 2006. "Practice Theory." In *Philosophy of Anthropology and Sociology*, ed. Stephen Turner and Mark Risjord, vol. 15 of *Handbook of the Philosophy of Science*, ed. Dov M. Gabbay, Paul Thagard and John Woods, 499–540. Amsterdam: Elsevier.

———. 2007. "Practice Theory." Division I Faculty Publications. Paper 43. http://wesscholar.wesleyan.edu/div1facpubs/43.

Rutheiser, Charles. 1999. "Making Place in the Nonplace Urban Realm: Notes on the Revitalization of Downtown Atlanta." In *Theorizing the City: The New Urban Anthropology Reader*, ed. Setha Low, 317–41. New Brunswick, NJ: Rutgers University Press.

Sacks, Michael. 2003. "Suburbanization and the Racial/Ethnic Divide in the Hartford Metropolitan Area." http://academic.research.microsoft.com/Publication/11620090/suburbanization-and-the-racial-ethnic-divide-in-the-hartford-metropolitan-area (accessed June 18, 2011).

Sales, Teresa. 1998. *Brasileiros longe de casa*. São Paulo: Cortez Editora.

Sánchez Jankowski, Martín. 1991. *Islands in the Street: Gangs and American Society*. Berkeley: University of California Press.

Santiago, Silviano. 1994. *Stella Manhattan*. Trans. George Yudice. Durham, NC: Duke University Press.

Sartre, Jean Paul. 1957. *Existentialism and Human Emotions*. New York: Citadel Press.

Schein, Louisa. 1999. "Performing Modernity." *Cultural Anthropology* 14 (3): 361–95.

Scheper-Hughes, Nancy. 1983. *Death without Weeping: The Violence of Everyday Life in Brazil.* Berkeley: University of California Press.

Schulgasser, Daniel. 2002. "Newark and the New Jersey Performing Arts Center." Unpublished manuscript.

Schwartz, Jonathan. 1998. "Comment: High School Classmates Revisited: Sherry Ortner and Philip Roth." *Anthropology Today* 14 (6):14–16.

Schwartz, Larry. 2005. "Roth, Race and Newark." *Cultural Logic* 8. http://clogic. eserver.org/2005/schwartz.html (accessed April 12, 2008).

Scott, James. 1992. *Domination and the Arts of Resistance: Hidden Transcripts.* New Haven, CT: Yale University Press.

Shanahan, Michael, Michael Finch, Jeylan Mortimer, and Seongryeol Ryu. 1991. "Adolescent Work Experience and Depressive Affect." *Social Psychology Quarterly* 54 (4): 299–317.

Sheriff, Robin. 2001. *Dreaming Equality: Color, Race, and Racism in Urban Brazil.* New Brunswick, NJ: Rutgers University Press.

Shipler, David. 1972. "The White Niggers of Newark." *Harper's* 245:1467–77.

Sidney, Mara. 2003. "The Case of Newark, USA." In *Understanding Slums: Case Studies for the Global Report on Human Settlements.* New York: UN Habitat, Developing Planning Unit.

Silverstein, Paul. 2005. "Immigrant Racialization and the New Savage Slot: Race, Migration, and Immigration in the New Europe." *Annual Review of Anthropology* 34:363.

Simpson, Jennifer. 1996. "Easy Talk, White Talk, Black Talk: Some Reflections on the Meaning of Our Words. *Journal of Contemporary Ethnography* 25 (3): 372–89.

Skidmore, Thomas. 1993a. "Bi-racial USA vs. Multi-racial Brazil: Is the Contrast Still Valid?" *Journal of Latin American Studies* 25:373–86.

———. 1993b. *Black into White: Race and Nationality in Brazilian Thought.* Durham, NC: Duke University Press.

Souza Alves, José Cláudio, and Letícia Ribeiro. 2002. "Migração, Religião e Transnacionalismo: O Caso dos Brasileiros no Sul da Florida." *Religião e Sociedade* 22 (2): 65–90.

Spiro, Melford. 1982. *Buddhism and Society: A Great Tradition and Its Burmese Vicissitudes.* Berkeley: University of California Press.

Stearns, Carol, and Peter Stearns. 1989. *Anger: The Struggle for Emotional Control in America's History.* Chicago: University of Chicago Press.

Steedman, Carolyn Kay. 1986. *Landscape for a Good Woman: A Story of Two Lives.* New Brunswick, NJ: Rutgers University Press.

Stewart, Kathleen. 2007. *Ordinary Affects.* Durham, NC: Duke University Press.

Stoler, Ann. 2001. "Matters of Intimacy as Matters of State: A Response." *Journal of American History* 88 (3): 893–95.

———. 2004. "Affective States." In *A Companion to the Anthropology of Politics*, ed. David Nugent and Joan Vincent, 4–16. Malden, MA: Blackwell.

Stone, Robert. 1998. "Waiting for a Lefty." *New York Review of Books*, November 5, 38.

Storper, Michael. 2000. "Lived Effects of the Contemporary Economy: Globalization, Inequality, and Consumer Society." *Public Culture* 12 (2): 375–409.

Suarez Findlay, Eileen J. 1999. *Imposing Decency: The Politics of Sexuality and Race in Puerto Rico*. Durham, NC: Duke University Press.

Taussig, Michael. 1987. *Shamanism, Colonialism, and the Wild Man: A Study in Terror and Healing*. Chicago: University of Chicago Press.

———. 1999. *Defacement: Public Secrecy and the Labor of the Negative*. Palo Alto, CA: Stanford University Press.

Taylor, Diana. 2003. *The Archive and the Repertoire: Performing Cultural Memory in the Americas*. Durham, NC: Duke University Press.

Telles, Edward. 2004. *Race in Another America: The Significance of Skin Color in Brazil*. Princeton, NJ: Princeton University Press.

Thoits, Peggy. 1989. "The Sociology of Emotions." *Annual Review of Sociology* 15:317–42.

Thomas, Lorrin. 2010. *Puerto Rican Citizen: Historical and Political Identity in Twentieth Century New York*. Chicago: University of Chicago Press.

Thompson, Becky Wangaard. 1992. "'A Way Outa No Way': Eating Problems Among African American, Latina, and White Woman." *Gender and Society* 6 (4): 546–61.

Throop, Jason, and Keith Murphy. 2002. "Bourdieu and Phenomenology: A Critical Assessment." *Anthropological Theory* 2 (2): 185–207.

Tolman, Deborah. 1994. "Doing Desire: Adolescent Girls' Struggles for/with Sexuality." *Gender and Society* 8 (3): 324–42.

Torres, Maria de los Angeles. 1998. "Transnational Political and Cultural Identities: Crossing Theoretical Borders." In *Borderless Borders: U.S. Latinos, Latin Americans, and the Paradox of Interdependence*, ed. Frank Bonilla et al., 169–82. Philadelphia: Temple University Press.

Tosta, Antonio Luciano de Andrade. 2004. "Latino, eu?: The paradoxical interplay of identity in Brazuca literature." *Hispania* 87 (3): 576–85.

Trabasso, Tom, and Asli Ozyurek. 1997. "Communicating Evaluation in Narrative Understanding." In *Conversation: Cognitive, Communicative and Social Perspectives*, ed. Talmy Givón, 269–302. Typological Studies in Language 34. Philadelphia: John Benjamins Publishing.

Turner, Patricia. 1993. *Heard It Through the Grapevine: Rumor in African-American Culture*. Berkeley: University of California Press.

Twine, France Winddance. 1998. *Racism in a Racial Democracy: The Maintenance of White Supremacy in Brazil*. New Brunswick, NJ: Rutgers University Press.

Urciuoli, Bonnie. 1996. *The Semiotics of Exclusion: Puerto Rican Experiences of Race, Class and Language in the U.S.* Boulder, CO: Westview.

Vaca, Nicolás. 2004. *The Presumed Alliance*. New York: HarperCollins.

Vasconcelos, José. 1997. *La raza cósmica: Cuadernos del centro* (1925). Heredia, Costa Rica: Centro de Estudios Generales, Universidad Nacional.

Venkatesh, Sudhir. 2008. *Gang Leader for a Day*. New York: Penguin Press.

Wacquant, Loic. 1991. "Making Class: The Middle Class(es) in Social Theory and Social Structure." In *Bringing Class Back In: Contemporary and Historical Perspectives*, ed. S. McNall, R. Levine, and R. Fantasia, 39–64. Boulder, CO: Westview Press.

———. 2004. *Body and Soul: Ethnographic Notebooks of an Apprentice-Boxer*. New York: Oxford University Press

Wade, Peter. 2004. "Images of Latin American Mestizaje and the Politics of Comparison." *Bulletin of Latin American Research* 23 (3): 355–66.

Wagley, Charles. 1957. *Plantation America: A Culture Sphere*. Caribbean Studies Symposium Proceedings. Seattle: University of Washington.

Warren, Jonathan. 1997. "O fardo de no ser negro: Uma anlise comparativo do desempenho escolar de alunos afro-brasileiros e afro-norte-americanos." *Estudos Afro-Asiáticos* 31:103–24.

Warren, Jonathan, and France Winddance Twine. 1997. "White Americans, the New Minority: Non-blacks and the Ever-expanding Boundaries of whiteness." *Journal of Black Studies* 28 (2): 200–218.

———. 2002. "Critical Race Studies in Latin America: Recent Advances, Recurrent Weaknesses." In *A Companion to Racial and Ethnic Studies*, ed. David T. Goldberg and John Solomos, 538–60. New York: Blackwell.

Waters, Mary. 1999. *Black Identities: West Indian Immigrant Dreams and American Realities*. Cambridge: Harvard University Press.

Watson-Gegeo, Karen Ann, Geoffrey Miles White, and Andrew Arno, eds. 1990. *Disentangling: Conflict Discourse in Pacific Societies*. Palo Alto, CA: Stanford University Press.

Weber, Max. 1958. *The Protestant Ethic and the Spirit of Capitalism*. New York: Talcott Parsons.

Weiner, Bernard. 1985. "An Attributional Theory of Achievement Motivation and Emotion." *Psychological Review* 92 (4): 548–73.

Werneck, José Ignácio. 2004. *Com esperança no coração: Os imigrantes brasileiros nos Estados Unidos*. São Paulo: Augurium Editora.

Weston, Kath. 1995. "Do Clothes Make the Woman? Gender, Performance Theory, and Lesbian Eroticism." *Genders* 17:1–21.

White, E. Frances. 2001. *Dark Continent of Our Bodies: Black Feminism and the Politics of Respectability*. Philadelphia: Temple University Press.

Whitten, Norman E., and Arlene Torres. 1998. *Blackness in Latin America and the Caribbean: Social Dynamics and Cultural Transformations*. Bloomington: Indiana University Press.

Wikan, Unni. 2008. *In Honor of Fadime: Murder and Shame*. Chicago: University of Chicago Press.

Wilkins, Amy. 2008. *Wannabees, Goths, and Christians: The Boundaries of Sex, Style, and Status*. Chicago: University of Chicago Press.

Williams, Patricia. 1997. *Seeing a Color-Blind Future: The Paradox of Race*. New York: Noonday Press.

Williams, Raymond. 1973. *The Country and the City*. London: Oxford University Press.

———. 1977. *Marxism and Literature*. London: Oxford University Press.

Willis, Paul. 1977. *Learning to Labor: How Working-Class Kids Get Working-Class Jobs*. New York: Columbia University Press.

Wilson, William J. 1990. *The Truly Disadvantaged: The Inner City, the Underclass, and Public Policy*. Chicago: University of Chicago Press.

Winant, Howard. 1992. "Rethinking Race in Brazil." *Journal of Latin American Studies* 24 (1): 173–92.

———. 1994. *Racial Conditions: Politics, Theory, Comparisons*. Minneapolis: University of Minnesota Press.

Yamamoto, Eric. 2000. *Interracial Justice: Conflict and Reconciliation in Post–Civil Rights America*. New York: NYU Press.

Zukin, Sharon. 1996. *The Culture of Cities*. Malden, MA: Blackwell.

Index

Abbott school districts, 83
Abu-Lughod, Lila, 331n8
adversarial outlook, 382n6. *See also* hardness
Aeriel, Natasha, 271, 275
Aeriel, Terrance, 271, 275
affect: in African American–Brazilian relationships, 162; in African American–Latino relationships, 141; in African American–Puerto Rican relationships, 82, 120, 124, 132; and Americanization, 43–44, 286–89, 307–8, 314; and authenticity, 306–7; and black women's aggression, 266; of Brazilians, 186; and conceptions of practice, 7–13; and cultural sampling, 208; dimensions of, 260; and emotional and body labor, 216; and emotional-cultural schemas, 70; epistemological considerations of, 29, 30, 33; in evaluative judgments, 317; in home, 80; in Latino-black relations, 249, 257; of migrants and return migrants, 307; in multicultural capitalism, 151; and relationship narratives, 233–35, 238; and nation-state racial projects, 104; and neoliberalism, 28, 288, 318–24; and Newark's image, 59, 62; ordinary, 158; performances of, 338n17; and perspectives on race, 4; in Portuguese-Brazilian relationships, 189; in public, 280, 316; and Puerto Rican Blackness, 297; and Puerto Rican self-help, 95; in race-talk, 185; and racial democracy, 22–24, 31, 32, 42, 139, 167, 173, 195; and racialization, 283–89; and racism, 172; research on, 6, 40, 41; in sex work industry, 232; stereotypes of, 198–201, 205, 208–9, 240–45, 256, 284; subjectivity of, 258; and urban emotional commonsense, 14–15, 18–19; of white middle class, 73. *See also* emotional style; emotions; feelings; sentiment
affirmative action, 371n5
Africa, 171, 240, 339n20. *See also* pan-Africanist alliances
African Americans: and affect, 12, 186, 283; and aggression, 43; and appearance, 214; associations with welfare dependency, 237; Brazilian and Portuguese attitudes toward, 186; and Brazilian culture, 159–63; Brazilian perceptions of class, 153–57; and civilizing manners, 251, 252; claiming of Brazilians, 193; cultural sampling by, 206; difference from blacks, 172; at East Side High School, 164; emotional-cultural schemas of, 69–71; emotions of, 101, 132; and failed US racial system, 167–73; and "feel" of Newark, 41–42,